The Complete Book of

Sportfishing

THE COMPLETE BOOK OF SPORTFISHING has been originated, designed and produced by AB Nordbok, Gothenburg, Sweden.

Editorial chief: Göran Cederberg
Graphic design: Munir Lotia
Consultant: Jan Olsson
Translators: Robert Blohm
Cheryl Eliasson
Olle W. Nilsson
Jerry Petterson
Peter Steensen
Jon van Leuven

Artwork

Anders Engström: pages 38–39, 50, 65, 90, 93, 96 (top), 100, 115, 116, 117, 119, 121, 156 (right), 178, 191, 214–215, 262.
Peter Grahn: page 26.
Tommy Gustavsson: pages 200–201, 202, 206, 206–207, 208, 216–217, 218, 222–223, 227, 228, 276, 277, 279, 281.
Gunnar Johnson: pages 42, 44, 45, 46, 47, 49, 52, 58, 82, 83, 96 (bottom), 97, 98, 101, 104, 105, 106, 108, 109, 112, 129, 130, 131, 132–133, 134–135, 147, 152, 155, 156 (left), 163, 168, 184, 192–193, 196–197, 198, 205, 219, 220–221, 224, 226, 234, 236–257, 260, 261, 263, 267, 268, 269, 270, 271.
Munir Lotia: pages 55, 129 (right).
Lennart Molin: pages 136–137, 138–139, 140–141, 142–143, 153, 154, 159, 169, 170, 210, 229.
Ulf Söderqvist: pages 20, 22, 28, 30, 34, 35, 51, 56, 57, 61, 62, 64, 185.
Nordbok: pages 16, 17, 18, 19, 21, 23, 24–25, 33.

Photography

ABU Garcia: pages 40, 41.
Peter Bang: page 76 (left).
Erwin Bauer: pages 51 (left inset), 66, 67, 72 (top), 77 (top left), 140, 162, 180 (left inset), 204.
Rudolf Bischoff: pages 14–15, 95.
Kenneth Boström: pages 263–266.
Bill Browning: pages 74 (left), 75 (center), 84 (top), 127, 177 (inset), 180, 182 (right), 186, 189, 195, 199.
Göran Cederberg: endpapers.
Johan Dahlqvist: page 72 (bottom).
Gunter Fröhlich: page 182 (top right).
Jan Grahn: pages 75 (top), 78 (right), 80, 88–89, 92, 118, 218.
Peter Grahn: pages 78 (left), 79, 86–87, 113 (right inset), 118 (inset), 122, 146 (left).
Hermann J. Grubl: pages 32, 74 (right), 77 (top right).
Jens Ploug Hansen: pages 36–37, 48, 53, 59, 69, 71, 73, 75 (bottom), 76 (right), 77, 81, 83, 84 (bottom), 85, 95 (inset), 99, 105, 109 (left), 113 (left inset), 114, 120, 126, 137, 138, 140 (top), 142, 143, 145, 146 (right), 148–149, 150–151, 155, 157, 166, 167, 169, 170, 171 (top), 172, 173, 179, 182 (left), 201, 211, 215, 218 (top), 226, 231, 272–273, 275 (top).
Christian Hvidt: pages 180 (right inset), 181 (inset).
Heinz Jagusch: pages 68, 103, 106, 111 (inset), 113, 181 (right), 187, 213.
Bengt G. Johansson: pages 267, 268, 270.
Christer Johansson: pages 51 (right inset), 59 (center and right insets), 70, 94 (left), 107, 109 (inset), 144, 176–177, 183, 258–259.
Jan Johansson: pages 174–175, 214, 222, 225, 274.
Gunnar Johnson: pages 242–257.
Inge Lennmark: page 33 (inset).
Åke Lindau: pages 91, 94 (right), 109 (right), 111, 153, 161 (bottom right), 181 (left), 191, 209, 230, 275.
Henry Lundgren: pages 232–233, 235.
Mike Millman: pages 124–125, 161 (top).
Jan Olsson: pages 63, 64, 65, 151, 156, 158, 163, 164, 165, 171 (bottom).
Janne Olsson: page 46.
Jan-Erik Sjöberg: page 8.
Leif Wiklund: pages 6–7, 41 (top).
Mikael Zachrisson: pages 277, 278.

Nordbok would like to express sincere thanks to the following special advisers: ABU Garcia, Bertil Ekholm-Erb, Olof Johansson, Benny Lindgren, Normark Scandinavia AB, and Bengt Öste.

Published by Grange Books
An Imprint of Grange Books
Limited
The Grange
Grange Yard
LONDON
SE1 3AG

Reprinted 1993

British Library Cataloguing in Publication Data
The Complete Book of Sportfishing.
1. Angling
799.1'2

Typeset by Bokstaven Text & Montage AB, Gothenburg.
Reproduction by Reproman, Gothenburg, and Offset-Kopio, Helsinki.
Printed in Spain 1993 by LITOPRINT, S. A.

ISBN 1-85627-312-1

The Complete Book of Sportfishing

Grange Books

Editor

GÖRAN CEDERBERG is an experienced sportfisherman and a contributor to Swedish sportfishing journalism. As the project leader for this book, he has planned and organized it, guided the authors, edited their material and collected illustrations, in addition to writing Chapters 1 and 10.

Authors

ERWIN BAUER is a legendary wilderness journalist and photographer. He has written diverse books about sportfishing and collaborated on large works, besides being a contributor to *Outdoor Life*. He has added sections on American fishing conditions in Chapters 3 and 6.

KENNETH BOSTRÖM is a professional rod-builder and a devoted fly-fisherman with great experience from Scandinavia, Iceland and Alaska. He has contributed for years to Swedish fishing magazines. The section on building and renovating rods in Chapter 9 is his work.

COLIN DYSON is a well-known sportfishing journalist, editor of the British journal *Coarse Angler*, President of the Pike Anglers' Club of Great Britain, and one of the sport's leaders in his homeland with experience from Europe and America. He has written Chapter 4.

GÜNTER FRÖHLICH is editor of the West German journal *Der Fliegenfisher*, and also contributes to sportfishing journals in Scandinavia, having thorough knowledge of fly-fishing in both Europe and the United States. He has written most of Chapter 7.

JENS PLOUG HANSEN is an internationally recognized sportfishing journalist and photographer, contributing to several European journals, and the author of some twenty books about sportfishing as well as parts of various international publications. Most of Chapters 3 and 6 are his writing.

JOHN HOLDEN is one of the world's leading experts on surfcasting and has written around twenty books, many articles about coastal and sea fishing especially in *Angling Times*, and for journals in Germany, France and the United States. His contribution is Chapter 5.

BENGT G. JOHANSSON is a long-time contributor to Swedish fishing journalism, and has published a comprehensive book on how to make fishing equipment. Being also a designer of lures and rods, he has added the section on lure-making in Chapter 9.

JAN JOHANSSON is a notable leader in salmon fishing and the author of some books about it, as well as of numerous articles in Swedish and Norwegian sportfishing journals. He has written the section on "Heavier Fly-fishing" in Chapter 7.

GUNNAR JOHNSON is editor of the journal *Flugfiske i Norden* (Fly-Fishing in Scandinavia). He has also contributed well-known illustrations and innumerable articles to both Swedish and foreign books and fishing journals. The text and pictures in Chapter 8 as well as most of the other watercolors in this book are his.

OLLE W. NILSSON has been editor of the Swedish journal *Sportfiskaren* for about thirty years. Known chiefly as a fish biologist, he has written some ten books and various articles in Swedish, English and German journals. Chapter 2 is his contribution.

Contents

Foreword

Whatever their language and nationality, sportfishermen around the world are united by one thing—the passion for fishing with a rod, line and hook. Perhaps the sources of this enjoyment should be sought in our ancient, inherited instincts. When all is said and done, not many generations separate us from our primeval ancestors. For even if our clothes and customs mean culture, we are still wild enough in genetic terms. As such "civilized savages", we experience deep satisfaction in feeling a fish gobble our deceptive baits, and the same excitement makes us fight the fish with everything our age has to offer by way of rods, reels, line and bait. These are the result of thousands of years of practical fishing, not to mention the latest in industrial high technology.

A profound, genuine sense of nature and its diversity is often essential for what we call, rather vaguely, "fishing luck". This depends, in fact, more on knowledge of the prey's life and environment than on the harvest of chance. Water makes up 70% of our earth's surface, a realm which is mostly hidden to us, and what goes on inside it is largely up to guesswork. We must therefore take advantage of every trick if fish are to be duped by our clever baits, well-laid hooks and imaginative fly-patterns. In other words, sportfishing takes place entirely on the fish's conditions—we always have to try and lure the fish somehow into biting. The greater our knowledge, the better we succeed. Yet much of the challenge surely lies in this very uncertainty: can we imitate the fish's natural prey so well that it mistakes our lies for the truth? Here is a question at the heart of the joy of sportfishing.

Fish species and aquatic surroundings are almost endlessly varied throughout the world, and the development of equipment and techniques has not gone equally far in all countries. Consequently, our impressions of what constitutes modern sportfishing may change as we travel. In spite of that, the methods of fishing are frequently universal, giving us plenty of opportunity to learn from each other. A growing awareness of where the fish live, how they behave in different environments, and when they are active enables us to understand the basic similarities. The more one knows of this astounding range, the greater one's possibilities of becoming a good fisherman, and thus of enjoying the fruits of sportfishing. To such an extent, we are indeed blessed with fortune. And so the adventure goes on . . .

Göran Cederberg

There is a common saying—or hope—among anglers that any time spent fishing is not deducted from one's allotted life span. If so, there is an extraordinary number of opportunities all over the world to keep a sportsman busy and to postpone the inevitable, perhaps forever . . .

Erwin Bauer

The history of sportfishing

There are probably as many reasons for fishing as there are sportfishermen. Most of us, though, will agree that the experience of nature is at least as important as the catch itself. In our efficient and often stressful society, sportfishing is a valve that gives millions of practitioners rest and release from daily cares. Perhaps, too, it is a way of getting back to our roots somewhere in a distant past, while feeling the satisfaction of seeking our own food in nature's great, sometimes generous, pantry.

Through newspapers, radio, TV and other mass media, ideas spread faster today than ever before in history. Methods which have long been tested, and found effective under certain conditions, tend to be diffused at an ever quicker pace around the world. Experience from the United States is applied in Europe, and typical European methods such as angling have begun to catch on in the States during recent years. In southern and central Europe, ever more eyes are directed toward Scandinavia for new and more profitable methods of fly-fishing. And when it comes to trolling in lakes or the sea, America has shown the way for fishing in other parts of the world.

How sportfishing will look in the future is hard to predict exactly. But in order to understand the national variations in equipment and technique at present, it can be useful to take a deep dive into human history and see how fishing started long ago.

These old tools of bone were used by fishermen in northern Europe 8,000 years ago.

The first hooks

Man has taken his food from nature for hundreds of thousands of years—hunting, fishing, and gathering plants to supply his daily meals. The strongest and most inventive people lived longest, and this constant fight for survival inevitably also shaped their relationship to the surroundings. Creativity was not only a sign of ingenuity, but rather a necessity under difficult circumstances of existence.

We know very little about how the first human beings fished, but they must have soon discovered the enormous food resources in lakes, seas, and running waterways. These consisted of shellfish, mussels, and seals, as well as fish. No doubt people began to catch fish by using their bare hands, then gradually learned that sharp pins and other primitive fishing equipment were far more effective. Scientists are not at all sure which equipment was used before around 30,000–40,000 BC, but archaeological finds indicate that three main kinds were employed later. Spears served primarily for fishing in shallow lakes and rivers, and in the sea to catch, for example, seals. Woven nets and various sorts of traps were placed in the richest fishing areas. The third type, which is also most interesting for sportfishermen, was the hook. Exactly when and where hooks were adopted is unknown, but it was probably in southern Europe about 30,000 BC. These barbed hooks were made chiefly of bone, but presumably also of wood. The hooks were fastened on a line made of animal sinews or thin, tough plant materials such as roots, vines and certain grasses. They were baited with worms, mussels, small fish, or whatever else might attract the big ones to strike.

As the millennia passed, hunting peoples turned into more or less settled farmers. Thus, they became less dependent on wild animals, and domestic beasts provided new economic security. Yet peasants never managed to tame fish, and it was natural that fishing continued to be very important as a food supplement.

The development of angling

Archaeology proves that the art of angling was relatively refined as early as 7,000 years ago. Among the finds are floats which were cut from bark and used in fishing with hooks. Three thousand years later on, Egyptian paintings showed how to fish with a rod, top-knotted line, and hook. This is the first evidence that people actually practiced a kind of fishing which, at least superficially, was quite similar to the angling of today.

From fishing with natural bait, it is not a big step to using artificial bait, and we can safely assume that long ago there were, for instance, model fish whittled out of wood. Another likelihood is that people soon realized how closely the natural prey of fish can be imitated by hairs and feathers.

"Already the old Greeks . . ." as the saying goes—and what would sportfishing be without them? It was Theocritus who, about 300 BC, wrote the first literary description of fishing with hook and rod.He spoke of using a "bait deceitfully dangling from the rod", and there is good reason to believe that fishing for enjoyment was first done in ancient Greece. Theocritus and his social class certainly had no need to fish for food.

By around 200 BC the Chinese had developed sportfishing so far that silk lines and metal hooks were being employed. At the same time, the Macedonians fished with artificial baits made of hair and feathers. Such down-hooks, more like jigs than flies, were doubtless just as effective as the ones we now use. How far advanced these people were, and not only in terms of culture or education, is clear from the fact that iron hooks began to be manufactured in Europe only three centuries later, in the middle of the Iron Age.

This Egyptian painting, about 4,000 years old, is probably the most ancient portrayal of angling known today.

The complete angler

Even if mankind has derived great pleasure from fishing throughout its long history, regular sportfishing belongs to the past 450 years. This is the art of fishing with hook, line and rod for pure enjoyment and leisure. A milestone in its own evolution was *The Treatise of Fyshynge Wyth an Angle*, published in England in 1496. Probably written by a nun, Dame Juliana Berners, this work was part of the *Book of St. Albans*, which told the nobility and other "gentlemen" about hunting, fishing, and other elite pastimes of the age.

The "treatise" dealt, however, not only with techniques and methods, but also with the fisherman's relationship to nature. It had an enormous influence on the development of sportfishing for more than two centuries afterward, and became a source of inspiration for later writers of better-known works on the subject. According to its viewpoint, the sportfisherman should also be a nature-worshipper, philosopher and idealist. The sport was to be developed to perfection and a real fisherman ought to make his own rods, lines and artificial bait, as well as being able to collect and use different kinds of natural bait correctly. The harder a fish was to catch, the greater was the sport of fishing.

Just 150 years later, in 1653, appeared Izaak Walton's *The Compleat Angler*, subtitled "The Contemplative Man's Recreation", which is a classic known all over the world today. Together with

Here begynnyth the treatyse of fysshynge wyth an Angle.

The first page of Dame Juliana Berners' "Treatise of Fyshynge wyth an Angle", from the original edition in 1496.

The complete angler himself, Izaak Walton, is shown here with his fishing equipment. This drawing was on the title page of the jubileum edition exactly 200 years after his first edition of 1653.

Charles Cotton's chapter on fly-fishing from 1676, the book has been published in more than 300 editions until now.

Walton's work aroused interest with its presentation of methods for fishing with rod, line and hook. It also established sportfishing as a tradition for the first time. Fishing solely for enjoyment, and thereby valuing the experience of nature at least as highly as the fishing itself, became a popular idea along with the term "sportfisherman". Development of equipment and methods for sportfishing was one objective, but nearness to nature and "the great adventure" was another important ingredient in fishing. The farther away—and harder to fish—a body of water was, the more sporting the activity became. A true sportfisherman was, to a large extent, a "hardship romantic".

Equipment and its long evolution

Fishing gear and techniques developed rather slowly from the mid-seventeenth century until the early nineteenth century. The main reason was, of course, that sportfishing still had only a few practitioners and these stuck to old traditions. Top-knotted lines made of horsehair, long clumsy rods of jointed wood, and relatively simple tied flies were their customary armament.

Even if one could occasionally buy reels of multiplicator type during the early nineteenth century, fishing continued until the heyday of industrialism to resemble Izaak Walton's approach in the 1600s—priority was given to the experience of nature. The only pioneering change in equipment concerned the hooks. Around 1650, their durability began to be improved by hardening. They were still fashioned by village smiths, but gradually the needlemakers took them over, turning the old handicraft into a large-scale industry. As a result, hooks also became lighter and suppler, although they remained pretty crude by today's standards.

The Englishman L. Lloyd was not only a famous bear-hunter, but also a passionate sportfisherman who spent happy summers by Scandinavian waters. This drawing from the Norwegian salmon river Namsen was in his book "Scandinavian Adventures", Volume I (1853).

With the industrial revolution in the mid-nineteenth century, equipment saw an ever more rapid development. Technical innovations and mass production offered wholly new opportunities for sportfishing by people other than "nobles and gentlemen". The winds of change also brought new techniques and methods of fishing. It was now that people began to seriously question Izaak Walton's ideas of 200 years before.

Thus sportfishing, a pleasure of the privileged until around 1850, began to attract an ever wider public in both Europe and the United States who were interested in fishing with rod and hook. New types of fishing waters were "discovered", and eyes were opened to nontraditional kinds of sportfishing, especially in the sea. The old lyrical ideals of nature were regarded by many as snobbish, and different groups of sportfishermen took shape.

The fly-fishermen, who had almost exclusively fished with dry flies and "classical" wet-fly patterns during the nineteenth century, were those who held most firmly to Waltonism. They considered a correctly prepared imitation of a natural insect to be, from the sporting standpoint, far superior to fishing with live or dead bait—an opinion which survived long into our own century.

Yet it was also the fly-fishermen who mainly advanced the development of new and more purposeful equipment, not least in regard to rods. These went through several stages of improvement in the early 1800s. For example, experiments were conducted with different kinds of wood, such as hazel, hickory, lancewood and greenheart, in order to find the perfect rod material. The first split-cane rod was created by an American violinmaker in 1846. This gave bamboo a breakthrough as rod material, and revealed a method of construction that outdid all earlier ones. Split-cane rods were not only comparatively light and easy to handle, but also gave a longer cast. Despite their many advantages, the method took another quarter-century to become effective enough for profitable mass production.

Developments proceeded in other areas as well. Multiplicator reels had to wait for some time into the nineteenth century before they began to be used by a larger group of sportfishermen, and then primarily in America where they proved popular in sea-fishing, for striped bass among others. These early bait-casting reels were both clumsy and sluggish, giving a relatively short cast. Nor were they helped by being used together with thick, unpliant lines of cotton and linen. Some attention was therefore paid to developing new and better lines. The success in manufacturing oil-impregnated silk lines in the 1870s was regarded as a big step forward, since the casting length could thus be tripled.

Towards modern fishing

Although adequate techniques of making rods and lines were invented during the nineteenth century, reels (and principally bait-casting reels) were still a serious problem. Heavy casting-weights were needed to reach out to the fishing grounds. So it was good news when the first spinning-reels came onto the market in the early 1900s. The prototype of today's spinning-reel was created at Bradford, England, in 1905. Things went fast after that, in view of its obvious advantages. Most important was the longer cast, but it also made the troublesome backlash—common with the multiplicator type—easier to avoid.

Coming to the years before World War II, we find two innovations that have been perhaps the most decisive promoters of sportfishing around the world during the past three decades: synthetic lines and the glass-fibre rod. These thin, flexible lines offered even the novice a chance of learning rather quickly how to cast, with no real problems. The glass-fibre rod's durability and low cost meant that one did not have to suffer a hole in the pocket to try fishing.

Popularity has stayed with the glass-fibre rod, no doubt mainly because it is easy to mass-produce and therefore cheap, but also due to its continual improvement. However, with the rapid development of artificial-fibre materials at present, we can expect that glass-fibre rods will be replaced by even better types in the future. This was first indicated in the mid-1970s, when the first carbon-fibre rods appeared. These were lighter than glass-fibre, and indeed reminiscent of the split-cane rod's superb casting properties, but their initial prices were terrifying. It took a while before they could compete, yet they then caught on strongly, first among fly-fishermen and next with spin- and spool-fishermen.

New materials will always influence the rod market. A declining group of sportfishermen still considers the split-cane rod to be unbeatable in casting ability and drilling feel. Others have high hopes that the new materials will yield revolutionary rods with amazingly light weight, fine balance and optimal casting power. The rods now being produced from carbon-fibre, boron, glass-fibre, and various mixtures of these, have at any rate brought us a good way along the path to perfection.

A further field of development is that of artificial baits. Perhaps the main link between the fish and fisherman, baits have also become more effective and suitable. Not the least successful have been rubber and plastic imitations, which now occupy a firm place in the equipment of most sportfishermen. Jigs are another much-adopted type and, in many cases, they have replaced both spoons and spinners. The general trend is an increasing preference for rubber, plastic, and feathers, since these have proved very catch-yielding.

Using hair and feathers to imitate the natural prey of fish is a tradition two thousand years old, so it is no accident that those materials have retained their popularity. But the fly-patterns have naturally diversified and evolved during this long span of time. The constant effort to improve catching ability has given fly-fishermen a deep interest in entomology. Flies must be as similar as possible to the fish's natural prey, and "classical" patterns have consequently lost importance in favour of many new designs—not least the nymphs, streamers, and so-called lure animals.

We cannot speak of sportfishing's development without recognizing the crucial role of boats, which enable us to reach new fishing grounds and raise our effectiveness. During the past twenty years, boat-fishing has become ever more common on both lakes and seas. New methods of fishing have emerged, particularly in the surface and middle layers, while new species have caught the sportfisherman's interest. Many boats are also specially equipped for trolling and big-game fishing; even special types of boats are manufactured for sportfishing. Moreover, the echo-sounder, once used almost exclusively by professional fishermen, has come to be an important tool of the sport for locating fish.

Environmental conservation

The industrial revolution, which made it possible to manufacture better and more effective fishing equipment at relatively low prices, has also led to destruction of the natural environment at an ever-increasing rate. Pollution of water and air, in many places around the world, has killed off sensitive fish species such as the sea trout.

With the spread of "civilization", conflicts between nature and culture have become ever more tangible. Our enormous energy needs, for instance, are satisfied by the expansion of hydroelectric power plants. Cities grow continually with houses and roads built in areas which once held waters rich in fish. Agricultural overfertilization has given us dead bottoms in lakes and the sea. Water diversion, dredging, dams, and other direct interference with natural waterways have changed the living conditions for fish. Finally, changes in the chemical content and temperature of water have done much harm to sportfishing. To find fairly undisturbed water, the sportfisherman must go ever farther out into the "wilderness".

Fortunately, one can also hear rising voices against uncontrolled pollution in both Europe and the United States. In addition, many of the deteriorated fishing grounds are being "restored". This and the implantation of fish have created far better conditions for sportfishing. In some places, especially in America, an effort has been made to create completely new fishing

Salmon fishing has had an exclusive aura even in our century. Depicted here in the lovely landscape of Scotland is a fisherman landing a fine day's catch, attended by his gillies.

areas in the sea with artificial reefs. Thanks to the erection of huge amounts of concrete, macadam and rubber tires in especially favourable spots, a bottom environment has resulted where fish thrive and a very high class of fishing can be enjoyed.

Why sportfishing?

The thought of competitive fishing would probably make Isaac Walton spin in his grave. This says quite a lot about the transformed relationship between fish and fisherman which has emerged during the past three centuries. Prize and specimen fish are now an important part of sportfishing all over the world, not least for anglers. Most fishing magazines publish lists of record fish caught, and results of different kinds of competitions. Even many manufacturers of equipment proudly display pictures of "dream fish" caught with their gear. The great upsurge of seafishing in our century also led to the foundation of a special organization in the United States in 1939, the International Game Fish Association (I.G.F.A.), chiefly for collecting information about record fish caught at sea, as well as in fresh waters during recent years.

But sportfishing means not only catching fish—it involves a closeness to nature which few other sports can match. For some people, it is the joy of catching many and big fish; for others, it provides a good time together with friends. Certain practitioners appreciate the solitude of quiet waters far from the daily ratrace, while a lot of us want to taste the great adventure at sea far from land. The competitive element in hunting large or specimen fish can be attractive, or the calm and contemplation may be enough without caring about the catch.

Which type of fish is preferred, and what kind of water the line is to get wet in, are matters of individual choice. The important thing is not what distinguishes us, but a common interest that unites us. Whoever has become an avid sportfisherman possesses a hobby that lasts for life and can be varied almost indefinitely—whether by actively fishing, by sitting at the fireside with an exciting book about fishing, by making one's own equipment, or by dreaming oneself away to a favourite stretch of water during the dark winter evenings.

Fish and their world

The water environment

To understand the life, habits, and behaviour of fish—in general, their manner of functioning and reacting—it is necessary to know something about the medium they live in. When we sportfishermen, for instance, discuss the right fly or lure, we easily forget those limitations and possibilities which are determined by the water.

Water is a unique medium in several ways. The water molecule, a combination of two hydrogen atoms and one of oxygen, is remarkably stable—and among the more common substances on earth, water is the only one which exists as a gas, liquid, and solid alike. It also has the peculiar property of being most dense at a temperature higher than its freezing temperature: for pure water, these are 4°C (39°F) and 0°C (32°F) respectively. This is of decisive importance for the survival of fish and other aquatic organisms during winter. The same property makes ice float on water, forming an insulating layer in lakes, rivers and coastal areas. Again, this property makes possible the thermal stratification and seasonal turnover of water masses in lakes in cold climates, which is essential not least to fish.

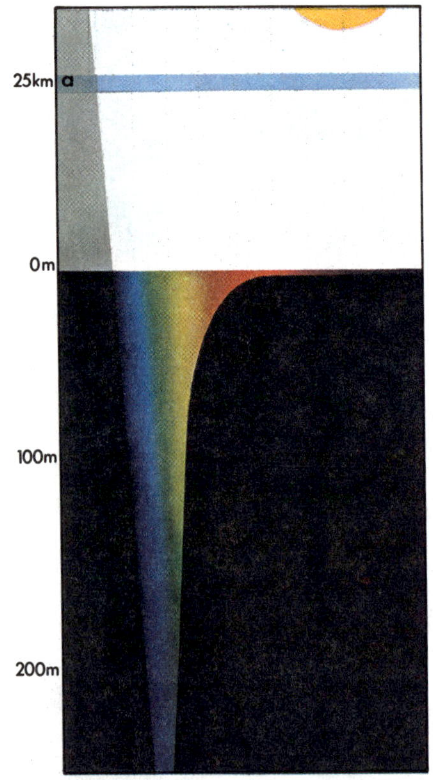

The earth's atmosphere absorbs some of the sunlight that passes through it. Its ozone layer plays an important role by reducing the dangerous ultraviolet rays. When the light enters a body of water, even more is absorbed, depending on the rays' wavelengths. In pure water blue-green light penetrates farthest, but even this part of the spectrum becomes too weak to allow photosynthesis of plants at depths below about 100 m (330 ft). Therefore, it is vital that nutrients in deep water are brought up to the surface, where the sunlight is stronger and they can be utilized by plant plankton and algae.

Water as a mixture

Completely pure water does not exist outside the laboratory. All natural water contains various substances. In "fresh water", these are mainly the so-called buffering system, or carbonate complex, of carbonic acid with carbonate and bicarbonate. This determines whether the water is acid, neutral, or basic, as measured by its pH value which, chemically, shows the proportion of hydrogen ions. Neutral water has pH 7, while lower values mean acidity and higher ones mean that the water is basic (alkaline). Lakes and rivers usually have higher pH values in limestone areas than in regions with little lime in their soil.

Whereas lake and river water is said to be fresh, sea water is called salty (saline). Between fresh and salt waters, there are many intermediate types. In some inland seas, such as the Baltic, we speak of brackish water. Water containing less than one gram of dissolved substances per kilogram (litre) is considered fresh, and all higher amounts define salt and brackish waters. Sea water generally contains about 35 grams per kilogram (also termed promille, parts per thousand).

Light in water

Light conditions in water are very different from those in air. Even in the clearest lake or ocean water, sunlight is reflected, scattered and absorbed, so greatly that only about 1% remains at a depth of 150 metres. In muddy and turbid waters, the light cannot penetrate more than a few metres. These differences in penetration naturally have a great effect on, for example, the ability of fish to see a lure.

Apart from its limited penetrating power, light is essential to the organisms in water. They depend on light not only for warmth and the energy used by plant photosynthesis, but also for the oxygen and organic substances which are produced by green plants. This "primary" production is mostly confined to the surface layers—in the sea, chiefly waters over the continental shelves and shallow banks.

Sound in water

As a medium for sound transmission, water is far superior to air. The speed of sound is 330–340 metres per second in air, but 1,400–1,550 metres per second in water, depending respectively on the atmospheric pressure and the salinity.

The world of water is, therefore, by no means silent—even if we sportfishermen often have that impression. Living above the surface, we seldom hear sounds from underwater, mainly because their waves are extinguished at the surface. Investigations with modern hydroacoustic equipment show that water can be compared with a good record library, in which fish are responsible for much of the sound production!

The water cycle

Water covers about 71% of the earth's surface, and the total volume of water on earth is estimated to be more than 1,450 million cubic kilometres. About 94% of it is in the oceans, 4% is fresh water, and 2% is in ice-fields and glaciers, only 0.001% being in the atmosphere. Most of the fresh water is involved in a perpetual circulation process driven by heat energy from the sun. This worldwide cycle has several main stages.

Water evaporates continually from the oceans. The vapour is

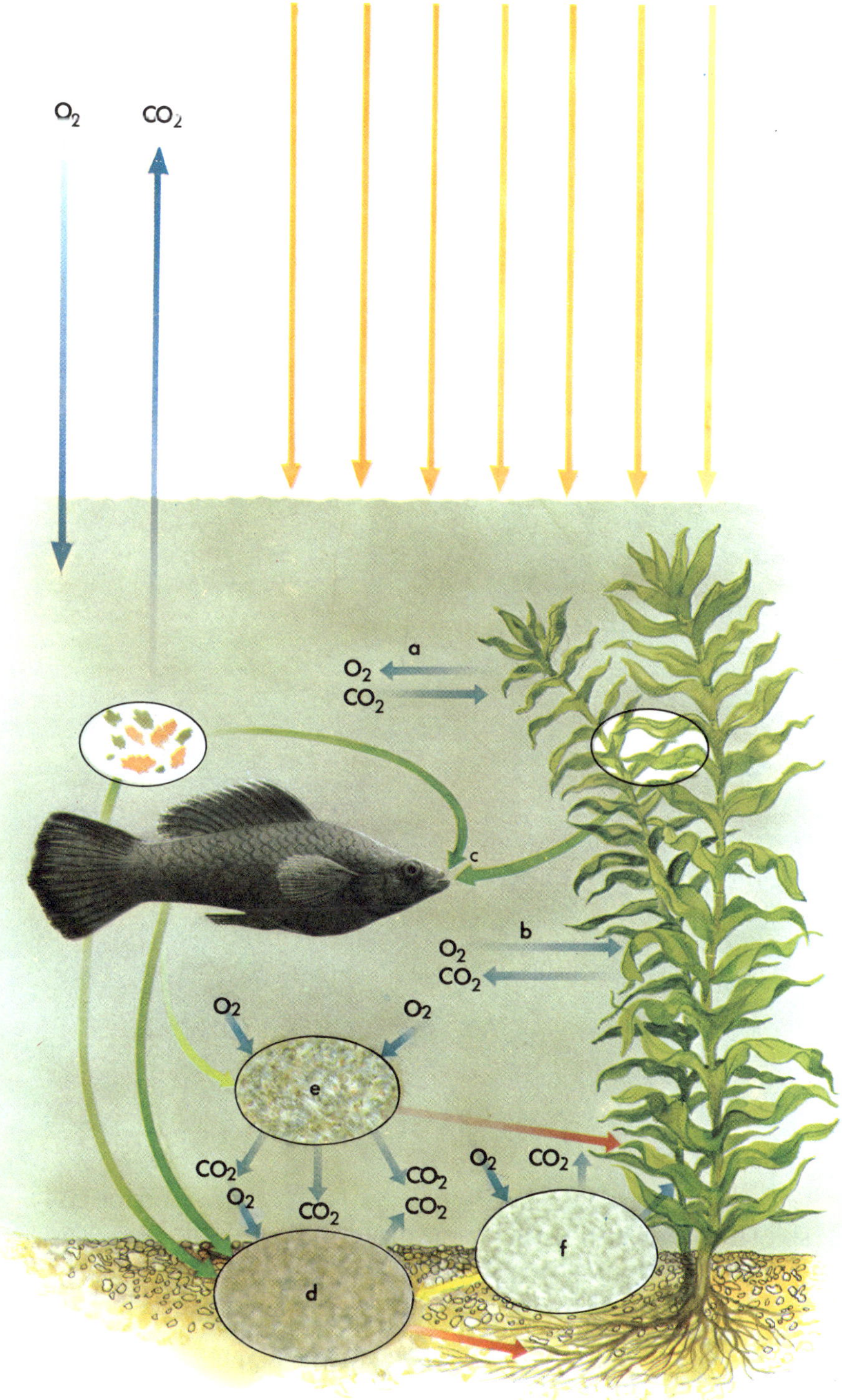

In nature there is a continuous circulation of energy and matter. In this schematic diagram of photosynthesis are shown dead organic material (green arrows) and the cycles of oxygen and carbon dioxide (blue arrows), of nitrogen compounds (yellow arrows), and of inorganic nutrients (red arrows). The many different processes must balance each other in order to create a healthy environment. Light energy causes photosynthesis in plants, absorbing carbon dioxide and giving out oxygen (*a*). Respiration is an opposite process, utilizing oxygen and producing carbon dioxide, while releasing energy (*b*). Herbivorous fish eat plant material (*c*). Excrement, urine, and dead plant parts collect in the bottom sediment and are broken down by bacteria (*d,e,f*). This breakdown uses oxygen, and gives out carbon dioxide along with the nutrients which were taken up by plant roots and leaves. Thus the circulation is completed.

carried by winds, condensed by cooling, and precipitated as rain, snow or hail. About 1 metre of water evaporates annually from the ocean surface, and 90% of it goes directly back into the sea by condensation over the surface. The rest is blown over the continents and yields a highly variable precipitation. Most of this evaporates from lakes, rivers, vegetation and the land, then returns to the sea. Of what remains on the continents, nearly all forms a run-off of water from the land to the sea, as the final stage in the circulation process.

Circulation and stratification

Besides the global water cycle, many other circulation processes and currents exist in oceans and lakes. The currents transport heat and dissolved materials, which are very important for fish and other aquatic life. Ocean currents flowing from subtropical latitudes bring warmth to vast areas of the northern Atlantic and Pacific Oceans. Vertical currents raise cool waters as well as nutrients from the depths of oceans and lakes to their surfaces.

The surface currents in both oceans and lakes are driven chiefly by the winds. Further forces behind currents are the changes in atmospheric pressure and water density, and the tidal force caused by gravitational attraction of the sun and moon. Changes in water density are due to changes in water temperature, which are greatest in the deep lakes of the temperate climatic zones. Here, as already mentioned, the water masses are thermally stratified and turned over in a seasonal cycle, between autumn and spring, as follows.

During summer, the warmer water in a lake is least dense and forms a surface layer. This stratification lasts until autumn, when the water cools down and the whole lake has an even temperature. But since water is most dense at 4°C, additional cooling in winter makes the coldest water least dense, so it forms a surface layer. The winter stratification lasts until spring, when the water is warmed from the surface and the lake's temperature evens out again.

Thus, during both its summer and winter stratifications, the lake has two relatively stable water masses, with very little exchange between them: the surface layer (epilimnion), and the bottom layer (hypolimnion) where few or no nutrients can be produced because of the weak sunlight. These are separated by the thermocline, a zone of very stable water, whose temperature may vary by up to 10°C (18°F) within a few metres of depth. This forms a barrier not only against mixture of water between the surface and bottom layers, but also against wind-driven circulation and the oxygen supply from the atmosphere to the bottom layer. During the summer stratification or "stagnation", rather serious oxygen deficiency can therefore occur, especially in highly productive lakes where much oxygen is needed for the breakdown of organic material.

In sea water, however, as its salinity increases, the temperature of maximum density decreases below 4°C. At the same time, its freezing temperature decreases slightly below 0°C. In highly saline water, these temperatures become virtually equal. As a result, when such water is homogeneous, ice cannot float, and no water freezes until the entire mass has cooled down to the freez-

All life on earth depends on the sun. Solar radiation is not only turned into nourishment of green plants, but is also the energy source for circulation of water and air throughout the world. Water warmed by the sun evaporates into the atmosphere, is transported by wind, and eventually falls as rain or snow. On land, it flows in rivers and other waterways back to the sea, where it circulates in currents until it evaporates again.

ing point. Nor does any stratification or turnover occur here as in lakes.

In brackish waters—especially those with much fresh water, like the Baltic—a surface layer with low salinity tends to stratify over a bottom layer of higher salinity. Only the surface layer takes part in the vertical circulation. Below this is the saltwater thermocline, or halocline. Water below that has little or no seasonal variation in temperature and salinity. Consequently, the water above the halocline is generally well-saturated with oxygen, while the bottom layer is often deficient in, or totally devoid of, oxygen.

Fish habitats

The kinds of environment inhabited by fish are indescribably numerous, ranging from the smallest brooks and ponds to the widest oceans. We must therefore limit them to the three main types of fish ecosystems: lakes, running waters, and seas. Between these lie many intermediate kinds of habitat which will also be omitted. Our present concern is primarily with the waters in temperate climatic zones.

The lakes

Lakes can be classified in various ways. Here we do so on the basis of their production of organic matter. Oligotrophic lakes, low in nutrients, are relatively deep and contain few organisms. Eutrophic lakes, rich in nutrients, are fairly shallow and produce abundant organic life.

What determine a lake's production are chiefly its basin, precipitation or catchment area, and climate. As a rule, the most oligotrophic lakes are located in regions of poor archaic rock, while the most eutrophic ones lie in lime-rich regions. Lakes in the populous parts of the Western world are becoming ever more eutrophic, as they gain nutrients from domestic sewage water and farmland drainage water. These increasing nutrient flows, as we shall see, are a serious threat to the salmonid fishes—although at present they somewhat favour the so-called eutrophic species, notably a number of carp (cyprionids).

Life in a lake

The animals and plants in a lake depend greatly on its nutrient state. Both their number and species may differ widely between a eutrophic and an oligotrophic lake. However, both types of lake have common biotic features.

Plankton is a vast group of small floating organisms whose movements are more or less affected by currents. This is especially true of the plant variety (phytoplankton), while some of the animal kinds (zooplankton) are active swimmers. Most of the zooplankton live in the lake's free waters, called the pelagic zone. Several of them, such as copepods and species of *Cladocera*, make vertical migrations diurnally, coming up to the surface at night and returning to the depths by day. This migration phenomenon is not yet understood, but is apparently related to sunlight. As we shall see, plankton provides an important food for almost all young fish, and the main food for a number of fish species.

Nekton are usually defined as the organisms which swim, and in particular the strongest ones which can navigate at will. So these are primarily fishes, but other animals such as crustaceans and swimming birds may be called nekton as well.

Benthos is the group of organisms attached to, or resting in, the bottom. They live in the bottom sediments or depend in other ways on the bottom for their life and their food supply. Especially in the lake's littoral zone, this environment is very diverse and often stressful, requiring different adaptations. For example, species living on steep, wind-exposed, stony bottoms must be able to resist mechanical pressure. They frequently have a rather flat body, and sometimes have claws, suckers, or friction-pads, just as do many animals in running water. By contrast, the species living in a calm bay with a bottom of clay or mud can be relatively fragile. They need only take up enough oxygen to survive the oxygen deficiency which commonly occurs there. This protected environment has generally high primary production of plants by photosynthesis. Its benthic species are often numerous, including worms, mollusks, crustaceans, and insects in various stages of development.

The littoral zone of a lake is the richest in species, despite its diverse habitats. As one moves out to increasing depth of water, the species become fewer because the environment is more strenuous, although they tend to have more individuals since there is less competition between species.

In a eutrophic lake, benthic plants mainly form the rooted vegetation of the littoral zone. The shallow waters near the shore are inhabited by heliophytes—plants with long stems which stretch their upper parts over the surface. Outside these are rooted plants with floating leaves, whose flowers do not stretch over the surface. And beyond those are submergent rooted plants, living completely underwater. This deep vegetation is usually the least developed in eutrophic lakes, but the most important in oligotrophic lakes.

Food chains in a lake

The primary producers in lakes are green plants. Enabled by their chlorophyll to create nutrients through photosynthesis from solar energy, carbon dioxide and water, they are self-feeding in a sense, but still depend on external supplies. Above all, they need bacteria to break down dead material, providing them mainly with nitrates. Thus, strictly speaking, bacteria should be regarded as the basis of the "web" of food chains in lakes.

The food chains in a temperate lake. Such chains need not be straight from the primary consumers to final consumers. Interrelated with each other, they often form a complicated food web in the environment.

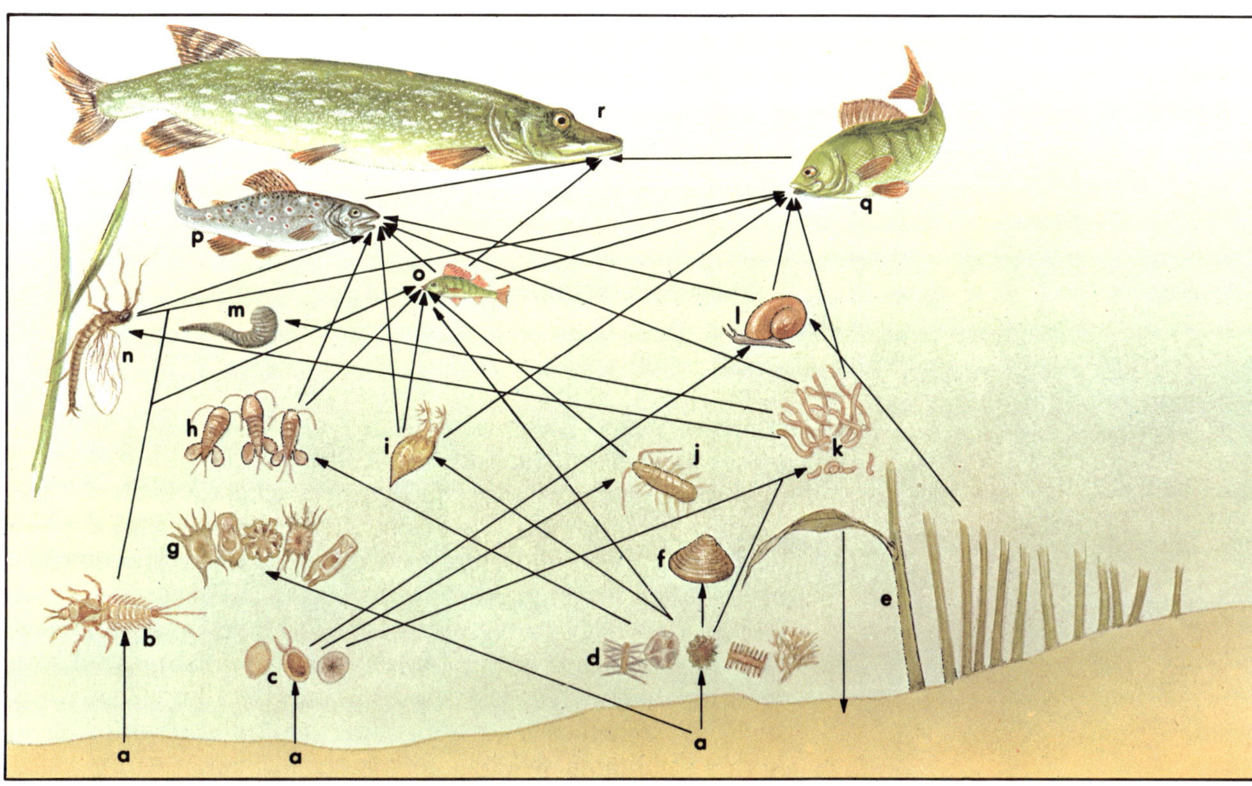

a detritus
b mayfly larva
c benthic algae
d phytoplankton
e riparian plants
f mussel
g rotifers
h *Cyclops*
i water flea
j water louse
k bloodworms
l freshwater winkle
m horseleech
n mayfly
o perch fry
p trout
q perch
r pike

Green plants are the first stage in this web. Next come plant-eating animals, the primary consumers. These have to choose between living and dead plant materials. How much of each they consume is largely unknown to us. Bottom-living herbivores, at depths so great that sunlight is too weak for green plant growth, certainly must eat dead material that washes or falls downward. Probably this is also the chief diet of herbivores in the shore zone.

The third stage in the food web consists of carnivorous animals which eat the herbivores. They may be eaten by other animals—primarily fish—as a fourth stage, and so on. Any simple sequence of organisms on these different stages is a food chain, but most animals have a varied diet including several food chains, so the chains are interwoven in what is often a very complex food web. This can also change with time: for example, most fish eat zooplankton when young, and later turn to bottom-dwellers, while some species like carp may eat plants in adult life.

Where are the fish in a lake?

Fish inhabit nearly all of the habitats or biotopes in a lake. Their species and individuals tend, however, to be most numerous in the littoral zone. Of course, plankton-eaters such as whitefish, feeding mainly in pelagic waters, are much less bound to the littoral zone than, for instance, trout which find their chief food there.

Shown here is a "fictitious" lake, marked with sure-fire fishing spots: (*a*) stream and river inlets, (*b*) marsh edges, (*c*) points of land, (*d*) stream and river outlets, (*e*) tree overhangs, (*f*) sunken rocks.

As in the sea, many factors influence the locations of fish in a lake. Frequently important is the water temperature. This makes a fish like pike, relatively adjusted to cold water, stay on shallow bottoms in spring and autumn, but move to deeper and cooler water in summer. Conversely, perch love warmth and head for the areas or layers that have the highest temperature in every season, often even if the difference is just a few tenths of a degree.

As stated, trout are primarily adapted to the littoral zone. And we can be sure of finding them there almost throughout the year, as long as we do not define the inshore region too narrowly.

Running waters

Depending on their sizes and amounts of flow, running waters are described as brooks, creeks, or rivers. In terms of the speed of flow, their different parts may be classified as pools, rapids, waterfalls and so on. A pool is a section of more or less standing water between rapids or streams. We also speak of the neck of a rapid or waterfall—meaning the upper part—and of its foot, the lowermost part.

The land drained by a river is called the *drainage area*. *Watersheds* are heights which divide different drainage ages. The amount of water flowing per unit time through a cross-section of a watercourse is known as the *discharge*. This is commonly measured in cubic metres (thousands of litres) per second. The discharge per unit of the drainage area is called the *drainage*, commonly measured in litres per second per square kilometre. The *water-level* is the height of the water surface in relation to a certain basic level, and can be read on an instrument graduated in centimetres.

Life in running water

In lakes, as mentioned above, zooplankton provides the main primary production. But running waters tend to be very unfavourable environments for these floating organisms. The plankton found here have usually been washed out from lakes and slow-moving (lentic) waters.

In running water the green plants are mostly mosses, lichens and algae, covering the stones on the bottom. Only in slow-moving parts of a brook or river are there any higher aquatic plants of importance to primary production. Yet this production can be surprisingly great, indeed among the greatest known in any ecosystem. The reason is that running water constantly brings substances which are needed by organisms and removes their waste products. Such effective turnover allows organisms to produce far more than their numbers would suggest.

However, running waters are extreme and stressful environments, often forcing organisms to adapt. The flattened bodies and hooks which enable insect larvae to hold onto rough surfaces of stones, are even more essential here than, as we have seen, they are on steep lake shores. Many insect larvae in streams, such as stoneflies and sedgeflies, typically have flattened bodies—although whether this is an adaptation to the water

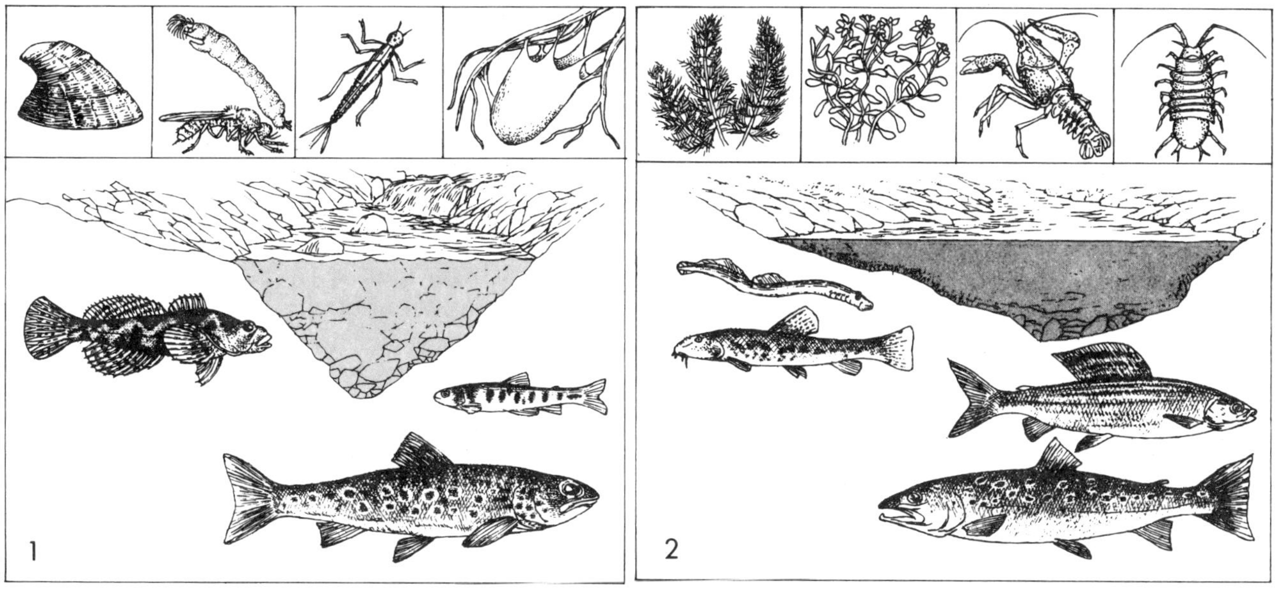

A temperate river begins high up in the mountains and runs into the sea, where fresh and salt waters merge. (1) The source water, cold and oxygen-rich, flows down in an often rocky furrow. The animal life is adapted to these surroundings—swimming well like the salmon and trout, making good use of calm waters as the bullhead does, and so on. Smaller bottom-dwellers hold onto rocks with their diverse organs for gripping. (2) Farther down, the current weakens in deeper water, which still has plenty of oxygen, over a bottom of stones with patches of sand or gravel. The species are more varied here than upstream.

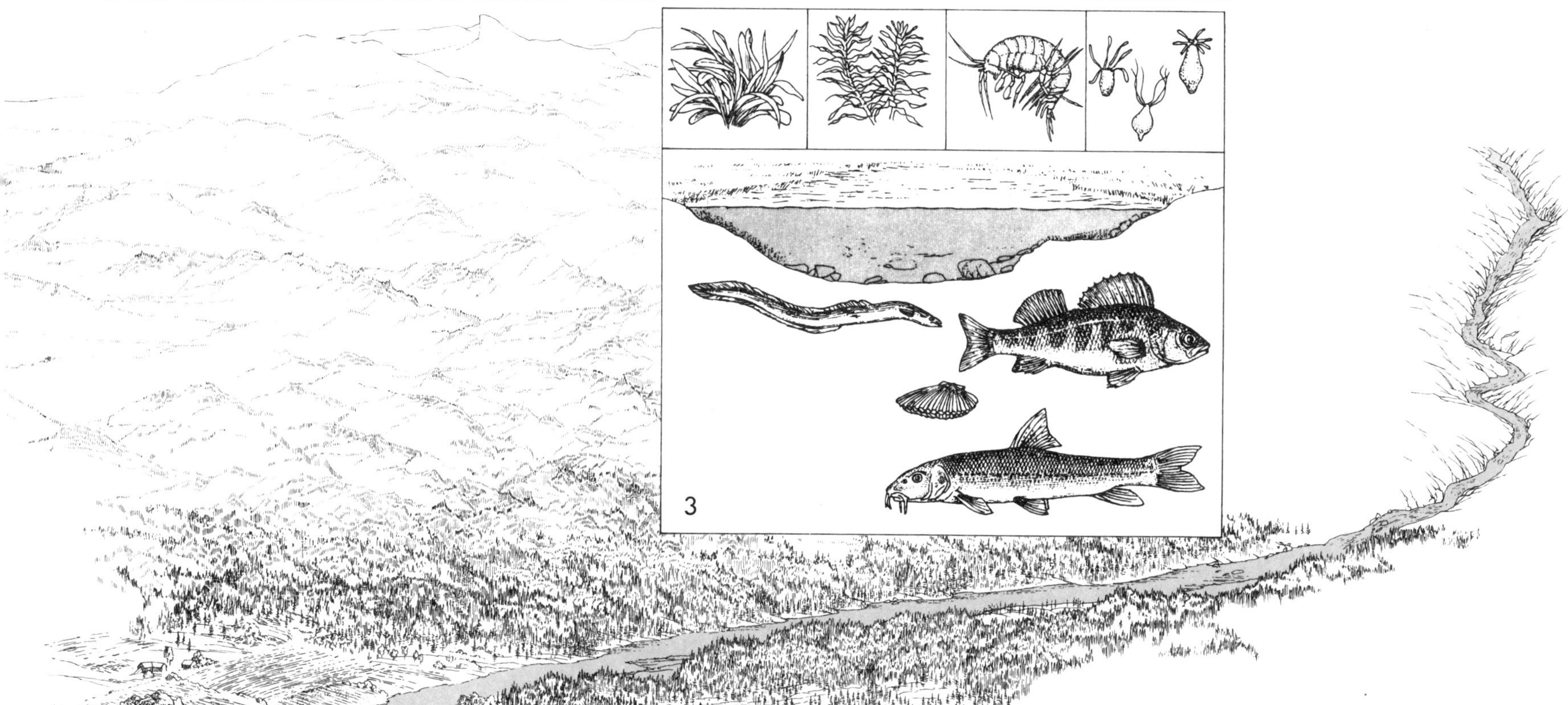

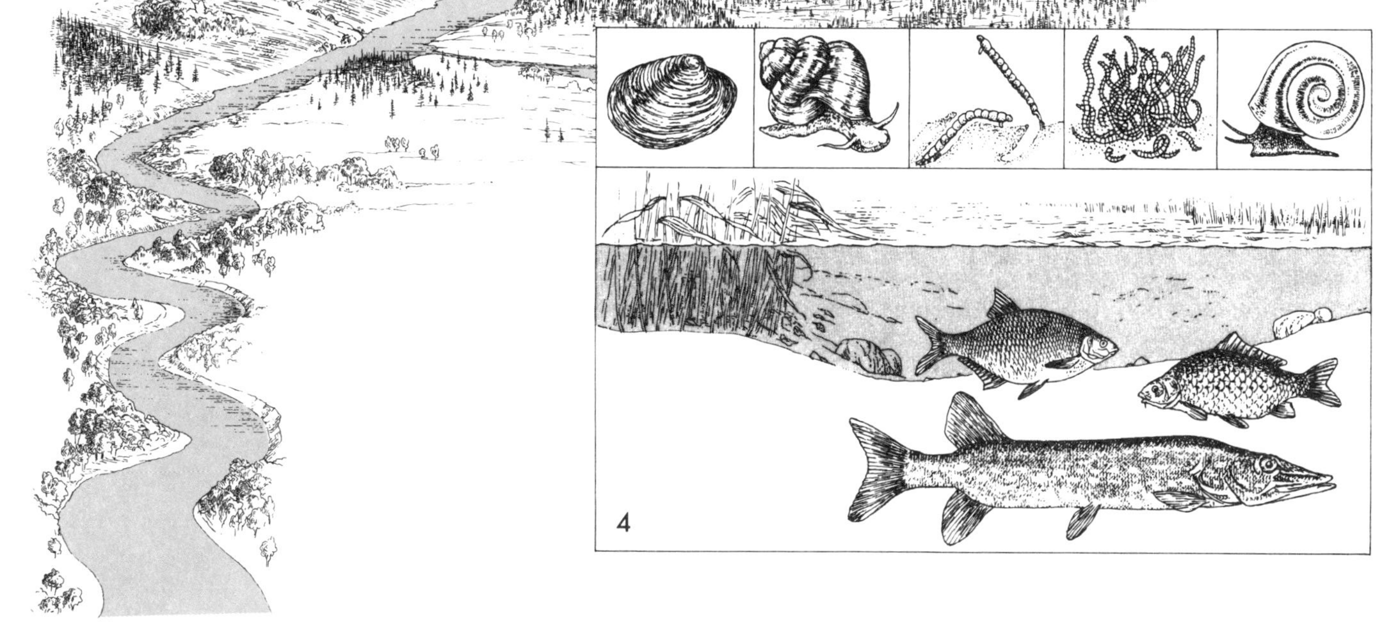

(3) In the lower midriver regions, the bottom is mainly of sand and gravel, while the current is usually much weaker. Perch and eel are among the common fish species here. (4) The river's lowest reaches are rather like a pond, with turbid water flowing slowly over a muddy bottom. Reeds and other rooted plants line the shores. Vegetable and animal species abound. Most of the fish are slow and have a high body profile, such as carp and—the commonest fish predator here—pike.

pressure, or to the need of creeping into crevices for protection from the current, is uncertain.

Among other adaptations of animals in running water to avoid being pulled off by fast currents, the protruding parts of the body are reduced in size by, for example, some mayfly larvae. Several species of articulated animals hold on by means of a silk-secretion produced in their salivary glands. The risks of being washed away can also be lowered by a weight or load: thus some sedge larvae make "houses" with sand and grains of gravel. Fish, too, are adapted to the high pressure in running water, and the species living in fast currents usually have the most streamlined bodies.

Organic drift

The living or dead organic material carried by running water is known as organic drift. This is a mixture of insects and larvae which have fallen onto the surface, plankton washed out from lakes, animals pulled off the bottoms, and so on. Organic drift is consumed partly by a kind of benthic organism called *filtrators*. These gather food from the drift fauna by using various catching devices, which are rather simple in some species, but may be quite complicated—such as nets with meshes so tiny that they can even catch bacteria!

The greatest organic drift usually comes from lakes and other slow-moving waters. They also tend to have the most filtrators. In turn, there follows a rich fauna of predatory animals which live on the filtrators. Thus the drift, filtrators, and predators "cooperate" by forming a food chain, as efficient as a factory. Particles of water-borne nourishment, as a rule too small to interest fish, are parcelled into the filtrators—and when these lose their grip on the bottom, they are packaged into the predators.

Since this process occurs mainly below lakes, their outlets are highly productive parts of running waters, and popular places for fish as well as fishermen. In fact, many stream-living fishes use the drift in much the same way as the filtrators do. Instead of hunting for prey, they choose a strategic spot in the flow and take whatever comes along. This behaviour is typical, for instance, of young salmon and river trout, of rainbow and brook trout, and to a certain degree of grayling and char in running water.

Fish habitats in running water

Most kinds of fish that live in fresh water can be found in running water. Many freshwater species alternate between lakes and running water. Moreover, all such fish are territorial.

A number of fish inhabiting fast (lotic) waters are anatomically adapted to the flow. Frequently they have more or less streamlined bodies. Salmonids like trout and grayling are adapted to relatively fast currents in this and other ways, although the grayling generally prefers somewhat slower water than the trout, which also resembles salmon in this respect. Several species, however, are bound to the bottom and often seek cover behind or under stones, as do bullheads and sheat-fishes (*Silurus*). Carpfishes (cyprionids) and pike tend to live in the slower parts of brooks or rivers.

The habitats of fish in running water do not obey any other strict rules, since the species and their adaptations create enormous variation. Here we have chosen to show the probable stands of trout in a river with sections of differing water speed.

This imaginary stretch of current shows normal places of fish stock: (*a*) deep pool, (*b*) small rapids in surface pool, (*c*) surface pool, (*d*) deep rapids in surface pool, (*e*) shallow chalkstream, (*f*) calm neck of the pool.

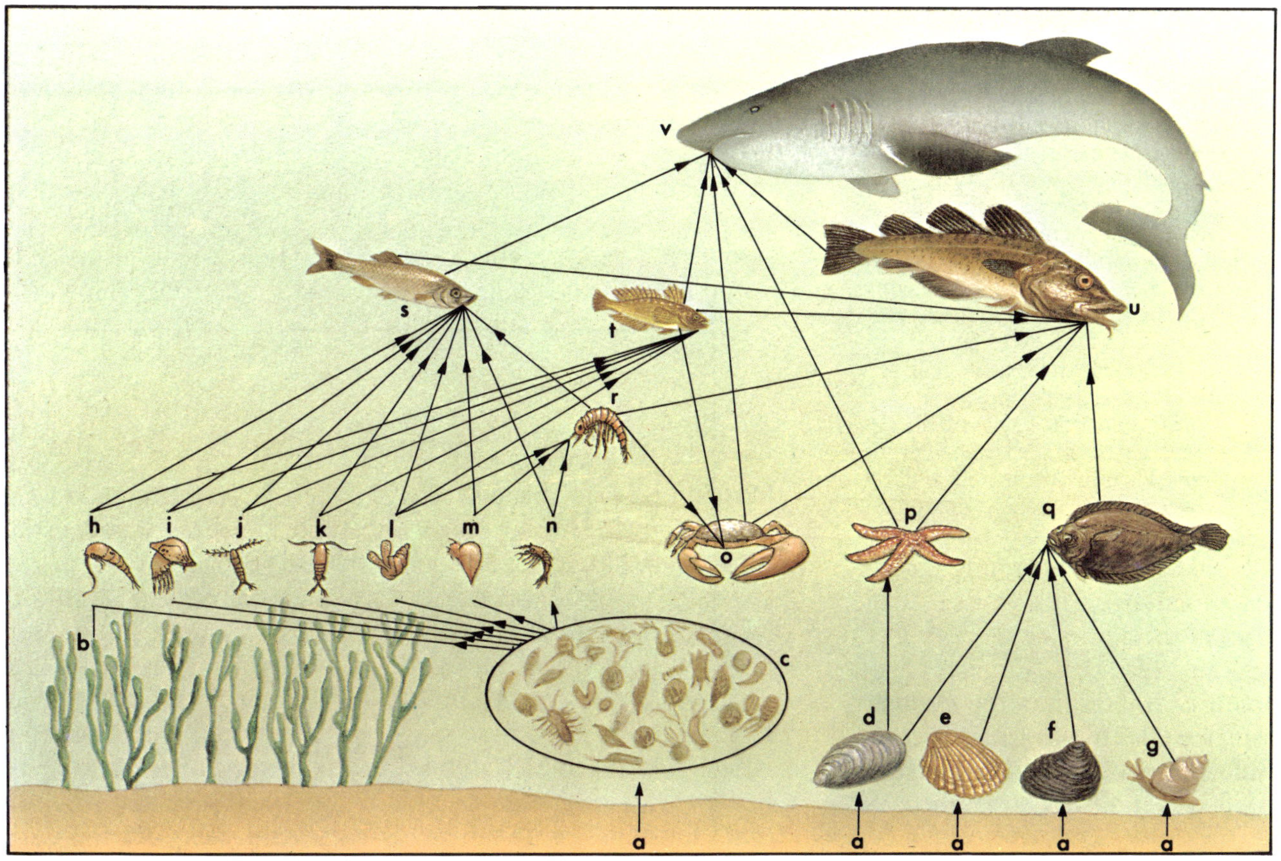

a detritus
b kelp, sea grasses
c phytoplankton
d blue mussel
e cockle
f mussel
g *Hydrobia*
h-n zooplankton
o crab
p starfish
q flatfish
r shrimp
s herring
t goby
u cod
v shark

Food chains in the sea resemble those of inland lakes, but depend more directly on photosynthesis by plants. Here too, many food chains are interwoven and form a complex food web. Zooplankton are very important for nutrition; the copepod *Calanus finmarchicus* is even regarded as one of the world's principal food animals.

The sea

Due to the extent of the world's oceans, and their average depth of about 3,800 metres, marine organisms have far more living space than do the terrestrial ones in what is usually a limited inhabitable area. Yet the seas are comparatively poor in species of life. They contain only around 160,000 of the million known animal species on earth. Two thirds of the latter are now insects, which hardly exist in the sea.

As in lakes, the sea is divided into different zones. Its pelagic zone of open water actually consists of two zones or regions. The *neretic* (near-shore) zone, corresponding roughly to the littoral zone in lakes, includes waters over the continental shelves out to a depth of about 200 metres, beyond which lies the *oceanic* zone. The greatest environmental variations are found in the neretic zone—shores, beds of seaweed, estuaries, banks, the coral reefs of southern seas, and so on—as well as the greatest numbers of species and individuals, not least of fish.

Marine life

Animals and plants that live entirely in the pelagic zone are described by marine biologists as *holopelagic*. Among them are about 200 species of animals and practically all microscopic algae. Organisms that mainly inhabit the pelagic zone, but are bound to the bottoms in benthic zones during certain phases of their lives, are called *meropelagic*. These include some 1,000 animal species, such as most jellyfish.

Between the meropelagic animals and the true *benthic* animals are many transitory forms. For instance, herring live pelagically as adults, but their eggs hatch on the bottom. Cod hatch eggs in the pelagic waters, but begin benthic life as adults. Even plaice and other flatfish develop initially in the pelagic zone. Indeed, it is there that most of the marine benthic animals have their larval stage.

Marine organisms are divided into plankton and nekton, as in lakes. Phytoplankton (planktonic algae) are responsible for nearly all primary production in the sea. The most important kinds of phytoplankton, besides diatoms, are dinoflagellates. These are also familiar in lakes, and provide one of the chief particle foods for copepods, which in turn are the staple food of herring. Dinoflagellates are notorious for their appearance in vast quantities, especially in tropical seas, where their red-brown shells colour huge areas of water and form a "red tide".

To the sea's main zooplankton belong copepods such as the species *Calanus finmarchicus*. This is perhaps the leading animal nutrient on earth, and it lives in almost all oceans, from the

The varied habitats along this coast are a result of wind and water movements. Three main habitats can be recognized: (1) A rocky shore, most exposed to waves, consists of cliffs and boulders and gravel. It has diverse niches for plants, animals and fish, depending on the water depth. (2) On shallow beaches continually influenced by the tide, animal life must be adapted to the extreme conditions which can occur with long dry periods or offshore winds. (3) Farther in, near a river mouth, the environment is more protected, and beaches often consist of sand or clay with scattered stones.

surface down to about 3,000 metres. In addition, the euphausids—or krill—are virtually unsurpassed at filtering microscopic algae, and thus have immense value for marine food production. The nekton in the sea consists of fish, cuttlefish (cephalopods or octopi), mammals and birds.

While the pelagic marine animals number only some 3,000 species, there are about 150,000 species of benthic creatures, which live mainly in the neretic zone at depths less than 200 metres. The Arctic and Antarctic seas are much poorer in species than the tropical seas. Such distribution of species is largely dependent on the temperature, which itself depends on the latitude and the great ocean currents.

Fish habitats in the sea

Marine organisms seem to have an almost boundless adaptability to their environments. Fish exist at almost all depths, although the numbers of species and individuals are greatest in neretic waters. This zone offers them a wide range of choice from shore regions, seaweed beds, and estuaries to offshore banks. The specific habitats of marine fish depend, for example, on the water depth, salinity, current, and the bottom material (substrate). Most obvious are cases like the flatfish, whose body shape is adapted to the bottoms where they live—or the mackerel and tuna, which are built for high speed with torpedo-shaped bodies, and swim freely down to great depths. Generally the habitats of the neretic zone can be divided into waters within, and waters beyond, the islands or skerries that lie off a coast. Some typical habitats in the former region are shown by the accompanying illustration.

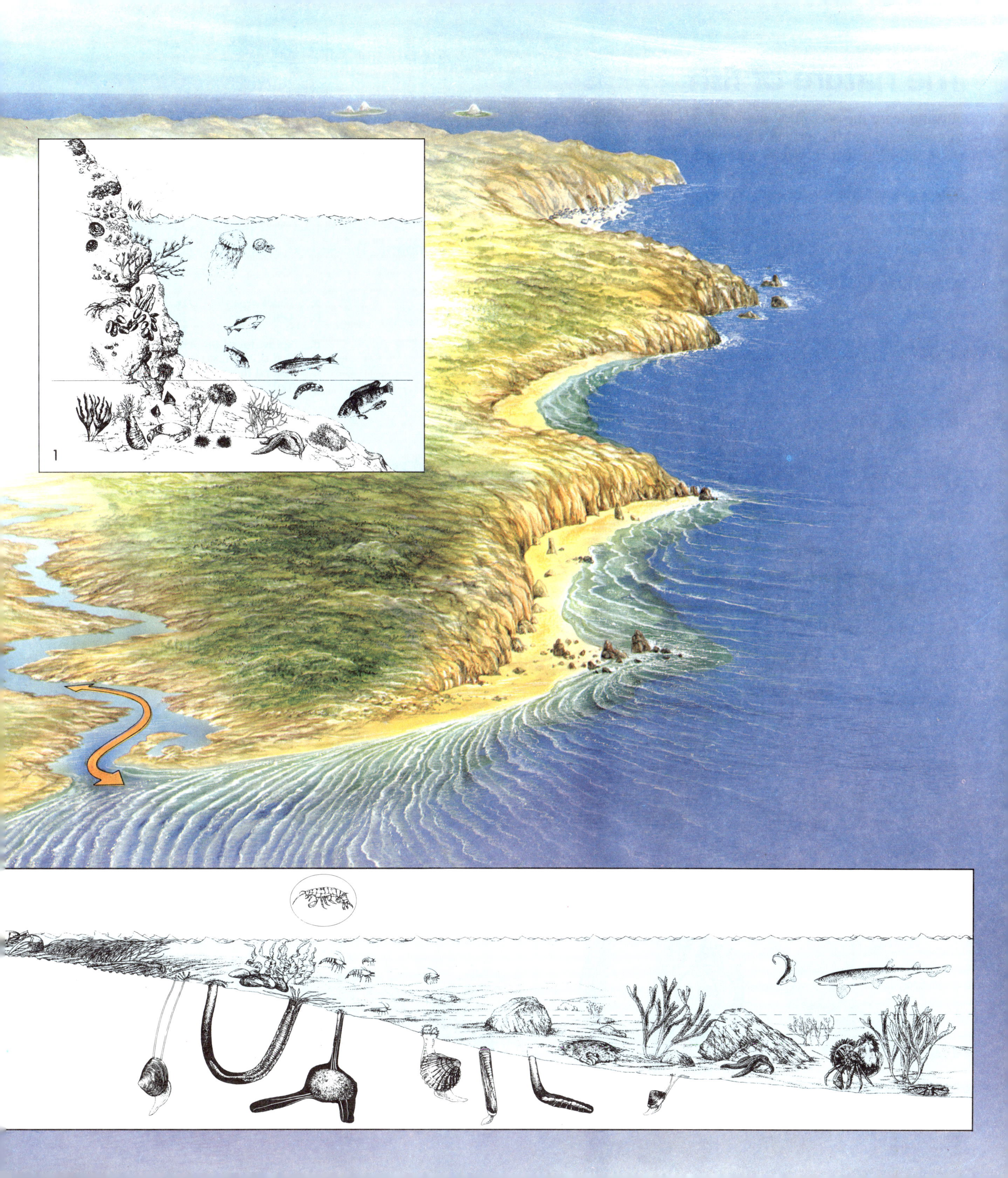
1

The nature of fish

Turning from the biotopic surroundings of fish to the animals themselves, a sportfisherman also needs to understand many aspects of their structure, senses, and behaviour. These have a very long history. When the first fish appeared on earth about 500 million years ago, they were something quite new in the animal world, a daring experiment of Mother Nature. They were the first organisms with bony parts inside their bodies, and are therefore the oldest vertebrates. Although rather low on the vertebrate scale in terms of complexity, they can thus be called high on the animal scale as a whole.

A fish may be defined briefly as a water-living vertebrate with fins and with respiration by means of gills. We thus leave aside some fishes which have no visible fins or respire through lungs. There are three main categories of fish: cyclostomes, cartilaginous fishes, and bony fishes. The first are very primitive, including lampreys. The second are also an old group, such as

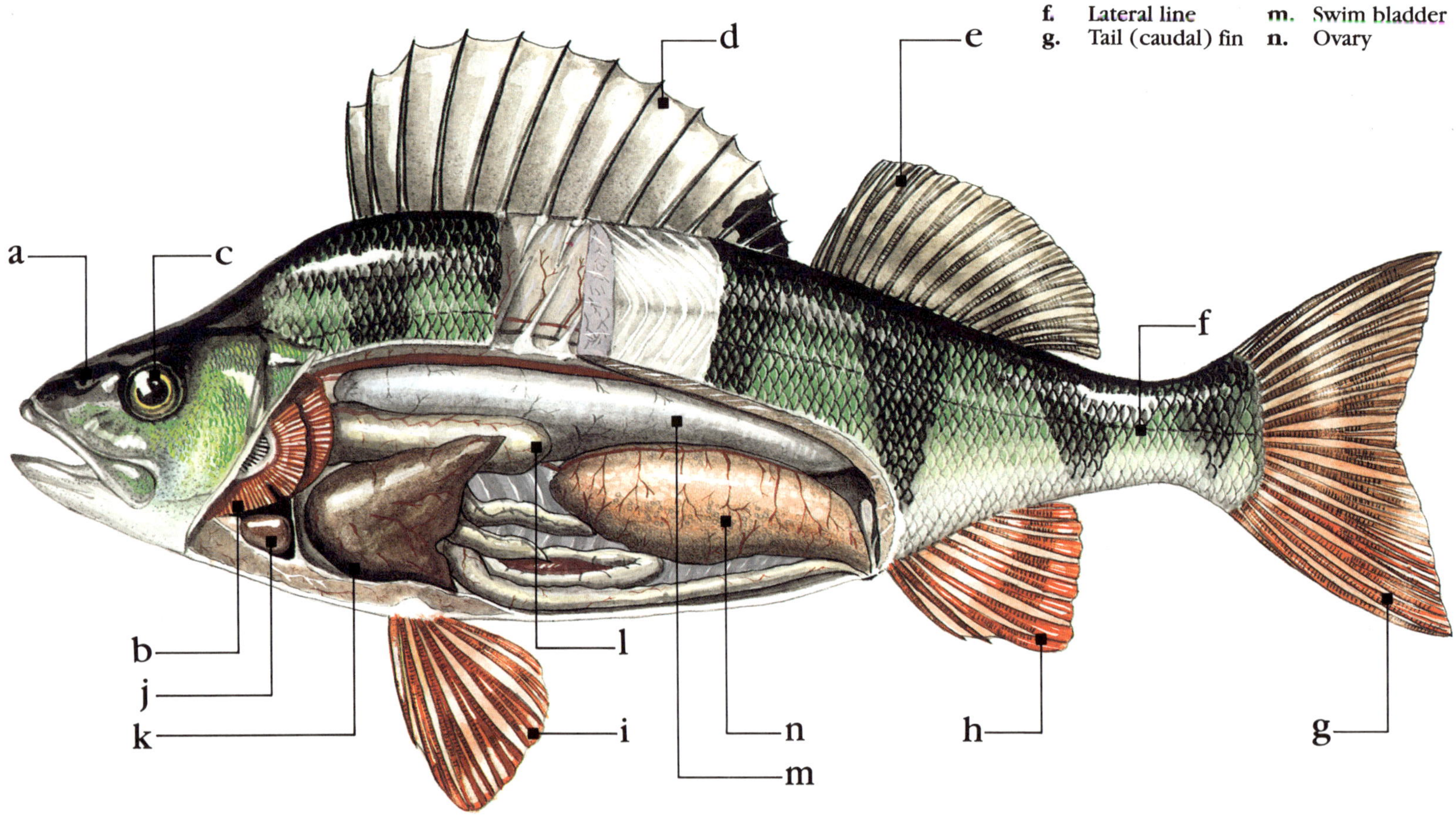

a. Nasal organ
b. Gill
c. Eye
d. Spiny dorsal fin
e. Soft dorsal fin
f. Lateral line
g. Tail (caudal) fin
h. Anal fin
i. Pelvic fin
j. Heart
k. Liver
l. Stomach
m. Swim bladder
n. Ovary

Gill

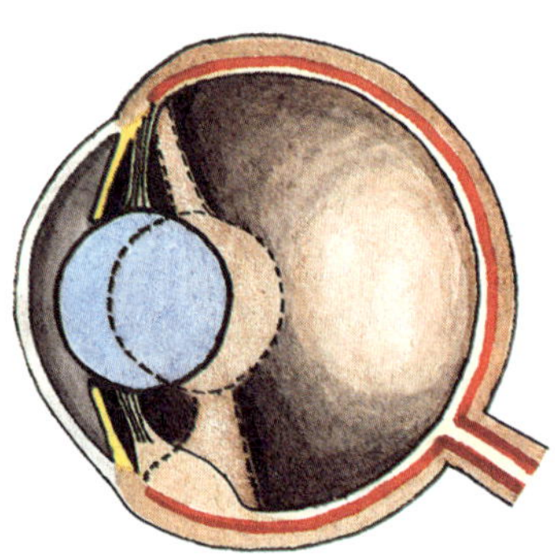

Eye

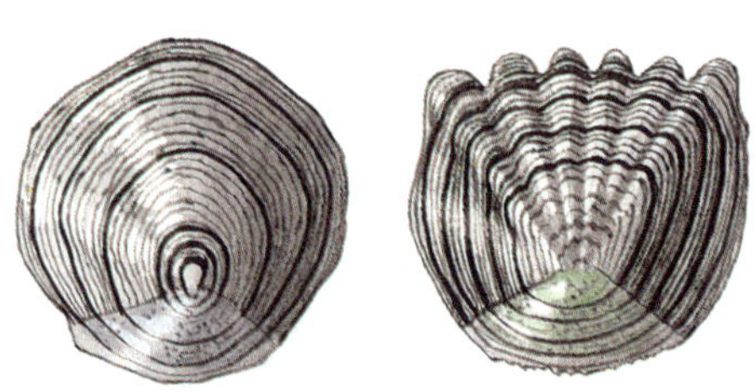

Cycloid scale and ctenoid scale

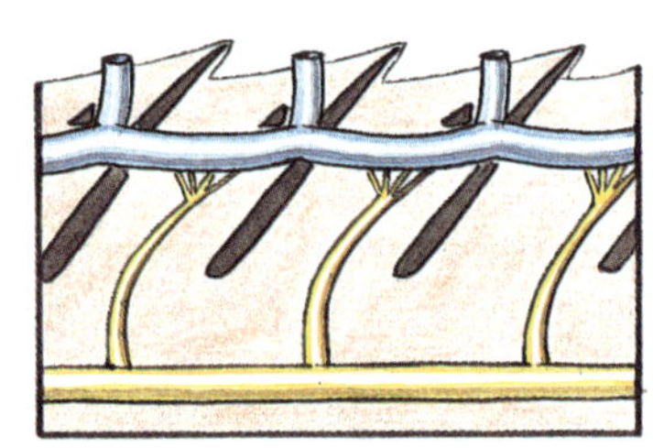

Structure of lateral line

sharks and rays. Today, however, ninety percent of the world's fishes are bony.

A fish's structure

The appearance of fish is extremely diverse, and some species do not really look like fish. Still, they are all variations of a simple "basic model" which is best seen in a typical bony fish.

The fins are the exterior part of the body which, perhaps more than any other, characterizes "real" fishes. They consist of folds of skin, stretched on a network of fin rays, which may be soft and branched (soft rays) or stiff (spine rays). These are usually articulated at the base and fastened on muscles, so that they can be turned down or spread out according to need. The dorsal fins, anal fin, and tail (caudal) fin are unpaired—but the pectoral and pelvic fins are paired, corresponding to the front and hind legs of a higher vertebrate. The epidermis, a fish's uppermost body cover, is almost entirely of living material, unlike that of mammals. Thin and transparent, it secretes a slimy mucus which gives less friction in water and protects against bacteria and parasites. A sportfisherman, therefore, should never damage this mucus by putting dry hands on a fish that will be returned to the water.

Under the epidermis lie the scales, which are ossifications in the cutis. Some fishes, such as perches, have cogged and striped (cosmoid) scales, whereas salmonid fishes have smooth and uncogged (ganoid) scales. The scales grow at the same rate as the fish does, with new layers forming at the periphery of old ones. The resultant growth zones, or annual rings, can reveal much about the fish's life history and, for many species, they can be used to determine its age.

As is well known, many fishes are silvery at the sides. This lustre is caused by light reflection from a substance called guanin, released from the backsides of the scales and from special colour cells in the cutis. There are thousands of these "chromatophore" cells in a fish's skin. Each has its own pigment—red, orange, yellow or black—and the fish can change colour by spreading out or concentrating the pigment. Numerous fishes also develop spawning colours which come from other pigments.

The skeleton of a fish includes its cranium, spine, and all the bones that make its body and fins stable. The cranium combines the brain-pan with the mouth and gill parts, while mobile skeleton-bows are attached to the underside of the brain-pan. The spine gives stability to the bones in the unpaired fins, but the paired fins have their own bones attached loosely to the shoulder bones.

In a fish, contrary to mammals, the teeth lie not only in the jaws but also in the roof of the mouth cavity. All these teeth tend to be long and sharp, often awl-like, since their purpose is just to hold the food until it is swallowed. This is an adaptation to gill-respiration since, if they were used to chew food, the fish could be choked. Some species also have teeth on the tongue. Plant-eating fish have broad, flat throat-teeth for grinding food.

The gills consist of thin-skinned, blood-rich filaments supported on stiff arches. On the arches' sides facing the mouth cavity are the so-called gill rakers, a filtering mechanism for collecting small food particles. The gill rakers are highly developed in species that eat mainly plankton, such as herring, whitefish, some chars and other filter-feeders.

A swim-bladder does not exist in cartilaginous fishes, but all bony fishes have at least a rudimentary one. In herring and salmonoids, it is an "open" swim-bladder, connected with the foregut by a narrow duct. But in cod and perch, for example, this connection degenerates after the fish hatches, resulting in a closed swim-bladder. It then holds an amount of air which is controlled by special gas-glands that secrete gases into it. The swim-bladder serves partly as a hydrostatic organ, adapting the fish to the water pressure. Fish with a closed swim-bladder are usually the most sensitive to variations in water pressure. Many fish have a special connection between the ear and the swim-bladder, which thus also functions as a kind of hearing aid. Some species even use it to produce sounds.

The senses

A fish's brain is an enlargement of the anterior end of the spinal cord. It consists of the forebrain, midbrain, and cerebellum. The forebrain receives the nervous impulses from the olfactory (smelling) organ. This is a pair of pits in the nasal area, connected not with the mouth cavity but—in most fish—to the outer skin through two openings. The sheat-fish, or wels, has smelling organs at its tail as well, since it lives on dark and muddy bottoms where visibility is poor.

Fish have taste-buds on the tongue, as we do, yet this is not their only taste-organ. Similar organs exist in the barbels of fish such as most cod, and on the bellies of, for instance, cod and carp.

The main purpose of smell for a fish, like terrestrial animals, is to detect food at a distance—and probably also enemies or companions. Taste is primarily used to investigate the quality of food. In water, however, all the substances causing sensations of smell and taste are dissolved, making it hard to distinguish the two. Nonetheless, these senses are clearly well-developed in many fish. For several of the salmonoids, smell must be quite important for orientation, and we know that most fish can distinguish between sweet, salty, sour, and bitter tastes. Among the real specialists in smelling is the eel, which has been proven able to detect even a few molecules of a smelling substance.

The midbrain is the centre of vision in a fish. As mentioned earlier, sight is restricted differently in water than in air. Even in the clearest waters, it is impossible to see very far, and the eyes of fish are not adapted to do so. When at rest, they are accommodated for near vision. To see at a distance, their lenses must be drawn back by a special muscle, and cannot change shape like those of humans.

Due to the location of its eyes, a fish's binocular vision—ability to see objects with both eyes—is limited to a narrow field in front of it. Consequently, fishermen must try to place their baits and flies there in order to have the best chance of getting a bite. The refraction of light at the water surface has two crucial effects on a fish's ability to see out of the water. First, objects above the water

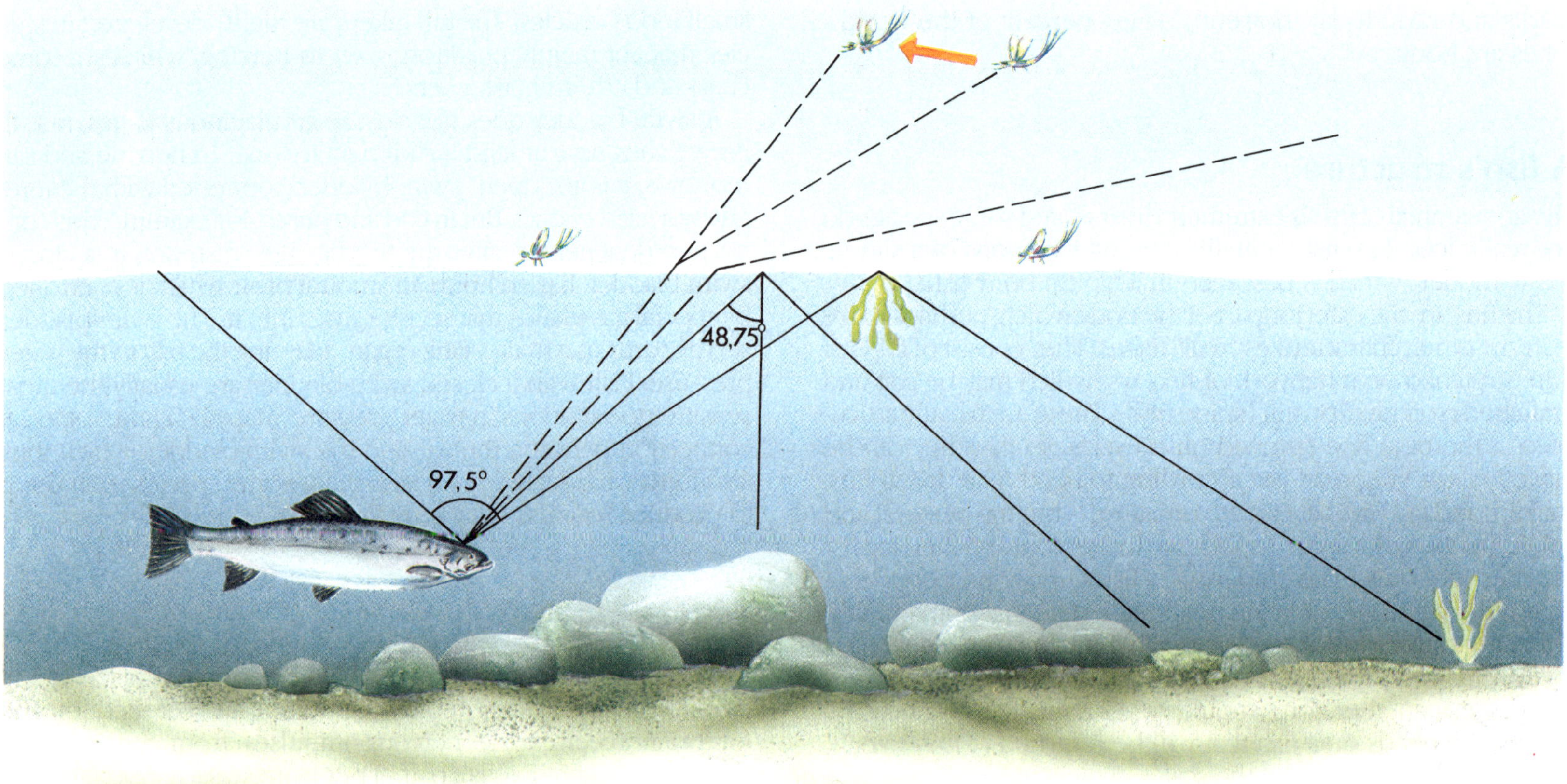

An object on or above the water surface looks different to people than to fish, which see it as higher up than it actually is. The fish's field or "window" of vision is like an inverted cone with a tip angle of about 98 degrees.

appear to be higher up than they actually are. Secondly, they are all compressed into a cone-shaped field of light, with an angle of about 98 degrees where the apex reaches the fish. So the fish sees them as if through a round window in the rest of the surface, which simply reflects the underwater world like a mirror. In particular, when the fish tries to see along the upper surface, it thus gets a faint and distorted picture which may be blurred by reflections. This fact explains the old belief of fishermen that there is a "dead angle" near the surface, preventing fish from seeing a man who stands low enough on the shore. Yet in spite of these restrictions, sight is the main sense of many fish. Several species have excellent vision, and a number possess well-developed colour vision which, indeed, may be very important for those living in a bright environment.

The cerebellum coordinates a fish's muscular movements, as well as impressions from its inner ears (labyrinth) and its lateral-line organ. Since fish have no external ear, auditory meatus, or middle ear, they were long thought to be virtually deaf. But we now know that many fish hear quite well, especially those having a connection between the inner ear and the swim-bladder, which can amplify sounds underwater. Although most fish lack this connection and can probably hear only low-frequency sounds, these are the dominant sounds in water.

The lateral line has been regarded as a mysterious organ of fish. In most species, it is a rather clearly marked line in the epidermis, running from behind the head to the base of the caudal fin, often continuing onto that fin. This is the external part of a mucus-filled canal beneath the skin, opening outward at intervals in pores that pass through or between the scales. Inside the canal is a series of sensors, connected to a nerve that runs under it. Recent studies suggest that this organ works like an echo-sounder for long-distance "touch" sensations. It registers vibrations of very low frequency, caused by animals' movements and reflected against other objects in the water. The organ's main purpose may thus be to warn the fish against enemies or obstacles, especially in the dark when it cannot see.

In this context, a fish's ability to feel pain is also significant, not least as regards the ethics of sportfishing. We hook and play our fish for fun. Naturally we are encouraged by the fact that a pike or perch, having been damaged by the hook but escaped back into the water, may strike again at the next cast. Yet this hardly means that it has not suffered. Otherwise fish would never have learned to survive in the struggle for existence. Even if its smaller, simpler brain makes a fish less sensitive to pain than higher vertebrates, there are many indications that different fishes have a varying sensitivity to pain. Apparently, too, stress and excitement can reduce this sensitivity. But in any case, we sportfishermen must always avoid playing a fish longer than necessary, and should immediately kill the ones we plan to keep.

Registration of pain is probably the main purpose of the touch papillae which are spread all over the skin surface of a fish, not unlike our own skin. Thus fish have direct organs of touch, in addition to their long-distance lateral-line organ as noticed above. Touch is, indeed, the most fundamental sense of animals. Ability to feel the temperature of the surrounding water is obviously important for a fish. It gives the fish a chance to escape from unfavourable or dangerous conditions of heat or cold. This sense is also essential to the spawning process, migrations, and other aspects of the fish's life cycle. It is highly developed in many species, and some can register variations of only a few hundredths of a degree, if these occur fast enough. We know little about where and how the temperature sense functions in a fish, but the touch papillae must partly serve this purpose. The lateral-line organ and taste organs may be involved as well.

Digestion, respiration, and excretion

A fish's teeth have the primary purpose of holding prey. While herbivorous fish do grind plants with their pharyngeal teeth, the food is not chewed but usually swallowed whole. Fish have no salivary glands, so the food is digested in the alimentary canal, stomach, and intestine. The length of the intestine in fish is mainly adapted to their diet, being usually short in prey-hunters and long in plant-eaters. As for the other digestive organs, fish—like higher vertebrates—have a liver, gall bladder, pancreas, thyroid gland and thymus.

The gills serve the same function as the lungs of land-living animals, bringing oxygen into the body and releasing carbon dioxide. In many saltwater fish, the gills are also secretory organs for getting rid of excess salt. But most of this secretion passes out with the urine through the kidneys, which also regulate the water balance and, in part, the salt balance.

Reproduction, growth, and age

Among the cartilaginous fish, several species are viviparous: the eggs are fertilized in the oviduct, and the fetus develops mainly or entirely in the female's body. In sharks, fertilization occurs when the male places sperm in the female's genital opening with his ventral fins which, at spawning time, are changed into copulation organs.

Most species, however, have external fertilization. The female lays eggs (roe) in the open water or on the bottom, where they come into contact with sperm released by the male. Many fish, notably marine species, spread their eggs and sperm rather randomly, so that fertilization is often accidental. Their large numbers of eggs, though, normally ensure that the population is maintained.

Salmonids and many other species have a very practical spawning behaviour. The female digs a pit with her fins to lay the eggs in, and the male releases sperm over them at the same time. Then the eggs are covered by a layer of sand or gravel. This greatly increases the chances of fertilization, so the female lays comparatively few eggs. In general, the number of eggs (fecundity) is related to the chances that the eggs will be fertilized and that the fry and young fish will survive. The smaller the eggs are, and the less "care" is given to them and the fry, the more eggs are laid—and conversely.

The age of maturity in fish is very diverse. In salmonids, it is often 2–5 years. Eels mature only at 10–14 years. In temperate climates, fish usually spawn just once a year, and during a particular season. Some fish, such as the Pacific species of salmon, spawn once in their lifetime: they all die after the first spawning.

Before hatching, the fetus is nourished by the yolk-sac. This contains the remains of the egg material from which the fish develops. What is left of it, the newly hatched fry consumes before beginning to hunt for food. The fry often show no resemblance to adult fish. In some species, like eels, the development from fry to adult is as complicated as the metamorphosis of insects.

Contrary to mammals and birds, fish continue to grow for nearly their whole lives, provided that they get enough food. An older fish should thus be larger and heavier than a younger one, given the same food supply. But since the food resources differ widely between waters, there is no clear equation between age and size of fish. A small darkish trout in a brook may well be older than a big silvery trout in a lake. If the former is moved to a food-rich lake, it will probably become a big silvery trout within a few years. On the other hand, if a trout from the lake were placed in a brook, it would certainly not survive long.

Shoals and territories

Even fish which normally live alone are found in large groups at particular times of year, as when spawning or eating a temporary concentration of food. Other fish have a rather constant tendency to gather in groups. When numerous fishes of the same species live together almost permanently, with coordinated behaviour, they are said to form shoals. These occur mainly among pelagic fish such as herring, mackerel, and vendaces.

What advantages do fish enjoy by living in shoals? Several possible ones have been pointed out. A shoal enables the fishes to detect dangers more easily, escape more effectively, and defend themselves by performing coordinated manoeuvres. It may also resemble a gigantic individual which enemies do not dare to attack. But this depends on the kind of enemies it is exposed to. Instead, it may attract predators from a distance. They may do more harm by swimming right into the shoal and biting at random—a method of assault used by marine hunters such as mackerel and barracuda. Probably shoaling behaviour should be explained by the social instincts of fishes within certain species.

By contrast, territorial behaviour involves aggressiveness. The fish establishes an area which it considers its own, to be defended against intruders. Fish in slow-moving waters do so almost ex-

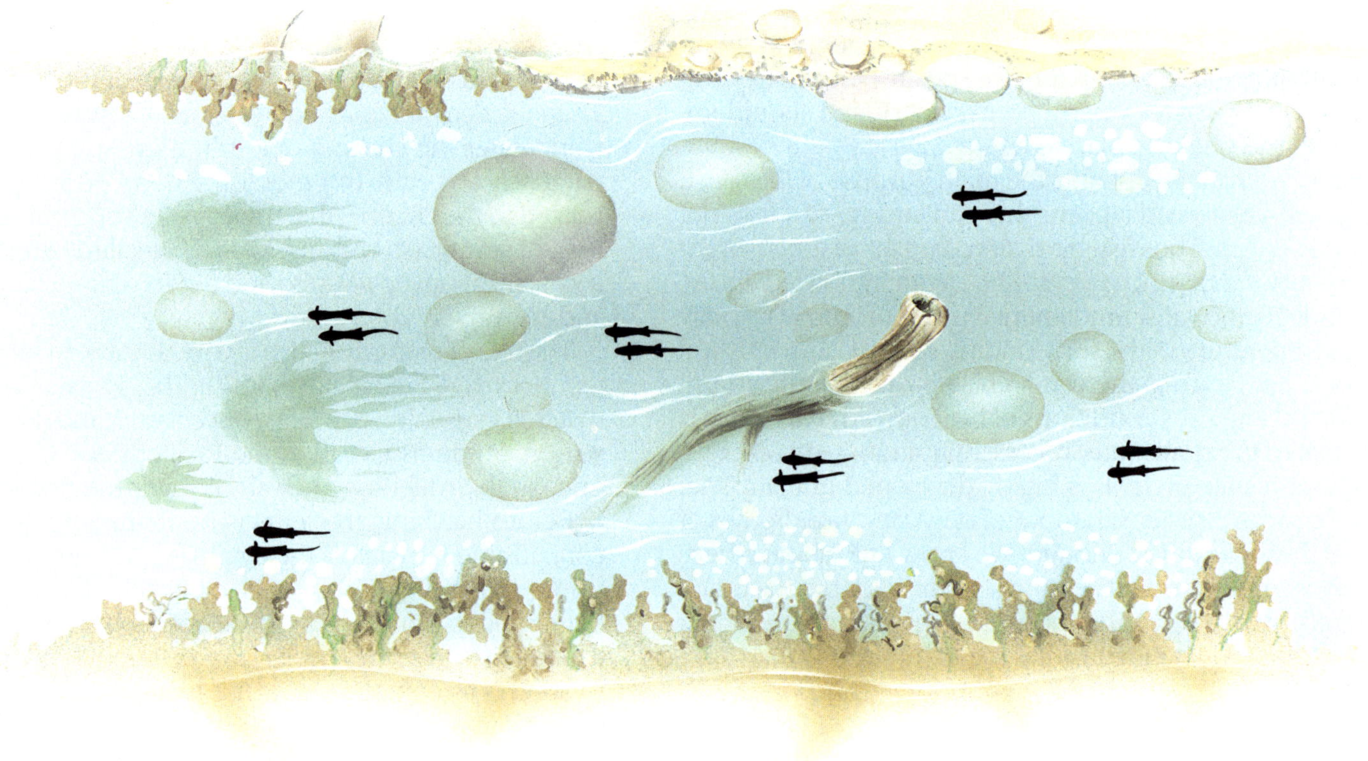

Territory is marked primarily by the males. If they cannot see each other easily, for example because of the bottom conditions, their breeding territories are smaller than when the bottom is smooth and visibility is good.

clusively while spawning. But stream-living fish such as salmon are much more territorial, often for long periods over their whole areas of growth and feeding as well as spawning.

Some species defend territory by, for example, biting the intruder or whipping it with their tail. More usual, and no less effective, is "threat" signalling or behaviour. Trout threaten by raising certain fins, lowering the bottom of the mouth, spreading out the gill lids, and assuming a particular body position.

The main purpose of territorial behaviour is apparently to reduce competition for food. It spreads the fishes over the bottoms so that they can utilize the nourishment efficiently, as long as food particles are not too scattered. This behaviour is also most common among species which normally live in environments with a concentrated food supply, ranging from Arctic streams to tropical reefs.

Migration

Virtually all fish undertake some sort of migration during their lives, for a variety of reasons. They may go in search of richer feeding grounds, suitable spawning bottoms, or more favourable levels of water temperature and salinity. Some need to make only short migrations, whereas others may have to travel hundreds or thousands of miles—even across oceans, in the case of tuna and Atlantic salmon.

Fish that migrate between sea and fresh waters must be able to tolerate not only the journey, but also the adjustment to life in water of very different salinity. Some species, like Atlantic and Pacific salmon, are "anadromous", spawning in fresh water and growing up mainly in the sea. Others, such as eel, are "catadromous" and do the opposite. Most die after their first spawning, as with the eel and Pacific salmon, although several Atlantic salmons survive to spawn as many as four times.

These extreme migrators are particularly interesting for their ability to orientate. How can the Atlantic salmon, after wandering thousands of miles, find its way back—not just to a home river or brook, but to the very stream where it was born—when the time comes for spawning? There are no definite answers yet. Studies indicate, notably for Atlantic and Pacific salmon, that navigation by the sun plays a role, as it does for migrating birds. This means taking "bearings" and compensating for declination, like our use of a compass. Laboratory experiments with a model sun have revealed this ability at least in some species of salmon.

Still, the sun cannot be the sole means of orientation for such fish. Once a salmon returns to the coast near its home river, it presumably seeks other guidance, and a likely aid is its sense of smell. We know that several species of fish can distinguish clearly between different fresh waters, and can remember the smell of their home river for a long time if it has been impressed on them when young. Scientists have recently suggested that migrant fish are guided by the smell-substances (pheromones) which their own species produce, and even by the smell of excrement which they deposit enroute.

Diurnal rhythm and diet

Like all animals, fish have a twenty-four-hour cycle of activity. This is easily seen from their alternation between hunting food, or eating it, and resting. Sportfishermen in temperate regions know, for example, that trout in summer are usually hungriest at dawn and dusk. Similarly, plankton-feeding fish migrate diurnally between different water layers, mainly following the zooplankton which rises to the surface at night and sinks back to the depths by day, seemingly in response to the light level.

As to eating habits, fish employ the common principle of saving energy: they seek a maximum quantity of food with a minimum of effort. Even if different types of food are equally accessible in equal amounts, the fish economizes by choosing the biggest food particles—up to a size which is hard to swallow. On the other hand, the more food is available, and the bigger the fish, the more careful it becomes in choosing its nourishment. This is familiar to sportfishermen: in waters with plenty of food, inducing the big ones to take our lure or fly can be almost impossible! Most fish have definite preferences in food. But if the supply of its favourite meal becomes too scarce to be worth hunting for, a fish must naturally lower its standards. When faced with a real shortage, it may even accept food that would normally have been scorned. However, the dietary pattern can be complicated. Fish also tend to become accustomed to a certain type of food, and blind to anything except what they are presently gobbling.

At the opposite extreme is their reaction to food that causes discomfort or injury. Recent investigations of such "negative training" show that fish learn very quickly to avoid disagreeable food. This includes, of course, a baited hook—and there is no doubt that discussions of "hook-shyness" are justified, although by no means all avoidance behaviour proves that the fish has previously been hooked. A fish's exact choice of food is nearly always related to the competition among fishes, both within and between species. After all, competition for food is probably their most important kind of mutual interaction. When the number of individuals in a given species and water area increases, the demand for food becomes ever more pressing. The weakest fishes may then stop growing or die, and sometimes a whole population is stunted. In northern climates, this phenomenon is conspicuous in perch and char.

Another result of increased competition is that the fishes which cannot compete strongly for their favourite food are forced to eat items far down on their preference list. This is particularly true of closely related species: the most reliable sign of competition is that their food choices are very similar when the supply is good, but quite different when it is sparse. Thus we sportfishermen, for whom preferences of food among fish are significant, can make serious mistakes when we try to judge them by what the fish have been eating. If we find the same food in a number of stomachs, this does not prove that the fish are competing—and if we find different foods, it is risky to conclude that they are not competing.

Predation

The most radical way for fish to compete is to eat up their rivals. When this occurs within a species, we often call it cannibalism. In more general terms of biology, it is an instance of predation, which plays important roles both within and between species. The fish most exposed to predation are usually the newly hatched fry. They are frequently consumed by all fish in the neighbourhood. The fry's chance of being eaten depends, among other things, on how fast it grows in size and swimming ability.

To the individual prey-fish, there is certainly no benefit in being swallowed. Nonetheless, the predator and prey often interact in a manner which may be of value for the population of prey-fish as a whole. If a population of predators—such as big trout—is introduced into water with a population of prey, like small char or whitefish, the immediate effect will be an increased mortality among the prey. But this leaves more space and food for the remaining prey increasing their chances of survival and growth.

The predators can make ever more use of the prey until a maximum equilibrium, or sustainable, yield of prey is reached. If the predators go beyond that point, their catches will decline even if they hunt more intensively. In terms of the human predator—fishing with commercial equipment—this is what we call "overfishing". The difference between the fish predator and the human one is that, while the fish reduces the prey population from the "bottom" by mostly taking small and young prey, the human reduces it from the "top" by catching larger and older prey.

Threats against fish

Apart from overfishing, humans have increasingly endangered fish life by altering the watery environment. The two main ways of doing so are with chemical substances and physical structures.

Contamination of fishing waters

Not least for us sportfishermen, it is a sad fact that fish—and notably many of our most attractive species—belong to those organisms which have suffered extremely from the modern use of water. Before industrialization and advanced social development in the Western world, human effects on lakes, seas, and running

If a fish goes too far with the principle of saving energy, it may ultimately have difficulty in swallowing prey that are too large.

waters were negligible. Not until large factories were built near rivers, to obtain water for manufacture and to dispose of waste products, did pollution begin to destroy fishing habitats on a serious scale. This damage soon accelerated with the construction of pipelines from toilets and other facilities into lakes and rivers, as well as with the exploitation and drainage of farmland.

Such industrial, municipal, and agricultural emissions contain solid pollutants, suspended and dissolved material, oxygen-consuming substances, plant nutrients, and poisons, including heavy metals and petroleum products. Normally, water and its organisms have a great capacity to neutralize pollutants. This "self-purification" means that the bigger particles are deposited on the bottom, and the organic substances are decomposed (broken down) by microbes. In the process, however, oxygen is consumed and, if there are too many pollutants, the result is an oxygen deficiency which may kill most of the fish and other organisms in the water.

Pollutants from industry often destroy fishing waters faster than do those from sanitary facilities. Enormous damage is done by paper mills and mining works—in the latter case, chiefly with heavy metals, oils and sludge. From ironworks and mechanical plants come phenols, metallic salts, and other poisonous substances which can kill fish directly. Farms produce nutrients that speed up the eutrophication of lakes and rivers, and may severely harm the fauna along seashores by, for instance, causing "blooms" of algae. The sea also receives petroleum products from ships.

In recent years, the growing knowledge and awareness of these dangers have led to much improvement in water purification, and in making industrial processes less pollutive. The outlook is thus brighter in some places, but not in the developed world generally. A new and awful threat to fish has lately arisen: the airborne emissions of sulfur and nitrogenous substances, due to ever more burning of petroleum products and coal. In Europe and North America, this is causing widespread acidification of natural waters—both directly and through their precipitation of poisonous elements, mainly mercury and cadmium.

Regulation of waterways

Nearly every type of large-scale water use requires some mechanical interference with lakes or rivers. This is, as a rule, to the disadvantage of their fish. In many Western countries, water is regulated chiefly for hydroelectric purposes. These have resulted in tremendous change to thousands of rivers and drainage areas, mostly with deteriorating conditions of life for fish and other fauna. Species which depend on running water for their spawning and early development, in particular salmonoids such as Atlantic and Pacific salmon, rainbow trout and river trout, have suffered most.

Such regulation usually has the immediate effect of cutting fish off from their spawning areas, for example with dams. Long stretches of stream are dried up by leading the water through tunnels. Most processes which begin in the water and affect the fish indirectly, however, proceed very slowly and their ultimate consequences lie in the more or less distant future.

With the regulations of lakes that are normally needed for generating extensive water-power, fish are influenced primarily by the fluctuations in water level. The difference between high water with summer damming, and low water with winter discharge, can be great in the northerly climatic zones: a hundred metres or more. As a result, large shore areas are dried up, and most of the bottom fauna in the littoral zone die—notably the bigger crustaceans, molluscs, mussels and others.

When river reservoirs are created by hydroelectric power stations, the flow disappears and is replaced by lentic waters, at best separated by some rapids. The food supply may not be damaged as much here as in regulated lakes, due to the more moderate water-level fluctuations. But the latter are frequently "short-term", every twenty-four hours, and the environment then becomes very unfavourable for salmonoid fish. River reservoirs do favour the so-called lentic species such as pike, perch, and carp. However, increased predation—mainly by pike—is often an important cause of the salmonoids' disappearance.

Equally serious for salmonoids is the withdrawal of fresh water for industrial and municipal uses. This also commonly involves regulation, even if the water level fluctuates less than at power stations. Still, it generally leads to a catastrophic decline in salmonoid populations.

Life in water is more or less sensitive to acidification. Water that is not acidified must have a pH of at least 6. Below this value, life is harmed, and it becomes impossible at pH values under 4.5.

Fish conservation

Many of the measures taken to preserve and promote fish populations belong to the scope of environmental and water conservation. Today, the concept of fish conservation or management is broad and diverse. We shall consider it in a more limited and direct sense: the ways of specifically protecting and maintaining fish populations as well as getting the best sustainable yield from them.

The basic condition for meaningful fish management is a good knowledge of the given water, its biology and problems. To estimate the population size and structure, some kind of sample-fishing is normally done with nets. Biological studies indicate the food supply for the fish, while analysis of the water yields information about its chemical and physical qualities.

Practical management includes the introduction of fish and prey organisms. This may be a one-time event, to create fish populations such as salmon, trout or pike-perch. Repeated introduction, known as put-and-take stocking, is undertaken when the fish are not sure to reproduce. A third type of stocking is the introduction of species as food for more valuable fish, naturally according to the latter's preferences. In Scandinavia, for example, salmonoids such as trout and char are promoted by introducing small fish like smelt and stickleback, or various crustaceans.

In oligotrophic waters, the nutrient supply can also be improved by fertilizers such as phosphate. Another kind of management, with recent importance due to acidification, is the liming of waters, which must be repeated indefinitely in most cases.

A somewhat controversial approach—in order to decrease or wipe out undesirable fish so that valuable species can thrive, primarily for the benefit of sportfishing—is to treat the water with a fish poison, rotenone, before stocking. This has met some opposition from conservationists, since rotenone also kills certain benthic and planktic animals. However, rotenone is broken down fast in water, and usually affects only the adults among these animals, so that they soon begin to recolonize. Such poisoning began in the 1950s but is much less common today.

In order to prevent widespread acidity damage, lakes often have to be limed. This should be done regularly for best results. Shown here in a "normal lake" are the places suitable for liming: (*a*) streams and other inflows, (*b*) mossy banks and coniferous shores, (*c*) coves with poor circulation, (*d*) stony bottoms, (*e*) breeding bottoms, (*f*) underwater springs.

One of the principal kinds of conservation in fresh water is fishing itself. If a fish population is to grow well and allow maximum yield, there must normally be a rational fishing of all species in the water. This reduces some populations and leaves more food for others to grow rapidly. In turn, it enables us to fish for ever younger, and thus more numerous, individuals. The numbers of individuals in a population, of course, tend to be smaller at older ages with higher natural mortality.

In lakes where no versatile fishing occurs, the balance between different species is often greatly disturbed. Today, this is obvious in many lakes, because the earlier commercial and household fishing has given way to sportfishing for a few attractive species. A consequence is that, where the uninteresting fish are abundant, they can multiply rapidly, and usually at the expense of the very species important to sportfishing.

A further kind of fishing for purposes of conservation is directed only against those that compete with the species we want to promote. Here, too, it is essential to use effective commercial equipment. The results tend to be best at times and places of gathering among the fish, especially for spawning.

Until now, we have described only those types of management which deal with fish and their populations. Quite distinct is the improvement of fish environments. In running water, this includes the removal of obstacles to fish migration, the building of fishways and fish-ladders, the construction of pools, stream concentrators, resting places for fish, and artificial spawning areas. It may even involve planting trees on riverbanks, in order to create shade during high summer and promote insect life.

In lakes, this form of conservation consists mainly of reducing the heavy aquatic vegetation, which is a problem in many eutrophic waters. Other methods are to build spawning areas for different species, and to increase the oxygen content with technical devices. Also important, but usually very expensive and complicated, is the restoration of bottoms that have been destroyed by pollution.

Biotope management means improving the environment for fish. A good example is this stretch of current, shown before and after restoration. To improve the fish's opportunities for breeding and growth, so-called current concentrators have been built. These make the water flow more balanced during, for instance, spring floods or strong rainfall. As can be seen, the biggest stones have been left to create stocking places. Only material that was in the stream originally has been used. Since the water must pass through the narrow openings, its speed increases, which improves its uptake of oxygen and also helps to keep the breeding bottoms clean. Moreover, the faster water digs out the bottom, giving fish more space to live in during low water too.

Spinning with artificial bait

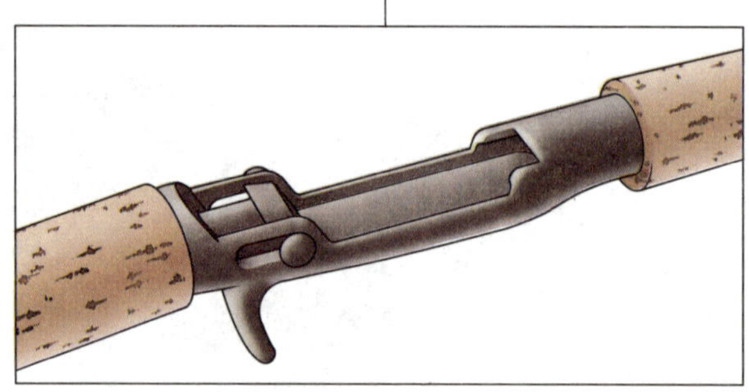

Outwitting a predator with spinning and bait-casting tackle, convincing it to take an artificial lure instead of its natural prey, evokes a special excitement in a sportfisherman. The very same excitement has probably existed for thousands of years, ever since the first fisherman dressed a hook with feathers, hair or fibre and tossed it out to an unsuspecting fish. Even though our ancestors were fishing for survival, the challenge and excitement were undoubtedly the same as today's angler finds in luring an unwary fish with plugs or spoons.

On a lucky day a fish can strike the instant the lure hits the water or even while it is sinking down to the bottom. But most fish do not take the lure until it is retrieved.

Predators hunt shallow as well as deep, but they generally live and take most of their prey at the bottom. It is up to the fisherman to know how lures look under water, how they cast, how they sink and how they "swim". Fishing with fixed-spool and multiplier reels, then, is the art of placing the right lure at the right water depth. Fishing involves more than just a good rod and reel and a feel for casting; it also involves knowing the various lures for different fish species and for deep, shallow, calm or fast flowing water.

Fishing with a rod and reel has different traditions in different parts of the world, but the foremost influence has always been American bass fishing. Decades before the first modern artificial lures were cast in European waters Americans had already developed a tradition of fishing with an array of spoons, spinners, plugs and jigs. It took a long time before some of these innovations came to Europe and some, trolling plugs, jigs and soft plastic lures, did not appear in Europe until the 1970s.

Rods

Twenty years ago most fishing rods were made of fibreglass. Many of today's rods are made of graphite and boron or of composites made from all three materials. New materials, kevlar for example, are constantly being developed. In addition, graphite rods are being strengthened with new materials such as silicon carbide "whiskers", a product introduced by Daiwa.

It looks as though graphite rods are going to dominate the market. These rods weigh less, stop faster after casting, and are more sensitive to the movement of the lure than the almost old-fashioned fibreglass rods. These new graphite rods, however, have the disadvantage of being relatively fragile and must be treated accordingly. All things considered, fibreglass rods must be considered the most versatile. Rod manufacturers have become more competetive during the past few years, each claiming that just their composition of fibreglass and filling materials is the best. A rod with 80-90% carbon fibre, however, is not necessarily better than one containing only 75%. It is mainly the design and construction of a rod that determine its qualities.

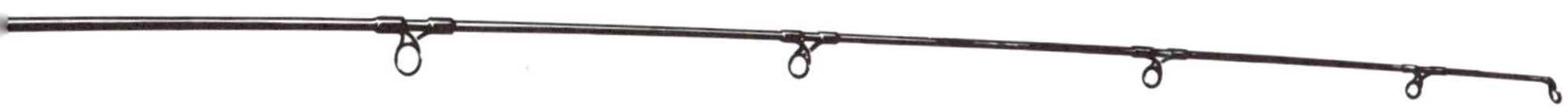

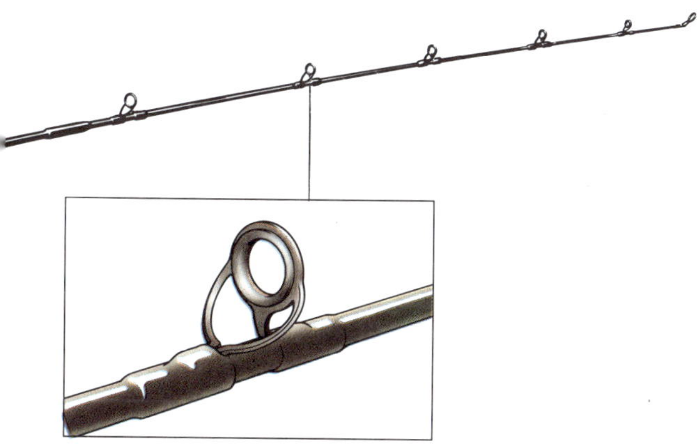

Three types of rods for casting and spinning. At the top, a two-handed rod with a fixed reel seat and large guides facing downwards. In the middle, a single-handed spinning rod. At the bottom, a two-handed casting rod with a recessed fixed reel seat and small, upward-turned guides.

A rod's action determines its performance during casting and when fighting the fish. At the top, a rod with slow action. In the middle a rod with medium followed by a tip-action rod, also called fast-action. At the bottom, a rod with very fast action.

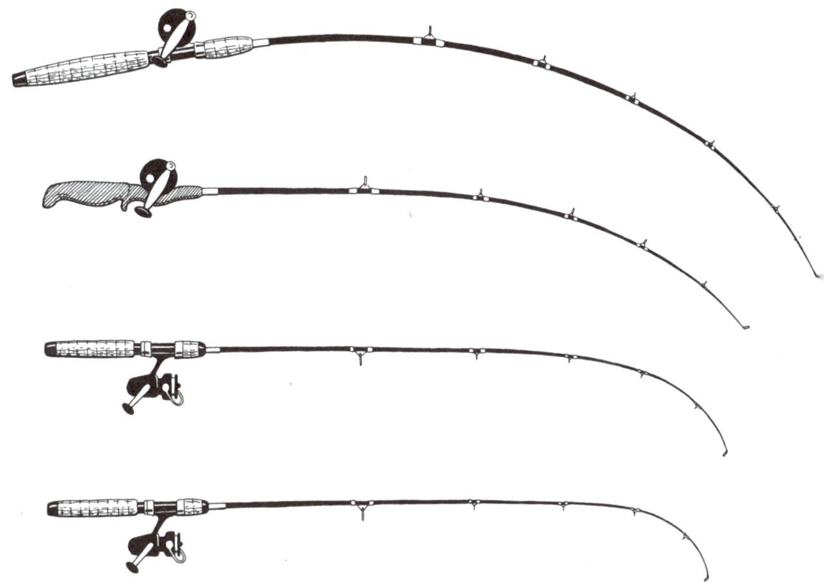

Action and length

A rod's action, or how it responds when casting and playing out a fish, is determined partly by the thickness of the rod and partly by how the material is used.

Slow action describes a rod that bends along its entire length. It casts accurately, has the backbone to wear out a fish and the resilience to withstand dives. Unfortunately, they are often not strong enough to set the hook well and they require an experienced angler.

A medium-action rod has more power for setting the hook as well as the backbone and stiffness necessary for high casting precision. Only the tip half of the rod bends when playing the fish.

Fast-action rods bend in the upper third section. They have good casting qualities, set the hook fast and hard and have backbone, but do not cast accurately. Because the action is in the tip one-third of the rod, these rods are less sensitive during retrieval.

Extra fast action means that only the top one-quarter of the rod bends. This type of rod has fantastic casting abilities and is often used for competition casting and surf casting, but this means that little action is transferred down the rod to the hand grip. For surf casting using natural bait, a slow-action rod is often used instead.

It should be remembered that the rod action does not indicate what casting weight the rod is suited for.

The rod's strength and its ability to cast various weights are determined by the tapering of the tip and the diameter of the rod as well as the mixture and use of the component materials. Throughout the years manufacturers have used several simple but effective systems to choose the right rod. Some designate the casting weight, such as 14–28 grams (1/2–1 oz) which means that the rod is strong enough to cast lures of that weight. As a rule, lures weighing 8–10 grams (1/4–3/8 oz) and as much as 35 grams (1 1/4 oz) can be cast on such a rod. But the casting weight limits cannot be stretched too far. Other manufacturers use a number system, often dividing rods into four weight classes. For example, class 1 would include ultra-light rods with casting weights of 2–10 grams (1/16–3/8 oz). Class 2 weights are 10–20 grams (3/8–3/4 oz), class 3 are 20–30 grams (3/4–1 1/8 oz), and class 4 includes casting weights of 40–100 grams (1 1/2–3 1/2 oz). The classes give no information about the length of a rod.

Some fishing situations call for particular rod lengths and for that reason it is a good idea to follow a few general rules when choosing a rod. Boat fishing often needs a shorter rod for light lures and slightly longer rods for heavier lures. Fishing in a small river or stream is often best with a longer rod so the lure can be kept free of trees, bushes and grass along the shore, and to provide better control of the lure in the current.

Large open water areas require a longer cast and with it a longer rod. In general, a long rod casts better than a short one, even if both are designed for the same casting weight. Long rods are more sensitive to sudden movements of a fish when being landed, but when fishing under low hanging branches a long rod will only get in the way.

Rods for trolling are often stiff, making them unsuitable for casting. Their main purpose is to distribute the tension along the line and lure while wearing out the fish. Rods for trolling with downriggers in lakes and coastal waters are usually medium action, 8–9 feet long with 10–12 ring guides.

Telescopic rods are practical for travelling anglers, but many of a rod's good qualities are lost in the construction. For the travelling fisherman a 4–5 sectioned rod takes up the same amount of space but offers the angler greater satisfaction.

Handles and reel seats

The shape of a rod's grip depends in part on the reel, which may be a fixed-spool reel (spinning reel), a closed-face fixed-spool (spin-casting reel), or a multiplier (bait-casting reel). Longer rods almost always have longer handles so the angler can cast with both hands.

Handles are made of a variety of materials and are covered with foam rubber, cork, or other comfortable materials. The reel seat is mounted at the handle and holds the reel in place. Rods designed for multiplying reels mostly have fixed reel seats, but spinning rods can have either fixed or sliding reel seats, and can even consist of only two rings (sliding bands) so the reel can be placed anywhere on the handle.

Guides

An angler wants to have the best possible contact with the lure in the water. Because too many ferrules can make a rod less sensitive, ferrules are being improved. Metal ferrules, for example, are being used less and the butt end of the blank extends into the grip, with the reel seat resting almost directly on the blank to provide the best contact with the hook and the fish.

Many miles of line glide through the guides in a day's angling, but it is always the same 1–50 meters (3–160 ft). The guides are there to reduce friction and to protect the line from wear. The guides must be durable so they aren't damaged by the microscopic grit that is often reeled in on the wet line. Besides this, the guides must be lightweight and not so stiff that they affect the rod's action and weight. They should also distribute the tension of the line along the entire rod. The rod and its action can be adversely affected by too few or too many guides.

A few decades ago guides were made of chromeplated steel, agate, tungsten carbide or ceramics. Today, most guides are made of aluminium oxide, silicon carbide or Hardloy. Although guides made of these three materials are generally called ceramic guides, they have nothing in common with the older guides that were actually made of ceramics and that can still be found on cheap saltwater rods. Even the diameter of the guides is important. Rods with spinning reels need guides with a larger diameter than those for bait-casting and spin-casting reels. If you are fishing with a spinning reel on a rod with small-diameter guides, the strength of the cast is reduced and the lure's action is taken up in the rod before it has reached the reel and the handle.

Multiplier reels

The predecessor of the modern multiplier reel was built by a Kentucky watchmaker and silversmith named George Snyder at the beginning of the 1800s. This explains why the first casting reels were often called Kentucky reels. Snyder had succeeded in making a reel where the spool rotated around its axis several times for every turn of the handle. The development of these reels continued and other brands also entered the market, but it was not until the 1920s and 30s that the more refined reels began to be manufactured. The last few decades have completely revolutionized multiplying reels. Trolling reels for salmon, pike or muskellunge, for example, are usually multipliers. But they are now remarkably simpler in construction than a standard multiplying reel, and most important of all—there is a good drag system. The spools are often made of metal and are therefore not suitable for casting. On the other hand, they are often reasonably priced—a point that should not be taken as criticism.

Multipliers rose to the peak of their popularity before World War II. After the war, spinning reels began to dominate the market, as they could cast better than multipliers with the new, thin nylon lines. American bass fishing still leads the way in the development of lightweight reels. Without bass fishing, improvements in multipliers would have progressed much more slowly. On a fixed-spool or spinning reel, the spool rotates only when

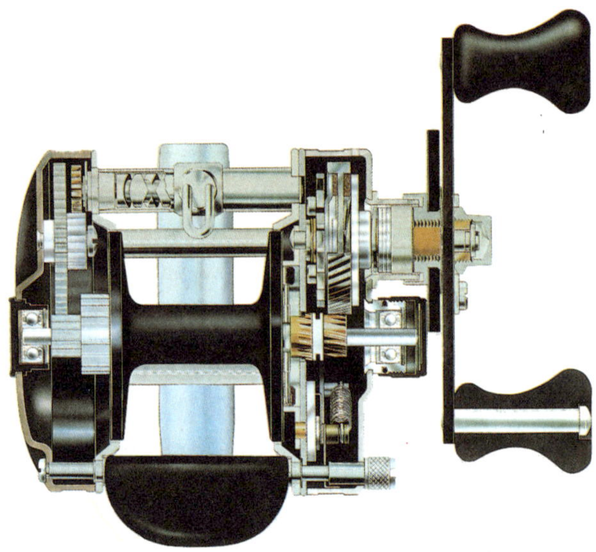

The first multiplier reels were introduced in the beginning of the 1800s. They were much simpler in construction than today's reels. The illustration above shows an x-ray of the classic Ambassadeur 5000. At the right is a more technically advanced multiplier with magnetic brakes and other special functions.

the drag is used. On a multiplier, or bait-casting reel, the spool rotates during both casting and retrieving, which means that the energy of a cast is transferred to the spool, resulting in a tendency to backlash. The backlash problem made the multiplier a beginner's nightmare, even though it was often the choice of experts. There are many parts in a multiplying reel. Getting the best results from these reels in terms of long casts with small, light weight lures demands a skilled angler with a sensitive feel for casting.

Many reels are equipped with level-wind devices that are activated during the cast. Many manufacturers now make reels with level-winders that can split into two halves when the spool is engaged. When it's time to reel in, the spool is automatically set in gear and the level-wind is activated.

The drag on a multiplier is usually the type called star drag, so named because the screw that adjusts the drag is shaped like a star. Multiplier reels with magnetic brakes have become very popular during the last few years. They prevent backlash when the spool is rotating during casting. Because the strength of the brakes is adjustable they are recommended for beginners wanting to avoid line tangles.

Fixed-spool reels

Fixed-spool reels became popular after World War II when nylon lines became available. The first fixed-spool rod was patented in 1905 by an Englishman named Illingworth. This reel, called the Illingworth reel, worked in principle just like the fixed-spool reels we use today.

Today's reels come in almost all sizes—from small lightweight reels for ultra-light fishing to the "coffee grinders" used for heavy surf casting and salmon fishing. These reels have a spool axle that runs parallel with the rod. When casting, the line is drawn over the edge of the spool, and in retrieving it is caught up by a bail arm that lays the line on the spool. The advantage in using this type of reel is that it is easy to use and makes a low-friction cast. The result of reduced friction is a longer cast. It is important, therefore, to correctly fill the spool with line. Small reels use thin line, larger reels heavier line.

The drag is an important detail on a reel. When the fish bites the brake is set in action and the line can run out. The drag is composed of one or more disc drags, often of teflon, that rub against each other when the drag is on. If the reel releases the line unevenly the drag is not functioning properly—the line should be released in a smooth and fluid motion. On most reels the drag adjustment knob is placed on the back edge of the spool house, but on some reels it is placed on the spool itself.

The gear ratio of reels can vary, but the most common are between 1:3 and 1:6. A gear ratio of 1:3.5 to 1:5 is usually best for spinning. It is generally an advantage to have a lower gear ratio when a large fish must be played out.

There are many movable parts in a fixed-spool reel. The spool house must be able to rotate freely and easily when the bail lays line on the spool. Reels with two to three ball bearings have the smoothest action and are the most durable.

An anti-reverse device prevents the spool from rotating backwards. On some reels there is a click signal that indicates when a fish has taken the line—a definite advantage when trolling.

The open design of a fixed-spool reel makes it almost friction-free and suitable for very thin line. It is also possible to control the release of the line manually by holding a finger on the line. The line can be stopped by pressing it against the spool.

A new type of fixed-spool reel, called an Autocast, has recently been introduced. With this reel the bail does not need to be picked up on manually. Instead, by holding the line, and a small lever at the same time, the bail arm is positioned automatically.

Closed-face spinning reel

Closed-face spinning reels are basically built like other spinning reels, except that there is a cone-shaped cover over the spool and the spool house. The line runs out through a hole in the cover, creating a small amount of friction as the line is first drawn across the edge of the spool and then centered to run through the hole.

Closed-face spinning reels are equipped with a push-button line release. Precision casting demands that the angler be in control the instant the line-release button is pushed and the line runs out.

There are two basic types of fixed-spool reels: open face and closed face. At the top is a cross section of an open-face reel. The drag adjustment is situated in front of the spool, but, as shown in the smallest picture, the drag knob can also sit behind the reel house. The reel at the right is a closed-faced fixed-spool reel with star drag.

There are both advantages and disadvantages with these reels. They do not make long and accurate casts, but they are reliable and easy to use. Unfortunately, they seldom have good drag systems. On the other hand, closed-face reels are excellent for fishing in poor visibility and in the dark, as well as in dense vegetation, because grass and other debris do not get trapped in the spool. Many fishermen regard closed-face reels as those best for beginners.

Spinning or bait-casting reels?

An experienced sportfisherman seldom hesitates when choosing a reel. A novice, though, can be easily influenced by the mechanical functions found on many multiplier reels. Before choosing a reel, both the advantages and the disadvantages should be considered.

Spinning reels are best for light tackle casting, but can be used for up to 100–150 (3 1/2–5 1/2 oz) casting weights. They are excellent when casting against the wind, they are simple to use and require a minimum of maintenance and service.

It is hard to cast light lures of 1–4 grams (1/28–1/8 oz) with a multiplier reel. Every now and then they backlash, particularly when casting against the wind and the wind suddenly takes the spoon and spinner while the spool continues to rotate. It is often necessary to keep a finger on the spool when casting, particularly when the lure hits the water, making the reel unsuitable for night fishing. When retrieving, a multiplier reel provides better control and contact with the lure and its movements than a spinning reel does. Multipliers are best suited for casting with heavy lures and for playing large fish.

In other words, an experienced fisherman who likes mechanical components would probably choose a multiplier reel. Another experienced angler who prefers a simple and reliable reel would probably choose a fixed-spool reel. Beginners often start off with a closed-face spinning reel, but soon want a fixed-spool reel to increase their casting distance.

Lines

Most lines are made of nylon monofilament. This synthetic fibre was discovered by DuPont in 1937 and was first received with much scepticism by anglers who were used to natural fibre lines. The raw material, nylon, is extruded through holes of different sizes, after which the threads are cooled and then drawn across heated, rotating wheels to stretch and align the molecules so they become stiffer, stronger and less elastic. Although the process may sound simple, it is actually rather complicated.

There is a wide variety of lines available today, differing in manufacturing as well as raw material and quality control. Unfortunately, there is little consumer information printed on packages of line, apart from the diameter and the breaking strain.

In general, the thicker a line is, the stronger it is. Strength is given in pounds and kilos. Super and extra strong lines are processed from better-quality raw materials, the molecular structure is homogenous and the line is inspected. Inexpensive lines

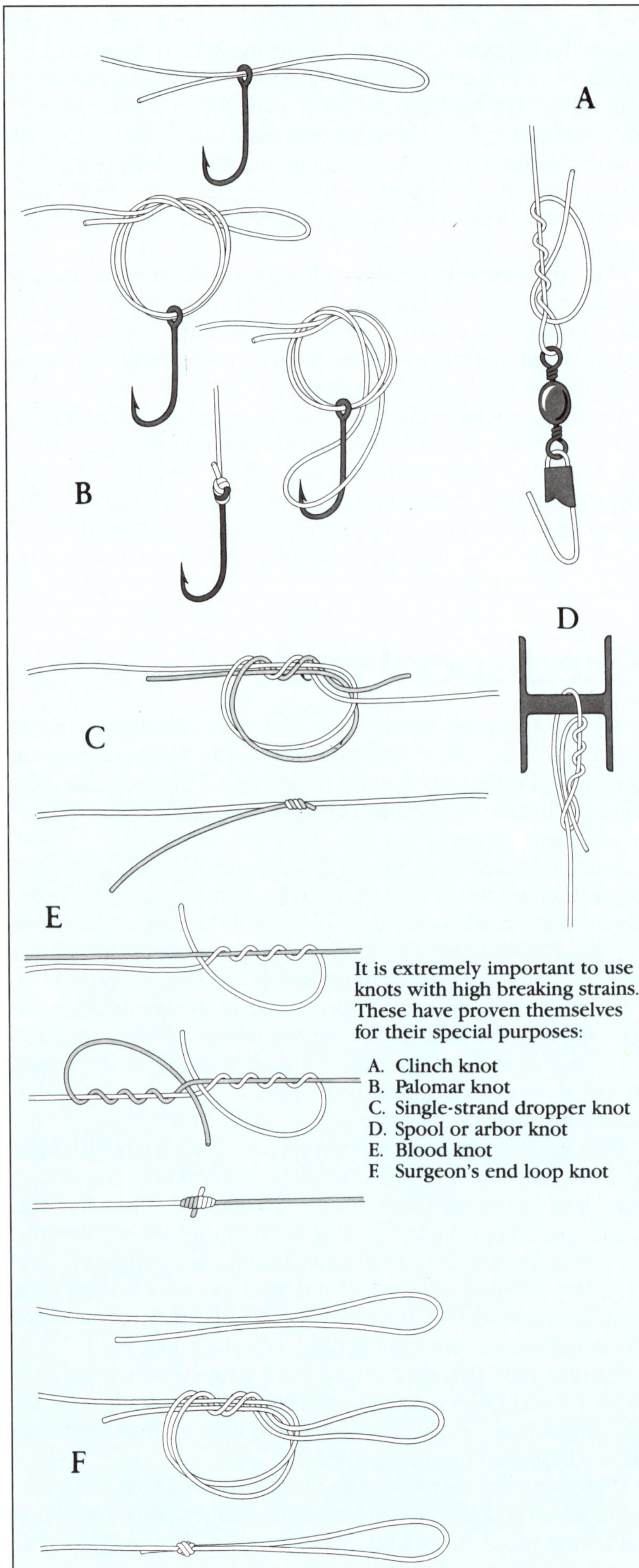

It is extremely important to use knots with high breaking strains. These have proven themselves for their special purposes:

A. Clinch knot
B. Palomar knot
C. Single-strand dropper knot
D. Spool or arbor knot
E. Blood knot
F. Surgeon's end loop knot

are produced from cheap raw materials and are subject to minimal quality control for breaking strain and diameter. This means that the breaking strain of an inexpensive line can be irregular, even if the diameter is constant. Fortunately, fluctuations in breaking strain seldom vary more than 10–15%, but abrasion and knots can cause a further reduction in strength.

Knot strength varies from line to line. An ordinary overhand knot decreases the breaking strain by up to 50%. Even the most specialized knots reduce breaking strain by 5 to 20%, emphasizing the fact that only special-purpose fishing knots should be used. Durability is also an important line quality as a damaged guide, for instance, creates enough abrasion to damage a line, and a few snags and catches on the bottom also quickly reduce the line's breaking strain. Lines usually stretch about 15–30%, even more when they are wet. For that reason most sportfishermen usually prefer lines with little elasticity. Stiffness is another quality worth consideration. While some anglers like a stiff line i.e. as a leader for flyfishing, others prefer softer, more supple lines that stack better on the spool.

Monofilament line is almost transparent, although it is often coloured during manufacturing, resulting in green, blue, red or white line. Line can also be processed so it becomes fluorescent. These lines glow in ultraviolet light, a feature that gives the angler better control of the line when trolling or in poor light. Opponents of fluorescent lines believe they frighten the fish.

Both knots and water can quickly lower the breaking strain of a line. Abrasive guides or bottom snags and scrapes against branches and rocks can all reduce a line's breaking strain. When actually being fished, a 10-kg (20-lb) line may in fact have the strength of only a 5-kg line (10-lb). Other factors leading to diminished strength can be sunlight, gases released from aerosol cans or exhaust fumes.

There are other materials, such as braided dacron, that are not often used for casting. Dacron line is almost impossible to use on fixed-spool reels, but is used for trolling with multiplier reels and for certain kinds of multiplier reels, particularly those used for zander and walleye, northern pike and muskellunge. A dacron line has almost no elasticity, which explains its sensitivity and its strength in setting a hook. There are also several types of wire including leadcore lines that are used for trolling.

Test line and line classifications

During recent years there has been an increasing interest in line class fishing. Internationally, nationally, and at the club level, notices of fish hooked on lines of particular breaking strains are prominently posted. The inspiration behind this concept is the International Game Fish Association (IGFA). IGFA has made an enormous effort to register fishing records throughout the world.

The line classes recognized for "light tackle" are 2,4,8,12,16,20 and 30 lbs, or the equivalent of 1,2,4,6,8,10 and 15 kilos. For a record to be accepted the fish must have been hooked according to predetermined rules on a line of a test strength not exceeding the designated class. The lines used in such fishing undergo very rigid quality-control testing and must meet stricter requirements than "normal" line, because no manufacturer wants to be represented by a line that might not measure up to its designated test strength during line class fishing. A 6-kg (12-lb) test line, for example, has a breaking strain of 5–5.5 kg (11–12 lbs) when wet, and it will break before it has reached a 6-kilo test strength.

Some thoughts on line

A good-quality line is worth the investment even though low-price offers for 500, 1000 or 2000 meters of line may seem attractive. Because the major line manufacturers continue to improve their products you generally get more for your money by staying with an established brand. Buying from a store with constant turnover is also a good idea, as the line is always fresh. Stay away from line that has been in a display window—it may have been damaged by sunlight. Change line often, at least once or twice a year, even if you do not fish constantly.

It's a good idea to discard the first 4 or 5 meters of line after each fishing trip, as this is the part of the line that is subject to the greatest wear and tear. Check your line regularly, for example when you are retrieving, by letting it run through your fingers. It's then easy to notice any scrapes or abrasions that call for a change of line.

Never let a line wind onto a reel under heavy tension. After bringing in a large fish or snagging on the bottom it is not at all unusual to wind in the line and leave it on the reel until the next outing. But a line has a built-in memory and it shrinks to its original length before it was stretched. In the worst scenario, a contracting line can split the spool, which is usually made of synthetic material. Another good habit to develop is to remove the lure from the line after fishing. When the lure is left on the line, the knots tighten even more, and the line's breaking strain is reduced even further.

The right equipment

Water, species and fishing method, along with personal preference, determine an angler's fishing tackle.

Ultra-light fishing for small species calls for a short light rod, from 150–180 centimeters (4.5–6 feet) long, a small reel carrying a line capacity of 100–125 meters (108–135 yds), and a line diameter of 0.10–0.23 mm (2–6 lbs) test strength. Choose a rod with a casting weight from 2 to 10 grams. This tackle is best for fighting small trouts, bass and pikes. It is particularly suitable for boat fishing, for smaller ponds, rivers and streams.

Light spinning tackle is a supple rod about 6.5–7.5 feet long with a casting weight of 10–20 grams, a small reel and 0.23–0.30 mm (6–10 lbs) diameter line. This is a good basic tackle combination that provides enormously satisfying fishing, but it is also reliable when fishing for trout, bass, small pike or salmon. A lightweight rod with an extra long handle for two-handed casts gives extra strength and control.

A classic, all-round tackle consists of a rod of 7–9.5 feet with a casting weight of 12–28 grams (1/2–1 oz), a medium-sized reel and 150–180 meters of 0.25–0.35 mm diameter line (6–15 lbs). This tackle has the necessary strength for casting medium-sized plugs, spoons and spinners and it can even wear out heavy opponents like pike, salmon and lake trout.

For boat fishing the most practical rod is 6.5–7.5 feet long, also with a casting weight of 12–28 grams. It takes less space but it has the same good qualities. With an extended handle for two-handed casting these rods are extra powerful.

If heavier tackle is needed for trolling or casting with heavy plugs, or for playing in really big fish such as salmon and large pike, a special-purpose rod is usually called for. These rods can be from 6.5 to 10 feet long, depending on whether they are used for trolling from a boat or for beach work. There is always an extra-long handle as they are made for two-handed casting.

Casting techniques

There are many different ways to cast. The most important are the side cast and the overhand cast. Besides these, there are several special casts that are determined by the situation, as when there are branches, bushes or trees behind the person casting. The dynamics of casting—the movement, acceleration and the instant of line release—are the same, however, whether the angler has chosen a spinning or spin-casting reel, or a multiplier. Each type of reel, though, requires its own special grip on the rod.

In side casting the lure should hang about 30 cm from the tip of the rod. The rod is drawn horizontally backwards, either to the

The side cast

left or right, depending on which hand the caster is using. When casting, the rod is first lifted forward and a bit upwards at the same time that the line is released. If casting from the right side and the lure lands too far to the right, the line was released too soon. If the lure is delivered too far to the left, the line was released too late. When the lure drops straight in front, the cast was perfect. Side casting is not an accurate cast, but it is the easiest and often the most powerful.

An overhand cast is far more accurate. The angler stands with his face turned in the direction of the cast and the lure dangles about 30 cm (12 in) from the tip-top. The target spot is sighted with the rod and with an accelerating motion the rod is brought to a vertical position, 12 o'clock. The weight of the lure arches the rod so that the tip of the rod is at a 3 o'clock position. At the same moment, the rod is cast forward and the line is released. If the lure lands with full force right in front of you, the line was released too late. If it drops softly in the same place, either the cast was too weak or the line was released too early.

Overhand casting is not very suitable for shallow water because there is often more slack line in the air than with a side cast. A side cast provides much faster contact with the lure when retrieving. The overhand cast can be slowed down, either by holding the line with a finger, as on a spinning-reel, or by pressing the thumb against the spool, on a multiplier reel.

The overhead cast

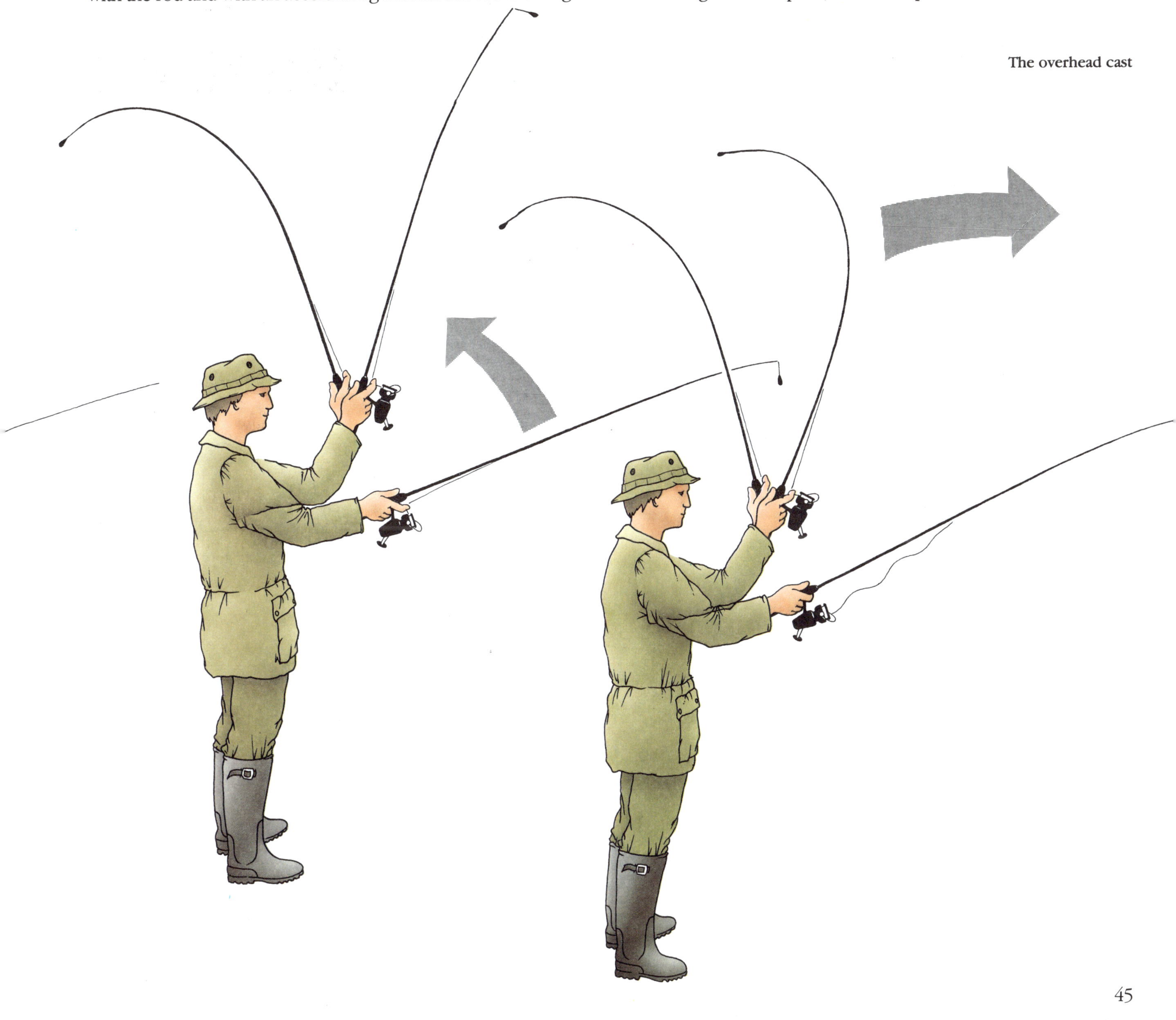

When fishing and casting for particular fish or in a particular spot the cast should be aimed directly over the target but a few meters further out, so the lure does not splash and frighten the fish. The lure must then have time to sink to the depth where the predator will see it and strike.

Backhand casting is a special cast that is used in a confined space, as in a boat, or where branches hang in the way. In this situation the cast is "over the opposite shoulder".

The underhand cast can be necessary when there are branches or bushes behind the angler. The cast is not a very long one but it is useful along shorelines and banks with heavy vegetation. The best reel for underhand casting is either a spinning or a

Both hands are used on a two-handed cast, resulting in optimum casting results.

The underhand cast

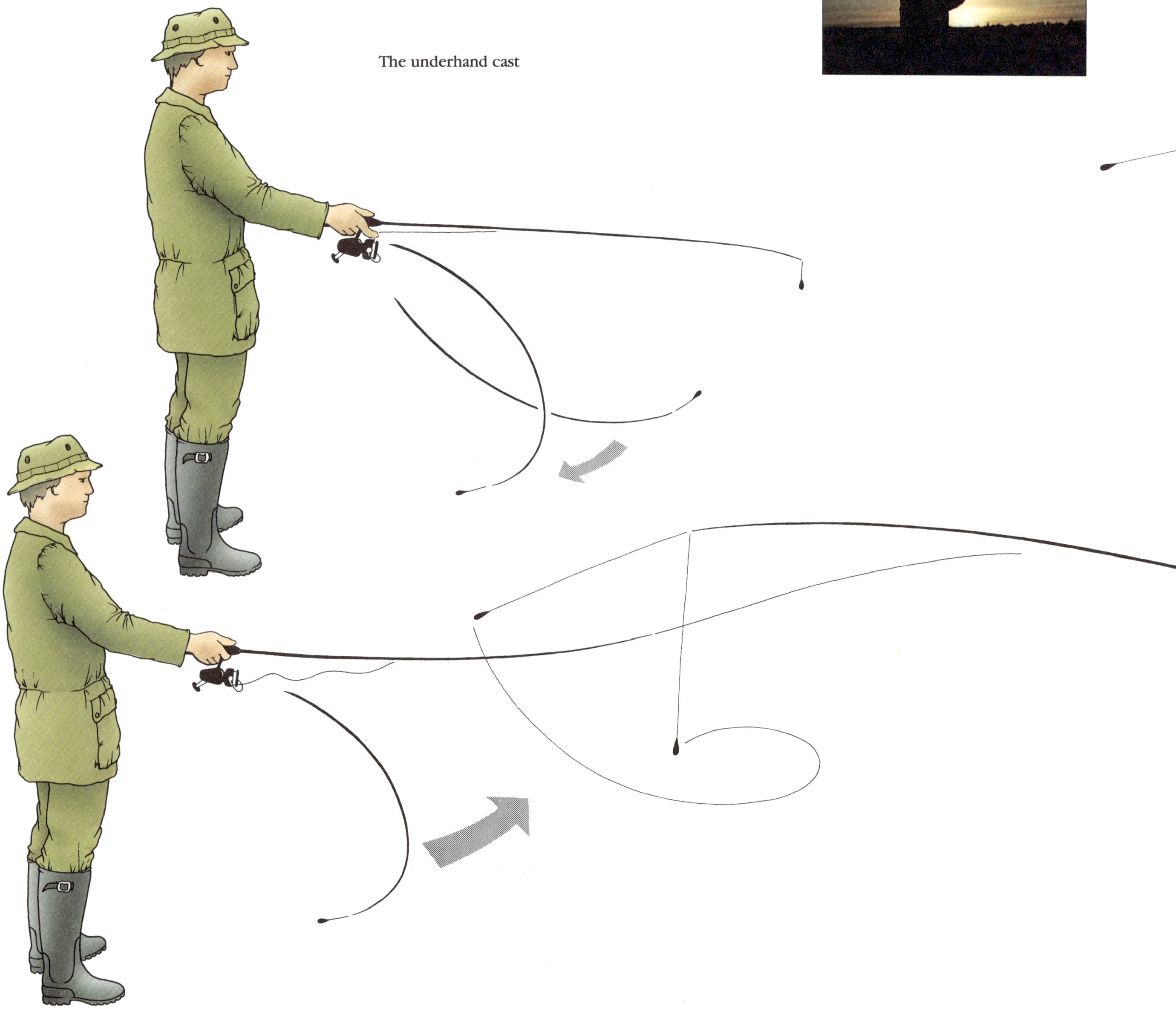

closed-face fixed-spool reel. Underhand casting with a multiplier reel demands a skilled, experienced angler. Boat fishing, when the angler must stand up to cast and often has a fellow fisherman behind him, is another situation when the open space in front of the angler is used for an underhand cast.

More powerful casts follow basically the same pattern, but use more body and arm action and a two-handed cast.

One of the most common problems when casting with a fixed-spool reel is too much line on the reel. Long sections of line spin off quickly and get tangled. Shortening the line can be a simple solution to this problem. A cast that is too short can be caused by too little line on the spool or too light a lure. Small line guides can also explain a cast that is too short.

On a multiplier reel, the most common problem is usually poor braking qualities on the spool, resulting in backlash. The solution is to increase the drag on the magnetic brakes. If this does not help, the line might be too stiff, since the reels are not suitable for light casting weights. On reels without level-wind, kickback and tangled lines can be avoided by using the thumb and forefinger to spread the line evenly on the spool. Another reason for poor casting can be line that is wound too loosely on the spool when fishing with a jig, for instance. When recovering line with a lightweight lure the line should be held between the thumb and forefinger and a slight pressure should be exerted.

The two-handed cast

Artificial lures

This description applies to all lures that imitate natural bait, including a variety of fish and worms. Plastic jigs and worms that are impregnated with scents synthesized from natural bait are a category of lures that are difficult to identify as natural or artificial. Even though artificial lures imitate a predator's natural diet, they can never be an exact copy, as predators often strike at fish that are sick or injured or in some other way behave strangely in their natural environment.

Artificial lures broadcast signals or stimuli that predators recognize and react to. Shape, colour and movement are the main signals that induce a fish to strike, but even size, texture, smell and sound can trigger a reaction. Manufacturers attempt to include as many of these stimuli as possible in their artificial products. When a lure maintains its popularity year after year, it does so because it attracts fish in many different situations. Toby, Rapala, Mepps, Heddon and Dardevle are names of artificial lures that have proven themselves with sportfishermen for decades and that continue to attract fish in all latitudes.

An artificial lure moves through the water in a certain way with a certain recovery speed. When the retrieval speed changes, the lure's swimming action also changes. A really good lure is just as tempting to a fish at one speed as it is at another, leaving the angler in complete control over the movement of the lure and its attractive qualities. Artificials can be roughly categorized as spoons, spinners, spinnerbaits, plugs and jigs. There are many other artificials available, of course, many of them developed in the USA for bass fishing.

Because sportfishing has developed in both North America and Europe, using different methods and fishing for different species, differences in terminology are unavoidable. This is particularly true of jigs. What an American would call a jig would be classified as a jig, a pilk or a pirk in Europe, where all of these lures are widely used for fishing in lakes, rivers and the sea.

Spoons

The largest group of artificial lures is called spoons. They were given this name because many of these metal or plastic lures are actually spoon-shaped.

Spoons are found in many shapes and forms, including round, oval, or elongated and often slightly S-shaped, to imitate various baitfish. The oval and round spoons are best for calm water. They swim with a rocking motion but because they rotate when they move faster, they are not suitable for fast flowing water. In fast, rippling water (as well as in water where predators feed on small fish that dart about rapidly), narrow, elongated and often slightly S-shaped spoons are used. The more S-shaped a spoon is, the more it swings out to the sides, emphasizing its swaggering movement as the water passes over its concave surface. Because these spoons must be in motion to attract fish, they are not effective in still water. With no current to make them swim, they must be retrieved at a rate that is much too fast for calm water.

In between these two groups there are spoons that work well with both fast and slow retrievals. Two classic examples are Toby and Dardevle.

Spoons are found in many varieties, but all have the spoon shape that gave them their name.

Spoons can be made of thick or thin metal; they can be compact and heavy, or large and ultra-light. A good spoon will cast well, sink quickly, have an enticing swim and be able to bring a fish to the hook. When it comes to casting short distances, for instance in ponds, brooks or streams, the spoon's fish-like swim is its outstanding characteristic. For longer casts from piers or beaches or against the wind, the spoon's easy cast is what makes it so popular.

Deeper water calls for heavier, more compact spoons that sink quickly to the right depth and stay there during retrieval. Shallower water and even some light currents are best fished with lighter spoons with fish-like swims. It is almost impossible to get heavy spoons to swim with life-like action in deep water.

A realistic, enticing swim should be the number one priority in any type of water. The key to success in fishing with spoons is to sink the lure to the fish's depth and then move it at a speed the fish can accept as natural.

Spoons are popular because they are easy to fish with, and effective. They send out signals that attract fish and they set solidly when the fish takes the hook, whether an expert or a novice is working the rod. In general, a spoon with very lively swim hooks fewer fish than those that swim evenly through the water. But on the other hand, it is quite often just that lively, irregular swim that tempts a fish to strike.

Weedless lures

Spoons can be protected so they do not hook as easily on underwater vegetation such as seaweed and lily pads, or on roots or stones.

Spinners are often effective because they send out vibrations that travel through the water and attract fish from a distance.

The hook is protected by a thin thread of wire or a piece of very stiff nylon line. Weedless spoons are perfect for fishing in thick vegetation, but they do not work as well as an open hook because the weed guard protecting the hook often gets in the way when the fish bites.

Pirks or diamond jigs

Metal lures that are very compact, slender, and heavy for their size are called pirks, pilks, diamond jigs or jigging spoons. These lures have a slow, even swim that attracts fish through relatively fast retrieval or by moving the rod. Their advantage lies in their outstanding casting ability, which explains why they are often used for fishing in deep water and for making long casts.

On a smaller scale, these pirks are also used for ice fishing, where they resemble food fish that predators find hard to resist. Pirks are made of brass, iron or lead.

Standard spinners

A spinner is really a spoon that rotates around the body when it is retrieved. Spinners are most suitable for fishing in shallow to medium-deep water.

While a spoon can induce a strike when retrieval is stopped, a spinner tends to sink like a stone if there is any slack in the line. It works only during retrieving.

Differences in size and shape, however, can vary a spinner's action. A very compact, heavy body sinks deep; a thin, light weight body has a shallow swim, as do oval or round spoons; and a long, slender spoon swims deep in the water but needs a fast retrieve. A thin spoon and a light body combine to produce a shallow-draught spinner that swims even when retrieval is slow. An important aspect of a spinner's action is its size. In order to sink deep it may be necessary to weight the line in front of the spinner or to choose a spinner with a heavier body.

A spinner uses a technique quite the opposite of a spoon—it does not resemble a small fish. A spinner's attractiveness depends mainly on the sound waves and the flashes of colour it transmits. In order to improve their spinners, some manufacturers have made holes through the blade. These holes are designed so the spinner sends out extra-strong sound waves that are reproduced as pressure waves in the water.

The spinner's large surface area in comparison to its weight means that it takes a longer time to sink before retrieving can begin. This slow sinking rate makes casting upstream a very effective method for hooking predators. By casting upstream and reeling in as the lure drifts downstream, the spinner moves a little faster than the current and rotates at the same time. Although this cast is best left to skilled anglers with sensitive feel for the spinner, it is extremely effective because the lure suddenly and very naturally appears in the water before the fish has time to react. A downstream cast gives the fish more time to become suspicious.

Lead-headed spinners

A lead-headed spinner looks like any other spinner except that the body is placed in front of the spoon. This change in balance means that the spoon continues to rotate even when retrieval stops and the spinner sinks in the water. The spoon keeps rotating even if the recovery is very slow. By dipping the spinner's head in lead, the spinner can also be used in deep water because the spoon's rotation is not affected by the weight of the body.

Lead-headed spinners cast well and sink quickly. By mounting the body asymmetrically at the shoulder and shaping the body like the keel of a boat, line twist can be avoided. These weighted spinners are understandably the best for trolling, but they are also excellent for fishing in fast flowing water with deep pools and channels.

Lead-headed spinners normally have treble hooks, but many varieties have single hooks for natural bait such as strips of fish. This "cocktail" is particularly tempting to zander/walleye.

Other types of spinners

For decades American bass fishing has been the source of development for new fishing methods, new types of tackle and artificial lures. Bass fishing takes place under extremely varied conditions in many kinds of water, including swamps, overgrown ponds, impoundments and reservoirs. Bass actually thrive in warm water with abundant bottom vegetation. It is just this plant growth that has so often made the standard artificial lures impossible to use, and has stimulated the development of specialized lures. These lures are seldom used by European fishermen.

Spinnerbaits are one type of artificials that look like spinners. They are shaped like open safety pins with a non-rotating spoon placed on the upper arm. The hook and body sit on the lower arm and because it is fished in water with lots of weeds, a single hook is used, turned up in jig fashion. The hook is protected by the upper arm and often by a thick skirt of deer hair or plastic. This spinner is designed to avoid snagging on the bottom and collecting weeds on the hook. It hooks much more successfully than a weedless lure. Spinnerbaits are most useful when trying to locate a fish. Once the fish is found and has shown some interest in the lure, many anglers change to a better-hooking artificial.

Spinnerbaits come in a variety of shapes. They make a relatively good cast, they swim equally well when retrieved slowly or rapidly, they sink quickly, but they do not hook well.

Buzzbaits are made basically like spinnerbaits, but they have a spoon that rotates like a propeller. They are made for spinning over the tops of aquatic vegetation that grows almost up to the surface, and for fishing in shallow water. When being retrieved the propeller rotates at the surface, making movements and pressure waves that resemble a baby bird or a frog. The propeller can have two or three wings and the arm can be mounted with two propellers. Either treble or single hooks are used. One type with only one arm looks like a standard spinner with a propeller mounted in front of the body.

Plugs

Plugs are artificial lures designed to simulate a fish's natural food. Because they are three-dimensional, no matter which angle a predator sees a plug from, it looks like a small bait fish. Even the size and movements imitate small bait fish. Most plugs are made of plastic, some are made of balsa wood. They usually carry from one to three treble or double hooks.

Plugs can be put to more use than spoons and spinners and can even float or sink. Many plugs have a bill placed slightly in front of them, sometimes like a lip, that functions as a shovel or a bill in clearing the way for the plug under the water when retrieving the cast. The design of the bill and the speed of the retrieval determine how deep a plug will sink. The construction and design of a plug enable it to work deeper water than a spoon or spinner, and a plug can be weighted for deeper casts. When retrieving a spoon or spinner, the pressure on the line and the angle of the rod tend to lift them up in the water but the plug's design allows it to continue to swim at a constant speed during recovery.

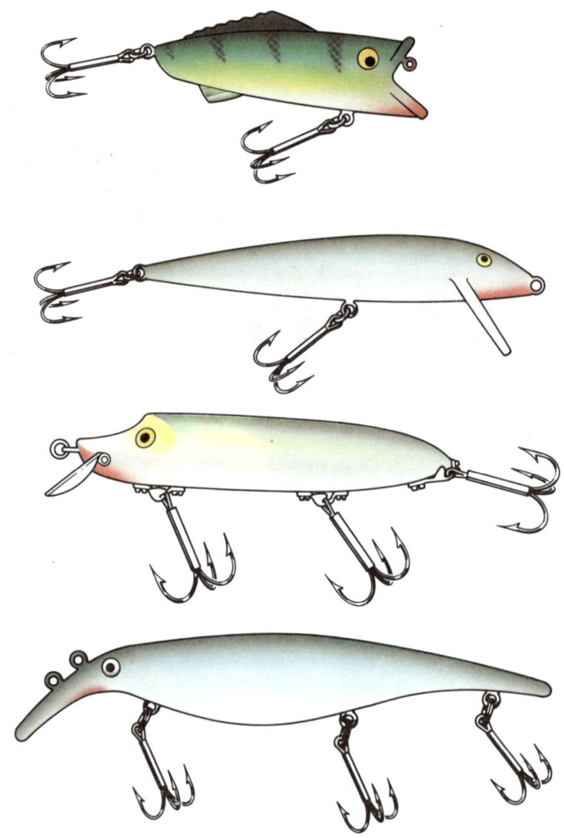

Four types of plugs that have proven themselves irresistible around the world:
Whopper Stopper
Rapala
Hi-Lo
Swim Whizz

Most plugs are calculated to work at a predetermined depth, but the faster a plug moves through the water, the deeper it goes. Some plugs can be adjusted to work at various depths. The Swimm Whizz and the Believer for example have two eye rings for attaching a line. When the line is attached in the upper eye, the plug goes deep with lively movements; when the line is in the lower eye, the plug has a shallow draught with calm movements. The Cisco Kid is an example of a plug with a flexible metal lip. The more the lip is bent the livelier and the shallower the plug swims. The more horizontal the lip stands, the deeper and calmer it moves.

Some plugs, such as ABU Garcia's Hi-Lo, have a movable lip that can be adjusted for five different depths. The upper position gives the deepest action and each adjustment lower on the scale raises the plug's action in the water. When the lip is at the bottom position and pushed completely back, the plug swims right at the surface.

Most plugs, such as a Rapala, have only one eye to tie a line with. Many small, lightweight plugs are most active when attached with loop knot. The bigger plugs can be tied to the line with a tight knot or attached with a snap swivel.

The plug's three-dimensional shape and realistic swim make it the artificial lure that best imitates a fish's natural food. It is more versatile than a spoon or a spinner because it can be fished at almost any depth from the surface to the bottom. Northern pike, bass and lake-run brown trout are a few of the species that find plugs attractive.

Floating and sinking plugs

A floating plug is a good all-round plug that can be fished at the surface or down to 10 meters (32 ft). When there is slack in the line the plug rises to the surface, only to retreat back to the depths when retrieving starts again, creating a very realistic movement to attract predatory fish. Floating plugs are very handy in slow to moderate currents where the water is not too deep. In ticklish situations,, such as water with heavy vegetation, trees or rocks, it is a good idea to let the floating plug be caught up in the current and carried to the fish's feeding spot before retrieving the line.

Sinking plugs more closely resemble spoons and spinners because they can be fished in water from 5–15 meters (16–48 ft) deep. If a plug is properly sunk and if the recovery is slow enough, it will work along the bottom until the recovery speed increases and lifts it up.

Other types of plugs

Minnow Plugs are fish-like plugs about 5–20 cm (2–8 in) long that are copies of a predator's natural food. These floating or sinking plugs are probably the most commonly used.

Short, compact plugs are primarily made for lightweight casting. Called crank baits, these plugs have excellent casting qualities. They come as either floaters or sinkers with long or short bills for various depths—from about 5–8 meters (16–26 ft) deep and up to the surface. Many plugs in this group have built-in rattles which create noise as the plug is retrieved. These sonic plugs can also be used for trolling.

The largest plugs are for trolling. They are awkward to cast and require heavy tackle. Since big fish go for big prey, these plugs are excellent for trolling through large areas where there are big fish to be caught. Using these large plugs is also a selective process—the angler is out after big fish. In spite of their weight, these plugs can be cast in confined fishing spots with shallow to medium-deep water. A magnum plug resembles a standard plug, but is specially made for trolling for salmon in the rivers of western North America and in the sea. These trolling plugs can fish at depths of up to 15 meters (48 ft), depending on the trolling speed and the sinkers used.

Surface plugs

Surface plugs are a special type of floating plugs made especially for bass, pike, muskellunge and other predatory fish when they feed in shallow water or at the surface during the summer. Fishing with these lures provides some of the most fascinating experiences an angler can have because the fish are at the surface and then can be seen taking the lure. A great deal of skill is necessary to set the hook at the exact instant that the fish strikes.

There are many kinds of surface plugs. The most common have one or two propellers that rotate during retrieval, churning up the water at the surface. Once the right retrieval speed is reached, the propeller action and the lure make a lively and tempting combination. The body of these prop lures is shaped like a cigar, and they swim smoothly through the water.

Without the propellers and at the right recovery speed, this cigar-shaped plug swims from side to side. It should be played in with a series of consistent, even tugs on the lure.

A special type of plug has wings on either side in the middle or at the front end. The wings make the plug lurch back and forth so water shoots out at the sides like the movement of a frightened baby bird.

Another special plug has a notched head. It sprays water in front of it when the rod is worked with a hard but consistent jerking motion.

These surface plugs are all small or medium-sized and can be used on bass, pike and muskellunge. Pike and muskellunge have their own special, surface plug called jerkbaits. These have long, slender bodies with flat hips, giving the plug a fast, smooth and easy gliding motion when it is reeled in with an irregular jerking action. On some jerkbaits there is a metal disk extending downwards from the tail, to help keep the lure slightly deeper during retrieving, while lures without this weight work at the surface. These plugs are usually a good size and need special tackle consisting of short, sturdy rods and multiplier reels filled with braided line. When cast, these plugs land with a big splash. They should be retrieved erratically, an effect best achieved by jerking the rod to the side, or even better, to the surface of the water.

All surface plugs used for pike and muskellunge fish best when the predators are actively feeding at the surface in water temperatures of at least 16–18°C (61–64°F). If bass fishing, the water temperature must be higher. Surface plugs can give good results even at depths of 5–6 meters (16–20 ft) in areas with thick aquatic vegetation. Predators often lurk in the cover of vegetation waiting for small birds and fish that usually appear in the early morning and in the evening.

Jigs

After World War II jigs became a more common sight in the tackle boxes of many American fishermen. In spite of the jig's being one of the world's oldest lures, it had previously been used mainly for saltwater fishing. The increased use of the jig coincided with developments in light tackle fishing. Once again, it was bass fishing that paved the way and first used the jig. Since then, the jig has become accepted for other types of fishing and is now regarded as one of the best lures for pike, walleyes, trout and even salmon, as well as bass.

The jig is a compact and heavy lure. It offers little resistance in the air and can be cast with precision. Jigs sink quickly and do not have built-in movements; however they can be easily used by beginners. Jigs should be reeled in with a hopping, jerky rod action.

Thanks to the upward-turned hook, jigs can avoid bottom snags. Fish are hooked securely, often in the upper jaw. Jigs are also inexpensive, perhaps the most inexpensive of all lures, as a half dozen jigs cost as much as one spoon or a single plug.

A jig is basically a hook with a long shank that is bent at a right angle just before the eye. The head is made of lead and is cast at a right angle so the eye of the hook protrudes either from the top of the lead head or from the middle of it. The placement of the eye is what gives the jig its balance in the water. On jigs used for casting, the eye is placed slightly forward on the head. On jigs for ice fishing, the eye of the hook is placed exactly in the center of the leaded head for vertical alignment. Jigs are grouped according to the shape of their head, which can be shaped like a ball, a banana or a keel; they can be metal-lipped as on plugs, or they can have a rotating blade that is mounted either on the hook or on the underside of the leaded head.

A compact, lead-headed jig is fished at the bottom with a jerky retrieval to give it an irregular, bouncy swim. The body is usually made of hair, feathers, soft plastic or rubber.

Right: Several different jigs that fish find irresistible. Large predators such as walleye/zander are attracted to large jigs with pliable rubber bodies, while smaller species such as perch mostly prefer smaller jigs covered with hair or feathers.

A jig's body can be made of a variety of materials. Hair-covered jigs are made of deer hair; feathered jigs are made of hackles and soft, texturous marabou feather. Soft bodies of silicone as well as plastic worms have expanded the choices available since jig bodies can be cast in so many different ways. The bodies can also be made or skirted with different kinds of nylon, synthetic fiber, mylar or tinsel. The bodies of the most common saltwater jigs are made of deer hair and are often called bucktails.

Jigs come in almost all sizes and weights, from less than one gram (1/28 oz) to several hundred grams (10 oz). The smallest are called micro-jigs.

The correct terminology is not really to spin in a jig but to work it in. Jigging involves activating the lure to look as lively and tempting as a small feeder fish, a frightened fish, or a fish trying to hide. The rod can be shifted from left to right when reeling in, but this movement probably decreases the contact with the jig, which is exactly what is needed to detect a bite and set the hook. The best indicator of a strike in calm water is often just a wiggle in the line!

Even while the jig is sinking it is important to maintain contact with it, as a strike can come before it has reached the bottom. As long as the jig does not kink the line, it is best to tie the line directly to the eye of the jig's hook. Snaps and swivels may make the fish suspicious.

The soft and pliable silicone bodies on some jigs are often torn to shreds by the fish. For that reason, it is a good idea to take a good supply of extra bodies along. The colours on plastic bodies can bleed and even melt if they come in contact with some other plastics. So be sure each coloured jig is kept in its own plastic bag. It should be noted that some lure boxes are described as "worm proof", which means they are specially made for storing plastic jigs.

Some jig bodies are impregnated with various scents to stimulate a bite. By being injected with an enticing scent a jig can slightly increase its hooking potential. The scent is injected into the body, but this "striking oil" can also be wiped on or rubbed in. A streamer made of fish flesh can be hung on the jig to give it a more natural smell and consistency. Some sportfishermen use a little bait fish hooked through the top and the bottom lips. Zander/walleye find this jig especially attractive.

Plastic imitators

Plastic worms are imitations of leeches and worms that are often made of silicone. They were developed for bass fishing, but can be used successfully for pike, zander/walleye, small muskellunge and trout. Fishing with these plastic worms is similar to jigging.

Jig hooks can be used for the worms, but they must be weighted as little as possible so they do not lose the life-like action of the swimming leeches that are a predator's major natural food in many waters. Special hooks are available for plastic worms, along with advice on how they can be threaded on the hook to minimize the risk of snagging in weeds. A stiffer rod is necessary not only for the weeds but also to set the hook firmly. The worms can carry up to three single hooks and can be weighted with split shot sinkers.

Soft plastic and rubber material is perfect for natural-looking imitations of freshwater animals, salamander, frogs, larvae, crabs and fry, that are threaded on a single hook with small sinkers. The same technique is used for artificial grains of salmon eggs and fry. Without a doubt natural bait is best for trout, steelheads and salmon, but plastic imitations can do in a pinch. Small rubber roe are also used for ice fishing.

Sinkers

In order to fish an artificial lure effectively, it is sometimes necessary to use a sinker. Small, lightweight lures such as floating plugs often need extra weight for casting and for reaching the bottom, where 90% of all fish live. It is also possible to cast with flies, but lead weights are needed for casting weight and to take the fly to the bottom. Trolling (without a downrigger or diving planers) usually calls for sinkers. Large floating plugs that are used for pike must also be weighted to work the bottomregion.

For good casting qualities a sinker should be aerodynamic. For good movement in the water, it should be hydrodynamic. The very lightest-weight sinkers are small lead shots that are split in half and squeezed onto the line. They come in weights of a fraction of an ounce or gram to several ounces or grams. The best split shots are soft enough to be pressed onto the line with small arms so they can be opened up and used again.

Split shot is added directly to the line. An alternative is to tie a leader just in front of the lure, using a blood knot. The shots are then squeezed onto the leader, as many as are needed. The length of the leader depends on how far off the bottom the lure should be.

To add more weight to the line, choose a type of sinker that uses a rubber band (Rubbercor), a little plastic stick (Catarina) or a pair of wings (Clasp). Sinkers with rubber bands cause the least wear on the line.

Large lead weights that are designed to sink the lure to the bottom should be long and slender so they do not get caught on the bottom. These can be fished from a moving boat or trolled in shallow water, but they are also very useful for salmon fishing in rivers with stones and rocky outcroppings. They are attached to a leader 30–120 cm (12–48 in) in front of the lure.

The same "sinking line" that is used for nets can be used when fishing in flowing water. A length of sinking line weighs from 5–10 g (1/8–3/8 oz) and is useful not only for fishing with nightcrawlers, but also for sinking small plugs, flies or other lightweight lures to the bottom. The advantage in using sinking line is that it does not get caught as easily on stones and rocks.

Another sinker that is both fast and effective is a lead ball with a hole through the middle. The sinker is strung on the line above a swivel to keep it from sliding down the line.

These examples may make it seem common to use a leader with a sinker. In practice, however, the leader has a tendency to flip up and get itself entangled in the line and the lure. As most anglers will tell you, this problem can be easily solved with the help of an American invention called a Bait Walker that every angler can make himself. Bait Walkers are for fishing from moving boats or for slow trolling. The device is a single, heavy wire that is bent at an angle. The lure is attached to the upper arm with a piece of line. The fishing line is tied to a loop in the wire and the lead is cast around the lower arm to ensure that the lure and the sinker keep their distance from each other.

For pelagic fish or fish swimming in water from 10–20 meters (32–64 ft) deep, more substantial sinkers are necessary if the fish are to be trolled. These heavy sinkers, however, are no pleasure to fish with and the angler finds himself fighting the sinker just as much as the fish. A solution to this dilemma is a trolling device called a diving planer that is designed to dive deep under the water. Divers are attached directly on the line and the lure is adjusted to fish 180–300 cm (6–10 ft) after the planer.

To fight a fish without the diver, or to fish in deeper water at an increased speed, a downrigger must be used.

Hooks, swivels, rings and leaders

The hook is the light-tackle fisherman's most important detail, but it is often the piece of equipment given the least attention. What good are a rod, a reel, a line and lure that function as a perfect "casting machine" if the hook is weak, the point is not sharp enough, the connecting rings are weak—or if the fish can cut the line!

Hooks are available in more than 50,000 different shapes and sizes. They can be basically grouped as single, double or treble hooks. A single hook is commonly used with spoons, pirks and jigs, while double hooks are used sometimes with plugs. Treble hooks are the preferred hooks for artificial lures, even though they do not work as well as single hooks. When the force of a strike or of setting the hook is distributed over three points, none of them penetrate as well as when that same energy is concentrated in just one point. The popularity of treble hooks can probably be blamed on the psychology of fishermen—if one hook is good, three hooks must be better! Experience has shown that treble hooks get more bites but lose more fish, while a single hook gets fewer bites but lands more fish.

Certain artificial lures are designed for fishing with either single or treble hooks, some even for double hooks. A jig is a traditional single hook lure, while plugs are traditionally treble hook lures.

The parts of a hook

The parts of a hook are the eye, the shank, the bend, the point, the gap and the barb. These parts can vary in shape and description, bearing names such as Hollow Point, Needle Eye, Kirbed Shank, and Reversed Point. In general, the names stick to the point—a round eye exactly that, a tapered eye has a tapered wire for an eye, and so on. Hooks with points curving inwards are usually for natural bait and hooks with straight points are for spinning with artificials.

Hooks vary from size 28, only a few millimetres long, to size

The parts of a hook:
A. Eye
B. Shank
C. Bend
D. Point
E. Gap
F. Barb

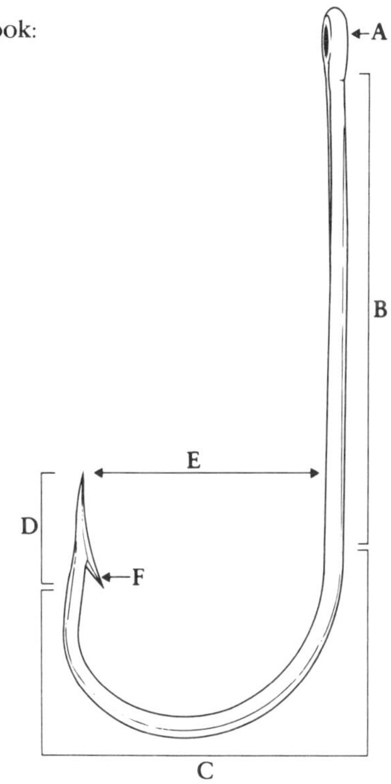

18/0, which is a rugged shark hook. As the scale stretches from 28 down to 0, the hooks become large and larger, and as the scale progresses from 1/0 to 18/0 they continue to increase in size.

Hooks are made of wire of carbon, steel, or stainless steel. The wire is tempered in various ways so that some hooks are soft and some are hard. Some hooks are tin/nickel-plated for salt water, others are bronzed for use mainly in fresh water. Hooks can be coloured blue or red or gold. Blue or brown hooks provide camouflage; red hooks are used for red lures that look like boiled shrimp or the larvae of the mosquito *Chironomidae*; gold hooks are used to make artificials extra attractive.

Most fresh factory hooks seem sharp and pointed at first glance, but the criterion for a sharp hook is if it can dig into a fingernail. If it cannot, it needs to be sharpened with either a whetstone or a file. Big hooks are sharpened with a file, smaller ones with a whetstone. After each strike or bottom snag the hook point should be checked and sharpened if necessary.

Split rings, swivels and snaps

Split rings, round or oval-shaped, are mounted either on the hook or the swivel. Oval connectors give the hook the most flexibility. This piece of equipment is usually the first bit of tackle to rust, so it is wise to keep a good supply in your tackle box.

A swivel is a thrust bearing used to connect the line and the lure. They were designed to eliminate the line twist that is commonly caused by rotating artificial lures. They come in many shapes and forms for different types of fishing. One special kind of swivel that is used with artificial lures has built-in ball-bearings to make it even more effective when trolling.

Snap swivels are used to make changing lures easier and faster. Once the snap is attached to the line, the lure can be changed by opening and closing the snap rather than tying a new knot. A snap, however, makes the lures more visible and even slightly heavier. The size of a snap should be kept to a minimum, especially when using small lures. A large snap can immobilize lightweight lures and perhaps make the fish skittish and suspicious. Snaps come in many shapes and sizes. Some are almost self-locking and are reliable when put under pressure, but others are weak. No-knot fast snaps are the very smallest snaps, designed for the quick changing of fliers or suspended lures.

Leaders

Leaders are not only for fishing predators with mouths full of sharp teeth. They are also useful when the last few meters of line are constantly being worn and abraded, when being dragged over rocks, boulders, branches and roots, i.e. when trolling. Casting is also hard on a line. Using a leader with a smaller diameter than the line makes the lure move more naturally. When fishing with a fluorescent line an effective technique is to use ordinary line which has less visibility on the one or two meters of line that are closest to the lure.

A leader is made either of strong monofilament or of several strands of wire that are covered with nylon. Pike, muskellunge and other fish with sharp teeth can fight and bite hard enough to damage the line or even to break it off. By tying a strong piece of line (25–40 cm with a breaking strain of 20–30 kg) at the end of the line, the fish has something to sink its teeth into.

Wire leaders are probably the most durable, but they are much more visible than nylon leaders. Both leaders can easily be made yourself. A nylon leader requires a snap, a swivel and a suitable piece of line. A wire leader is made from sleeves, a swivel and a snap. A simple method of forming a loop in the end of a coated wire is to twist the tag end around the standing part of the coated wire 5–6 times and then heat it with a match. Pre-tied leaders are available at all bait-and-tackle shops.

Some sportfishermen prefer solid wire, often piano wire leader, because it is easy to work with and does not need sleeves.

An extra-long leader is called a shock line and should be able to withstand the heaviest strains. It can also function as a leader. Shock line can consist of 3–4 meters long monofilament line tied directly to the fishing line. These extra meters of line receive the worst of the wear and tear caused by casting. It is important to remember that 50–100 cm of shock leader on the reel demands a powerful cast.

Spinning techniques

Many an angler's first fishing experiences are snags on the bottom, and lost lures. To compensate, the lure is retrieved so high that it never enters the fish's field of vision. It is a known fact that fish spend most of their time on the bottom and that is where the lure must go.

Spinning is often a matter of getting the lure down to the bottom. One way to do so without losing the lure is to use a count-down system. This approach works well with sinking lures such as spoons, spinners and sinking plugs. It also works with the addition of a sinker weight 4–6 ft up the line from a floating plug. After the cast, the lure lands on the surface of the water where it begins to sink and continues to take line off the reel until it has reached the bottom. When the line begins to slack the lure has reached the bottom and it is time to begin the retrieval. To find out how deep the water is, begin counting as soon as the lure hits the water: 21,22,23 . . . until the line is slack. Then begin retrieving. On the next cast, let the lure sink for one less count before retrieving. The idea is to count the lure down to the right depth and then spin it in, knowing it is passing over the bottom at exactly the depth where the predators are. This is a reliable method of getting to know the fishing water as well as an indirect method of learning its depth. Assuming that the lure sinks at the rate of one meter per second, that is the same amount of time it takes to say the number twenty-one. If the lure has reached the bottom by the count of 27, the water must then be 7 meters deep.

This deep measuring system is not always necessary—it takes only a little practice to learn how quickly the lure sinks, when it should be retrieved and how deep to fish.

If searching the bottom does not produce any fish, try fishing a little higher up, perhaps even up to the surface. Some predators are known to hunt in stages, first at the bottom, then in the middle, then just under the surface. The count-down system makes it easier to try your luck at these different levels.

Even though artificial lures are designed to swim in a certain pattern when they are retrieved, a varied retrieval is still important in attracting fish. Sometimes a fish strikes at the exact instant the retrieval stops, making the lure start sinking to the bottom. A predator interprets the lure's action as that of its prey, and the fact that it seems ready to escape stimulates the predator to strike. Injured or sick fish also display this run-and-hide behaviour pattern. By creating a varied pattern of reeling in and stopping, the lure imitates the hesitant, jerky action of a little fish swimming or feeding on the bottom.

The line can be retrieved in a great many ways. Instead of stopping the retrieval, it can be slow one moment and rapidly increase its speed during the next. The rod can be raised and lowered so the lure rises and sinks in the water.

The illustration on the left depicts spinning in water that is nutrient-poor. In nutrition-rich water as at the right, abundant aquatic vegetation can make it necessary to fish from a boat in order to get close to the fish.

In fast moving water, a pause in the retrieval leaves the spinner or spoon standing still in the water. Action can be transferred to the lure by lifting the rod and then sinking it again so the lure drifts back with the current to where the fish is.

When the lure is 10–20 meters away the rod can be shifted alternately from left to right, giving the lure the action of a weak or injured fish trying to protect itself.

The following rules can be applied to fishing in shallow and medium deep water (1–5 meters). Use lightweight spoons with large surface area that move easily and have a lively swim. Use lightweight spinners with big spoons and thin bodies. Use sinking or floating plugs that do not dive too deep. Most medium-sized floating and sinking plugs are made for depths of 1–5 meters.

Most problems occur in deeper water, usually 6–12 meters. As an example, imagine a cast of 25–40 meters and let the lure sink deep. After the first 5–10 meters of line are retrieved, the line will have been lifted 6–12 meters above the bottom and will no longer be in a fish's striking zone.

In order to keep the lure effective, reeling in must be stopped periodically so the lure has time to sink back to the bottom—probably as often as every 5–10 turns of reel. Retrieving in this way guarantees that the lure is working the bottom effectively.

Currents put additional pressure on the lure. Because the surface current is always stronger than the bottom current, it is not enough to use a heavy spinner or spoon that can penetrate at the bottom. In this case it is better to use a lighter lure and cast it diagonally across the current, or even up against the current, and give it a few seconds to sink. By the time the current has carried the lure right in front of you, it is down at the bottom and the retrieval can start.

Knowing where a predator feeds is not the same as getting it to strike. Besides the necessity of trying out different types of lures and colours, it is just as important to experiment with different retrieval techniques. Retrievals can be fast or slow; they can be jerky or provocative, as when the lure is rapidly moved in to the fish, after which its speed is increased so the lure dashes away from the fish just like a frightened fry. One technique that is often successful is to let the lure swim slowly towards the fish and then quickly withdraw it. It is just as important to let the fish see the lure from different angles, so the fish is "bombarded" by baitfish from all sides.

If a fish has struck at a lure, it may have been frightened and will continue to be timid. It is often a good idea to leave the fish alone for a while and return to it later.

Most predators have a natural feeding pattern in the same sense that we eat breakfast, lunch and dinner. These patterns, however, are affected by the weather, the feeding patterns of the prey, the air pressure and temperature, the phase of the moon, the amount of light, the pH value, the amount of oxygen in the water, and the time of day. With all these variables, it is quite understandable that if a fish does not react on the first cast, it might strike an hour or so later because the weather or some other condition has changed.

A number of external circumstances determine how fast the line should be retrieved. Water temperature is the most important factor. It determines where the fish will stay and how eagerly they will forage for food. Arctic char, North American lake trout and several other trout species are most active in cool or cold water. Northern pike, zander/walleye, perch and many other fish lose their appetite in cold water. They make little effort to take a lure that is too far away from them or moves too fast. When fishing these species in cooler water temperature, it is important to fish the lure slowly and to choose lures with lively action, even when using a slow retrieval.

In warmer water, a fast lure that broadcasts lively pressure waves, perhaps even a surface lure, is the best choice. In water with low visibility it is important to use a relatively slow lure with an enticing swim, a spinner for instance. Water that is both cold and cloudy is best fished with brightly coloured lures such as silver or the fluorescent reds, yellows or oranges, that provide a strong visual signal.

Droppers

Many predators can ignore a lure because it is too big. A predator's diet consists of the larvae and fry of fish, insect larvae or other little animals that are much smaller than the most minute spinner or plug. By attaching a leader with a fly above the spoon, spinner or plug, however, you get a good imitation of the fish's natural prey. Plastic imitation, micro-jigs or a variety of other flies can be used. Bass, trout, perch and even northern pike react well to this lure. Perhaps these predators cannot tolerate seeing the little "fish" about to feed, and take the fly for themselves. When perch fishing there is nothing that attracts fish more than two or three flies suspended like this above a lure.

Spinning with flies

Spinning with flies is a fishing tactic that should not be ignored. Lurking in the deep pools and hollows of rivers and streams are trout and salmon that might choose to bite only on a fly. In these situations it can be necessary to fish with flies on spinning tackle. A little sinker is mounted about one meter up on the line and the fly is cast so that it is retrieved by reeling it through the fish's feeding place. Using spinning tackle with flies is a slow process, very similar to fishing with a fly rod.

A rather popular and effective way to make long casts with flies is to use transparent spinning or casting bubbles that are filled with water to gain casting weight. These bubbles have two eyes. Thread a short piece of nylon line (about 60 cm) through the eyes and attach a swivel at each end so the bubble can glide along the line. After that, attach a leader (120–210 cm) to one swivel, along with a fly or other small artificial fish or an imitation larva. Tie the remaining swivel to the fishing line. Many sportfishermen attach the bubble by tying the line to one eye and the leader to the other. By using this method, however, the strike is not felt as clearly as when the bubble glides and there is direct contact with the hook.

Bubbles are also available at various casting weights, for example, 5, 10 and 15 grams of lead in a plastic pipe shaped like a cigar. Another type is shaped like a casting plug with a magnet, and the fly is attached to the magnet. When the plug hits the water a quick jerk with the rod releases the fly from the magnet.

Right: Tube flies and big streamers can tempt even finicky fish to bite, especially when used for boat fishing in large lakes and the game is different types of salmonoids.

When spinning with a fly, place the sinker 0.75 m to 1 meter in front of the fly.

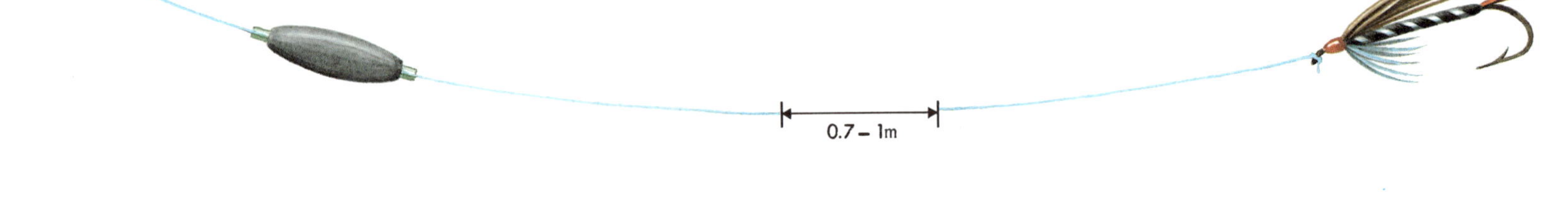

Trolling

The most effective method when fishing a large area is trolling. That means trailing a line and lure after a moving boat.

Trolling methods can be as simple as allowing a spinner or plug to stream after a boat that is being rowed. Or they can be as sophisticated as combing the area from a motor boat that is equipped with the most modern electronic equipment for locating the lake's depths, shoals and fish.

Large areas of many lakes are uninhabited by fish. For this reason, a fisherman who does not know a lake's depths, shallows and dropoffs is going to spend only a very small percentage of his time fishing effectively.

A navigation chart is very helpful because it shows the slope, edges and shallows where fish are most likely to feed. By using a chart, many areas can be eliminated and all efforts concentrated on areas with good fishing potential.

Many predators hunt at the surface at the same time of day throughout the year. Bass, trout, northern pike, salmon and sea-run brown trout search for food in shallow areas from 1–3 meters (3–9 ft) deep. The best way to fish such species is to troll with lightweight spinners and floating plugs. When trolled at a minispeed of 1.5 knots these artificial lures are life-like and enticing. Large, ultra-light spoons also produce an excellent, lively and tempting swim at this speed, and so do plugs if they are not sunk too deep. This type of fishing is called surface trolling.

During the summer it is very common to find lake fish in open water, where they go to stalk smaller fish. Trolling these waters involves locating fish in the pelagic zone. In fact, predators seem content to stay within a particular water level, so finding the right depth is the only way to catch them. The most successful approach to finding the right depth is to fish with several rods, each to test a different depth. A spoon can be used for the surface rod. A floating plug that dives to a depth of 2–4 meters (6–12 ft) is the right lure for the second rod. Diving and sinking plugs or lead-headed spinners are best for testing depths of 4–6 meters (13–20 ft). During the warm summer months fish usually retreat even deeper, i.e. to 7–10 meters (32–39 ft). At that depth the only lures that will work are medium-sized sinking and diving long-lipped plugs.

Using these four artificial lures the lake can be searched down to 10–12 meters (32–39 ft). If the water is clear, this method is more effective because the fish can see the lure from as deep as 15 meters (48 ft). When the fish actually strike the sportfisherman can pinpoint the fish's depth. This method of trolling can also be used at dropoffs and along shoals by locating the water depths on the chart and then fishing with plugs that sink to the right depth.

The basics of trolling

A few fundamental principles apply to trolling, whether from a rowboat, a motor boat, or even a boat with an electric motor. One is to use a rod holder. This very important piece of equipment should sit securely in the boat and preferably be permanently installed. The rod should sit snugly in the rod holder and yet provide quick access to the rod when a fish strikes. Rod holders can be made of simple metal of plastic piping, as long as they can be mounted on the boat. Many varieties of portable rod holders are also available. The most practical of all portable rod holders is without a doubt the Down East—it not only meets all the above requirements, but it can be mounted on most small boats.

A gently zig-zagging or curving course is the best to follow. Using two or more rods, this course creates a natural situation where the lure on one side swims faster while the lure on the opposite side slows down. When turning, make sure the turns are wide so the lines do not cross. Two to four rods can be fished at the same time.

The line can be thrown with a light casting action or the spool can be released so the forward movement of the boat pulls the line off the reel. Short lines are best for trolling, but they should not be so short that the area is not properly covered. Long lines means less control in working the lures. In trolling, the vibrations at the tip of the rod are a sign that the lure is moving well. Besides this, short lines set the hook much better.

A rule of thumb for trolling with artificials at the bottom is that the amount of line you have out should be 50% more than the depth you are fishing. The only time more line is advisable is when the water is crystal-clear and the fish are shy.

It is worth the time it takes to experiment with different lures until the right one is found. After that, the day's "favourite" can be used instead of the others. There are times when spreading lines throughout the area is the most effective trolling technique. There are other times when running the lines closer together is more attractive to the fish, because the lures resemble a small school of fish.

When it is windy it is important to keep the lines close to the water so the wind cannot blow slack in the line. If the line is not taut the signs of a strike are lost. In order to have complete control of the situation once a fish has been hooked, the other lines must be retrieved before the final fight starts.

Deep trolling

Fish spend most of their time close to the bottom at depths of 5–15 meters (16–48 ft) or more. Unfortunately, very few lakes are so clear that there is good vision to those depths. If you are familiar with a lake's depths or you have a sonar, a lure can be sunk first to 5 meters and then an instant later be sunk to 10 meters or more. The best way to keep the lure consistently on the bottom and to be sure it is moving at the right depth is to weight the leader in front of the lure. One of the easiest ways to sink a lure is to use deep trolling tackle or an American invention called a "Bait Walker". The following is an extremely effective rig for fishing bass, trout, northern pike or zander/walleye.

Begin with a three-way swivel and tie 60–200 cm (2–7 ft) of nylon monofilament to one eye of the swivel and to a floating plug. This piece of line will function both as a leader and as a shock line and will bear the brunt of the wear and tear from any rocks or ledges that may get in its way. In the lower eye of the swivel, tie a 30–100 cm (1–3 1/2 ft) long mono line with breaking strain slightly lower than the fishing line. At the end of this piece

Suspended fish can be difficult to locate when they are feeding. It is necessary to fish at different water levels until the fish are discovered. The best method is to fish lures at different depths, 3, 6 and 9 meters, for example. When a fish takes one lure, the others can be placed at that depth.

Deep trolling along the bottom is a proven method of fishing northern pike and other fish, both with artificial lures and with natural bait. One type of deep trolling leader is shown in the inset. Floating plugs should be used to reduce the risk of bottom snags.

of line tie a sinker, around 30–75 grams in weight, that will keep the plug down at a trolling speed of 1–3 knots. In the swivel's third eye tie the fishing line. This rig is guaranteed to keep the plug right over the bottom the entire time you are fishing. It functions to a depth of 10–15 meters (32–48 ft) and sees to it that the plug stays on the bottom even when fishing at 4–5 meters (13–16 ft) one minute and 15 meters (48 ft) the next. It is important to use floating plugs because they swim free of the bottom. In addition, the plugs should have a smooth, streamlined swim, not one that trips along the bottom and risks getting caught.

A simpler version of this rig can be made by tying a 1-meter-long leader to the fishing line and letting the line run through a slip sinker. This rig keeps the lure working the bottom, but there is a greater risk of abrasion on the line.

Trolling with a downrigger

Casting and trolling with weighted artificials covers a depth limited to about 10–15 meters (32–48 ft). At depths of 10–20 meters (32–64 ft) a diving planer can be attached to the line 2.5–4 meters (8–13 ft) in front of the lure. These divers are used to pull the lure down to deeper water, but when the fish is played in, the resistance of the diver, often made of metal or plastic, is added to the strain on the line. Previous generations of sportfishermen had to add heavy lead sinkers to their lines when they wanted to troll in deep water. Thousands of big northern pike, North American lake trout and salmon have been fought, along with sinkers weighing 3–5 kg (6.6–11 lbs), on heavy saltwater tackle—a type of

A downrigger is a spool with wire line and a boom with a pulley, through which the wire passes. Most downriggers are also equipped with a rod holder, depth counter and drag system. A downrigger rod should have medium action and be arched in a J-shape when properly set.

sportfishing that was very satisfying but that involved more muscle than sport. The downrigger gave deep trolling a more sporting nature. In North America, where the downrigger originated, there is a divided opinion as to where the first downrigger was made. Some say it was made by west coast salmon fishermen; others maintain it was invented for fishing North American lake trout, a fish that can weigh over 45 kg (100 lbs), in the large, cold, deep lakes of the north.

The downrigger's simple construction makes it possible that it was made in several places, each quite independent of the other. One thing is certain, and that is that today's sophisticated downriggers were developed in the Great Lakes area during the last two decades. Downriggers come in small, portable sizes that are manually operated, as well as in electric versions with computerized control. The Great Lakes, thanks to enormous conservation efforts and the massive stocking of various salmon species in a surprisingly short time, have developed into what are probably the world's best freshwater game fishing.

The salmon species that were stocked were chosen carefully so there are always fish available in shallow as well as deep water throughout the season. And regardless of whether boat fishing is near the shore or in open water, most of the salmon are taken with the aid of a downrigger.

The first downrigger in Scandinavia was introduced in Sweden in the 1970s. The use of downriggers is increasing in all Nordic countries, especially for fishing salmon. Even in other parts of the world, in salt water as well as fresh water, the downrigger is used for fishing deep water.

A downrigger is made of a spool carrying a wire line and a boom with a pulley, through which a single or stranded wire is run. Most downriggers are equipped with a drag system, a line counter, and a rod holder. The sinker is placed at the end of the wire and a line-release is attached either to the wire or to the sinker. Extra line-release can be placed higher up on the wire if several lures are going to be trolled from the same downrigger.

The fishing line is held by the line-release, anywhere from 3–30 meters (9–96 ft) away from the lure, depending on the depth of the fish, visibility in the water and other factors.

The weight of the sinker is determined by each individual downrigger. The heaviest sinkers weigh about 6 kg (13 lbs). They are often torpedo-shaped and have fins.

The importance of an echo sounder for finding the right depth cannot be overemphasized. It also helps to locate predators that often live at particular water depths. With this information, you can troll one lure slightly above the fish, another under it and two at the same depth as the fish.

Downriggers can be used on any size boat. The rod is placed in the downrigger's own rod holder or right next to the downrigger. Specially designed rods are available for use with downriggers to provide extra strength in setting the hook when there is a strike. The reel used is generally a multiplier. A relatively thin line is used, but it must be able to withstand the strain of trolling at 3–4 knots.

The line-release must be perfectly adjusted. It can be made of clips or a spring that is released when a fish strikes, freeing the line for the angler to play the fish with the rod. When the climate warms up each year, predators retreat to water temperatures that better suit them. They can sometimes move as deep as 30–50 meters (96–160 ft). A temperature indicator fixed to the downrigger-cable can tell you the temperature at the lures' location.

Electronic equipment

The simplest way to measure the depth is by dropping a string tied to a lead sinker. A small plastic marker is knotted at each meter of the string, and when the sinker hits the bottom, measuring is simply a matter of counting the plastic markers. This method, however, is a time-consuming and lengthy process to use very often.

Electronic equipment for measuring depth has made sportfishing and especially trolling much more exciting and effective. There are several different types of sonars. There are systems that flash, LCD systems, graphs, and colour sounders. The flashing sounder is the least expensive and gives a very clear picture of the

Big Fish
Big Fish
RYDS 580 BF

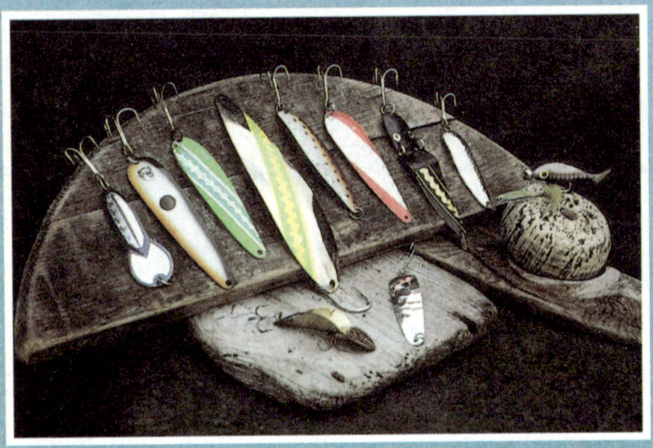

Above: A sonar is an excellent aid in locating fish. The sonar display shows the depth, bottom structure, thermocline and the spots where the fish are. The graph sonar in the picture shows, among other things, that there is a fish just to the left of the ridge.

Right: A downrigger uses a sinker weight to take the lure to the required depth. The fishing line is attached to the downrigger's line-release. The distance between the lure and the line-release can vary from 3–30 meters. Lower to desired fishing depths. When a fish strikes, the fishing line releases from the sinker. The sinker is then retrieved so the fish does not get tangled in the wire during the fight.

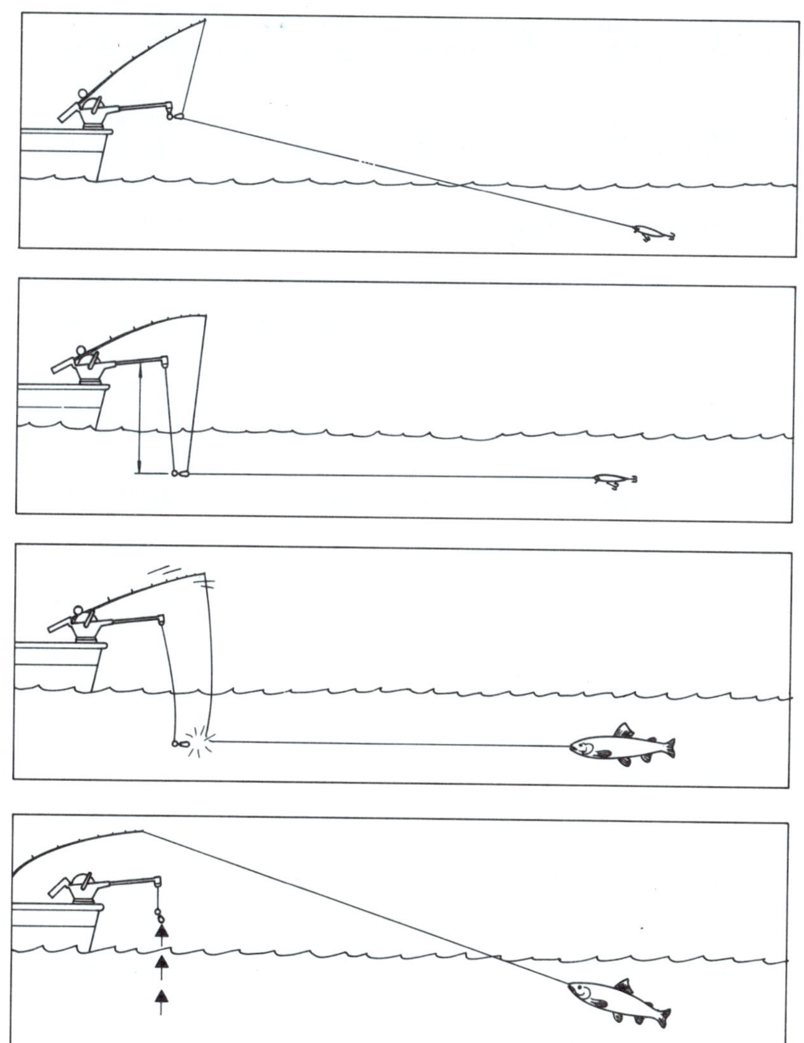

Left: Specially designed boats are often used for trolling. Normally 4–6 rods are trolled at the same time. The technique makes it possible to fish for species that feed in the pelagic zone as well as bottom-dwellers. Two types of very effective trolling lures are shown here. In the upper inset are light spoons mainly used only for trolling. In the lower inset are various plugs working well during different boat speeds.

depth as well as the composition of the bottom, whether it is rocky, sandy or muddy. Some of the more sophisticated flashers can also indicate schools of fish or individual fish and are equipped with signals that sound when a fish is found or when the bottom gets shallow. This information is displayed in the form of light signals on a disk.

A graph recorder registers all information on a paper roll. This type of echo sounder can give information on depth, bottom structure, shoals, submerged tree trunks, small fish, predators, the thermocline and currents. Video sounders use more advanced technology but provide the same information, in colour. Other electronic equipment that can be installed to make fishing easier is a gauge for measuring water temperature and an instrument to measure trolling speed.

The catch

Sportfishermen of North America may be the most fortunate in the entire world. Nowhere else do so many excellent game species of fish exist so widely in fresh water, as well as in the surrounding seas. Furthermore, the future of fishing remains fairly bright. Although pollution, acid rain, and the unregulated sprawl of human development have degraded once fertile waters, most rivers and lake systems remain pure enough to sustain healthy fish populations. Serious fishermen and a modern conservation ethic have combined to save many waters from destruction.

Bass

Probably the most important game species is the largemouth bass (*Micropterus salmoides*), also locally called green bass, green trout, and black bass. Originally a native of the southeastern United States, west to the Mississippi River, the range of the species has been gradually expanded (by stocking and waterway engineering) to any suitable waters from southern Canada southward to Honduras and Cuba, and including all of the United States, even Hawaii. Bass have been successfully introduced in Morocco, Kenya, southern Africa, Italy, Spain, Portugal, France, and in a few places in southern Germany. In Europe, however, a fish of 1.5–2.0 kg (2 1/2–4 1/2 lbs) is considered large.

Largemouth bass once thrived best in weedy, shallow lakes, in swamps and river backwaters (oxbows) because these habitats assured them an ever-abundant food supply and protection from predators. They were usually found in water less than 6 meters (20 ft) deep; below that rooted vegetation would not grow. But during the last half of the 20th century, largemouths have adapted to the deeper water-supply reservoirs of middle America, to millions of farm and ranch ponds, and especially to the deep impoundments behind large hydroelectric dams of the southern and western United States. Largemouths still grow heaviest and fastest in the rum-coloured lakes, sloughs, rivers and bayous of Florida where specimens weighing 4–5 kg (10 pounds) or more are most common. The all-time record of 10.09 kg (22 1/4 pounds) was caught in adjacent Georgia in 1932. If that record is ever exceeded, some biologists believe the new trophy might come from one of the reservoirs in southern California where the growth rates are high.

The "father" of American bass fishing was a medical doctor who (in 1902) claimed that "inch for inch and pound for pound, the black bass is the gamest fish that swims". That is not exactly true, yet the popularity of this freshwater species is understandable. Bass are easy to catch, but not *too* easy: a definite asset. They are powerful when hooked, fast swimmers and frequently jump out of the water. Far from the tastiest on the table, they are nonetheless good to eat. But best of all, bass are available. No sportsman anywhere in America lives very far from good bass fishing water.

The largemouth has two close relatives that are favourites of fishermen. Most numerous of these is the smallmouth bass, or bronzeback (*Micropterus dolomieu*). The other is the spotted or

Largemouth bass

Kentucky bass (*Micropterus punctatus*), which has a very limited range in the southeastern part of the United States.

When of comparable size, smallmouths probably are livelier, stronger, warier game fish than largemouths. Not nearly so adaptable to stocking and transplanting, smallmouths prefer cleaner, colder waters, usually farther north in the Great Lakes region, in New England, and eastern Canada. The best populations occur in lakes with rock or gravel bottoms where there is considerable wind and wave action, but without dense vegetation. However, largemouths and smallmouths do share some lakes where the habitat varies from one area to another. Smallmouths also populate many clear, free-flowing streams (sometimes together with brown trout) that have clean gravel or bedrock bottoms and a gradient (drop) of from 4 to 25 feet per mile (0.75 to 5 meter per km). Stream or river smallmouth bass are at least as game as trout of comparable size. The record smallmouth bass of almost 5.5 kg (12 pounds) was taken in 1951, in Dale Hollow Lake, Kentucky. The two largest known spotted bass weighed 4.10 kg (9 pounds) each.

Perhaps no game species anywhere are taken on such a variety of tackle and under so many different conditions as are freshwater basses. In springtime both species move into shallower waters anywhere, but especially along the irregular shorelines of lakes to spawn. Then anglers can cast for them either by wading or from small, maneuverable boats, with light tackle. One effective technique is to use a flyrod with floating bugs, or "poppers", which imitate frogs or water beetles.

But most often bass tackle means either a spinning rod and reel, or a shorter, stiffer bait-casting rod and a level-wind, multiplying reel. The latter combination was developed in America especially for bass fishing and is still the one most widely used for most of the fishing season, to cast a bewildering variety of lures or plugs that weigh 10–25 grams (3/8 ounce to 3/4 ounce).

After spring spawning, and as the water temperature gradually rises with summer, bass seek deeper and deeper water and/or the shade of more dense vegetation. There is also a tendency in some large lakes to gather in schools. Therefore lures that run deep when retrieved are necessary. To cast into vegetation sometimes as thick as sauerkraut, weedless lures (with guards covering the hooks) are used. A serious bass fisherman's tackle box will contain several kinds of weedless lures (usually spoons), jigs, plugs (with wooden or plastic bodies to imitate small forage fishes), spinners and soft, supple plastic worms, that may be used alone or in combination with jigs or spinners.

Often from mid- to late summer, the most difficult part of catching bass is finding them and that may mean exploring much water area in as short a time as possible. The result has been the development of the modern "bass boat", a light, swift watercraft with a shallow draft and containing either two or three swivel seats (to accommodate two or three fishermen) for convenient casting in any direction. Boats are also equipped with sonar devices to determine water depth, an outboard motor, a small electric motor to propel the boat slowly while casting, a live well, an anchor, and a cooler or live bait container. Some fishermen prefer to use live crayfish, minnows, salamanders, or other natural baits rather than artificial lures.

For fishing smaller water, say ponds and swamps, or rivers, bass fishermen use everything from canoes and johnboats which can be transported atop their autos, to one-person inflatable fishing tubes. The latter have become increasingly popular because they permit an adventurous angler to test waters that others cannot reach by wading or in larger boats. They fish not only for bass this way but for other game species as well. The writer has recently used fishing tubes widely over North America and this has opened up an entire new world of exciting sport.

Bluegill

Distributed in most warmer waters throughout America live many members of the sunfish family (*Centrarchidae*), to which the basses above also belong. Most are brightly coloured, many are too small to be worth catching, and since some hybridize, positive identification may be difficult. The most important family member is one that rarely weighs more than 0.5 kg (1 lb) but which is surprisingly game on ultra-light flyfishing tackle. It is the bluegill or bream (*Lepomis macrochirus*). In many areas it is both exceedingly abundant and unwary enough to be easily caught. No sophisticated tackle or angling experience is necessary to catch many. No wonder it is a favourite everywhere.

Bluegills prefer calm, somewhat weedy waters where they can both feed on aquatic insects and hide from the bass and pike that prey on them. They are more likely to be found exposed in more open places, close to shore, early and late in the season as well as early and late every day. Bluegills are among the most frequently caught fish through the winter's ice. But spring is the best time of all to quickly hook enough for a delicious banquet.

When lakes begin to warm, bluegill concentrate in shoal water sometimes barely deep enough to cover them. There they scoop out clusters of honeycombed nests that are easy to see in clear water. Then for two or three weeks the bluegills patrol these nests and lay eggs in them. They will also quickly strike

Crappie

almost any kind of small trout fly that is cast nearby. A wise fisherman will catch as many of these spawners as he possibly can because the species is exceedingly prolific. In fact they often overpopulate many waters and stunting is a result. The heaviest bluegill ever caught (in Alabama) weighed 2.15 kg (4 3/4 lbs).

Judged by the sheer numbers and total weight, the twin species of crappies would lead the list of freshwater fish caught and eaten every year in the United States. Also members of the sunfish family and roughly similar to bluegills in size and shape, white (*Pomoxis annularis*) and black (*Pomoxis nigromaculatus*) crappies differ in that both are sought almost entirely for food rather than for sport. However, crappie fishing is almost everywhere a gregarious or family pastime and this may more than compensate for any lack of game qualities in the two species.

Both crappies are carnivorous, surviving entirely on crustaceans, insects, and especially on smaller fishes. White crappies are more tolerant of turbid conditions and are found in greatest numbers in murky lakes and reservoirs. Black crappies need clearer, purer waters and tend to be most abundant in the northern Midwest and Great Lakes states into southern Canada. Both are school fishes, travelling and feeding in groups in which all are about the same size.

Because they are attracted to sunken debris, deadfall, and brushpiles, fishermen seek out these places, anchor their boats nearby and dunk live minnows around the edges. In fact, some addicted crappie fishermen build their own underwater brush havens by carrying old logs and slashings out onto winter ice, then allowing it to sink when the lake ice thaws later on. The locations of crappie havens may be marked for future fishing with small buoys. Only the simplest of tackle—a cane pole, line, small sinker, and cork float—are necessary to catch crappies around a productive brush heap. Fishing at night is often better than during daytime, especially during the heat of summer.

Catfish

North American waters contain several species of catfish, some of which may average less than 0.5 kg (about 1 lb) (such as brown, black, and yellow bullheads) to one that occasionally reaches 45 kg (100 lbs) (the shovelhead or flathead catfish that is usually taken on set lines, without rod or reel). Of all this family (*Ictaluridae*) only the channel catfish will ever strike artificial lures and be regularly captured on sportfishing gear.

The best thing about channel cats (*Ictalurus punctatus*) is that they lurk almost everywhere in both moving and impounded water. Long, usually silvery, with forked tails, a channel catfish hooked on spinning tackle in a river is a very worthwhile adversary, especially if it weighs four or five pounds or more. Like most other catfish, this one feeds more actively and strikes more freely at night, particularly on such natural baits as crayfish and minnows allowed to drift downstream with the current into deeper pools. The record channel catfish, 26.30 kg (58 pounds), was caught in South Carolina in 1964. At any size it is such a good, popular food fish that the species is being raised commercially on fish farms.

Channel catfish

Walleye and zander

The walleye or walleyed pike (*Stizostedion vitreum*) is another American species with a modern range much greater than its limited original home area of southern and central Canada, plus the Great Lakes in the United States. Probably its savory flesh, much more than its sporting qualities, has encouraged fisheries to introduce the species far beyond its original territory.

This is one species that prospers far better in larger bodies of water than in smaller lakes. In fact, it reaches its greatest abundance in northern lakes from Lake Erie on the U.S.-Canada border northward through Manitoba. But the fact that it is comparatively easy to produce walleyes in hatcheries has resulted in a good supply of fish elsewhere. The average-size fish taken by sports anglers is between 0.5–1.5 kg (1–3 lbs). Any walleye over 2 1/2 kg (5 lbs) is a very good catch and beyond 5 kg (11 lbs) is well worth bragging about. The record walleye stands at 11.34 kg (25 lbs) and was landed in a Tennessee lake where the species had been stocked.

Walleyes strike readily on many natural baits as well as on some of the same lures cast for largemouth and smallmouth bass, and then retrieved deep along the lake bottom. Except occasionally at night, walleyes do not venture far from rocky or hard bottoms and it is a waste of time to seek them elsewhere. Once hooked, walleyes wage dogged, if unspectacular struggles to escape. The best advice to walleye fishermen is to always fish for them slowly, deliberately, and with patience. Concentrate efforts during early mornings, late evenings, or on rainy days.

Zander (*Lucioperca lucioperca*) is a game species that is highly regarded in Europe. It is common throughout Scandinavia and

Zander

central Europe and has been stocked in several areas in England where, however, it is not very popular because it is regarded as competition for the local match-fishing species. Zander thrive in murky lakes except for the Baltic Sea, in canals, and along slow moving rivers. It is only during spawning that zander are found in fast flowing water. Pike and zander are seldom seen in the same waters except for the Baltic Sea because the zander prefer muddy waters with an abundance of smaller fish where pike, mainly visual hunters, cannot survive. Because zander have exceptional eyesight in dark and murky water, they are typical night feeders, waiting for dark before they begin hunting.

A zander hears his way to his prey, detecting pressure waves made by the movements of smaller fish as they stir up sand. The prey is then stalked and attacked from behind. Many casting techniques are based on knowledge of this hearing, feeling sensitivity. Artificial lures are very effective in fishing zander, once the sportsman has mastered the art of sinking the lure to the bottom. The lure must have a life-like swim that sends out enticing sound waves and it is an advantage if the lure can occasionally bounce off the bottom, sending out even more vibrations. The zander should now come swimming after the lure, trying to bite it. A strike can have exactly the same feel as when the lure snags on the bottom, so be careful! A common problem in fishing zander is that the fish gets a crooked bite on the hook.

All kinds of lures can be used for casting in shallow water, but plugs that take an occasional bounce off the bottom give the best results. Spinners with lead head are excellent, as are spinners that transmit strong sound signals. Jigs can be extremely tempting to a zander and have an even better effect if a small bait is attached.

Weighted lures, plugs for example, are used for deep water. Even though zander feed on smaller fish, experience has shown that medium and large plugs are excellent for deep trolling, particularly during the cold months of the year.

Zander hunt mainly on the bottom but at night, especially during summer, they move higher up in the water to hunt school fish and can then be fished with plugs.

Wire leaders are not necessary for zander. A line diameter of 0.30–0.45 mm (12–20 lb) is strong enough for a leader, but because there might also be pike in the same water, many anglers use a wire leader anyway.

A zander's cartilaginous jaw makes it hard to hook. Needle-sharp points are vital on the hooks, which explains why treble hooks on lures are often replaced with thinner ones. Zanders are tenacious fighters, they are usually difficult to pull up from the bottom, and they are renowned for suddenly jerking and diving just when it looks as though they are finally close to the surface and worn out. The average zander fished in normal water weighs 1–3 kg (2–6 1/2 lbs). Fish weighing 5–10 kg (11–22 lbs) are trophy fish, while a zander over 10 kg (22 lbs) is rare. The record weight, however, is just under 20 kg.

Northern pike and muskellunge

Esox lucius, the northern pike or jack or jackfish, is circumpolar in distribution. In the New World it is by far most common all across Canada and in central Alaska. Not always a favourite because of its very bony skeleton and because it so often strikes when an angler is seeking lake trout or some other game species, the jack is nonetheless a splendid game fish. Usually hungry enough to strike, it is powerful, active, and sometimes even acrobatic after it is hooked. For decades the muskellunge has played a dominating role in American sportfishing. Sportsmen have literally hunted the species, resulting in overfishing in many places and extremely small populations in others. For that reason fishing for northern pike, which was once relatively unimportant, has now become very popular. Bait-casting is the usual method, but many Americans have adopted European fishing methods such as fly-casting and the use of both living and dead bait. The writer believes that trophy hunting for pike—deliberately stalking only the largest jacks of more than 10 kg (20 lbs)—is among the most exciting of all freshwater angling.

More than fifty different names have been applied to the muskellunge (or muskalonge, maskininge, or tiger musky) (*Esox masquinongy*), which is the largest member of the pike family. Like the northern pike, it has an elongated body about six times as long as it is deep. A resident of rivers, lakes, and occasionally smaller streams, muskies prefer quiet, shallow to medium depth waters where large areas of both submerged and emerging weeds grow. The original range of the species is only a fraction of that of the northern pike, being limited to chains of lakes in Wisconsin, Minnesota, Ontario in Canada, and other isolated populations in the St. Lawrence River and the Great Lakes, and in southern Ohio and Kentucky. But the muskellunge is so renowned as a game species, and its mystique so widespread, that its range has been increased artificially to meet sportsmen's demands.

Northern pike

Anglers seek—often stalk—muskies and northern pike in the same way and with the same tackle which is sturdier than that used for the basses. The basic gear is a stiff bait-casting rod, often with a long handle for two-handed casting, plus a level-wind bait-casting reel. Because of the formidable teeth of both species, fishermen usually insert a short wire leader between the line and lure.

Lures tend to be larger than those employed for bass and weigh between 20 and 35 grams (3/4 and 1 1/4 ounces). When retrieved, most imitate the swimming motion of small prey fish and the speed of the retrieve is varied to render the swimming more life-like. Some of the most exciting action comes suddenly when a lure or plug, which resembles a small mammal or large frog, is retrieved erratically on the surface, through weed beds where muskies lurk. The resultant strikes are often explosive.

Many pike and muskies are lost because they are not securely hooked. Both have hard, bony mouths and it is necessary to "set" the hooks solidly beyond the barbs or the fish easily escapes. The larger ones are landed by gaff or with a deep, long-handled net.

Unlike most other fishing which is readily available widely across North America, going after pike and muskies means travelling north into wilderness areas. This requires camping out or lodging in one of the many fine Canadian wilderness resorts that cater to trophy anglers. The best seasons for both are late springtime (June across southern Canada) and autumn, from mid-September until the northern lakes begin to freeze. Often there is a period during August when fishing especially for muskies is exceedingly slow. Once it was believed that pike and muskies stopped feeding altogether at this time because they were shedding teeth. We now know that this is untrue. The fish simply retreat to deeper, cooler water until temperatures begin to fall in September.

Although larger specimens have been reported from time to time, the recognized world-record muskellunge weighed almost 32 kg (70 lbs). It was boated in the St. Lawrence River, New York State, in 1957. The North American record for northern pike also was caught in New York (Sacandaga Reservoir) in 1940. It almost surpassed 21 kg (46 lbs).

Another much smaller and less popular pike, the chain pickerel (*Esox niger*) inhabits ponds and sluggish rivers of the eastern and southeastern United States. The largest pickerel ever weighed was 4.25 kg (less than 10 lbs).

Northern pike (*Esox lucius*) is one of the most widespread game species in Europe. Its range extends from the clear Arctic lakes of northern Scandinavia to the rivers and lakes of northern Spain and Italy, and even to the Baltic Sea, where it preys on herring in the brackish water and grows to a substantial size.

The large distribution area of the northern pike accounts for the substantial differences in its behavior. In the northernmost lakes that are ice-free only during the summer, the fish are most active during the bright, sunny summer days, when they hunt about two meters below the surface. Summertime farther south means that pike retreat to colder water.

Northern pike are found in fresh water almost everywhere, in streams and rivers, impoundments formed by dams, and in large lakes and reservoirs. Their life cycle is uncomplicated; early in the spring they come in along the shoreline to spawn. As the temperature rises, they head out for deeper water, where they remain until they return to the shallow feeding ground in the fall.

A northern pike is a perfectly formed freshwater hunting machine. With its jungle camouflage, it can lie undetected among the reeds and other bottom vegetation, ready at any moment for a sudden attack on a smaller fish. It is also a cannibal and does not hesitate to attack one of its own species. The remains of 3–4 kg (6 1/2–9 lbs) pike and salmon have been found in the stomachs of pike weighing 15–20 kgs (16–22 lbs).

Pike are basically visual hunters, a fact that makes them an exciting challenge to fishermen, as they usually live in very clear water.

Success in shallow water calls for fast-rotating, light spinners, lively plugs and light spoons. Heavy artificial lures that sink to the bottom are just what the doctor ordered for fishing deep water. Heavy spinners, especially lead-headed, sinking plugs, and heavy spoons are all effective.

Northern pike alter their activities to suit the water temperature. For that reason it is important that lures move slowly in cold water. In warmer water a lure that gives a fast retrieve is an asset.

Large pike have been known to take small lures, but as a rule it is a waste of time for a pike to go for small fish time after time when one large prey would fill his stomach nicely. It stands to reason then that small lures attract small pike, but the bigger the lure, the bigger the pike. The northern pike's hunting instinct is so strong that small pike have been known to attack lures that were at least half their size. The lure can be made more tantalizing for the pike if it is retrieved by an erratic series of starts and stops so the lure's sudden spurts imitate a small bait fish trying to escape a predator. Northern pike seem to be stimulated to bite by seeing the lure time and time again. When an angler knows this and knows that a pike is nearby, it is important to continue casting in the same spot, perhaps even changing to another artificial lure with a different swim, colour and size, because suddenly, after 5, 10 or perhaps even more casts, the pike has finally become so irritated (or perhaps entranced) by the lure that its resistance is worn down and it takes the hook.

The colour of an artificial lure is important. Every body of water has its "own" colour, but lures can generally be divided into two groups—the naturals and contrasts, such as red-white, red-blue, red-yellow, blue-white, and the fluorescent colours, which show up more clearly under ultraviolet light. Fluorescents often bring good catches in cloudy, dark water or in weak light. Silver, copper and brass are always a good bet for a strike.

A northern pike has several hundred sharp teeth that can easily cut through fishing line, making it necessary to fish with a leader. A mouth opener and disgorger can also be useful for getting the hook out. In Europe, pike are known to reach weights of 20–25 kg (44–50 lbs). Fish weighing over 20 kg (44 lbs) are landed each year, especially in southern Germany, Austria, and Switzerland, and Eastern Europe. Even in Scandinavia a 20 kg (44 lbs) pike is hooked nearly every year in spite of the Baltic Sea's brackish water. In North America, where most pike weigh 2–5 kg (4 1/2–11 lbs) and a 5–10 kg (11–22 lbs) landing is a trophy winner, these European pike are regarded as monsters.

Perch

Perch (*Perca fluviatilis*, in US *Perca flavescens*) is, despite its insignificant size, a marvelous game species when hooked on light tackle. This explains its popularity in so many countries. It's found in a few places in the northeastern United States where it plays a minor role among game species. In Europe the perch is found in almost every spot of fresh water that has suitable conditions—from the smallest ponds to the biggest lakes, rivers and reservoirs.

Although perch can be hooked on natural bait, it is a fish that is easily attracted to artificial lures. Small spinners, spoons and in particular jigs are all-enticing to this black-striped predator. Red is a perch's favourite colour, even though lures with strong colour contrasts—yellow, red-white and especially black—can also tempt it to strike.

Theories about the striking periods of perch have been discussed for years. One theory is that the closed air bladder is the cause. The air bladder acts as a kind of stabilizer that equalizes pressure by taking in or releasing air, but since the perch's air bladder is sealed, it cannot carry out these functions as other fish do. The "air pressure" theory claims that fluctuations in air pressure are bad for a perch and make it reject a fisherman's lure. Stable air pressure, either high or low, is considered best for perch fishing. Changes in air pressure are also related to the weather conditions and to changes in light that perhaps have a indirect effect on perch and their prey. Although no one knows the answer, one thing is certain—perch have distinctive striking periods. In big lakes, in particular those abundant with bleak and roach, perch go through typical striking periods during which they hunt and feed senselessly. During these times even in the worst of conditions, perch can show an interest in artificial lures. It is interesting to note that when one perch has been lured to the hook, there is a good chance that others in the school will follow suit. This chain reaction has been observed in small lakes, ponds, and in flowing streams, where the smaller perch often swim together in schools while the larger fish range over more water but usually stay within the same fishing areas.

Perch

The method of retrieval depends on how willing the fish are to bite. There are times when perch strike at everything, and other times when only special lures will tempt them. It is always important to sink the lure to the bottom and to vary the retrieval speed there. Sometimes you can see the fish, or sense it passing by the lure a time or two—then you must tempt the fish to bite with alternating patterns of small jumps and hops while the lure is being quickly reeled in, allowed to slacken, and reeled again.

There are simple ideas that always bag fish. One of these, for example, is using small dropper flies, preferable in glowing colours, that can more than double your chances of a fish and that work extremely well for school fish. A little red fly attached to a leader just after a hookless lure can indeed provide surprisingly good fishing. Perch can also be caught on a dropper loop leader with feathers, plastic baits, nightcrawlers and strip baits. A jig is probably the best lure for perch. The compact head helps it to sink quickly in the water, while the body material, made of marabou feathers, deer hair rubber or plastic, give the jig a pulsating rhythm as it is "jigged" by short, quick, back-and-forth rod action. By jerking the tip of the rod the vibrations are transferred to the jig, leaving the perch faced with a delicacy it can seldom resist.

In lakes, perch are usually found along dropoffs and along shoals where they stage attacks against smaller fish. In small lakes perch are often found in deep pools, but occasionally here, too, in rather shallow water. In fast flowing water perch seek out calm, deep, underwater troughs and holes, generally located between deep pools and shallower water.

Perch bite just as feverishly when it is warm as when it is cold. It is this behaviour, in combination with tenacity as a fighter, that has made the perch so popular. This little warrior of a fish provides many fine moments with a rod and reel while it provides excellent practice. Perch weighing 100–500 grams (3–8 oz) are the most common. Fish weighing more than two kilos are so rare they are the fish of a lifetime!

Striped bass

The story of the striped bass (*Roccus saxatilis*) in America is one of both despair and success. Not too long ago it ranked among the most important of all marine game species, often entering brackish or fresh water as it cruised in vast numbers along the entire Atlantic Coast from the Gulf of St. Lawrence southward to Florida. Casting in the surf or trolling just offshore for stripers was the highest quality sport. Striped bass were so highly regarded that the species was successfully introduced across the continent into the Pacific where the species now prospers from San Francisco Bay north to the Columbia River.

But the Atlantic populations of striped bass have been seriously depleted, if not actually doomed, by the terrible pollution in the Hudson River and in Chesapeake Bay, both of which are important nurseries for the species. Too great a commercial harvest may also have taken a toll.

But a success story, arguably, is that striped bass have been successfully landlocked by fish scientists and now thrive in many of the larger reservoirs across the southern half of the United States. That fact is good, but the stripers seriously compete with largemouth bass, to which they are not related. In fresh water stripers are caught either by trolling, usually with downriggers, or by casting toward roving schools with heavy spinning or bait-casting tackle.

The largest striped bass ever captured by a sportfisherman weighed 35.60 kg (78 1/2 lbs) at Atlantic City, New Jersey in 1982.

Striped bass

The record landlocked striper was hooked in an impoundment of the Colorado River, Arizona, in 1977. This one weighed over 27 kg (60 lbs). White bass (*Morone chrysops*), a purely freshwater relative of the striped bass, are abundant in Lake Erie and in other large impoundments. Success in catching them tends to be erratic but when feeding they are easily taken in great numbers. The record white bass was from a North Carolina lake and weighed almost 2.7 kg (6 lbs).

Rainbow trout

The family *Salmonidae* is very well represented in North America. The rainbow trout (*Salmo gairdneri*) is native to the west coast of North America, was not only established all across the continent but also has been stocked widely around the world. Today either the rainbow or the brown trout may be the most widespread game fish on earth.

There are both migratory and non-migratory races of rainbow trout and from locality to locality these vary greatly in appearance, behaviour, and growth rates. The migratory rainbows are known as steelheads and average much paler in colour than their cousins. They are silver in hue. Steelheads and non-migratory rainbows that live in large, deep lakes reach a much larger size than those that live year-round in American rivers. The chief difference between rainbows and other trout is that rainbows are essentially fish of very fast water.

The rainbow trout was first brought to Europe at the end of the 1800s where its principal use was as a stock fish. No one knows today where the first rainbows came from, but the rainbow trout found in Europe have the characteristics of several American rainbow species as well as the cutthroat trout.

Through the years, many rainbow trout have escaped from their original artificial lakes and ponds to natural waterways. In several countries stocking natural streams and lakes is no longer allowed but the fish still somehow manage to escape and have been found among hatchery-reared brown trout and sea trout when they were released in streams.

There are very few places in Scandinavia where rainbow trout are known to spawn in natural water, and even fewer places where the young grow naturally to maturity; the competition from the brown trout is too much for the rainbow.

A rainbow trout can tolerate higher temperatures than a brown trout; it grows faster, and tends to be cheaper to raise for stocking. The fish that are now slipping out from stocking ponds or mixed in with other species originate from hatcheries that often concentrate their efforts on growth, the time of spawning, and colour—factors that could be considered detrimental to the rainbow's natural life cycle when they escape the hatcheries and swim freely in natural lakes and rivers.

All rainbow trout, if it is possible, try to migrate to the sea where they quickly take on a much paler hue. This is the case in the Baltic Sea area, particularly in southern Sweden and Denmark. It is possible that these rainbows carry genes from the migratory rainbows, the steelheads. During the springtime in these parts of Scandinavia there is an increase in shining silver "steelheads" that are on their way to spawn and then return again to the sea.

Rainbow trout ▲

▼ Steelhead

While the brown trout prefers to spend its time in hiding places and along the shore where it feeds, the rainbow is a fish of the open water, often seen accompanied by other rainbows. This gregarious behavior could possibly be bred in the fish hatcheries, where many fish live together in a small area. The rainbow prefers a diet of insects, larvae and small animals and sometimes even of young fry. The brown trout's diet is on a larger scale, including frogs, crustaceans and minnows.

Whether fishing for rainbows or for brown trout in very fast water the technique is just about the same. The rainbow trout is hooked in stream passages, deep holes and among bottom vegetation. Spinners, small spoons and plugs as well as weighted flies and different kinds of natural bait are all good choices. Rainbows feed at twilight. They are much fussier about their food than the brown trout are, and can be very hard to please.

Rainbows seem marvelously content in lakes. So much so that several countries have created trout ponds and stocked them with rainbows. The British have successfully stocked reservoirs where an abundance of rainbows now makes fly-fishing from the banks and by boat a very popular pastime.

In Scandinavia, especially in Sweden, there are several hundred natural lakes that have been stocked with rainbows. Many local sportfishing associations contract their own gravel pits, ponds and lakes that are stocked with rainbows for their members.

Cutthroat trout

Another American trout that has *not* been widely or successfully stocked beyond its range is the cutthroat (*Salmo clarkii*) of the Snake and Yellowstone river drainages in Wyoming, and elsewhere in the western mountains. Searun cutthroats are found in river estuaries from Alaska south to northern California. The species readily hybridizes with rainbow trout in Rocky Mountain lakes. Many different races of cutthroats occur and except for the bright red slash marks on the throat, the colourings and markings vary widely. Cutthroats of the Yellowstone country, which are pink, blackspotted and with golden fins, are among the most striking of all. It is the writer's opinion that the cutthroat is not nearly as wary nor as hard to hook as the rainbow trout.

Eastern brook trout

Nor is the eastern brook trout or squaretail (*Salvelinus fontinalis*), which (especially in spawning colours) may be the most exquisite member of its family. Males at spawning time are one of the few freshwater fishes colourful enough to be compared with the fishes of coral reefs. Their most distinctive markings are the pure white edges of the fins.

When the first settlement of America began over three centuries ago, brook trout abounded in many of the pure freely flowing woodland streams of the eastern United States and Canada. But clearing the land for farming and cutting the forests caused

Cutthroat trout

Brook trout

so much siltation and increased the water temperatures enough that today brook trout barely manage to survive in only a few remote streams in the United States. The species requires cold water and cannot tolerate temperatures much above 21°C). Some good brook-trout fishing still exists in the more remote lakes of Maine, but for the best of it, a fisherman must explore farther north into Labrador and wild eastern Quebec.

The eastern brook trout was introduced in Europe at the end of the 1800s, along with the rainbow trout, but because the rainbow trout was more suitable for fish cultivation, little interest was shown in the eastern brook trout. Some fish farms still maintain small quantities of this fish.

As a result, the eastern brook trout now lives "wild" in many of Europe's clear and cold brooks, rivers and streams where there is fast moving water at low summer temperatures. Sometimes fish as long as 40–50 cm (16–20 in) are hooked, but average small eastern brook trout are 10–25 cm (4–6 1/4 in). Although insignificant as a game species, this trout is still a keen opponent.

Landlocked Arctic char

Arctic char

Farther north still, in the Keewatin District of Canada's Northwest Territories, the brook trout's close cousin, the Arctic char (*Salvelinus alpinus*), still makes annual spawning runs every summer into many Arctic rivers. Char fishing is doubly rewarding because it carries an angler into some of the loneliest, still unspoiled regions of the western hemisphere. Breeding colours of male Arctic char are almost surreal, varying from pure scarlet to scarlet and black or scarlet and gold. On the Pacific side of the continent, especially in Alaska, the range of much paler Arctic char overlaps with another native char, the Dolly Varden (*Salvelinus malma*), which is not nearly as sporting a fish.

Dolly Varden ▲

▼ Seagoing Arctic char

In Europe, the Arctic char appears in several different forms. A landlocked Arctic char is found in Norway, Sweden and Finland, on Iceland and Greenland, in certain cold, deep lakes in Ireland, England, Scotland and Wales, in alpine regions, and in the northern USSR. There is a migrating char that is found along the coast of central and northern Norway, on Svalbard, Greenland and Iceland, as well as in North America. This species does not grow as fast as its cousins in northeastern Canada, so a European fish weighing 1.5–3.0 kg (3–6 1/2 lbs) is considered large. The only place heavier Arctic char can be fished is on Greenland, where there are some individual streams that boast fish of 6–7 kg (12–15 lbs).

The landlocked Arctic char have their own special characteristics. Although these fish seldom grow to a significant size, there are places in Sweden, Norway and Finland where weights of 4–9 kg (9–19 lbs) have been recorded. In alpine regions and in Great Britain stunted populations are found, seldom weighing more than 0.5 kg (1 lb).

Wherever it is found, Arctic char is a very popular game fish. In deep lakes they are usually hooked on small live bait or lures that are either trolled or spinfished very deep.

In Scandinavia the method of trolling is often a group of small spoons attached in convoy fashion, the last vehicle being a fly or a single hook, i.e. baited with a worm. These same lakes see action during the winter also, when eager ice fishers test their skills using small shiny pirks or a jigging spoon that carry a baited hook or a fly suspended above the artificial bait.

In alpine regions Arctic char are fished during the coldest part of the year, using artificial lures early in the spring, but natural bait also. Non-migratory fish are found in some rivers in Scandinavia. It is not unusual for the Arctic char in nearby lakes to wander into these river estuaries during the long, light Nordic nights, and to swim far up the rivers. Arctic char are fished with spinners and small spoons. They doggedly follow a lure, which makes it possible to use the old trick of changing the treble hook to a little red or dark coloured fly on a leader trailing line about 5–10 cm (2–4 inches) behind the lure.

The migrating Arctic char move up the rivers during the summer. When newly arrived they can be hooked on spoons and spinners, but in most cases fly-fishing is an effective method in clear rivers. In Arctic rivers where glaciers have made the water cloudy, Arctic char bite on spinners, spoons and plugs that are cast into backwaters, holes and stream passages. The fish is a good fighter and will always give you and your tackle a good workout. It is a temperamental fish with highly geared fighting instinct and the fact that it is one of the world's best-tasting salmon has given the Arctic char enormous popularity throughout its fishing waters.

North American lake trout

North American lake trout

The North American lake trout (or togue or mackinaw) (*Salvelinus namaycush*) lives today in a vast territory from the Great Lakes northward, completely throughout Canada and extending into parts of Alaska. Therefore its range widely overlaps those of other trout and game species. The writer has taken lakers in the same waters as walleyes, northern pike, Arctic grayling, rainbows, brook trout, and Arctic char. Although all the other trout are best and most enjoyably taken by fly-fishing and with artificial flies, or on light spinning tackle, the deep, cold habitat of lake trout requires other methods. Perhaps nine in every ten lakers are captured by trolling over deep reefs and rock formations. Only when briefly spawning in the shallows can they be taken on lighter gear. In Europe, northern Sweden is one of the places where transplanted North American lake trout can be found.

Pacific salmon

The fact is not very well known, but all of the five species of American salmon can be taken, at least at some times, on sportfishing tackle. The writer has even caught all of them on a flyrod. However, the chum or dog salmon (*Oncorhynchus keta*) and the humpback or pink salmon (*Oncorhynchus gorbuscha*) are not highly regarded as game species. Nor often is the red or sockeye (*Oncorhynchus nerka*) although it certainly deserves to be. With good reason the most sought-after of the Pacific salmon are the king (or chinook or tyee) (*Oncorhynchus tshawytscha*) and the coho or silver (*Oncorhynchus kisutch*).

Humpback salmon

Red salmon ▲

Chinook salmon ▲

Coho ▲▼

The life history of kings and cohos is very well known. All Pacific salmon hatch from eggs deposited in cold, clear streams or rivers and the young salmon soon migrate to the sea where they spend from three to five years, gorging on the ocean's bounty and growing rapidly, before returning to their natal streams to spawn and die. But the cohos and kings are fair game while living in salt water, as well as for a brief period after they return to fresh water and immediately before the serious spawning begins. Fishing during the latter period with light tackle is by far the most exciting although deep trolling from a seaworthy craft is the normal way to seek salmon in salt water.

King salmon grow to substantial size and are strong fighters whenever or wherever hooked, from coastal British Columbia to the Bering Sea. They strike on a variety of salmon plugs, flashy metal spoons, spinners, feather jigs, and natural baits such as herring, and even on streamer flies in fresh water. Cohos also will strike all of these but the species is never more challenging, more acrobatic or more thrilling than when hooked on a flyrod, soon after it re-enters fresh water. In fact there are few game species in the entire world that can match the coho cavorting in a wild Alaskan river.

Among the more remarkable achievements of fishery biologists has been the successful introduction in recent decades of chinook and coho salmon into the Great Lakes system along the United States–Canada border. Now these two species also migrate yearly from natal feeder streams into these large bodies of fresh water (instead of into the Pacific Ocean) and back again to spawn. The result has been a busy sport fishery that almost matches the original.

Atlantic salmon

Taxonomists consider the landlocked salmon of northeastern United States and adjacent Canada to be structurally the same as the Atlantic salmon (*Salmo salar*). But nonetheless this superior, highly prized game fish is greatly different in its restricted habitat and in the method of fishing for it. Long ago in distant prehistory, Atlantic salmon were isolated by geologic changes from their access to the sea and since then have managed to survive without annual migrations to the ocean, in a few deep, cold, wilderness waters. Their range has even been extended by fish culturists to other lakes in New England and Canada as well as to Argentina and Chile. Most are taken by trolling, but late-evening insects hatched on many waters make fly-fishing as effective as it is exciting. Spinning also pays off when landlocks feed in shallower lake edges. Many of the early, now famous American trout-fly patterns were designed originally for landlocked salmon.

A 9–10 pound landlock is a real prize taken on any kind of tackle. Even in Europe landlocks can be found in a few rivers and lakes. The very large Gullspång salmon has its origins in Sweden's Lake Vänern, which is western Europe's largest lake. This salmon can actually weigh up to 18 kg (40 lbs).

In Europe salmon have been important to sportfishing for several hundred years and a great deal of fishing knowledge has naturally evolved around "the king of freshwater". The salmon's natural distribution area stretches from the north of Spain to Greenland. Salmon is easily recognized by its slender body and the forked tail that provides such a welcome grip when it is being landed. Another characteristic is the shape of the gill filaments. Salmon can weigh as much as 36 kg (79 lbs), but a salmon over 15 kg (33 lbs) is a rare sight almost everywhere, except in the Norwegian rivers, which are renowned for perpetually producing salmon of over 20 kg (44 lbs). Salmon are hatched in spawning grounds in rivers and live for 1–5 years in fresh water before they wander out to sea, where they grow rapidly and put on weight. Young salmon spend their youth off the coasts of Norway and the Faeroe Islands, along Greenland's west coast and in the Baltic—quite a distance from their natal streams. After 1–4 years in the sea, salmon make the return migration back to fresh water. The return trip upstream is a long and dangerous one, where a good number of salmon wind up in nets or on hooks. Once returned to their native streams they must pass deep pools with slick surface water and the sophisticated lures of sportfishermen and probably force a waterfall as high as 3 meters (10 ft). Unlike the Pacific salmon that die after spawning, only a few Atlantic salmon die, leaving the majority to return to the sea. After a year or more in the sea, the salmon will again make the long upstream migration.

Atlantic salmon swim upstream from early in the spring until summer, the time of the migration varying between different countries and latitudes. In the British Isles salmon start their upstream journey in February and March, but in northern Norway they do not begin until the middle of June. The big salmon come first, followed by the smaller, 1–3 kg (2.2–6.6 lbs) salmon. Well into the season it is not unusual for a large salmon or two to make a late arrival.

Once the salmon have swum up the rivers and streams they stop eating. All stomach activities stop, and all energy is divided between the development of the reproductive capacity and the preparation for the long journey to the spawning grounds, where spawning begins late in the fall.

What makes a salmon take a lure in fresh water is something no one can say with certainty. Much evidence suggests it is at first a matter of a striking instinct retained from the sea, followed by "irritation" caused by the duties of territory maintenance, and finally, seasonal aggression, as it is now very close to the time when a salmon must chase other males away from the spawning place. By this time the salmon, silver coloured on their return from the sea, have become intensely coloured and dark.

Atlantic salmon strike with the most determination when they have just migrated upstream. Early in the season the water is cold and salmon prefer the deep parts of the streams, deep pools and trenches. They rest at the bottom, where the current is the weakest, and it is here one should fish for salmon. Big, heavy spoons and plugs, often lead-weighted, are fished deeply and persistently where the salmon is thought to be. It may strike at a first cast, maybe the fiftieth, or the one-hundredth, maybe not at all. A good angler knows the local conditions and fishing techniques. Fishing at the lower end of a stream involves choosing the right time of day, when the salmon wander up into the stream. Fortunately, fishing is also a matter of luck.

In the summer the water levels decrease and the temperatures rise. Salmon move to their lairs in the shoals, preferably at the edge of the current. A fresh run salmon is often found at the tail of a pool where the currents converge. Because these pools are the first resting places after migrating, salmon often fight with each other over the places. At this time the fish might be aggressive and take the lure. This is a good time for fishing with lightweight spoons and plugs, since they do not necessarily have to be fished

Atlantic salmon

at the bottom, even if the chances of a strike improve the closer the lure can get to the fish.

When the water warms up in the streams and the water level has sunk even more, many fly-fishermen begin using small flies and floating lines. Anglers using spinning tackle usually give up, but most of the time it turns out that by fishing close to the surface, with small spinners and spoons while imitating the movements of a fly, the salmon strikes. Most anglers cast diagonally or downstream depending on the fish's location, the current and the depth. Fishing upstream is actually very rewarding, especially with spinners. If you can work a spinner against the fish's lies and then get the lure to change direction, or escape, you can often get the salmon to strike. The technique demands a lot of practice but is extremely effective in many streams.

What colours attract salmon? This question bring on lively discussions. At the beginning of the season spoons or plugs in silver, gold or copper are decidedly the best. Later in the season fluorescent red plugs such as a weighted Rapala can be colossal "salmon killers" when fished in the right hands.

When in the rivers and streams, salmon continue their wandering. They spend most of their time resting and can stay in one place for several hours, days, or weeks before they resume their journey. In this situation be careful, take extra care not to startle the fish, but keep working the spot. It is not unusual for a salmon to see the same lure every minute, every hour without paying the slightest attention, and then suddenly, after several hundred casts from the persistent angler, it strikes.

Lake-run brown trout

Lake-run brown trout (*Salmo trutta lacustris*) are found in many clear, deep lakes in Europe, primarily in Scandinavia and the lakes of the Alps. In order to survive, they need cold water in combination with feeder streams that make good spawning grounds.

Lake-run brown trout

Under optimal conditions a lake-run brown trout can weigh as much as 5–10 kg (11–22 lbs). Trophy fish weigh 10–20 kg (22–44 lbs). These fish may vary a bit in appearance, but a genuine lake-run brown trout is shiny silver with perhaps a trace of bronze or gold, enhanced by black, cross-like spots.

In the lakes, these trout hunt smaller fish in the open waters. Smaller trout usually stay closer to shore where they feed on insects, larvae and small animals. When lake-run brown trout reach a certain size their diet changes to perch fry, bleaks, small roaches and several other species. At this stage the fish can also be cannibals and their growth is rapid. The trout must now be fished in open water, when they are a much more formidable adversary.

When the ice melts in the spring the lake-run brown trout swim at or near the surface where the water is warmest. As the water temperature continues to rise, the fish retreat to deeper water. Late in the fall they return once again to the surface waters and can be seen in areas where muddy river waters run out into the lakes.

Trolling at the surface with spoons and plugs is best for spring fishing. As the fish go deeper, heavy sinkers and lures are needed. Fishing in, under, or just over the thermocline can produce good results. In the fall, trolling at the surface or in shallow water is again the best method.

There are many areas where smaller lake-run brown trout, those between 0.5 and 1.5 kg (1–3.3 lbs), feed in the shallows or rise to the surface after insects and larvae. Some of the classic fishing areas for lake-run brown trout are the large lakes in Ireland and similar lakes in Scotland, where the fish are called the brown trout, or brownies. In these lakes the fish, by whatever name you choose, are caught on flies, or small trolling plugs, or by casting in aquatic vegetation and along ledges and sand banks at depths of 1–5 meters (2–16 ft).

Sea trout

The sea trout (*Salmo trutta fario*) is a seagoing brown trout. It is found from northern Spain to northern Norway, on Iceland and the Faeroe Islands, in Great Britain and Ireland. It feeds in the sea, but during summer and fall, or during winter at the latest, it migrates up brooks, rivers and streams to spawn. Although there are regional variations, the sea trout closely resembles the salmon in appearance and behaviour. The sea trout has a shorter, rounder body. The head is often small and the tail fin not so forked. In spite of these differences, many experienced anglers cannot tell at first glance which of the two they are fishing, especially if both species are found in the same water. The only reliable way to distinguish between the two is to examine the scales and the gill filaments. While salmon often travel long distances from their birthplace to their feeding grounds in the sea, sea trout do not venture far from the coast. Recent studies have shown, however, that the sea trout are capable of migrating many hundreds of kilometers, even though they generally do not travel as far as the salmon.

Seagoing brown trout

After 1–5 years of growing up in their native environment, sea trout wander out to the sea where they spend 1/2–5 years before they make the long return journey back, often to the same place they were hatched.

The sea trout's original territory is around the North Atlantic, where there are still abundant clean, oxygen-rich rivers and streams for spawning. These same rivers and streams—in which the sea trout wander upstream to spawn and downstream to regain their strength in the sea—are the very places where sea trout have now become popular game fish. In Great Britain, Ireland and Norway and in several parts of Denmark, sea trout are not fished on their return to the sea after spawning. In neighbouring Sweden, however, fishing activities continue throughout the spring. Several rivers in Sweden, among them the Mörrum, are well-known for their excellent and relatively good quality sea trout, fished in the spring.

As soon as the fish move up to fresh water they become very cooperative, which explains why sea trout are known as typical fly fish, even though spinning is the predominant method in many areas.

Sea trout bite best at dusk, at night, and early in the morning, when they move into shallower water, and can be hooked on small spinners, spoons and wobblers. An angler's knowledge of the fish's feeding spots and its ranging habits in fresh water can be the difference between a good catch and none at all.

After the fish have been in the stream for a while, they lose their striking instinct and are influenced instead by other trout in the water. They can become irritated and aggressive and may chase away smaller fish as well as other trout. This is also the time when a sea trout can be hooked on artificial lures. Evenings and the hours after dark continue to provide the best fishing. It is not until fall, when the water level rises, the water carries more silt and begins to cool off, that fish can be caught in the middle of the day. This late in the season, though, sea trout are more aggressive, as spawning approaches and they fight with each other over the best spawning places. This is the most difficult time to get a strike, but an aggressive fish may just be mad enough to take at a little spinner or plug. After spawning, sea trout return to the sea, and during the spring months they are once again eager to bite.

As a rule, sea trout eat very little during the stay in fresh water. Flies and nightcrawlers are just as effective as artificials, which explains why you can just as well fish with a weighted fly once you have located the sea trout.

When spawning is over sea trout quickly fill their stomachs. In many streams and rivers they eat small fish, crustaceans and even frogs before they return to the sea. They remain at sea for one or several seasons before they again swim up the waterways to produce the next generation of sea trout.

In Great Britain and Ireland, and in Norway too, sea trout are found in lakes through which their spawning river runs. Here it is common to troll at the surface with floating plugs and spoons. Sea trout in these lakes follow established routes through the lakes. Knowing these passages increases an angler's chances of a good catch. In lakes, the sea trout strike best on flies.

Sea trout have been successfully introduced in South America—in Argentina, Chile and Tierro del Fuego—where the population has increased nicely and has reached an average weight of 3–6 kg (6–13 lbs). In 1958 the fish was planted in several river systems in the northeastern United States and in Canada. It is also found in New Zealand.

Brown trout

Brown trout

The brown trout (*Salmo trutta*) is a native European species that has been successfully transplanted to many other parts of the world, including the USA (1883), New Zealand, Pakistan, India and South America. The brown trout is biologically the same species as the sea trout and the lake-run brown trout, but it is non-migratory and lives in fast flowing water.

These three fish are quite different in appearance. The brown trout is often recognized by its small red spots. There are also strains with many black spots, and some that are almost completely light brown with only a few red spots. It is almost impossible to identify a brown trout if it shares the same waters as sea trout. The only certain identification is an analysis of the fish's strontium sulfate level, as sea trout contain large concentrations of this compound.

Brown trout grow more slowly than the other two trout, even if hatchery fish have produced the same rate of growth as the sea trout and the lake-run brown trout. Brown trout living in lakes with an abundant food supply increase in weight, but are then classified as lake-run brown trout.

Brown trout spawn in autumn and winter. Their rate of growth varies from stream to stream and with differences in climate and types of water. Water conditions can vary from the cold, almost sterile, Arctic streams to the nutrition-rich waters in England, Yugoslavia or Denmark. The brown trout eat an all-round diet of insects, larvae, small animals, fry, other brown trout, frogs and even small rodents. The brown trout cannot tolerate the high temperatures that a rainbow trout can, and it is a territorial fish, choosing a lair and chasing other fish away from it.

Much of today's spin and fly-fishing knowledge is based on fishing for brown trout. They have excellent eyesight and can detect colours, but studies indicate that their colour perception readjusts at dusk, at night, and as the amount of light decreases and increases at dawn.

Small spinners, spoons, plugs, jigs and flies—just about any type of lure—can be fished. A large brown trout usually feeds on smaller fish which means that a plug, an imitation fish, is a good choice.

Casting upstream is generally a successful technique in fast flowing water. As the lure is carried downstream by the current, it is presented to the fish as naturally as possible before the fish has time to be suspicious. This technique works best when the retrieval is well controlled. Just like other predators, brown trout react to bright colours when the temperature falls. Red is especially effective. During part of the winter the fish feed on fish eggs that float with the current through the spawning grounds, which might explain the phenomenon of the colour red. Brown trout often eat the eggs of their own species, or of other fish such as the rainbow sea trout, "steelhead", and even salmon.

In many small streams with meagre vegetation brown trout reach weights of 100–300 grams (4–7 oz) and seldom larger, but in water with better nutritive qualities they weigh 0.5–2.0 kg (1–4 1/2 lbs) and sometimes more. Because brown trout claim territories, the size of the population in a stream is often regulated by the number of lairs and hiding places available as well as by how much the stream is fished.

Huchen

Huchen (*Hucho hucho*) is a salmon that lives in the Danube River and in many of its tributaries, especially those in Austria, southern Germany and Bulgaria. It has been successfully introduced in Yugoslavia and Morocco.

For the last several decades the huchen has been threatened by pollution in its natural territory, a problem which has not been enhanced by siltation and the closing off of their spawning grounds. Although these salmon are known to weigh over 50 kg (110 lbs), today a fish of 10–20 kg (22–44 lbs) is considered big.

The season starts in the late fall in the deep pools and holes of the clear rivers. Huchen are fished with artificial lures that go deep down to the bottom. A jig-like lure with a lead head and an artificial body is common, but heavy spoons and sinking plugs are also used.

Hooking the fish

Too many fish have been lost because the drag on the reel was adjusted either too tight or not tight enough, letting the fish fight itself off the hook or break the line. Fish are also lost because the hook was not set properly, a problem that often occurs when the reel releases line at the exact instant the fish strikes.

When retrieving, the line should form an angle with the rod and the drag effect should be adjusted so the fish can be hooked exactly when it strikes. A predator can behave either violently or cautiously, but under all circumstances it is vitally important that the point and the barb penetrate the fish when it bites. The hook is then set by pulling the rod backwards as quickly and with as much determination as possible, and then maintaining even pressure on the line.

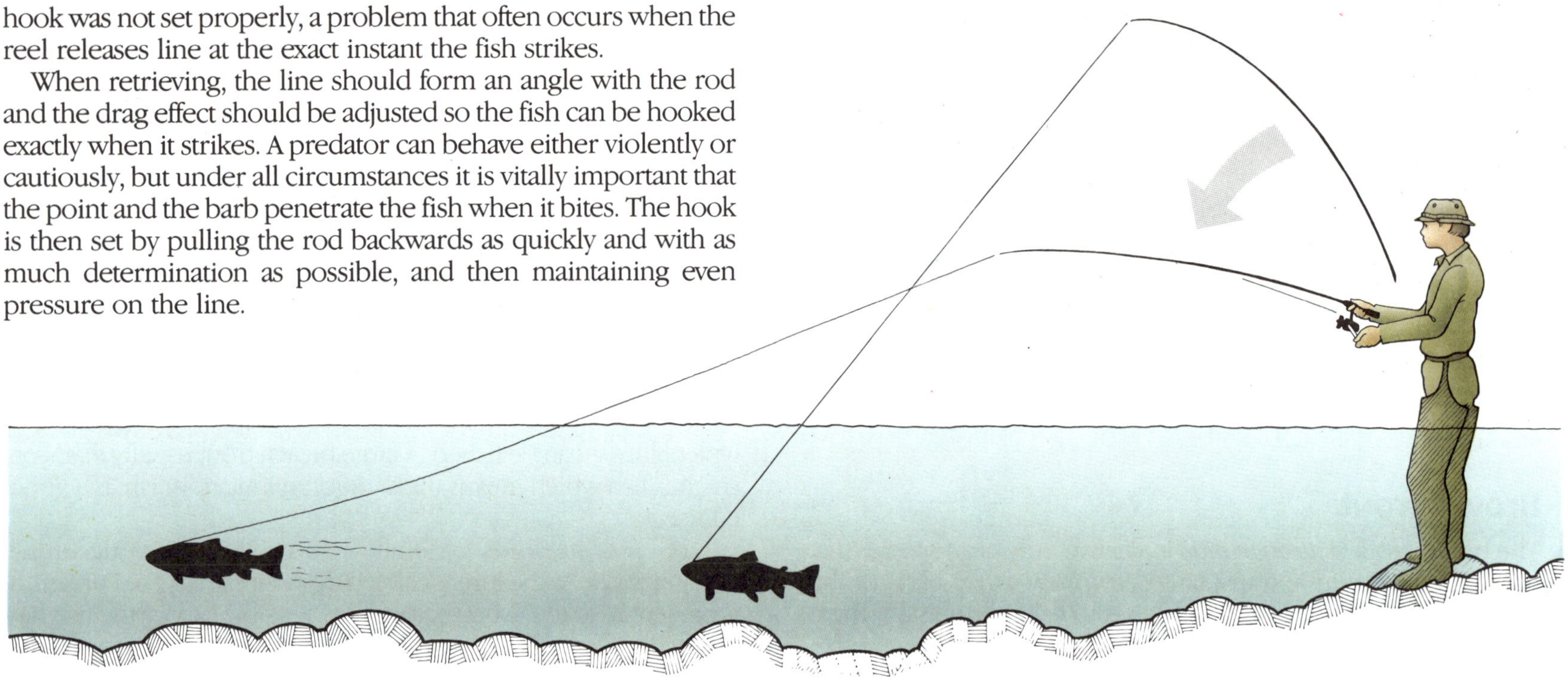

Above: A sudden run can free the fish, particularly if it is close to the tip of the rod. To avoid losing the fish, quickly lower the rod to the surface of the water.

Below: Another critical situation during the fight is if the fish jumps at the surface. Here also, the best reaction is to quickly lower the rod to decrease the tension on the line.

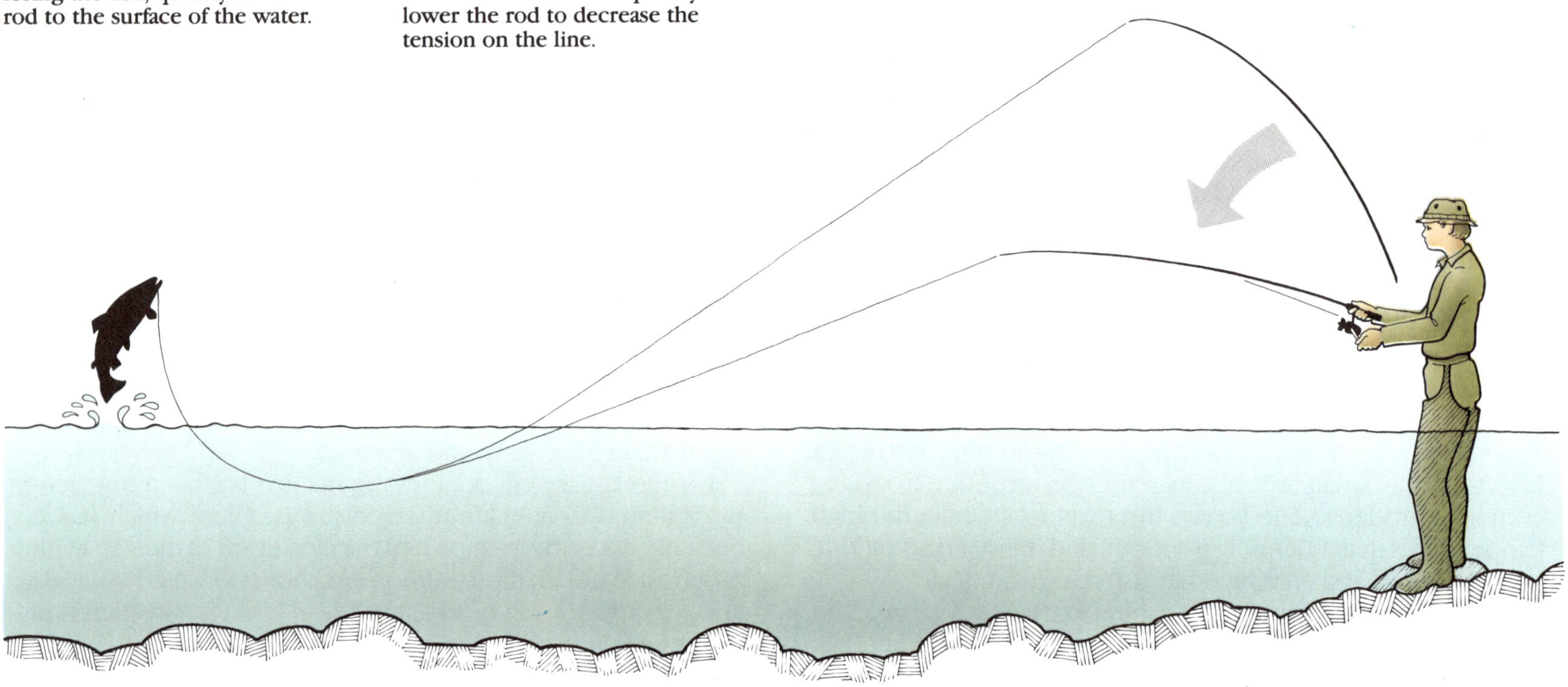

The strength of a strike varies depending on the length of the line. A long line demands more power to compensate for the line's elasticity. On a short line the hook can be set with a quick jerk of the arm.

The purpose of playing in the fish is to bring it securely to land, not to see it thrash to the surface time and time again. A fish fights so violently because its natural sense of balance, normally controlled by the air bladder and sense organs, is disturbed. Once this has happened, the fish tries with all its might to stabilize itself again.

It is important to keep an even, constant pressure on the fish. If it is poorly hooked, the barb may not have penetrated or the hook's point may have caught in loose skin. The wrong pull on the rod may lose the fish.

When a fish jumps it is best to follow it by lowering the rod in the hopes of reducing the shock effect on the fish. If the fish looks like it wants to thrash at the surface or try to run on a short line, putting the tip of the rod in the water can sometimes help. When a fish twists off a hook it is often caused by a combination of its own weight, slack in the line as a result of the jump, and the fact that the fish beats the water with its head.

Big fish are pumped in slowly by lifting the rod without reeling in any line. When the top of the rod is lowered again, the line should be reeled in.

Above: While fighting the fish it is important to maintain even pressure on the line, as it is impossible to know how well the hook is set. Too much or too little tension could free the fish.

Below: The best way to tire a big fish is to slowly pump it in towards you. Lift the rod without reeling in line, and then sink it while taking home line.

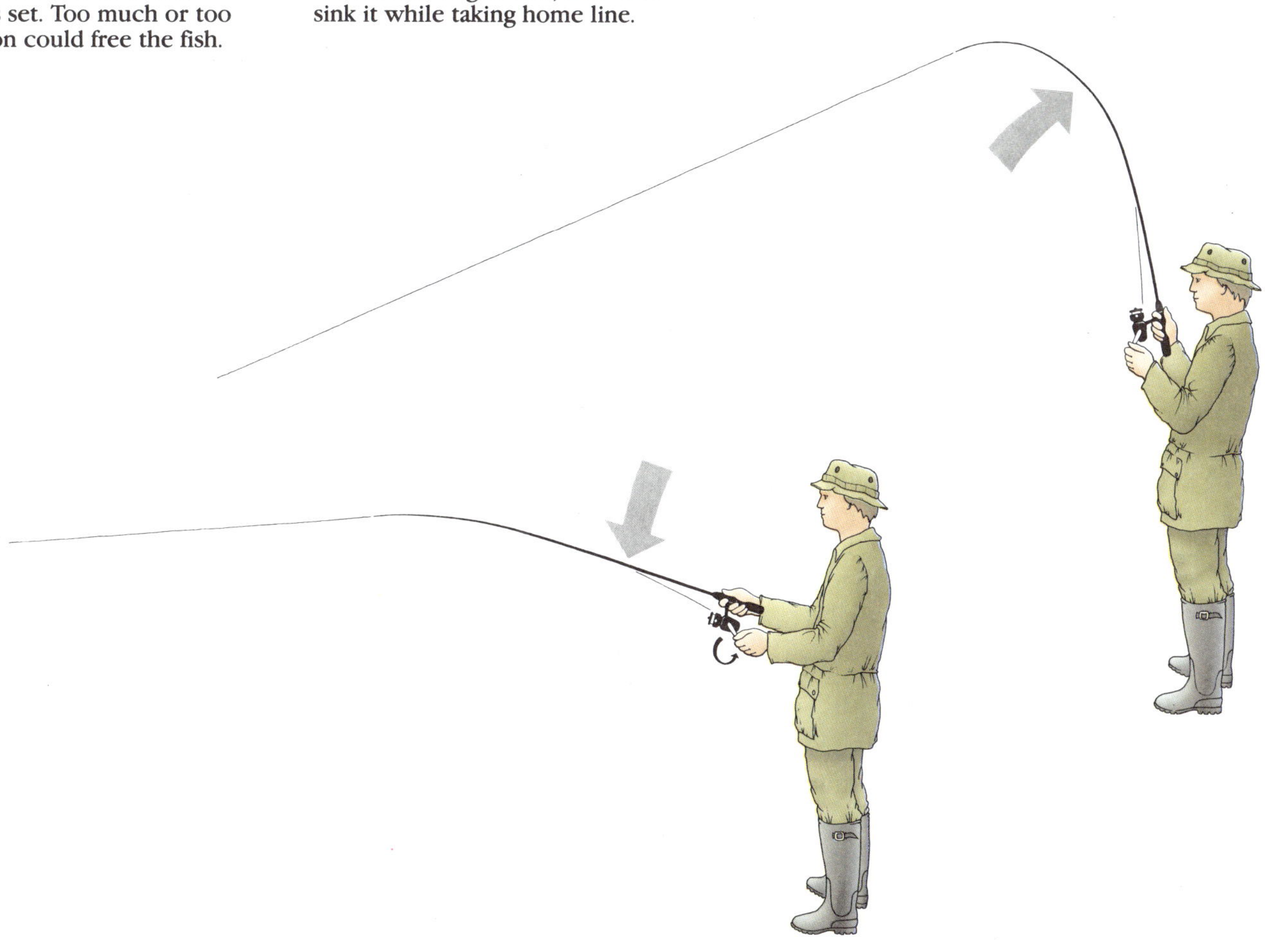

Landing a fish

When the fish is finally worn out, it can be landed with a net or a gaff. Other methods are to slide the fish on land or to take it with your hands.

A good net can have a long or a short handle. A shorthandled net is used for fishing in rivers and streams. It should have a floating frame so it can also be used when wading. Longhandled nets are used for boat fishing but they are also used for beach fishing when it is difficult to get close to the water and the fish. In fast flowing water the net is held behind the fish so the current spreads out the net and helps to slide the fish into it.

A gaff is a giant hook attached to a pole. There are no barbs, so it is easier to penetrate the fish's skin. Gaffs are made with short or long handles. They are used for large fish and are very popular in Scandinavia, where they are used for salmon, sea-run trout, northern pike and zander. In other places, Great Britain for one, nets are more traditional and gaffs are reserved for salmon and northern pike. Salmon are normally gaffed in the neck, the jaw or the tail, northern pike in the neck or the jaw.

A special salmon-tailer is used to land salmon. This piece of equipment is actually a snare made up of a long shaft, a cable and a spring-steel bow. This noose is drawn about one-third of the way over the salmon's body, from the tail end. As the salmon-tailer is drawn against its body, the noose closes over the salmon, holding it tight by its tail. On a smooth beach of sand, gravel or small stones, it is usually easier to slide the fish on land. This is done by walking slowly up the beach, backwards, keeping a constant, even tension on the line, and sliding the fish up onto the beach.

Fish can also be landed by hand from a boat or from the shore. Salmon are usually carried up on land by the tail. Northern pike and walleye can be lifted up to a boat or onto the shore by getting a good hold on the fish's neck.

Perch, small bass and other small fish can be landed by carefully and evenly swinging the line onboard.

Larger bass can be landed by placing the thumb in the toothless lower jaw and supporting the grip with the index finger. The bass can then be lifted without thrashing.

Regardless of the equipment being used to land a fish, never forget that many fish make a last desperate attempt to get free, even though they may look completely exhausted. Many beginners have felt confident enough to increase the drag on the reel and force the fish in closer. And many fish have regained their freedom during the final seconds of battle because the tension on the line was too tight.

Returning the fish to water

There are many different reasons for returning a fish to the water. The fish might be too small—that is, under the legal limit for its species. There might already be too many fish at home in the freezer. In many fishing waters there are also strict limits on how many of each species can be taken. In addition, there is a growing feeling that the future of fishing will benefit if most of the fish caught, some say all of them, are released back into the water.

Above: Always hold the net under water when landing a fish, as it is easily startled and will try to break away. To further reduce the risk of losing the fish, hold the net behind the fish and let the fish glide into the net.

Below: A gaff is used to land large fish. Northern pike are usually gaffed in the lower jaw.

Above: It is quite common to land salmon by hand when the beach is shallow and free of vegetation. The salmon is grasped by the tail and carried up on land.

Below: To keep from damaging a fish's sensitive slime layer, hands should be wet before touching the fish. An exhausted fish has the best chance of survival if it is held vertically in the water until it shows signs of recovery.

It is important to know how to return a fish so it will survive. Studies have shown that if a fish is not put back in the water properly, the survival rate is extremely low. The most common cause of death is an increased amount of lactic acid in the blood. While it is battling the hook, the fish utilizes all its energy, including its oxygen reserves, with the resulting effect that the fish suffocates. The growth of bacteria is another common cause of death. The layer of slime covering a fish is its protection against infection and if this is damaged, the fish can be attacked by bacteria and viruses. Fish that are hooked in deep water are sometimes retrieved so quickly that they do not have time to equalize the pressure. Just like a diver, they get the bends and cannot survive after being returned to the water. The hook or hooks can also injure and maim fish, especially if they sit deep in the throat, the gills or the stomach. A fish hooked in a large artery seldom survives.

Many fish die because the hook is not removed carefully. Hooks without barbs and single-pointed hooks increase a fish's chances of survival. The best way to remove a hook is with a long-handled plier or a fish-hook remover. If the hook is set deep in the throat it is important not to put strain on the line as the hook could then penetrate the heart, located just behind the pharynx. Northern pike and other large fish have mouths brimming with teeth, making it often necessary to use a mouth-opener. This piece of equipment is actually a steel spring with two arms that can be inserted in the fish's jaw. When the spring is released the jaw is opened and it is comparatively easy to remove the hook. If the hook sits very far back in the mouth it can be removed by inserting a pair of pliers backwards, between the gill arches, to reach the hook.

A fish's chances of survival are greater in cold weather, and in cold water rather than warm water, because cold water contains more oxygen. If a fish is to be released, it is best to remove the hook while the fish is still in the water. But if the fish is already out of the water, the risk of damaging the slime layer is decreased by wetting the hands before touching the fish.

When releasing a fish in flowing water it is essential to hold its head against the current, and in still water the fish must be held vertically. When the tail begins to flip, the fish is ready for release. But keep a sharp eye on the fish. If it turns bottom up, catch it and hold it vertically again. For some fish, it takes several minutes or more of this procedure to insure the best chances of survival.

If the fish is hooked deep and it is difficult to remove the hook without injuring the fish, it is probably best to cut the line at the hook, or to break off the hook with tongs. The fish will suffer less from the hook than from the injuries sustained in removing it. Connective tissue will grow around the hook and it will eventually fall out of its own accord. Besides, unless the hook is made of stainless steel, it will rust away.

Bait-fishing

ABU garcia
Cardinal 4

One of the fascinating aspects of angling is how the sport has developed differently in various parts of the world. There are sound reasons for the differences, mostly environmental or climatic, but what is becoming more and more appreciated is that everyone can learn something useful from everyone else. Simply by studying the angling magazines of many lands, it is possible for even the nonlinguist to see how ideas and approaches are beginning to travel around this planet.

My attitude during travels is always "When in Rome, do as the Romans do". I have not played the angling missionary. Instead I have tried to learn what others do and why, and to see which bits of it can help me to catch more and better fish, and enjoy myself more—for that is what the game is really all about. I have learned the joys of catching fish on lures, an area where the Americans, Canadians and Scandinavians reign supreme. I have seen the competition fishermen in my country discovering with awe and deep respect the differing pole-fishing skills of the Belgians, French and Italians. I have seen the compliment returned, as the Continentals have suddenly realised the awesome capabilities of the British with rods and reels and float tackle, especially at long range. Everyone is much the better for it.

When pebbles are thrown in European ponds, the ripples spread a long way. On my last trip to America I met a Canadian outdoors writer who begged me to send him a book on English float-fishing methods. Why? "Because there's an English guy float-fishing for steelheads with night crawlers, and he's emptying my river!" Even the Americans' faith in lures is being slightly eroded as they learn that some of the British and European methods of pike fishing, with live and dead fish, can be deadly for their predators. The magazine In-Fisherman has devoted much space to it in the past two or three years, and their staff of expert anglers all seem to be converts.

In my own country we perhaps export more ideas than we import. It is not because the English are particularly clever. It is simply that a certain development which began way back in the 1950s transformed our own angling scene. We saw the birth of the specimen hunter, and of specimen-hunting groups. Small groups of people, mainly interested in carp at the beginning, got together to pool ideas on how to catch big fish. Big carp were considered virtually uncatchable. Even when they were hooked, they could not be landed on the tackle then available, without a great deal of luck. The British record was 26 lbs, and thought to be invulnerable. In a short time it was 44 lbs, and now 52 lbs. So much has been learned about carp that absolute beginners have caught fish over 30 lbs, and the old record mark is surpassed almost every week.

The carp-fishing advances led to the formation of groups interested in other species, and similar progress was made. Nothing comparable was going on in other countries, and the knowledge gained was exportable. If memory serves me right, Dutch carp anglers were the first to benefit, and they also helped by

sending back valuable information. Where are we now? The huge carp of Lake Cassien, in southern France, have proved easily catchable. No carp on earth is invulnerable!

So, what are these methods which are so applicable elsewhere? My role in this book is to cover some of the most interesting developments for a number of different species. It can only be a sample selection, but I will try in the main to cover methods which are adaptable for species other than the ones the methods were developed for.

Equipment

For fishermen who have to live on a limited budget, fishing tackle is usually a compromise. It is possible to make one rod perform several functions, though not with maximum efficiency. Some anglers get around the problem by concentrating on one or two aspects of the sport. Only all-rounders like me end up with their homes becoming almost copies of the tackle shop down the road!

When I knew I had to write this section of the book, I looked at my tackle collection with some despair, wondering how to summarise the requirements, and even whether readers in all countries were familiar with the way we British classify our rods—by the test curve, which is expressed in pounds weight or fractions of pounds.

Rods

Briefly, we are talking about the weight required to pull the tip of a rod round into its full, natural curve. The test curve can range from mere ounces up to about 3 lbs, the heavier end being the most powerful.

The test-curve system arose in the days when most anglers used split-cane rods, which could be damaged if misused, with stronger line than the rod was designed to take. The old formula for deciding the right line range was 2.5 times the test curve, with a margin of error of plus or minus one third. Thus the ideal line for a 2-lb test curve rod would be 5 lb breaking strain, but it would also take up to 6.6 lbs or as little as 3.4 lbs.

Even though modern materials have outdated the formula, it remains a reasonable guide. Nowadays the danger lies in having line which is not heavy enough for a rod. It would break before the rod could achieve its full curve. Overloading modern rods is much less of a danger than it was with split cane. They are virtually unbreakable in normal use, certainly at the stronger end, and it is quite common to see anglers using 3-lb test curve rods with 12- or 15-lb line, sometimes even stronger than that. I do it myself, for pike fishing and for carp.

To complicate matters further, it is possible to have two or more rods with, say, 2-lb test curves which are totally different in performance. Modern materials like carbon fibre and boron, and fibreglass before those two came on the scene, enabled rod-blank makers to build different actions into the tip sections. We can now have fast taper, medium taper, slow taper and compound taper, and they are all good for some jobs or bad for others.

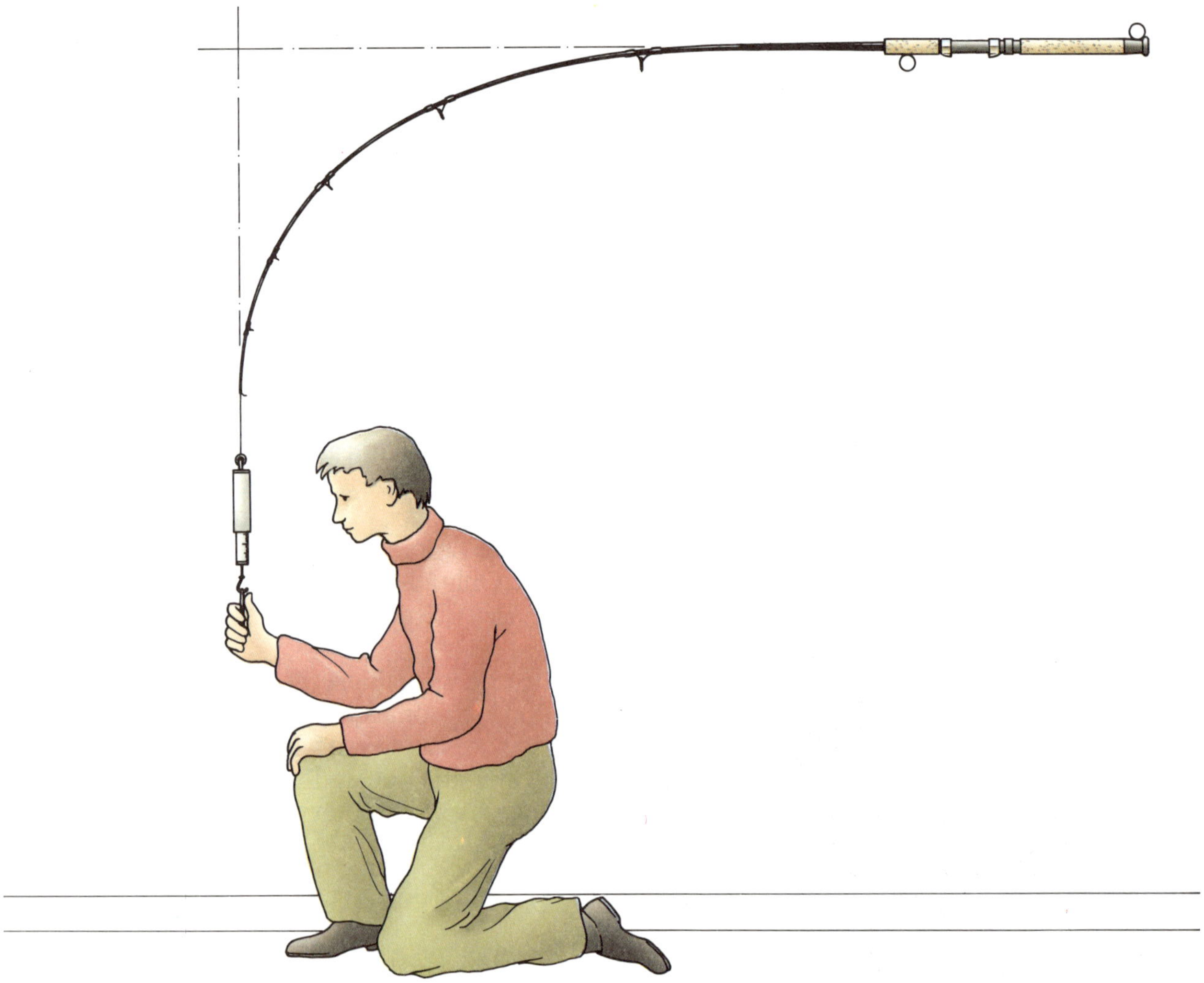

The test curve shows roughly which line strength should be used for a particular rod. To determine the test curve, load the rod top until the rod bends at ninety degrees. The simplest way is to fix the rod horizontally on a wall, and pull down the top with a scale, until the rod top points vertically toward the ground. Then the test curve can be read off on the scale.

Compound and fast-taper rods are better for casting big weights a long way, and are better at striking the hooks home at long range, but they are less pleasant to use when playing fish. Medium and slower-taper rods are much better for close work, and I will try to draw attention to this when describing the rods I use for the species and methods discussed later on.

For all my fishing these days I use carbon rods, but there are still much cheaper glass rods available which have similar specifications. They are, unfortunately, heavier and usually much thicker in profile. For pike fishing I have several carbon rods, varying from 11 to 13 ft in length (3.5 to nearly 4 metres) and from 2.5 lbs to 3 lbs in test curve. They will all cast big baits quite easily to 50 or 60 metres, if required, and a 12-ft rod with a 2.75-lb test curve will cast much further than that. I also use a 13-ft rod with a 3-lb test curve, mostly for one method I describe later: long-range fishing with a vaned float. The length facilitates lifting line off the water to control the float, and also helps striking. It has the power to drive hooks home at long range.

The same rods will also serve as long-range carp rods, and no doubt a really expert caster could put a bait over 100 metres with the two most powerful. For then they are casting the weight in the compact form of lead, and only a small bait which offers less resistance in the air.

Much lighter rods of 1.25- to 2-lb test curve, and with a more medium taper action, are more suitable for carp fishing at closer range. Carp are extremely powerful fighters, and very fast swimmers too. Rods with plenty of action are better able to cope with the shock of sudden plunges, especially when a big fish is hooked at close range or, as sometimes happens, when they really start to fight once they have been brought in under the rod tip.

In waters with lots of tough weed, or other obstructions such as sunken trees, it is necessary to hook carp and prevent them from achieving full speed. That means hooking them and holding on hard, and with powerful rods a great many are lost simply because the hook tears out. My 1.25-lb test-curve rod, 11 ft long, bends almost double in these circumstances when using line of around 10 lbs breaking strain, but it loses fewer carp than any of the others.

For smaller predators than pike, I prefer 11-ft rods of 1 to 1.25 lbs test curve, and a nice through action is preferred, especially for soft-mouthed species such as perch. The same rods are also right for still-water work for such species as good-sized bream and tench. For eels, however, carp or pike rods in the 2- to 2.5- lb class are necessary.

Much lighter rods are required for stick-float and waggler fishing, which I will be describing. They are classified as match rods in Britain, whether or not their owners fish competitively. Nowadays they are usually 12- to 14-ft rods in carbon or boron, and light enough (usually 5 to 8 oz) to hold and fish with all day, without undue fatigue. They are made for use with light lines up to 3 lbs, with hook lengths of 1 to 1.5 lbs—sometimes less, 12 oz or even 8 oz. The choice depends on the size of fish expected.

Many companies make them, but they boil down to two basic types. Stick-float rods are made with solid inserts in the tip section. It makes them nice and snappy in the action, good at lifting line off the water and hooking the fish with a mere flick of the wrist. Waggler-float rods do not have inserts and have much more of a through action, mostly because waggler-float anglers have to strike with a long sweep of the rod to take up loose line. Tip-actioned rods sometimes break light line with that sort of strike, so the rod must be softer to absorb the shock.

Reels

The best advice is always to buy the best you can afford. For the types of fishing I do, I use fixed spool reels almost exclusively, relying on the quality makers like ABU (Sweden), Mitchell (France) and Ryobi, though the once cheap and nasty products of the Far East are vastly better in quality these days.

My one departure is a closed-faced reel for stick-float fishing. I began to use them when the ABU 505 came out years ago, followed by the 506 and 507. They were made for spinning, but were perfect for one-handed operation with match rods. Unfortunately they had to be adapted in various ways, and I did not find a suitable alternative until Ryobi produced their Mastermatch CF1 in 1986. Line does not stray into the works, and it comes out of the reel smoothly.

Floats

Obtaining good stick floats and peacock-quill waggler floats might be a problem in some countries, though most seem to import English-made sets these days. The stick floats come in sets of the usually required sizes, the biggest taking around six no. 4 shots. The most popular waggler floats are those taking 1, 1.5 and 2 SSG shots, though smaller ones taking 1 to 2 BB are sometimes used at close range.

Line and hooks

Line makes are very much personal preferences, and there is lots of good line available now, mostly from Germany or France. It is the same with hooks, though for match rods the new chemically sharpened makes in sizes 22 to 18 are the most popular. I use size 14 up to 8 for quality fish, and rarely use bigger than size 8 trebles for live and deadbaiting for pike. In my experience one needs

Floats are best stored in certain boxes, keeping the different types in view.

bigger trebles only on lures, which my section of the book does not cover. For carp it pays to use specially made, extra strong hooks in sizes 10 to 6, occasionally bigger for large baits or extra large carp. My favourite hooks are Mustad (Norwegian) or Kamasan (Japanese), plus Partridge (England) for specialist purposes.

Accessories

Among the vital accessories, I would stress the need for a good-sized landing net, big enough to easily enclose the size of fish you are after. I have one 40 inches wide for pike, and a 24-inch for quality fish of other species. For those who wish to keep and return their catches unharmed a good keep-net, in knotless mesh, is required, with a minimum length of 6 ft (two metres), though I prefer longer ones of around 3 metres, with plenty of width.

More and more pike anglers are adopting the English habit of returning their catches to fight another day. Most are returned straight away, but for those who wish to retain an extra-large fish while they get organised for photographs a large keep-sack is essential. This is made from rot-proof nylon with holes punched through and with a draw-string to close the neck. Pike, and also large carp, lie perfectly quiet in it for long periods, probably because they are disorientated inside a dark sack. In a keep-net they will constantly try to escape, and damage themselves.

Modern anglers surround themselves with a variety of accessories, often well-adapted to diverse fishing situations.

Most fishermen properly equip themselves for unhooking fish, using one of a wide variety of hook disgorgers, but many pike anglers are not so well-equipped in this regard. One vital requirement is a long pair of lock forceps, which can remove hooks from anywhere inside a pike's mouth without the angler's fingers getting anywhere near the sharp teeth.

Some writers will advocate cutting equipment to snip through wire traces if a pike swallows hooks down its gullet, but I think this is criminal. Most of us accidentally deep-hook a pike now and again, but it is easy to remove a swallowed hook safely by using a specially made long disgorger. At the business end it has a slotted tube protruding from a wide bush, which is also slotted. One can slide the slot down the trace until the tube picks up the three arms of the treble hook. A little push will remove the hooks, and the points are then masked by the wide bush as the implement is withdrawn. It is a clever invention, yet simple, as most good inventions are.

It also helps to know how to handle a pike, which makes the unhooking job much easier. The old spring steel gags to hold the jaw open are now redundant. The best way is to slide a gloved hand inside the gill cover and towards the point of the jaw before taking a firm grip. The hand is outside the jawbone, clear of the teeth. Lifting a small pike off the ground, or a large pike partially off the ground in that way, forces the jaw open, making hook-removal with the free hand a simple task. It is even easier with a friend there to assist. I am now so confident with this method I no longer use gloves.

Obviously I cannot mention all of the items which anglers find useful, but in looking through my accessories there are some things I certainly could not do without. Most of them are items for bite detection systems, which I will come to in a moment.

Baiting needles have a multitude of uses, but one thing I would be lost without is PVA tape and string. This product of space-age technology could not look more ordinary. The tape looks like a strip of plastic and the string looks like string. But it melts in water, and it has many uses. It can assist long casting, tying back a bait to the main line and allowing the lead weight to lead the way. I do not like to hook dead fish baits for pike too firmly, so I tie the tails tightly to the line with PVA to make sure they don't come off during the cast. Some of the tackles I mention later can tend to separate during the cast, cutting down on casting distance. PVA will hold them together, swiftly melting away once the tackle is in the water. Other uses are mentioned later in the text.

Shown here is an Optonic bite indicator, with a double system: both light and sound signals indicate the bite. When fishing with two rods, it also shows which rod the fish is on.

Bite indication systems

Now to those bite indication systems. There are several different set-ups, all of them perfectly efficient, but the best are dual systems—audible and visual. Electronic bite alarms are highly sophisticated now, but the best make is the Optonic. These serve as the head of the forward rod rest, and when running line moves a wheel on which it is resting, it moves an interior paddle. This breaks a beam of light, causing the battery-operated mechanism to bleep. It also activates an LED (light-emitting diode).

If two Optonics are being used for two rods—the most common set-up in my country—the light instantly tells the angler which rod is in action: important, for very often the first sign of a bite is a slight tightening of the line, which can cause just one quick bleep. The light, however, stays on for about eight seconds.

When a taking fish swims off, the Optonic bleeps and flashes as the line runs over the wheel. The angler even knows how fast or slowly it is swimming. If the rest of the set-up is correct, however, the Optonic can also signal slack line bites, caused (depending on how the terminal tackle is arranged) when a fish swims towards the angler.

The angler needs some way of ensuring that slack line is pulled backwards over the wheel, and a typical method is the "drop-off" arm. It is clipped to the rear rod rest, and comprises a length of brass rod with a polystyrene ball and adjustable clip at the front end. This is clipped to the reel line immediately below the spool of the reel, whose bail arm is left open.

One of two things can happen to the drop-off arm when a fish takes the bait, depending on which way it swims. If it swims away,

the line is pulled out of the clip, and the arm falls off to hang straight down. If the fish swims towards the angler, the arm will fall backwards. Either way the angler instantly picks up the rod, engages the bail arm, reels up any slack line, and strikes as soon as he feels contact with the fish.

For anglers with Optonics, the drop-off arm is more of a back-up system of bite indication. For those who do not have costly electronics the drop-off arm is a perfectly satisfactory bite indication system in its own right, though it has obvious limitations for night fishing.

Another efficient bite detection system which works with or without electronics is the monkey climber set-up. The indicator can be made quite easily from any light plastic tubing. Herb containers are ideal. It is placed on a metal spike, usually a spoke from an old umbrella, mid-way between the reel and the butt ring on the rod. How it works depends on the length of the spike. On a short spike, a normal bite from a fish will cause the indicator to lift and fall off or, in the case of a fish moving towards the angler, to drop down. If a spike long enough to reach above the line level is used, a running fish will take line off the spool, causing the indicator to rise and fall on the spike like a toy monkey on a stick—hence the name.

In my experience both the drop-off and monkey-climber systems are excellent for the more powerful species such as pike or carp, but they offer rather too much in the way of resistance when we are fishing for the smaller and more shy species, such as bream, or roach. Such fish can, at times, detect even slight resistance and let go of the bait before the angler can strike.

The best alternative in this situation is the angled spike. Here the indicator is much lighter, often a simple cylinder of metal foil, which will fly off the spike without the fish feeling anything. Some of my eel-fishing friends rate this system more highly than any other, and I certainly prefer it for bream and roach.

Rod rests

It does not take much skill or imagination to make some of the bite detection accessories, but the rod rests themselves are both excellent and cheap to buy. The rules in some countries allow the use of two or even three rods, and dual and even triple rod rest systems are available. They have been christened buzzer bars, mainly because the front rests are made to take the Optonic sensor heads, though a more standard type of forward rest can be used instead. Lots are made, and all have one essential characteristic. They are designed to allow line to run freely through them.

To those who have not tried using more than one rod at the same time, it will seem like a recipe for chaos once a big fish has been hooked. But having two rods together does not mean that the baits are together. One can be to the right, the other to the left, or one close in and one way out. When a fish is hooked, the usual response is to knock the other rod off the front rest and let it sink down into the water, still propped up at the other end. The line sinks to the bottom, and is not usually tangled up with the fish on the other rod. The biggest problem can arise if fish take both baits almost simultaneously, but that is fortunately a rare event!

An often-used type of bite indicator is the swing-tip. This movable part is fixed at the end of the rod top and begins to move when the fish bites.

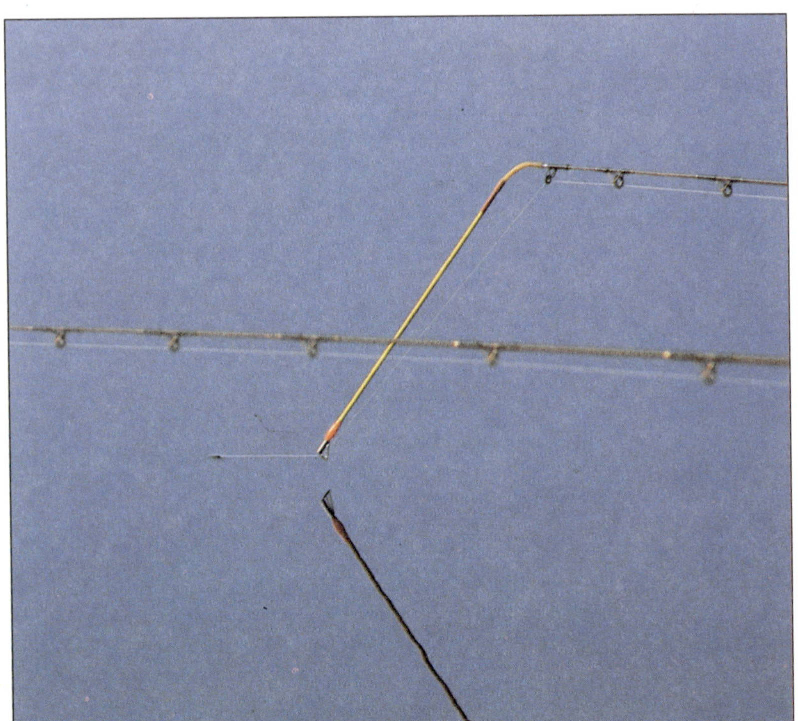

These rod holders are only for one rod, but there are others which can hold several rods, such as that shown on the preceding page.

Pike frequently take live or dead bait with pleasure. The inset picture shows two different categories of bait: a freshwater whitefish (above) and a piece of mackerel filet (below).

Angling for pike

Most fish eat other fish if they get the chance, but anglers think of predators as those species most likely to be caught on fish baits or imitations of live prey. Pike, zander, walleye, muskellunge, bass, catfish and the perches, together with members of the salmon and trout families, are the obvious species.

My particular speciality is the pike, using both live and dead fish baits. While I shall concentrate on this predator, readers will hopefully see how the same principles and methods can be adapted for their favourite species. In some cases I will suggest how that is done.

Livebaiting is a universal method; deadbaiting less so. It is most widely practised in England, I believe, where the knowledge that pike would scavenge for dead prey fish was revealed in books several centuries ago. For some reason, though, the method was forgotten until its rediscovery in the early 1950s. Anglers found that pike would eat not only dead fish of the species known to inhabit the water, but alien species too. It led them to the use of sea-fish like herring, mackerel, sardine and smelt, and the latest "in" bait is horse mackerel.

We are also seeing more use of exotic sea-fish, imported for our immigrant population from such places as the Caribbean. These are fish with different shapes, smell and colouring, and no matter what the colour, it was also found that most fish dye easily in solutions of cold-water clothing dye. So, we could turn them gold, yellow, red, even blue—the colour which the experts tell us that fish can most easily see at great depth. Deadbaiting fitted easily into our system of fishing for pike, which relies upon three key senses—sight, smell, and the ability to detect and home in on vibrations. All three are exploited by the angler, sometimes simultaneously. Nowadays we even have lures which smell!

The whole approach is littered with questions. Why, for example, do we need so many different types and smells and colours for deadbaiting? The short answer is that experts have discovered that pike have the ability to learn that dead fish can mean danger. If they have been caught on mackerel several times, they may not

A hook disgorger can be an essential accessory if the hooks sit deep down in the pike's throat.

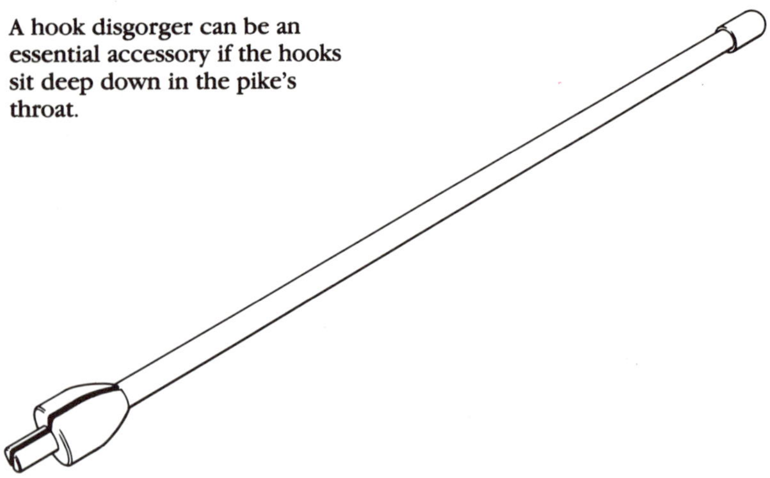

take it again. New baits always seem very effective for a season or two, and then decline.

Pike seem less able to learn about live fish. They eat them so often without problems, and even if they are capable of learning that live fish sometimes have hooks in them, they could do little about it. They still have to eat! The assumption that pike may be wary, however, has influenced the development of terminal tackles and methods of bite detection. Any of those detection systems can be used with the methods I am about to illustrate.

Bottom fishing with deadbait

The basic way to present a deadbait is simply to cast it out to lie on the bottom, attached to one or two treble hooks (depending on bait size) and a wire trace, which is vital for all types of pike fishing. Without wire—usually 18 to 20 lbs breaking strain—a pike will easily bite through the line and may later die from swallowing the hooks.

This method is simple enough, and there is little to alarm the pike. Because the pike can swim in any direction, causing the line to tighten *or slacken*, the bite detection system must be capable of showing "drop" bites. I prefer drop-off indicators for pike, since they either fall off when a pike swims away or drop back if it swims towards the angler. Either way, he can tell immediately that he has some action.

For longer casting, or to hold position in flowing water, it is necessary to introduce a lead weight to the tackle. I use weights of at least 10 oz and up to 30 oz. You can never get drop-bite indication by fishing this way: the lead weight acts as an anchor point, and a running pike takes line through it, no matter which way it swims.

Bottom fishing with livebait

Both methods can also be used with a livebait, but the hooks would be reversed, with one through the lips of the bait and the other in the back near the dorsal fin. Yet the bait will just swim away and keep on going, you may think. In fact it won't. When such species as bream or roach are used, they have a very obliging habit of swimming over the shallows and down the shelf into the deeper water, right where the pike is likely to find them. There they stay put, for some reason. On canals and drains, freelined livebaits, as we call them, consistently find the deepest part of the water to hide in.

Obviously it is a difficult method requiring constant attention, and it cannot work where there is weed. The angler must allow the bait to take line until it stops, before setting up his bite detection system, and he must watch like a hawk for both types of indication, especially the drop back. It is not an easy method to master, but it has consistently caught big pike.

Presenting a livebait on or close to the bottom is often effec-

The most common method in pike angling is to fish with deadbait, which must lie still on the bottom. Shown here are two types of tackle, with and without sinker.

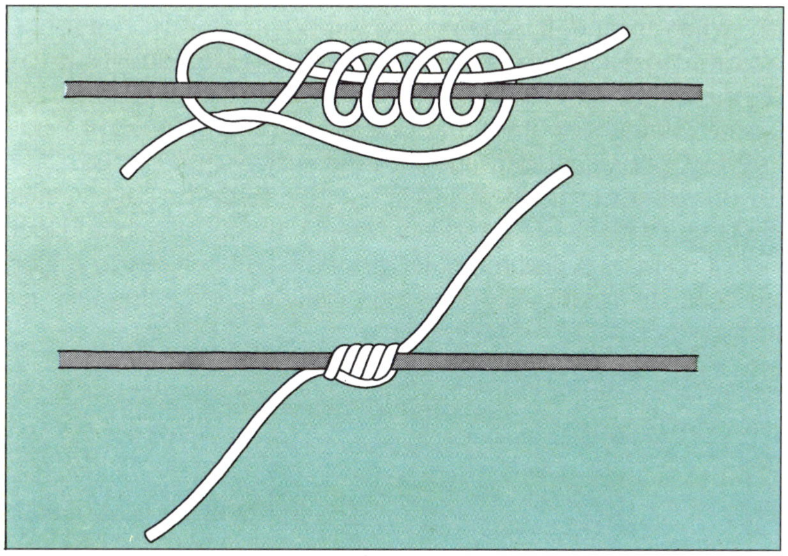

Stop knot

When fishing with livebait, the hooks should be applied rather differently than with deadbait. Shown is a paternoster tackle with sunken float, which keeps the bait fish at the same distance from the bottom regardless of the depth.

To prevent the bait fish from hiding on the bottom, a float or a piece of polystyrene can be placed right in front of it. This makes the fish keep trying to move downward, which stimulates pike to strike.

tive. When we involve a lead weight, the best method uses a polystyrene float, which prevents the fish burying itself if there is weed or debris on the bottom. It makes the fish lift up in the water whenever it tries to rest, and it keeps trying to get back to the bottom. This constant up-and-down movement is very attractive to the pike! The reason for the small-diameter plastic tubing jammed into the swivel eye of the weight is to reduce the risk of casting tangles.

Where bottom weeds or snags are a problem, there is what we call the "sunken float paternoster" method. This can present a livebait at any pre-determined distance from the bottom, within reason, simply by varying the length of line from the lead weight to the top eye of the upper swivel. This method incorporates a double wire trace, for if the bait should swim and tangle with the line above, a taking pike would bite through it. Using a short wire trace to the fish, and a longer wire trace above, eliminates this problem.

The reason for covering the connecting point with silicone tubing is to reduce the risk of tangling on the cast or when the fish swims around. It is a very clever approach, for the bait fishes the same no matter what depth of water is involved, and it is great for presenting tethered baits in known hotspot areas. Also, by using the sliding stop knot, the polystyrene ball float can be adjusted to give visual indication on the surface, if required. One obvious disadvantage is that, when a pike takes the bait, it takes everything with it—float and lead weight. In theory it should feel a lot of resistance, and might let go of the bait before the angler can strike. In fact it rarely does, especially when feeding very actively.

This type of sliding tackle makes no resistance when the pike takes the bait fish. It also gives the bait greater freedom of movement, which works well when the pike are sluggish.

Nonresistance tackle

When pike are less actively feeding, it can pay to present a bait with more freedom of movement, which makes it more attractive, on a tackle arrangement that offers no resistance. The latest is an amalgamation of the ideas of several clever anglers. With this method a running pike leaves the float and the lead weight where it is, and once the line has come out of the clip at the rod butt, it feels no resistance at all.

The angler can suspend a dead bait, but it is really best for a livebait. It can swim about a lot, because the line is not particularly tight, and can also move the float. The bait cannot reach the float to tangle with it, if the lower trace is shorter than the line from float to curtain ring. In theory it can tangle with the line or the upper trace, but it seldom does. The upper trace is just a precaution. When bites from pike are hard to come by, this type of presentation usually outscores any other rig. It has caught me many big pike.

Buoyant bait

Before moving to baits with surface floats, I should mention another method of fishing a dead bait off the bottom, when the bait has been made buoyant in one of several ways. Injecting freshwater fish with air, with a hypodermic needle, is one way to achieve it. Sea baits tend not to retain air, but one can tie a suitably sized polystyrene ball to them, or push varnished rods of balsa wood down their throats.

This method takes advantage of the pike's sight and smell senses. The eyes are mounted for forward and upward vision when a pike is in the normal swimming position, and it is likely to see a bait off bottom more quickly. Many times an off-bottom deadbait will be taken when one on the bottom is ignored, but it can also work the other way around.

Caution is always needed in loosening the bait from the pike's jaw, since the needle-sharp teeth can cause serious injury to your hands.

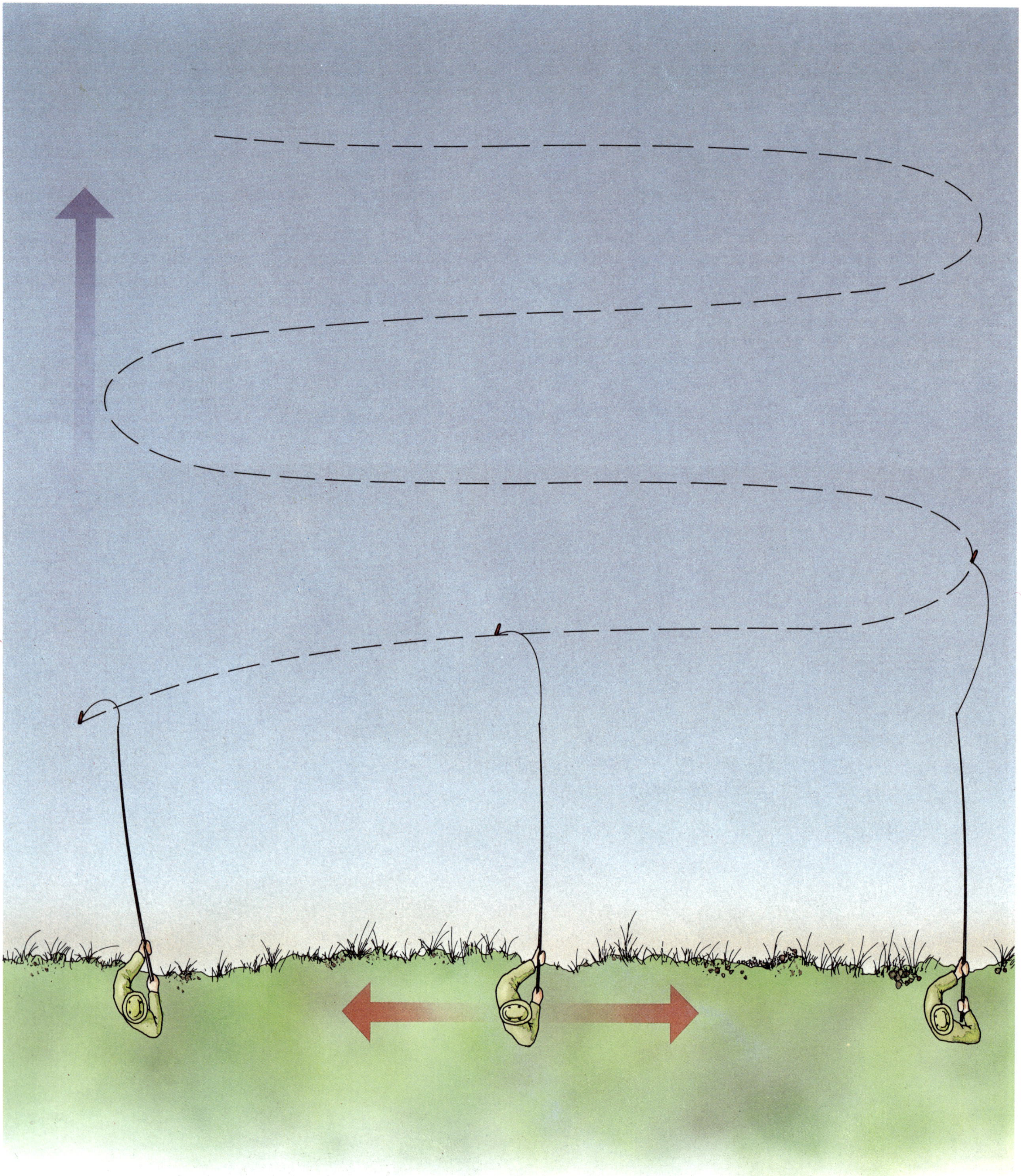

Left: When fishing with a drifting float, you must have the wind at your back. By going back and forth slowly on the shore, you can make the float cruise like a sail over the water surface. The greased line can also be steered so that the bait covers, for example, shallow and deep edges up to 100–150 metres out into the lake.

Drifting floats

It is all a question of finding what is best on the day, and frequently they will go for baits suspended from surface floats. Long ago we fished with huge, round floats, which were very inefficient, offering considerable resistance to a taking pike. Now floats are much more sophisticated, and one relatively new float method is remarkably effective.

Surface floats for live or dead baiting are mostly cigar-shaped, with holes down the middle. Ideally the float should be only just big enough to support the bait and the lead on the line, and the line above the float should be greased to prevent it from sinking.

Below: This shows how the tackle for drifting float can look. The float itself is cigar-shaped with a hole through. The bait may be either live or dead.

If it does sink, it immobilises the float, and sometimes the bait will tangle with sunken line. Normally such floats are cast in to drift around a particular area, though a good-sized livebait can be made to swim upwind if the line between float and rod is kept reasonably straight. If a bow develops in the line beyond the float, a livebait will immediately feel the resistance from it and swim away from that resistance—back towards the angler.

Inevitably anglers began to think of ways of float fishing in a more controlled manner, and the vaned drift float was conceived and finally perfected. Originally the idea was to send a bait under perfect control down-wind, with the vane acting as a sail, the angler simply releasing greased line as fast as the float would take it up. It was soon realised, however, that the float was capable of much more than that. It can also be made to act like a yacht to tack across the wind, right or left, depending on how the angler controls the line.

Thus it can be made to patrol right along the nearside shelf of a lake, then sent out to search the open water on a slow zigzag course. It can cover all the water a plug or spoon angler can cover, presenting a perfectly natural live or dead bait—much more likely to be taken, at times, than a flashy piece of metal or plastic. Then it can go on to search areas beyond the reach of the lure angler or even a long-casting dead-bait angler. I have fished drift floats at about 300 yards, though to be sensible 80 to 150 yards should be about the maximum.

The method of operation depends on the wind direction, but the manoeuvres previously described are possible only with the wind directly behind you. The line *must* be greased. Cast out and the let the wind catch the vane. It will soon be going downwind, but if you want the float to tack across wind you simply stop the release of line. A bow will develop to the right, or left of the float. If it develops to the right, the float will slowly skate to the right and, if bankside vegetation permits, the angler can simply walk along with the float as it covers the chosen area. When it has gone as far as it can (or as far as you can go), let the float out another 10 or 20 metres, then lift as much line as you can off the water, by raising the rod high, and walk to the left. This creates a bow to the left of the float, and the float will skate left, searching new territory.

In this way vast areas can be searched, including the always promising margins of islands, sunken mounds or ledges which the competent angler should know about. Modern graph and digital recorders, like the Lowrance Eagle and others, make the mapping of waters very easy. Conversely, a boat angler can use a drift float to fish around known features and also towards the bank, especially reedy bays which so often hold pike and other predators. It is a very versatile and productive method, best used on waters which are mostly 3 to 7 metres deep.

On such waters I would fish a bait at half to two thirds the average depth. And I can hear you saying, what about waters which are shallow within maximum casting range and much deeper further out? Often this can be overcome by using the dissolvable PVA tape I mentioned in the tackle section. If you want to fish a bait four metres deep and the float has to go over shallows two metres deep, you set the tackle to fish four metres. Then tie a simple slip knot in the line, say 2.5 metres above the wire trace, and tie the trace swivel to the loop with PVA tape or string. Usually the float will get out over deep water before the PVA melts, dropping the bait down to the chosen depth.

Another way is to drift out with a balloon. You slip a paper clip onto the trace swivel and put an inflated balloon into the clip. Tying the balloon to the clip with PVA ensures it will stay on while you cast. When the balloon has taken the tackle to the required distance, the PVA will have melted, and one sharp jerk of the rod will make the balloon break free. The bait drops down to the required depth and the float takes over. This method can also be used to take most of the other tackles I have described to distances beyond those the angler can reach by casting.

Live or dead baiting?

These are just some of the more effective methods for live and dead baiting for pike. Before going on to suggest how the same or similar methods can work for other fish, I should comment on the success rates of both methods. Some claim they are equally effective, but that is not my experience. Having looked through the last 200 pike I have caught over 10 lbs, I see that about two thirds took livebaits, even though deadbaits were used just as often.

It is claimed that deadbaits tend to catch the biggest pike, and for some that is true. Of my pike over 20 lbs, however, livebait has also caught a few more than deadbait, including my biggest pike of 30 lbs 12 oz. For numbers of pike of all sizes, I strongly suspect that lure fishing wins, but that subject is covered elsewhere in this book. To get the best out of pike fishing, pike anglers anywhere should learn to fish all three methods efficiently.

One final tip, before moving on to the smaller predators—a method of casting deadbaits long distances without having them fly off the hooks, or having them hooked so firmly that it is difficult to strike them into a pike. We call it an ejector rig, for obvious reasons. The ejector takes all the strain of the cast, for the bait is hanging from it via a loop of strong line tied to the tail. Immediately after the cast, the pole rubber straightens out, getting rid of the loop. Thus, lightly hooked bait can be delivered much further than it could be cast if only the hooks were taking the strain.

Smaller predators

Some of the live and dead baiting approaches for pike have been developed from methods first employed for small predators and scavengers like the perch, zander and eel. Other predatory fish which grow to similar sizes as perch and zander are obviously vulnerable to similar methods.

Perch

A standard livebaiting method for perch was the starting point in the pike fishing section, and it is an exceptionally good way of presenting small livebaits like minnows and gudgeon, or the small live smelts which are available to many Continental anglers.

Both big perch and zander are extremely wary of resistance, and this tackle eliminates that as far as possible. Once the line has come out of the clip at the rod butt, the predator is free to run, taking the line through the swivel eye at the top of the sunken float. For presenting a small, lively bait in a fixed position, I think this tackle is hard to beat, though less satisfactory for fishing from a boat.

I envy my colleagues in such countries as Sweden, where perch grow much bigger than my personal best, a fairly modest 3 lbs 7 oz specimen. That perch came on a boat trip which produced three perch over 3 lbs and several others over 2 lbs, a feat virtually impossible in my country today. Good perch fishing has almost disappeared, thanks to disease and pollution in some waters where they once thrived.

I am jealous of those who can still catch perch in large numbers and of good quality. I still keep trying that float tackle and the sunken float method with little livebaits, catching the occasional nice perch, or hopefully putting out a lobworm. Lately I have tried the small spinner, lure and jig methods which produce so many fine perch for the Dutch and other Continentals, but have not yet caught anything big.

Smaller predatory fish, such as pike-perch, can be caught by about the same method as pike.

Zander

As for zander, they have been spreading slowly through my country since the 1960s, and there is growing interest in them. It was natural for our anglers to fish for them in much the same ways as for pike, with small live and dead baits. The methods, or scaled-down versions of the livebaiting in the pike section, are all effective.

Just as many zander fall to small deadbaits presented on the bottom. Slim-shaped fish like little chub or dace are the best baits, followed by roach or rudd. An unlikely-looking but extremely effective bait is a section of a small eel. One of around 30 cm will cut into three nice baits.

Having studied zander fishing in several countries, however, I like the Dutch methods best of all. Their long, slim floats are perfect for slicing through the waves in choppy conditions, yet offer little resistance when a zander takes them under. The floats lean with the wind, looking as though they are going to slide under any second—even when they have not done so for several hours!

The other main method of the Dutch is effective for many predatory species, as well as zander. Casting a long way with a lip-hooked livebait, and recovering it slowly along the bottom, produces many fine zander, some of them bigger than many of us can even dream about.

I was surprised when I watched some of their experts using this method. I thought they would be raising and lowering their rods, causing the bait to flutter up and down in an erratic manner, as when pike anglers sometimes fish a deadbait. Instead they were virtually fishing as the fly-fisherman recovers line, stripping it steadily through their fingers and pausing only occasionally to put loose line back on their reels.

All the while they are feeling with their fingers for the often delicate pluck from the zander, and also watching the tips of their soft-actioned rods for the slightest tap. I wondered if the same method of presenting a bait would work for pike, until they hooked several which bit through the line, Unfortunately, zander will not tolerate wire traces! When I tried it back home in England, I discovered that it would catch my pike, too, though there was none of the gentle plucking that the Dutch were feeling for. The first pike to fall to this method almost pulled the rod out of my hands.

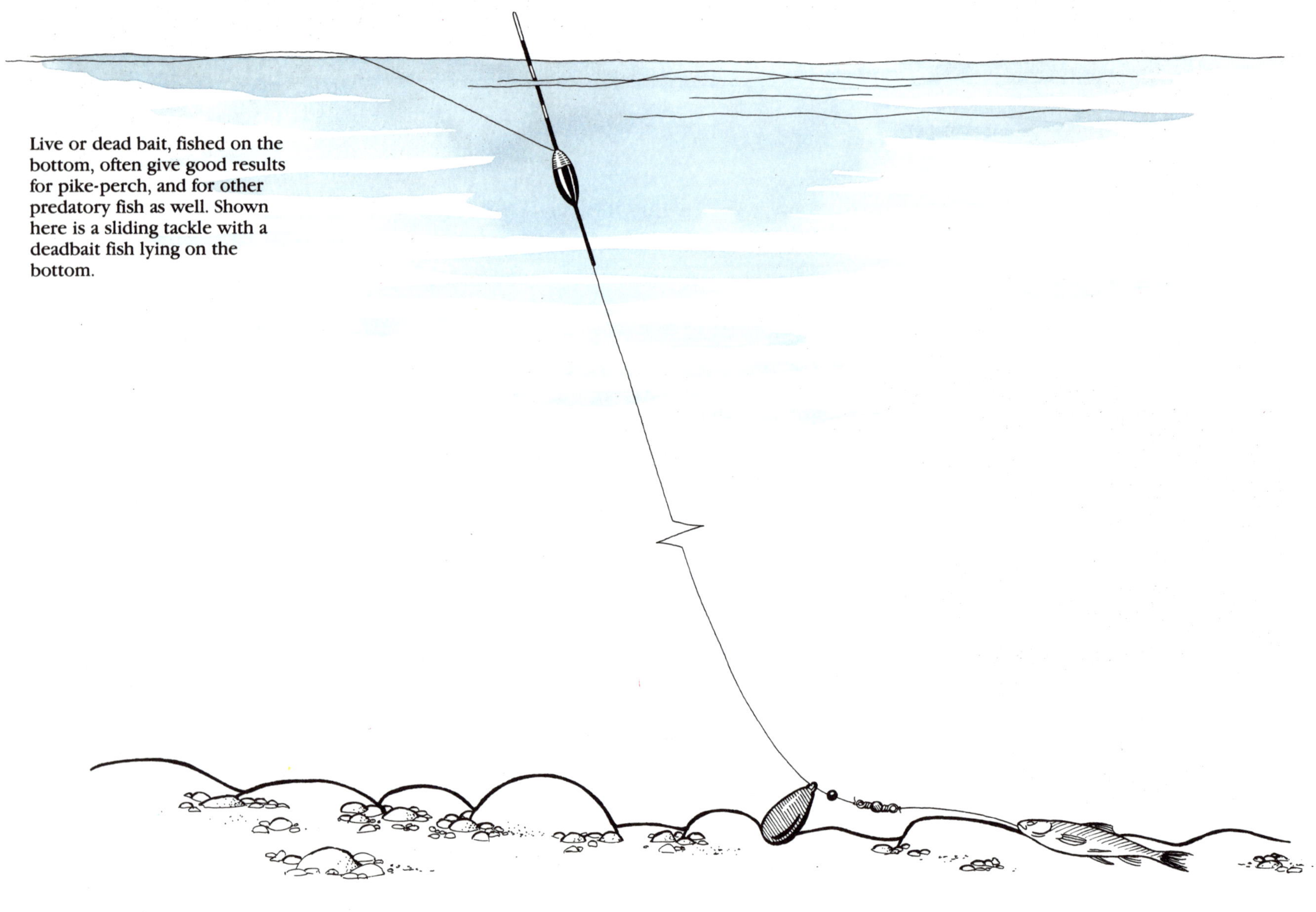

Live or dead bait, fished on the bottom, often give good results for pike-perch, and for other predatory fish as well. Shown here is a sliding tackle with a deadbait fish lying on the bottom.

Eels

Much of my angling career has been dedicated to finding ways of *not* catching eels. They are not my favourite species, though I have recently come to appreciate them smoked in Continental restaurants—a remark which will horrify some of my friends who devote all leisure time to their pursuit, and have amassed tremendous knowledge of this remarkable creature. According to a biologist I heard on the radio, it can detect just one drop of a concentrated liquid flavouring if dropped into a volume of water the equivalent of Lake Constance!

My friends seek the female eels, which penetrate much further into our systems of rivers and canals than the males, which mostly stay around the estuaries. The females push on, as elvers, right up into the fresh headwaters, and find their way overland or through drainage systems and tiny streams into remote lakes and ponds. There they grow large until they are overcome by the urge to migrate back to the Sargasso Sea for spawning. It is thought that the really big eels are those which either lose the urge to migrate, or cannot find a way out of the water they got into as elvers.

Who knows? There is more mystery about this fish than any other, though anglers have certainly developed some excellent methods for catching them, and locating the waters where they

The eel is a greedy yet shy predator.

Illustrated below is an eel tackle for soft or vegetated bottoms. The fish pieces can also be attached to an ordinary sliding tackle without bamboo pin.

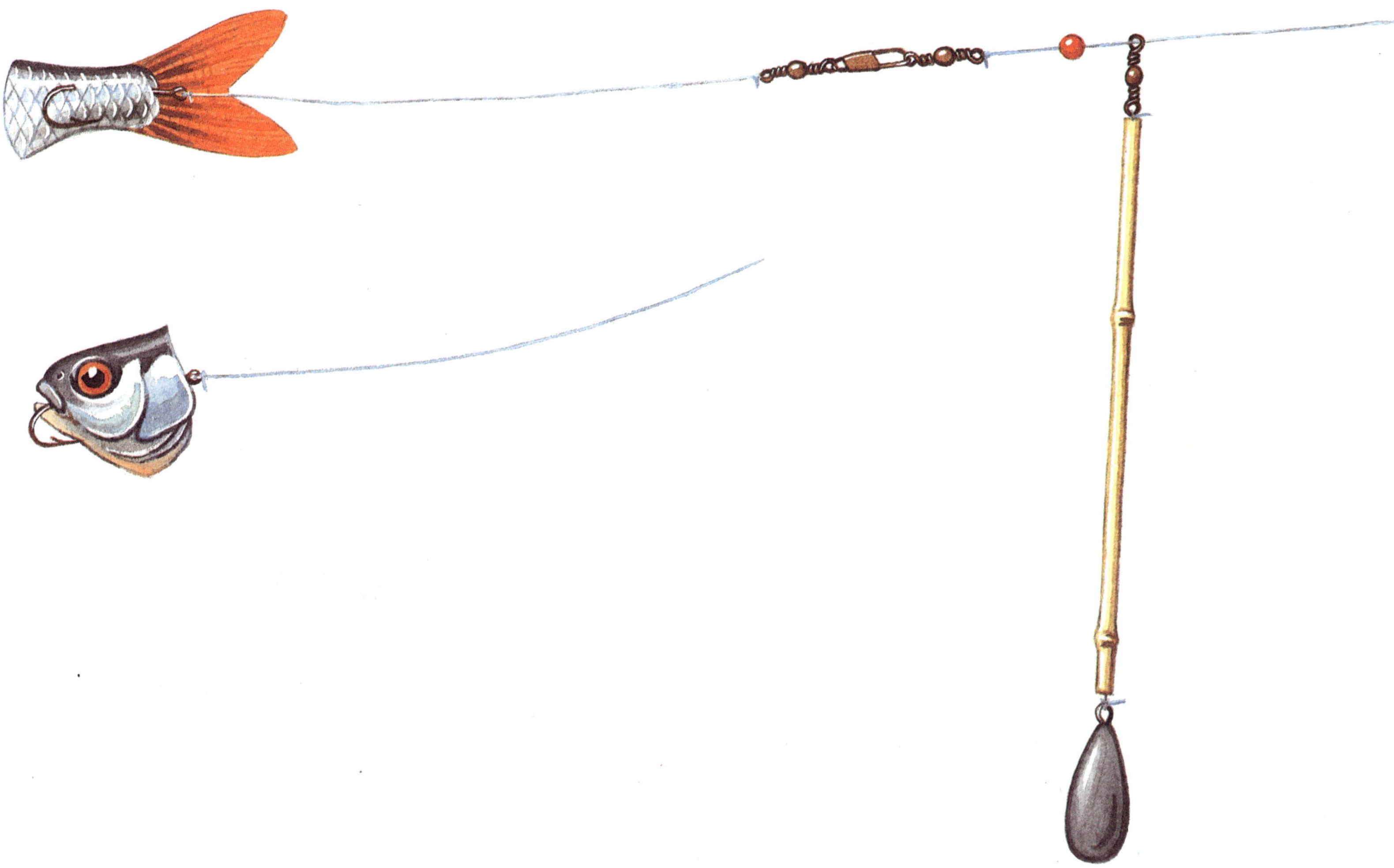

are likely to grow large. They favour fairly shallow, weedy lakes which are full of small crustaceans and lots of small fish. Shallow waters warm up more quickly than deeper ones, and since eels are most actively feeding when the water is warm, they grow more rapidly.

The biologists recognise that there is only one *Anguilla anguilla*, but anglers see two types when it comes to catching them: large-headed and small-headed. Why eels have evolved with either large or small heads is hard to imagine, but they have, and the size of their mouth varies accordingly. The first thing an eel angler does when he catches his first fish from a new water is to note which type it is, for the remaining population are likely to be the same. If it is small-mouthed, then nobody has yet come up with a better bait than the humble lobworm. The "big-heads" are also vulnerable to deadbaits, especially sections like the head and tail.

Anglers use baiting needles to present head and tail baits. These can be clipped to a terminal tackle, which is a good method for use on very soft or weedy bottoms. On hard bottoms an ordinary lead weight would replace the cane stick. For lobworm fishing the same system can be used.

Wire traces are not always used for eels, especially with worms as bait, though it is important to strike at the first sign of a bite to ensure hooking the eel in the mouth. One useful approach for eels is to use a swimfeeder instead of a standard lead weight. The feeder can be packed with pieces of chopped fish, often an effective attractor for a species which relies greatly upon its sense of smell when hunting for food.

Nightcrawlers can also be effective prey in eel-fishing. Shown here is a gliding tackle whose hook can take one or more worms. In the lower left corner are shown three types of sliding tackle.

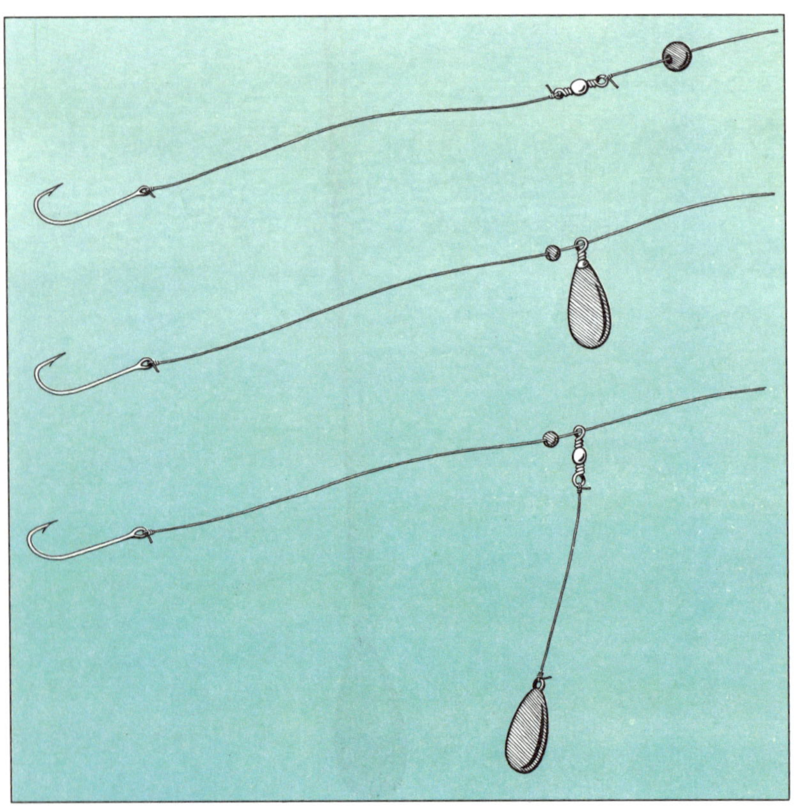

Carp

Many anglers claim that the carp is the most intelligent of all freshwater fish, and others say with equal conviction that it is among the most stupid. Both, I suspect, are correct. In countries where carp are way down the order of anglers' priority—America and Canada, for example—they *are* easy to catch. In the rivers of some Continental countries, like Spain, they are suicidally easy, and readers could no doubt add to the list.

Why should they be considered so clever in other places, like most of Britain and Holland? Perhaps it is because in those countries the carp and the pike are the biggest fish by far, and attract considerable specialised attention. While the Americans and Canadians are obsessed with predators, and have several varieties of large and hard-fighting game fish to concentrate upon, much of Europe has carp or pike at the top of the list.

The fact that carp is a good fighter and can reach a relatively high weight has helped to make it a very popular sportfish in many parts of Europe.

History of carp fishing

It is in Britain that the carp has received the most specialised attention over the last thirty years. Prior to that, carp were considered virtually uncatchable because the fishing tackle available could rarely land them, even if they were hooked. Only a handful of carp enthusiasts were making any progress, until the great breakthrough came in 1952. Richard Walker, the doyen of British anglers, designed a split cane rod with the power to land large carp. In that year he almost doubled the British record with a fish of 44 lbs from a tiny 3-acre lake in Herefordshire. Suddenly big carp *were* catchable, and Walker's feat set in motion a bandwagon for carp which is still rolling. More and more waters were stocked with carp, and today it seems rare for a week to go by without the capture of carp over 30 lbs.

One fact to emerge over this time is that, the more people fished for carp, the harder they became to catch. Although I am by no means a carp specialist, I have personal experience of this. I was once fortunate to fish a lake which held carp and had never been fished before. I caught nearly 200 lbs of carp up to 5 lbs or so, on the most simple of methods: float-fishing with sweetcorn. The second time I fished with sweetcorn, I caught a lot less, and after a few visits it became difficult to get a bite on that bait.

It seems crazy to suggest that every carp in that lake had either learned from direct experience that sweetcorn meant trouble, or that those which had not been hooked had been frightened off by the wary reactions of those which had been caught. But I believe it to be true, and I doubt if I could find a carp specialist in my country who does not believe it too.

The whole history of the sport backs it up. One of the earliest methods was simple, floating breadcrust, which carp would engulf with relish. Once caught, however, they would start nudging large crusts with their noses, eating only the small pieces which broke off. Anglers began fishing a small piece of crust attached to a larger piece, with the hook in the smaller section. That worked for a while, until the carp also got wise to that trick. Since then it has become a recognised fact that carp, and especially large carp, do have the capacity to "remember" that they have been caught on a particular bait, and that they can retain the memory for a considerable time. No other fish I can think of has this capability so well developed.

The other big difficulty is that carp become extremely wary of anglers' terminal tackles. It was found, for example, that when sucking in a bait they could detect and take alarm at the stiffness of strong nylon monofilament line, and promptly eject the bait. Previously people had thought that the carp would not take the bait because they had seen the thick line, but Richard Walker again proved this wrong. He could get positive bites using braided lines much thicker than monofilament, and even easier to see. The difference was the suppleness of braided line. It allowed carp to suck in the bait without feeling anything to cause alarm.

These are just a few examples, small pieces of a giant jigsaw puzzle which forms a 30-year picture of the development of carp fishing. Going through every development is impossible here, but it is easy to summarise the challenge.

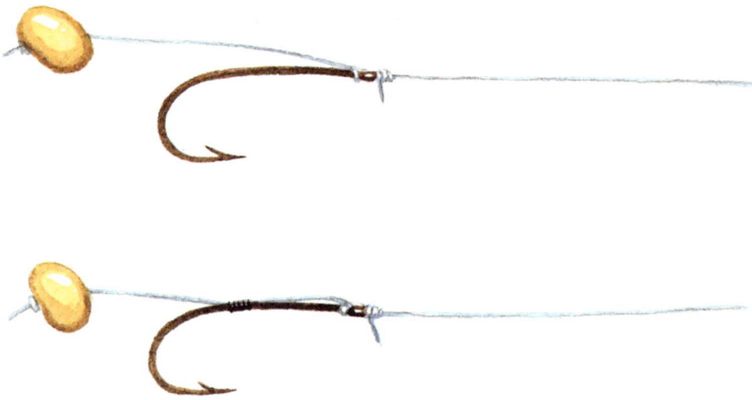

Whether or not carp are considered intelligent, the methods of catching them have become ever more refined. Shown above is the method called "stringer", and at left are two variants of the ordinary Hair Rig.

The Hair Rig

Anglers were faced with a fish which could learn quickly about baits and terminal tackles. They have had to learn how to fool carp with new baits and new tackles, and how to stay ahead of the game, developing something else as their quarry gets wiser. And we are still talking, in some cases, about the same carp. Some of the fish which were in that small Herefordshire pool in the 1950s are still there today, more than 50 years old. Many waters stocked since then still hold their original carp.

So, for brevity, I must leap over years of development and explain the situation today. I will describe some of the modern methods and the thinking behind them, starting with the invention of arguably the most important step forward ever made in carp fishing—the "Hair Rig".

Baits are tied to the hooks via a short length of fine monofilament line of, say, half a kilo breaking strain, though we now know that heavier braided lines work just as well. This shy fish tentatively sucks and blows at the bait, and detects no cause for alarm.

Many other examples of this bait have been thrown into the water by the angler, and this carp has already taken some of them, sucking them in, crushing them with the powerful pharyngeal teeth in the throat and swallowing. This next bait seems no different. It does not seem to be anchored to the bottom by the weight of a large hook and strong line, so in it goes. The hook follows. Alarm bells ring in the brain of the fish, and in the same instant the bite detection mechanism of the angler is activated. The fish is as good as caught.

The Bolt Rig

Very often the Hair Rig is used in tandem with another tackle, now known as the Bolt Rig, another brilliant invention which completely reverses original thinking on the need for extreme sensitivity in terminal tackles. The sensitivity is in the Hair Rig, which fools the carp into taking the bait, but then total insensitivity takes over.

Anglers have scanned the brains of carp, and surprisingly found them wanting. They are clever, certainly, but can only "think" about one thing at a time. It was found that if a carp picked up a bait, pricked itself on the hook and, at the same time, encountered the enormous resistance from a heavy, fixed lead weight, its first reaction would be to run away.

The first time I tried it, the effect was almost frightening. One moment the shallow, weedy pool was all peace and tranquillity. The next it was mayhem. There was a huge explosion as a carp took my bait and bolted. A big bow-wave mapped its course across the pool, and my reel was backwinding at crazy speed as the fish took line. It turned out not to be a particularly big fish, at 13 lbs.

In many, perhaps most cases when using the Bolt Rig, the carp actually hooks itself against the weight of the lead. Even if lightly hooked, or not hooked, it is too obsessed with running away from danger to think about trying to eject the hook. The method is so efficient it catches carp even when the angler is not there. He can come back from the pub or local shop and reel in his prize, raising large question-marks about his sportsmanship and the validity of the Bolt Rig method.

Many think it is not fishing at all, and I tend to agree. I mention it only to show how far carp angling has "progressed" as a result of modern thinking. It has possibly gone a bit too far, and the early Bolt Rigs were real killers. If a carp managed to break the line, it was doomed to tow around a large fixed weight. Anglers now fish in such a way that, if the line breaks, the lead will easily pull off.

A Bolt Rig can be an incredibly effective weapon in carp-fishing. When it is used in combination with a Hair Rig, the fish often catches itself.

Mass baiting

I turn to other modern approaches which carp anglers everywhere will find useful. Where carp are numerous and little fished for, some of this will be irrelevant. The old baits like bread, crust, worms, and partly boiled potatoes will still catch them, and tinned sweetcorn will be deadly. But where generations of fishing have made them wily, the essence of the game is to find a likely bait and educate them to take it with confidence.

Many approaches have worked, including mass baiting with a vast variety of edible matter. So much is introduced, usually for a long time before the bait is used on a hook, that the carp become used to eating it with confidence. It virtually becomes part of the natural diet, and when a carp is finally caught on the bait, it has lost the ability to connect its capture with that bait. It has eaten so much before without experiencing a problem, and it will eat so much afterwards, until it is caught again. This is how the old bait-recognition problem has been overcome to a large extent.

Below left: It is often a matter of finding a bait that the clever carp can take without fright. The inset picture shows how corn is put on the hook.

Below right: Fish can be accustomed to a certain bait by mass baiting (chumming).

Particle Bait

When particle baits, as we call them, begin to succeed, they remain effective for a long time. One such bait was and still is the humble peanut. Soaked overnight in water, peanuts swell up to more than twice their original size, and once carp are educated into taking them it is a long time before they stop. I fed 4 lbs of peanuts into a certain lake every time I fished for several months, while catching on another bait. When I eventually tried them on the hook, the results were spectacular. It worked for two seasons, when I gave up out of sheer boredom.

The same approach works with so many other particles—virtually every type of bean, for instance. Black-eyed beans are deadly, especially if boiled in soup like tomato or oxtail for added flavour. Take a look around a health-food shop and see how many other beans and peas there are. They have all caught carp. Look in pet shops for the seeds fed to birds, like hempseed and maple peas which, like many of the others, have to be boiled before use. There's wheat, and maize, the latter requiring soaking for several days until it starts to "brew". Peanuts led to tiger nuts, another truly deadly bait. The list is endless. Even lupin seed, too small to be used on a hook, catch carp if fed in sufficient quantity. The angler puts a ball of clay or even chewing gum on the hooks, and embeds the seeds in that!

Pellets

Health shops and pet shops are by no means the only source of particle or mass baits. Supermarkets sell carp baits by the sackful, though they think they are selling processed pellet food for cats and dogs! These are small to medium-sized baits in all sorts of shapes and with all kinds of flavours, and carp go crazy for them.

These baits float, of course, but prolonged introduction of them will see the carp coming up for them like silly rainbow trout in a fish farm. That also makes trout pellets a viable carp bait too. Like cat and dog food, they are processed for use on the hook by dampening them and keeping them in a plastic bag for a few minutes. They soften enough to take a hook without breaking up. Carp fishing with floating particles is very enjoyable, much better than sitting around with a bolt rig and a bait on the bottom.

Boilies

Various high-protein products intended for human consumption are mixed together, using eggs as a binder, and rolled into small balls. These are then boiled for about a minute to give them a hard outer skin so that only the carp can eat them. Certainly it stops smaller fish nibbling at them. Food dyes are used to make them in different colours. Every type of concentrated food flavouring has been used to make them taste and smell differently.

The whole business has become so scientific it has gone beyond me; I cannot be bothered to study it. The theory, however, is that carp will eat high protein and somehow recognise that they are benefitting from it. Most anglers seem to believe that, and carp demolish boiled baits by the million every year. We can now buy different mixes, adding only the eggs and perhaps a bit of water, choosing our own flavour and colour, bottles and packets of which are also sold by the million. Some understand the game well enough to make their own mixes, and many businesses have sprung up to supply them with a bewildering number of ingredients. These include Casein, Lactalbumin, Sodium and Calcium Caseinate, Meat Protein, Soya Isolate, Soya Flour, Wheat Gluten, Wheatgerm, Equivite, Codlivine, Fish and Shrimp Meal, Molasses Meal, Peanut Meal, Meat and Bone Meal . . . The list is endless.

The baits are so good, beginner anglers can almost walk into a shop and come out again as instant experts. But this is expensive and, I believe, often unnecessary. Unless your carp have become as shy as those in British waters, I would suggest you work your way through all the beans and peas, nuts, raisins, sultanas, luncheon meats, seeds and cat and dog foods, by which time you will be at least 100 years old!

If you must go into boilies, though, the basic method is the same—feed a lot in to get the carp used to taking them. And they can be made buoyant to fish just off bottom or on the surface. Pop them into the oven to bake for a short time. They swell up, so make a few smaller boilies for the oven. The standard sizes of boiled baits are 14 mm and 18 mm.

Different bait-rigging methods

Virtually all the baits I have mentioned can be fished by hair-rig or bolt-rig methods, and that is certainly how I would prefer to use the harder baits like boilies, peanuts and tiger nuts. Softer baits lend themselves to hair-rigging too, but can also be fished on the hook. It is important, when using baits direct to the hook, to keep the point of the hook exposed, or bites will be missed. Only the very soft baits, like bread and crust, can be used to mask a hook completely.

The method for hair-rigging baits should be explained in more detail. Originally anglers used fine monofilament lines of about half a kilo breaking strain, but I mostly use braided line much stronger than that. It is flexibility which matters, not the thickness. I tie a piece 40 to 50 mm long to the bend or eye of the hook, with a loop on the end. Special baiting needles are available to pull that loop through the bait or baits (baiting needles for pike fishing will also do the job), and they are held in place for casting by putting something through the loop. I often use a piece of grass stalk, or a very short piece of strong monofilament line.

Often fished in conjunction with hair-rigged baits is a method which has been christened a "stringer", which is particularly effective with boilies, though it works with other baits as well. We thread baits onto dissolvable PVA string, putting a knot below each bait to prevent it slipping. When we have, say, five baits at short intervals, the PVA is tied to the bend of the hook. After the cast the PVA dissolves, leaving a nice line of baits leading up to the one on the hook. A lot depends on which end of the line a carp comes across first, but there is a 50/50 chance that it will suck in five baits without having any cause for alarm or concern, and run into deep trouble with bait number 6! Even if it does not work in

Carp become harder to catch in a given body of water, the more they are fished for. This is why sportfishermen around the world have such varying experiences of this type of fishing.

that way, it is an excellent method of getting baits into the exact area one wants to fish. We are baiting up with great precision with every cast.

In deciding which of many different ways to present a bait for carp, the key factor is the exact nature of the bottom. Very often there is a layer of soft silt, like liquid mud, into which baits can totally disappear. Sometimes there is soft weed or even more formidable weed. Carp will root around no matter what the bottom is like, and can find baits buried in weed or silt, but I prefer to make the hook bait visible if I can.

One method for silt bottoms is to present a slow sinking bait which will stay on top of the silt, and one way of doing it is to use a weight which only just sinks. We use a drilled piece of hardwood on the line, weighted with just enough lead to make it sink very slowly. When I make mine, I wrap sheet lead round until I get it absolutely right, then I glue it into the hardwood.

Buoyant bait

An alternative which is particularly useful in bottom weed is to make the bait buoyant instead, so that it can be presented at any chosen distance from the bottom. Bread crust was probably the first bait to be fished in this manner, but it is now commonly used with those oven-baked boilies I mentioned. Big worms can also be fished like this, simply by injecting them with air from a hypodermic needle. On some waters this can be a very effective method indeed.

On shallow waters, buoyant baits can be presented on the surface, by lengthening the distance from the bait to the lead weight. Whether it works depends on your carp. If they are not shy fish, they will probably take it, especially if other pieces of crust without hooks in them are fed to get them going on the bait. Wary carp will probably mop up all the loose offerings and ignore the one with the hook in it. I think they sense that it is anchored, and that it should be drifting with the wind like all the other pieces! In that case, one should present a bait which is drifting with the loose offerings, and this can be done in a variety of ways.

Some anglers still use bubble floats which, when partially filled with water, can be cast a long way. Others use a drilled piece of hardwood similar to the slow-sinking device mentioned previously, only without the lead weight. For close range, a simple piece of peacock quill fastened with two float rings will suffice. There are also self-cocking balsa floats, loaded in the base with either lead or brass, which I prefer against the bubble float for long-range work. They have swivel rings at the base and the top, and can be used to drift a bait if the line goes through the top ring, or for an anchored surface bait if sufficient line and a lead weight are tied to the bottom ring.

All these methods can be used for drifting bread crust, but using them with cat and dog food pellets tends to be more exciting and productive. Pre-baiting campaigns will get the carp used to coming up for these baits, which come in a variety of shapes and sizes, and in many different colours. They are easy to prepare for the hook, as previously described; and where carp have never seen this method before, it can be used with deadly effect.

Where carp *have* been caught a number of times, however, they become extremely wary, and adept at identifying which of the many particles has the hook in it. The last time I tried it, on a lake I had not fished before, I was delighted to see the carp come swirling to the surface within minutes of throwing in some loose samples. They cleared them all up in a short time, but when I cast a bait among a second helping of samples, they took them all except the one on the hook. Obviously they had seen cat and dog food before, but no true carp angler would consider such fish uncatchable. Difficult, maybe, but not uncatchable.

One of my friends got the idea that his carp had come to recognise the drilled hardwood float he was using, and caught a few by adapting a piece of driftwood he found at the waterside. Others came to the conclusion, however, that the really crafty carp were detecting the line running from the bait, and that was a rather more tricky problem to solve. Somebody did it eventually by inventing a different type of controller. It was designed and weighted to float at half cock and to dangle a bait on the surface with the line held off the water.

That requirement of keeping one step ahead of the carp has led fishermen into developments undreamed of by the early carp-fishing pioneers. Where it will all end, I do not know, but I take my hat off to some of those now involved in carp fishing. They are arguably the cleverest and most innovative anglers in the world.

Above: Floating bread-crusts are often an effective bait for carp. Shown here is a tackle with sinker, allowing you to adjust the distance between sinker and bait.

Below: This shows a sliding tackle with the sinker anchored in the bottom. A floating ring, in the inset picture, holds the line over the water surface by standing at an angle.

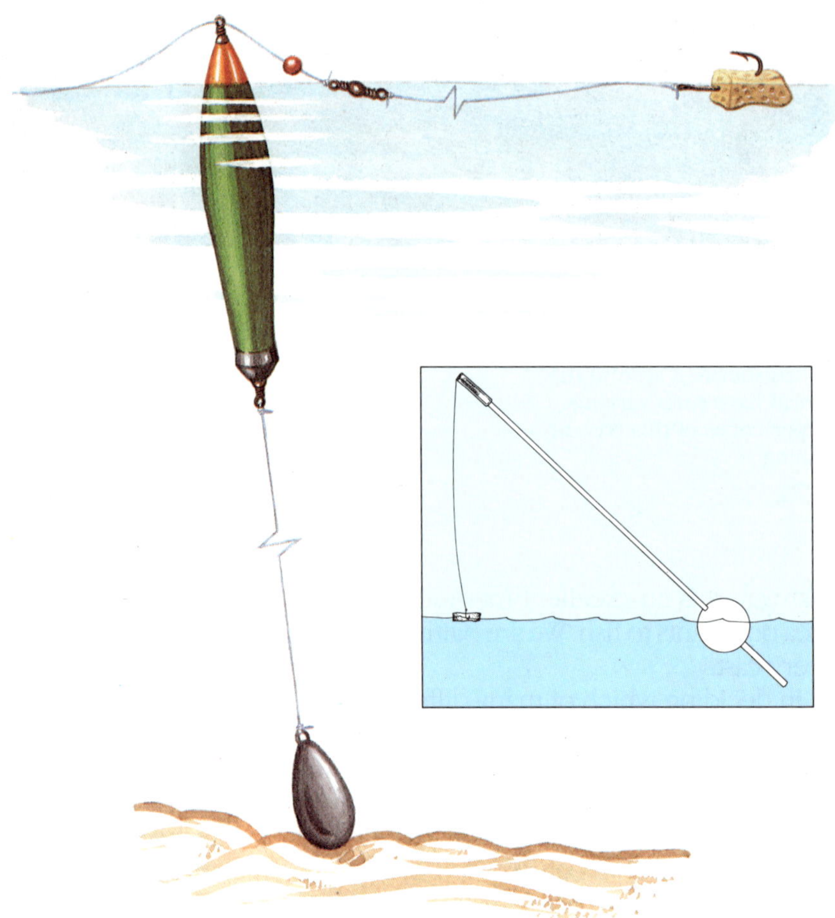

Match fishing

Having described some of the approaches for predators, scavengers, and carp, it is time to switch from discussion of particular species to methods which have been developed for most of the other species. These can be seen in the key elements of British match fishing.

Englishmen have become recognised as leaders in the methods of rod and reel float fishing, certainly by all the European and Scandinavian countries which compete in the CIPS World Championships. England made a tremendous impression while winning the team title in Italy in 1985 with long-range float fishing. Even before that, England had produced several individual world champions using rods and reels, which alerted everyone to their potential, and were easily the most consistent team for several years before the breakthrough win in Italy. That victory greatly accelerated the export of British floats and tackle to most if not all the CIPS member countries.

Match angling has given rise to an amazing development in equipment and methods, but these are well worth knowing even for noncompetitors.

A stick float can be used to catch a great variety of whitefish.

But exporting the tackle is one thing; exporting the knowledge of how to use it to maximum effect is quite another. I will attempt to do that, for it will help both competition anglers and those who fish only for fun.

Two floats in a variety of sizes are the basis of our match fishing, together with a method which is not allowed in competitive events in some other countries—the swimfeeder. Nevertheless, the latter method will catch a lot of good fish for anglers anywhere in the world, and I cannot think of a single species of fish which will not fall to either stick float, waggler float or the swimfeeder. So let me look at them in more detail.

Stick floats

These are normally floats made from balsa wood with heavy cane in the base—usually two thirds balsa, one third cane. Some are made with piano wire as the base, and more recently aluminium rod. They are for use on slow- to medium-paced rivers *only*, and are attached to the line with tight silicone-rubber sleeves just below the tip and at the base.

They are designed for easy and accurate casting with fixed-spool or closed-faced reels. With practice they can be easily controlled in all except very windy conditions, especially downstream or facing winds, when other methods often have to be used (described later). They are employed to catch large numbers of whatever shoal fish inhabit the river—roach, dace, bream, chub, ide, gudgeon, bleak or perch, plus whatever else might be present, like the occasional carp or barbel. Even pike will sometimes snatch a bait intended for other species.

The keys to success with the stick float are good control and precision feeding of the swim with whatever bait you wish the fish to take. To deal with control first, the first essential is to make the float travel downstream in a perfectly straight line. Imagine a nice calm day in an area where fish can be caught at close range, for example right off the end of a 4-metre match rod. A light float could be dropped in at the rod end and, with reel disengaged, the flow would take the float down in a straight line at the speed of the current. Often that is the right speed to present the bait, but sometimes the fish take better if the bait is either slowed down or held back from time to time.

Slowing down is done in different ways. Line comes more slowly out of a closed-faced reel, for example, than it runs off a fixed-spool reel with the bail arm open. Some anglers let the line run through their fingers to slow it down with friction. Others, including myself, sweep the rod upstream immediately after the cast, trap the line with a finger on the spool, and then move the rod slowly in a downstream direction to follow the float. In this way the speed can be controlled precisely; but when the arm has travelled as far downstream as it can go, you have to release the line, sweep the rod back upstream and repeat the process. With practice it can be done very smoothly.

Precisely the same kind of control is needed when you want to fish further out. The job becomes progressively more difficult the further out you go, and you probably need a bigger float carrying more lead shot. If a float starts skating sideways when you try to control it, you need a bigger float.

When fishing at a distance, the biggest control problem is that a bow develops in the line between rod tip and float. This will cause the float to skate or impede the strike when you get a bite, so the bow has to be eliminated. The correct method is to stop the line coming off the reel and quickly lift the line in an upstream direction to straighten it out. This may have to be done two or three times each cast, and it is a useful trick to try and do it just before the float reaches the part of the swim where you are getting the bites. If you cannot control the float properly all the way down, then the aim must be to control it in the parts of the swim which really matter.

This brings me to the important point of feeding the swim, which is done, obviously, to gather the fish together and get them feeding where you can get at them. We use maggots or the chrysalis of maggot (which we call casters). Sometimes we feed only hemp with maggot or caster on small hooks—usually size 18 or smaller, unless the fish are really big.

If the water is deep and strong-flowing, the feed must be packed in groundbait to get it down. If the target is a groundbait-loving species such as bream, we will use it anyway. One useful trick for stick-float fishing is to feed two areas, one close in and another further out. If you feed just one spot, the fish can become wary as their numbers diminish, and leave the area. By keeping two areas going, you can take two or three fish from one spot and then rest it for a while by fishing the other area. This tactic produces a bigger catch in the long run, and it is called "nursing the swim".

As you will see from the left-hand side of the shotting diagram, the basic approach is to be lightly and evenly shotted for slow water, which presents a slowly falling bait to catch fish at all levels.

Right: Two types of stick float are shown here, followed by a sinker diagram with different ways of leading the line. The tackle at left, with lead shots evenly distributed over the line, is standard for fishing in slow-flowing water. At its right are two variants for deeper and faster-running water.

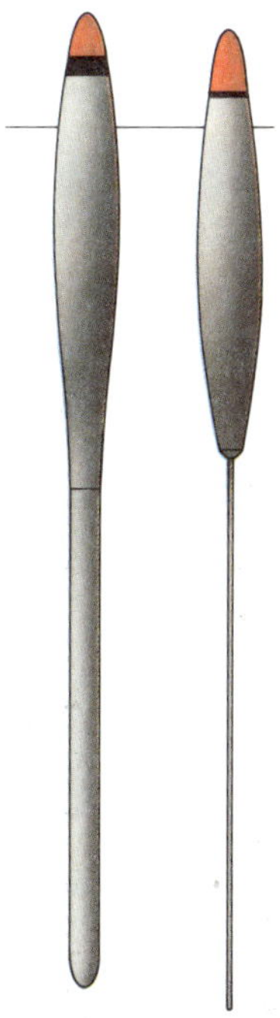

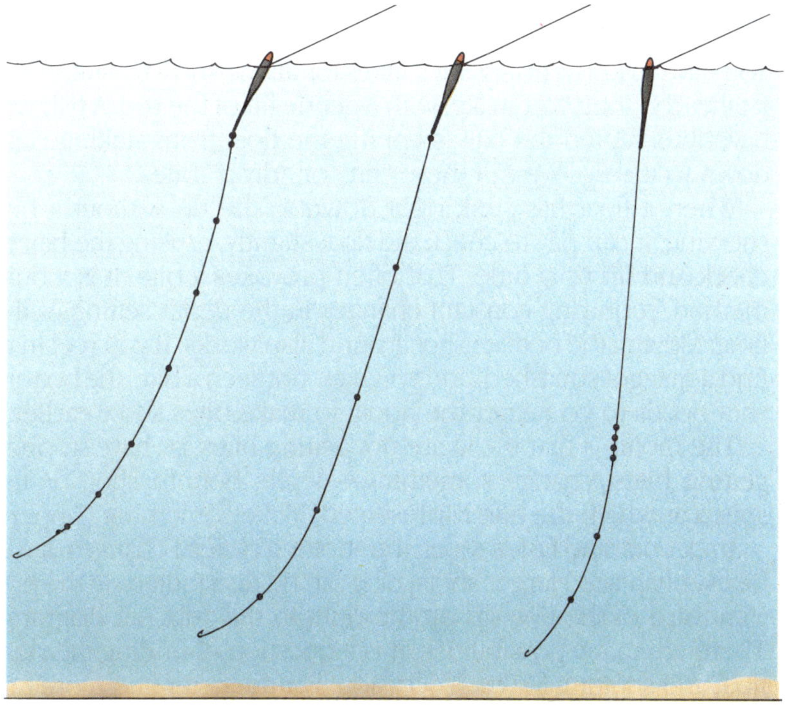

Below: It is important for the float to drift downstream in a very straight line, and at the same speed as the water. In some circumstances it can be effective to brake the float now and then, or to completely stop the drifting for a moment.

You have to know how long it takes for all the shots to sink, and if it takes too long you strike, with a gentle lift of the rod. A fish will have intercepted the bait, stopping the float from sinking right down to the tip. We call these "lift" or "drop" bites.

When a float has sunk right down to the tip without a bite showing, it can pay to check the float slightly, causing the bait to check and lift up a little. That often provokes a bite. It is a busy method, requiring constant changes in the depth setting of the float. Moving the bottom shot around also works. If you reel in to find a maggot squashed, and you have not seen a bite, the bottom shot needs to go nearer the hook, to make bites show earlier.

The motto is that if you are not getting bites, or have stopped getting bites, change something—depth, bottom shot, or the speed at which the bait is presented. Make something happen!

In deeper and faster water, the shotting pattern changes. It can be evenly placed larger shots, or it can be distributed on the bottom third of the line (as on the right in the adjacent diagram). There are many possibilities. It is a question of finding the right float and shotting for each occasion. For the faster and more turbulent water, the wire-stemmed stick float usually proves more stable and easy to control.

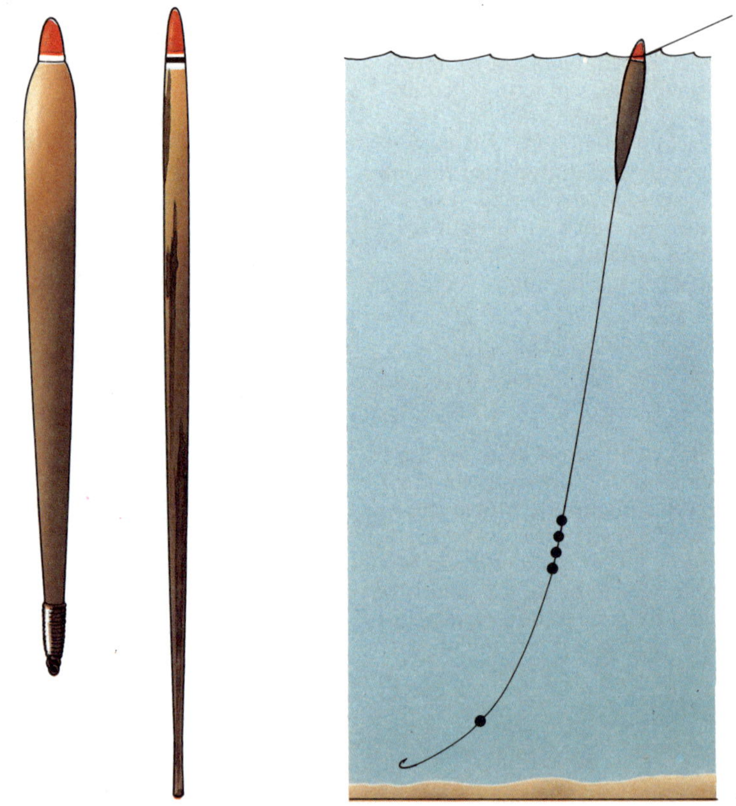

The balsa float is a variant of the stick float, used in deep and strongly flowing water. The tackle at left shows how the shots should be placed in clumps, about a metre from the hook, with one shot halfway toward the hook.

Balsa floats

I know I have not mentioned these before, but they are really an extension of the stick float for use in deeper, heavier flowing water. Being all balsa, they carry much more lead shot—up to four SSGS—and these are fished in a group about 1 to 1.25 metres from the hook, with a single shot below, half way to the hook.

These floats are controlled as previously described, at a speed as slow as possible. Baits can be small, with small hooks, or big on bigger hooks. They are commonly used to fish bread, luncheon meat or wasp grubs for big fish.

One of my friends has taken large catches of ide from fast-flowing Swedish rivers with this method. Another uses it in Canada with lobworms, or night crawlers as they call them, for several species including steelheads.

Waggler floats

Waggler is the collective name for floats which are attached via the bottom end only, but in the main they are made of various lengths and thicknesses of peacock quill. Sometimes they have balsa bodies at the base, the sole purpose of which is to increase the amount of lead shot they take. The more shot they carry, the further the floats can be cast.

Unlike stick floats, the waggler is employed on both rivers and lakes. By using a small bottom ring not much bigger than the diameter of the reel line, together with a stop knot, it can be fished as a sliding float to cope with very deep water. If the water is, say, six metres deep, one cannot cast a fixed float to fish at that depth with a four-metre rod. A sliding float overcomes that problem, but here I must confine myself to the basics.

The main method of fishing them is to have most of the shot load a given float can carry on the line at either side of the float ring (or on the hook side of the float if it is fished as a slider). Two large shots are used to lock the float in place, with only a few small shots down the line.

On rivers, when an awkward wind prevents the angler performing properly with a stick float, a small straight waggler can be used instead. It would be cast beyond the line to be fished. Then the rod tip would be pushed below the surface and the float reeled back sharply to (*a*) bring it to the area to be fished and (*b*) sink the line under the surface. Then you just allow line to run off the reel and the float to run downstream, watching for the usual signs of a bite. It cannot be controlled as well as a stick float, but with the line underwater it does at least run down in a straight line. It can catch in conditions where a stick-float angler is beaten, but it is not as versatile.

Another use on rivers is to fish beyond the distances which can be fished with a stick float. It is important to choose a size of float which can easily be cast to the required distance. Here it can be very effective indeed, especially on slow to medium-paced waters which are not tremendously deep.

Mastering the waggler can be difficult, especially if the wind is strong enough to create a big bow in the line. If that is the case, the line has to be sunk as previously described, but this creates a problem. There is so much tension on a long length of sunken line that the float will be trying to go under all the time, even when a fish is not biting. The hook or lower shot touching bottom will make it start to drag slowly under. The same happens if there is any check on the line leaving the reel.

One answer is to use a thick-topped float on rivers, and undershot it so that more of the top sticks out. With a bit of luck you can get it to go downstream without dragging under too much. If it does drag under slowly, ignore it, for it won't be a fish. Feed some more line and the float will pop up again. If a fish takes the bait it will stop the float's progress, and the current will push it under *quickly*. That is the time to make a long, sweeping strike.

Long-range river fishing with line sunk is the most difficult waggler method to master, though most of the time conditions allow us to fish the line up top. This is much more efficient. The float does not try to drag under at all, and if too big a bow develops in the line, it can be straightened in much the same manner as described for the stick float. I had a lot of trouble mastering the waggler until I watched some of our international-class anglers fishing it. They did not bother too much about large bows in the line. They watched for the float to disappear, then made long sweeping strikes to get rid of the bow. Often they would take the rod through a 180-degree arc *and* make several rapid turns of the reel handle before making contact with the fish. For some reason fish seem to hang onto the bait a long time with this method. My theory is that the flow creates tension between fish and float, preventing the ejection of the bait.

Here we see two different waggler floats and their method of use. At left in the sinker diagram is a typical tackle for fishing at medium distance in lakes and streams. The tackle at the centre is good for brooks and canals. The tackle at right, with a large float, suits fishing at long distances in rivers and big lakes. Naturally, the fishing distance is limited by how far out you can cast the food, either by throwing balls of it or by using a bait sling.

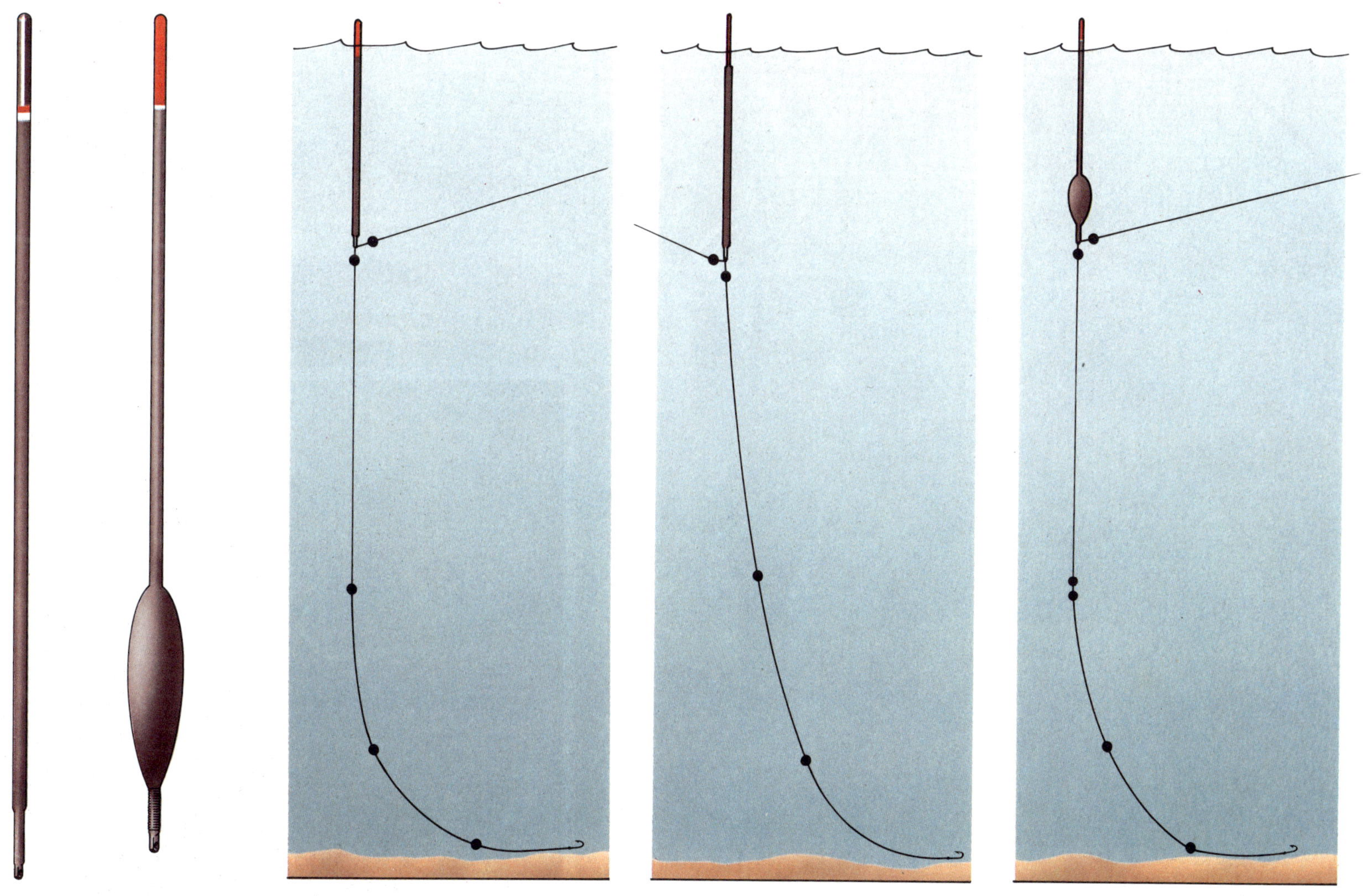

Right: Waggler floats, intended for still waters, have an extra-thin top called an insert. Shown here are two types of waggler floats with insert, and how they should be used.

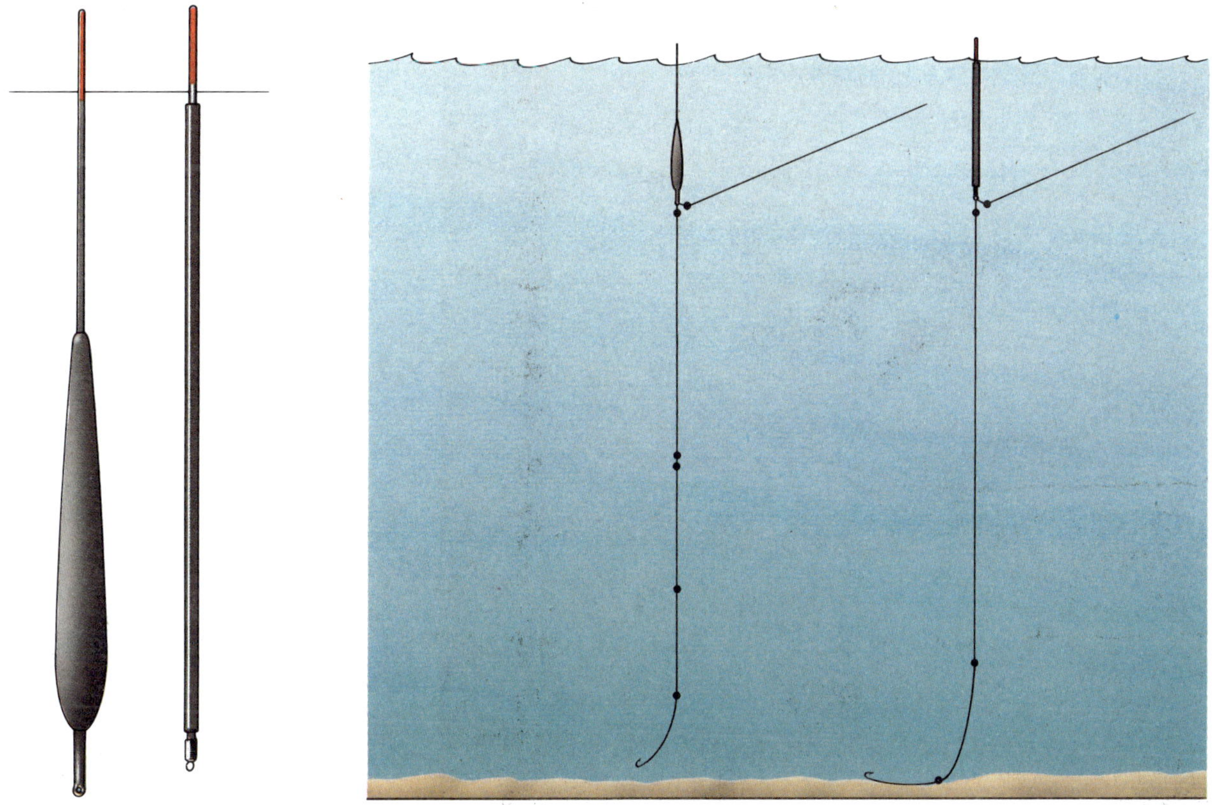

For closer range on lakes and canals, the function of wagglers is basically the same, though there are differences. They are always fished with the line sunk to get it below the influence of any surface drift, and the length of the floats assists this purpose. Because there is no significant flow on lakes, apart from water movement caused by the wind, there is no problem with sunken line. But since there is no flow to help push a float under when a fish bites, the stillwater/canal waggler has to be more sensitive.

A stillwater fish trying to pull under a thick-tipped river float would feel the resistance and let go. We therefore fish the floats with thin inserts in the tips to reduce that resistance. We let a thin piece of peacock into a thick piece, or sometimes use different materials like cane, reed, or even bristles from nylon sweeping brushes. It depends on how far away we are fishing. The nearer in we are, the more thin and sensitive the tip can be. It is a question of sorting out what we can see properly at a given distance.

The big advantage with slim inserts, apart from offering less resistance when a fish takes them under, is that they emphasise the bite which comes as a bait is slowly falling, or is picked up off the bottom along with the lower shot. The tip will either stick way out of the water longer than it should, or suddenly climb out of the water to register an unmistakable lift bite. A shot as small as a number 8 will sink about 8 cm of nylon brush bristle. So when a number 8 is lifted off the bottom, that bristle will lift up to 8 cm—difficult to miss!

The one time thin tips don't work on still waters is when the wind has set up a considerable undertow. The top water is going one way and the bottom water in the opposite direction. With bait and shots on the bottom, a thin-tipped float will drag under. Then it is a question of finding a float with a tip thick enough and buoyant enough to stay up top.

Left: Like all sportfishing, bait-fishing is a fine way to relax by green, idyllic waters. A popular sportfish is tench, seen in the inset here.

Left: Wagglers are the floats to which the line is only attached on its lower part. This type of float can also be used as a sliding float, and—unlike the stick float—it suits both calm and running waters.

Right: The purpose of a swimfeeder is easier feeding of the fish. It is filled with the same kind of bait that you have on the hook, then both are cast out to the same spot. In running waters, a trail of lure bait is laid, leading the fish to the hook.

I can remember using waggler floats in such countries as Holland, France, and Italy before such floats had been seen in those countries, and I got some very strange looks from fellow anglers—until they saw what the floats could do. In Italy, on Lake Garda, I was catching species of fish I had never even seen before, like sunfish and small catfish. I have since caught such species as bluegills and crappies in America, where European float methods are still virtually unknown.

The message is that the methods are universal. On rivers, lakes or canals, they will catch whatever is there, and that is certainly true of the next method—the swimfeeder.

Swimfeeder

The swimfeeder is nothing but a piece of weighted plastic tube, with or without caps at each end, but few "inventions" have been taken up with so much enthusiasm, or caused more controversy. The "Plastic Pig" is one of the less complimentary descriptions from gifted float anglers, who have seen some of their traditional skills eroded by the feeder. It has turned hopeless anglers into occasional catchers, occasional catchers into regular catchers and regular catchers into super-stars. In the right hands it can turn virtually every bite into a fish on the bank, and it can attract bites when float anglers are struggling.

As the name suggests, its function is to deliver feed—samples of whatever is being used on the hook. Because it is attached to the line, it delivers both hookbait and feed to the same place, with pinpoint accuracy. Gone are the days when the two had to go out separately, requiring great skill in the accurate throwing of groundbait, working out where the bait had some to rest on the bottom and casting onto it.

Now all those things are achievable with just one accurate cast. If there are fish in a river or lake which will take whatever you want to offer on the hook, they are vulnerable to the feeder, no matter what species they are. The method is deadly and simple, though not so simple as many seem to think. It is possible to fish the feeder badly or extremely well, and as usual it is the thinking angler who gets the best out of it.

A basic swimfeeder tackle is, in this case, the type with enclosed ends, the upper cap being removable, and it is full of holes. This type is designed to be loaded with loose feed—maggots, casters, hemp or any other bait small enough to be washed out through the holes. Imagine what happens when the feeder is cast to the chosen spot on a river. Some samples of feed fall out on impact, and others come out as it falls, creating a trail of

Types of bait are innumerable, but maggots are among the most popular.

bait on the bottom to lead fish into the main baited area. As cast follows cast, the trail of bait is consolidated, and lots of bait is scattered where the feeder comes to rest at the top end of the swim.

Large numbers of fish can be congregated in this area, and as they feed with ever-growing confidence they inevitably find the one bait with the hook in it. As they disappear towards the net, they are replaced by other fish coming up the bait trail. They are on a sort of conveyor belt to captivity. So simple, so deadly—providing the angler knows how to detect and hit the bites.

That used to be the major problem. Anglers developed rods with slender, flexible tips made from fibreglass, and watched them keenly for the bites, which could be anything from tiny flickers to great big pulls. We still use those slender tips, but the rest of it is redundant. The type of bite which registers today is both unmistakable and almost impossible to miss.

The secret is in the weighting of the feeder. I cast in with a lead strip which I think may just about hold bottom, but hoping that it will not hold. If it does not hold, the rod tip will tell me, for it will simply move back and forth in tune with the feeder bouncing along the bottom. I will drop just one large lead shot in the feeder and try again, adding one more shot each cast until the feeder stops moving after it has hit the bottom. Only when I have got this weighting exactly right will I bait the hook and fill the feeder with feed. Now only two things can make the feeder move—a bit of debris coming down with the flow and wrapping itself round the line (which we just have to put up with), or a bite from a fish.

The tackle is so finely balanced that a bite, even from a very small fish, dislodges the feeder and makes it roll. As it does so, the tip of the rod starts wagging violently from side to side. We have found that there is not even any need to strike. Just lift the rod and reel in. The fish is invariably on the hook, either because it never felt any resistance or because it could not eject the bait. I am not sure which, but I think it is the former.

It has been found that the best place to cast on a river is slightly upstream, so that the feeder is immediately opposite the angler when it hits bottom. It also pays to have quite a large bow on the line between the feeder and the rod tip, which is angled straight out or slightly downstream. Releasing some slack line helps the feeder to hold with less lead weight—logical, if you think about it—but the bow also facilitates an alternative method, which is to fish the feeder on the move.

By finding out how much lead weight will make the feeder, hold it follows that removing one or two weights will make it move. If there is a big bow in the line, the feeder will move directly downstream instead of across the current. Fish are suspicious of anything which appears unnatural, and baits moving across the current are unnatural.

A moving feeder is fished when the stationary feeder stops working properly, usually because the fish have become wary and dropped downstream. As the feeder moves, the rod tip will also move, but slowly and rhythmically. When a fish takes the bait, that slow movement becomes a rapid flapping, an unmistakable signal to lift the rod and reel in as before.

The open-ended swimfeeders are fished in much the same way, but are balanced with large shots nipped on to the line which links the feeder to the main reel line. They are for use with groundbait—standard bread crumb holding samples of the hook bait or, increasingly common nowadays, the fancy mixes developed by Continental match anglers. Groundbait is used only if the target species responds to it, bream being the outstanding example.

Some species, like chub, run away from groundbait sometimes, though I do not think it will be long before groundbait is developed which will appeal to most species of fish. Carp anglers' experiments with bait flavours have revealed that certain smells appeal rather too much to other species. This does not please them, but competition anglers are nowadays rediscovering what the carp anglers found. Strong, fruity flavours appeal to lots of different fish in warm water conditions, while spicy, curry-type flavours work best in colder water. Pretty soon they will isolate exactly what smells attract which species. Vanilla, for example, is already known to be a marvellous bream attractor, and maple turns on tench. The Americans are finding smells which attract predators. It is a field where there is much to learn.

It should go without saying that both types of swimfeeder are effective on still waters, for most of the same reasons as they work on rivers. The main differences are that bite detection is not as easy, and the proportion of bites successfully struck is not as high. Here we do have to rely on slender fibreglass rod tips, and watch for the tiniest of movements, especially in winter. An alternative, especially for those who seek big fish on still waters, is to employ an electronic bite-alarm system and/or a sensitive butt indication, for example a fold of metal foil on a spike.

Another problem for the stillwater feeder angler is managing to cast into the same area every time, especially at long range. One useful tip is to cast to the required spot, and then coat about a metre of line from the reel with ladies' nail varnish. On every subsequent cast it is then easy to see whether one has cast too far, in which case reel back—or not far enough.

How much lead is used on feeders? River flow conditions vary from slow to extremely fast, and because of the water pressure on the line, the amount of lead required also varies according to both depth and distance. On the rivers I fish, as little as 0.25 oz, sometimes 4 oz, with 1.5 to 2 oz the most common weight, are used. I also have to contend with tidal waters, where the flow is either increasing or diminishing. This requires constant adjustment if full efficiency is to be maintained.

Clearly it is difficult to find one rod to cast the full range of weights efficiently, but I can get away with two: a nice, easy-actioned 11-footer for the lighter work, and a stiffer version of the same length for the heavy leads.

In order to attract the maximum number of bites, many anglers fish with light hook lengths. They may have something like 6-lb line on the reel for safe casting of the weight, but the breaking strain of the hook length may be only 1 lb or 1.5 lb. There is a potential problem, here, especially with the more powerful species such as carp and barbel, though big bream and chub may also be involved. When these fish take a bait with gay abandon, they can smash the hook length if the weight of the lead is too great. If it is finely balanced, as previously described, the big fish merely dislodge it, and the line remains intact. If it is too firmly anchored, however, the line will break. Once the initial shock has been absorbed, the remaining problem is to play the fish efficiently and very carefully. A rod powerful enough to cast 3 oz is not the ideal weapon with which to play good fish on light line.

Another point to consider is the choice of line itself—not the breaking strain but the diameter. Several makes of line are now said to be "extra strong". That is, it may break at 6 lbs but is actually the same diameter as 3.5 lbs. I am suspicious of some, but one make from the German company Bayer (brand name Ultima in my country) has proved to be excellent for the feeder. Line diameter can make a big difference to the amount of lead required to hold bottom, and generally the less lead the better.

One can use the lesson about line in the fine balancing of the feeder. For example, when you think you have almost got the weight right, the job can be perfected simply by propping the rod a little higher, taking as little as one or two metres of line out of the water. A feeder which is slowly moving will then hold. Similarly, if you want to make a holding feeder move, then lowering the rod rest may do the trick.

On still waters, of course, the weight used is dictated only by the distance you want to cast, though in deep water I would use more lead, rather than less, simply to get the feeder to the bottom more quickly. Feeders are bought with light, medium and heavy lead strips, but additional lead strips can be purchased or made.

Coastal fishing

Welcome to the world of coastal fishing, a branch of angling that attracts millions of enthusiasts worldwide who cast from surf beaches, steep shingle banks, cliffs and estuaries. Here the fish are truly wild: free to migrate, unmanaged by man, and their lives and feeding patterns are strongly influenced by season, weather and biological cycles.

To be successful, the coastal angler must be skilful, self-reliant, and well-versed in marine natural history. Unlike his inland colleagues, he cannot rely on fish stocking programmes and waterside management. Techniques such as groundbaiting and swim preparation are generally impossible due to the vast areas of seabed swept by waves and currents. There are very few opportunities to wean fish onto special baits—as in modern carp fishing, for example—and it is extremely rare to enjoy the advantage of pinning down the shoal's precise location for more than a few hours.

Sea species are continually on the move, feed only on natural plant and animal material, and are highly sensitive to their surroundings. Changes in water temperature, barometric pressure, water clarity and spawning cycles mean that sometimes it is easy to locate and catch your fish, while on many more occasions tempting a single bite calls for talent and persistence. However, that is all part of coastal angling's huge appeal and we would wish it to be no other way.

Wherever I go in the world, people ask how the sport varies from country to country. Apart from obvious differences like species of fish and local environment, coastal angling is remarkably uniform. Tactics developed for, say, cod and bass surfcasting in Europe would catch channel bass in America or *maigre* on the Atlantic coastline of Africa. Similar parallels exist for just about every type of beach structure, fishing technique and category of fish. Yes, you'll have to use specific baits and adapt to new water conditions and fishing times; but the basic mechanics are the same.

With this in mind, I have deliberately steered towards the major technical aspects of coastal angling. Paramount among these is casting, for unless he can place a bait well over the 100-yd mark when necessary, an angler is at a severe disadvantage. Of course there are times when the fish are close in. Sometimes they are literally beneath your feet. But in the longer term, the man who has the option to cast a long way enjoys the highest catch rate.

Learning to cast properly is therefore a priority. With today's tackle and a few weeks of sensible practice, that's no problem. The next step is to assemble the correct terminal rig for the waters and species in question. Insist on using the finest quality baits. And finally, study the life cycle of your selected quarry along with its preferred season, tidal pattern and habitat. In summary, the winning formula is to be in the right place, at the right time, with the right bait. But then, that's true of any kind of fishing!

Equipment

Choosing the right rod for coastal fishing is quite difficult because of the need to combine long-distance casting power with the ability to detect bites and fight a heavy fish. A rod designed with a very stiff handle and fast tapered tip will throw a sinker well over 250 yds, but it may be unable to detect a small bite. On the other hand, a beautifully light and responsive fishing rod might lack the power to propel bait the full distance.

Inevitably, then, rod design is a compromise between these basic requirements. Modern materials like carbon fibre help to bridge the gap, but the angler must still be aware of that fundamental clash. The majority of newcomers to the sport make the mistake of buying a rod that is far too stiff and powerful. Thus equipped, they find it impossible to learn proper casting and fishing techniques.

Shore fishing rods fall into three categories: general-purpose beachcasters for 4–6 oz sinkers; spinning rods that handle lures weighing up to about 4 oz; long, light rods for delicate techniques such as float fishing in harbours. The first rod on the list is by far the most important, because it can handle over 90% of coastal fishing requirements. For some anglers it will be the only kind of rod ever needed.

Coastal fishing often calls for long-distance casting, and one needs a rod that can take weights of 100–150 grams. In order to feel even cautious bites, the rod must have a relatively soft and sensitive top, but its midsection should be strong and fairly stiff for casting the bait far enough.

Beachcasters

Today's casting rods are either about 12 ft long with the reel attached in traditional fashion, or in the 13–13.5 ft class with the reel set low near the butt cap and controlled with the left hand. The rod blank is constructed of "semi-carbon" (a mixture of glassfibre and carbon fibre). All-carbon rods are not popular because, although excellent for casting, they suffer from excessive stiffness at the tip, which lowers bite sensitivity and also reduces the range of sinker weights that can be cast properly.

Despite a great deal of controversy and opinion about the merits of tapers and actions, for most anglers there is nothing to be gained by straying from a medium-fast tapered tip coupled to a stiff, but not rigid, butt section. The design ensures plenty of speed and power for casting extremely long distances, but still compensates for casting errors. The action suits every common style of casting, including the *pendulum* technique. Being quite slim, the tip of such a rod will detect the smallest of bites; the centre section is flexible enough to fight big fish in comfort. Using modern materials, designers can incorporate all this power and precision in a rod weighing less than 16 oz.

Rod rings are selected to suit multiplier reels, fixed spools or a combination of the two. For maximum performance, specific ringing for one type of reel is recommended. A multiplier rod would have 7–9 rings graded down from 30 mm diameter at the butt to 12 mm at the tip. For a fixed spool reel, 3–4 rings from 50 mm to 16 mm are better suited to the large coils of line that are thrown off the spool during the cast. Combination or "hybrid" ringing adopts a middle route: 5–6 rings from 50 mm to 12 mm offer adequate performance and control for anglers who like to use both fixed spool and multiplier reel on the same rod.

Spinning rods

Casting plugs and metal lures is an essential aspect of coastal fishing for anglers in many parts of the world. The right choice of rod depends on lure weight, casting range and size of fish. In the majority of cases, a 9–11 ft rod balanced to cast 1–4 oz does an excellent job. Since bites are much easier to detect in lure-fishing than on legered natural baits, tip sensitivity is not as important and therefore all-carbon rods are popular. Extremely light and well balanced in the hand, they blend power, casting speed and the ability to handle big fish on relatively light lines. Virtually all serious lure-fishing is done with the fixed spool reel, so the blank should be ringed with large-diameter rings, and not too many of them.

Float-fishing rods

Float fishing is not generally popular with coastal fishermen, and cannot be used in shallow water anyway. However, for presenting baits in midwater alongside rocks, as well as in harbours and other deep-water fishing stations, float tackle not only catches more fish than conventional tactics but also avoids heavy tackle losses in rocks and weeds. The heavier forms of float fishing may require several ounces of lead, in which case a normal beachcaster serves well. But for lighter sport with, say, sinkers up to 2 oz, a special rod should be used. Powerful freshwater fishing rods are worth considering: pike and carp rods about 12 ft long with a test curve of 2–3 lb have all the casting power and strength you need.

Reels

Probably 90% of coastal anglers use fixed spool (spinning) reels because they are easy to operate and do not backlash. For serious long-distance casting with 4–6 oz of lead, the multiplier (conventional) reel is smoother, stronger in the gears and drag, and more precise in its control over a fish. From the casting point of view, if used properly, it does give a slight but worthwhile improvement in distances.

Fear of backlash is the only reason why so many anglers do not use multiplier reels. Old-fashioned reels were notoriously difficult to control, but today's purpose-built casting multipliers with centrifugal or magnetic casting brakes are so good at smoothing the flow of line that only the worst of casters can possibly induce serious tangles.

Because a fixed spool reel's performance is related to the amount of line friction it creates during the cast, the spool should be as large as possible. Ideal examples are the Mitchell 486, 489 and Penn Spinfisher 850SS for heavy-duty fishing, and the Spinfisher 650SS for medium work.

The best multiplier reel for any given situation is the model with the smallest safe line capacity and the lightest spool. Whether or not it actually spills from the spool, every inch of line wound onto a multiplier reel rotates during every cast. Heavy spools create high inertia at the moment of release, followed by high momentum (flywheel effect) in the middle of the cast. These create the ideal conditions for backlash to develop. For general fishing with 12–15 lb test line, small reels like the ABU 6500GR, 7000C and Pen 970 are excellent. For heavier duty, ABU9000 and Penn Magpower 980 are still controllable with lines up to 35 lbs provided that the control system is correctly adjusted.

On both types of reels, the following features are absolutely essential for coastal fishing: strong gears; powerful but smooth drag system; corrosion-resistant construction; easily available spare parts and servicing. If you are interested in tournament casting, choose a multiplier such as the ABU6500GR that can be modified to conform to "CT" specifications. Among other things, this means replacing the level wind system with a plain crossbar, and re-tuning the magnetic brake to allow higher spool speeds.

Lines

Because line is the only link between the angler and his bait, which might be over 150 yds away, it must be absolutely reliable. Surprising as it might seem, it does not need to be of particularly high breaking strain. Under normal circumstances, 12–18 lbs is adequate. Only rarely are stronger lines necessary for hauling big fish out of heavily weeded ground, and for battling species like sharks that weigh several hundred pounds.

Fairly light lines make sense for two main reasons. First, the thinner the line, the farther you can cast. A cast of 100 yds with 25-lb line would increase to 130 yds if the line strength were reduced to 15 lbs. In addition, strong lines are wasted because a beach-fishing rod is very bad at generating tension. By pulling as hard as you can with the most powerful beachcaster, it is practically impossible to produce more than 3 lbs tension at 100 yds distance. Even at 25 yds, it takes a very strong man to develop 10 lbs of pressure on the hook. Of course there are other factors involved, but even so it does mean that lines over 15 lbs breaking strain cannot be exploited other than in exceptional circumstances. All they do is cut distance and increase the size of the required reel, which in the case of a multiplier inevitably leads to poor control.

Monofilament nylon is the only valid choice. Medium-grade lines are usually the best investment. Obviously you cannot rely on the cheap ones; on the other hand, the advantages of premium-grade brands are difficult to realise on the beach. In addition, beach fishing is very hard on a line, so you need to change it after about a dozen sessions anyway. Price is therefore an important consideration.

Sinkers

An efficient sinker for coastal fishing must be well streamlined so that it flies cleanly through the air, and also capable of being anchored firmly to the seabed when necessary to counteract water currents and waves. A great deal of research into the subject has resulted in two main types of sinker being popular around the world: the bomb and the inverse pyramid. Although still common for fishing over sandy bottoms, the pyramid is fast becoming obsolete in regions where long-distance casting has increased its influence, for there is no doubt that the streamlined bomb is far superior in flight. Fitted with fixed or swivelling grip wires, it can also be made to hold firmly in the seabed under the worst of conditions. A bomb's performance is further boosted by replacing the short wire tail loop with a single wire about 4 in long. The tackle becomes more stable in the air, and its seabed grip improves by about 30%.

Most beach rods are nominally rated as 4–6 oz, but nearly all of them produce peak performance with a sinker weighing 5–5.5

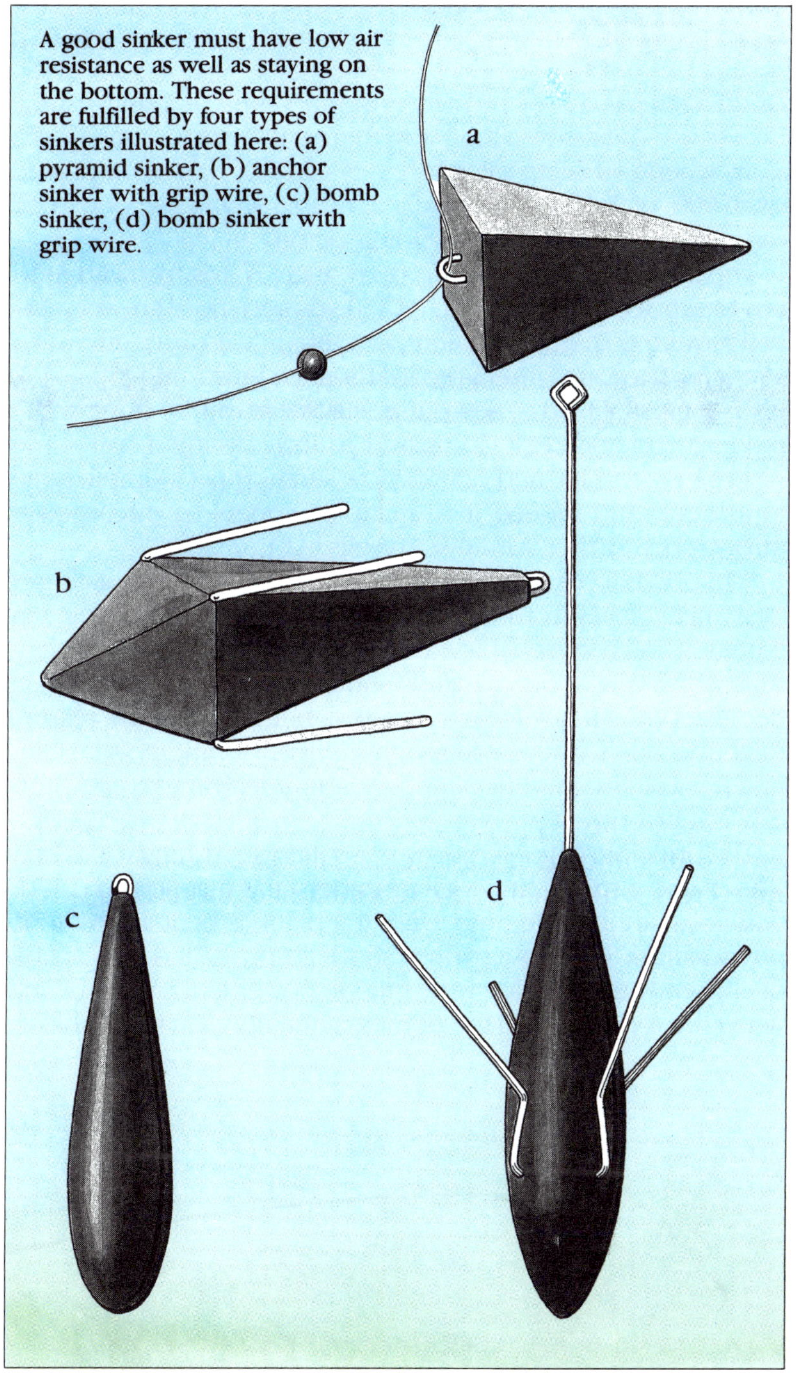

A good sinker must have low air resistance as well as staying on the bottom. These requirements are fulfilled by four types of sinkers illustrated here: (a) pyramid sinker, (b) anchor sinker with grip wire, (c) bomb sinker, (d) bomb sinker with grip wire.

oz. Because of this, 5.25 oz (150 g) has become the single most popular weight for long-range fishing and has been adopted by many tournament casting associations as the standard competition sinker. Anybody wishing to learn how to cast long distances would be well advised to practise with 150 g to the exclusion of all other weights.

Lures and float tackle are weighted with drilled bullets or small bombs. Sometimes it is more economical to use substitutes such as pieces of scrap metal or spark plugs when casting onto very rough ground. Because long casting is seldom a factor here, there would be no advantage in a streamlined bomb anyway. The only other sinkers that may be necessary for coastal fishing are wired bombs in the 6–8 oz category for exceptionally rough water and strong winds.

The hook shown at left is a Mustad Seamaster, one example of a strong thick-wire hook. At right is a thin-wire Aberdeen hook for discreet presentation of small bait.

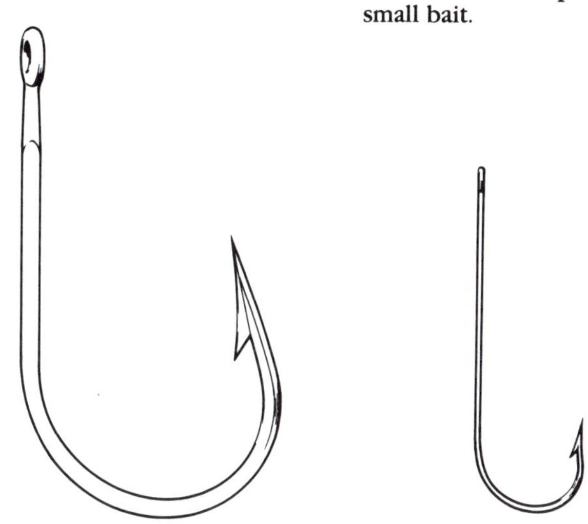

Hooks

It is impossible to say exactly which hooks should be used for coastal fishing. The type that suits, say, bluefish in American waters would be inappropriate for a similar-sized fish like the cod of North-West Europe. However, hooks can be neatly divided into two broad categories: fine wire types where the emphasis is towards superb presentation of delicate baits; and a heavy-duty construction in which sheer strength outweighs nearly every other consideration. The former is typified by the Aberdeen hook with its long shank, round bend and rather fragile-looking wire. Of the latter, the Mustad Seamaster is the classic example. Sizes are dictated not so much by the weight of the fish as by the size of bait. Provided it is of the correct type, a small hook often outperforms a big one. For one thing, owing to the long casting distances involved, a small hook is so much easier to sink beyond the barb.

Traces

An enormous number of trace designs exists, most falling into either the paternoster or the running leger groups. On the paternoster, between one and three hooks on short fixed snoods are attached like the branches of a tree to the shock leader. The sinker is clipped to the bottom. Running legers carry a single hook on a fairly long piece of nylon or wire attached to the leader. The sinker is free to slide up and down the line by means of a link swivel or clip-on boom device. The idea is to present a biting fish with the minimum of resistance and thus to encourage shy species to feed more positively. Whether it achieves that any better than a paternoster is open to debate among experienced anglers. Many would argue that the length of the trace is a far more important factor.

Bait clips

Bait clips are a vital accessory for long-range fishing. The clip is fixed to the leader and linked to the hook bend prior to casting. Thus, bait and hook lie close alongside the leader during the tackle's flight. Distances are improved because air drag is reduced; baits themselves are shielded from damage. As soon as the tackle hits the water's surface, the clip and hook are disconnected, and the trace streams out in the currents in the normal manner. Without doubt, this simple piece of bent wire is one of beach fishing's major innovations.

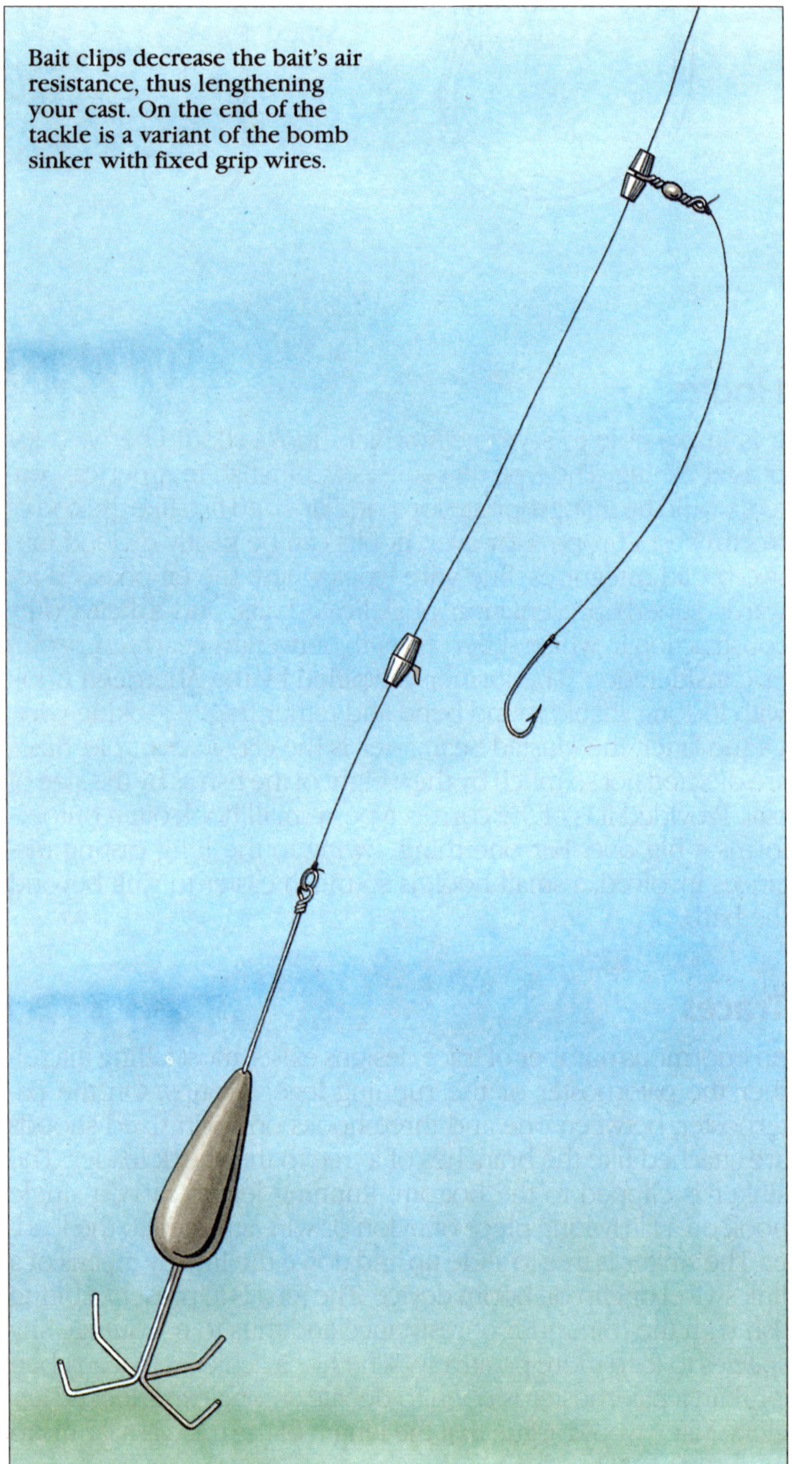

Bait clips decrease the bait's air resistance, thus lengthening your cast. On the end of the tackle is a variant of the bomb sinker with fixed grip wires.

Casting

Good casting is one of the most important skills of coastal fishing. Unless you can throw a long way, there will be many, many occasions when you fail to catch fish. It is said that 10% of the anglers catch 90% of the fish—and so far as coastal angling is concerned, casting ability is often the deciding factor.

The average angler casts no more than 75 yds. Yet with modern beachcasting tackle, casts of 150 yds and more are very easy and require no particular talent, and certainly no huge amount of strength. The tournament record distance for casting 150-g sinkers is almost 300 yds—so you see just what can be done with a modern rod and reel! Compared to that, casting a bait somewhere between 100 and 125 yds now seems quite a simple target to achieve. And indeed it is: many beginners have learned to throw much farther within six weeks.

Why 100-125 yds as a target distance? Catch statistics gathered over many years from around the world strongly suggest that there is a link between that particular zone of the seabed and the most consistent sport. Why this should be so is open to debate because of the many factors involved; but whatever the reasons might be, that's where you are more likely to find good fishing under most circumstances, and therefore learning to cast properly is a priority.

The principle of good casting is as follows. A fishing rod is both a lever and a spring. It is vital to understand that no rod can do both jobs at the same time. Until the blank is bent almost to its physical limit, it acts as a springy shock absorber and is incapable of efficiently transferring your muscle power to the sinker. Only when the rod is bent to the point that the fibres in the blank are

"locked" under full tension does it become an effective lever. Only then will the rod transfer maximum power to the sinker and produce the desired acceleration. All good casting techniques—including South African and pendulum casts—are founded on the same principles: first to "lock" the rod blank fibres and then to inject full muscle power, which is immediately and fully transmitted to the sinker and terminal tackle. The importance of this two-stage system cannot be overemphasised, because it is the one and only way to produce long-distance casts.

Practise your casting on a field or on a beach at low tide. Avoid combining casting practice with fishing, because to begin with it is essential to concentrate on developing the right technique. Trying to catch fish at the same time is too distracting.

Set up your rod and reel, tie on a shock leader of 40–50 lbs nylon, and attach the sinker. There is no need to use a trace. The shock leader should be long enough to ensure that at least six full turns remain on the reel spool when the "drop" (the length of line between rod tip and sinker) is correct. A drop of about 4–6 ft is a good basis to begin with, but do be prepared to lengthen it if your casts fly consistently low and left.

Stand with your feet comfortably spaced and angled. Prepare the reel for casting and check that the leader is not wrapped around the tip ring. Reach back (away from the casting direction, that is) and throw the sinker onto the ground at its full extent from the rod tip. The tip itself should lie no more than 6 inches from the ground. Be sure that your left elbow is at shoulder level or slightly above, while the right arm is comfortably extended away from your body. Now, look up into the sky in the direction in which you intend the sinker to fly.

Concentrate very hard on the imaginary target in the sky, and pull the rod with your right hand in exactly the same manner as you would throw a javelin or a stone. The rod itself must move forward on its long axis, as if it were a spear—that is, moving in a straight line, not around in an arc. Your left hand will automatically and naturally extend away from your body and drift slightly upwards. As the right hand pulls the rod forward, begin to transfer your body weight from the right leg to the left.

The result of this action is, firstly, to tense the fibres of the rod blank so that they begin to lock. In other words, the rod begins to bend against the inertia of the sinker. And secondly, to bring the weight of your body into action so that it assists in the rod-bending process.

When this is complete, you will naturally arrive at a position with your right arm bent as if ready to throw a punch, and the left

Basic casting technique

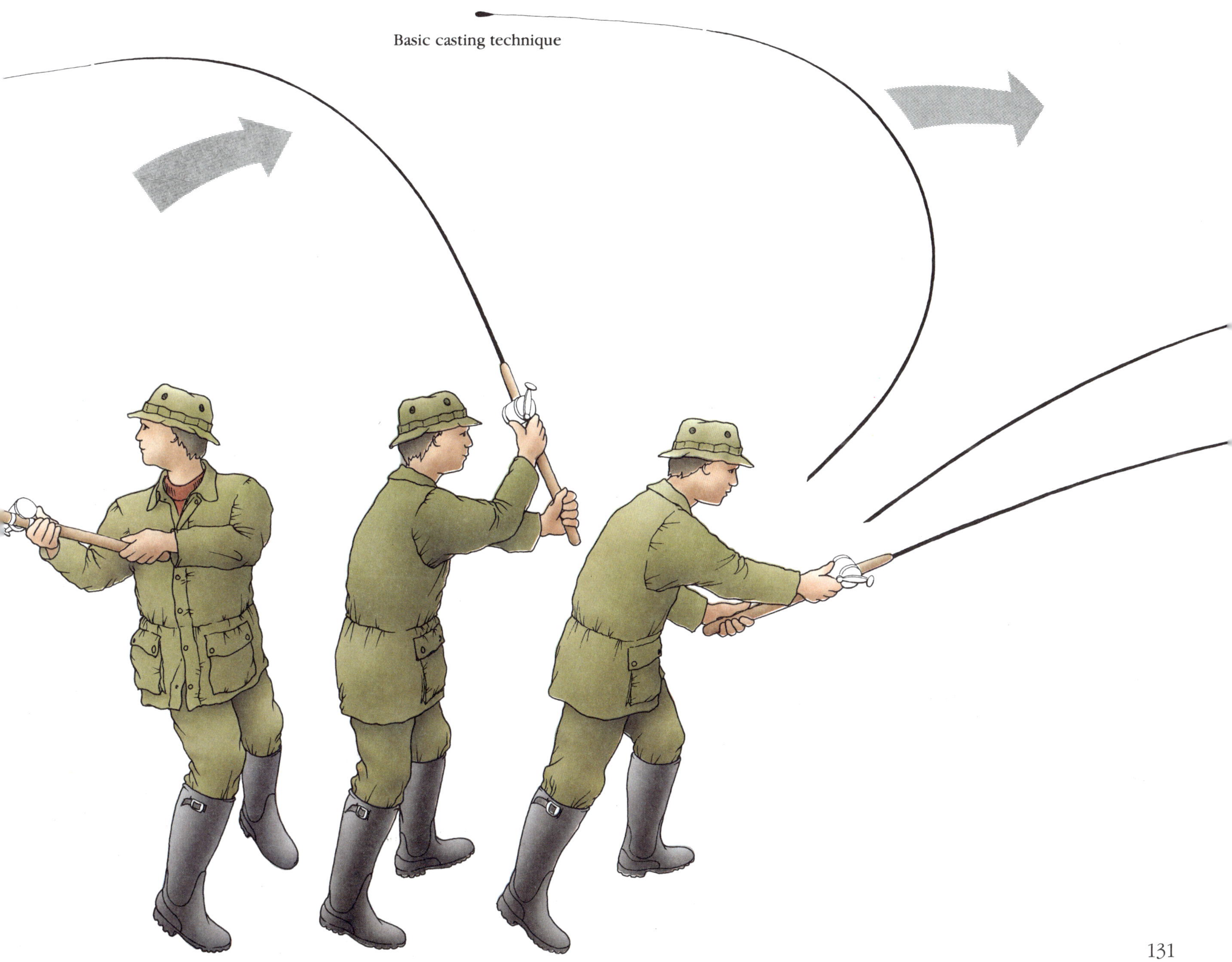

extended and therefore able to pull down towards the bottom left-hand corner of your rib-cage. Even though the movement which occurred earlier seems short and without power, it has still generated enough tension to transform the rod into a reasonably efficient lever. So, conditions are now satisfactory for you to begin accelerating the sinker towards maximum speed. This is achieved very simply: pull down strongly with the left hand while at exactly the same time your right hand punches upwards and forwards. Of course, this second phase of the cast is a smooth, unbroken continuation of the previous step. Do not slow down or hesitate between the two.

Obviously the punch/pull action will flip the rod over as in any traditional casting style. But because the blank was pre-tensed, your muscle power is employed much more effectively, and as a consequence the sinker flies higher, faster and therefore much farther. When should you release the line? Don't think about it . . .it is a natural reaction that requires no conscious thought so far as most anglers are concerned. In fact, consciously trying to time and control it are the best ways to ruin the procedure. Let line run out until the sinker hits the ground; then, in the case of a multiplier, be sure to brake the spool to a halt before the reel has a chance to backlash.

The South African cast

Despite huge improvements in rods and reels, the style of casting developed in South Africa at least 30 years ago is still capable of holding its own with modern techniques such as the Pendulum. The South African cast is nothing more than an extended version of the sequence of exercises learned so far. Its power is derived

South African cast

from a virtually identical preload and punch/pull action; in fact, the only mechanical difference is that the South African caster swings his rod through a much greater arc, and in doing so extracts maximum speed and power from his leg, back and shoulder muscles.

The illustration highlights the expanded power stroke: this is achieved by gradually building onto the layout position used in the previous exercises. The aim is to use as much body power and acceleration arc as possible, because in this manner both the rod and the caster's body are made to work at peak efficiency. However, never extend the action to the point where you feel uncomfortable and unbalanced. An arc of 270 degrees is large enough to generate casts well in excess of 200 yards. Notice that as the rod arc is increases, a longer "drop" is employed. The angle between rod tip and leader is also adjusted, in order to maintain smooth lift-off for the sinker and to build up a fairly high preload pressure quite early in the cast.

An ordinary beachcaster rod responds fairly well to the style, but lacks sufficient tip length to extract maximum distance when the layout arc approaches 270 degrees. True South African style rods tend to be at least 13 ft long (13.5 ft is a recommended average for casting and fishing) with a fairly fast tip, stiff butt and medium-fast central zone to the blank. The reel is attached about 9 in from the butt cap and controlled with the caster's left hand. Using a reel in this position is quite awkward at first, but certainly repays the effort in longer casts, less pressure on the reel, and greatly improved control and power build-up. Multiplier reels are a popular choice; the style is probably the best of them all for casting a fixed spool reel.

The Pendulum cast

Modern in concept, exciting to watch, and currently the style of casting that holds virtually every tournament record, the Pendulum is actually no more complicated or difficult to learn than the South African cast. Like the South African, it shares the same principles that we used in the basic casting exercises: in its regular fishing format, the Pendulum is nothing more than a modification made to the layout. Instead of being laid out on the ground, the sinker is swung pendulum-fashion to a starting position in mid-air. The relative angle of the sinker, rod, leader and the caster's body combine at that position to generate higher inertia (which preloads the blank better) and also extends the arc of movement (which contributes extra power and acceleration), so that when the time arrives for the final punch/pull of the arms and shoulders, the rod is able to transfer almost 100% of the available energy to the sinker. Distance and control are greatly enhanced.

Setting up the pendulum swing

The Pendulum cast should not be attempted until you have mastered the basic exercises. Unless the preload and punch/pull phases are so well practised that you can cast a sinker consistently beyond the 120-yd mark, there is nothing to be gained by switching to the pendulum swing.

Pendulum cast

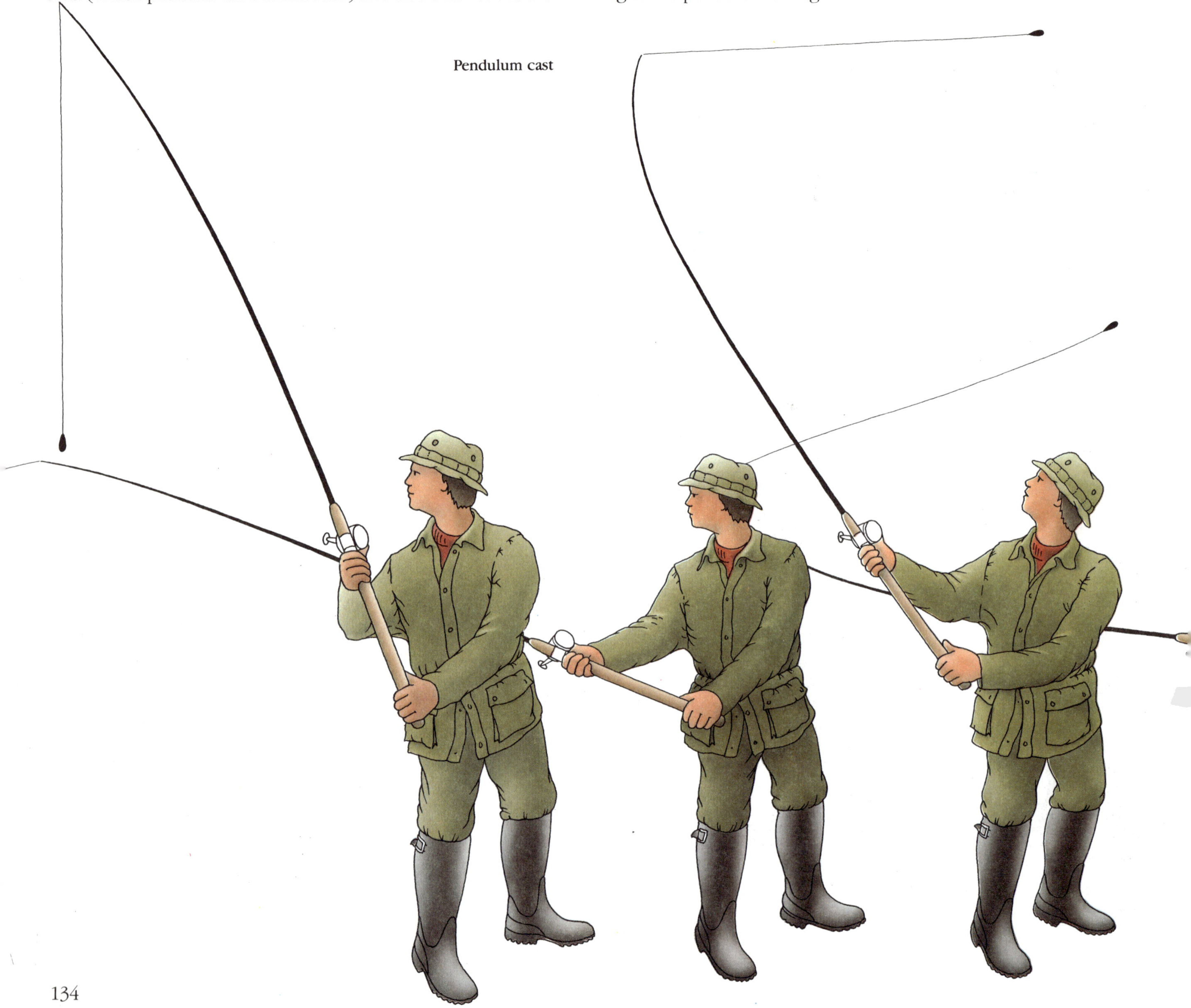

Feet position and general stance are the same for Pendulum casting as for the basic exercises. To make the new cast, first adjust the drop to about 6 ft: this gives a steady, fairly slow pendulum swing that is easy to time and control. Begin the action by pushing outwards with your right hand. The sinker will swing away from you, rising to approximately eye level. Now without moving your right hand, *push downwards on the rod handle with the left hand*. The push is transmitted to the rod tip and then to the leader, with the result that the sinker swings through a reverse pendulum arc that brings it past the rod, past your right shoulder and out of sight somewhere beyond your right shoulder. As it rises to the maximum height, the leader loses some of its tension. The sensation that you get is of the sinker having suddenly "disappeared".

Actually, it is hovering almost stationary in mid-air . . . and that is the signal for the next stage of the cast to begin. It is a very simple process: all you do is turn your head and look into the air towards the imaginary target used in the previous exercises. The right hand pulls the rod forward, spear-throwing fashion; then the hands and arms finish the cast with the normal punch/pull action.

Yes, the preload and power stroke are exactly the same as those you have already mastered in the preliminary exercises—that is why it is so important not to introduce the pendulum swing until the main casting action is so familiar that it becomes automatic. So if things go wrong, remind yourself that the main difference between the two styles of casting is merely the starting position of the lead. Power flow, timing and release are identical.

Fixed spool and multiplier reels are equally well suited to Pendulum casting, but for maximum response with the former reel you should choose a rod with a slightly stiff tip and plenty of flexibility in the central zone. The reverse is the case for a multiplier: flexible tip and fairly rapid mid-zone generate peak performance.

The best Pendulum casters use either a 12-ft rod with the reel set approximately 28 in from the butt cap, or a 13–13.5 ft rod with the reel attached in the low, South African position. The big mistake is to use a long rod and a high-set reel. It is a sure formula for poor distances, backlashed line and a thumb burned by the reel spool as it slips midway through the cast's power phase.

Coastal fishing techniques

Considering the world's enormous variety of coastlines, water conditions and species of fish, you might well think that thousands of different techniques would be necessary to cope with them all. For example, surfcasting for channel bass along the eastern seaboard of the USA seems to bear no relationship to cod fishing from the shores of Europe. In reality, both the techniques and the species of fish have much in common. Tackle and tactics are broadly identical; the fish feed in much the same manner, and respond to similar water conditions and weather. Similar parallels exist with all kinds of fish and virtually all locations. In short, variations on the coastal fishing theme are far fewer than one might at first imagine.

These similarities are neither coincidental nor unique to coastal waters. They reflect nothing more than the selection process that is at the foundation of the natural world. In essence, the network is founded on the interrelationship of plants, plant-eating animals and predators (known as a food chain), and on the fascinating way in which nature always fills every environmental vacuum.

Channel bass migrate towards the coast to feed on mullet which in turn feed on planktonic life forms that thrive in shallow salt water. Cod move inshore to hunt whiting, shrimps and crabs, all of which feed on microscopic plant and animal material. Thus, the natural roles of bass and cod are basically the same. And because they can find more food when waves and winds stir the inshore waters, the best fishing times tend to be during rough weather with a powerful surf running. Furthermore, the rod, reel and terminal rig developed for cod fishing is ideal for channel bass as well.

The message to the coastal angler becomes clear: by approaching the sport from the natural history angle, fishing is so much simpler and more predictable. It even pays to develop a plan of attack based on the kind of coastline rather than the species of fish. You can afford to do this because the tactics evolved for rock fishing in, say, Ireland work equally well in the West Indies. Baits will be different, as will the species of fish that grab them; but fishing tactics are almost exactly the same. A similar story applies to surf beaches, steeply shelving beaches of stones and shingle, estuaries and harbours.

Surf beaches

Surf beaches are typically broad expanses of sand washed by shallow seas and exposed to prevailing winds. In many parts of the world, the rise and fall of tide may result in anything up to half a mile between high and low water marks. Food creatures like sand eels and crabs either move in and out with the tide, or bury themselves under wet sand during the low water phase.

Flatfish such as flounders and dabs are happy in just a few inches of water and are therefore ideally adapted to live on surf beaches. Swimming just behind the water's edge, they move in and out twice daily with the tides and are not particularly sensitive to wave action or light intensity. Extremely bright sunlight and mirror-calm water may deter them, as will raging storms that they are physically incapable of handling, but in general such resident species are predictable in habit and quite easily caught.

These small fish fall prey to a wide spectrum of predators ranging from middleweights like the European bass to bluefish, channel bass, tope and sharks. Requiring fairly deep water to operate, and for all their weight and power being rather cautious unless driven into a feeding frenzy, these species do not come within casting range as regularly and as predictably as their prey. The habits of the European bass are not only classical but also mirror what happens with most other species regardless of where in the world's oceans they reside.

Bass are extremely wary of calm, clear water and daylight. In the absence of wind to stir the sea's surface or a swell to create underwater currents, they linger well beyond casting range and are not inclined to feed anyway. To fish a surf beach on a calm

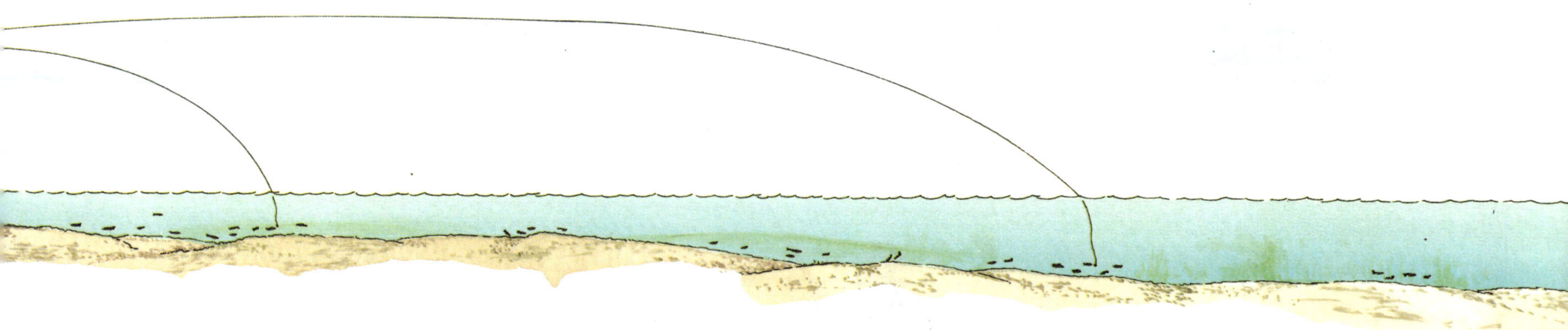

summer's day is usually to guarantee total failure.

At night, the same beach may be alive with fish even if the water is quite still and clear. Fish are less cautious and probably will move into casting range, but they still won't come really close to the water's edge. The value of being able to throw a bait well beyond 120 yds pays dividends under such conditions; sometimes it is the only way to get a bite.

The best fishing occurs when wind, swells and low light combine to produce a brisk wave pattern, plenty of underwater currents and reduced clarity. Now the bigger predators will venture into easy casting range in their hunt for small fish and other marine animals washed from the sand and generally disorientated by the swirling water. A 75-yd cast is long enough to drop your bait into the feeding zone; occasionally fish will move so close that they drive their prey literally onto the dry sand. If you wade only a few yards, fish may bump into your legs.

Long casts are frequently essential to good catches when you are fishing in calm, fair weather. Of course, if the light is weak and the water is turbid, predatory fish will venture closer to land in search of small fish, crabs, and other prey that leave their hiding-places. Casting lengths of around 70 metres can then be enough to reach the fish. But the only species which come very near land even in good weather are various flatfish that hunt, for example, lugworms and other saltwater worms. Further species approach shallow water at best under cover of dark and in hard wind, when the waves wash up food from the bottom. These may be reached with a cast of 30–50 metres. One should naturally also take account of local variations due to the tides, which in some places make a kilometre-sized difference between high and low water marks. A flatfish often caught in this coastal environment is the plaice, shown in the illustration inset.

Steeply shelving beaches

Steeply shelving beaches represent the midway step between the flatness of a surf beach and the sometimes vertical drop from rocks and cliffs into deep water. Fishing tactics and species also reflect that halfway stage to some extent. As a consequence, these areas of the coastline offer some of the best sport available and are extremely popular with anglers.

The steeper the angle of the beach, the closer together high and low water marks become. Sometimes less than 25 yds of foreshore are exposed on the lowest of spring ebb tides. The result, of course, is that fairly deep water is always available even if you cannot cast extremely long distances. And from the fishes' point of view, there is a definite increase in confidence prompted by having plenty of water to hunt and hide in. Put the two sides of the equation together, and you can see that steep beaches usually fish consistently well throughout most of the tidal cycle, and are less likely to be badly affected by calm seas and bright conditions.

In addition to flatfish and other small resident species, steep beaches are the natural zone for residents like rays and dogfish, and also attract migratory fish such as cod and bass. Indeed, almost every species is drawn towards them according to season. The fish population therefore lends itself equally well to mixed fishing as to specialist work for one species in particular.

The classic fish of the North Atlantic and North Sea beaches is the cod, *Gadus morhua*. For a vast army of anglers in Britain and Europe, it is the only species of coastal fish worth hunting. For most, the best sport comes during autumn and winter when migratory shoals move down from the far north; but in those more northerly regions of Scotland and Scandinavia, cod are present all year around. Several subspecies of cod are also involved, but they all fit into the same category as far as angling is concerned.

Sloping shores commonly offer the best fishing, since they have both good hiding-places for fish and free water to swim in. Moreover, this type of coast is relatively uninfluenced by tides, winds, and weather. Several distinct species may be encountered, ranging from bottom-dwellers such as cod and flatfish to mackerel and other pelagic swimmers. As the fish can come nearer to land here, long casts are not as necessary as, for instance, on long shallow shores. It can be an advantage to fish with two or three rods simultaneously, with baits at different distances from land.

Rock fishing

When a coastal fisherman refers to rock fishing, he usually means casting from a cliff into very deep water that runs right up to the rock face beneath his feet. The seabed might be of perfectly clean sand, although it is more likely to be a mixture of boulders, reefs, weeds and clean patches of sand or grit.

The huge advantage of rock fishing is that the underwater environment within casting range is virtually unaffected by tidal rise and fall. Even at low tide there may be 50 ft of water remaining, which makes fishing much easier even if you cannot cast very well, and also expands the options of technique. Legering is an excellent all-round method, but you can equally well use a float rig—impossible on a surf beach due to the water's shallowness. Spinning is probably at its most effective from the rocks, although of course it can be employed from virtually any beach when necessary. In addition to the direct angling benefits, the rock fisherman can also be confident that the underwater world is far more stable here than on any other type of coastline. Fish feel safe, and tend to feed longer and less cautiously.

Cliff fishing in deep water near land does not demand as much casting ability. The chances of a good catch here are high, since the fish are not particularly shy and they often hunt for long periods. The variation in species is usually wide, and fishing with several methods at the same time can be effective. In the free water layers, pelagic species such as mackerel, bass and garfish can be caught on artificial lures. Bottom-angling can take rays and sharks some hundreds of metres out, and closer to land it may yield cod or flatfish—as well as species that hide among big stones and in cliff crevices, such as ling, wolffish and conger eel. A few metres out from the cliff edge, float-fishing may turn up grey mullet.

Harbours and estuaries

Harbours and estuaries are interesting because you can often find a wide variety of fishing places within a short distance of each other. On a harbour breakwater wall, for example, there could be deep water on one side populated by a dozen species, and on the other a wide expanse of shallow mudflats or sand that attract fish only during the high-water period. The fast currents of an estuary mouth where bass and mackerel hunt small baitfish give way to lagoons and backwaters farther inland. There you will find shoals of mullet and flatfish that tolerate low salinity.

Of the many different kinds of coastal waters, harbours and estuaries are the most influenced by mankind. Jetties, pilings and dredged channels are common features of any industrialised area. Man's modification of the natural environment is not necessarily bad for fish or wildlife in general. Pollution aside, much of what we do to the coastline proves attractive to many kinds of fish. Some are weaned from their normal diets onto fish guts, waste products from food-processing factories, and all manner of free offerings. These factors play an important role in successful angling.

The habits of the conger eel are a fine example. In the wild, the conger is a shy, ultra-cautious fish that feeds almost exclusively on fresh meat—fish, squid and crabs included. The chances of luring one on anything less than absolutely fresh bait are small. But in harbours where congers have taken up permanent residence, their feeding habits switch towards scavenging. Discarded fish and guts thrown over the side of trawlers are so much more convenient than hunting live fish . . .so before long the eels give up the chase altogether. They also become accustomed to noise and the presence of man, thus losing a great deal of their natural cunning. There are probably more big eels landed from harbour walls than from wild rocky coasts, and the reason is easy to see.

Harbour installations and estuary mouths allow, within a rather small area, considerable diversity in species and methods. Palisades and log jams, for example, are full of hiding-places for shy eels. Flatfish are readily caught in the shallow water from the landward side of a wavebreaker. On the outer side, with currents in deeper water, frequent hunters are mackerel, pollock, and sometimes even cod. It is a fact that very big fish can be caught from wavebreakers, such as the shark shown at top in the illustration. Species like sea bass, cod and mackerel hunt in estuaries, while others unable to take strong current stay in the backwaters.

Baits for coastal fishing

The difference in catch rate between good and bad baits is huge. Even so, the majority of anglers pay nowhere near enough attention to their choice of bait or to its quality. Regardless of whether you use fish, worms, crabs or any other popular bait type, its freshness must never be compromised.

The most successful coastal anglers go to enormous trouble in digging or catching their baits; in fact, many devote more time to collection than to actually fishing. Once gathered, those baits are looked after with loving care. Worms are kept in aerated tanks of sea water; fish baits are frozen; crabs live in controlled conditions of humidity and temperature. This may seem unnecessarily fussy and complicated, but the results speak for themselves. Compared to ordinary baits bought from tackle shops of fishmongers, the experts' bait is at least twice as effective.

The basic problem with a sea bait is that, no matter how many worms go on the hook or how large the chunk of fishbait, it is still tiny compared to the vastness of the ocean. At best, the amount of attractive juice exuded by a bait is diluted millions to one in sea water. Most fish are exceedingly sensitive to such stimulants, but there is obviously a threshold below which they cannot detect what is on your hook. In the past, the only remedy lay with the bait itself. But today, science provides an excellent aid in the form of Biotrak. This natural blend of stimulants and attractors produces an exceptionally powerful biochemical "magnet" that draws fish from long range and stimulates them to feed. Anglers all over the world have already described Biotrak as the biggest step forward in angling bait technology during this century. My personal success rate has increased by 20% at least.

Fish baits

By far the most versatile of baits, fish are universally popular with coastal anglers. In many countries, they are just about the only baits considered worth using. They are presented in three ways: as whole fish, in large fillets, and as thin strips and cutlets. Choosing between them is a matter of logic—the bigger the fish you expect to catch, the larger the bait should be.

Most of the fish used as baits are freshly killed. Livebaiting is a relatively uncommon technique, due mainly to the difficulty in casting a live fish long distances, and sometimes of obtaining it in the first place. Sand eels probably account for 99% of the livebaits used in Britain and Europe; whether the live bait really is superior to a freshly killed one is open to argument. The main point to consider is that, live or dead, fresh meat is invariably superior to stale meat.

Key features of fish baits are strong scent and taste, plus a high oil and blood content. Mullet, mackerel, herrings, menhaden and similar species of renowned baits all have those qualities in common, and are therefore the preferred baits in almost every situation. Choose one from the list, or its local equivalent, and you will not go wrong.

Worms

Worms are an essential part of many a small fish's normal diet and therefore one of the most effective baits. Larger fish such as bass and cod probably regard worms as a tasty snack. However, in just the same way that we sometimes prefer a piece of candy to a full meal, they often grab a hookful of worms when they might otherwise not bother to attack a big fish bait. For cod particularly, a bunch of lugworms is the standard bait for autumn and winter

Both live and dead bait must be of good quality to attract these fish. A careful coastal fisherman gathers his bait personally to make sure that it is fresh. Small fish and various worms are popular bait for a large number of species.

Fish can be presented either whole or in pieces. The ling shown at right has bitten on a large fish filet.

shore casting. Similarly, ragworms are a deadly bait for bass.

Another advantage of worms is that, because they do appeal to a wide cross-section of the fish population, they are an excellent bait when you are fishing for whatever happens to turn up, rather than for one species in particular. Ragworms on the hook might give a mixed catch of flatfish, bass, eels, and dogfish, whereas a strip of mackerel would produce dogfish alone.

Crabs

The majority of bottom-feeding fish never miss an opportunity to eat crabs. The common green shorecrab of Europe, the ghost crab of subtropical seas, spider crabs, hermit crabs and many others are all superb baits for a wide range of species big and small. The intriguing point about crab baits is that, although nearly all fish eat hardbacked crabs as part of the normal diet, they are reluctant to take them from the hook. Some species ignore them altogether.

What you want are moulting crabs: either "softbacks" which lack an armoured shell, or "peelers" which are the pre-moulting stage when the old shell is beginning to loosen. It is generally agreed that peelers are slightly superior, probably because they exude stronger scents associated with the breeding cycle.

Peeled and soft crabs may be used whole or cut into chunks, depending on the kind of fish you are after. Even the legs can be peeled and threaded on to the hook point for extra attraction and to make the bait last longer. Most crabs are used in their freshly killed state, but they can also be frozen for use during the colder months when the moulting process does not take place.

Different types of worms are the standard bait for many people who fish over sandy bottoms. The inset picture shows the piles of excrement left on the bottom by certain worms, which can be found by digging under them.

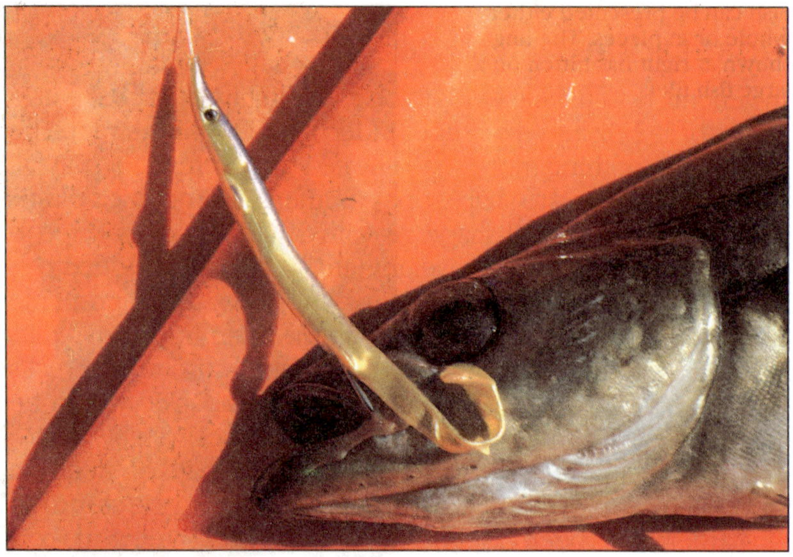

Left: Squid are often taken by large fish. As illustrated here, they can be cut in strips before going on the hook.

Right: For school-hunting fish in the middle water layers, the best attractor may be artificial bait. Red Gill, shown in the picture, is one of the most effective, being strongly reminiscent of sand-eels.

Squid

Squid is an interesting bait because, while generally less productive than fish, worms or crabs, it seems to select the bigger specimens. Bass fishing is the classic example. Sometimes by casting worm baits you'll enjoy bite after bite as small fish rush to attack, Throw out a big chunk of squid, and you may sit all day long without a bite. In fact, some specialist anglers are prepared to wait for days or even weeks on end, knowing that when they do get a bass it will be a big one. A similar pattern is evident with cod and the larger species of North Atlantic rays such as thornbacks and blondes. Unless you are fortunate enough to catch your own, choose fresh-frozen blocks of Kalamari or Californian squid available from fishmongers.

Artificial baits

On the worldwide scale, plug baits and the vast array of metal lures falling into the American category of "tin" account for a significant percentage of the *total fish* catch, but it would be wrong to consider them as rivalling natural baits so far as all-round coastal fishing is concerned. Probably 75% of the different *species* caught along the world's coastlines fall to legered natural baits.

The strength—and weakness—of artificial baits is that their greatest appeal is to shoaling predators like the European mackerel and its warmer-water equivalents such as the bluefish. While very different in size and ferocity, these two species fill a broadly similar ecological slot—that of an inshore predator which often herds shoals of baitfish into the shallows in a wild feeding spree. Throw a lure into the mass of hungry fish, and you simply cannot go wrong. However, the sheer numbers of such fish landed by serious anglers and holiday-makers should not be allowed to distort the true statistics of coastal fishing. Bass, cod, flatfish and many other species are relatively poor attackers of lures, and some show no response at all.

The choice of a lure for the shoaling predators is seldom critical. Anything bright enough to catch the fish's eye and heavy enough to be cast the required distance works adequately well. The Hopkins lure and other classics like the German Sprat are equally deadly for the more discerning European bass and cod, and the American striped bass. Plugs work well provided that they can be cast far enough and are able to sink to the required depth.

Of more modern lures, the Redgill sand eel stands supreme, being a renowned fish-catcher throughout the world for species large and small. Mepps and other vibratory/spinning blade lures are deadly as well, but lack the universal appeal of the sand eel. And finally, if you don't have any artificial baits but still want to spin-fish, try working a weighted strip of fresh mackerel or a freshly killed sand eel through the water. These natural offerings sometimes outfish plastic and metal, due no doubt to their blood and oil content.

Basic fishing rigs

Legers

It's worth remembering that very few species of fish cannot be caught on a natural bait presented on the seabed. The leger is therefore not only the most versatile and basic of rigs, but also the most successful of them all. Being compatible with long-distance casting techniques, it allows baits to be fished anywhere from beneath the rod tip to well beyond the 175-yd zone.

The paternoster and running leger illustrated are chosen to be effective as they stand, and also representative of the general design theme. Number of hooks on the paternoster, snood length and spacing, the provision of bait-restraining clips, and choice of boom are open to experiment. Similarly, with the running rig, you can vary trace length and breaking strain, hook size and type, and even the trace material. Nylon traces suit the majority of species, but tope, conger eels, sharks and other toothy predators demand cable-laid wire between hook and leader.

Float tackle

In general, float fishing tends to be in the lightweight class with a sinker of 1–2 oz and main line under 12-lb breaking strain. The float can be nothing more sophisticated than a chunk of polystyrene foam trimmed to shape, or a commercially moulded plastic cork float of traditional shape. As with the leger, you are free to adjust trace length, sinker weight, etc. to suit. Fishing depth is controlled by a stop knot fixed to the line at the appropriate point, and the float is free to slide up the main line to meet it.

Heavier versions of float tackle are extremely useful over rocks and weeds, where to cast conventional leger tackle would be highly expensive in lost equipment. With sinker weights over 4 oz, the best float is a partially inflated child's balloon tied to a swivel with a scrap of nylon. The swivel runs up to the stop knot when the rig has been cast, so that the bait is presented at the correct level, which in this case should be just above the bottom. The trick is not to over-inflate the balloon: a diameter of about 4 in provides adequate buoyancy, yet is still easy to cast quite far.

Artificial lures

Under most circumstances, the lure is attached directly to the reel line or by way of a short wire trace that wards off sharp teeth. The weight of the lure is enough to provide long casts and rapid sinking. Ideally, you should not add a lead sinker because if you do, almost inevitably some of the lure's action will be lost. But if you do need extra casting weight—and you always will with very light baits of the Redgill type—fix a bullet or barrel-shaped lead at least 2 ft away from the lure. Better still, space them 3 ft apart. The problem there is that lure and sinker tend to "helicopter" around each other during the cast, reducing distance and promoting line tangles.

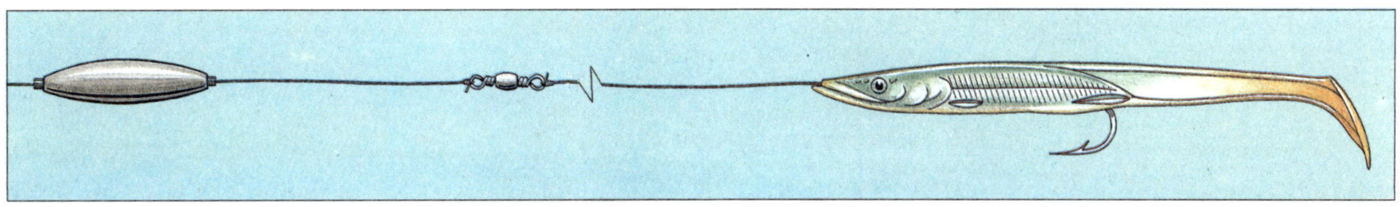

Above: Tackle for artificial bait, such as Red Gill, must be lead-weighted to get a sufficiently long cast. The lead sinker is placed 60–100 cm in front of the bait.

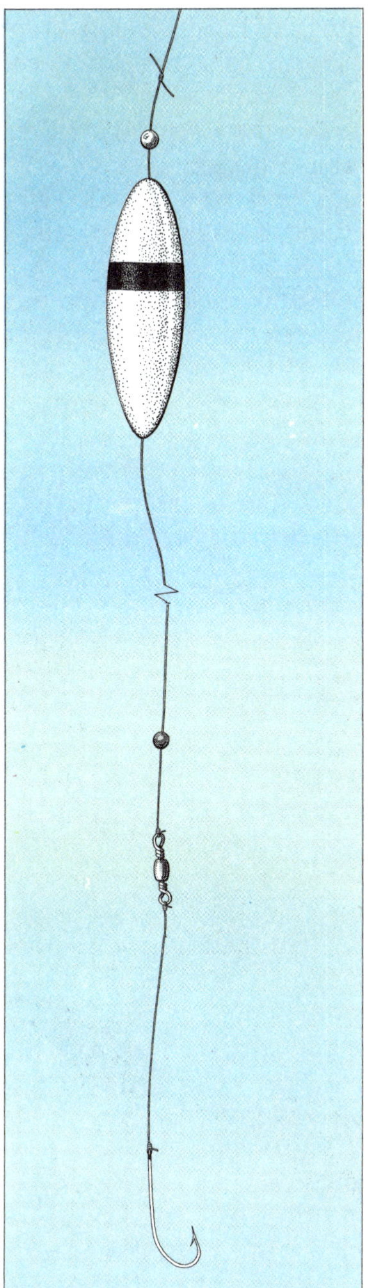

Left: Float-fishing is very useful when fishing over "difficult" bottoms where other types of tackle would always get caught on the bottom. Lead-weighting, snood length, and depth should be adjusted to the given conditions.

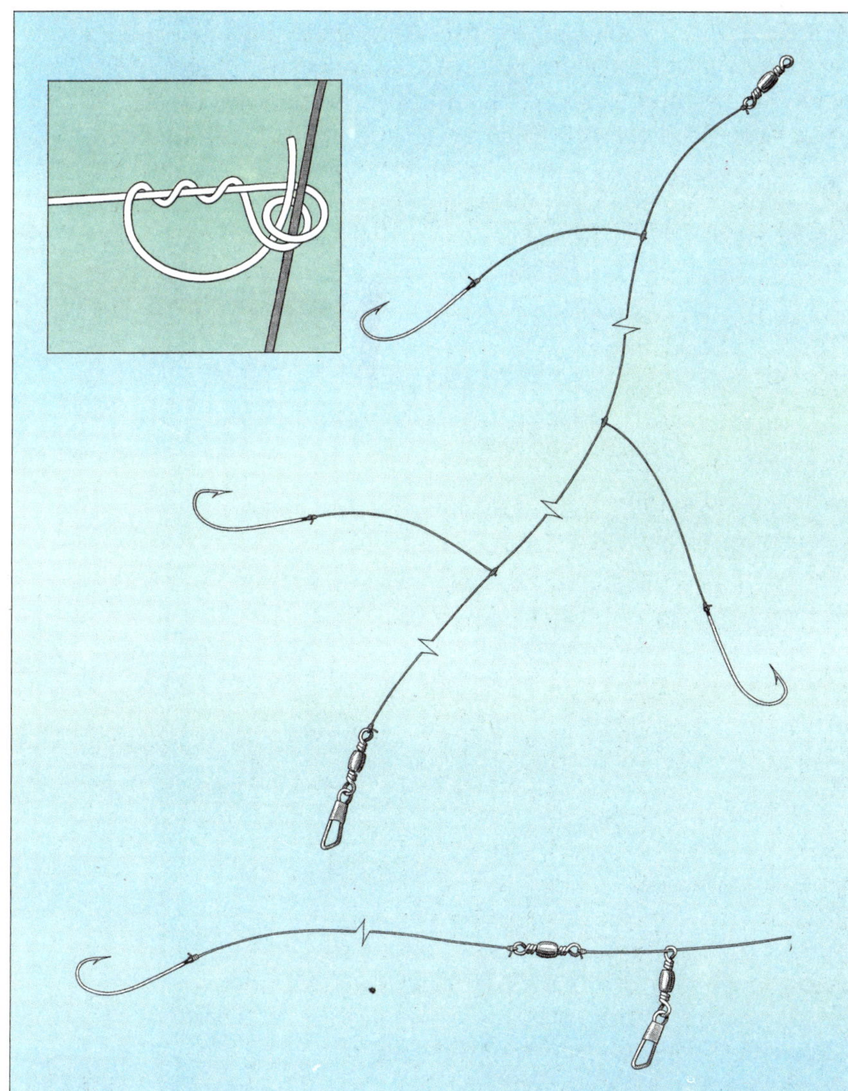

Right: A paternoster tackle normally consists of two to four simple hooks, apart from the sinker. The snood lengths and hook spacing can be varied according to the bottom conditions and the species being fished. Each snood is attached to the main line with a durable knot. On the other hand, sliding tackle consists of only a hook: as the name indicates, the line must be able to slide out freely when you get a bite, so that the fish does not panic. This tackle is most common when fishing for shy species like eel. On both types of tackle, the sinker is fixed in the swivel.

Sea angling

There is nothing like being at sea with your fishing tackle. It is like hooking the world and you never know for sure what you will get at the other end of the line or how big the fish may be. I wonder whether it is the chance for big or many fish which attracts anglers. Or is it the environment—the sunny days in the heat, the refreshing air, the good fellowship with like-minded anglers, or simply getting away from it all?

Sea angling ranges from the cold Arctic days with ice in the rod guides, cod and coalfish below the keel, and warm clothing to the pleasant bright sunny days near the coast with mackerel, flatfish or other species. Sea angling is the ultimate fight with huge fish, and big-game fishing for tuna, shark and marlin. It is also reef, bank, or ground fishing where anything from ling to conger and other unknown fish might attack—or in distant latitudes of the Caribbean where a tarpon empties the reel in explosions of shallow water. Sea angling is a passion like other types of angling. But whoever has not yet been out there and wants to experience the salt, gulls, and fish must be well equipped. All species of fish and areas are characterized by their own methods and conditions, but the fundamental methods and techniques apply wherever you fish in the world, and the fishing tackle is practically the same.

Equipment

The sea rod

In principle, sea fishing tackle can be divided into three categories: light, medium and heavy. The modern sea rods are usually classified with a weight specification by the numbers 6, 12, 20, 30, 50, 80 or 130 lbs ("lb" stands for one English pound), corresponding to 3, 6, 10, 15, 24, 37 or 60 kilograms. These classes reflect the line strength which fits the rod. A 30-lb (15-kg) sea rod should be used with a line whose breaking strain is 30 lb (15 kg). This classification is made according to the system which the International Game Fish Association (IGFA) has drawn up for the registration of record fish caught on different lines—from those with a breaking strain of 2 lb (1 kg) to those of 130 lb (60 kg).

Sea rods are built of either fibreglass, graphite, or a combination of the two (known as composite). The most common is the fibreglass type. The ideal length is 5.5–8 ft (170–240 cm). When standing in a boat to fight big fish, a stand-up rod is best used. Most fishing with pirk or jig demands a strong rod, not too long, particularly in deeper water, whereas bait fishing on the bottom requires a longer and softer rod. The rods have different actions: slow, medium, and fast action. Most people prefer the slow-action rod for light sea angling because it is easier to control and fight the fish with this type of rod.

The sea rod has several parts: a butt, handle, reelseat, foregrip, blank, and guides. Some rods have a mid-section ferrule, while others are joined in the handle.

The grip is either of wood, fibreglass, artificial materials, or light-alloy metal, the last being used mostly for trolling. The reelseat should have two reelseat lockers. The foregrip must be 20–30 cm long, which leaves the hand more space when fighting the fish. The foregrip is usually made of cork, foam or mouseskin.

The blank generally has 4–7 guides: either the roller-guide type, Aftco, the ceramic type, Fuji, or chrome-plated brass guides held in a chrome-plated brass frame. The roller guides are specially designed for trolling and fast-swimming fish, to minimize friction and wear on the line, which passes continually through the guides while fighting a fish. The guide rings fit on the rod with one or two wrappings, and the finish consists of rod varnish.

The sea reel

There are two types of reels: the fixed-spool reel, and the multiplier reel with either star or lever drag. A fixed-spool reel is used for light sea angling, spinning and trolling for smaller species. The reel's construction with several power-transmitting axles is a weakness, as is the line capacity. A multiplier reel has either a star drag like Penn Senator, or lever drag like Penn International. The

Above: Equipment for sea angling is usually classified from ultra-light (IGFA class 6 lbs) to heavy (class 130 lbs). At left is shown a light outfit of class 20, and in the centre a very light one of class 12, each having a multiplier reel with star drag. At right is a medium-light outfit of class 50 with a lever-drag reel.

principal difference is that the star drag consists of several brake discs which press against each other when the drag is activated, unlike the lever drag which functions like one large disc so that the entire brake capacity is transferred. The lever drag reel's brake disc is much bigger than the disc of the star drag reel, and thus more solid. It is more expensive to change, but lasts longer and offers a more stable and gentle braking. The lever drag is activated like a clutch by the help of an arm which is both the drag and clutch arm, while the star drag reel has a separate arrangement for connecting or disconnecting the reel spool.

Which type of reel to choose depends on the fishing and the species. The trolling reel should be of the lever drag type. Bottom fishing and fishing with jig or pirk can be practised with both types, but preferably with a reel which has a spool of artificial materials—not metal, which makes it heavier.

Smaller sea reels can be equipped with a level wind for better and easier placing of the line on the spool. Sea reels are classified from 1/0 to 16/0, but also with the specifications 12, 20, 30, 50, 80 or 130 lbs, which correspond to the IGFA classes. It is possible to use a 50-lb (24-kg) line on a 30-lb reel. In common sea angling for smaller species, most anglers use tackle in the IGFA class 6–30 lb (3–15 kg), and if necessary also 50 lb (24 kg). The best reel size for lighter bottom fishing, and jig and pirk fishing, is from 1/0–4/0. The reels have different gear ratios from 1:2.5 (normal) to 1:3.8 (high speed). It is harder to fight a fish with high than with normal gear ratio.

Lines

Nylon lines were first used by sea anglers after the end of World War II. Nylon was a trademark of the American Du Pont factory. Until the war began, lines of vegetable origin were widely used. But soon, nylon monofilament line ousted the natural lines. Today nylon monofilament lines, dacron (artificial braided) lines, and wire are the commonest types.

Nylon monofilament line, the most popular, is cheap and quite strong. It does not decay and has a high breaking strain. The disadvantages are mainly that it is easy to damage and is very elastic with an elongation around 20–30%. It also loses some strength when wet and near the knot. Moreover, the breaking strain is reduced by strong sun exposure. The lines are transparent, coloured or fluorescent, and the last kind offers an excellent line control when, for example, trolling. Some lines are classified with a guaranteed breaking strain—the line breaks at the pressure which is printed on the packing or line spool, such as 20, 50 or 80 lbs (10, 24 or 37 kg). These lines are used for the potential record fish or particular tournaments or championships. The lines usually cost a bit more than unclassified ones.

Dacron line is braided like a hollow tube. It stretches less than 10%, loses no breaking strain when wet, and is much more knot-strong than nylon monofilament line. It has practically the same diameter as nylon monofilament line, because it is spun and hollow, the air inside the tube being under pressure. It also lies better spread on the reel spool. The line is used for trolling and sometimes other forms of fishing. Its weaknesses are the price and the fact that damages on the line are not as easy to detect as on nylon monofilament line.

Wire lines are divided into single-stranded wire or several-stranded wire having 7 or 49 strands with or without a nylon coating or leadcore line. Single-stranded wire line is used as a downrigger line (Monel) or when fishing in deep water with a strong current. It has a high net weight, resists the current, and has no elongation. It is not easy to spread properly on the reel spool, and breaks easily if a kink occurs. This line is for specialists. Several-stranded wire is mostly used for the downriggers. Leadcore line is made of a solid strand of lead within a braided covering. It is used for deep-water trolling.

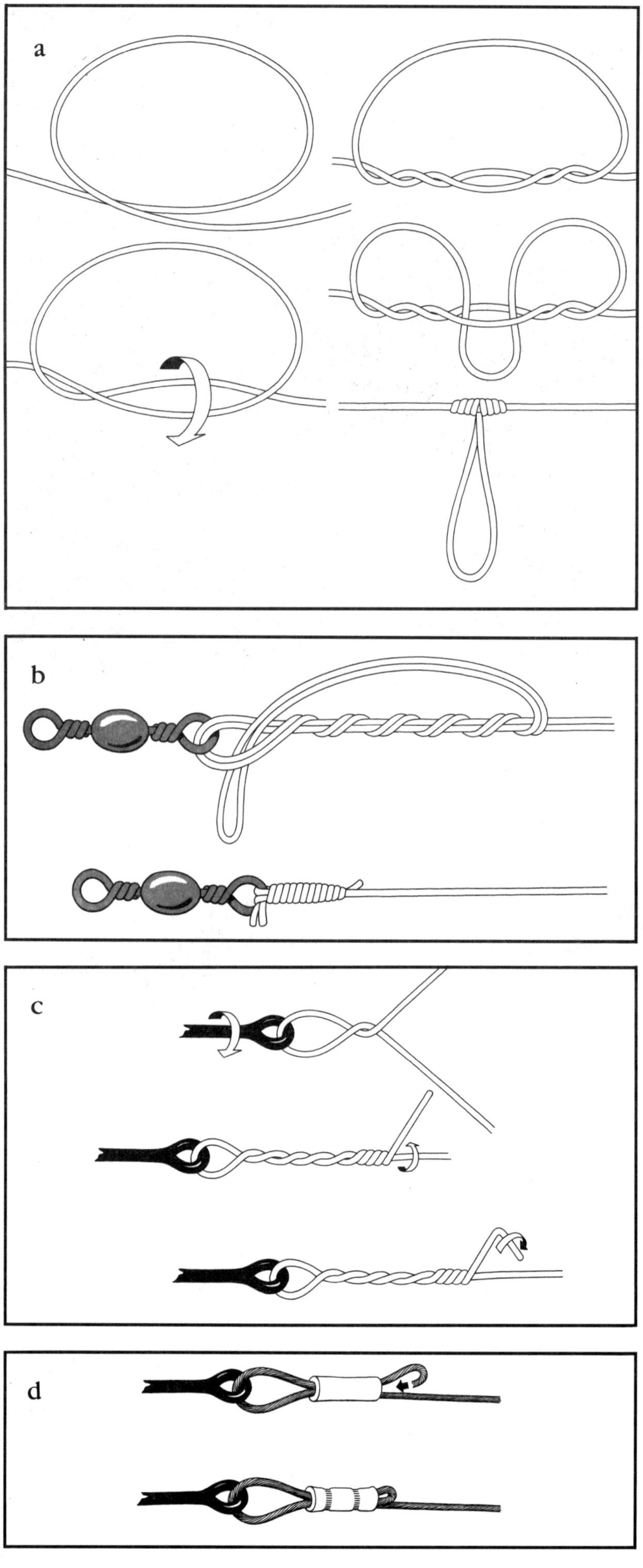

When fishing at sea, lines and terminal tackle must be knotted and joined simply and effectively. A general rule is to use no more knots than absolutely necessary.
(a) Dropper loop.
(b) Double clinch knot.
(c) Haywire twist (for single-stranded wire).
(d) Wire sleeves (for several-stranded wire).

Fishing methods

The fishing takes place from either a drifting or anchored boat. Some species are attracted by baits which are trolled.

The fishing method used depends on the local species and bottom conditions. Fishing from a drifting boat is both for pelagic species, which swim in the open water, and for species of bottom-dwellers. This method is particularly rewarding if the bottom is diverse—with sand, rocks, gravel and varying depths that attract different species. The current and wind may make drift-fishing difficult, and it is necessary to be at anchor. The bait moves too fast for the fish to catch a glimpse or smell of it. When the boat is at anchor, only a limited fishing area can be covered, in fact only the area below and close to the boat. On the other hand, this provides contact with species which do not normally take moving baits. Anchoring is preferably in areas with reefs, grounds, banks, wrecks, or the edge of an underwater slope or ground. Pelagic species can also be taken from an anchored boat.

Trolling is a method which covers a much larger sea area than other fishing methods. It can be practised on the surface or in deeper water by using downriggers: special lead-charged devices to which the lines and the baits are attached by the help of a release mechanism. When the fish takes, the line is released and the fish can be fought directly on rod and reel.

Trolling takes place in a range of environments: on the western American coast for salmon, and in the warmer sea regions where a number of species are attracted by baits which are trolled in the surface, but also in Northern waters as for mackerel.

Lures and artificial baits

Lures are imitations of the fish's natural food. To make the fish take, the lure must have a certain pattern of movement. Among the most used lures for sea hunters are the Norwegian pirk or Diamond jig, and similar jigs and soft plastic artificial worms, besides flies of feathers. For lighter fishing, spoons, plugs, and spinners are fine. The Norwegian pirk is a metal imitation made of either lead or brass. The pirk appears in most tackle shops in a weight range from 25 grams to around 750 grams (1–26 oz). It is mostly used for jigging. The bottom is searched by pumping or jerking the pirk up and down in moderate movements above the bottom when the boat drifts.

Pirks are particularly popular in the Northern waters, as for cod, coalfish (Am. pollock) and pollack. They can also be used in the warmer regions for reef species which rely on vision in the hunt for food. A pirk's body, surface and construction are individ-

Fishing from a drifting boat, for example over sunken rocks, is usually done with artificial bait. The catches are commonly fish of the cod family.

ual. The bigger its surface compared with its weight, the livelier it moves in the water. Norwegian and Swedish pirks have for decades been the model for several types of pirks on the market.

Since fish are attracted by a pirk, its colours influence the catch. In shallow water, red and yellow pirks are very effective and popular, whereas in deeper water you will experience the best pirk fishing with either bright and shining pirks or chromium-plated ones.

Some species which react to a pirk also take smaller artificial soft plastic imitations, feather flies and other artificial imitators which are always placed above the pirk or jig. Use 1–3 artificial imitations depending on the species you are hunting, and on whether you want to feel the fight with each single fish or just prefer to haul fish on board. It often happens that several fishes are landed at the same time, when small imitators are used above the pirk. Such imitators are normally coloured hooks with a skirt of plastic, rubber, feather or hair. They can also be imitations which look like the local prey, like British sand-eel imitations or Norwegian rubber eels.

Among the smaller artificial lures is the Norwegian mackerel spoon, widely used all over the world. But as in pirk fishing, it is the depth of the fishing spot that determines which colour the lure or feathers should have. Red, white, yellow and silvery colours are effective for fishing in shallow waters.

The jig is one of the artificial lures which are very productive in almost all kinds of bottom-fishing. A jig can be moved and jerked without being snagged, because the hook has an upward bend. It can also be fished considerably slower and livelier than the pirk. When fishing for carnivorous fish in shallow water, the jig is an excellent fish-tempter. With practically the same results, both pirk and other artificial lures and jigs can be used for spinning both from a drifting or and anchored boat.

Trolling demands other types of bait with a built-in movement pattern which must be properly adjusted to the trolling speed. Neither pirk nor other artificial lures and feathers are suited for trolling, unlike the jig which is very catching when trolled.

Natural baits

Natural baits are used particularly for species that hunt with the sense of smell, but also for those which rely equally on smell and vision. Natural bait is everything from fresh strips, or fillets of fish, to whole fish—dead or living—and shrimps, crabs, mussels, or snails. Worms, particularly lugworm and ragworm, are very effective baits. Natural bait should be presented to the fish so that it tempts both by smell and movements. The bait must be placed properly on the hook in order to produce the movements, and the hook must be secured so that the fish can swallow it.

To fish effectively with natural bait, it may be necessary to anchor the boat—not least when the fish stay in a limited area, as around wreckage.

Fresh bait is best: the older a bait becomes, the less it attracts. Gradually its smell washes out in the water, and soon the whole bait must be renewed.

Mackerel, sardine and herring have a very penetrating smell that makes them excellent baits all over the world. Shrimps and crabs are excellent for bottom-feeders which usually feed on them or on shellfish. Squids are used in strips or slices or whole. Mussel meat sends out a particularly strong smell, but it can be difficult to place on the hook. Use something like a hairnet to hold the meat. When the meat forms a small ball, close the hairnet and place it on the hook.

Live bait fishing is effective anywhere. A living bait tempts not only by its looks, smell and consistency, but also by its movements. It can be extremely productive in some waters with suspended hunters, whether these are cod, shark, coalfish, groupers or tuna-related species. Note, however, that live bait fishing is prohibited in Norway.

Terminal tackle and hooks

The terminal tackle is the angler's link to the fish. It must be able to resist the wear and tear from the bottom, rocks, gravel, pieces of wreckage, and sharp fish teeth. The leader, or trace material, is of nylon monofilament line, single- or several-stranded wire, with or without a nylon coating. For many species, a wire leader is needed, but the majority can be caught on a nylon monofilament leader.

The leader should be tied simply and effectively, with few knots. It must be able to be lowered to the bottom and catch fish, yet without getting tangled or failing to alert you if a fish swallows the bait. In general, traces for bottom-fishing and fishing in open water can be divided into the paternoster rig, the driftline trace, and the running leger tackle.

The first of these is commonest. It consists of the rig's main line with one or two short traces, on which the hook is placed. This rig is used for artificial lures as well as pirk and feather flies. It is possible to add more traces or loops if preferred, for instance, in mackerel fishing or other shoal fishing where several fish take at the same time. The paternoster rig is knotted with

Paternoster tackle with artificial bait

Paternoster tackle for natural bait

blood knots. The short traces have to be around 8–12 in (20–30 cm) long.

The driftline trace is just a horizontal paternoster rig. It has one or two loops with hooks which are fished close to the bottom. Both rigs are used in drift fishing.

The running leger tackle is the best when fishing from an anchored boat where you fish near grounds, wrecks, underwater slopes, or on sandy bottom—for ray, shark or flatfish. The advantage of this trace is that there is a direct contact with the hook. When the fish takes, it has a chance to retire or move away without feeling the resistance from the lead. Consequently the trace is ideal for shy fish or species which need time to smell their way to the bait and return for cover with it. It is just when the fish retires for shelter that the strike must be made. Many species, such as shark and skate, seize the bait and then swim for some metres before swallowing it. This manoeuvre is only possible with the running leger, since a firm piece of lead might awaken the suspicion of the fish and make it spit out the bait.

Booms, made chiefly of wire, may be very useful to present the hook and bait better. But the sea angler's most important accessories are the swivel connecting the main line with the leader, and the snap swivel which is used as a link between the rig and lead or the main line and sinker.

The knot for the trace follows the blood-knot principle. If the rig must have thick nylon monofilament line of 1.0–1.5 mm, then use a pair of wire sleeves and crimping pliers. The thicker the trace line, the harder it is to make a solid knot, and wire sleeves are often the right solution for more powerful rigs.

Wire leader is necessary for some fishing. The wire resists the teeth of fish and the wear from rocks and pieces of wreckage on the bottom. A wire leader is made with wire sleeves which must fit the nominal diameter of the wire. A pair of pliers is needed for perfect fitting, and the best type is naturally one designed for this purpose.

From time to time, you will have to use more specially designed leaders. For instance, it is common to use a baited pirk which suits Northern species like cod, halibut and wolf-fish. It is also possible to place a hook in a trace below the pirk when the

Running tackle with boom, also usable as driftline tackle

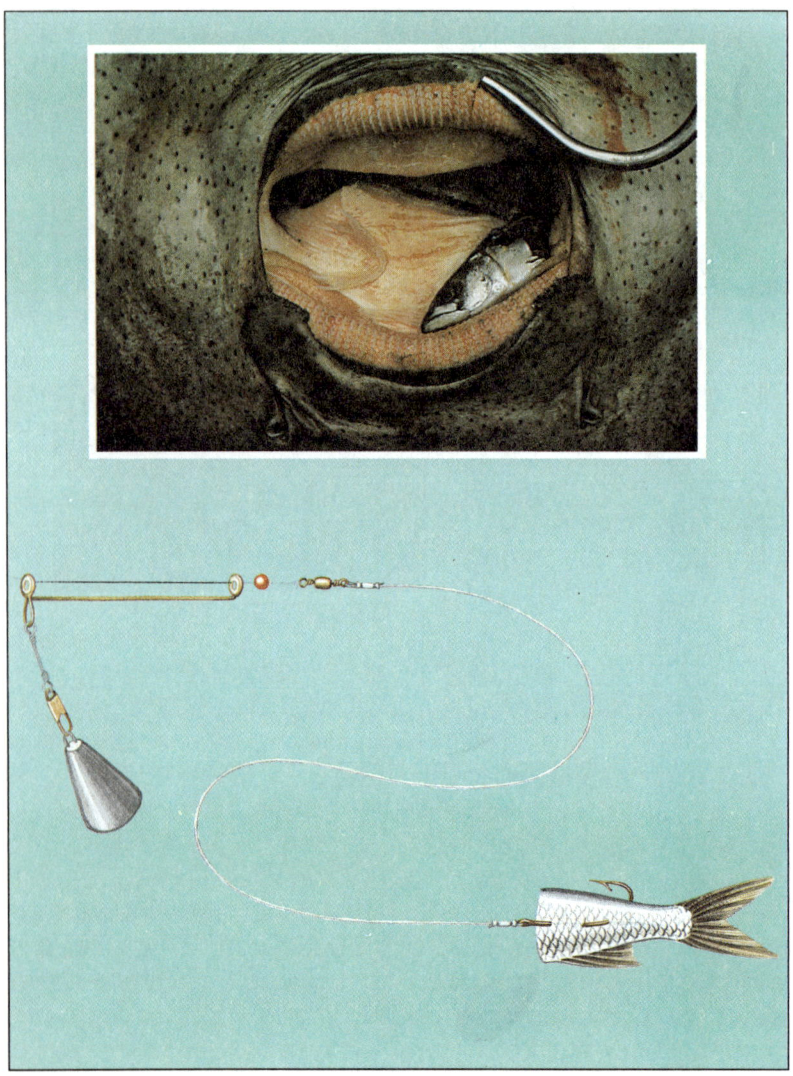

As many as 20,000 hooks are available for various species and fishing methods. Here is a selection that will go a long way.

With any choice, the main point is that a hook should be sharp to penetrate properly even in hard-mouthed fish.

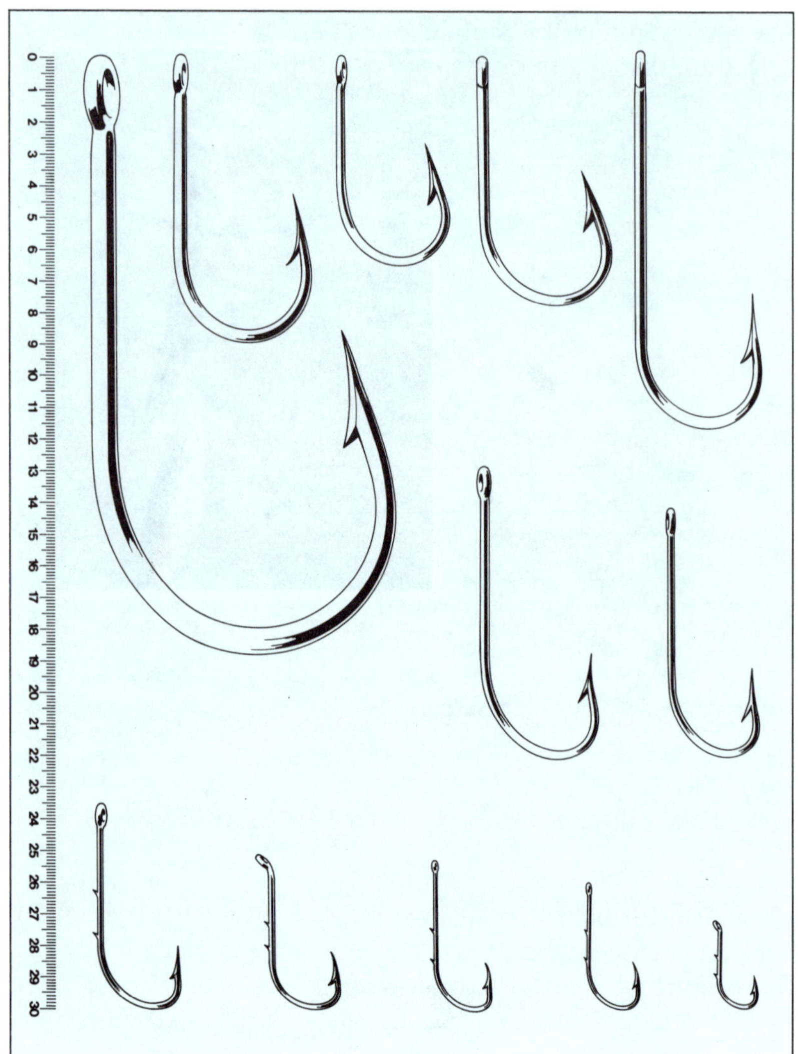

treble hook has been removed. In this case the pirk will be an attractor for the fish, which can more easily glimpse the natural bait.

Teasers and attractors are often used for sea-angling traces, and a teaser or attractor can be put onto every trace. But this is only worthwhile when you fish from a drifting boat, and in waters with a good current or wind. Smaller attractors and teasers are used for flatfish. Small pearls and buttons are fitted onto the flatfish trace and, if mistaken for a snail or mussel, they persuade the fish to take the baited hooks.

The three-way swivel is not very handy in modern sea angling, since every eye of the swivel demands a knot. To use a three-way swivel, three knots must be tied, instead of one or two. But a three-way swivel can be helpful in connection with a plastic tube which is pulled over the line loop and placed on the swivel's eye. The plastic tube acts like a boom and holds the hook out from the main line.

There are many types of hooks designed for different fishing methods and species. Commonest is the O'Shaughnessy hook, which penetrates the jaw of both hard- and soft-mouthed fish, providing a firm hold on the fish in motion. Mustad's Beak hook has a slight in-curved point and is particularly good for keeping a firm grip on the bait and hooking the fish. Long shanked hooks like the Aberdeen type are good for flatfish. The small bend of the hook makes it easy for the fish to swallow the bait. The shank juts out and removal is simple.

Nothing beats a hook which has been sharpened so that it penetrates the jaws of any fish. But not even the sharpest hook works if the knot is too weak or damaged. In other words, the perfect tackle for any sea angler must work perfectly even in the weakest links.

With a rod belt and shoulder harness, one can fight huge fish in a standing position. To use a shoulder harness, the reel must have two lugs for fastening the quick-release snaps.

Accessories

It is sometimes difficult to fight a large fish for a long time, particularly in heavy sea on a slippery deck. Helpful here are a couple of accessories: rod belt, kidney and shoulder harness. The rod belt consists of a "cup" and strap. The idea is to place the rod butt in the "cup" and spread the pressure from the bend rod over a larger area. The shoulder harness is a vest-like garment that fits across the angler's shoulder and is used for larger fish—such as shark and tuna—but only in combination with sea reels that have two harness lugs which are clipped into the quick-release snaps of the shoulder harness. By the help of a rod belt and a shoulder harness, one can fight fish up to around 100–200 lbs (50–100 kg) while standing with no other help.

A tackle box is a great advantage: it can store a sizeable selection of pirks, hooks, swivels, artificial lures, feather flies, mackerel spoons, pliers and rigs. Some of the biggest tackle also have space for a couple of extra spools or reels.

On charter boats, there are gaffs and scoop nets on board. But if you decide to set out on your own, it is important to remember either a net for smaller species or a gaff for the bigger ones. Big fish require a long-handled gaff, and it is essential to bring a pair of leather gloves for seizing hold of line or leader, as well as hauling the fish on board for release or to be kept.

Chum

Sea-angling environments vary widely—from protected bays and oil rigs to artificial reefs and deep oceans, from areas with strong tides and currents to open water, from sand and clay bottoms to rocks and stones.

Many species which react to natural baits can be attracted to a boat by the use of natural baits: mashed mackerel, pieces of herring, sardine or similar fish, or other species that can be chopped and served overboard.

This method, known as rubby-dubby or chum, is used in many ways. The most popular chumming is for shark, which are attracted and led to the baited hooks by the trail's scent in the water. It is also possible to chum from a boat, anchored where the chum slick will tempt those in the deep—or by placing the chum can on the anchor rope, which can attract fish to the baited hooks on the bottom. Chum is widely used in tuna fishing, where small pieces of fresh fish or live bait are thrown in the water and attract the tuna to stay around the boat.

Chum is used for numerous species. Flatfish are attracted to the boat by lowering a riddled can (chum pot) of dog or cat food to the bottom. By shaking the pot occasionally, an immediate trail is washed out of it, drawing flatfish. The same method is widely employed for eel, on a larger scale for species like cod or ling, and in southern waters for local species which normally take bait. Chum gives superb results when it comes to conger, ling and muraene, which lead a solitary life in the underwater rock clefts and caves, leaving only when they sense food.

Ground-up or mashed fish is put into an old potato bag, a big net, or cans made for the purpose, which are placed onto the boat at the water line. In every method of chumming, the trail in the water must be continuous. If broken, it can make the fish lose track of the baited hooks.

Strike, fight, and landing

A fish takes an artificial lure or bait because this is mistaken for a natural one. Consequently a strike is needed to hook the fish before it realizes the error and spits out the bait. Some fish hook themselves, but others require an immediate strike, particularly the deep-water species. The rod is lifted moderately, and it is important to maintain a tight line to the fish and to begin fighting it with regular pumping movements. Be sure to keep the same bend and pressure on the rod and fish during the fight. The fish must be able to take line if it suddenly dives. The reel drag has to be adjusted according to the line's breaking strain. After a while the fish comes closer to the boat and, when it appears in the surface, it is landed with a scoop net or a gaff, or—if it is small—just lifted on board with the line and rod.

When fishing with natural baits, the fish must have time to swallow the bait before you strike. A lot of anglers make a strike when they feel the fish, but that is too early. It is unnatural for the fish to have the bait torn out of its mouth when barely tasting it. Give the fish plenty of time, feel cautiously that there is good contact with the fish before making the strike, and far more fish will be landed.

A modern sportfishing boat needs some basic equipment to function effectively. The main aid to finding fish quickly is a sonar. Shown at right is how a paper-driven graph recorder "sees" the bottom. Under this can be seen how the bottom really looks and where the fish are. A compass and navigator are also important boat navigation instruments. So is a VHF or AM/FM marine radio.

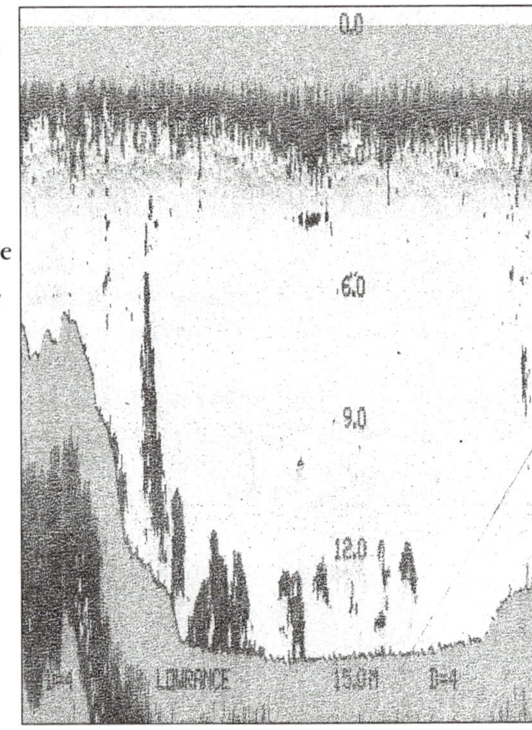

LCG recorder

Compass

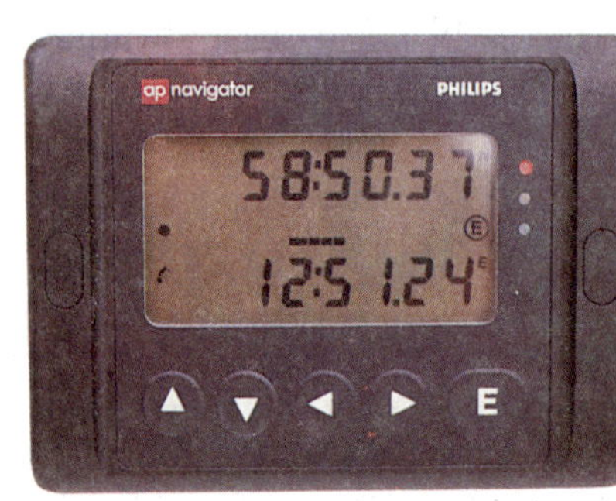

Navigator

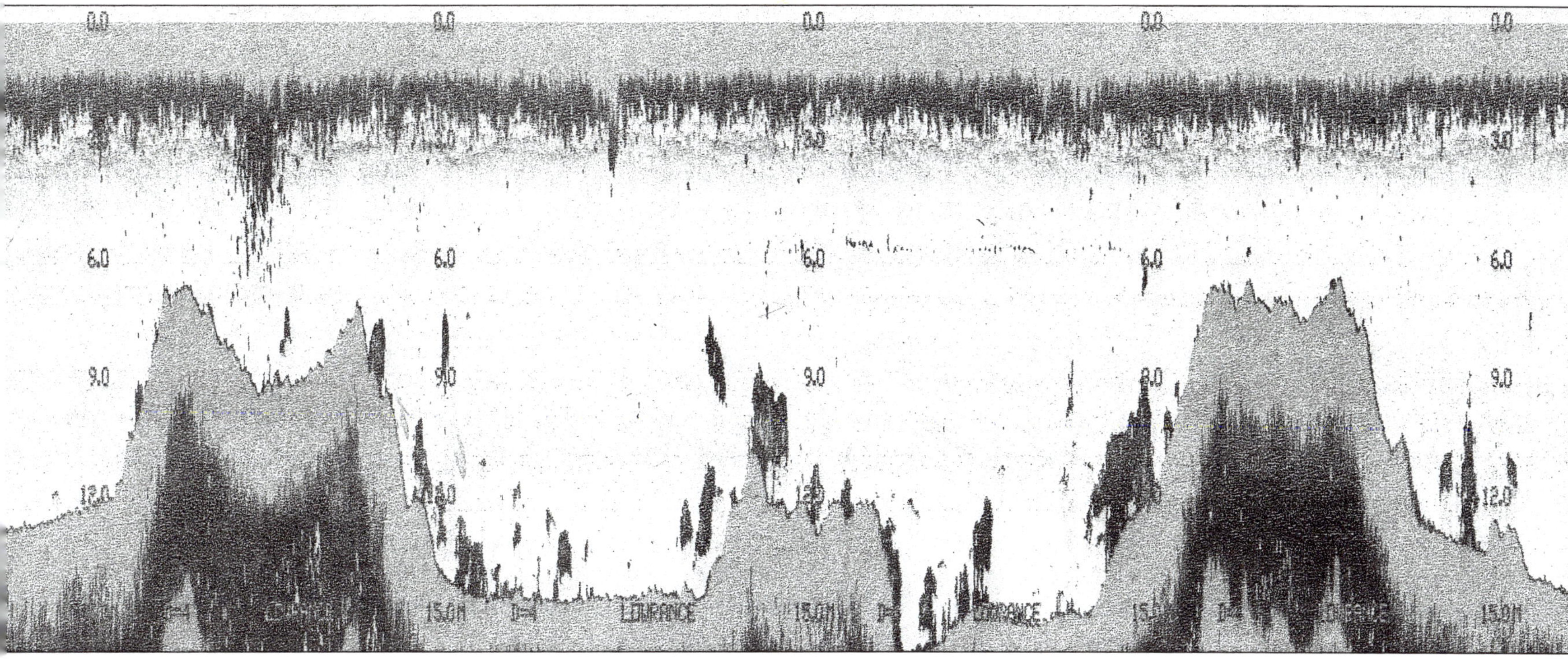
0.0
3.0
6.0
9.0
12.0
15.0M
LOWRANCE

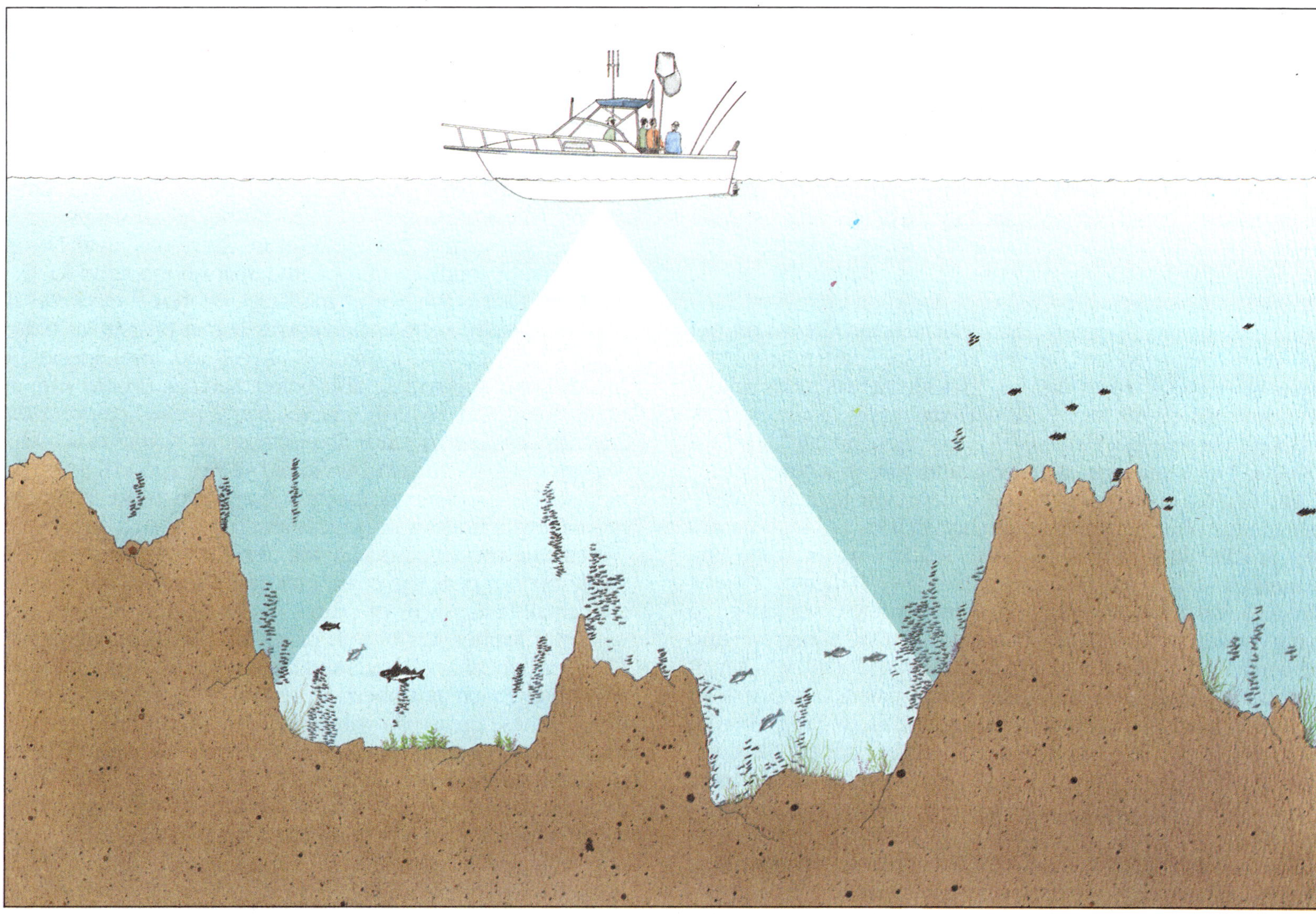

The sea angler's challenges

The sea is rich in species, from the Arctic and temperate zones to the subtropical and tropical regions. Some species migrate every year over long distances from feeding to spawning grounds, but it is mainly the water temperature that determines whether a fish takes. The bottom conditions vary from sand to rocks or gravel, and most types of bottom attract their own fish stock.

Only a small part of the sea's total surface is used by anglers, namely the part nearest to the coast. The exception is trolling for the southern high-speeders like tuna, marlin and sailfish, which are mostly caught in the surface over depths of more than a couple of kilometres.

In the northern Atlantic lives a special stock of excellent game fish: cod, coalfish (pollock), pollack, flatfish, conger, spurdog, tope, wolf-fish, ray and skates, ling and mackerel. Of these fantastic fighters, quite a few can be met in southern waters, like the Mediterranean Sea. There are varying stocks of cod near the coast and in deeper water, but also elsewhere in almost pelagic shoals that hunt mackerel, smaller coalfish, herring and so on. They take both natural and artificial baits. The coalfish is a strong pelagic fighter. The small fish appear near the coast with a strong and stable current, whereas the bigger fish operate further at sea and often in midwater, at spots where the sea angler seldom comes to fish.

The pollack stays closer to the coast and does not migrate as much as the coalfish, but it is a splendid fighter. Like coalfish, it goes wild for artificial baits but seldom for natural baits. The flatfish species—dab, flounder, and plaice—are met on shallow water and in bays and fjords, where they are caught on light tackle and worms or fish pieces as bait. The turbot lives in deeper water. The king of the Atlantic, the halibut—a close relative of the Pacific halibut in the North Pacific—was once common in Norway, Scotland, the Shetlands, Orkneys, Faeroe Islands and Greenland, but has been decimated by commercial fishing, particularly long-lining. It weighs up to around 600 lbs (300 kg), yet today halibut of more than 60–80 lbs (30–40 kg) are rarely caught on rod, although commercial fishing fleets occasionally land a fish of 100–200 lbs (50–100 kg). It takes natural baits or a baited pirk.

The ling is a codfish which feels comfortable in deeper water. Its main distribution is around the British Isles and in the North Sea. Smaller ling can be found in shallow water, while ling around 20–40 lbs (10–30 kg) are met in 50–200 metres of water. Wrecks serve as a magnet for ling: here they find cover and good living conditions. In warmer waters like the Gulf Stream, we find the conger, which feels at ease in both deep and shallow water, as long as it can find cover near rocks, pieces of wreckage or a stony bottom. It weighs up to 200 lbs (100 kg), and the angling record is over 100 lbs (50 kg), taken in the English Channel where the biggest are landed. The conger is only taken on natural baits, often from an anchored boat as it needs time to smell its way to the bait.

The wolf-fish occurs in Arctic and Scandinavian waters, where it is popular game. It prefers a rocky and stony bottom, and eats shellfish which it breaks with its strong jaws. There are three species: a blue deepwater species and the spotted wolf-fish, which are particularly common near Greenland, and the striped wolf-fish of Scandinavian waters and the North Sea. The blue wolf-fish weighs at most 80 lbs (40 kg), the spotted wolf-fish 60–70 lbs (30–35 kg), and the striped wolf-fish 30 lbs (15 kg).

Among the smaller species we find the spotted dogfish, which is abundant around the British Isles and in the Mediterranean Sea, notably on sandy bottom where it sometimes prevents other forms of fishing by attacking the baits. The spurdog appears in shoals near almost all European coasts, in addition to North America's Atlantic coast. It is greedy and prefers natural bait. The tope hunts in the same area, is often located in shallow water, and also occurs in sandy bays with only a few metres of water and a good current. It weighs up to 60–80 lbs (30–40 kg) and is known to be an excellent fighter on light tackle.

Ray and skate are widely distributed along some coasts and in deeper water, where they prefer bottoms of sand, clay or gravel. The largest skate species weigh up to 200 lbs (100 kg). They have been pursued by both commercial fishermen and anglers in many places, and the stock has drastically declined. The British Isles are best known for their skate stock. Other large skate species include *Raja oxrinus* and *Raja lintea*. Among the smaller ray species, commonest are the thornback ray and some other species which seldom weigh more than 20 lbs (10 kg) and mostly have local distribution. The monkfish, in the same family as the shark and ray, is distributed around the British Isles and the Mediterranean Sea, where it lives in shallow water. Ireland has produced unusually large monkfish in some of the bays on the west coast.

Many of the North Atlantic species are also met in southern waters, where new species offer further possibilities for sea angling. Both garfish and mackerel are distributed in all European waters. In southern Europe, the Spanish mackerel looks almost identical to the Nordic mackerel, but horse mackerel also hunt pelagically. *Lophius piscatorius* is met on regular bottom types. There are also a number of reef and coral species, sea bream being the widest distributed, such as *Brama raii*, and other shiny and reddish species like *Pagellus centrodontus*, *Pagellus erythrinus* and *Spondyliosoma cantharus*, which seldom weigh more than a few kilos but give a good fight on light tackle. The muraene is met on stony and rocky banks and grounds with underwater cracks and caves.

Near the rocky coasts you will also find the wrasse and, on sandy bottom near the coast, gurnard. These southern fish all take small baits, slices or pieces of fish, and sometimes small colourful feather jigs or soft plastic or rubber imitations. On Madeira, the Canary Islands and the Azores, new species appear continually, such as amberjack, several groupers and jacks. But even in these areas you will meet more Northern species like mackerel, tope, and species of redfish and brosme, which has a southern development area here.

Along the American east coast, other game fish have meant a lot to the development of American sea angling. Cod and pollock appear—as in Scandinavia—on grounds, banks and wrecks. On deeper water, there are ling and cod as well. Due to the heated currents, warm-water species occur farther north than in the similar latitudes of the East Atlantic: for example, bluefish and striped bass which are caught off the coast. Southward near the Carolinas and Florida, other species are found—jacks, crevall and horse-eye, black drum, snapper, and black sea bass.

On artificial reefs, rocky banks and grounds, there are diverse species of sea bream and large groupers, not to mention amberjack. The species are all attached to certain environments. The most extraordinary are the "flats"—huge areas with shallow water in southern Florida and Key West, the Bahamas, near several islands in the Caribbean, and along the American Gulf coast. Some of the world's best light-tackle fishing has seen the light of day here.

Several challenges are open to the sea angler—but the species naturally vary according to the climate, bottom conditions and water temperature. Shown here are a halibut (below at left), a small shark (centre) and a cod (right); at right is a ray.

The "flats"

Bonefish, tarpon, permit, barracuda and snook belong to the species which appear on the flats with a strong tide and "islands" of mangrove. The flats are rich in crabs, shrimps and other shellfish and prey which are on the menu of carnivorous hunters. The water is crystal-clear and the weather baking hot. The fish can often be spotted either as large black shadows or when their fins stick out of the water. This is the paradise of small boat anglers and light-tackle enthusiasts, as well as of fly-fishermen.

Imagine yourself slowly drifting near the edge of the mangroves or in a shallow bay, when the shadow of a 60–80 lb (30–40 kg) tarpon is revealed 40 yards (35 metres) from the boat, out of range. You drift closer to the fish, and are eventually sure that a crab can be placed even nearer, sunk to the bottom, and led into the fish's field of vision. Or a large bushy streamer might be cast so precisely that it lands a few inches from the jaw of the tarpon. Suddenly the fish moves towards the bait, opens and closes its jaws, and at once feels the hook and the resistance from the rod and line. The fight begins, maybe for a few seconds, or even 30 seconds, in explosions of water, followed by a furious run which hardly no drag resists. Hundreds of metres of line are torn off the reel and, despite powerful leaps, the fish is able to make headway at top speed without leaving the angler much control over the fishing tackle. Nine out of ten fish recover their freedom. And you might get only one chance to fight a fish for a few minutes. There is no doubt that the tarpon is among the most desired quarry on artificials (fly, spoon, plug) and natural bait.

The season varies for different species. Water temperature, current conditions, and the phase of the moon are very important ingredients in the fishing. It is unimaginably important to be in the right place at the right time—indeed, timing is more valuable than the best guide. On the flats, fishing goes on throughout the year except during a few months, since the flats stretch along the coasts of two continents.

Spinning is used for a few species with small plugs, lures, spoons, jigs and spinners. But in most cases living bait is more rewarding, for instance small crabs which are put on a single hook, or small living shrimps. The method is simple: cast in the direction where the fish appears, and let the bait sink to the bottom in its field of vision. Give it time to pick up and swallow the bait, then make a strike. The boats used in such fishing mostly

Channel bass or redfish are also seasonably plentiful on warm-water flats at flood tides.

These species require a leader of strong nylon monofilament, not wire. On the flats in a few metres of water you may also experience barracuda and lemon shark. Spinning for barracuda is done with either long slim lures or a special plastic tube rig with one or two hooks, either single or treble hooks. This tube must be around 8–12 in (20–30 cm) long. The barracuda is as shy as the other species, and dislikes anglers and inexact casts. It demands a

The "flats" are fished with small boats and light gear. Artificial bait is sometimes used, but the usual choice is natural bait such as shrimp and crab, while fly-fishermen use streamer flies.

belong to the local fishermen or guides who are specialists—with a few exceptions—in scanning the water and finding fish. So you are normally in good hands.

Most large tarpon are taken by drifting or still-fishing with natural bait such as crabs, mullet, shrimp or saltwater catfish. Slow trolling is effective along the Florida Gulf Coast. But these tactics simply cannot match stalking the fish in shallow water and then casting to them with salt-water bait-casting rods, with spinning rods or flyrods. The nylon leader must have a breaking strain around 20–40 lbs (10–20 kg). Hook sizes 1/0–6/0 are the most common, but most anglers use 4/0.

Not the least of the inshore fishes is the bonefish, the gray ghost of the flats. This is one game species that an angler sees before, during, and after the strike. Bonefish feed across the vast tidal flats surrounding Florida and many Caribbean islands, usually arriving with a flood tide. They are easily visible (with polaroid glasses) in the clear shallow water, but they are also very nervous in such an exposed environment.

Most bonefish are caught by casting a live crab or other natural bait in the path of a feeding fish, with spinning tackle. But it is far more challenging to hook a bonefish upward of 5 lb (2.5 kg) on an artificial lure, especially on a flyrod and streamer fly. If a bonefish strikes, it immediately races away in a powerful, breathtaking run for the safety of deep water. If a fisherman survives that first run, playing and landing a bone is not too difficult. They are poor food fish and, like tarpon, all should be released after netting.

The bonefish appears in shoals and can be taken on a hook size 1/0 or 2/0 on a nylon monofilament line with a breaking strain around 10–20 lbs (5–10 kg). It seldom weighs more than 8–10 lbs (4–5 kg), and fish of 2–5 lbs (1–2.5 kg) are commonest. Normally some weight of lead is attached in order to extend the cast, because the longer you cast the better chance you have to hook a fish on the flats.

The permit (pompano) is a more round and strongly built fish which prefers stony, rocky or coral bottom on the flats. It has both shrimps and crabs on its menu, or sometimes a small jig.

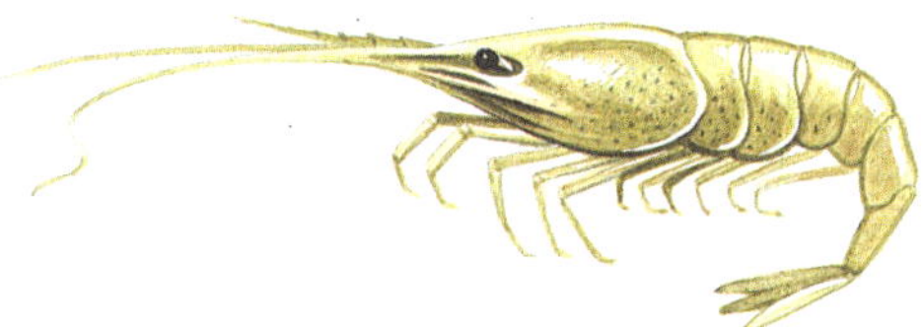

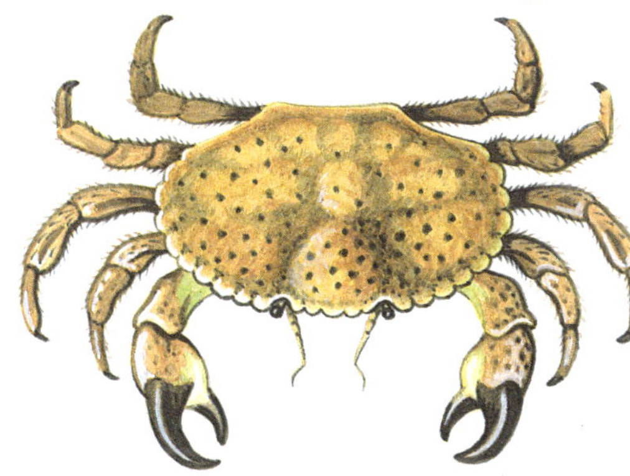

Fly-fishermen find the "flats" a paradise. Few other places in the world enable one to hook such big and battling fish on fly-fishing equipment.

wire leader, either single- or several-stranded, around 8–12 in (20–30 cm) long. Lemon shark is often caught on natural bait but sometimes also on artificial lures.

Fly-fishing the flats

It is on the flats that a fly-fisherman can make his dreams come true. Tarpon strips the reel of line in a few seconds. Bonefish make a fly reel sound like a dentist's drill at its highest number of revolutions. The flats are a genuine paradise for fly-fishermen. But no paradise without a snake: the fly-fishing requires the strongest and best fishing tackle available. Precision, skill and strong fishing tackle, knots and connections are the only way of getting a fish. A good guide is not enough. Also caution, alertness and attention are important qualities. You do not have to make any blind casting, and you may not spot more than 5–15 fish of which you only get to fight a few each day. So the casts must be precise. Some records have been landed with only 5–10 metres cast, but the longer and more precisely you cast, the better your chances.

Special saltwater tapered fly-lines are available. Bonefish of 2–10 lbs (1–5 kg) can be caught on fly tackle class 6–9 as long as the reel has a backline capacity around 220 yds (200 m) and an adjustable drag, preferably lever drag, for instance Marryat, Pflueger, Fin-Nor, Hardy Sunbeam or Scientific Anglers. I recommend a Pflueger Medalist which is one of the best in its price range for this special fly-fishing.

Even more important is the tackle constellation for tarpon. In this field of fishing, you will usually hook larger fish, and thus need a comparatively short vigorous rod designed especially for tarpon. Class 11–12 is the commonest, with different corresponding shooting-head or weight-forward fly-lines. It is strong tackle but you will hardly get to cast that many times a day. Smaller tarpon of 10–20 lbs (5–10 kg) can be taken on lighter tackle. The 4/0 flies are used for large fish and usually 1/0 for smaller ones. The leader should have a breaking strain around 20–30 lbs (10–15 kg).

Bonefish can be outwitted with smaller flies, often size 1/0 or even smaller. Pink shrimp imitations have been popular, but new fly-tying materials like Fishair have changed the traditional bonefish fly patterns. Often the best is a fly with wings twice as long as the shank. Retrieve the fly in varied shrimp-like movements. The permit seldom takes a fly, but it does so without warning and, though shy, it sometimes requires a few precise casts before it attacks the bait and explodes in the surface. Barracuda can be taken on large flies of colourful materials, such as Fishair, and a leader of piano wire around 4–6 in (10–15 cm). Snook and spotted sea trout are always ready to attack a fly.

There are flats along the American east coast with mangrove swamps, crystal-clear lagoons and tropical heat. Here, too, you will find other species which can be taken on fly, like striped bass, bluefish and fluke. Yet it is not only a question of whether the fish takes the fly, but also whether you are good and persistent enough with the fly tackle to tempt the different species which are normally caught on artificial and natural baits.

Big-game fishing

The dream of the big fish haunts all sea anglers. A fight lasting for hours, the excitement of feeling a power which suddenly interrupts the ocean's silence, and the victory—these are some of the ingredients which make sea anglers hunt the big one. And hardly any other fish has its several hundred kilos of pure muscle which take the bait and vanish like a locomotive at top speed, partly in the water and partly in mid-air, on an unknown course.

It was that dream which beguiled anglers at the end of the eighteenth century, when the first tarpon and tuna were landed in the United States. They were not large fish by today's standards, but real monsters in those days. Eventually the prey became bigger, and early in our century the first striped marlin was caught. In the twenties, the American author Zane Grey overpowered a marlin of more than 1,000 pounds—a great breakthrough.

At that time, the first tuna were taken not only in American waters, but also in the English North Sea and in Denmark. Tuna fishing expanded during the thirties in both the United States and Northern Europe. Fishing tackle managed to cope with giants which grew up to 380 kilos. Then, too, a French angler caught tuna in the Bosphorus, and the first tuna was to be landed in France during the forties. The sea angling organization IGFA, established in 1939, made rules and regulations for modern sea and big-game fishing: hard rules meant to ensure the correctness of records. After a few years, approval was denied to Zane Grey's fish, which had been damaged and attacked by shark during the fight. It was not until 1952 that IGFA could acknowledge a marlin of over 1,000 pounds.

In the fifties and sixties, big-game fishing became very popular and the tackle had gone through various phases of renewal and development. In Europe, the French angler Pierre Clostemann gained much status for sea angling; he was undoubtedly the "godfather" of French big-game anglers for years, and inspired thousands to take up fishing, as did Michael Lerner during the interwar period in the USA. The Great Barrier Reef's outstanding marlin productivity was discovered, and the Australian Alfred Dean excelled with a white shark of more than 1,000 kg.

American anglers were then looking for new territories—the Bahamas and Hawaii. European sea-angling pioneers reached

the Canary Islands in the sixties, and soon turned them into a centre for big-game anglers from all around the world. The first shark centre had been founded in England already during the fifties. Madeira's possibilities were noticed in the sixties, and the marlin fishing of the Azores began in the early eighties. Meanwhile, thousands of reels have been emptied, rods broken, battles lost and victories won—yet new line is always being wound on, and new rods are being made everywhere. For old monsters and even bigger new ones are waiting to be confronted . . .

The boat

Fishing can be done from almost all types of boats, and in fact several big-game species have been caught from rubber boats or smaller craft of 15–18 feet. But to guarantee safety, space for tackle and outfit, and the angler's comfort, most fishing takes place from boats of 20–60 feet, equipped with outriggers, rod holders, a fighting chair, flying gaffs, nets, and often a so-called tuna tower. There are also modern navigational instruments, and a water-temperature gauge: many of the prey in big-game fishing are hot-water lovers which hunt and live in the surface waters.

It is hard to define the difference between big-game fishing and fishing for large species. Moreover, the former term includes fishing for halibut, skate, and shark from 30–40 kilos upward. But in big-game fishing a variety of other species is landed as a by-catch, such as wahoo, kingfish, dorado, dolphin and barracuda—although it is possible to adjust the tackle and bait for fishing of the intended species.

The fishing tackle

The fish is big and fast, and has quite a lot of water under its belly. You will also notice a difference in the fighting spirit of the species. The fight lasts from a few minutes with a small blue shark, to hours of dueling with tuna or marlin. Big-game fishing requires tackle in the IGFA class of 30, 50, 80 or 130 lbs (15, 24, 37, 60 kg). For marlin and gigantic bluefin tuna, tackle of 80–130 lbs (37–60 kg) is used. Smaller marlin and tuna (bigeye and yellowfin), as well as broadbill swordfish, are challenged with tackle of 50–80 lbs (24–37 kg), whereas 30–50 lbs (15–24 kg) is used for smaller shark, tuna, sailfish and striped marlin.

The rod is specially designed for this heavy-duty fishing. It has a stainless light-alloy metal butt, solid reelseat and roller guides of the trademark Aftco, Mildrum or Fin-Nor. Trolling rods are designed and made stronger than common sea-angling rods for bottom fishing. Different traditions in sea angling and big-game fishing have resulted in the development of rods which have the same classification but do not have the same action or bend. For stand-up fishing, the California style rods with extended foregrips and the longer butts are superior to the traditional trolling-rod.

The reels are stoutly built and offer high line capacity. Level drag reels are preferred by the majority for trolling purposes, because of reliability and smoother running of the drag, which is able to endure the punishment from fast-swimming monsters with their desperate hanky-panky. Among the classical star drag reels you will find Penn Senator, while the best-known level drag

Boats for big-game fishing are specially equipped for stressful conditions. The outrigger, rod holder, landing gear, tuna tower, and advanced navigation instruments are typical aids.

A fighting chair is often needed for landing really big fish. At each side can be seen "trolling rods" with their reels.

The reels used in big-game fishing must be strongly built, with space for several hundred metres of line. Shown here is one of the lever-drag type.

reels are Penn International, Fin-Nor, Everol, Gladiator, Mitchell, Daiwa Tournament and Shimano Triton. Mitchell, Daiwa and Shimano are also producing traditional star drag reels.

Lines are used according to the line class you have chosen. Nylon monofilament lines are the most common. The fluorescent lines provide better line control. Braided line of dacron is still the favourite of many big-game anglers, but is not often the type used on modern charter boats.

Fishing techniques and methods

The fishing is done from either a drifting or an anchored boat, with some kind of natural bait or live baitfish—particularly for bottomfeeders like shark and tuna, besides swordfish. Trolling is the most widely used fishing method in big-game fishing, and a large range of species responds to the artificial or natural baits which are dragged behind the boat.

Fishing from a drifting or anchored boat is normally combined with the use of chum or rubby-dubby, which especially attracts shark species. The chum is made of large pieces of fish and live baitfish. These also attract tuna to the boat and the baited hooks which are placed at the different depths.

Chum is excellent in shark fishing, and three or four baits can be located at different depths—for example, one just below the surface, one at 10 or 20 metres, and one at 50 metres. The slices of fish and the scent form a trail in the water, helping the shark to find its way to the boat. Also other species like dorado, bonito and mackerel are attracted by the rubby-dubby. The shark leaders are located at different depths with the help of a float, such as a balloon or plastic container, which is put onto the main line. You use fresh bait and fishes ranging from sardine to mackerel pieces, a bonito or a small slice of tuna.

Trolling is a very efficient method for covering large fishing areas at sea, with artificial baits dragged 20–50 metres behind the boat, where the boat averages 5–12 knots depending on the species, water temperature and local bottom conditions. The teasing effect of trolling consists of the interaction between the vibrations from the engine, screw and wake, which somehow imitate the movements of hunted or hunting small fish in the surface. As many of the species are pelagic surface hunters, they are provoked by these vibrations before they discover the baits, which are trolled behind the boat and thus easily taken.

Usually 3–6 lines are trolled at the same time, depending on the species. In tuna fishing, it is normal to use 4–5 baits; for marlin, only 3–4. It is also quite common to use teasers or attractors, which are artificial baits without a hook. These lures are placed between the others, or immediately behind the boat. With the help of the teaser and its signals in the surface, the hunters are attracted.

Most species have their own preferred bait, colours and trolling speed, together with the line length behind the boat which makes them take the bait. Big-game fishing is usually done from charter boats or private boats where the skipper and crew have a passion for just this kind of fishing, and you will experience an expertise in preparation of the bait and rigs, not to mention a knowledge of the local waters' favourite bait types. However, the artificial baits have to move relatively straight through the water, making a strong wave of bubbles, a so-called "smoke". If the lure has too much movement—for example in hard weather with big waves—or if it has a wrong or weak construction and body, it must be changed.

Natural baits are widely used, such as a rigged mullet or ballyhoo, small bonito or other firm fishes. Generally the trolling speed is identical for baits, and the local conditions determine whether to use natural or artificial baits. In many places, natural bait is still the most common, since it is cheaper than artificial baits and, as a rule, also more giving. Sometimes live bonito is used as bait for marlin. The bonito is caught and immediately put on the rig, then released back into the water, whereupon the boat makes 3–5 knots with the bonito swimming behind the boat.

The spreading of the lines, and the baits' mutual placement, have to be perfect. The same applies to the drag of the reel, which must be adjusted so that the fish is hooked properly in the crucial seconds of the strike. And when fishing with natural and live baits, the adjustment must be so fine-tuned that the line gives when the fish takes. The fish swallows the bait on the spot before the strike should be made. In all parts of the world where big-game fishing is practised, the skilful crews and skippers possess these finer points of knowledge.

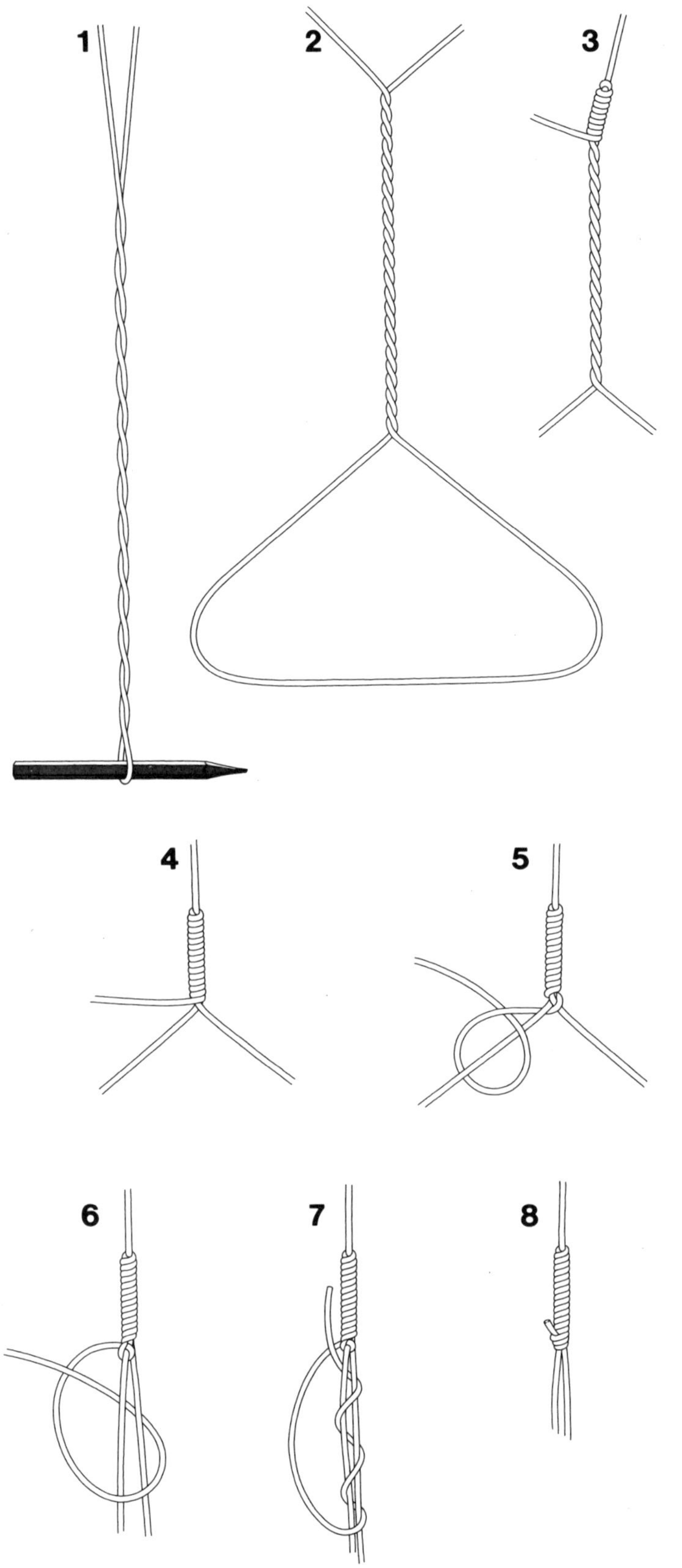

The Bimini twist is the safest knot in big-game fishing. It is hard to tie, but very durable.

Bait and rigs

Natural bait is anything from pieces or slices of fish to a whole fish—which is either used from a drifting or anchored boat, or else trolled. Artificial baits are anything from plugs to jigs of different kinds, such as Japanese feather jigs, jetheads, knuckleheads, softheads, konaheads, and flatnose lures. These baits have a head of metal or artificial material, perhaps with an in-built weight of lead, besides a skirt which covers one or two hooks. The leader must be only 30 feet (9 metres) long, when using tackle in the range 30–130 lbs (15–60 kg), if you want to be able to participate in tournaments which are held according to the IGFA rules or to register a fish as a record. Single- and several-stranded wire, and nylon monofilament line, are the required leader material types.

It is allowed to use a double line which must not exceed the length of 30 feet (9 metres) in the IGFA classes 30–130 lbs (15–60 kg). The combined length of the double line and leader should not exceed 40 ft (12 m). The double line becomes especially important during the end of the fight, when there are some crucial moments with the fish in the surface and the risk of breaking the line. Thanks to the double line, it is possible to put the first turns on the reel spool and add extra pressure on the fish.

There are other IGFA rules for big-game fishing leaders in the class of 6, 12 and 20 lbs (3, 6 and 10 kg), but only a few use such light tackle for the wild monsters of the deep.

Shark fishing

Fishing for shark includes—among other species—porbeagle, blue shark, mako, and hammerhead shark, which are the most common in the world. Most shark species rely mainly on the sense of smell when hunting, whereas mako and porbeagle shark use their vision.

The fishing of most shark species can be done from drifting or anchored boats, and improved by using chum or rubby-dubby. The hammerhead shark can also be trolled and caught on natural bait or, less often, artificial baits. In some places it is common for the mako shark to take trolled artificial baits.

Shark fishing requires wire leaders, either of several-stranded wire with a breaking strain around 100–400 kg, or a shorter piece of 3–6 feet (91–182 cm) of single-stranded wire such as piano wire with a breaking strain around 50–150 kg. The latter's advantages are that it is cheap, easy to change and, not least, hard-wearing against sharp teeth. These sometimes make their way in between the single threads on a several-stranded wire, but cannot do so with a single-stranded wire.

Blue shark and mako are distinct hot-water species which live in the middle of the free water. By contrast, the porbeagle shark feels at ease in the temperate zones, and sometimes it seeks shallow water. Most records for porbeagle shark come from the north coast of Cornwall in southwest England. Its main distribution area is around the British Isles, but it can also be met in subtropical areas of the North Atlantic, as well as on the east coast of North America.

Shark fishing is often done from a drifting boat. An important part of it is chumming, which attracts sharks to the boat. Here we see a chum bag (at left), a tackled baitfish (above right), and a mako shark about to be boarded (below right).

Below: The principles of drift-fishing. On one side of the boat, a chum bag hangs in the water to lay an attractive slick of fish debris. The tackle is laid out on the boat's windward side to fish at various depths by means of large floats.

The hammerhead shark can be found both far off the coast—often as large individuals—and as smaller species staying in shallow water, notably near rock coasts, skerries and reefs.

Tuna fishing

There are several species of tuna, the most common being bonito, albacore, bigeye and yellowfin, and bluefin among others. The tuna is an eternal migrant or hunter. Lacking an air bladder, it is forced to swim from birth until death. Usually it forms shoals, with the exception of bluefish tuna which, most of the time, are on their own or together with a few family members.

The tuna hunts in the upper water layers and takes smaller fishes, which it chases to the surface. Here the tuna shoals are revealed by diving seagulls. Under such circumstances, the tuna is on a frantic hunt, and takes both artificial and natural baits. On grounds, underwater slopes, and other areas where the tuna hunts, it can be taken on live bait which is fished in deep water, for instance 50–100 metres. Also trolling with artificial baits can persuade the fish to take. Since tuna have only small teeth, all trolling leaders are of nylon monofilament line with a breaking strain around 50–200 kg. The commonest for tuna weighing around 50–150 kg is a breaking strain of 100–150 kg.

Tuna are attracted to the boat particularly by Japanese feather jigs or other colourful baits, which skate in the surface and make a good "smoke". Sometimes several tuna are attracted to the

Trolling with artificial or natural bait is the commonest way of attracting tuna to strike. It is also the most rewarding method for various species of billfish.

lures and, at the same time, it is common to troll four baits behind the boat. The tuna takes smaller jigs, and the odds are better if a teaser or attractor is placed above the bait.

Fishing for billfish

These species consist of black, blue, white and striped marlin, spearfish and swordfish. The species appear in subtropical and tropical waters, except that swordfish can also be met in the temperate zones.

Not only are all of the billfish extremely powerful, but some are splendid jumpers when newly hooked.

The various marlin species can be caught on live bait from a drifting or anchored boat, but the commonest method is trolling. For blue and black marlin, trolling takes place with a rigged fish like mullet, mackerel, bonito, dolphin, bonefish or smaller tuna. The artificial baits are usually large konaheads, knuckleheads, flatnose lures or similar types. Sometimes, in pure excitement and hunger, the fish attacks smaller baits such as jigs and small softheads which are normally picked out, for example, for white marlin or sailfish.

Striped marlin is often taken on medium-sized or smaller baits. The white marlin usually takes small jigs, softheads, or rigged slices of fish or small fishes such as ballyhoo. There are several species of spearfish, but these are a rare and accidental catch.

Another member of the billfish family, the swordfish, although probably widespread in all the world's oceans, has always been harder to catch than marlin or sailfish on sport fishing tackle because it lives in very deep water. But recently pioneering sportsmen from New York to Florida, as well as in southern California, have discovered new techniques to catch giants by drift-fishing far from shore on calm nights. But sometimes it appears in the surface. It is then called a sunbathing fish and may take a lure which was actually chosen for a marlin. The same happens with a rigged bait such as mackerel. A speciality developed by the Americans is casting with live natural baits for sunbathing swordfish, and this method has already yielded many fish.

Night fishing for swordfish in 40–100 metres of water has proved to be the most effective method. Dead or living bait, for instance squid, is fitted with a cyalume stick, or injected with a luminous chemical fluid. This is because the swordfish seems to have extraordinary night vision and responds to bait which emits light in the water.

The sailfish—characterized by its enormous dorsal fin, the sail—is usually caught on surface skating lures, but also on small rigged natural baits: fish either whole or in pieces or slices, fitted to a jig or other small lure. Both marlin and sailfish may follow the lures for hundreds of metres or more. Sailfish in particular do so, and their curiosity is what makes it possible to attract them

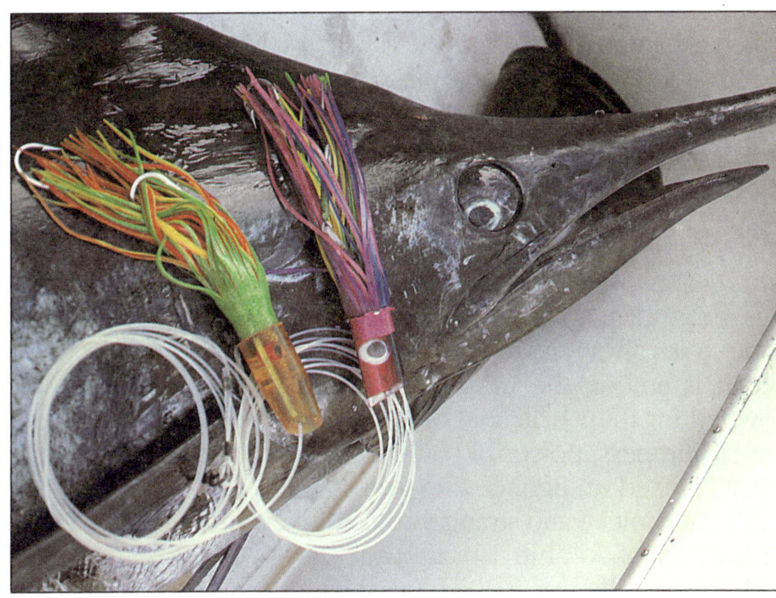

Shown below at left is a rigged mullet. At right are some types of artificial bait, primarily for billfish. Above is a newly caught marlin.

close to the boat and use the bait and tackle you prefer. This sometimes applies to the white marlin as well.

The billfish has, instead of sharp teeth, small rasping teeth on its bill. Consequently, a wire leader need not be used for the fish. Most anglers use leaders of nylon monofilament line. Only in waters with other species, such as wahoo, barracuda or mako shark, is a wire leader used—mainly piano wire. The breaking strain of a nylon monofilament leader should be around 100–300 kilos for black and blue marlin, and 50–100 kilos for white marlin and sailfish.

A couple of decades ago, most of the trolling lures for billfish were rigged with a single hook, resulting in the loss of many strikes. Today the rig has been developed and, instead of one single hook, it is better to place two single hooks in the lures, one of which is hanging freely. It is fitted with a several-stranded or single-stranded wire or nylon monofilament line, and is adjusted in order to ensure that the bait's movements in the water are satisfactory.

Other species

Wherever two or more serious fisherman gather in America, debate soon turns to what exactly *is* the greatest game fish of all. Some votes always go to the dolphin fish, *Coryphaena hippuras*, which is among the most exquisite of all game species. Renowned for their brilliant colouration, they are swift and spectacular jumpers, powerful battlers on any tackle, but especially when hooked on light casting gear.

It is a primitive and strangely beautiful experience to encounter a school of dolphin fish far out at sea. Moving closer you spot dark shadows darting in the blue water below you. Troll or cast a lure—any lure—toward the shadows and lightning will strike at once. Dolphin fish strike savagely, without hesitation and immediately catapult into the air.

But a myriad other game species inhabit lagoons, beaches, estuaries and rivers where sleek charterboats and costly tackle are not necessary to pursue them. In subtropical and tropical waters king mackerel, wahoo, and large barracuda can also be tempted to take. The wahoo is considered to be the fastest fish in the world. In shallow water near the coast, there is sometimes an opportunity of catching bluefish, dolphin and other species. Give these a go if you get a chance and they are present—all such species are grand fighters if they are caught on the right tackle.

The take, strike, and fight

After many hours on the sunny sea, the silence is broken by a marlin or tuna which suddenly makes the reel drag scream aloud. In that instant the fight begins. The crew has to rewind the other lines and the skipper manoeuvres the boat in an accurate interaction between the angler and the fish. No fish is landed without skilled teamwork on board, from the moment when the fish takes the bait until when it is gaffed or perhaps released. To a great extent, the skipper's and crew's skills are what determine the day's catch.

The fight with smaller species can be carried out while standing with a harness or shoulder-harness, for example with tackle of 30–50 lbs (15–24 kg). This is an exciting challenge but requires good weather. Larger species call for a fighting chair. In some places, the fish has to be released and the skipper is a master at manoeuvring the boat close to the fish, in order to free the hook and let the fish regain its freedom. A fish cannot survive if it is released after a long-lasting fight. The key to the fight is unvarying pressure on the fish, while you let the tackle do the hard work and you have the knowledge of using the reel drag, as well as knowing the fundamental techniques and the breaking strain of the line.

The big game fish of the sea may take many hours to strike—but when they do, everything must go right, down to the last detail.

Good teamwork is required to give the fight a happy conclusion.

Registration of records

The registration of a record is important for every fishing centre and skipper, due to the perspectives of advertising a good and productive fishing location. The international angling organization IGFA operates on a world-wide basis with record registration. If a record fish is to be approved, it must be caught, fought, weighed, and shown to meet the outer conditions and rules drawn up by IGFA. Application forms and information can be obtained from the organization's home address: IGFA, 3000 East Las Olas Boulevard, Fort Lauderdale, Florida 33316, U.S.A. If you are a supporter and member of IGFA, you also support the development of modern sea angling and contribute to the preservation of the species in the salty environment.

The dream of the really big catch has been fulfilled. Now the fish need only be boarded, weighed, and possibly reported as a record to the IGFA.

Birds and fish

Not even one percent of the world's sea surface is visited by anglers. The fishable parts of the oceans seem particularly enormous when you set out on them, and sometimes you cannot stop wondering whether it is possible to find the fish out there. But if the skipper, crew, and angler are attentive to all the signals which indicate fish in the water, you have a good chance.

Sea maps show grounds and banks near the coast where the current runs, carrying cold or hot water and food. These are usually excellent spots. Whirlpools normally form good conditions for either warm or cold water which attract different species. A lot of species prefer the warmest water, and modern boats are commonly equipped with water-temperature gauges because only a slight change in the water temperature determines whether the fish is present or not.

Most important are the seagulls and other birds—scouts of the ocean which are constantly on the lookout for something to eat. The ocean might look quite empty and dead, but in fact it is more than just alive. Suddenly the first gull arrives, then others follow and start to attack the surface, taking the smaller fish which the big carnivorous species chase up from the depths. The big ones are what interest us. Always use your eyes at sea, and several pairs of eyes are better than a single pair, though the skipper and crew should have hawk's eyes on the ocean.

Seasickness and clothing

Next to fishing madness, the worst disorder you face is seasickness. Against this, some general rules and reliable medicine are the following. Get plenty of sleep before the expedition. Avoid alcohol, coffee, and bitter drinks such as lemon juice. Drink sweetened juice instead. Eat lightly but often. Bring sweet fruits. Get some fresh air from time to time and keep yourself occupied. Avoid the smell of smoke and diesel. If seasickness begins, try to think of something else. Seasickness tablets are a comfort for some people, but do not take any tablets which you have not tried before, since some brands have side-effects such as attacks of weariness. Quite a few sea anglers have fallen fast asleep and missed the whole expedition after taking a couple of tablets. If you are used to a certain brand of tablet, stick to it.

As regards clothing, I recommend that you use "thermo" clothing in colder climates. Instead of one thick pullover, use a number of thinner items in cold weather. It is the air between the individual layers that insulates and keeps you warm. Also bring hot drinks like soup or tea, and plenty of digestible food.

In southerly regions, it is important to protect yourself against the sun and heat. Polaroid glasses, sun-tan oil with a high sun factor, and a cap are all essential aids. Also bring a T-shirt, and a shirt or thin jacket with long sleeves for protecting your arms against the sun. In the tropics, the best fishing apparel is a light, airy set of "pyjamas" which protects the body from the sun. Bear in mind that sunbeams are twice as strong at sea as on land, because of the water's reflections. This indirect radiation is quite high.

Fly-fishing

To describe fly-fishing merely as a very successful method of catching fish would hardly express the "specialness" of this type of fishing. It would be equally superficial to see in fly-fishing only the elegance of the sport. Certainly, the floating lightness of a perfect cast is elegant, and the seeming weightlessness of flying lines is an aesthetic sight. But there is much more to the concept of fly-fishing and to its deeper essence.

Fly-fishing is the most natural way of fishing in the world—it takes part in the processes of nature. A fly-fisherman closely observes what is happening in the water. Thus he acquires an insight into the rules of nature and learns how to get along with them. He relies on a phenomenon which is widely developed in nature and is played upon in ever-changing variation, namely illusion. He makes use of extremely varied works of mimicry: his "flies" imitate the familiar forms by which fish recognize their prey. His knowledge of the patterns of nature is therefore the basis of his success.

How far back in time the roots of this type of fishing stretch, we can only guess. The first primitive attempts at catching fish with feathers and hair-covered bone hooks were ancient. But do they go all the way back to the earliest beginnings of fishing with hooks? The use of the fly-rod was already well known to the Macedonians, who were described by Claudius Aelianus in the first century A.D. For them, such fishing had already outgrown its elementary purpose of catching fish.

Ever since then, fly-fishing has occupied a strong position in the sport of angling. By the time it reappeared in the "Treatise on Fyshinge wyth an Angle", written in 1496 by the legendary Dame Juliana Berners, fly-fishing in England had already changed its character to fishing for pleasure and become a sport for gentlemen. Occasionally, other and even older fragmentary accounts from the dim history of Central Europe have come to light about fishing with the "feather-rod" and its refinement.

Generations of anglers have ardently devoted themselves to fishing with the fly-rod and pondered over what they were doing. With almost scientific earnest, they have followed the many-faceted life of the water and studied the fundamentals of their passion. Our modern-day fly-fishing culture is the sum of the collected enthusiasm of centuries. With its store of wisdom in numerous publications, its sensitive portrayals of nature, and its nearly confessional autobiographies, fly-fishing now has at its disposal a unique gold-mine of literature.

Fly-fishing first bloomed, without a doubt, in Great Britain. From England, the impulses spread—mainly in the last century—to bear fruit in many parts of the world. The English style influenced fly-fishing in the whole of Europe, and far into our own century. In North America, however, the development was stormy. In less than a hundred years, completely new styles arose, characterized by unconventional thinking but also by the influences of the landscape and rivers. This "American way of fly-fishing" has, on the other hand, long been fruitful for fishing and fly-tying in Europe, and has influenced the development in many other countries.

In Central Europe, fly-fishing has experienced its first real break-through in the last few decades. In Scandinavia, it has been undergoing an explosive expansion during the past decade. Still, only in Western Europe including France, Great Britain and Ireland is fly-fishing today popular in the truest sense of the word. In the British Isles, for example, two million anglers, especially in quiet waters, take advantage of every chance to pursue this beloved sport. The majority of European anglers remain rather reserved towards fly-fishing.

In Central Europe, where the possibilities are restricted by high population density, water regulation and pollution, not even the waters with salmonoid fish are used solely for fly-fishing. The basic reason for this is a nearly insurmountable obstacle, which makes the average angler uncertain: fly-fishing is generally considered to be both complicated and expensive.

Fly-fishing is not only easy to learn, but also a very natural way of approaching fish with imitations of their food—all sorts of insects that live in or near water.

How could such an idea have arisen?

For one thing, fly-fishing has always been surrounded by an aura of exclusiveness—not because of any "elitism" among fly-fishermen, but simply due to their enthusiasm for the sport. Perhaps their abundant literature has been interpreted wrongly—anything about which so much has been written must be terribly complicated . . . But that would be a special kind of irony, for nothing could help the novice at fly-fishing more than does its collection of fundamental knowledge and practical information.

Fly-fishing means watching, stalking and lying in ambush, which presupposes the virtues of the hunter: alert senses, self-control and the ability to react. It is an active, creative type of angling, which offers everything one could ask of sportfishing—excitement, playful casting motions and breath-taking battles. It is an immediate, intensive experience of nature and anyone who once gets caught up in it soon becomes enthralled.

Possibly more than any other type of sportfishing, fly-fishing can be cultivated and pursued like an art. But its basic techniques and tactics are no harder to learn than any other method of fishing. In order to fly-fish with pleasure, you need be neither especially talented nor rich. You need only a genuine interest in nature and a moderate ability to become enthused. In a word, you need to be a fisherman.

Modern fly-fishing

Anyone who has not yet tried fly-fishing will be surprised by how varied fishing with the "flying lines" can be. Today as in the past, the salmon-type (salmonoid) fish are the focus of fly-fishing techniques and tactics. With wet and dry flies and nymphs, however, not only can trout, grayling, Arctic char and other salmonoids be caught, but many other types of fish as well. If bucktails, streamers or muddlers of the right size are added to the list, then the number of fish-types can be further enlarged to include even the true predators, like perch and pike.

Fly-fishing for salmon, which has been a classic domain for years, will not be included here but, because of its importance, is dealt with in Chapter 7. Likewise, the type of saltwater fly-fishing especially popular on the American coasts is discussed in Chapter 6. We shall first take up fishing with wet flies, dry flies, pupae, nymphs, and streamers. The division into these categories has generally been accepted, but is probably rather arbitrary. Even though they can rather easily be kept separate, the patterns—like the fishing techniques—necessarily overlap to some extent.

Such topics are avidly discussed by true fly-fishermen, particularly when discussing the definition of fly-fishing. There are many who, in their eagerness, tend to interpret fly-fishing a little too narrowly, arguing that fly-fishing is fishing with imitations of flies. Imitations of other types of food important to fish, such as minnows, amphibians, leeches and other large fantasy patterns, are not "flies" but "lures", and fishing with such large patterns cannot be considered fly-fishing.

Although water insects certainly contributed to the early development of fly-fishing, and are still by far the most important today, fishing with streamers cannot be disregarded from the ranks of fly-fishing. Besides, the size of the patterns is no criterion at all. Life-sized imitations of, for example, stone fly nymphs belonging to the European dinocras or perlode species, or the huge "hellgrammites" of the Western part of America, are larger than many streamers. Wet-fly patterns of stone flies are, by the way, genuine classics: they were referred to by Dame Juliana Berners as early as 1496. The definition of our flies, however, is concerned with quite different qualities.

If the many fundamentally different types of flies are compared with each other—from a tiny midge pattern to a voluminous pike-streamer— their common character becomes clearer. All true fly patterns are similar in two important respects. They are built up, taking into consideration their optical attraction and function due to their silhouettes, colours and movements. Secondly, they are so light that they can be just cast out, using a special fly-line and an appropriate fly-rod.

With this definition it is easy to rule out the kinds of bait that lack these characteristics. That is, lead-headed jigs covered by feathers and hair, which could just as easily be used with a light spinning rod. Seen soberly, this kind of fishing has as little to do with fly-fishing as tying a fly on water-filled casting bubbles or on a sideplaner.

In fly-fishing, the featherweight fly is cast with the help of the weight of the line. And it is fishing with such flies, in combination with a fly-rod and fly-fishing line, that constitutes fly-fishing. Nothing else! Modern fly-fishing should, perhaps, rather be called "fly-line fishing", with reference to the "flying lines", as the archaic German terms "Flugangeln" and "Flugschnur" remind us.

Fishing with wet fly

Fishing with wet flies is the oldest form of fly-fishing. Long before the first attempts to fish with dry flies, which float on the surface, wet flies were common. So many old patterns have been handed down to us that the collection in Ronald's book, *Fly Fisher's Entomologie* (1836), seems almost modern. Considering the ability of these old English patterns to catch fish, they have lost none of their value even today. Not a few of today's sportfishermen, on both sides of the Atlantic, take particular pleasure in fishing with these classics.

Wet-fly fishing is as effective as it is interesting. No wonder, for salmonoids in most waters satisfy 80% of their nutritional needs under the water surface. Many cyprinoids feed entirely underwater. Over the years, modern nymph fishing in Continental Europe and North America has replaced the traditional method of fishing with wet flies. In Great Britain and Ireland, however, wet-fly fishing, especially in the lochs, is as popular as ever.

Fly-fishermen have constantly tried to make their patterns imitate the many distinctive stages of life seen in water insects and small crustaceans. Especially attractive are the soft and less jagged flies which move in the water in a way that makes them look alive. The most successful fishermen use flies which, in size and shape, most closely resemble the season's most abundant food source. There are relatively innocuous "all-round" types which are always worth trying. Wet flies are sometimes mistaken by fish for drowning land insects.

In running water, wet flies are mostly used alone, just under the surface of the water or deep down. In the classic style, they are cast across the stream and fished downstream. It is important that they be allowed to freely follow the stream and then, at the end of their drift, be brought gently back using the "wet-fly swing". It is recommended that each cast be completely fished out, as it is often in the last phase that the fish takes the fly. It can be very exciting to offer the fish a fly that is cast upstream, a technique that requires a good eye and quick reflexes.

In shallow water it is best to fish with floating line, while for

Wet flies often give the best chance of getting a bite, since 80% of the fish feed under the water surface. The soft-feathered flies fish best when they drift freely in running water, or are retrieved slowly with small jerks in a lake.

deeper water a sink-tip or a sinking line is better suited. A rod with good action, 8–10 feet (2.5–3 meters) long, and a line class of 5 to 6, best fulfill the requirements for guiding the fly and handling the line.

In still waters, wet flies are presented with active movements. After the cast, they are moved only slowly, perhaps with some small jerking motions. To fish deeper pools, sinking line is used as well. For large, open water surfaces, a rod more than 9 ft (2.7 m) long should be used. Flies fished near the surface allow a taking fish to be seen easily, as it often breaks the surface of the water at that point. When the swell becomes apparent, the hook has to be set by carefully, but firmly, lifting the tip of the rod and stretching the line at the same time. In deeper waters, a nibble is felt as an uncertain tug or as a definite jerk, and the fish can then be hooked in the same way. In fishing downstream, the fish often hooks itself.

Fishing with dry fly

Fishing with dry flies is attractive to most fly-fishermen. For many, this is simply "fly-fishing". The reason for its popularity is obvious. Everything that happens while fishing with dry flies, from the service to the take, happens out in the open. This appeals to our visual orientation as beings—we are "eye animals". In addition, there is a bit of a game in it, with excitement and a great deal of show appeal. Dry-fly fishing is elegant and entertaining, and has all the advantages that any method of angling could offer. One can soon become addicted to it!

In spite of all this, it is not necessarily the most difficult form of fly-fishing. Where the cast should land is easy to see, and a faulty serve is discovered immediately. Provided that the fisherman has a good knowledge of insects, the preferences of the fish are not hard to adjust to. The initial motivation for dry-fly fishing was observation of the activity on the surface of the water. The insect world's various stages of development and, especially, the life cycles of aquatic insects have set their marks on the flies and tactics used in dry-fly fishing. Constantly dealing with these problems has certainly promoted interest in entomology among fly-fishermen.

Dry-fly fever broke out in the middle of the last century in the chalk streams of Hampshire. This method was first described by George Pulman in his *Vade Mecum of Fly Fishing for Trout* (1841). Dry flies from that period are known through James Ogden, who was considered a leading expert on tying dry flies during the early epoch. Within fifty years, dry-fly fishing had reached its full flowering in southern England. Next it became a cult in the wake of Halford's book, *Floating Flies and How to Dress Them*. This, in turn, inspired Theodore Gordon, who founded the American school of dry-fly fishing and initiated the dry fly's triumphant march into his part of the world.

In the nearly 150-year history of the dry fly, its innumerable and enthusiastic followers have refined this kind of fishing and invented new variations. Midge imitations—tied with down to No. 28 hooks—on the one hand, and large dry flies for pike and bass, on the other, show the breadth of variation. Because of the differing landscapes and kinds of fish and insects, adapted patterns and styles have arisen. But the general principle of dry-fly fishing is simple: fish that rise up to the drifting insects on the surface of the water are offered artificial flies. The classic example is when the fisherman has identified the natural insects being taken

Dry-fly fishing enables one to follow the whole process of how fish take, thus adding much to the method's excitement. By studying the insects that fish prefer, one can easily get an idea of which patterns best make the fish rise.

and, with a corresponding imitation, lures the fish in its hunt for food.

The more closely an artificial fly—and even the method of presenting it—correspond to its model, the quicker it is taken. The presence of insects on the surface of the water depends, to a large part, on definite stages of the aquatic insects' life cycle. At the end of their larval stage, the nymphs come to the surface of the water, where they shed their casings in order to complete their life cycle as winged insects. When ready to lay eggs, they return to the water. Fish will rise to both the hatching and spawning insect. Even terrestrial insects that fall into the water are readily taken by the fish. In many areas, precisely these are of great importance for dry-fly fishing, especially in the western United States. There are, indeed, many flies which take their patterns from terrestrials.

The ideal circumstances exist when the fish are active on the surface of the water. When there are no rings on the surface, proven parts of the river can be tried on chance. But the pattern must then float well, and be offered either on the surface or sunk just under it. Floating line with a long leader should be used.

In running water, flies are usually presented up or across the stream. This is also the best way to approach rising fish without being seen. The fly is placed upstream and allowed to freely drift down towards the position of the fish. Everything depends on a very exact cast, correct drift and, naturally, the right choice of the fly. The choice is better made by observing the insects in the water than by trying out different patterns.

The stage between the cast and the rising of the fish is the most exciting part of this kind of fishing. Will the fish rise? If it rises, will it take the fly? If it does, then a not too energetic tug on the line is in order. A stretched line is often enough for the diving fish to hook itself firmly.

For dry-fly fishing, depending on the depth of the water and the type of bottom, a rod of 7–9 ft (2–2.7 m), in AFTM-class 4 to 6, is best suited. By using the lightest classes of line, the most discrete casts are achieved. These lines, are, however, much more affected by the wind, so fishermen who have not quite mastered their use should use heavier lines to begin with.

Catching fish with dry flies is scarcely a Herculean task. Anyone able to cast out around 10 yds (m) of line can learn to do it in a few hours. Achieving great proficiency is a long, yet fascinating, process.

Fishing with nymph

Fishing with nymphs is by far and away the most exacting, thrilling, and effective method of fly-fishing. Still, it is often misunderstood, mastered by few fly-fishermen, and thus practiced in a primitive manner.

Nymphs imitate the pupae or nymphs of aquatic insects. Strictly speaking, they represent the aquatic part of the life cycle of the mayfly or sedge fly and its form at the time of hatching. Imitations of other kinds of related mayflies, as well as of other two-winged insects, can be used. Even all sorts of water beetles (amphipoda) can be used. In fishing with nymphs, the most important point is not which species is being imitated, but that a correct, naturalistic

When fishing with nymphs, a correct presentation is often more important than the pattern used. It is essential to bring home the fly in the way that insects naturally move.

copy of the species is presented. Whether the fish then "misunderstand" our imaginative but necessarily imperfect imitations is, of course, another matter!

Fishing with nymphs started at about the same time as dry-fly fishing. The initiative was taken by G. E. M. Skues in the southern English town of Itchen. There he discovered that brown trout, extremely hard to catch, were partial to the hatching mayfly nymphs which drifted just below the surface of the water.

In 1895, Skues began to experiment with casting wet flies upstream, and gradually reduced them to the first modern nymphs. Over forty different, strictly imitative, nymph patterns can be traced back to him. He described his nymph technique for catching trout just under the water surface in various prominent publications, such as *Nymph Fishing for Chalkstream Trout*. Ernest Schwiebert, one of the great American nymph fishermen of the younger generation, emphasises in his mammoth work, *Trout*, the fruitful correspondence between Skues and James Leisenring, the man who gave American nymph fishing its first important impetus. Another Englishman, Frank Sawyer, was able to introduce to European nymph fishermen in the 1950s a completely different, yet brilliant technique for deep-water fish. Sawyer's patterns were lightly weighted, but even he consistently fished only when he could see the fish. He thought of reducing a few nymph types to their most elementary imitative fly forms, which perfectly matched the requirements for this type of fishing. His "Pheasant Tail", the classic mayfly type, is among the most fished nymphs in Europe today.

In fishing nymphs, depending on the type and activity of the fish, the patterns are fished just below the surface of the water, in midwater or just above the bottom. Presenting the fish with patterns that match the behaviour of their models is essential. In running water, this means drifting or with some slight movement—but never unnaturally pulled against the stream. In still water, however, nymphs are drawn like wet flies.

The most elegant way to present the fly to a "nymphing" fish is up or across the stream. For fish taking nymphs just under, and the fly presented on, the surface, the take can easily be seen: the fish exposes itself quite clearly. When fishing the middle layers, a very well-trained eye is needed to see the take, even under the most favourable conditions. When fishing nymphs deep in the water, the take can only be sensed by a nudge on the line or when the tip of the line stops. Then the hook has to be set at once.

Near the surface or in the middle layers, nymphs should be fished on floating lines. Special nymph-tip lines make it easier to see the take. For deeper waters, a sink-tip line is recommended, even though the take can be harder to notice with this kind of line. Sinking line should only be used for lake fishing, where the line is continuously taken in, allowing for constant contact with the nymph, thereby making it easier to feel the take.

There are also a number of presentation techniques with float-

Fishing with a streamer is an old method of imitating small fish and other, larger prey. Above at right are two streamers from the 1730s, used by Lapp fishermen in the Arjeplog mountains of Sweden.

ing line for deep water. But real depth can only be achieved by using extremely long leaders and heavily weighted nymphs. This presupposes, however, an absolute control over the line, and much experience is needed to feel the take under these circumstances. This type of fishing with weighted nymphs seems to be a special type of wet-fly fishing, rather than real nymph fishing.

A sensitive rod at least 8 ft (2.4 m) long, and line in class 4 to 5, are best suited to nymph fishing. A line that is as light as possible helps to achieve a discrete presentation and unhindered drift. In still waters, however, this aspect is meaningless.

Nymph fishing can be the most elegant and artful form of fly-fishing. Depending on his style and how the nymph is fished, a fly-fisherman's skill and sportsmanship are readily revealed.

Fishing with streamer

Streamer fishing is often thought to be a new kind of fly-fishing. But older patterns are known which imitate larger fish. They come from fishermen who had no access to metal and, therefore, arduously fashioned hooks from bone or horn. Such ancient streamers have come down to us from many different parts of the world. Fishermen in the mountainous regions of Swedish Lappland, 250 years ago, were still using extremely simple feather-clad "streamers" tied to hooks of reindeer horn. These ancient minnow imitations were still used 150 years ago to catch large brown trout in the roaring rivers near the Arctic Circle at the same time as fishermen in western Sweden were catching Atlantic salmon with sophisticated English salmon flies.

Other prototypes of streamers are known from New Zealand. The Maori were fishing with feather-clad bone hooks long before Europeans, at the end of the last century, had even brought trout and salmon to their islands. It is interesting that streamer fishing in the world-famous trout waters of New Zealand continued later with such distinction. Many extremely effective modern streamers, for example the Matuka types, come from there.

Modern streamer fishing progressed primarily through the efforts of North American fly-fishermen. Thus, most of our patterns come from the New World. The popular Bucktail patterns can be traced back to the "Bumble Puppies", which Theodore Gordon developed around 1880 on the Neversink River. The fact that it was this same Gordon who laid the foundations for American dry-fly fishing is a well-known example of the openness and versatility of the American fly-fisherman.

The term "streamer fishing" is, to be sure, rather limiting. Today's outstretched streamers basically imitate only one small fish, or minnow, among the many contemporary large flies which vary enormously in their appearance and effectiveness. So, too, are many of the other patterns close imitations of natural prototypes—such as muddlers, sculpins, and leeches. There are, as well, pure fantasy flies which are effective merely due to their colours and movements. The boundaries are flexible.

The goal of streamer fishing is to catch fish species which feed on larger prey. Fishing with large patterns requires, therefore, special rods, line classes and leaders. Unweighted larger flies can be cast and fished without great difficulty only if the weight of the line can bear them and the rod is strong enough. Rods with good action and powerful tips from line class 7 and up are the most suitable for streamer fishing. The minimum rod length is 8 ft (2.4 m), but even longer rods are better. Depending on the type of water and method of presentation, floating lines, sinking tip lines, or sinking lines are fished.

In running water, streamers are fished according to which patterns are used and which type of fish is found on the surface, in the middle layers, or on the bottom. A suitable fly is served across or, perhaps, a little upstream, so that it can drift down, at the correct depth, towards the fish. By mending the line against the flow at the right time, a natural drift is achieved. Accented movements give the fly life. Large flies with life-like movements can yield good catches, even in still waters. Each cast is fished until the line is stretched out, and is then reeled in slowly against the current. If the fish cannot be seen, which is normally the case, then exact knowledge of their habitats is important. The best results are achieved when the fly is allowed to drift with the flow of the river down to the activity area of the fish, or when the fly is flopped down at just the right speed in front of the fish.

In still waters, the drift of the fly is easier to control. The fly is guided according to the temperament and behaviour of the fish in question—slowly or extremely fast. Often, the sound of the fly landing will cause fish to start biting.

Streamers and other large flies greatly expand fly-fishing's possibilities and open up areas which were barely fished before. When fishing for salmonoids, the streamer should only be used for the really big ones. In trout streams it is hardly worthwhile using such large flies except, perhaps, for unwanted predators. The negative attitude of many fly-fishermen towards streamer fishing is unwarranted. Responsible streamer fishing—or, more precisely, large fly-fishing of all kinds—has exactly the same qualities as any other kind of fly-fishing.

Equipment

In sportfishing circles, the opinion is still held that the equipment for fly-fishing should be both extensive and expensive. Like many other misconceptions about fly-fishing, this myth must be refuted. With two rods, two reels, an extra spool, five lines, various leaders and a few dozen kinds of flies, just about any situation can be met. It is only for salmon fishing or for large ocean fish that special complementary equipment is necessary. A good all-round outfit contains the following, in addition to a range of wet flies, dry flies, nymphs and streamers:

1 rod	7.5–8 ft (2.3–2.5 m)	AFTM line class 5
1 rod	8.5–9.5 ft (2.6–2.9 m)	AFTM line class 7/8
1 reel	1 extra spool	AFTM line class 5 and 40 meters backing line
1 reel	2 extra spools	AFTM line class 7/8 and 120 meters backing line

Shown here are some one-handed fly-rods made of split cane, with a traditional basket creel, net, and fly-box.

1 floating line	DT or WF	AFTM line class 5 and 40 meters backing line
1 sinking tip line	DT or WF	AFTM line class 5 and 40 meters backing line
1 floating line	DT or WF	AFTM line class 7 and 120 meters backing line
1 sinking tip line	DT or WF	AFTM line class 7 and 120 meters backing line
1 sinking line	DT or WF	AFTM line class 8 and 120 meters backing line
10 leaders	tips 0.16–0.35 mm	leader line

A wide assortment of fly-fishing tackle is available today. This does not make the choices easy for a beginner, and an expert should be consulted if there is any uncertainty. In the course of time, a standard has been attained, which—especially for rods and lines—could not have been dreamed of two decades ago. And with this tackle, which need not be the most expensive, beginning is not at all difficult.

Everyone, even those who only want to "give it a try", should be advised to stay away from really cheap equipment. Unsuitable "beginner's tackle" has doomed many a promising attempt at fishing with flies to failure. Good quality is to be recommended, and has the best value in the long run.

Ever since American tackle manufacturers agreed to standardize fly-lines and were able to get these AFTM-classes accepted throughout the world, combining tackle has become exceedingly easy. The manufacturers' recommendations need only be followed in order to match the line to the spool or vice versa. Elementary knowledge of the requirements a rod must fulfill is sufficient for putting together good fishing tackle.

Fly, leader, line, rod, and reel are the five elements that make up fly-fishing tackle. The requirements for being functional are easy to outline: the tackle must be suitable for its purpose, each individual part must reliably accomplish its task, and all parts must be balanced harmoniously in relation to each other.

Flies

The total number of types of flies being fished today, and whimsically tied wet flies, dry flies, nymphs, streamers and large flies, cannot possibly be surveyed—new patterns come into existence daily. The main principle of this fantastic creativity is infinite variation. Indeed, it is a challenge to ever more modifications. In order to realize their own ideas and observations, real fly-fishing enthusiasts tie their own fly-patterns.

Fly-patterns have been, and still are, an eternal theme for all fly-fishermen. Flies and their natural prototypes are, for fly-fishermen, at least as fascinating as the catch. Fly-imitations are manufactured completely by hand, and good flies are therefore expensive. Quality is always important in buying flies. Carelessly tied flies, or those made of unsuitable material, are rarely worth their cost when fished.

The hooks must be of the finest quality. If, for example, the steel is too hardened, there is a risk that they will break. This can already be noticed when bending down an unnecessary barb with fishing pliers. But if the steel is too soft, the hook can possibly straighten itself out when the fish is played. The gap of the hook must also be in correct proportion to the length of the point, so that good durability and hooking qualities are achieved. While long hook shafts make long, streamlined streamer forms possible, they give rise to extremely unfavourable levering effects when playing the fish.

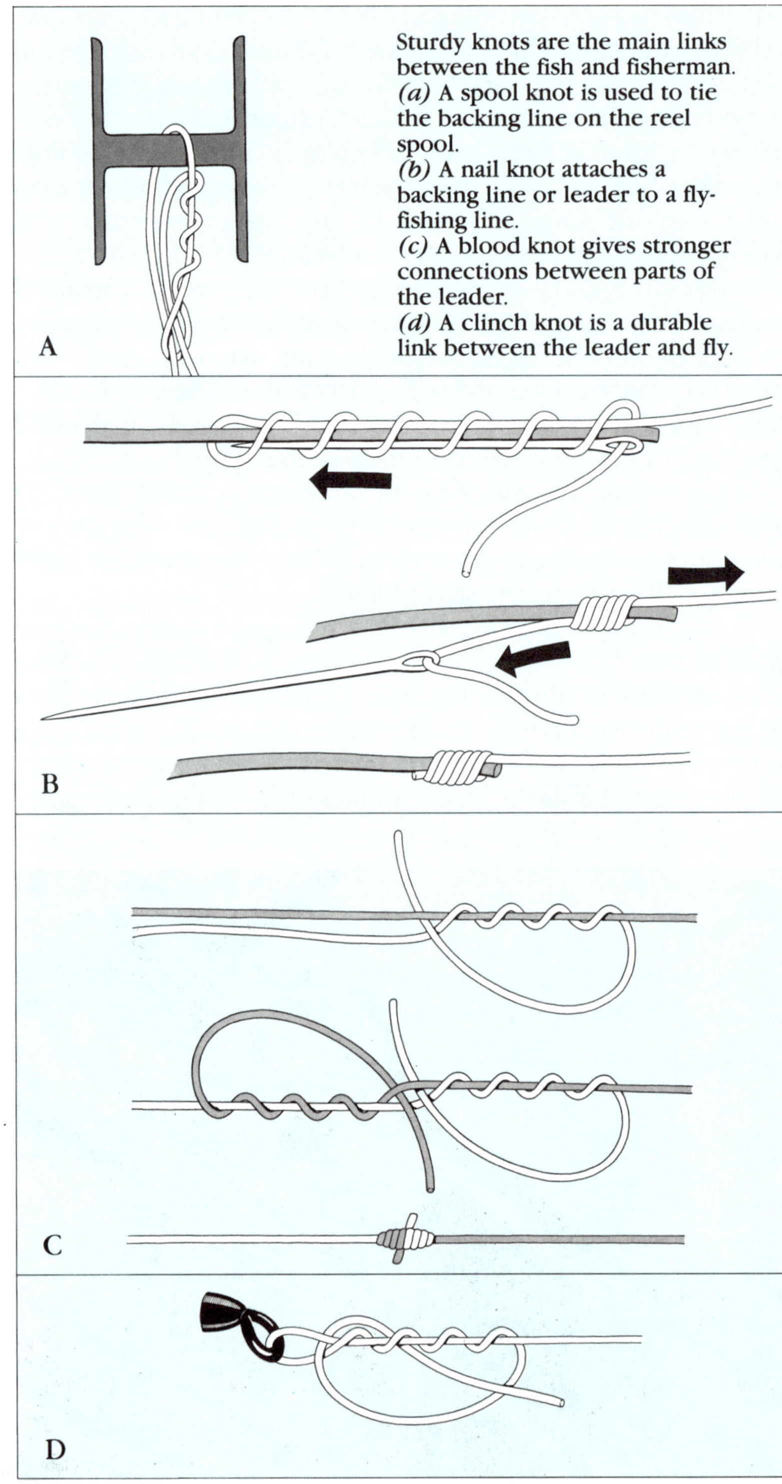

Sturdy knots are the main links between the fish and fisherman. *(a)* A spool knot is used to tie the backing line on the reel spool. *(b)* A nail knot attaches a backing line or leader to a fly-fishing line. *(c)* A blood knot gives stronger connections between parts of the leader. *(d)* A clinch knot is a durable link between the leader and fly.

The proportions of the fly—its wings, hackle, body and end lengths— must all be right. Imitating patterns must reproduce the characteristics of the prototypes. Dry flies must be able to be presented feather-light and float correctly. Wet fly patterns should sink quickly, without having large weights affecting their movements.

The effectiveness of flies is indeed, to a great extent, dependent on the conviction with which they are fished. But primarily it calls for a discerning method of tying, attentive to function and correct usage.

Leaders

The connection between fly and fly-line consists of the leader. Fly-leaders have a number of different functions. Especially for dry-fly fishing, they must be long enough to mask the relatively thick fly-lines. Their tips must be thin enough to present the fly but, at the same time, strong enough to manage a spirited battle. They must also be able to be cast well even when the wind is blowing, to roll over in harmony with the fly-line, and to be laid out either stretched or in an arc.

Today, nearly all leaders are built up within certain limits, according to a variable schedule. From the thicker upper parts, which provide a smooth transition to the tip of the fly-line, they taper in steps (smoothly, in the case of all knotless leaders) down to their thin tips. About 60–70% of the length of the leader consists of the stronger upper part, which conveys the power of the cast. The other 30–40% is split between the tapering part and the tip. The latter should be at least 50 cm (20 in) long for dry-fly fishing, preferably longer for wet-fly and nymph fishing.

Leaders can easily be tied as required by using sections of monofilament nylon line. The material used for leaders should be smooth and easily knotted, but under no circumstances should it be limp. Secure and lasting knots, which give good tapering, can be tied with sections that vary by 0.05 mm in diameter.

Leaders of 8 to 9 ft (2.4–2.8 m) can be used for most waters. Fly-casts (leaders), following the formula "Rafale", given by Charles Ritz over 30 years ago, are still to be recommended. The good qualities found in these types of leaders are hard to surpass, even for modern leaders.

Ready-made leaders are available in the most varied versions: pre-tied or knotless, flat monofil or in sections including braided line/leader connector, braided butt section, and tippet. The advantage of braided leaders lies in their greater flexibility and even more delicate unwinding. Their disadvantage is a certain delicacy and, if self-tied, their complicated construction.

Leader tips must always be adapted to the size of the fly. With patterns under hook-size 16, if a flexible rod is used, lines as small as 0.12 mm can be used. If larger fish are to be caught, then, for the sake of sportsmanship, leader tips smaller than 0.18 mm should not be used. For wet-fly fishing with larger patterns (hook-size 8 to 4), a simple, suitably strong length of monofil will suffice as a leader. When fishing with sink-tip or sinking line an extremely short leader can be advantageous. In this way, the fly is reliably brought down nearer to the bottom by the deeply sinking tip.

In spite of the fact that it has recently become fashionable to glue the upper end of the leader to the tip of the fly-line, or the fly-line to the hollow braided end of the leader, a simple knot is still an unbeatable method of linking line and leader. To the tip of the line, an approximately 12-in (30-cm) length of 0.45-mm monofil line is knotted, and then the desired leader. If this length becomes too short through constant changing, a new one is tied on. This is easily accomplished, even while fishing. The "improved clinch" is the best knot to use for fly-fishing. It is easy to tie as well, and is completely reliable.

Fly-lines

In fly-casting, the type of line is of vital importance. It is what gives the casting weight and is, therefore, a vehicle of transport for the fly. So that fly-lines can move elegantly, be held up in the air and be cast accurately, they must be built up in a special manner. Their profiles are tapered according to the laws of aerodynamics.

Modern fly-lines are the result of decades of experiment and research. They should cast extremely well, cut through the air, roll up without any problem and, because of their smooth surface, have good projectability. While fly-fishermen were opening up new fishing waters and territories, fly-lines were continually being improved upon. At the same time that all-purpose line was being developed, many special-purpose lines arose, which make it possible for the modern fly-fisherman to appropriately outfit himself for any kind of fishing.

Fly-lines are manufactured according to AFTM-standards, in fifteen different weight classes. The classes, meaning the casting weights, for all lines are determined by weighing the outermost 30 ft (9.14 m). Lines up to class 3 are extremely light and are only usable for the finest kinds of fishing on windless days. Classes 4 to 6 cover most normal dry-fly and wet-fly fishing needs. For streamer fishing, a somewhat heavier line is recommended, which allows perfect casting even with large flies. Classes 10 to 15 are used for salmon and large, saltwater fish.

The casting characteristics of fly-lines depend on their profiles, or tapering:
(a) **Level line.**
(b) **Double-taper line.**
(c) **Weight-forward line.**
(d) **Saltwater-taper line.**
(e) **Shooting-head line.**

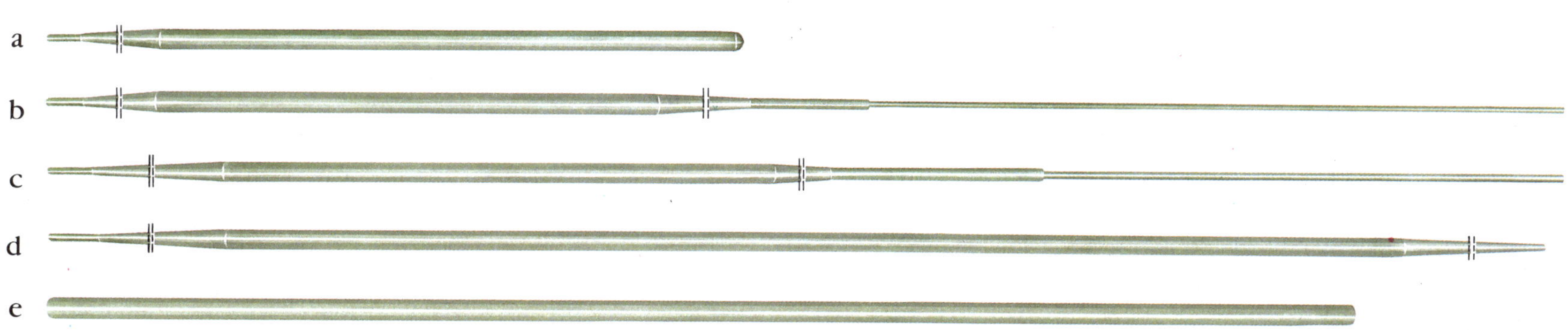

If the old-fashioned "level line" is disregarded, there are two main types of line: double-taper line (DT) which narrows down at both ends, and weight-forward line (WF). The DT-line has an even calibre through the middle, which tapers down to a tip at both ends. This narrowing towards a tip not only provides the transition to the leader, but is important for casting and for insuring that the fly will land delicately and precisely. Because of its symmetric construction, a DT-line can simply be reversed when one end is worn out. This type of line, being easy to cast, is among the most popular.

On WF-lines, the casting weight is concentrated to a limited area at the front end of the line. The tip of the line merges into this 26-ft (8-m) long belly, which tapers off to a thin shooting line. WF-lines were developed primarily for long casts. There are many different variations of WF-line. Lines with very concentrated weight up front (bass and saltwater tapers) are especially good for fishing large, wind-sensitive flies. Lines with extremely extended belly (WFL = long belly) function like DT-lines for short casts, but have the advantages of WF-line for long casts. Shooting lines (ST = shooting taper), finally, are simply projectile-like lengths of line, which are fastened directly to special shooting lines and are used for long-distance fishing.

For dry-fly fishing, as well as wet-fly and nymph fishing in shallow water, floating lines (FL = floating line) are used. For deeper waters, lines with tips that sink (F/S = floating/sinking line) or purely sinking lines (S = sinking line) are used. Compared with the latter, the many types of sink-tip line offer significant advantages. Inasmuch as they are available with sinking tips of different lengths, targeted fishing is possible, even at greater depths, while they are also easily controlled because of the floating-line parts. F/S and S-lines come in different sinking classes; slowly sinking lines are suitable only for still waters. The faster the water flows, the faster the line must sink.

We should also say a few words about the colour of the lines. During the cast and drift, light-coloured lines are much easier to follow than discrete darker-coloured ones. Floating lines and the floating parts of sink-tip lines must be easily seen, even under bad lighting conditions. And this is important for successful fishing! Any imagined fright effects on the part of light-coloured lines can safely be disregarded.

Fly-lines are nearly always 27–30 yards (25–27 meters) long. Even though the whole length is seldom completely used and is long enough for most fights, all lines are attached with a backing line, as well. This reserve line also functions as filling on the reel, so that the fly-line is not wound in too tight coils.

Monofil backing line must be avoided as it has a tendency to get tangled up. Braided Dacron is better suited, as it is, despite its small diameter, quite strong and durable as well. A long running fish must absolutely be played from the reel. Dacron line, taken in by hand and allowed to fall loosely on the ground, usually tangles itself into an unmanageable clump which is impossible to disentangle and often leads to the loss of a hard-running fish. The best type of backing line is synthetic coated Dacron line. This material is somewhat thicker, however, and takes up more room on the reel.

The fly-rod is not only for fighting fish in a sporting manner, but also for casting out line softly and correctly. A fly-fishing rod is thus the chief piece of gear, and must be chosen with great care.

Fly-rods

The fly-rod is a casting tool, which functions as an extended arm in the placement of the cast line when casting out the fly. It is, moreover, a fighting tool in the battle against a hooked fish. As a casting tool, its job is to convey the motive energy to the line without vibration. The rod must be able to smooth out all of the irregular forces which accompany the action of casting, so that the line reels out smoothly and can land in the desired spot. It must also be sensitive, so that even delicate impulses can be transmitted and received—yet it must be strong enough to bear the calculated line class, while being able to stand up to the fight.

Until the mid-1950s, fly-rods were exclusively made of bamboo by the split-cane technique. Since then, synthetic rods have taken over the market. After a brief heyday of solid and tubular fibreglass rods, an era of "high-tech" fibres was introduced by graphite rods, a development which is still expanding rapidly today. Thanks to these materials, ever more advanced manufacturing methods and tapering fly-rods have appeared. Their action, strength and damping ability leave nothing to be desired, while turning casting into child's play. Each rod bears information as to which AFTM-classes can be used, which makes it much easier to put together useful, harmonious equipment.

With the development of artificial fibres, it seemed that the age of beautiful, hand-made bamboo rods was gone forever. But in the last few years, split-cane rods have experienced a veritable renaissance. In central Europe, it is mostly the private, individual rod-makers who have influenced the modern split-cane rod, giving it a quality and precision that scarcely existed earlier.

Fly-rods are classified according to their performance, the so-called "action". Top-action rods have their greatest flexibility at the top of the rod, whereas full-action rods distribute the forces equally along their length. In between are numerous half-action rods. Most modern rods are more or less decidedly half-action types, and these are the easiest to cast with. The action of the upper third of the rod is at work with relatively short lengths of line. It is only with the heavier loads—when the rod is allowed to work harder—that the action is spread out along the whole length of the rod and thereby transmits even greater casting power.

Currents of fashion are not lacking in fly-fishing, and they affect everything from styles of casting and fish-trends to rod construction. The Alpine style of casting, influenced by Hans Gebetsroither, long caused the length of European fishing rods to shrink. Rods of 6–7 ft (1.8–2.4 m), short and relatively stiff, were "in". Such rods are, of course, first-class instruments for this modern, energy-saving style of casting, but their shorter length is a disadvantage while fishing. The same applies to their stiffness, which allows for thin leaders only if a completely controlled counter-thrust is to be accomplished.

The fly-reel serves mainly to store the line, but it must also have an effective drag system if and when a really fighting fish strikes.

Now the pendulum is swinging in the opposite direction. More and more fishermen are rediscovering the advantages of longer and more flexible rods. The extreme case of this development is the "long-soft" rod, an extremely long rod for use with very light line classes. Even a trend towards ultra-light fishing, with correspondingly light midge-rods, can be seen. Fishing with such toys often goes beyond sportsmanship, as they no longer allow for short, fair fights. It should be not fashion trends, but practical demands and a sporting attitude, which set the standards of fly-fishing.

The fly-rod must correspond to the conditions under which it will be used. Not only the length and line class, but also the size of the expected catch, the type of water and the natural surroundings should be considered. Rods under 7 ft (2.1 m) are only practical while wading; but even then, they do not make guiding the line any easier. A universal length is 8 feet (2.4 m), but longer rods are recommended for larger waters. For rod classes, the statements about AFTM line classes apply. For graphite rods, however, various line classes are often indicated. The beginner should choose the heavier line classes, because controlling the heavier line weights can be more easily learned.

The weight of a modern rod is never a problem, even for a poorly trained caster. Even long, one-handed rods in the upper line classes (8 to 10) weigh barely more than 120–140 grams (4.5–5 ounces) and are easy to fish with—assuming that the grip is logically formed to fit the caster's hand, which is important. The form of the handle is crucial as well. Lightweight rods, up to 8 ft (2.4 m) long, cast well with the index finger on the handle. To allow for this, a cigar-shaped handle is the most suitable. Longer rods and higher classes make the thumb-grip necessary, and here the "American standard" or the "fishtail" is better. For heavy, one-handed rods, a removable end piece (fighting butt) is practical, as it helps in tiring out a running fish. The stripping guides must guarantee a smooth cast. It is not particularly important if they are single-foot aluminium oxide rings or the traditional snake-loops, as long as their quality is good.

For most fly-fishermen, the rod is absolutely the most important piece of equipment. No other type of fishing requires the same kind of good relationship between the fisherman and his rod. The more the type of fly-rod and its way of functioning match the physical constitution and temperament of its owner, the better he can get along with it and develop his own possibilities.

Fly-reels

Hardly any other detail is given such different emphasis by fishermen as the fly-reel. Equipment "freaks" find their greatest joy in the fine points of an exquisite, sophisticated fly-reel, while less technically interested fishermen view their reels merely as practical line-holders. For lighter fishing, the type of reel makes little difference—as long as it does what it is supposed to do. In an emergency, a smaller fish can be played with loose lines. Fights with really strong fish, however, pose much greater demands—line capacity, braking ability, manageability and total reliability. Reel problems have often been the cause of the "big one that got away".

There are two basic types of fly-reels. The so-called "single-action" reels have a very simple construction. The line is rolled up onto a rotating spool, supplied with a handle. When the line is drawn off the spool, the handle turns backwards. A barely adjustable ratchet or an adjustable, stationary damper on the axle hinders overspin when the line is let out quickly. There are also models with adjustable and effective disc-brakes. The speed with which a reel can be wound up depends on the diameter of the spools and how much line is wound up onto it. Some reels come with multiplier functions. Easily managed antireverse reels have finely adjustable braking systems with gears. As the line runs off the spool, the handle stays still, or can be turned in the opposite direction. Leader breaks, from sudden stress on the line while reeling, can be avoided by correctly adjusting the drag.

Spools on normal reels usually turn inside a house, which gives it the necessary support. Reels of which one side is made up of the side of the spool must be very precisely manufactured if they are to avoid line problems. Reels made of synthetic materials have yet to solve this problem satisfactorily.

The requirements of a functional fly-reel can be summed up as follows. It should be as light as possible, rotate precisely, be relatively robust and have a line capacity which corresponds to the type of fishing at hand: for light fishing, fly-line and about 40 meters (43 yards) of backing; for heavier fishing, fly-line and 120 meters (130 yards) of backing. But the spool may only be filled to the point where no part of the line is touching the crosspiece. Easily changeable reels are needed, as well as a reliable and, above all, finely adjustable braking system. For single-action reels, using the rim for additional dragging with a finger is advantageous. Comfortably gripped handles and adjustment screws are necessary, as are smooth and line-saving stripping guides—preferably large and narrow—and a house which reflects the light as little as possible.

Besides all this, the reel must answer the needs of its owner, in placement for either right-handed or left-handed winding. Be sure that the reel is corrosion-resistant for saltwater fishing. When the type of fishing depends on the performance characteristics of the reel, quality reels are the only answer.

Clothing and wading equipment

How to dress for fly-fishing is not only a question of personal taste, but also a function of the prevailing circumstances. Harris Tweeds and a tie may seem pleasant on rivers running through the park-like English countryside, but are totally inappropriate in the thick underbrush along the banks of a river in Lappland or on a rubber raft trip in Alaska.

Fishing clothes need not be camouflaged, but should be discreet for tactical reasons, as well as comfortable and suitable for the purpose. Whether one prefers a fishing vest, or keeping equipment in a solid tackle-bag or in a back-pack, makes no difference as long as the items are easy to reach. A fisherman's style and behaviour are, in any case, determined not by the external details but by his attitude.

Due to the narrow radius of action in fly-fishing, the ability to fish while wading is very important, since the only limitations are then the water depth and the strength of the current. Even dyed-in-the-wool riverbank fishermen are occasionally forced to do some wading. Reliable wading equipment, which should not be neglected from the viewpoint of health, must insulate against the cold and guarantee firm footing as far as possible.

Whether hip boots or waders are chosen depends on the fishing method. Waders allow for fishing in deep waters, but are less comfortable than wading boots, especially if long stretches on dry land have to be covered in them. Thin materials mean less weight, but are less insulating. Even with heavy warm underwear, the heavy condensation on the inside can be very uncomfortable in cold water. Modern neoprene waders offer the most comfortable wading, as they are pleasant to wear, insulate exceptionally well, are light, quite robust and easy to repair.

The quality of the sole of the wader should be especially considered. Rubber soles are only slip-resistant when they have small steel cleats imbedded in them. The so-called Alpine soles, with Wolfram dubs, are of course quite slip-resistant, but their scraping along the bottom has a frightening effect on the fish. Felt soles are better suited, but wear out quickly. A rough piece of carpeting used as a sole is impervious to wear and unbeatable for gripping. Any good-quality wader can be cheaply "extra-equipped" by a shoemaker.

In strong currents, it is often not enough to have slip-resistant soles. Here, a wading staff is needed to act as a "third leg". Any shoulder-length, sturdy tree branch will do, but dead branches are unsuitably brittle. Naturally, the wading staff must be tied securely, as losing it far from shore can be disastrous.

Of the wading staffs offered for sale, the solid ones are best. Folding patent staffs, with internal rubber cord, are to be used only if their parts are held together by an absolutely secure construction. For the tip, I personally prefer a "silent" rubber stud to any kind of steel tip.

In still or slow-running water, where waders are no longer enough and boats are unavailable, a float ring (belly boat) adds new dimensions. Belly boats are made up of an air-filled floating ring (safest if it has two air chambers) which has a fairly comfortable covering with a place to sit. The belly-boater must have a breast-high wader on, as he is sitting approximately up to his waist in the water. Moving around is accomplished by the use of swim fins. Deflated and carried in a large bag, they can be used in any suitable water. This type of fishing, with a bird's-eye view of the water, has become ever more popular.

Other necessities

Among the rich assortment of accessories, we can only mention those which are a part of basic equipment. Some of what is not mentioned may well be useful, but is not absolutely necessary.

One thing which should definitely not be left out while fishing is good eye protection. Flies which have gone out of control—because of the wind conditions or a bad cast—can cause permanent eye damage. Therefore, a broad-rimmed hat or a cap with a low bill is not just for looks, but a minimum safety precaution. And flies without barbs are not only more fair to the fish, but less dangerous to ourselves as well.

A perfect type of eye protection is, naturally, any kind of glasses. Sunglasses, preferably polarized, are an advantage. They

Waders, fishing vest, landing net, goggles, and a broad-brimmed hat do not catch more fish, but they still belong to the basic equipment for a fully fledged fly-fishermen.

protect the eyes from the glare off sharply sun-lit water, reduce reflections from the surface of the water, and improve underwater visibility—from some angles considerably.

If a fly-fishing vest is desired, the number of pockets is not as important as how the pockets are adapted and how well they close. Less is lost from deep pockets than from wide, shallow ones, especially if they are closed with Velcro. Pockets which are on top of each other make the vest look grotesquely puffed-up, without adding to its practicality. Rear pockets are only useful if they can be reached. This is especially true for short wading vests.

Fishing bags need to be large enough to hold, not only fly-boxes and diverse small items, but also rain clothes or a sweater. Even here, oblong-shaped bags are preferable. They should be made of waterproof materials and be able to be closed well. A partitioned main compartment helps to keep things in order. Outside pockets which close tightly are a must. The shoulder-strap must guarantee that the bag can be carried painlessly and a belly-strap is needed to keep it from sliding around while bending over.

Fly-boxes should be chosen from models which protect the flies, provide a good overview, can be securely closed and float. For dry flies, boxes with partitions, especially if they can be opened one at a time, are good. Boxes with foam rubber protect the hooks, are easily scanned and, if they are large and deep enough, ensure undamaged dry flies. For nymphs and wet flies, even flat boxes can be recommended. Magnets are useful only if they hold properly. Fly-boxes with metal clamps are suitable only for streamers and larger wet flies—patterns which can be stored flat and whose hooks will not be damaged by them. Any kind of clamping system can be used only if it guarantees that the hooks remain undamaged.

There are special pouches available for storing completed leaders, but a billfold works too. It is more important to have a functional leader dispenser for leader storage, provided the various thicknesses are not carried on their separate spools. A good dispenser should hold four to six different thicknesses and should dispense monofil line easily and smoothly—but only when it is drawn out, not accidentally while in the bag.

A knife and scissors are indispensable. A good, sound knife is versatile and not only for killing and cleaning fish. Large scissor-pliers are handy for the careful removal of hooks, for cutting the line and, possibly, the trimming of flies. So as not to be lost, they are tied onto an elastic cord or a zinger retractor.

For those who are unable to carefully land a fish by hand, a short-handled or a trustworthy collapsible net can be chosen. In landing large fish, the size of the opening is not as important as the depth of the net. Wooden-rimmed wading nets, which are carried tied onto the back or on the side, are light and comfortable to use and are not only good for wading. On overgrown river banks, a free-hanging net can, of course, be a nuisance, and a patented river-net which has its own carrying case is better suited. For successful landing from high river banks or in deep water, long-handled models are preferable.

As regards the preparation of flies, many float preparations for dry flies are available. The liquid ones are best, as they do not affect the looks of the pattern and they function well once the solvent has evaporated. Amadou is excellent for drying wet flies, but even suede works well. Buoyant fats can be very effective for greasing leaders and lines. Leaders and slowly-sinking lines can be made to sink again by rubbing them with a little mud to remove the grease.

Casting techniques

The flying lines are what best characterize fly-fishing. Skilful casting technique fascinates through its rhythmical harmony. The movements of the caster seem almost to be playfully easy, a flowing elegance. In following the flow of the lines, the laws of gravity seem almost to have been annulled.

Wonderful to watch, but incredibly difficult to learn—that is a widespread belief among fishermen. And the fear of learning to cast is just what keeps most of them from experiencing fly-fishing. Still, fly-fishing is not a mystery but the result of a number of synchronized motions, each one of which can be accomplished as easily as running or swimming, once the main principles are understood.

Without doubt, being able to cast is important. Correct presentation of the fly presupposes, beyond all else, a successful cast. Real fishing is mastered only when a certain sureness in the cast is attained and need not be thought about. One thing is clear, however: one does not have to be a super caster in order to fly-fish successfully. There are plenty of prominent casters who, despite this talent, remain rotten fishermen—and extremely successful fly-fishermen who have but modest casting skills. For all their importance, the cast and the presentation are only a part of fly-fishing, though a thrilling part.

Nowadays, the opinion is often expressed that no one can properly learn to cast on his own. It is true that with practical instruction from an experienced teacher, beginning is much easier. But a course in casting is not necessary! Thousands of people have become enthusiastic fly-fishermen completely on their own. It is enough to have a portion of real interest in learning the main fundamentals of casting technique. After just a few hours of practice in a field, the first feeling for the rod and line is attained. And soon, any normally talented fisherman will manage an acceptable cast. At that point, he should go fishing—for there is no better way to practice casting than while fishing.

To emphasize once more: it's extremely important to have equipment that is perfectly coordinated. Matching the parts to each other is easy, if the manufacturers' information (according to AFTM) is taken into account. Which type of rod is best is something one discovers with time.

For beginners, a graphite rod with half-action, 7.5–8 ft (2.2–2.4 m) long, in class 5 to 6, and light-coloured fly-line are recommended. The highest AFTM line class for the given rod should be chosen, because then the weight of the line, even at short distances, is easier to master. At the end of the line, a rod-length, narrowing leader with a 0.20-mm tip is tied. For the very first tries, the fly can be left off—but under no circumstances the leader, as the narrowing leader takes up the powerful turn-over from the line and passes it smoothly along to the tip. If the first casts are successful, a light-coloured fly, with a hook size of 12 but without a barb, can be tied on. A "hookless" fly will not get caught in the grass, and is quite harmless upon unintentional contact.

Learning to cast

The basic process of casting is as follows. The moving casting mass is made up of the fly-line. The casting tool is the rod. Through a powerful lift, the rod is "loaded" and the energy is passed along to the line. In this way, the initial inertia of the casting mass, coming off the rod, is counterbalanced and the line is cast up in the air in an arch. By adding more synchronized energy during the back-and-forth movements, the line can be held up in the air, the speed will be increased, the line will become longer and controlled, and the fly can then be presented to the right spot.

In practice, this is easier to perform than to describe. Let us go out to a field and grope our way along to a feeling for rod and line.

The overhand cast

To begin with, the starting point: draw out 6.5–8.5 yards (6–8 meters) of fly-line, and stretch it and the leader out on the ground. The rod hand should have a firm grip on the handle of the rod, best with the index finger on the handle. The line hand takes hold of the line below the lower stripping guide and holds it in a clenched fist, at about middle height, so that the tightly stretched line loops forward over the thumb. The casting arm, with elbow relaxed, is held straight forward. The underarm is in line with the rod. The shoulder of the casting arm is drawn back a little and the body weight is on the corresponding leg. The foot of the other leg is pointing, a bit stretched out, in the direction of the cast. The tip of the rod is pointing somewhat downward.

The first exercise: with a strong lift, the rod is brought up from a horizontal to a vertical position. Stop the backward cast with flexed muscles. The line is lifted, follows the backward cast, flies backwards and is stretched out. Now the rod is brought back to the horizontal position with a forward cast. The line, once again, follows the movement of the rod, rolls forward over the tip of the rod and stretches out. Sink the rod and let the line become slack. The overarms and underarms are kept bent at the same angle to one another throughout the cast. The movement of the cast is accomplished only with the shoulder blades. Only when the line is slack is the casting arm brought forward.

The rod should be swung so that its tip swings in two parallel paths. During the backward cast, the rod is leaned slightly outward. The line flies by on the side of the rod and the caster. During the forward cast, the rod is straight up and down. The line rolls forward over the tip of the rod. It is important that the line-hand should follow the rod-hand's movements at the same relative distance. Only when the line is uniformly stretched, with a tight line between the line-hand and lower stripping guide, can the invested energy be completely transferred to the line and give it the necessary acceleration. The whole cycle of movement

Line treatment

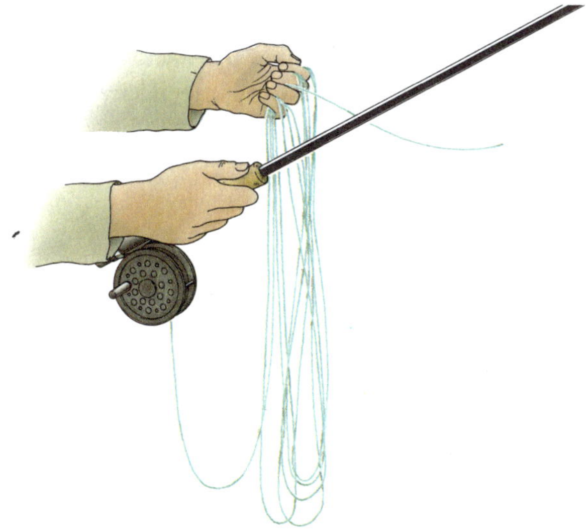

For casting and for all presentation techniques, it is important to be able to cope with loose lines. On overgrown river banks where the line cannot be laid out freely, or while wading where a strong current can take hold of a loose line, the line-hand acts as a storage place for loose line. There are a number of ways of keeping this line reserve ready for use.

The line is wound up in equally small loops. This technique is easy and practical. About 13 yds (12 m) of line can be held in uniform loops in the hand and be let out as needed.

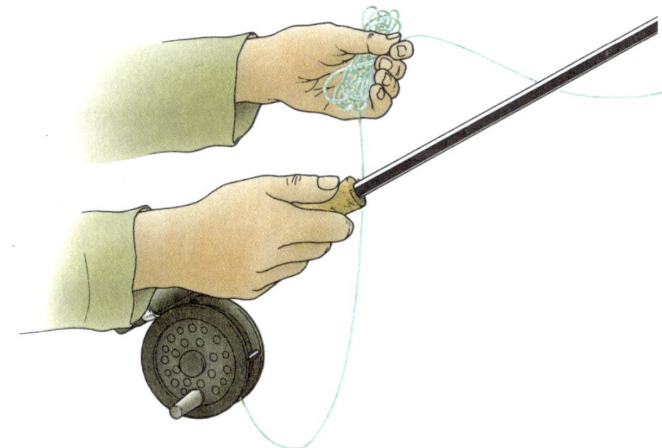

An elegant solution is to take up the line with the thumb and index finger, and to lay it over the index finger and the ring and little finger in "eights". The middle finger is left free. About 16 yds (15 m) can thus be held in uniform "eights" in the line-hand. By spreading the fingers slightly, the line can run out freely.

The line is retrieved in arbitrarily large, uniform loops and is held tightly. In this way, the whole line can be kept in reserve. To be able to allow the right amount of line to run out freely while casting requires a little training.

The line is laid into a "shooting basket" tied around the waist, where it lies in loose loops, ready for shooting or ready to be let out as required. Shooting baskets, previously woven but today made of collapsible canvas, are very practical for long casts, especially while wading.

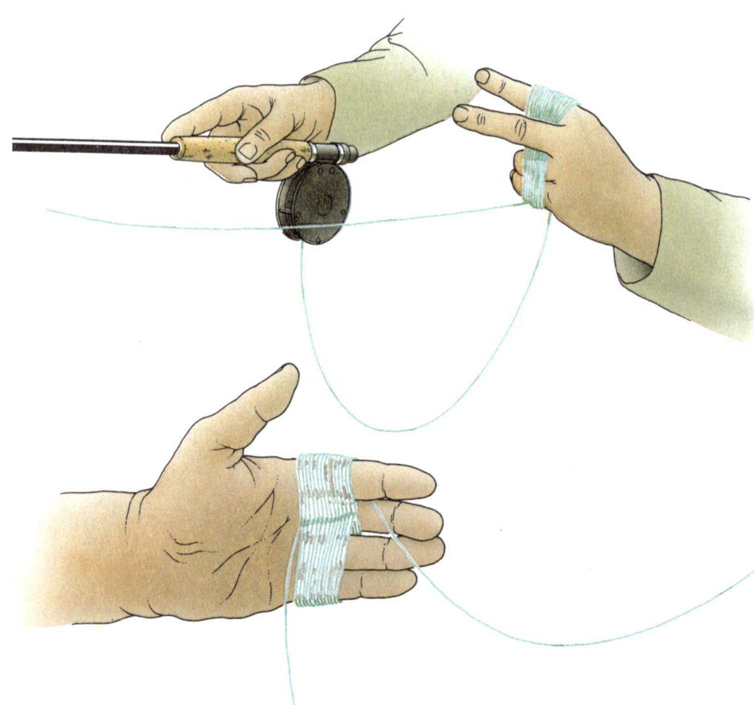

has to be even, quick and distinct, but with clearly separate movements. The vertical stopping point of the rod must be strictly adhered to. Not before the weight of the backward-flying line is felt in the rod—when it is stretched out—does the forward cast begin. Correct timing will determine whether the cast is to be successful or not. A forward cast begun too early, when the line is

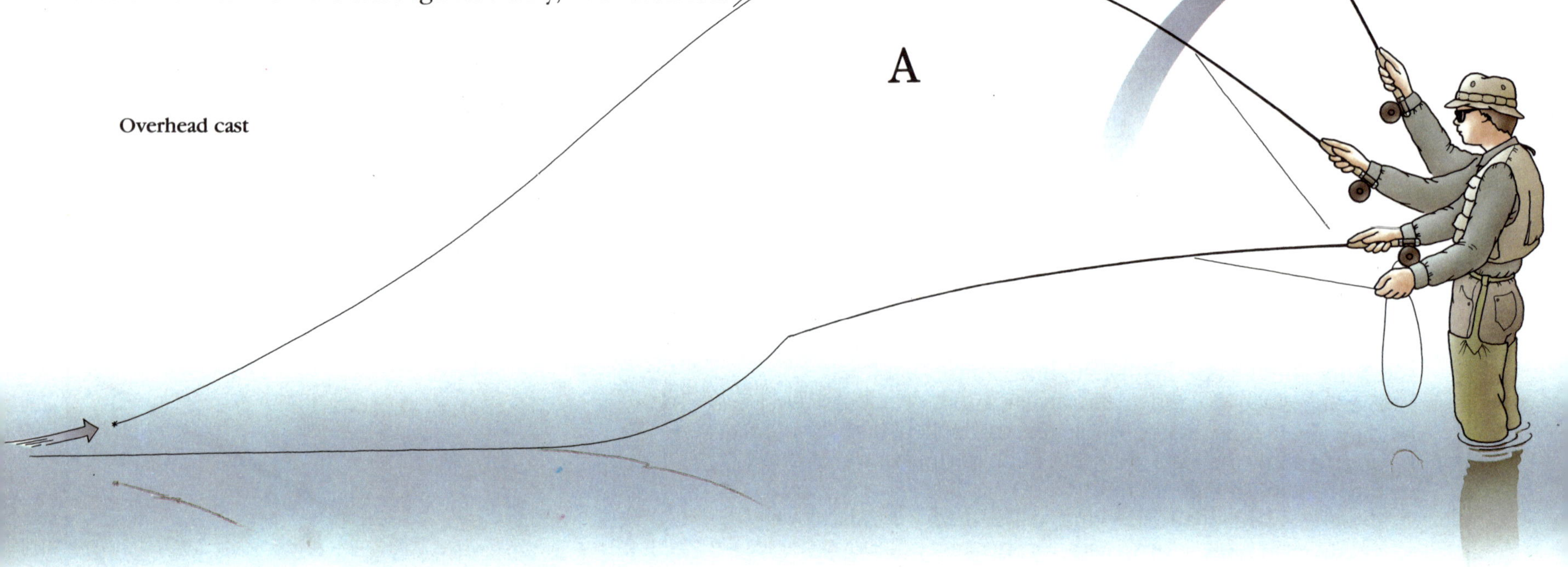

A

Overhead cast

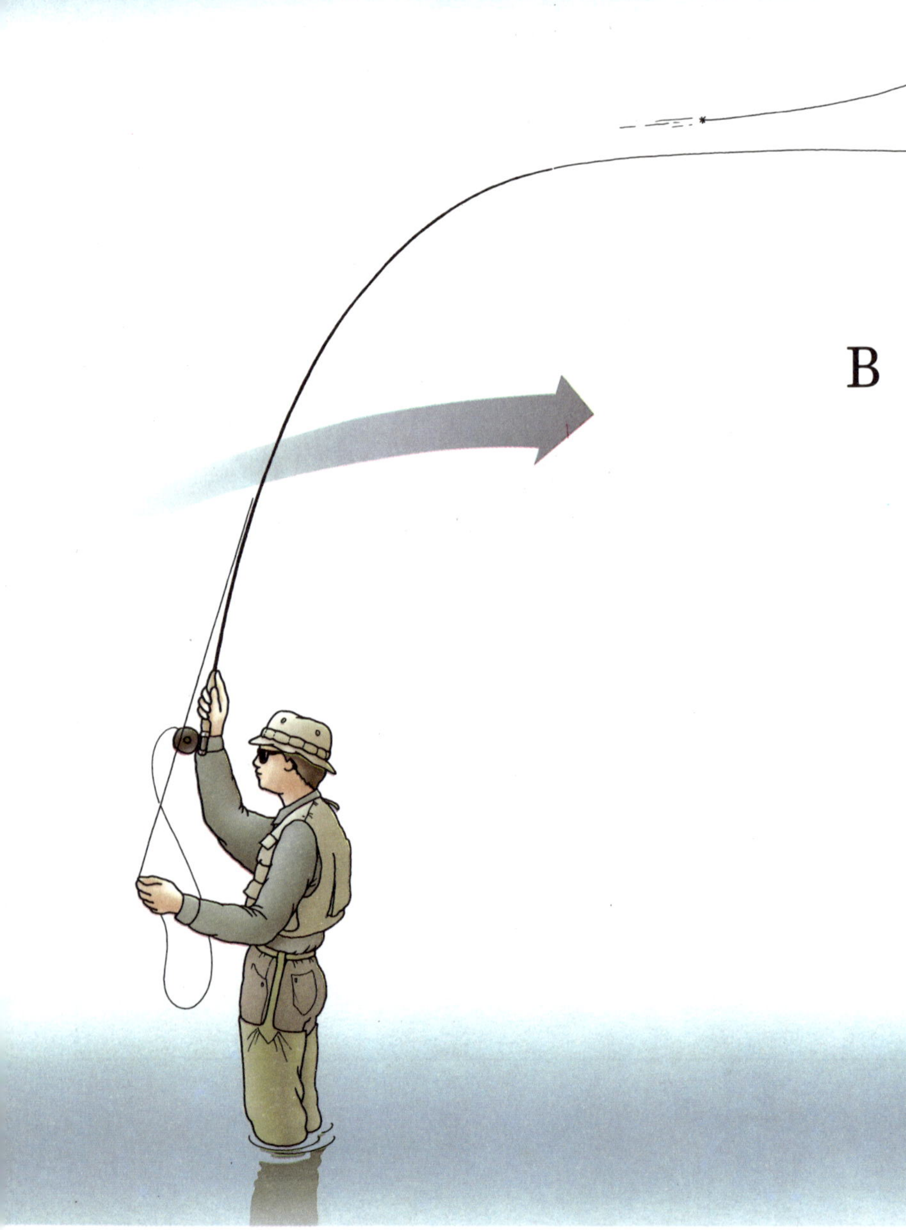

B

not fully stretched out, will result in a whip effect. This can be so strong that the fly is snapped off the line. If, on the other hand, the forward cast comes too late, the line will fall, perhaps touching the ground, and the cast will collapse.

After just a few casts, the weight of the line will be felt in the rod and a feeling for approximately the right casting moment will come. When the described cycle of movement is attained, and the line can be laid out straight and sure, the next exercise can be tried.

In the second exercise, the line is not cast forward, but is held up in the air in a "false" cast. The rod is now stopped with tightened muscles in an upright position, during the forward cast. The casting arm must still be bent. The line rolls over the tip of the rod and stretches forward. At this point, a new backward cast is initiated. The line accelerates to the next cast, and the rod is again stopped in an upright position. The line flies by on the side and stretches out to the back. Thereafter, a new forward cast is begun.

This "air-cast" can be repeated as long as desired, so that a feeling for the rod and line grows. When the timing of the casting movement is learned, an accentuated pendulum movement is attained, with which the line can easily be kept up in the air.

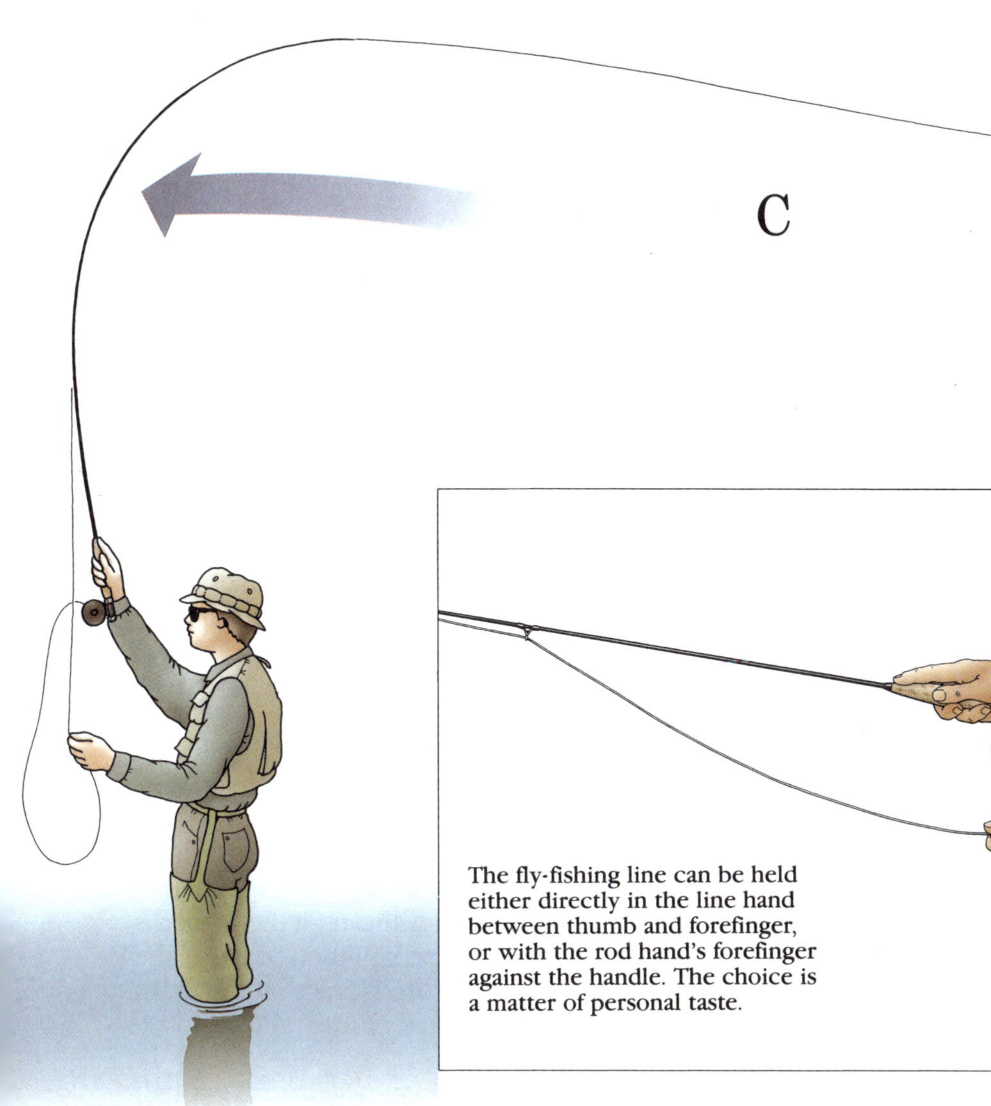

hand and the reel. Then the air-cast is begun, using the practiced line length. Through the powerful movements of the forward and backward casts, more energy is exerted on the line than it uses in its arching through the air. This extra energy is clearly felt when the line slackens—the line pulls at the line-hand. If the line is now let out a little, the loose line glides through the stripping guides. If this happens at the right moment—even here, correct timing is essential—the loose line is "shot" out.

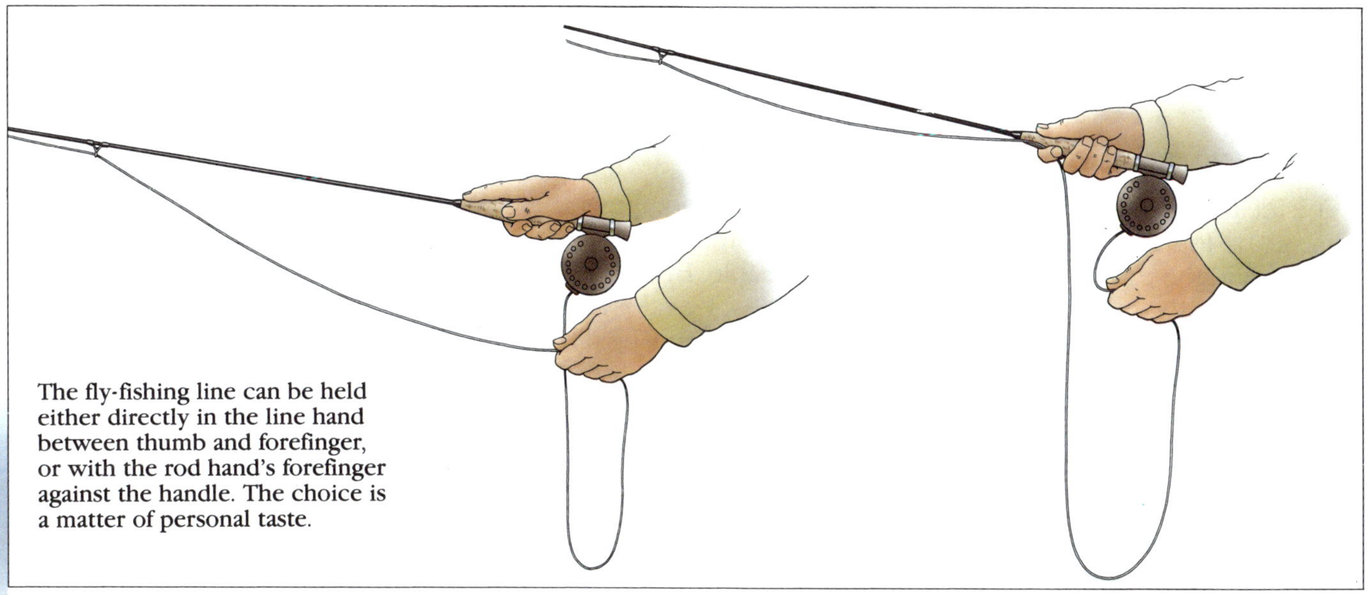

The fly-fishing line can be held either directly in the line hand between thumb and forefinger, or with the rod hand's forefinger against the handle. The choice is a matter of personal taste.

When the fly has been presented—after the line has been stretched out—the rod is lowered to a position slightly under the horizontal.

As soon as an air-cast with approximately 8.5 yds (8 m) of line is mastered, it should be practiced while moving about freely. This limbers one up and gives confidence. If the rod is leaned a little to one side, a side-cast is easily achieved, which may be necessary in some fishing waters. In the side-cast, too, the rod is handled as before. A side-cast is thus simply a more or less horizontal cast in the normal manner.

The third exercise entails trying to increase the distance of the cast by extending the length of the line. An extra 2–3 yds (m) of line are drawn out and, at first, held in reserve between the line-

This shooting out is not only important in lengthening the line during the air-cast. Even when presenting the line, the cast can be made a few meters longer by shooting out more line. It is also very important to a good service, especially in dry-fly fishing. In principle, a little slack line is shot out with every cast, so as to attain a soft, discreet presentation.

In presenting the fly, a point about 2 ft (60 cm) above the target is sighted in, and a forward cast is made to a horizontal position. When the pull of the stretched line is felt in the line-hand, the line is released and the rod lowered. The remaining energy is taken up in the shooting line and the fly lands softly.

It is important to practice feeding in and shooting the line, but a distance of 11–13 yds (10–12 m) is plenty to begin with. Once this distance has been fairly mastered, it will be no problem to successfully fish smaller bodies of water.

Casting variations and presentation

The ideal conditions for the first tour with fly-fishing equipment are to be found in the surface activity. The rising fish or their wakes and the exact place to cast are readily visible. By looking closer, what the fish are taking can be determined. Even for real novice fishermen, a debut under these conditions cannot be difficult. A practiced fisherman knows this much already—only the equipment and method of presentation are somewhat unfamiliar.

Naturally, during the first few days, it is wise to seek sections of water that demand no particular expertise in casting and presenting: free, even-flowing watercourses which have enough room for the back-cast. If the active fish are carefully approached going upstream, the right casting distance can nearly always be attained.

For presentation with stretched lines, the first thing to do is to draw out the correct length of line—a little more than is needed for the length of the cast. In principle, a little loose line is always kept in reserve while fishing. When wading, the loose line can simply hang down into the water. On shore, it is laid out on the ground. It must, however, be kept free of anything it might get caught up in, and be hindered from running out freely.

The correct distance is ascertained, the right amount of line is shot out in an air-cast and the cast is made upstream and across the current. When the fly is presented, a spot upstream from the active fish is sighted in. The sight is taken—as already mentioned—about 60 cm upstream and a little line is allowed to shoot out while casting. The line is let loose only when it is almost stretched out in the forward cast, with the rod sunk to a horizontal position. Shooting is achieved not by letting the line loose, but by letting it slip through the partially opened line-hand. This small amount of friction helps to keep the line stretched all the way out to the tip of the leader during the presentation. The fly is served delicately and can drift discreetly towards the intended catch.

After the fly has been served, the line is carefully squeezed tightly against the handle of the rod with the index finger of the rod-hand and, with the line-hand, the excess line is pulled in at the same rate as it drifts towards the fish. The tip of the rod is aimed at the fly and follows the drift. In this way, contact with the fly is always kept. When a fish takes, the line is stretched with a quick, but absolutely not violent, lift of the rod and the fish is hooked. If this stretching results in the often-mentioned strike, there is a risk that the leader will break. This is because the fish is hooked at exactly the same moment as it dives, and thus in the direction opposite to its movement.

There are several methods of casting, each with its own advantages in special situations. Particularly in stretches of water with great variations in current speed, the presentation can be made more elegant by varying the casting technique.

Moreover, if a modern and environmentally conscious way of fishing is used, with flies lacking the needless barbs, no power at all is needed to set the hook properly. If the fly is not taken, it is allowed to drift down a good way from the fish before a new cast is begun. The reason for the fly not being taken is mostly either a poor presentation or an inappropriate fly—or, often, both. A poorly executed cast and presentation are the main reasons a fly is ignored by the fish in dry-fly fishing. The presentation requires, therefore, maximum attention. The fly must drift with the current naturally and without drag. Under no circumstances can it plow through the surface.

With a stretched leader, this is possible only when there is an even surface flow. Where the speed of the current is irregular—as is usually the case—a better result is achieved if the leader is not stretched out in the cast. The current will then "eat up" the loosely floating curves of the leader before it drags on the fly. In some situations, therefore, it is essential to cast with a loose leader.

A *stop cast* is used in dry-fly fishing when the leader is enough to even out the differences of current in the casting area. Even in wet-fly fishing, the stop cast is usable: stopped flies on a slack leader sink more quickly. In fishing upstream, a stop cast can be advantageous—in fishing across or downstream, it is often indispensable.

A *serpentine cast* helps in dry-fly fishing to smooth out uneven current conditions and extend the unimpeded drift of the fly. If there is enough slack line ready for use, this is easy to achieve. During the shooting out of the line, the rod tip is whipped back and forth in short horizontal lashes. The line follows these movements and falls in curves onto the water. In this way, a stronger middle current, for example, takes up these curves before it can take hold of the fly.

In similar situations, especially when fishing downstream, a *parachute cast* can also be used. In the classic form of this cast, the rod is stopped at a nearly upright position and the line stretches forward at the same height as the tip of the rod. Then the rod is lowered towards the water and the fly is presented. With another lowering, two rod lengths of slack line can be laid out. In the "Gebetroither"-style parachute cast, the forward cast is stopped in nearly the same way as in the air-cast: the line shoots away at an angle upwards, and the tip of the rod is lowered almost to the surface of the water. The back part of the line lands first; the tip of the line and the leader land at the same time and drift downstream unhindered.

When fishing diagonally or almost straight downstream, the

line can be lengthened considerably after all of these casts by whipping out the fly-line afterward. A prerequisite for this is, once again, enough reserved line between the line-hand and the reel. As soon as the fly has landed, the slack line—just as in shooting—is laid out and the rod is whipped flatly and energetically upstream. The adhesion of the line on the water surface causes the slack line to collect in front of the top stripping guide; it can then be shot out in a medium-high forward cast downstream. For each lashing, the drift of the fly is extended by about the length of the rod. If a longer line is in the water, it is easy to "shake out" as much line from the top guide as desired, and thereby to extend the unencumbered drift of the fly.

Parachute cast

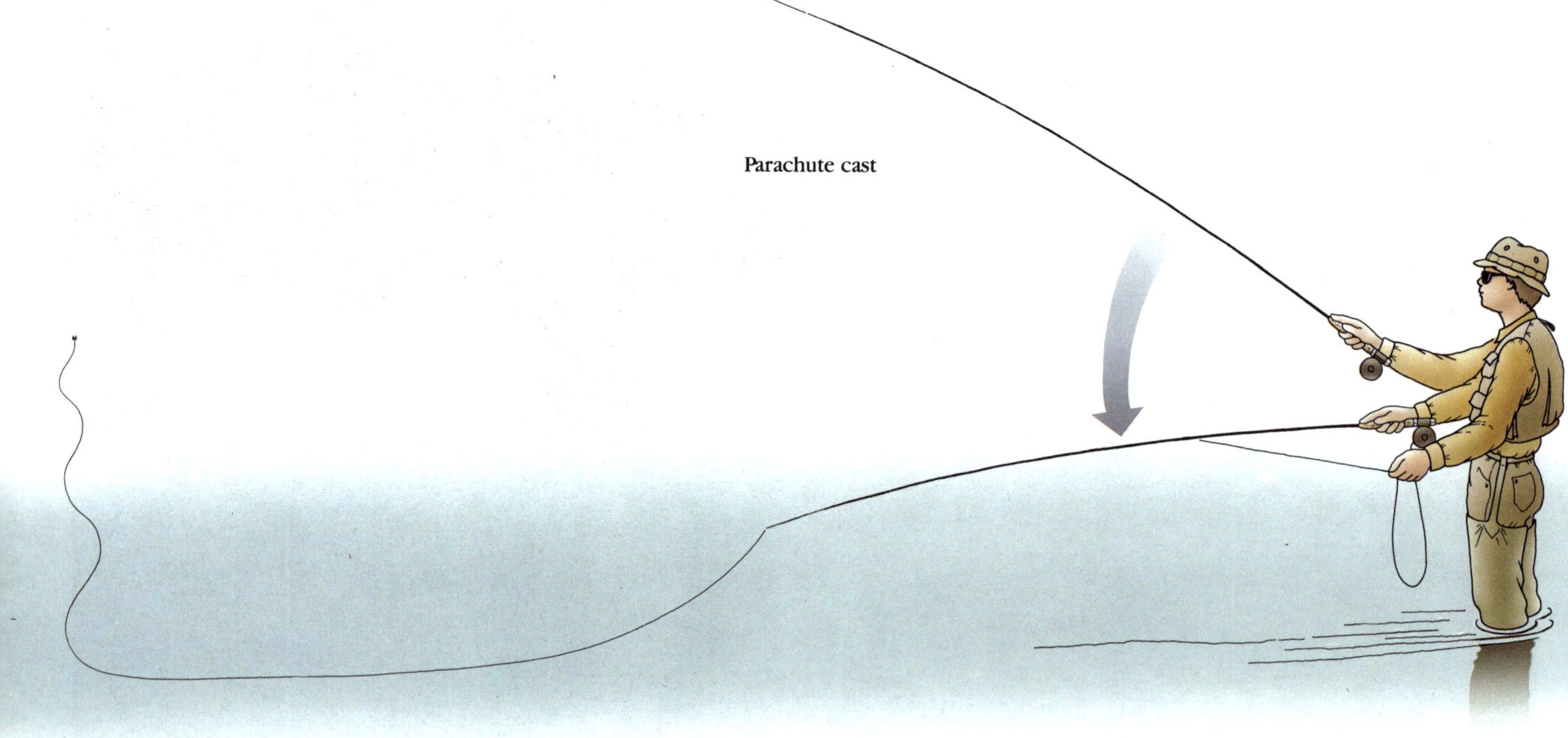

Serpentine cast

The *horizontal side-cast* is used in waters without enough room for overhead casting—such overgrown waters are often of primary interest. Medium-high and low side-casts are, in some areas, the most common ones. Often, even the area available for the back-cast is greatly restricted. By using a "backhand cast", situations are avoided where the fly could be caught during the back-cast. This is best achieved through a medium-high cast. With the target area to the rear, the right amount of line is laid out wherever there is enough room. For presentation, the casting arm is turned completely backwards, the rod is brought to a horizontal position, and the line is presented.

In areas where a back-cast is not at all possible, an exact cast can be made with a *roll-cast*. So that the line will strip smoothly during the roll-cast, about two rod lengths of line should be taken out with a little side-cast. Then the rod is lifted to a vertical position and whipped energetically down to a horizontal position. The line-hand holds the stripping line tight. The line follows the movement of the rod and rolls out onto the water surface towards the goal. By lifting the rod to the starting position and shaking it back and forth vigorously, extra length is added to the line in the air, and the casting distance can be extended. With several consecutive roll-casts and good coordination with the line-hand, casts of more than 13 yds (12 m) can easily be made.

A synthesis of side-cast and roll-cast can also be very effective in such situations. The necessary amount of line is drawn out using a side-cast, parallel and in front of the fisherman. The eyes are focussed on the target area. At the last back-cast, the rod is brought up in a flowing movement from a horizontal to a vertical position and is whipped towards the goal. The line, which is in the air, follows the direction of the rod's impulses and stretches out in an arch towards the goal.

The roll-cast is generally quite useful in many situations. Taking in the line with a "roll pickup" is especially easy when fishing upstream. The last few meters of line are simply allowed to drift towards the fisherman. The rod is then raised to an upright position and whipped forward to a medium-high position. The line is lifted to the side with a roll, stretches forward, and can be steered once again towards a new goal with an air-cast.

Small roll-casts can even be very suitable to use for shaking out extra line while wet-fly fishing. Impulses are sent lightly along the line, so that the roll dies out just before it reaches the tip of the line. The stretch is taken from the tip of the leader, and the fly can sink faster and freely drift away.

For dry-fly fishing, the fish should, if possible, not be allowed to see the suspicious leader. The fly must thus drift in front of the leader in the fish's active area. When casting across the current, this is still feasible with a straight, laid-out cast. For fishing upstream, it requires an arching cast.

A cast to the right is begun with a low or medium-high side-cast. Again, coordination of the line-hand is important to keep the forward-rolling arch intact. At the point of the cast—before the line has stretched out towards the goal—the power is removed from the cast by releasing the slack line. The energy which is needed to stretch the line is lost in shooting the line and it collapses. The result is that the fly lands in a more or less right-curving arch, and can drift away in front of the leader. The arch will be smaller, the earlier the line is let loose. If the shot is delayed until the line has started to stretch, the arch can be opened up to a right angle. After just a few casts, the feeling for the right timing will come.

A cast to the left can be accomplished in two ways. The first variation: the line is laid out in the direction of the target area with the shoulder of the casting arm lined up parallel, in front of the body and the presentation is made backhanded. This is quite comfortable. Otherwise, the cast is the same as for the right-opening arching cast. The second variation: to begin with, a medium-high normal cast is made, but with such power that the tip and the leader are completely stretched out and turn to the left. At this point, a little line is shot out, the rod is lowered and the fly allowed to land. In this variation, it is especially important to have the right amount of casting power and exact timing. A light head-wind is helpful.

Roll-cast

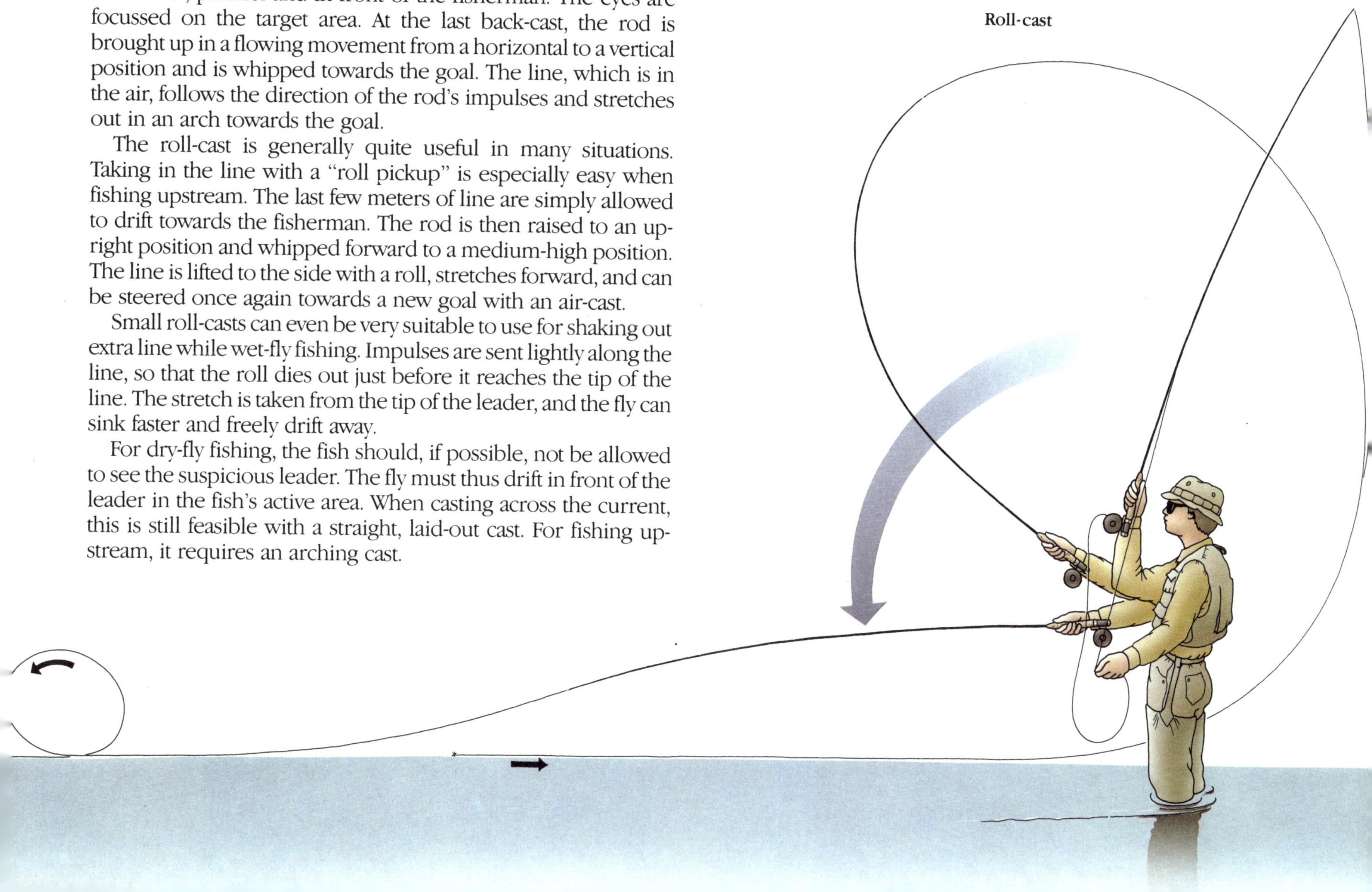

The double-haul cast

By handling the rod correctly with the right feel with the line-hand, a cast of about 22 yds (20 m) can be reached with modern equipment—much longer than what is needed in most running waters. The average length is 11–16.5 yds (10–15 m); for dry-fly fishing, even shorter. By contrast, in wider waters and especially on lakes, it is often necessary to double-haul. Not uncommonly, the chances of a catch increase with the length of the cast.

The difficulty of casting long while wading is experienced often enough. The deeper the water, the nearer to the water surface a line must, naturally, be cast. If the timing is not perfect, the line will touch the water during the back-cast, the rhythm of the cast will be lost and it will collapse. Similar problems arise, even with medium-long distances, when there is trouble with the wind.

The reason is that, with increased line-length, the weight of the line becomes increasingly important, because the rhythm of the cast inevitably becomes slower. With lowered speed, however, the weight of the line can only resist gravity to a certain degree. More energy is thus needed to hold the line in the air and completely control it. Long casts, and casts made in strong winds, succeed only if the line can be presented powerfully, quickly, and without letting its speed be reduced. This can only be accomplished by double-hauling the cast. Through the use of accented counter-pull with the line-hand, the tension on the rod can be increased, the speed of the line is increased considerably, and the line can be stabilized in the air-cast.

The *single-haul cast* is enough to give the line so much more speed that it shoots somewhat further in the cast. At the same time, it is a good first training point for the double-haul cast. The single-haul is begun at the same time as the forward cast, and aimed directly at the movement of the rod-hand. The line is pulled (hauled) with a quick, energetic movement diagonally downwards and released for the shot when it is at its tightest.

The speed of the line, accomplished by pulling, is clearly felt in the line-hand. The weight of the line, which has been increased by the extra speed, is felt against the thumb of the hand conducting the line. This pressure is, at the same time, the signal for the optimal moment to release the line. This is not only important for the presentation, but for lengthening the line during the air-cast. The result depends to a great degree upon the teamwork between both of the hands, and it takes a good deal of practice to achieve a feeling for the correct timing.

The double-haul cast is achieved simply by an added pulling sequence, which is begun together with the back-cast. The line is pulled in the rod's increasing upswing in the same manner as in the single-haul: with an energetic, diagonally downward pull. When the rod reaches its stopping point and the line is stretched backward, the line-hand follows the pull towards the guide and, using the forward cast, the pulling operation already described is applied. Once again, the line accelerates and stretches powerfully out to the front.

The double-haul is best practiced by using easy medium-length air-casts. At first, the pulling movements should be rather careful, with emphasis not on achieving great power but on finding the right timing between the two hands, together with a harmonious casting rhythm. When timing is right, the line will have a balanced and powerful flight. After this, more line can be let out with both the forward and backward pull and, with the increased length, a larger pull can be used. Only gradually can longer distances be successively achieved. Yet in general, after every cast, the right amount of line is taken in, so that the next cast can be built up from an easily cast length of line.

The double-haul cast is by no means notably difficult. Still, a great deal of practice is needed before it can easily be used. With the double-haul cast, not only can longer distances and troublesome wind conditions be mastered. Even slightly longer casts with the double-haul have advantages: they spare the casting arm, the motions are discreet, the line lengths are exact and, because of this, quicker and more perfect presentations are achieved.

Cast with double haul

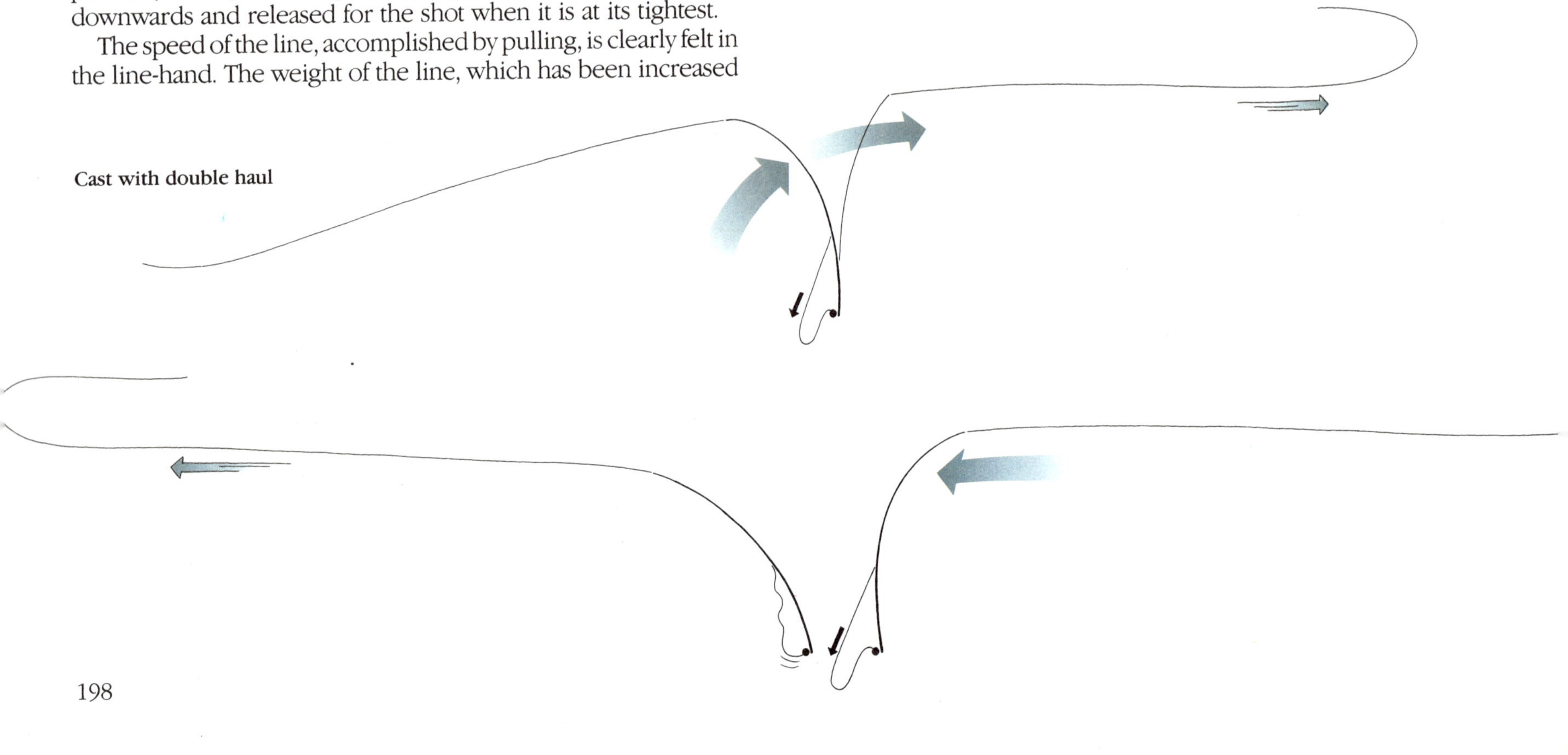

At the water

The goal of fly-fishing is simply to take advantage of what nature offers. Important for success are a watchful eye, correct interpretation of observations, and application of the appropriate techniques and tactics. A fly-fisherman must adapt to the type of water, the kind of fish, and their special way of taking nourishment.

Because fishing waters have such different characteristics, there are no general rules for fishing them. The breadth of variation is enormous. But three categories of water can be discerned, each making comparable demands on procedures, methods of fishing and equipment: streams and other smaller running waterways, larger running rivers, and the still waters of lakes. It thus seems appropriate to approach the necessities and possibilities of fly-fishing from these aspects.

Fishing in streams and small rivers

Many fishermen consider only this category to be worthy of fly-fishing. Such a viewpoint, like the term "fly-fishing waters", is misleading since successful fly-fishing is, in principle, possible in any type of water. On the other hand, it is quite true that streams and small rivers—especially in regions with salmonoids—offer the best conditions for fly-fishing. They have clear water and limited size, are therefore easily surveyed, do not demand very long casts, and are easy to wade in. Besides, salmonoids are particularly easy to fish for with flies, due to their habits of living and feeding.

The first principle for fishing in streams and smaller rivers is to be careful. Look first—then fish! Nowhere else do fish react to a blundering approach more explicitly, by simply ceasing to feed and then fleeing. Even careless conduct on the shore can spoil the fishing for many hours to come. Here, the threat from the enemy comes primarily from above, and a suddenly appearing shadow can act as a shock to a fish. It is pointless to even put out the line in an area of water where the fisherman has run around heedlessly. At best, the "inexperienced" young fish will then take a fly. Thus it is essential to avoid any kind of disturbance near the water.

Movements are made deliberately and slowly, taking advantage of every bit of cover. Where possible, one should sneak upstream. Well-adapted clothes allow the silhouette to merge into that of the shore and vegetation. By casting from as low a position as possible, an attempt is made to avoid the field of vision of the fish. Wading is done quietly and without disturbing the water, as concussion waves and sound carry a long way underwater. Particularly revealing are reflections, flashes from well-polished rods and gleaming fly-boxes. It is also best to shade sunglasses with a hat brim or the bill of a cap, so that no startling light signals can be sent out. The sun should never be at the back: shadows from the body, rod, and line are best kept away from the field of vision of the fish. Moving shadows across fully sunlit areas have

an extremely frightening effect. Only in half-shaded areas, especially in front of vegetation which is moving, is it proper to move around more casually. Shores that lack vegetation should be approached only as near as is required to fish. If necessary, the fisherman can crawl to a good casting position.

In shallow waters with smooth surface areas, the chances of being discovered too early are greatest. But even in deep waters with smooth surfaces, fine catches are quickly frightened away. Anywhere the fish can easily be seen, the fisherman himself is liable to be discovered if he behaves incorrectly. Only in fast running waters, with strongly broken surfaces, is the fisherman well camouflaged—but then the fish is, to the same degree, hard to observe.

Anyone fishing blind in streams and small rivers will make only the occasional catch by chance. The conditions do not allow for any kind of standard tactic. One must observe and constantly

adapt. It is this very variation which is the great attraction of such waters.

The activity of fish—their way of seeking food—depends primarily upon the existence of insect life. This affects everything that happens in the water. The choice of fly, and even the choice between dry fly, wet fly, nymph or perhaps a large fly, is guided by the tastes of the fish. It depends upon the way in which they are searching for food at the given moment. The most effective patterns are those which most closely resemble the current prey and those which are served like their originals—on the surface, just under or completely under the water. Observing carefully what the fish are taking at the moment is a much better method

When a fish in running water, like this trout, takes a drifting insect on the surface, it follows and rises to a point downstream of its holding position. So the fly should be cast some ways upstream of that point.

Here are some typical holding positions in small streams:
(a) Undercut banks with overhanging vegetation.
(b) Overhanging, shadowing tree branches that provide a sheltering "roof", especially if thick roots give further protection.
(c) At the front, sides, and rear of big stones. The pits formed behind stones are a common holding position.
(d) Soft bottoms with sedge borders in the backwaters are not typical holding positions, but trout often hunt there due to the great production of, for example, some mayfly species.
(e) Downstream vegetation offers much food, as well as some shelter and shade.

than random, fumbling attempts. The better the insect life in the water and its diverse forms are known, the more effective and better targeted the choice of the flies will be.

The surface activity of the fish is certainly the easiest to discover. It is, of course, difficult at times to determine whether the prey is actually being taken above or just below the surface, but the feeding behaviour of the fish will give accurate information about this.

A

B

C

D

E

If the fish are actually taking on the surface, then dry flies are the right choice. If the activity cannot be exactly determined, or if dry flies are persistently refused, then nymphs or wet flies, fished just in and under the surface, are the most effective. On the other hand, even seemingly quite passive fish can be enticed with a correctly served dry fly, if one knows where to find them. Judging the underwater activity requires a much more trained eye. Good visibility is necessary in order to clearly see whether they are taking in the middle depths. But the movements of the fish will settle the question: moving back and forth from the holding position, darting to the side or smaller risings from the bottom, for example, indicate that they are taking nymphs. If there is no life at all to be seen in the water, then a temptingly fished nymph or wet fly can give good results. The important thing is to find the holes and fish them right.

If the habitats preferred by the various salmonoids in smaller waters are compared, the really big brown trout are found in the hardest-fished places. These give food and camouflage at the same time—stream beds where the current is concentrated and beds that are protected by overgrown vegetation or undercut river banks, next to precipices, in pockets of current, next to large stones or underwater vegetation. Rainbow trout are not nearly as demanding in their need for protection. Even grayling and char will hold in the middle of a river, since they like whirlpools. In smaller waters, all larger fish prefer areas that are deep enough to provide camouflaged retreats. Not until the cover of twilight falls are larger fish found in very shallow water, when many areas insignificant in the daytime become interesting.

Whether fishing is done upstream, downstream or across depends upon the behaviour of the type of fish which is being sought, the local conditions and, not least, the fisherman's own ability to cast. It is most exciting and, perhaps, most sportsmanlike to fish only for really interesting specimens. But their habitats and the current conditions should always be carefully studied before a fly is presented to them.

The most common tactic in smaller streams is to move slowly upstream while fishing. The fisherman can thus come within casting range of rising fish without being discovered. In shallow waters, this is often the only successful method, regardless of whether a dry fly, wet fly, or nymph is being used. But the disadvantage is that backwaters, where the largest trout are frequently found, are approached straight on. If a large fish is to be enticed to take, it is always a good idea to go around the hole and try to cast downstream.

In upstream fishing, the line is laid out with a medium-high rod, if possible by casting a curve. When wading in the middle of the stream, both banks are reached equally well. If a cast is made straight upstream with stretched line, there is always the chance that the cast will fly over a fish which is holding there. The result will be panic. Even if the cast lands properly, the fish will not bite if others of the species give the alarm to flee. Straight presentations are possibly suitable in agitated waters, where the fish have to remain in the cover of the current and where their optical warning ability is restricted.

In somewhat wider sections and pools, casts across and down or straight downstream can be promising, but only if the cast can be made long enough or if it can be well disguised. Otherwise the fish are frightened away before the fly has even landed on the water. Only the grayling, in some rivers, have strong enough nerves to put up with the sight of busy anglers. Instead, they critically put flies and methods of presentation to the test and are very sceptical of the tips of leaders.

Correct presentation of the fly across irregular currents can only be accomplished with stop-serpentine or parachute casts. And it is not only dry flies that must drift away without dragging: even nymphs and wet flies work only in a natural, slack drift. If, on the contrary, they sweep away through the water on a line turning in the current, the result will be that the fish ignores the fly or simply takes flight.

Besides the nutritional supply, holding pools and the type of current have a strong influence on the often discussed "selectivity" of the fish. The faster the current, the less selective the fish are. In fast running water, they must react quickly or the possible nutrient will drift by and be lost. In intensive drifts of a single insect type, their field of vision can still be rather selective. Especially grayling manage, even in relatively fast and shallow water, to make a surprisingly accurate selection.

For dry-fly fishing in shallow water, the element of surprise can be used by casting very short. Critical fish are much easier to get to take, if they are given only a very short period of time to look the fly over. If the cast is made right at them or just to the side, they have little time to react. It is most effective to let the fish see the fly float down towards them. Sometimes, unwilling trout can be made to rise by using just such a "tough" presentation. In slow-moving waters and in pools, however, such tricks do not pay off. Exact casting, discreet presentation, and a drift as perfect as possible will bring success with large fish—when the fly is correct.

For the many tactics and techniques that are suitable for fly-fishing in streams and smaller rivers, lightweight, all-round tackle is best. Sensitive long rods of 7–8 ft (2–2.5 m), for line class 4 to 5, are just as usable for dry-fly fishing as for nymphs and wet flies. Small 7-foot rods are the shortest usable lengths, even for small overgrown streams, as they still allow the line to be presented where there is not enough room, while still being able to cast freely in shoulder-length vegetation. For the most part, a floating line will function well here, even for wet flies. Only in deeper rivers is there a need for an additional sink-tip. For the shorter-distance casting lengths which are needed here, DT-lines are suitable. Long leaders of 2.5 yds (2 m) are ideal.

Fishing with ultra-light equipment cannot be recommended at all, even for smaller streams containing salmonoids. This is not merely because low-hanging branches often result in lost flies, but because hard-fighting fish can only be landed after energetic battles. Not even a hand's-breadth length of line can be let out when a trout wishes to correct his mistake by fleeing. Therefore, leader tippets of 0.14 mm are the minimum. With this size, even extremely leader-shy fish can be fooled. Hiding defective presentation technique with extra light leaders is less than elegant. It is much better to practice casting and presentation in smaller streams in an area where salmonoids are found. This provides the angler with the best possible place in which to practice.

Fishing in larger rivers

Small waters, small fish; larger waters, larger fish—this rule of thumb describes the situation quite well. Not only does the idea of catching larger fish make the rivers containing salmonoids a challenge, but their very dimensions make completely different demands on the act of fishing them.

In wider waters, the fish are not nearly as evenly spread out as they are in narrower ones. Some stretches have noticeably sparse populations of fish, in others there are only small-fry to be found, and in still others only one kind of fish or another is represented. The reasons for this lie in the demands that different types of fish have on the environment and diet. But even if the demands are well-known, there is still a lot which remains puzzling.

The salmonoids' great need for oxygen sets certain limits on their spread in the waters of the temperate zones. In higher average water temperatures, salmonoids are obliged to stay in the fast-running parts (rapids). In the ever-cold high mountain rivers, this picture is erased. Here it is, above all, the availability of nutrients which influences where the fish are to be found. Besides the presence of insects, minnows are important in many rivers. And in the breeding rivers of the Pacific salmon, the choice of habitats and the way of feeding of the stationary rainbow trout and char are, naturally, influenced by the spawning cycle of the migrating types of fish.

Judging a large river correctly is not easy and, unless an expert is at hand to fill one in, this can only be accomplished step by step. The presence of insects gives the first, crucial information. It is not hard to see that even the aquatic insects are bound to definite areas. For many kinds of insects, hatching, swarming and egg-laying take place in certain areas and, therefore, make the fish active only there. Many types of birds, such as swallows, terns and gulls, give reliable information on the presence of insects. Stretches of water where birds circle and dive can be seen a long way off. These sections are always worth fishing. From great distances and in choppy water, very careful observation must be made to discover a rising or even a chase just under the surface of the water. A pair of binoculars (8 to 10 power) is a good aid, even in identifying insects.

If no insect life can be seen at all, there is the possibility of inferring the small animal life (and, thereby, promising fly patterns) from the bottom of shallow water areas. The areas of river bed which are temporarily dry, however, provide no reliable clues. In the deep-water areas, systematic trial fishing is thus seldom avoidable.

Rapids with large pebble bottoms and uneven currents, which provide pupae and larvae, living space and, thereby, food and sheltered grounds for the fish, are the most worthwhile to fish. Dark, algae-covered stretches, stony sections and deep channels should not be overlooked. Calm, deep currents are especially interesting just downstream from the running sections, which bring down larvae and insects in all stages. Moving sections where the flow of foodstuffs is concentrated are always good fishing grounds. The typical V-form can often be seen on the surface of the water. Many current "napes" (smooth currents just upstream from rapids), as well as pool inlets and outlets, show signs of this. It can also be very worthwhile to fish the inlets and, even better, the outlets of lakes and lake-like expansions in high mountain rivers. Many fish come to these places in search of food.

Fish are not nearly as frightened of shadows in large bodies of water as they are in small ones. If the current and depth permit, they can be approached within a comfortable casting distance by wading slowly. Yet their positions are often hard to determine, so the fisherman must wade out to a good casting position. Even so, considerable distances remain to be covered, and long casts from the shore can seldom be avoided in the larger rivers and streams.

Long, smooth rods of 8.5–9 ft (2–3 m) are ideal for larger rivers. They make it easier to use long lines, and facilitate line handling and presentation. Line in class 5 to 7 is a good all-round choice, light enough for dry-fly fishing and—this is especially important—not particularly susceptible to the wind. Floating lines cover surface fishing down to 3 ft (1 m) underwater. If deep-water fishing is necessary, quick sinking "wet-tip" or "wet-head" lines are better than pure sink-tips. Their floating head-lines allow for more goal-oriented line handling.

Naturally, the method of presentation depends on the structure of the water. In backwaters, where the surface is patched with many different areas of both still and running water, a line that is as short as possible should be used. The fly can be presented up or downstream or across. The important thing is to allow the longest possible drift, in order to give the fish time to take—regardless of whether dry flies or streamers are being fished. Only by using a stop cast, with a serpentine or parachute drop, can a dry fly be held long enough on the surface, or it can be allowed to drift along the shoreline. Only on a slack line can a wet fly drift temptingly, in the play of the current, into the relatively short-action radius of the fish in the backwaters.

In still-water areas, the fish are protected not only by the surface reflections, but also by the channels or, where the current permits, by water which has been forced up into so-called "cushions". Whirlpools, certainly, do not allow for any deep examination. If a good position has been waded to, all of the areas which are within reach should be well—that is, repeatedly—fished, before a new position is tried.

When dry-fly fishing in a calm running river, it is important that the current exerts no pull on the line, so that the fly can drift through the whole area of presentation without dragging. If, for example, trout are on the lookout just under the surface, they can immediately be seen in their feeding positions. It is easy to serve them the fly, because the necessary drifting distance is short. Fishing for fish deep down, however, means that the rod must be held out quite far and the fly served loosely, as the drifting distance will be long. Grayling, for example, almost always rise from the bottom, and the deeper and faster the water, the farther away from the feeding position the ring wake will be seen. Only when the fly is served long enough can they take it. Still, while grayling in shallow waters will only take the fly if it is in a very limited area, their "territory", a grayling in deep waters will nevertheless be willing to rise for a fly drifting by several meters to one side.

For fishing many large rivers, however, the wet fly is indisputably the most important. For presenting just under the surface or in the middle layers, the cast is preferably made a little upstream or across and down stream. The fly is presented lightly stopped, slightly upstream from the active fish or from the intended fishing spot. The fly can then sink freely. Just after presentation, the line is mended against the current to hinder any possible turning of the line when the current takes it. This mending is accomplished by whipping the top of the rod upstream, parallel to the surface of the water. This is timed so that only the part of the main line which is on the surface is lifted up and laid out in small curves upstream. The tip of the line with the fly should not move at all. By mending repeatedly, an unencumbered drift is achieved, until the line is stretched out downstream. Here, the pressure of the current forces the fly to the surface. This rising often causes violent reactions from the fish.

Whether a "dead" drift, without movements, or a pattern fished with small movements is the most effective depends, to a great deal, upon which insects the fish are taking at the moment—sometimes merely on the whims of the fish. The insects' behaviour in their various stages of development is definitely species-related. Anyone who is acquainted with them knows, for example, that mosquito pupae and many mayfly "emergers" drift without movement in the water, but that freely hatching mayflies strive to the surface with lively motions. Looking more carefully, and experimenting with some afterthought, helps considerably to further one's knowledge of the choice of patterns and methods of presentation.

When mending, the rod top is whipped quickly upstream, so that the main line is lifted from the water surface and laid out in soft bows, without affecting the leader and fly.

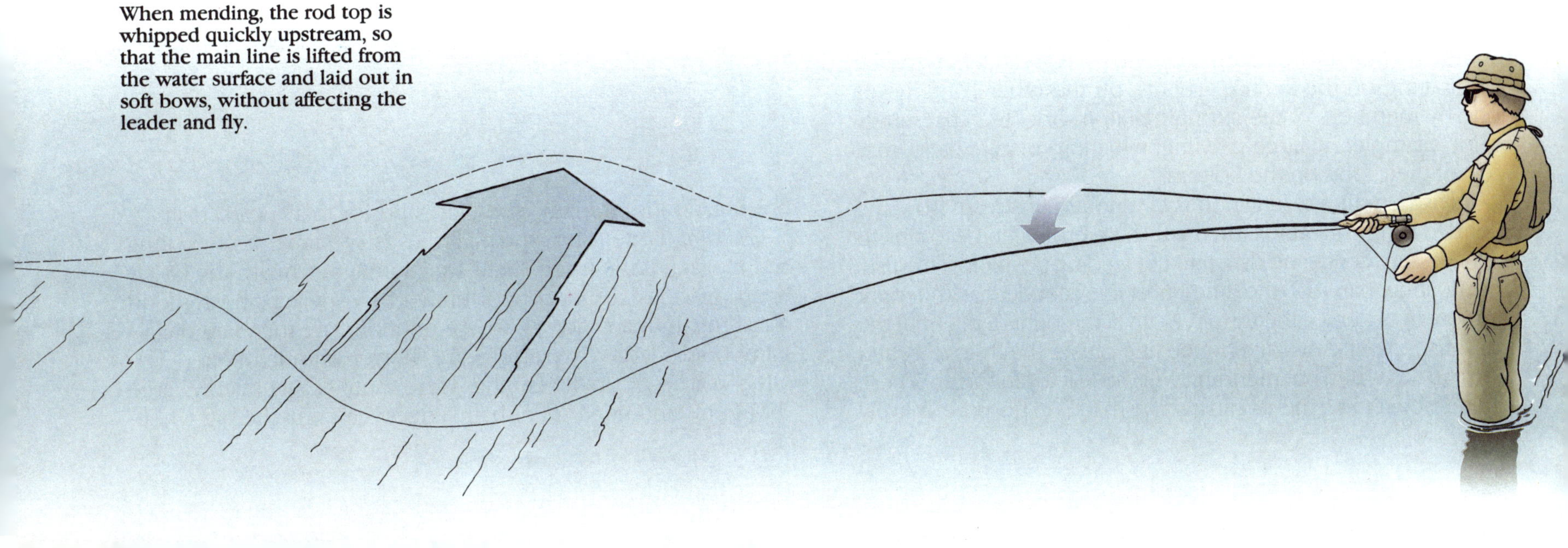

The depth of presentation is also important. Generally, it is worthwhile to come as near as possible to the way the fish are taking: that is to say, flies are served high to the fish near the surface and deep to the fish near the bottom. Trout in still-running waters can, however, even rise from great depths to take flies floating on the surface. This is, on the other hand, never done by members of the strongly bottom-oriented char family or, for example, by large grayling, which, in many waters, may seek all their food on the bottom.

Only when the presentation is far enough upstream from the intended fishing grounds can the fly have enough time to sink to the necessary depth and drift into the feeding position of the fish. The floating parts of the line must be mended at the right moment in order for the fly to remain at the right depth until the cast is fished out. Any curve in the line causes the fly to drag and to rise in the water, but mending will cause it to sink again. These up-and-down movements can also be made on purpose. A lively presentation is, in many cases, far superior to a "dead" drift.

Catching large fish with small flies is certainly most exciting and elegant. If the insect life is functioning normally, the larger rivers provide excellent opportunities for experiencing this kind of fishing. In many waters, where minnows are the main diet of salmonoids, large fly patterns are, however, much better. The same is true of dry-fly fishing. Here, only exaggeratedly large "hoppers" and huge "deer-hair sedges" can pull the big whop-

pers up from the bottom. In order to systematically fish all of the possible hiding places underwater, large flies are the most suitable—streamers, muddlers, woolly worms, and so on. This is where streamer fishing has its real use.

In larger flowing waterways, the fish positions are in more or less the same places as in smaller streams. Here they occur for example in front of drop-offs, behind stones, under overhanging trees and water plants, and where streams merge together.

Surface activity

Even insignificant movements in the water hint at surface activity. Active fish give themselves away by the bulges and small wave movements left on the smooth water surface, even if they do not break the surface. In the most common form of rising, different-sized rings, which do not necessarily correspond to the size of the active fish, show up on the surface.

While feeding just under the surface, fish show only their backs and tail fins, the so-called "head and tail". Large trout show their backs clearly, as do char and whitefish. When feeding on the surface, fish—especially large trout—clearly show their mouths, as well as their backs and tail fins.

Surface activity in fast, deep streams is often shown by grayling, char and trout breaking through the surface, due to the high speed with which they rise. Splashing "signs of turning" appear when the fish is hunting under the surface of the water (a false rise), as well as with actual rising.

Fishing in lakes

In the British Isles and Ireland, fishing with flies in still-standing water has a long tradition. The brown trout in the Scottish lochs, the lakes of Wales, the Lake District and, in the loughs of Ireland, even sea trout and salmon have fascinated fishermen for ages. Through many years of contact with these fish and the special conditions of their habitat, a quite independent classic style—a special way of fishing with flies—arose which, to this day, has retained all of its charm and effectiveness.

Thanks to the many newly-built dams, which are largely used also as commercial fishing ponds or "Stillwater Fisheries", such fly-fishing in Great Britain has been able to expand and become one of the most popular (as well as least expensive) types of fly-fishing today. T.C. Iven's book *Stillwater Flyfishing* (1952) was the first worthwhile guide to this interesting method of fishing, barely known outside the British Isles.

Most fishermen still have an enormous respect for lakes. Large bodies of water make many uncertain, and when the fish are not rising—the most common situation—it is easy to feel at a loss here. Fishing in still water offers only occasionally the amusement which makes the smaller fly-fishing waters so well-liked. Actually, a great deal of patience is required—and, above all, knowledge of how to fish lakes.

Smaller lakes, because of their comprehensibility, are very easy to begin with. If the fish are at all active, they will be caught—even by a beginner—with a deeply fished nymph, wet fly or streamer. Long rods, from 9 ft (3 m) up, with a line class of 6 to 9, give good range when fishing from the shore. Floating lines for dry flies, sink-tip lines for fishing just under the surface, and sinking lines for deep-water fishing allow diverse methods of presentation.

If no fish are on the surface, a search is made in a fan-shaped area extending out from the shore, using a deeply fished fly. Short casts are used to begin with, then the area is expanded more and more. If there is no reaction, the method is repeated fifty paces further along, and so on. After the cast, the fly is allowed to sink and reeled in, by jerks, a little at a time. Each cast is fished out, right up to the shoreline. Stragglers often do not bite until the last moment. Pulling the line in may vary from extremely slow to fast, depending on the way in which the pattern is supposed to move.

If there are neither inlets nor outlets, the open water can be fished against the wind, which causes wave movements that tend

Fly-fishing in still water is different in many ways from fishing in streams. Since the water area is often great, one needs a lot of persistence, casting ability, and caution. The methods differ too, because the fish in still waters spend less time in the surface layer. So to give the fish any chance of seeing our well-selected creations, the flies may have to be fished rather deep.

to concentrate the nutrients. Suitably deep, stony shores are better feeding places than steep cliffs. They provide good living space for insects and minnows, and thus attract larger fish. Tree-lined shores are always worth fishing, as there are always fish near them, even with offshore winds. Here, caution is advised, because even large fish come all the way in to the shore and are easy to frighten away. In many lakes, even small ones, the fish will stay in the deeper parts during the day and approach land when dark comes on. In twilight and at night, large fish such as browns and char can therefore be caught with dry flies.

In smaller, wind-sheltered waters, a float-tube can be used to easily fish those areas which are hard or impossible to reach from the shore. By sitting low in the water, no silhouette which can frighten the fish is formed. Active fish can be approached quite closely with caution. Even when fishing from a boat, it is always a good idea to remember to fish sitting down, so as to scare the fish as little as possible. Fish see a standing fisherman from much farther away than what a longer casting distance can compensate. This is also true when fishing from the shores of large lakes.

Areas with currents offer the best chances of a catch. On large bodies of water, even stronger movements are caused by the wind, which has to be taken into account. The narrows between islands, peninsulas, sounds and points are fine fishing places. In drifting boats, one finds the best chances of reaching areas of the lake where the fish are rising above or just below the surface. If the fish can be seen taking any kind of food, large areas should be fished by allowing the boat to drift with the wind. Fishing from an anchored boat is only worthwhile in places of proven value, such as inlets, outlets and areas with currents.

The most favourable is always a surface with ripples or waves. Glossy surface water is merely a disadvantage, especially for dry-fly fishing in bright sunshine. The fish have more time to study each pattern. Under these circumstances, it is hard to hide the leader well enough when it has sunk near the fly and lies submerged, although this sometimes can tempt the fish anyway by giving the fly a little life and movement.

In the classic style, fishing is done from a drifting boat in moderately deep water and casting with the wind. Long rods of 10–13 ft (3–4 m) are used, with floating line or, perhaps, "intermediates" and leaders, tied with three completely different flies in sizes 10 to 14. The foremost fly (tail fly) is fished deepest, but normally not more than 5 ft (1.5 m) under the surface. The middle fly (middle dopper) is above this, and the last fly (bob fly) moves on the water surface. The cast is made 11–13 yds (10–12 m) out, and the flies are then taken in with small tugs. Well-practiced fly control and a good deal of patience are needed in order to get trout to rise.

Three flies on the leader are, of course, not needed to catch fish: one is good enough. Casting against the wind from a boat

In most lakes, the fish stay deep during the day, but at dusk or night they enter shallow waters to search—sometimes wildly—for food.

has also proved itself, with both dry-fly and wet-fly patterns. Dry flies are presented about 16 yds (15 m) out, in a direction against the wind and allowed, if possible, to lie still. Assuming that the fly floats well, it can drift temptingly a few hundred meters behind the boat. If a fish should jump nearby, the fly can, without losing much time, be lifted up with the long rod and presented exactly, quite often with good results.

When a fish takes, the line must be stretched tightly at once. This requires constant concentration. Most "false strikes" are, in reality, "drowsy" strikes, a result of fishing for hours without the least feeling for it. When the fish are taking under the surface, one uses mayfly emergers, fished with a floating line and a leader which has been greased up to the last 20 inches (50 cm) or a prepared wet fly. When there are light wave movements, the fly need not be given any life. If there is no noticeable activity at all, systematic trial fishing is unavoidable.

Adjusting to depth, a longer sink-tip (wet-head) or a pure sink-line is used. Even here, the cast is made against the wind, and the fly is allowed to sink, then reeled in with small tugs. In strong wind and quick drift, it is enough to cast the fly out behind the boat and give it life with the tip of the rod. In deep-water wet-fly fishing, fish such as trout, grayling and char often hook themselves.

In choosing the fly, the insects in the water should always be the starting point for size and type. But not seldom, land insects play an important role. The greatest success is achieved by those who discover what sort of activity is going on, which is often hard to do in still water. For wet flies, classic and unassuming patterns of medium size are often best suited. A particularly successful pattern around the world is the simple Iven's "Black and Peacock Spider" which, in size 8, is effective even when the fish are actually out after small crustaceans. Fly-fishing in lakes is a real pleasure, and does not lack excitement as many people still believe. There are plenty of enormous fish to catch, even if they do not come easy!

Predators

It is exciting that fishing for pike and perch has slowly spread among European fly-fishermen. For most, the intelligent and temperamental perch and the explosive pike are still quite exotic. Many waters which should be interesting have thus remained obscure.

Even here, progressive American fly-fishermen are far ahead of the Europeans. Perch—above all, the black bass, which exists in many types and forms—is among the most popular sportfish and is fished ardently with fly. Especially enticing and enjoyed is fishing with "bass bugs", large "flies" with cork, deer-hair or synthetic bodies, which are fished "blubbering" on top of the water. Special WF-lines (bass bug tapers) with a belly, extremely

Fly-fishing for pike requires large flies with a clear silhouette. Extra long-shanked streamers tied with glittering Flash-a-Bou usually attract effectively.

concentrated on the line, make the presentation of such wind-sensitive patterns easier.

Surface-active black bass are mostly found in shallow waters and can occasionally be fished by sight. Because of this, the ever-alert fish cannot be alarmed by enthusiastic casting movements, or even by casting over them. Only when the fly lands discreetly, and is then set in motion well, is it possible to get black bass to bite. Even the European perch is easy to attract with a dry fly drawn across the surface—although, like small-mouth bass, they are much more attracted to wet flies, nymphs and streamers.

All perch hunt moderately quickly, are curious and easy to get to bite—but they are never imprudent. They react best to multi-coloured Marabou patterns, in sizes 4 to 8, which are fished slowly and deeply, yet as mobile as possible, with a sink-tip or sinking line. Laggers with folded-back fins can often be seen following the fly the last few meters, allowing themselves to be tempted. The easiest to catch are the medium-large fish found in schools, participating in their sensational hunt for minnows. Perch of this size and even larger ones often take small nymphs. Big perch, hunting alone, are usually found near small schools of fish, as they readily feed on smaller fish of the same species. Resting periods are always taken on the bottom. Even here, they can be fished with a fly near the bottom—as long as one has enough patience to find their habitats.

Even the largest European perch, the European pike-perch (zander), and its American counterpart, the walleye, are fished from the bottom. Large specimens of both will occasionally be found in schools. Like those which feed on minnows, they will bite best on medium-large, slowly fished streamers of minnow-type. Pike-perch sometimes bite voraciously. Because of their many sharp teeth, a 0.45-mm leader is the lower limit.

As opposed to perch, pike preferably bite on large, quickly fished streamers. Pike are typically ambushing predators—robust, with strong nerves and not easy to scare away. On the contrary, their attention is caught by making an extra loud presentation. In shallow waters, it is a good tactic to present the fly as loudly as possible, directly followed by a new cast to the same spot, then quickly pulling it in as soon as it has sunk. If the chosen pike is waiting in ambush, it will generally strike just as the fly hits the water. All too slowly fished flies are often followed with interest, but are taken only when one lets them "shoot" away. In clear water, this can easily be observed.

If the pike bites voraciously, it is nearly always hooked a long way down in the throat and is hooked for good. When the bite is more careful, the fish is often lost. Especially in the tough, tooth-filled upper jaw, the hook has a hard time piercing. The strike must be energetic, and this presupposes correspondingly robust equipment. Powerful 8.5-ft (2.5-m) rods of class 7 to 8 are right. The leader must be at least 0.45 mm. thick. Only steel leader (such as Berkley's Steel-on-Leader) are absolutely trustworthy when it comes to withstanding the murderous jaws of a pike. Pike under the minimum size can be unhooked without harming the fish or the fisherman by means of a long-handled disgorger.

Long streamers of 4–5.5 in (10–14 cm) are used as flies. Matuka patterns and similar small tied flies are fished even in this size without any problem. The most important is a clear silhouette. A little glitter (for example, Flash-a-Bou) also gives the fly a little life and lustre. Small salmon hooks in sizes 4/0 to 6/0 and special types with wide hook gaps, such as Mustad 3282, are ideal. In shallow waters, sink-tip lines are fished; in deep water, sinking lines are better.

Visible pike can seldom be fished. They are almost always lying in wait, well-hidden on the bottom. Finding typical habitats is, therefore, especially important. In running water, the pike is often found near the shore, in protrusions, under sunken driftwood, in back of concentrated water plants, and in the shelter of stones jutting out to the edge of strong currents. In lakes, their territories are found in clumps of reed and vegetation belts near steep banks. In quite a number of lakes—especially cyprinoid lakes—they can also be found out in the open water.

Pike fishing is a stimulating form of streamer fishing and, when it comes to excitement, can hardly be beat. Pike have everything one could ask of a sportfish—a stormy temperament, enormous strength and size. Anyone who has experienced this fish on a fly-rod, will, from then on, always be on the lookout to experience it again.

The cyprinoids, or carp family

For most fishermen, the first contact with carp fish is usually made by chance, in areas where carp often act as companions to the desirable salmonoids. In central Europe, there are mostly the ide, chub, dace, and other bottom-oriented river barbel. In North America, the places of many of these fish are taken by the wide-spread "suckers". If not before, then after the first contact with this kind of fish, it will be discovered that, from a sporting viewpoint, at least many fly-fishermen's disdain for them is totally unfounded.

Most carp fish, due to their way of living, are much harder to catch than salmonoids. They are slower and more careful when taking food, and the larger specimens are enormously timid. Feeling and taste play an important part in their search for food, especially in muddy waters. At the same time, they have much better eyesight than is commonly thought, and with optical stimulation—the fly—they can very well be tempted. This is easiest where the fish can be seen.

In running water, surface-active carp-fish take correctly presented dry flies and shallowly fished wet flies. The fly must, however, be presented very carefully and their slowness be taken into consideration. A counter-strike made too early will spoil everything and, if the carp becomes the least bit spooked, further attempts will be fruitless. It is even worse in still waters. Dry flies must be properly "breathed" down to the surface, and patterns which are fished underwater must be taken in with careful movements. The fish literally take in slow motion, and then only if the fly matches their expectations. At any rate, it is easier to follow and react to what is happening in the water.

Even greater demands are made on fishing with wet flies in deep and muddy lakes. Exact knowledge of feeding grounds and the behaviour of the fish, as well as patience, are prerequisites for successfully bottom-fishing nymphs. Fishing is done with a floating line and a correspondingly long leader or with a sink-tip line. After the cast, the line is allowed to sink, then the fly is taken in extremely slowly. It is hard to feel the bite, which is always very cautious. Any movement at the point where the line leaves the water can be an indication and should be answered by gently lifting the rod. Once the hook is set, it will stay put in the carp's leather-like mouth.

The rapacious asps are, through their predatory nature, completely different from other European cyprinoids. Their temperamental quest for food gives them away from great distances. Bleak breaking through the surface indicate that greedy asps are on the hunt. A fast, surface-fished streamer has good effect and makes fishing in their waters an exciting experience.

It is also interesting to fish for the skilfully swimming river barbels in the lower salmonoid regions. These bottom fish, which hunt in schools, can be found even in the deeper running waters. When they are feeding on the bottom, the glitter from their silver and gold sides is easy to see. This is the only time it pays to offer them a nymph.

It is possible to carefully approach an active school, near enough to cast, but the fly should be cast out only if the fish continue to feed. Here, the pattern itself is not as important as its being presented right on the bottom. The least movement from the drifting line tip indicates a bite. A counter-strike is made immediately. Afterward, these enormously strong fish defend themselves more violently than most salmonoids.

Fly-fishing for carp-fish is harder than most people think. But a properly presented fly, taken in with slow movements, often makes carp-fish bite—if only cautiously. But premature strikes are a common cause of lost fish.

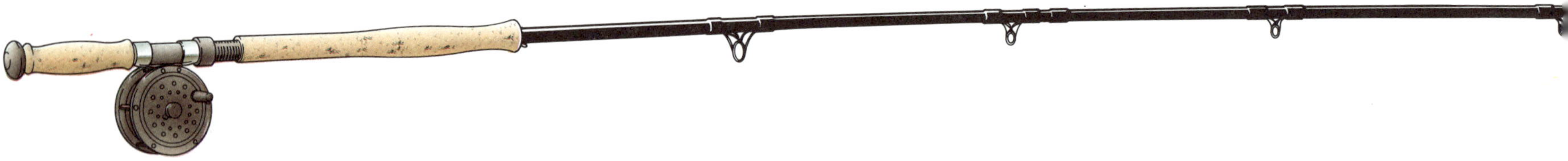

Heavier fly-fishing

Salmon and sea trout belong to a fascinating area of fly-fishing. There are many methods of catching these fish, but none can trigger off the same nerve-wracking feeling and atmosphere as does fly-fishing.

Atlantic salmon

The season

As a rule, the bigger salmon return first during the season, followed by the medium-size and smaller ones. The early-run salmon in Norwegian rivers can be very large, often averaging 10–12 kilos. Salmon are considerably smaller in the rivers of Great Britain, Iceland, Ireland and North America. But the autumn salmon in Scotland's rivers Tweed, Tay, and Nith can compete with the Norwegian ones in size.

The earliest ascent of salmon occurs in Scottish and Irish rivers—as soon as February 11 in some, and during February in most others such as the Tweed, Dee and Spey. The salmon season in the British Isles is not only the earliest, but also the longest. After it ends on the Tweed in November, for example, one can move farther south to the Camel and Fowey in Cornwall, where fishing continues until mid-December.

The season for spring salmon in Scotland runs from early spring to the end of May. Summer salmon, grilse and sea trout are caught during the next months. From September until the end of the season, autumn salmon are fished. Inland lakes with salmon and sea trout in Scotland and Ireland are also quite popular.

In Scandinavia, Norway has by far the greatest number of river salmon. They regularly run more than 200 rivers, or nearly a thousand if one includes all the minor waterways where small salmon and sea trout may run during times of heavy precipitation. June and July are the best months for salmon-fishing in Norway. The season now begins on June 1 for most rivers, such as the well-known Vossa, Laerdal, Surna, Orkla, Gaula, Stjørdal, Namsen and Alta. Late July and all of August are considered best for sea trout.

Only one river in Finland still has good salmon-fishing, the Tenojoki bordering Norway. The rivers emptying into the Baltic were once rich in running salmon, but have been blocked by hydroelectric power plants. Nor does Sweden boast many rivers with salmon and sea trout, but good catches can be made at times on the Mörrum, Emån, Ätran, and some others. The most interesting parts of the season are May to August for salmon, and September for fresh-run sea trout.

A lot of sportfishermen find Iceland the ideal place: its rivers still abound in running salmon, due to hard restrictions and bans on commercial net-fishing outside the estuaries. Although no larger than the state of Maine, this island has about fifty salmon rivers. Among the better known are Laxá in Adaldal, Laxá in Kjos, Selå, Nordura, Grimsa, and Stramfjordara. Some of the rivers also have plenty of seagoing char. As in Norway, the salmon ascend during summer.

Spain's salmon season runs from the end of March to the middle of July. The best times for fishing vary between rivers. On the northern Atlantic coast, there are sixteen important rivers, the best being the Sella, Cares-Deva, Narcea, Ason, Pas, Eo, Navia, and Canero.

French rivers, too, formerly swirled with running salmon, but most have been decimated by construction and pollution. The once famous Sienne, See, and Selune now yield no more than a few hundred salmon each year altogether. At present the best salmon waters in France are probably the Adour system, notably the Gave d'Oloron.

Steelhead

North America also has the best fishing in summertime. Around the eastern coasts, fine rivers for Atlantic salmon include the Narraguagus in Maine and the Margaree in Nova Scotia. Important in New Brunswick is the large Miramichi system with its tributaries—the Northwest Miramichi, Little Southwest Miramichi, the Cains, Dungarvon, Bartholomew, Renous, and Sevogle. In Quebec the Grant Cascapedia, Restigouche, and Matane are popular among American fly-fishermen. Newfoundland and Labrador are world-famous for salmon rivers such as the Humber, Portland Creek, Eagle, and St. Mary's.

In addition, several species of Pacific salmon run a number of rivers along the American and Canadian west coasts. Perhaps the main fly-fishing in these rivers, though, is for the steelhead, which offers a fantastic game with a one-handed fly-rod. Species of Pacific salmon can also be fly-fished in the rivers running into some of the Great Lakes.

Holding places

Inasmuch as the migration of salmon up the rivers is for the purpose of spawning and they do not feed during this period, it may seem that fishing for salmon is a strange kind of sport. But why do salmon insist on taking flies? Many think that the salmon has some sort of hereditary memory from its youth and therefore occasionally bites at a fly. Others believe that the recently ended fattening process at sea affects the salmon's biting reflexes.

Most, however, agree that it is a territorial defence mechanism which triggers off the biting reflex. This theory does seem the most probable, considering that salmon do not take flies during migration, but only when they have found suitable spawning grounds. It is thus important to know where suitable spawning grounds are found in the river.

Salmon fishermen speak among themselves of low and high water pools. In small, warm summer rivers, the salmon will often stop at places where the current is swift and there is plenty of oxygen. In large, water-swollen rivers, salmon are often found in the area between and within the outlets of pools. After heavy rains, when the rivers are swollen and muddy, salmon will usually be found very near to land.

Each river and section has its own form and character, which are the decisive factors for where the fish will settle. It is not enough that the current and the depth are right: the construction of the bottom is also important if the salmon are to get along in the pool. The river bottom in a salmon pool should consist of a mixture of fist-size stones, gravel and occasional large rocks. Around larger rock, holes are often formed, which are excellent resting spots for salmon.

The classic fly-pool starts upstream, at the end of rapids where the current evens out to a quieter pace and where the lower end accelerates and narrows to a nape. These pools often have a wadable side and a deep side with a sudden drop-off where the deep channel goes.

In low water, the salmon in this pool will have taken a place at the beginning of the pool, where the water is oxygen-filled. It can also be in the deep channel, near the steep side. The best fishing is when the river is medium-filled, because the fish can then be found anywhere in the pool. In water which is very high as well as muddy, the salmon are found very near to land on the wading side, sheltered from the hard current.

A good place to find salmon is where two streams meet. Here, they can be found either at the point where the streams come together or on the sides of the stream. River bends are also very good places, because salmon stop there during their migration upstream. Classic fishing places are always the narrows, where

Several factors determine where salmon are located on the way up a river to spawn. This stretch of river shows some typical holding positions in which salmon can often be found. At the confluence of a tributary with the main flow, fish frequently even stand in a V-formation. They may also occur some ways upstream in the tributary if it is salmon-bearing. Depending on how big the river is, they may stand both above and below the confluence. Other typical spots are just below rapids, where salmon tend to pause before attempting the obstacle—and at the necks above rapids, where they usually pause before continuing upstream. They also like to wait in the outer edges of the stream at the normal river-bends below rapids.

both salmon and sea trout stop to rest before continuing their journey upstream.

There are lots of different stopping places for salmon. But it is not at all certain that the same pool fishes just as well from one year to the next. Rivers change constantly, for example if the water has been abnormally high for a long period of time, or if there have been strong ice flows.

Below at left is the same stretch of river as above, but with little water flow. The salmon now stand where the current is fast and oxygen-rich.

The holding places of salmon in pools are at inlets and outlets, and in front of large boulders.

Casting with two-handed salmon fly-rods

Along the length of the river, both the current and the terrain change. In order to utilize the stream, from the viewpoint of fishing technique, it is an advantage to have different types of casts, which each have their own special areas of use. Of these, the switch, overhead, underhand and single Spey cast are the most important to learn.

The switch, or roll-cast as it is also called, is actually not a fly-cast at all, as the line is rolled out onto the water. Switch casts are very useful in cramped pools, where the vegetation makes it impossible to back-cast. The best use, however, of the switch cast is to roll the line up to the surface, before lifting it for a traditional casting method. For the switch cast, the line is stretched out on top of the water. The rod is brought up slowly, somewhat to the side, to a 1-o'clock position. Before the switch is begun, the rod is lowered somewhat more, so that the line is laid out in an arch, next to the fisherman. The switch is begun with a slowly accelerating movement of the rod. This movement is stopped when the rod is parallel to the surface of the water. The fly-line then rolls out onto the water.

The overhead cast is a basic technique for both two-handed and one-handed fly-fishing. This cast, however, has limitations as

Overhead cast with two-handed rod in practice

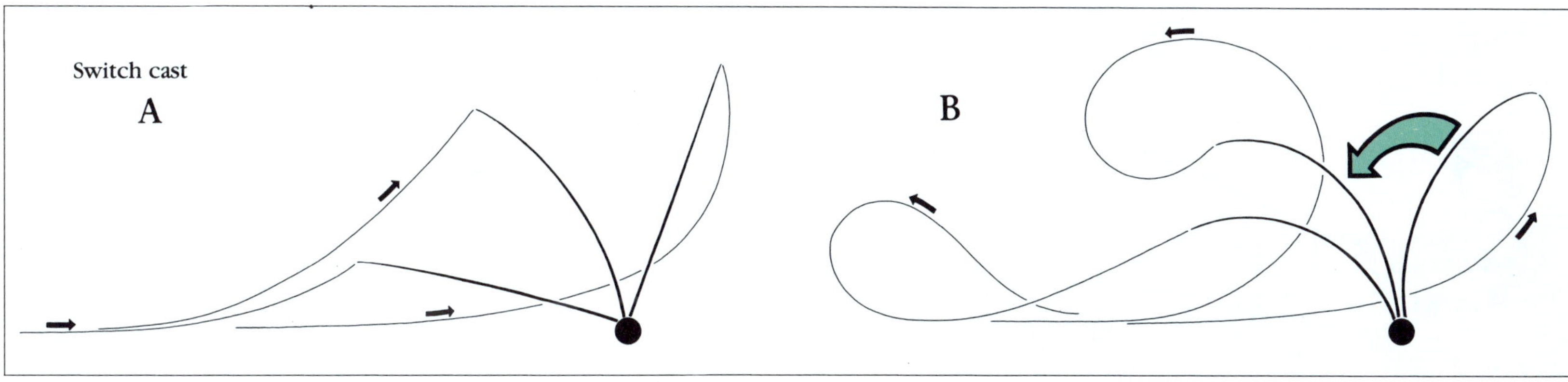
Switch cast
A
B

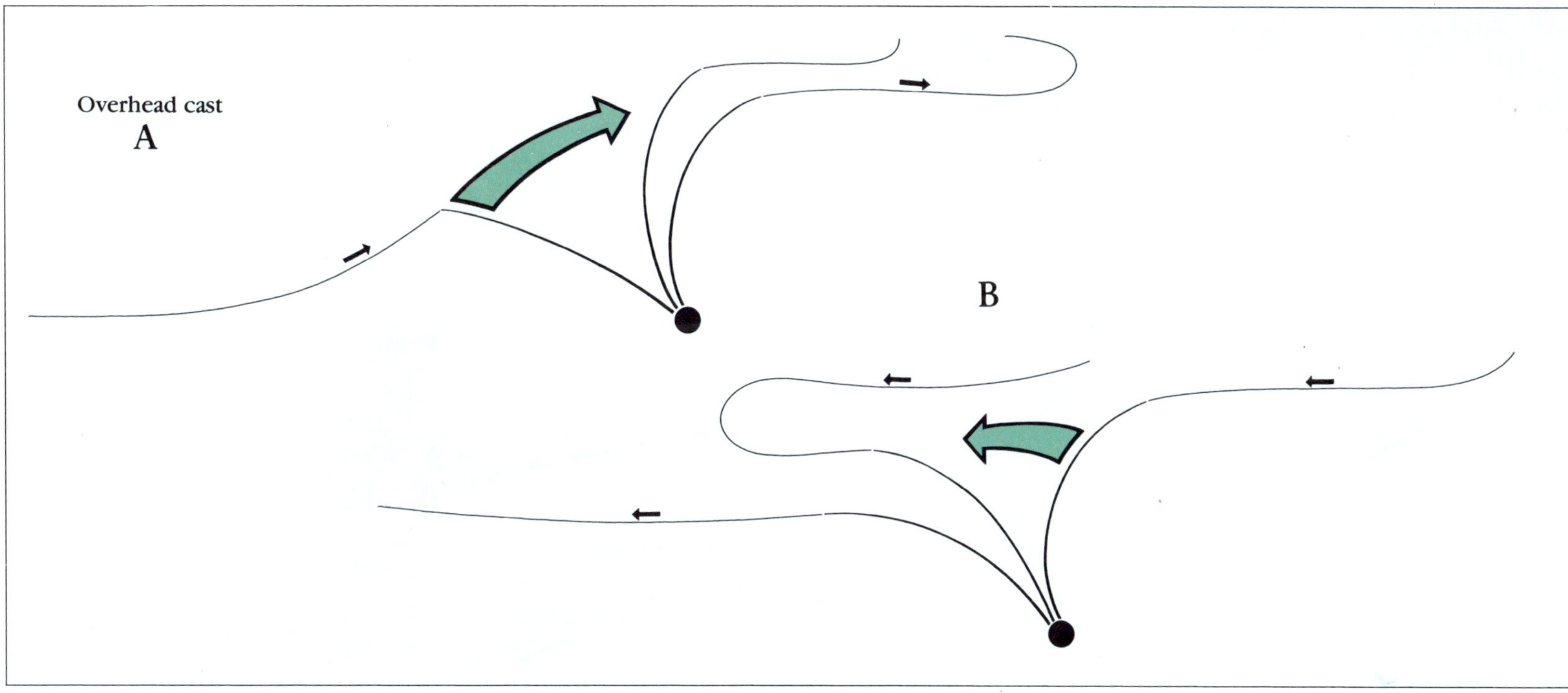
Overhead cast
A
B

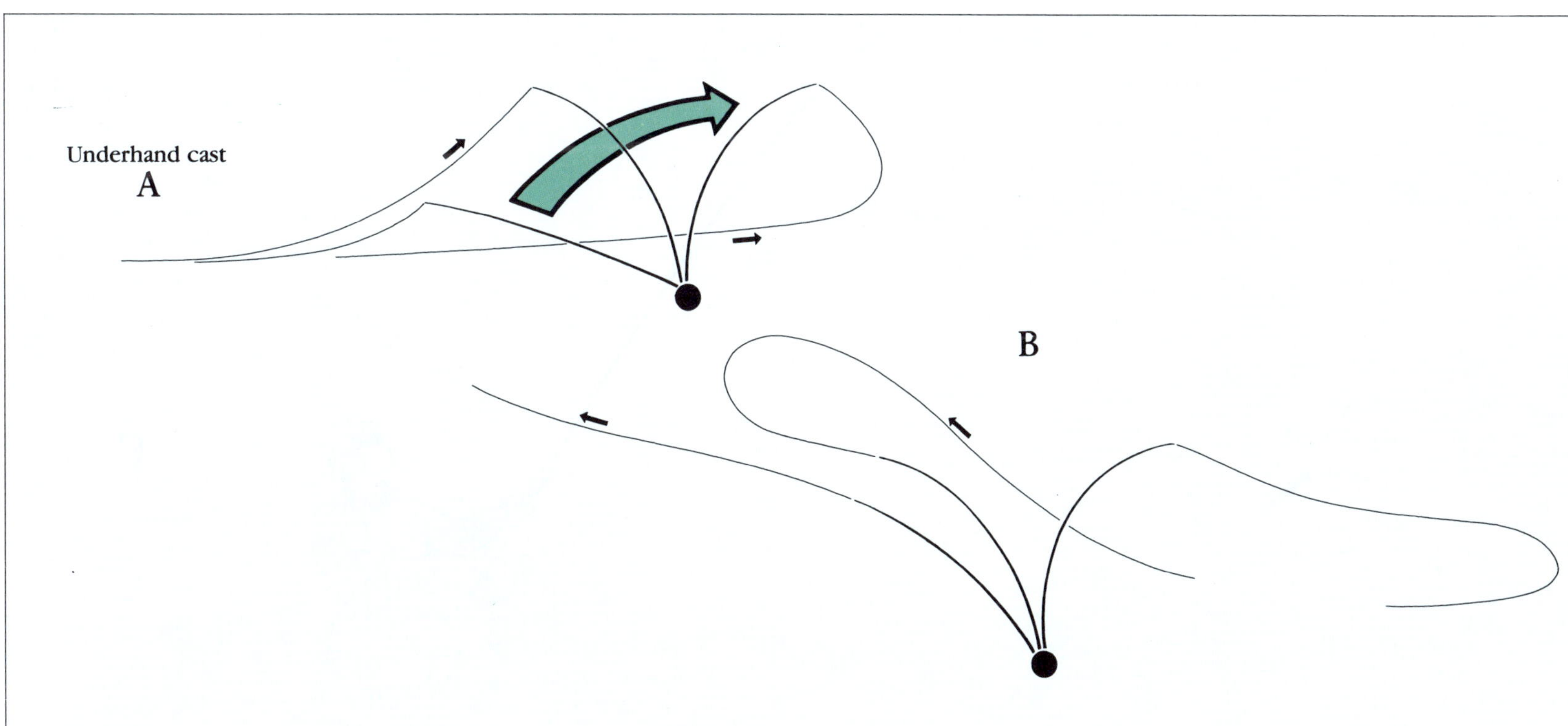
Underhand cast
A
B

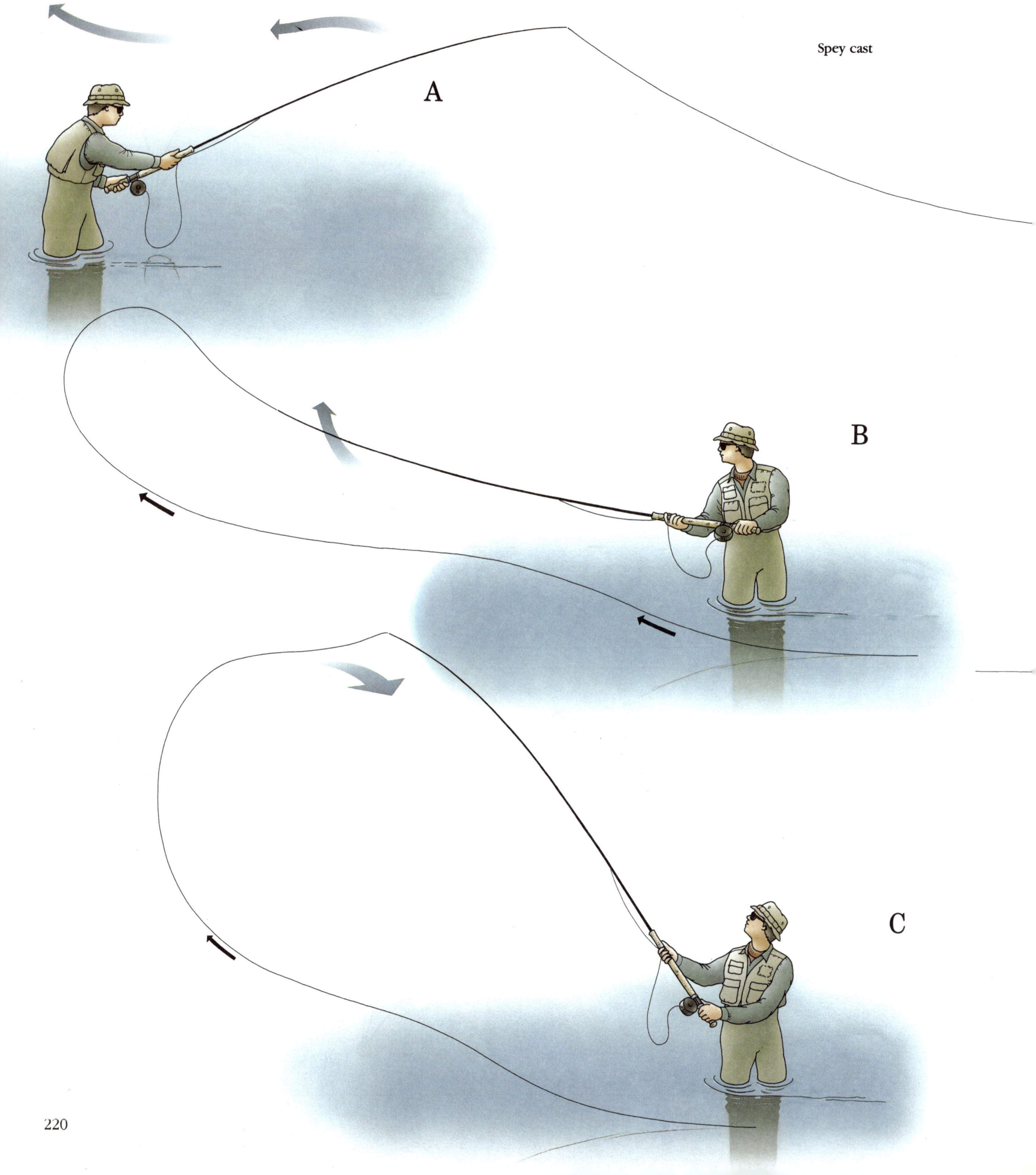
Spey cast
A
B
C

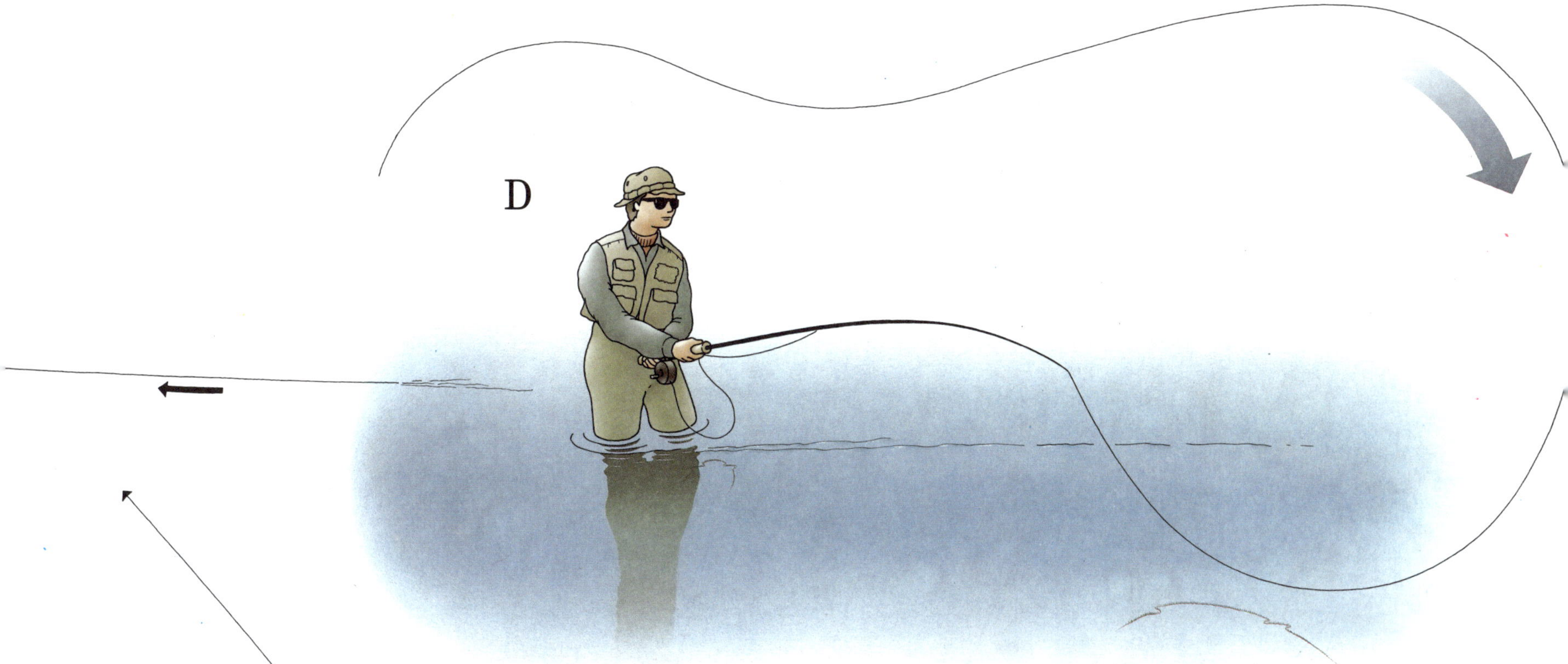

it requires a large area for the back-cast. The first step for an overhead cast is to lay the line, stretched out, on the surface of the water. The back-cast is started with a smooth, accelerating motion. The fly-line seems almost to be sucked out of the water. The rod is stopped in a vertical position, where a pause is made, so that the line can stretch out to the back. The forward cast is made with an accelerating motion. If the line is to be lengthened during the cast, it is shot out in the forward cast by letting loose the line that is being held in the fingers of the upper hand. In this way, the loose line is released and shoots out forward. When the back-cast begins again, the line is, once again, held tightly against the handle of the rod. When the required length has finally come out and the cast is angled out over the water, the rest of the loose line is shot out for the final presentation.

The underhand cast is one of the most elegant fly-casts. For many, casting with a two-handed salmon fly-rod is a difficult way of fishing. It is, therefore, important to find an effective, rhythmic and restful method of casting, which makes an extended fishing tour possible without requiring too much exertion. The underhand cast accomplishes this by using only one air-cast. When using the underhand cast, the fly-line is stretched out on the surface. The rod is stretched up, with its tip pointed towards the river, in an accelerating, circular motion. The fly-line, affected by this movement, will pass in front of the fisherman and under the rod. The stop is made in the vertical position. The forward cast is begun before the last 6–12 ft (2–4 m) have become stretched out. The highest concentration of power in the forward cast should occur when the rod is between the 11- and 12-o'clock positions.

The single Spey cast is, principally, a variation on the switch-cast. The big difference is that the fly is lifted and placed out over the river on the fisherman's outward side, instead of returning on the same level. The major advantage of the single Spey cast is that the fly does not get caught on the leader and that the cast is very useful in tight spaces, where there is not enough room for the fly-line behind the fisherman. The Spey cast is best accomplished with a floating DT-line. For the single Spey cast the line is laid, stretched out on the surface, downstream. The rod is stretched upwardly and out towards the river, in an accelerating motion, to about a 1-o'clock position. Instead of letting the line stretch out to the rear as in the overhead and underhand casts, the last 2–3 yds (m) of line are allowed to touch the water surface. The forward cast is thus drawn from the resistance in the contact of the line with the water. The concentration of power in the forward cast should be somewhere between the 11- and 12-o'clock positions. The whole cast should be accomplished in one single motion.

In the Scottish river Spey, it is common for salmon fishermen to alternate between a single Spey cast and a double Spey cast. If the fisherman is normally right-handed, the single Spey is used from the left bank and the double Spey from the right. The reason is that most fishermen generally have a strong and a weak casting side. Anyone who can easily manage to cast with both the right and the left hand does not need to bother alternating casts. It is enough to change rod hands.

Methods

Many fishermen seem to think that fly-fishing for salmon is possible only when the river is not too big or too cold. But nothing could be further from the truth. With the various types of fly-line on the market today, fly-fishing is the best all-round method for fishing for salmon, as long as the fishing is matched to the prevailing conditions. The most common methods of fly-fishing for salmon and seagoing trout are with sinking and floating line. To the classic methods, other and more local variations can be added: dry-fly, riffling hitch, backing-up, harling, dibbling and dapping.

Fishing with sinking line in a pool with varying current speed. At the inflow, where the current is fast, the fly is laid out askew downstream, so as to reach the right tempo—and immediately followed by a mending upstream. In the middle section, where the current weakens, the cast is laid across the pool without mending. At the outflow, the current regains strength and the cast is again laid out at an angle downstream.

Heavy fishing with sinking lines

Fishing for larger specimens is pursued in large, cold, high mountain rivers early in the season, for example on the Scottish east coast. But it can also be found during summer in rivers that are swollen by run-offs of melted snow or by long rainy periods.

When fishing for salmon in such rivers, the best chances are found in the zone between the bottom and the middle layers. Under these harsh fly-fishing conditions, a two-handed salmon fly-rod of 15–16 ft (4.5–5 m) in AFTM-class II, with powerful total action, is best suited.

In choosing between a WF and a DT fly-line, the latter is to be recommended for all two-handed rods. There are fly-lines designated "fast sinking" (S2) and "extra fast sinking" (S3) which are especially well suited.

The fly-reel for all salmon fly-fishing should primarily be reliable and large. It should, preferably, be able to hold, besides the fly-line, 165–220 yds (150–200 m) of backing in a line class of 26–33 lbs (12–15 kg). Depending on the size and weight of the fly, the diameter of the tip of the leader should be between 0.45 and 0.50 mm. As salmon are not particularly timid in large rivers, a leader length of 1.5–2 yds (m) is enough.

Salmon fly-fishing in large, cold rivers is a large-fly type of fishing, especially with tube-flies, Waddington, and Esmond Drury. The salmon are best attracted by colourful patterns. Special cold-water patterns, tied on tubes and Waddington, are the Garry, Green Highlander, Dee Royal, Black and Gold, Willie Gunn, and Tadpole.

In large rivers, salmon are generally found just below the swiftest currents. This means that they can also be found parked near the shore. Therefore, wading should always be done with care. It is often enough to wade out knee-deep, if one need go into the water at all. Many high-water pools are also fished from land.

Salmon are cold-blooded fish and, before the temperature has come up to 7–8°C (45–46°F), they are relatively slow in reacting. Thus the fly should preferably be fished slowly, which is best accomplished by presenting the fly as far as possible down and across the current. In slow-moving pools, the cast can be presented a bit more straight across the current. Fishing slowly and deeply must not be misinterpreted. The fly cannot seem to be lifeless in quiet pools, but needs to be kept in motion, since it is the drift itself which makes the fly interesting to the salmon.

What needs to be considered, when the cast has been fished out and the fly is hanging below the fisherman, is not to be in too much of a hurry to take in the fly, in order to make a new cast—something, by the way, which applies to both salmon and sea-trout fishing. It is often after a long drift that both salmon and sea trout bite.

Traditional fishing with sinking line

A little further along in the season, when both the air and the water temperature have risen, fly-fishing becomes richer in variation. The best chances to catch salmon and sea trout in water temperatures of 8–12°C (46–54°F) are in the zone between the middle layers and the surface.

More varied fishing requires a somewhat different choice of equipment if the season is to be fully exploited. Alternation between one- and two-handed rods is called for. In normal and small rivers, the length of the two-handed rod can be reduced, for example to 13–15 feet (4–4.5 m) in AFTM-class 9 to 10, meaning that the rod is somewhat more flexible than is needed for the heavy fishing in cold and large rivers.

The choice of fly-line for a river that has come up to 8–12°C is usually an intermediate (1) or slow-sinking (S1). The former is an extremely slow-sinking line, which stays just under the surface while it is being fished out. Slow-sinking (S1) is a normal sinking line with a broad area of use.

A smaller and warmer river requires longer leaders than in heavy cold-water fishing. A tapered leader length of 2.7–3 yds (2.5–2.75 m) is a good choice. The diameter of the tip can vary from 0.3 mm for the smallest flies in size 8, up to 0.45 mm for flies in sizes 3/0 with single hook. The most useful tip diameter for double hooks in sizes 6 to 2, which are the most common sizes at present, is 0.40 mm.

Many prefer one-handed equipment for this kind of fishing. This applies not least to salmon fly-fishing in North American and Icelandic rivers. In Norwegian rivers, however, one-handed equipment is more of a complement to the heavier two-handed equipment. One-handed equipment is even an extremely fine tool for both sea trout and for floating-line fishing for salmon.

For salmon and sea trout, the most useful lengths of one-handed fly-fishing rods are 10–12 ft (3–3.6 m) in an AFTM-class of 8 to 9. The rod should preferably be a full-action model, so that the fight can be taken out of a large salmon if necessary. For one-handed fishing, a WF-line has many advantages over a DT-line.

During this season, the choice of fly becomes richer in variation, both in size and pattern. A collection of single, double and treble hooked Drury flies in sizes from 8 to 3/0 is the most successful.

As to fly patterns, there is an old rule of thumb: if the sun is shining and the river is clear, then lightly coloured patterns will fish best, preferably with silver bodies and some green in the wings. Reliable good-weather flies are the Silver and Blue, Silver Grey, and Green Highlander. In cloudy and dark weather, dark and neutral patterns like the Grey Heron, Black Doctor, and Rusty Rat are good choices. When the river is swampy or brownish, the orange-coloured Garry and the dark-red General Practitioner are excellent appetizers. Night fishing for salmon is most popular in the rivers of Norway, where the choice is entirely black patterns like the Stoat's Tail, Black Tosh, and Black Shadow.

As mentioned, this time of the year offers larger variation in terms of fly and pattern sizes. If the pool has been fished well, using small and middle-sized flies, yet without result, it can be worth making a final attempt with a really large fly.

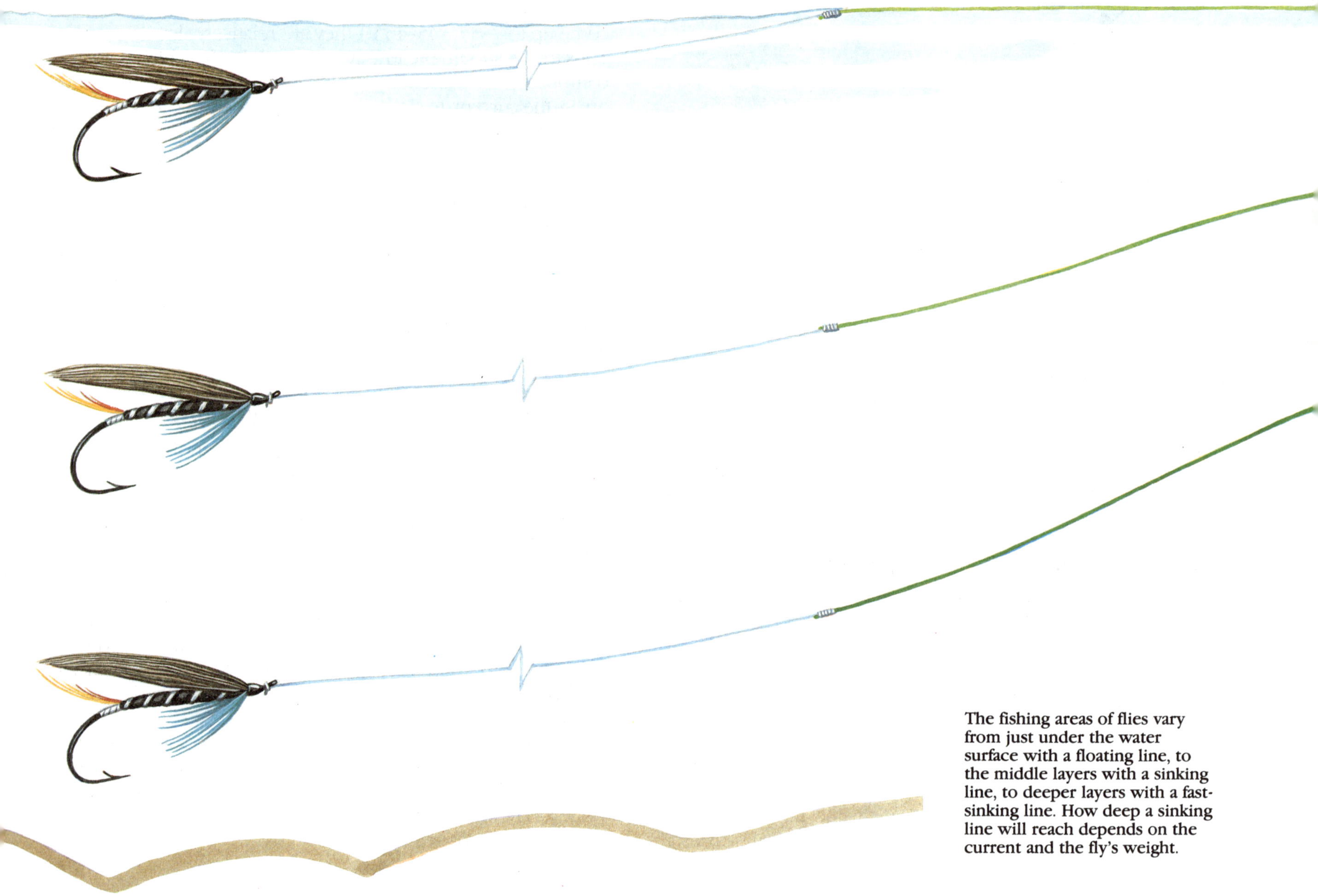

The fishing areas of flies vary from just under the water surface with a floating line, to the middle layers with a sinking line, to deeper layers with a fast-sinking line. How deep a sinking line will reach depends on the current and the fly's weight.

Fishing with floating lines

Many feel that this is the most sporting form of fishing for salmon and sea trout. The most famous floating-line fisherman of all times is the English salmon fisherman A.H.E. Wood. Between the years of 1913 and 1934, Wood landed no fewer than 3,490 salmon, most of them on greased line with small, surface-fished flies in the Cairnton Waters of the River Dee in Scotland.

Floating-line fishing is associated primarily with small and warm summer rivers, but this is only part of the truth. Fishing with floating line works extremely well, even when the river is cold, as long as it is not too deep. Willingness to bite usually increases, however, around 8–9°C (46–48°F).

When night fishing for sea trout in the clear rivers of western Norway, floating line is indispensable. Floating line is easier to lift up from the water for a new cast than sinking line, which can be quite important in pitch dark. By mending (lifting the line over against the current) floating line correctly, it is possible to fish a larger radius than with sinking line, where fishing is limited to the traditional 45° angle downstream. Sea trout bite on a high-fished fly better in the dark, as well.

According to A.H.E. Wood, the aim of fly-fishing is to try to show the fly to the fish from the side. Normally, therefore, the cast is laid out more straight across the current than when fishing with sinking line. The line is mended as soon as it shows the least tendency to bending while being fished out. In swift currents, it is, of course, impossible to both mend the line and show the fly from the side at the same time. In fishing pools with strong currents, it is thus better to present floating line, like sinking line, diagonally downstream.

For floating-line fishing for salmon and sea trout with small flies, a one-handed rod, 10–11 ft (3–3.3 m) long, is an elegant instrument. But even a flexible two-handed rod of 13–15 feet (4–4.5 m) has its admirers for salmon fishing. Appropriate floating line for one-handed rods is a WF-line in AFTM-class 8 to 9 and, for a two-handed rod, a DT-line in line class 10 to 11. Normally, a somewhat longer leader is used for floating-line fishing than for sinking line. A tapered leader with a length of 3–3.3 yds (3 m) with a tip diameter of 0.30 to 0.40 mm, depending on the size of the fly, is the most often used. The best fly-reel alternatives are in the light salmon classes, diameter 3.75–4 in (9.5–10 cm), the smaller reel being for the one-handed and the larger for the two-handed rod.

Floating-line fishing is at its most elegant when small flies in sizes 8 to 4 are fished. Often, sparingly dressed flies are specially tied for floating-line fishing: so-called low-water flies, where both body and the wings are shorter than on classic salmon flies. Famous low-water flies are the Blue Charm, Logie, March Brown, and Jeannie. To these, hair-winged patterns can be added, like the Munroe Killer, Red Butt, Hairy Mary, and Blue and Silver, which all are extremely effective.

Even if floating-line fishing is mostly for small flies, nothing forbids us to use larger flies. When night falls, a large dark fly, fished on the surface, is often a rewarding way of tempting a

Choosing a fly is often hard for salmon-fishermen. There are, as can be seen, any number of flies to select from, but too much emphasis is often put on the patterns. What matters most is the colour combination. The old rule can be valuable: bright patterns are best in fine weather and clear rivers, but dark patterns in bad weather and murky rivers. Orange-coloured flies are frequently the obvious choice in very brownish waters.

salmon. The periods of darkness in summer are also the time for sea trout. Then dark patterns are often chosen, such as the Stoat's Tail, Black Zulu, and Connemara Black, in sizes from 10 to 4 with double hook.

Floating-line fishing is also a fine weapon in the rivers of southern and western Sweden. Since these have humus-coloured water, flies with touches of orange, yellow and red are preferable for both salmon and sea trout. Successful patterns in, for example, the Emån, Mörrum and Ätran rivers are the Fiery Brown, Stuart's Shrimp, G.P., Strong Medicine and Fire Ball.

Fishing with dry fly

Fishing dry flies and riffling hitches are two American fly-fishing methods for salmon, which have their roots in the salmon rivers of the state of Maine and the provinces of Nova Scotia, New Brunswick, Quebec, Newfoundland and Labrador.

It cannot be said that this method of fishing has won any greater recognition in the rivers of Europe, though many attempts have been made in both the British Isles and in Norway. Many salmon have also been caught, but not so many that the popularity of dry-fly fishing and the riffling hitch can rival that of the traditional fly-fishing methods.

The one exception is fishing with dry flies for sea trout, mostly in Norwegian rivers like the Laerdal and Aurland in Sogn and Fjordane. There, dry-fly fishing for sea trout has a long tradition going back to 1902. It was then that the British Major T.T. Phelps, for the first time, fished for sea trout with a dry fly in the Laerdal. It is mostly small salmon of 2.5–7 lbs (1–3 kg) which are interested in a drifting dry fly. The same thing goes for sea trout, but this has not stopped sea trout of up to 17.5–22 lbs (8–10 kg) from being caught in the Laerdal and Aurland.

The riffling hitch, or "Portland hitch" as it is called, entails having the fly cross the surface over the current in a V-shaped wave. A half-hitch must be tied over the head of the fly. This method of fishing has proved effective, not only for North American salmon, but also in Norwegian rivers for salmon and small sea trout. A riffled fly, used for night fishing, can sometimes be as effective as a traditionally fished wet fly. Excellent flies with the riffling hitch are common hair salmon flies in sizes 6 to 10, tied on a thin, low-water hook.

The best conditions for both the riffling hitch and dry fly, when fishing for salmon and sea trout, are found during the summer months in rivers which are shallow, swift and clear.

Because fishing with dry flies for salmon and sea trout is mostly done up or across the stream, lightweight equipment is advantageous. A one-handed rod, 9–9.5 ft (2.7–2.8 m) long with quick action in line class 8, is a good choice. Such a rod, with floating WF-line and a fly-reel of diameter 3.5–3.75 in (8.9–9.5 cm), is a comprehensive combination for all such dry-fly fishing. The tapered length of leader should preferably be 3.3–3.8 yds (3–3.5 m) long and be 0.22–0.35 mm on the tip, while 0.30 mm is generally the most useful tip diameter.

Fishermen who use only dry flies for trout in high mountain waters will certainly react to the sight of large, thickly tied salmon dry flies. For salmon, it is, as it should be, American patterns

Above: The west coast of Norway not only has the world's finest salmon rivers, but also offers excellent chances of catching big sea trout on dry flies.

Below: The "riffling hitch" allows the fly to straggle across the current, giving fish the impression of a swimming animal. The fly should be knotted so that the snood comes out on the side which is towards the fisherman when fishing out.

which have received the most attention. This is mostly because of La Branche and Lee Wulff, whose books and articles have devoted much space to North American dry-fly fishing for salmon.

La Branche, in his time, marketed his own dry flies, the "La Branche" series, from which fly names such as Colonel Monell, Soldier Palmer, Mole Palmer and Pink Lady Palmer are still usable. Lee Wulff, still active despite his advanced age, is the inventor of the "Wulff" series, from which flies like the Grey

Wulff, White Wulff and Royal Wulff are well-known patterns.

If dry-fly fishing is to be fully practiced, it is important to utilize the sizes of flies in the right way. In swift currents, large flies in sizes 4 to 6 are to be preferred, while smaller sizes like numbers 8 to 10 are a better choice for slower currents.

In many small rivers of northern Scotland and in northern Norway, a method of fishing is used which has locally been named "dibbling". For dibbling, two flies are attached to the leader: an end-fly and a so called "dropper", which is tied a bit up on the leader. The idea of this kind of tackle is that the dropper, which is often larger and more thickly tied, is made to hop and "scratch" on the surface of the water.

Dibbling, or dropper fishing, is effective in shallow and swift small salmon rivers. The Komag River on the Varanger Peninsula in northern Norway is just such a river. Here, the local salmon fishermen have developed a refined type of dropper fishing, which brings in large catches every year.

Fishing from a boat

Fly-fishing from a boat is common in larger rivers, and in lakes to which salmon and sea trout migrate. In fishing these rivers, fly-fishing from a boat and harling (back-trolling) are most familiar.

Fly-fishing with a forward cast is accomplished by having the oarsman hold the boat against the current, while the fisherman works the fish-holding places. This method is common in, for example, the Alta River of northern Norway. In the River Tweed of Scotland, a method is also used whereby the boat is held in place in the stream with a weight which has been sunk to the bottom. Fishing from a boat is very effective in large and broad rivers, where the oarsman can position the boat so that the fly fishes correctly on top of the holding places.

Like casting from a boat, fishing by harling is a rewarding method in large rivers. By crossing with the boat back and forth, diagonally across the river, while the fly fishes above the holding places of the fish, even a wide pool can be effectively covered.

Practiced harling fishermen usually have three rods with different lengths of line out. The combination of baits may, for example, be fly, plug and spoon. But for pure fly-fishing, even three types of flies in different colour combinations and sizes can be as good. For harling, it is important to keep a distance to the shore and to let the fly fish out properly after each tack or "beat", because it is just at the turn that salmon usually take the fly.

Fly-fishing in lakes is accomplished from a drifting boat which is manoeuvred by the oarsman. Two main methods of fly-fishing are practiced from a boat: wet-fly fishing and "dapping".

Wet-fly fishing is done with a one-handed rod, 9.5–11 ft (2.8–3.3 m) long. It is best to use floating line or slowly sinking intermediate line. The British fish mostly traditional patterns, like the Black Pennel, Peter Ross, Soldier Palmer, Connemar Black and

Harling (back-trolling) begins highest up in the stretch of water to be fished. After each cross over the river, the boat is slipped a few meters downstream before starting the next cross.

Heckman Peckman, with different sizes—6 to 12 for sea trout. For salmon, a hair-winged salmon fly is also used, of which the Hairy Mary, Stoat's Tail and Munroe Killer are most popular.

Dapping is primarily a method for sea and lake-run trout. It usually occurs during the period when large, wind-carried insects land on the water surface. But dapping is not only dependent on natural insects and their season. Even when there are no insects, sea trout can be dapped. For dapping, rods of 16 ft (4.8 m) or longer are used. So that the wind will carry out the line from the boat, a light silk or nylon flossed line of about 3.8 yds (3.5 m) is spliced onto the back-line. On the end of this, a short leader of about 39 in (1 m) and 2.5–2.7 lbs (5–6 kg) strength is knotted on.

Naturally, insects as bait are the most popular in the Irish lakes. But in Scottish lakes, large hackle-flies are preferred, often being tied on a dry-fly hook of size 4 to 6. A healthy breeze is essential. The wind carries out the flossed line from the boat and, with the help of the rod, the fly is made to hop and dance on the tops of the waves.

Tiring out and landing salmon

How well is it hooked? How big is it? How will this all end? These are the three leading questions a fisherman asks himself when a salmon has taken the fly. Many fishermen call this sudden situation the "golden" moment.

Generally, one can say that the ways in which salmon take flies depend on the conditions of the stream. These determine how well the salmon is hooked. Sometimes the "bite" can hardly be noticed, though it may turn out to be a large fish which has taken the fly. The strongest bites are made in swift and heavy currents, where the fly is lying high up in the water while being fished out.

The salmon is a rewarding fish to hook. One need only tighten up on the rod and let the salmon hook itself with the help of the weight. To be sure, there are good and bad chances for hooking. With luck, for example, the salmon takes just as the fly turns in the stream, while it is being fished out. But the situation is more doubtful when the salmon takes a fly headed directly downstream. There is no good medicine for a strike straight downstream—one has to hope that fortune will smile and that the fish is hooked well enough.

When the salmon is being played, the rod should be held at a 60–90° angle, where there is not too much pressure on the leader and knots. The salmon tires faster if it also has to work against the rod. A lowering of the rod can be accepted in two situations: when the fish jumps, and on those special occasions when the salmon cannot be followed from land as it rushes down

One of the toughest situations with a big salmon which has taken the fly is when it rushes straight downstream and the terrain prevents the fisherman from following. A last resort—which has saved many dream fish—is to make the salmon turn upstream during the battle. Slack line, if quickly released and swept down past the salmon by the current, causes a pressure from the opposite direction, which may make the salmon start swimming upstream towards the fisherman.

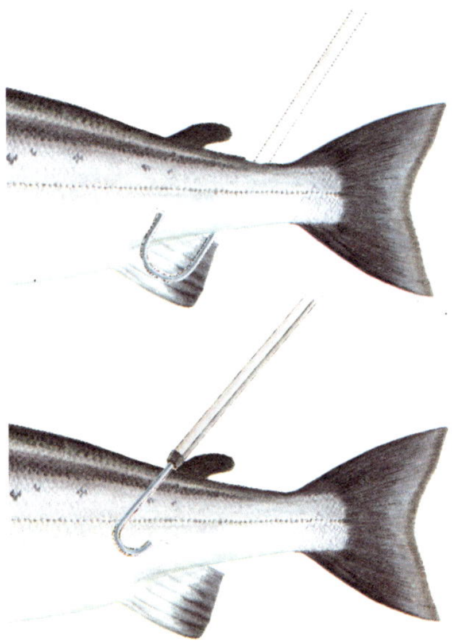

Here are three ways of landing a salmon. At left, a gaff hook is used, from below—if the water is deep enough—or else from above, which is the usual method if one is alone. At top, the fish is hand-tailed out of the water. Normally it is gripped just over the tail, with the little finger nearest to the fin. A woolen finger-glove gives better grip. At right, when the shore is long and shallow, the fish is most easily slid up onto land, then turned on its side, and finally hand-tailed.

the river. The latter situation is critical, but a lowering of the rod at the same time as loose line is being drawn off the fly-reel, so that the current takes hold of the line and presses the fish from downstream, can get it to turn upstream.

A salmon should be played with constant pressure. It is important to keep the fish moving with a stretched line and let it work against the stream. Drag lightly and let the salmon take the line, when it rushes out. As soon as there is a chance, the line is taken in with a minimum of frightening effect. If there is plenty of room on shore, the salmon can be tired out by simply walking back and forth, up and downstream, according to how the salmon is moving around—yet without using the reel too much in the process.

The most critical situation is when one has a lot of line out and the salmon becomes tired and turns itself against the current. Reeling in a tired, slanting salmon on a long line in a heavy current, while standing still, is virtually impossible with a fly-rod. Here, the only thing to do is to quickly move downstream, thus shortening the line. The line becomes loose for a moment, but the risk must be taken, because the salmon will go its own way anyhow if it cannot be followed.

Tiring out and landing a salmon is often a question of keeping calm, even when the situation becomes critical. The fisherman who can do it is also able to handle the most stressful situations in salmon fishing.

The first sign that the fish is starting to tire is when it goes slowly onto the surface and turns its shiny sides and stomach upwards. But never be too sure and believe that the salmon is ready for landing. Usually it still has enough strength for a couple of more short rushes before it finally gives in.

Each salmon pool is said to have its own special "landing places" where the salmon can be taken in without much effort. One should thus try to guide the salmon so that it can be landed in a good spot.

If one is alone, a spot with a long, sloping shore is the best alternative, making it quite easy to beach the fish. When beached, the fish should not be reeled in: it is best to "lock" the reel and back up onto land when the fish is a few meters away, so that the fish slides up on shore. It is also advantageous to put lateral pressure on the fish when it comes near land. This pressure often causes the fish to slide over on its side and lie there helpless.

To lift a salmon with a tailer, the loop is brought over the tail, then tightens under the fish's weight as the tailer is quickly lifted forward.

Then one can approach the fish, keeping the line stretched, and take hold of the tail section.

However, a river does not always offer such good possibilities for landing. The most difficult situation is when the salmon is below a steep riverbank over deep, swift water. If alone in this situation, a gaff is the best landing equipment to use. A tailer or landing net is also serviceable, but risky when a fisherman is standing alone with a large salmon in front of him.

When landing with a gaff from a high riverbank, the salmon has to be completely worn out. When the head of the salmon is nearby and facing towards the stream, in a left-handed cast pool, the rod is held in the left hand (in the right on the other side of the river), with the hardest possible press upwards, back and to the side. The salmon can then be guided into gaffing distance, and is gaffed either in the tail section or the head. For my part, I always gaff at the rear so that the tail will come out of the water first.

It is, of course, easiest—especially on steep riverbanks—to have two people during the landing procedure. The fisherman guides the salmon towards the one who is going to land it. In Scottish rivers the landing net is the most common landing tool. Even tailers have their advocates in many rivers. A tailer consists of a shaft with a handle and a wire which tightens to form a snare. The snare is looped just in front of the thick tail of the fish. Next, the tailer is lifted forward and upward. The snare tightens with the weight of the fish and, because of the shape of the salmon's tail, it holds securely.

When the salmon has come up on land, it should be killed immediately. This is best done by hitting the fish on the neck with a "priest".

The passion of fly-fishing

Finally, a vigorous warning. It might be best if you never even start fishing with flies—for if you do, you will never again be able to get the same thrill out of anything else! This type of fishing which touches the depths of our souls will captivate you, too. And once you have had a fighting fish on your sensitive rod, felt its wild attempts at flight in your line-hand, then you are emotionally hooked.

If you become a fly-fisherman anyway, it will transform your life as a sportfisherman. In time, it will also change your entire awareness of fishing, as you will see the aquatic world with new eyes. It is not for the prey that we fishermen of the twentieth century go out fishing, but as an expression of our hereditary natural instincts. And the finest a sportfisherman can experience is fly-fishing.

Fishing with a fly-rod is both ancient and very modern. Let us, then, with the inborn instincts which made us fishermen, enjoy life to the fullest in humble communion with nature, on a humanitarian level, freely and passionately.

Fly-tying

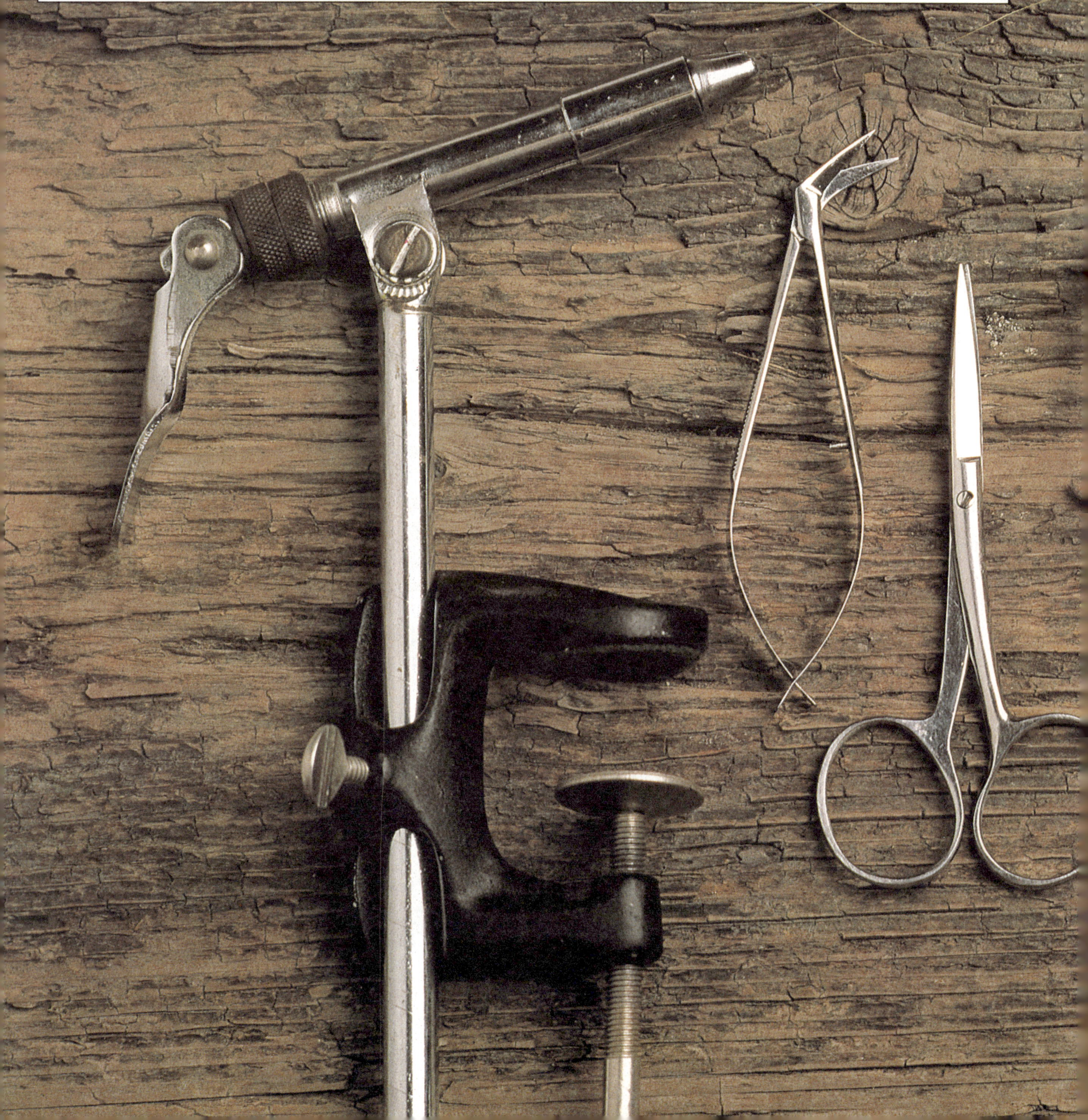

Tools

In earlier days, fly-tiers had to attach a silk gut leader or loop to the hook, since hooks of that period had no eyes. This was done simultaneously with the fly-tying, the hook being held "backwards" in the left hand with the hook bend pointing right to keep the silk gut out of the way. As the hook was held directly between the fingers, no fly-tying vise was used.

But as we nowadays use hooks with eyes, and thus do not have to get entangled with any leader tippet while tying, we choose to fix the hook to a vise, leaving both hands free. Furthermore, we use a number of small tools to facilitate the work. The previous pages show an elementary fly-tying outfit suitable for the beginner.

The fly-tying vise is the biggest investment. Vises come at different prices, but it is recommendable to select one of good quality from the start. The jaws have to be well-hardened so that they do not become worn out, but keep the hook in a firm grip. The jaws must also be adjustable to hooks of various sizes. Many tiers choose a vise with a spanner to be attached to the edge of a table, but I myself prefer a vise with a heavy plate, the vise being placed unfixed on top of the table.

The tying thread is kept in a bobbin holder, and it is a good thing to have several bobbins for different colours of thread. The weight of the bobbin keeps the thread straightened while tying, even when you let go with your hands. A bobbin threader makes it easier to put the thread through the narrow bobbin tube.

You need at least two pairs of small scissors: one very fine-pointed to cut silk, hackle fibres and other soft materials, and one pair of heavy-duty scissors to cut tinsel and metal wire. The dubbing needle is very useful as a "picking tool". A darning needle glued into a small wooden shaft makes a perfect home-made dubbing needle!

Hackle pliers are used to wind the hackle of the fly. The softly elastic jaws keep the hackle point in place while you put your forefinger into the bow of the pliers and, with a gentle hand, wind the cautiously stretched hackle feather around the shank.

To complete the head of the fly, half-hitches can be used. Most tiers, however, prefer the whip-finisher, an invaluable tool once you have mastered it. Whip-finishers can be purchased, of course, but are quite simple to make out of two safety-pins and a small wooden shaft. By looping up the tying thread to hooks A and C, then twisting the whip-finisher around thread B (so that A makes a circle around B), you get a "hidden" knot with turns of thread around its own party. Finally, loop A-C is threaded onto the hook eye, and the silk is gently unlooped from the tool, at the same time as you straighten the tying thread at D.

It is advisable to supplement your basic fly-tying outfit with tweezers and a hook hone. The tweezers can be used for a bit of everything, and the hone is a guarantee of always having properly sharpened hooks.

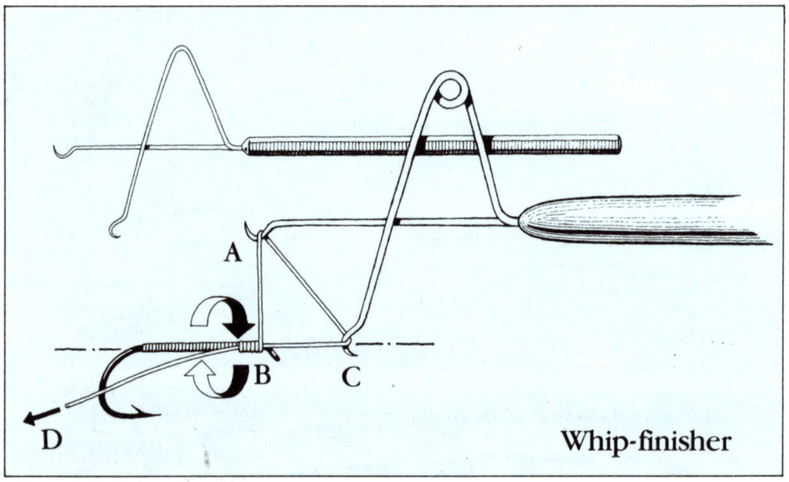

Preceding pages
To tie your own flies, a fly-tying vise is needed for holding the hook firmly. You also need two pairs of scissors, a pointed one for thread and other soft materials, and a stronger one for metal tinsel. Shown in the middle is a pair of hackle pliers, and to its right are models of bobbin holders. Next come a bobbin threader, tweezers and a hook hone. At bottom are a whip-finisher and dubbing needle.

Materials

Hair and feathers are traditional ingredients in flies, but recently a whole range of synthetic materials has come into use. Some of these are excellent—even if I still have a heart for Nature's own materials. Feathers, being available in numerous variations of colour as well as of length, softness and elasticity of the fibres, have great advantages as fly-tying material. To a large extent, the same is true of hair and fur from diverse mammals, although today these materials are often replaced by good synthetic substitutes. Many birds and mammals are threatened by extinction, a fact which also makes it urgent for fly-dressers to investigate and experiment with the new synthetic materials.

Classic hackle feathers normally come from domestic fowl. These we can use for our flies with a good conscience. Stiff hackles for dry flies are obtained from a cock's neck feathers, while for wet flies the softer hen hackle has the best qualities. Tails can be made of the long stiff fibres from a rooster's neck—or saddle hackle—but also of fibres from the tail feathers of cock pheasant, or long elastic hair from various four-footed animals like the badger.

Giving your fly its wings, made of sections from birds' wing feathers (so-called quill feathers), is an old trick. Wing feathers from small birds like starling, bigger birds such as poultry and ducks, and really big birds like geese and swans, are being used for this purpose. Hackle points or bundles of fibres from duck's shoulder feathers can also be used to form wings on a fly, as can bunches of hair from squirrel-tails or suitable hair from other furred animals. Flies with wings made of hollow hairs from roe deer or elk obtain extra floating ability.

In recent years, different types of poly-yarn have been used as wing material, especially in flies imitating certain mayflies and caddis flies. Various types of floss, wool, and silk, as well as poly-yarn, are employed for bodies, the material being wound around the shank. Strands of these materials, dubbed on a waxed thread, can be used likewise. The same technique with dubbing is used with fur from animals such as hare, opossum, mole and mink—to mention only a few of them.

Usually you can find feathers in all the colours you need, but it is also possible to dye hackle and other materials by using ordinary textile-colours. Fibres from suitable feathers are also fit for use as body material. Many popular fly patterns have bodies of peacock herl, for example. These herls come from the long, bronze-green fibres of the peacock tail.

Gold and silver bodies are made of tinsel—thin metal foil, cut into narrow strips and wound around the shank. If only a touch of "metal glitter" is requested, the fly can be ribbed with thin gold or silver wire, forming a sparse spiral over the body. The wire also makes the fly more resistant to sharp fish-teeth.

Today's fly-tiers almost exclusively use synthetic tying thread, thin and long-lasting, in most cases pre-waxed. It cannot rot and weaken the fly. Since it is thinner than the old tying silk, flies can be given a much more slender look. Fly-tying materials also include varnish and wax. Varnish is used to strengthen the fly between tying phases, and for lacquering fly heads. Wax is applied to the tying thread in order to make it sticky and enable fur, hair, and other dubbing materials to stay attached to the thread, when you make dubbed fly bodies.

To start tying your own flies, you don't need the whole range of materials. But with time you will accumulate piles of more or less indispensable plumage, furs, balls of wool, and so on. Most of these can be bought in fly-fishing shops, but a lot are to be found elsewhere, as in hosiery shops, woods and fields, or perhaps at the park-pond while feeding ducks . . .

Feathers and other materials which you bring home from woods and fields should be treated with great caution, to prevent you from getting bugs in your fly-tying box! It is also wise to put some anti-moth preparation among your materials, and to keep them in well-sealed plastic bags. Otherwise a crowd of hungry moths will have an orgy among the capes, feathers and furs.

Arranging a complete "shopping list" of all the materials required by the beginner is almost impossible. The picture on the previous page may indicate what are considered to be some suitable basic materials. Supplement your collection as you go along—according to the flies you need mainly for your own fishing.

Joining a fly-fishing club is always a good means of getting advice from more experienced fly-dressers. Some tying materials, such as high-quality cock capes, are rather expensive. But since one cape will be enough for hundreds of flies, you can make joint purchases within the club and divide up the material. Instead of buying one cape, you and a friend could buy two capes of different colours and share them. Thus both of you will achieve a decent selection of fly-tying materials with less delay and cost.

At top left are hen capes; to right, cock capes, one coloured red. Below these are a peacock feather, hare's-head skin, and various birds' body and wing feathers. At right under the hare mask are some fuzzy marabou feathers, and above is a long tail-feather from a male pheasant. In the middle are boxes containing hooks, fly-tying lacquer and wax, as well as silver and gold tinsel and tying thread. At left are orange-red neck feathers from golden pheasant, diverse animal hairs and pelts, and at right are squirrel tails in different colours. At bottom are fly-body yarns and shiny synthetic-plastic bands, known as lurex and Flash-A-Bow.

The parts of a fly

As in many other sports, fly-fishing and fly-tying have their own language, originating from English. Many words and terms have been kept, and others translated, in different countries. The adjacent illustration shows the names of parts of the fly.

A salmon fly consists of many components, each having its own name. This enables us to write down the tying description of a particular fly—the "recipe" of how to dress it. A common trout fly is simpler, but still described by the same features: wing, tail, body, rib or ribbing, hackle, and so forth. A small woolen tail on a fly is often called a "tag", and can even be part of a fly's name—for example, the well-known Red Tag.

The looks of a fly can be explained more easily if you indicate whether it has a throat or beard hackle, a front hackle or a body hackle. The last is sometimes also referred to as a palmer hackle.

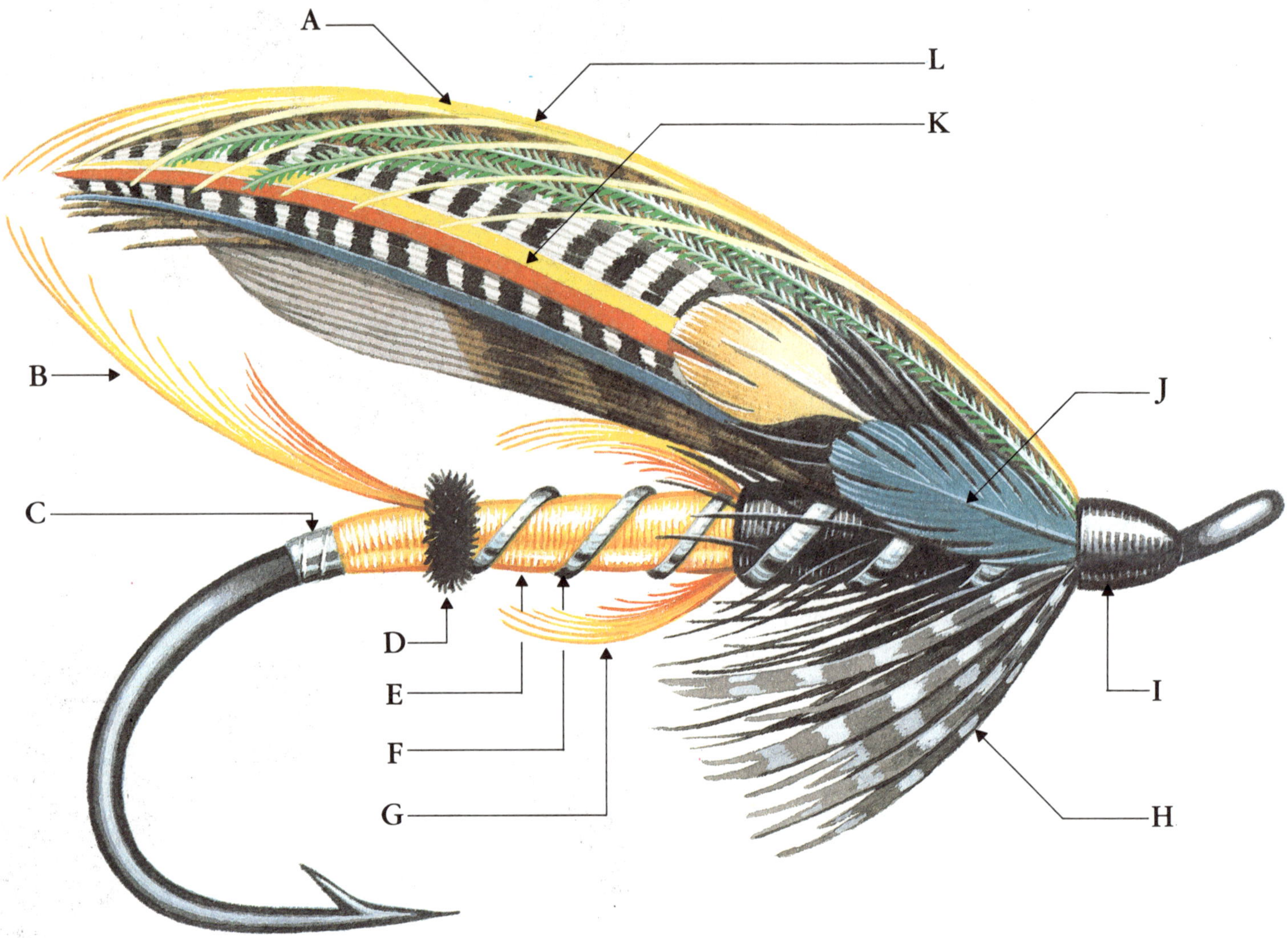

A. Wing
B. Tail
C. Tag
D. Butt
E. Body
F. Ribbing
G. Veilings
H. Hackel
I. Head
J. Cheek
K. Horns
L. Topping
M. Fronthackel

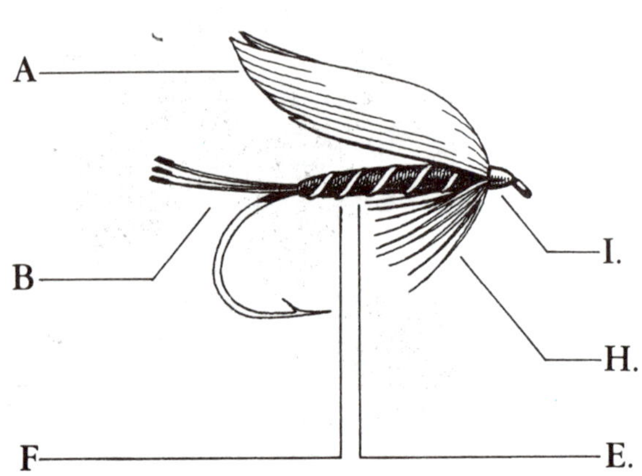

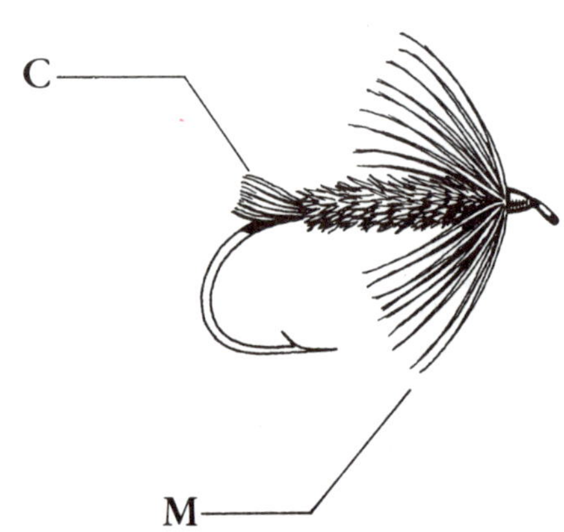

Basic elements of tying

The materials of a fly are attached to the hook by the support of the tying thread. While fly-tying, you will soon notice that only a few operations need to be performed with the thread. But the secret lies in knowing which methods to use, where and when, in order to obtain the desired result.

Normally the tying thread is used to accurately "pin" the material to a certain point on the shank. Yet sometimes, by making "sliding" turns with the thread, you can disperse the material *around* the hook shank. Let us look at some basic phases of tying, where the thread is used in different ways.

The tying thread is attached and "locked" to the hook by making a few firm turns around its own party (A). Cut the loose end close to the shank. Your thread is now well-secured and you can start tying in the various materials.

You finish the fly with a similar knot, the half-hitch (B). By using the whip-finisher tool mentioned earlier, you can make a "long half-hitch" (C), where the thread-butt stays hidden under the last turns of the tying thread. When cutting the thread, most fly-tiers cut as close to the whip finish as possible. This method creates a good-looking head on the fly. However, I myself prefer to leave a small stump of thread, about one millimetre, so that the whip finish knot will last longer if the thread shrinks during fishing.

How to make a sparse "transfer-spiral" with the tying thread is also illustrated (D). You use only close turns as you start and finish. The fewer turns, the more slender the fly. If you make some extra turns every time you complete a tying phase, just to be "on the safe side", you will always end up with a clumsy fly!

A "sliding" turn is shown in illustrations E, E_1. This is a convenient technique for spreading the material around the shank, for example when making a fan-shaped tail on a dry fly. You always use the sliding turn when you want to disperse the material on the hook. The technique in F, F_1 fixes the material very precisely—in this case the wings of a wet fly. These wings should not slide to the back of the hook. Put the paired wing sections together and grip them firmly between left-hand thumb and forefinger on top of the hook shank. Pass the thread up between thumb and wing, and down the other side between the rear of the wings and your forefinger. *Pull straight down!* Repeat once before releasing the wings.

In illustration G is a winged dry fly with its wings tied in the same manner, but pointing forward. After phases F and F_1, you raise the wings, form a coil of the thread, place it behind the wings, and pull. Repeat these "contra-turns" until the wings are

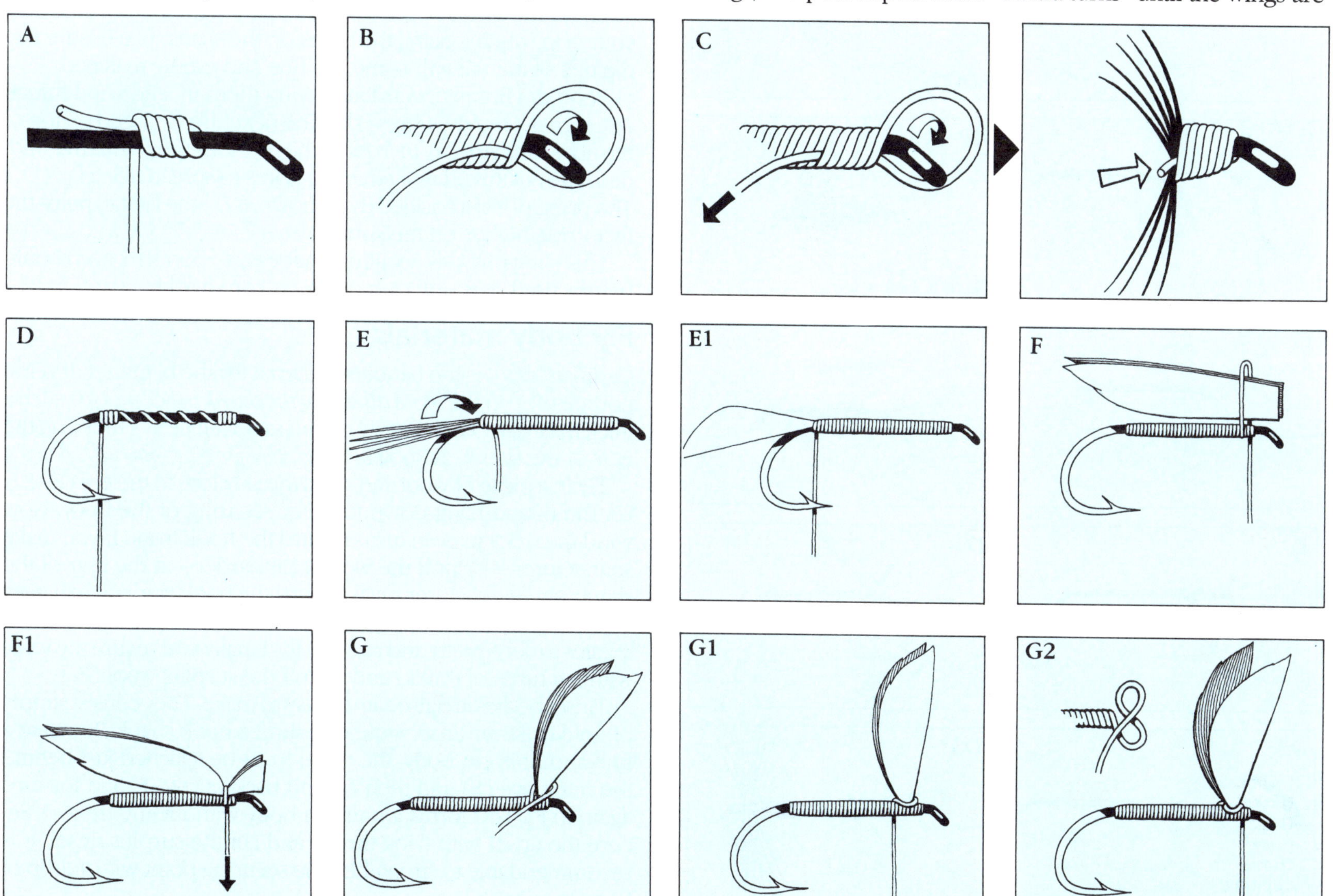

upright (G_1). Finally you can separate the wings by making "eight-turns" (G_2), which are contra-turns around each wing half forming a figure-of-eight.

The tail of a fly

The simplest tail is only a short stump of wool—a "tag" (A). It is not supposed to imitate the tail of any specific insect, and is mostly used in all-round patterns.

The purpose of the tag is to give the fly a higher "attention value". The tag makes the fly visible in water and gives the fish a target for the strike. If you put a colour-brilliant tag on a dry fly, the fly will be easier to observe for the angler as well. This is particularly handy when fishing at dusk or in rapid waters.

Attach the tying thread just behind the hook eye, leaving enough space between eye and thread for the hackle, head and wings. Place the tag material, such as wool or poly-yarn, on top of the shank and attach it by winding thread in close turns to the hook bend. Cut the tag at the back with a straight cut. At the front, however, you cut the tag material diagonally across, along the shank, to avoid a clumsy finishing of the fly and to facilitate winding the hackle later.

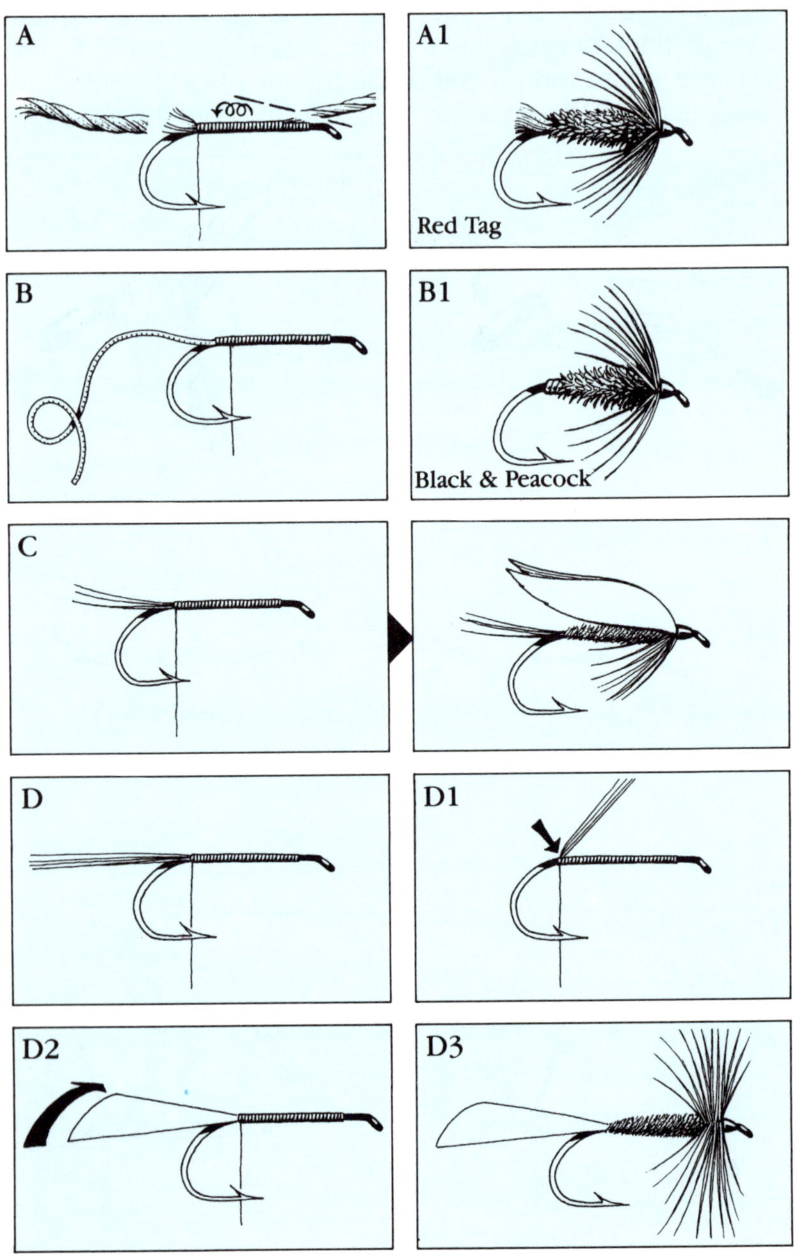

Another simple tag can be made of 2-4 turns of gold or silver tinsel at the rear of the hook bend (B). Here, too, you attach the material along most of the shank to avoid a "bumpy" fly body. Illustrations A and B show two examples of flies with tag-tails: Red Tag and Black and Peacock. These flies are not supposed to imitate any specific insect. On such flies, we use other materials to imitate the tails of the real insect.

The wet fly often has a tail of soft feather fibres (C). Tie in a tuft of fibres on top of the shank, just by the bend. Tail fibres should be soft and absorbing in order to give the fly life and movement in the water. Fibres from hen hackle are usually a good choice.

It is harder to tie in tails on a dry fly. One of their purposes is to help increase the points of footing of the fly. Consequently, we choose less absorbent and more elastic fibres for the dry fly tail. Long fibres from big cock hackle feathers are very suitable, as are hairs from several furred animals: the big, elastic hair of badger is one example.

Attach a tuft of about ten cock hackle fibres on top of the shank, and wind thread to hook bend (D). Make sure that all the fibres have the same length. This can be done easily by folding the fibres in a right angle to the stem before cutting or tearing them. Then all the fibres will have the same length. By not releasing your grip, when placing the fibres on the shank, you ensure that the tips of the tail will come out fine and evenly matched.

Bend the fibres upward after tying them in, and wind thread one turn *behind* the fibres (D_1). The next turn is placed on top of the fibres and *directly in front of* the previous turn. Thus the "hidden" turn of thread will force the fibres to spread like a fan (D_2). The principle of a hackled fly is shown at D_3: the fan tail helps the fly to ride higher on the surface.

This tying phase is not altogether easy to perform, and should be practised over and over again on bare hook!

Fly body materials

Ordinary wool is the handiest material for the beginner. It is important to tie in the wool *all along the shank*, since wool is such a thick material. Otherwise the result may well be a "bump" on the rear of the shank, as shown in E.

Tie in a piece of wool and wind thread close to the eye (E_1 -E_2). Let the thread hang down for later securing of the body. Now wind the wool in even turns toward the hook front. If you make sparse turns—or pull the wool a bit harder—at the rear of the shank, and wind closer turns toward the hook eye, you will get a fly body that thickens in front. This is called a *tapered* body, and creates a more pretty and realistic fly. Finally you secure the wool with 3-4 turns of thread and cut off the surplus wool (E_3).

Tinsel bodies are also rather easy to make. They consist simply of gold or silver tinsel wound around a hook shank. To make a fine and uniform body, the tinsel must be attached just behind the hook eye (F) and then wound backward to F_1 and forward again to F_2. This forms a uniform body without any "holes". Secure the tinsel with tying thread and cut the surplus tinsel. It is recommendable to strengthen the securing point with a drop of fly-tying varnish.

Dubbing bodies provide very fine flies. They are made out of fine fur, spun on a thread, which is then wound around the shank. If waxed, the thread becomes sticky and will hold the fur. Nail a small tack to a wooden plate, and place a well-waxed tying thread as shown in G. Pluck or cut some underfur from mole, hare, mink, or a similar fur pelt. Take away any guard hairs, and place the underfur in a very thin layer on top of the waxed thread. Old-fashioned tying silk is best for this dubbing technique. Fold the silk as in G_1, then twirl and spin the thread (G_2). The dubbed silk is attached to the hook at the bend, then wrapped around the shank, forming the body.

A somewhat simpler method of dubbing is to wax the tying thread itself, as it hangs from the hook, and stick the dubbing material firmly to the thread as you "spin" the fur by twisting the thread repeatedly between thumb and forefinger, as shown in H. Only twist the thread in one direction! Thus the soft hairs will form a narrow "tube" around the thread. H_1 shows how the body is made by winding the dubbed thread.

Dubbed bodies can hold microscopic air bubbles, making the flies especially enticing to fish. These air bubbles also increase the floating ability of a dry fly. Frizzled underfur is best for this purpose. Opossums have that kind of underfur.

Another important body material is herl, particularly herl from peacock tail feathers. It is the long feather fibres, covered with flue, that are called herls. Attach two or three herls to the hook bend (I). The size of the fly determines the number of herls. For a very small hook, one single herl will do. Herls are delicate and require a gentle hand to avoid cracking.

Spinning the herl with the thread (I_1) makes a fly more durable. Wind the herl and thread from the bend to just behind the hook eye (I_1-I_2). You can also attach the herl to the hook by giving the shank a very thin varnish layer.

By ribbing your fly with metal wire, you can strengthen the fly body. When using a rib, this should be tied in before the rest of the body material (J). Wind the body material *counterclockwise* (J_1) and secure behind the hook eye. Then wind the ribbing *clockwise* (J_2). The rib will "lock" the body material very effectively and the fly will last longer. The wire-rib also creates reflections in the water, making the fly more tempting.

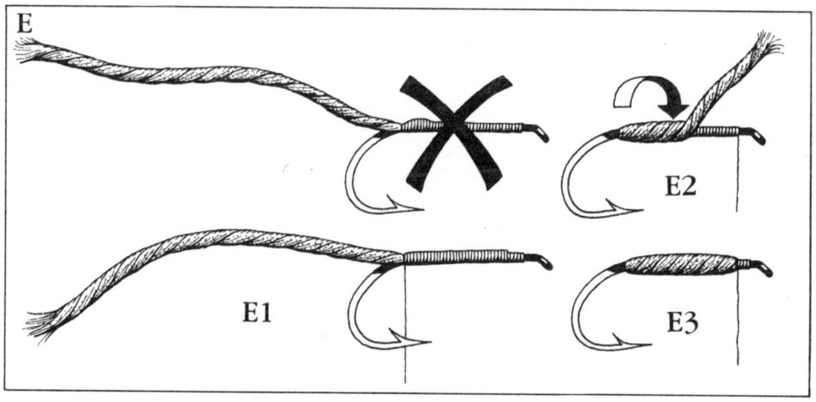

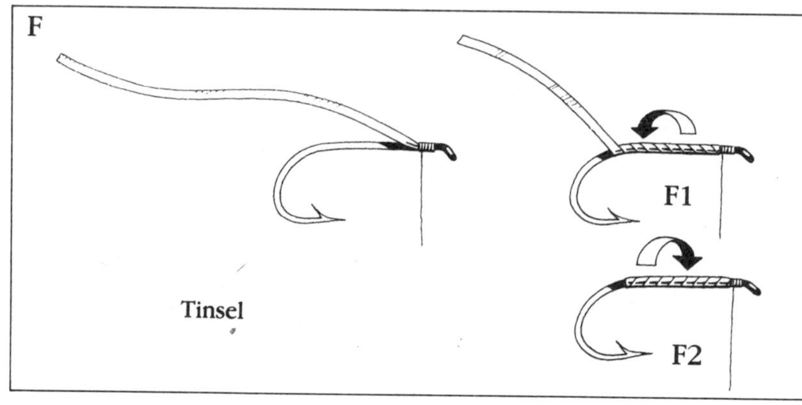

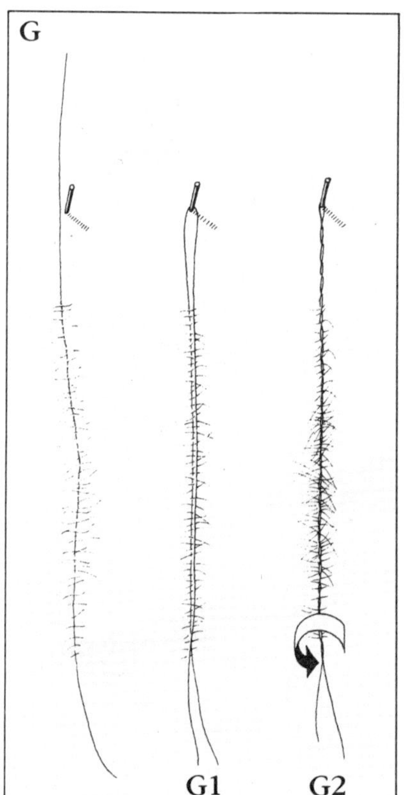

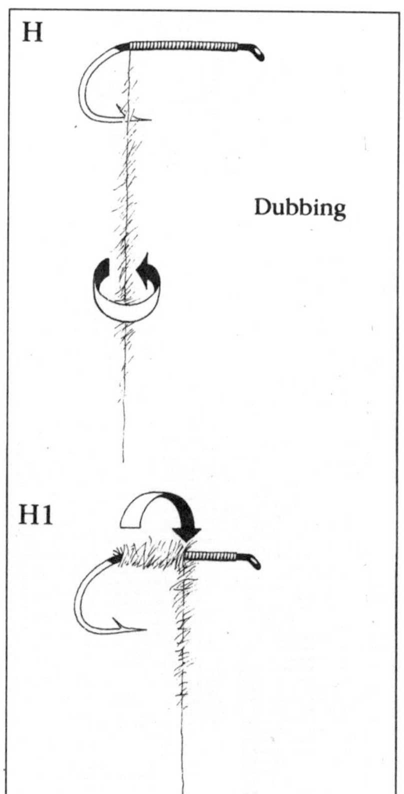

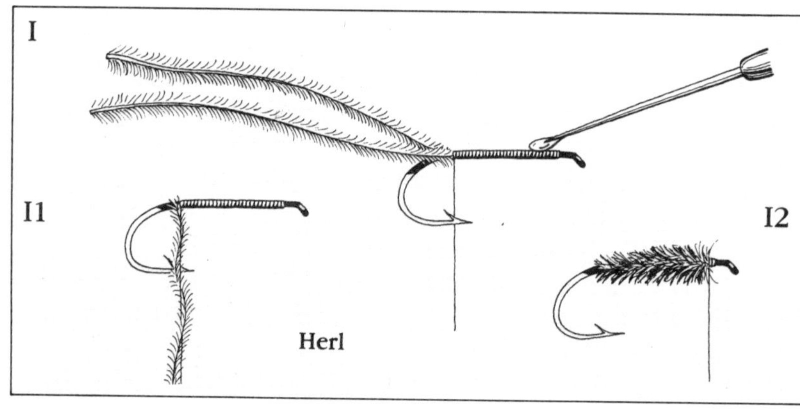

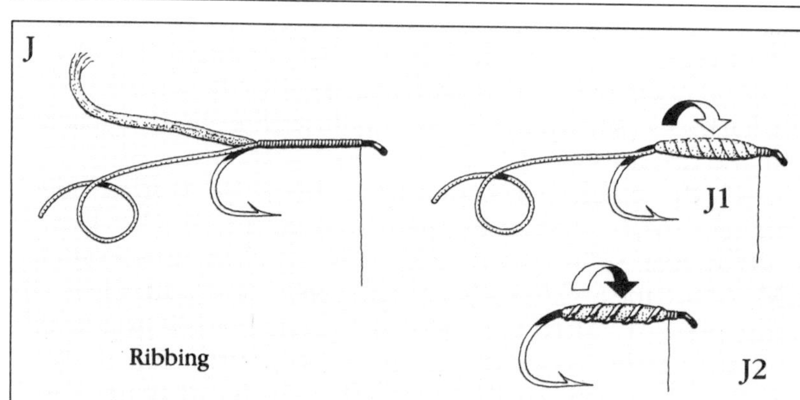

Wings

Classical trout flies often have so-called *quill-wings*. These are made of two equal sections, one left and one right, from wing feathers (A). On a wet fly, the two sections are placed with the concave edges together and the tips pointing inward. Tie them in as described.

Tying in quill-wings is difficult, but the wing sections might be easier to handle if you put some diluted varnish on the rear sides of the sections. This will make the fibres stick together.

You can also make wings of bunches of loose fibres (B). For this purpose, mainly shoulder feathers from different ducks, such as wood duck, are the best. Wings of loose fibres are tied in the same way as mentioned above. Use "eight-turns" to split the wings. Quill-wings are stiffer than fibre-wings. The latter are especially popular since soft-winged flies do not twist your leader when casting, as do quill-wings.

When imitating caddis flies, you can use wings made of tufts of hairs from roe deer or elk (E). These hairs are hollow and filled with air, which gives the fly extraordinary floating abilities. Hairs of this type are also suitable to trim with scissors.

Before being tied in, the cut hairs are placed with points downward in a so-called "hair-stacker": a small case, for example an empty cartridge or a pen cap (E_1). Tap the stacker on the table, the hairs thus being packed together at the case bottom. When you take out the hairs, the tips will be equally long and your wing will get a smooth rear edge.

Illustration F shows a long-shanked fly of the bucktail model. Nowadays such flies are tied with wings of many different materials, not just bucktail. Squirrel's tail, goat hair, and various synthetic "hairs" are a few such wing materials.

Hackles

Cock and hen hackles from domestic fowl are the only ones considered here. These hackles consist of feathers lying like tiles on top of each other, from a bird's head and neck down to its shoulder and back (G), with very small feathers at the top and getting bigger farther down. A cape of hackle feathers can thus provide you with feathers for all sizes of hooks.

Shown at H is a typical long, narrow cock hackle with stiff fibres, suitable for dry flies. At I is illustrated a hen hackle with soft fibres for wet flies.

Before tying a hackle to the hook, you prepare the feather by tearing off the lower, flueish fibres—the "down". You also remove a few extra fibres on the side of the stem which will be closest to the hook (see J). This simplifies the formation of a good-looking hackle, since the stem will mould itself around the shank from the first turn.

Attach the hackle perpendicular to the shank, convex side pointing forward. Secure the stem with eight-turns (K). Then bend the stem backward and make a few taut, close turns around it (K_1). Clutch the hackle feather by its tip with the soft jaws of your hackle pliers (L). Hold the pliers in a gentle but taut grip, and wind the hackle around the shank in close turns. Secure the point with thread and cut the surplus (K_2). The hackle fibres now

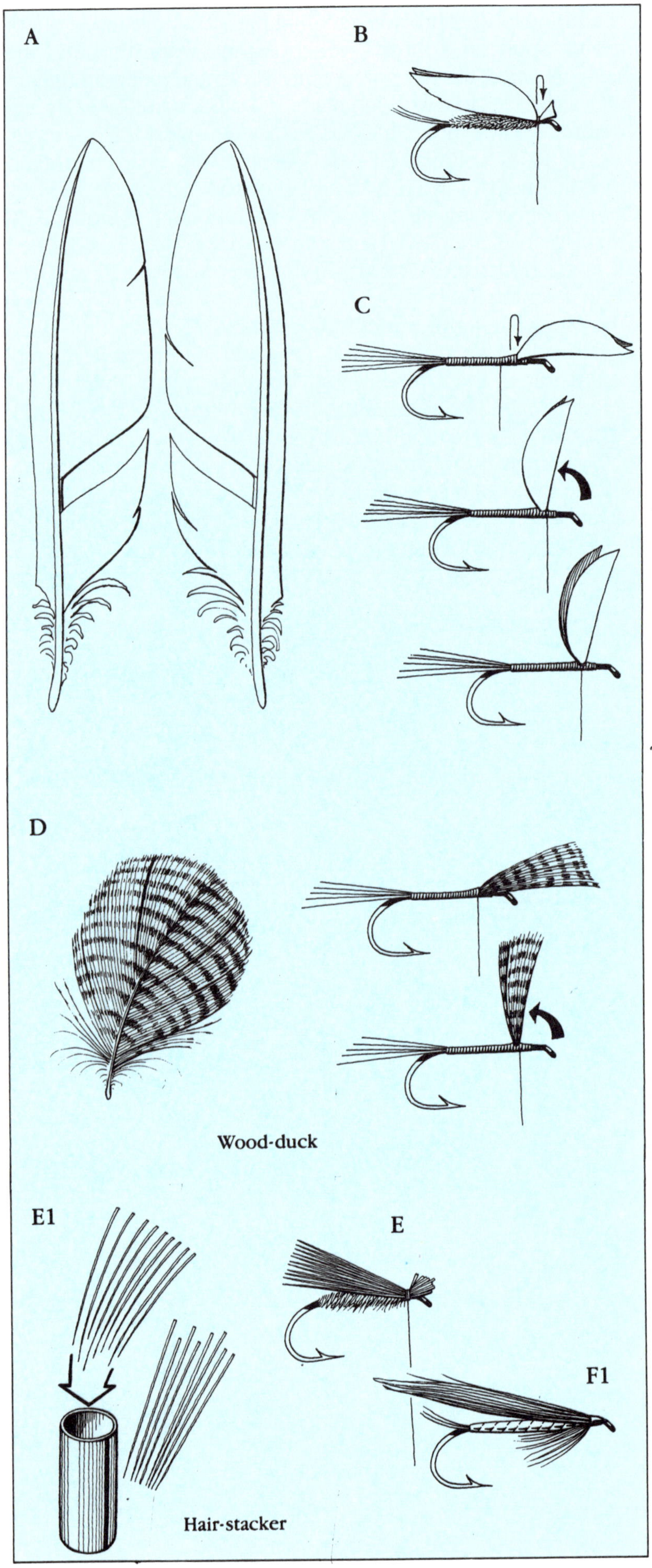

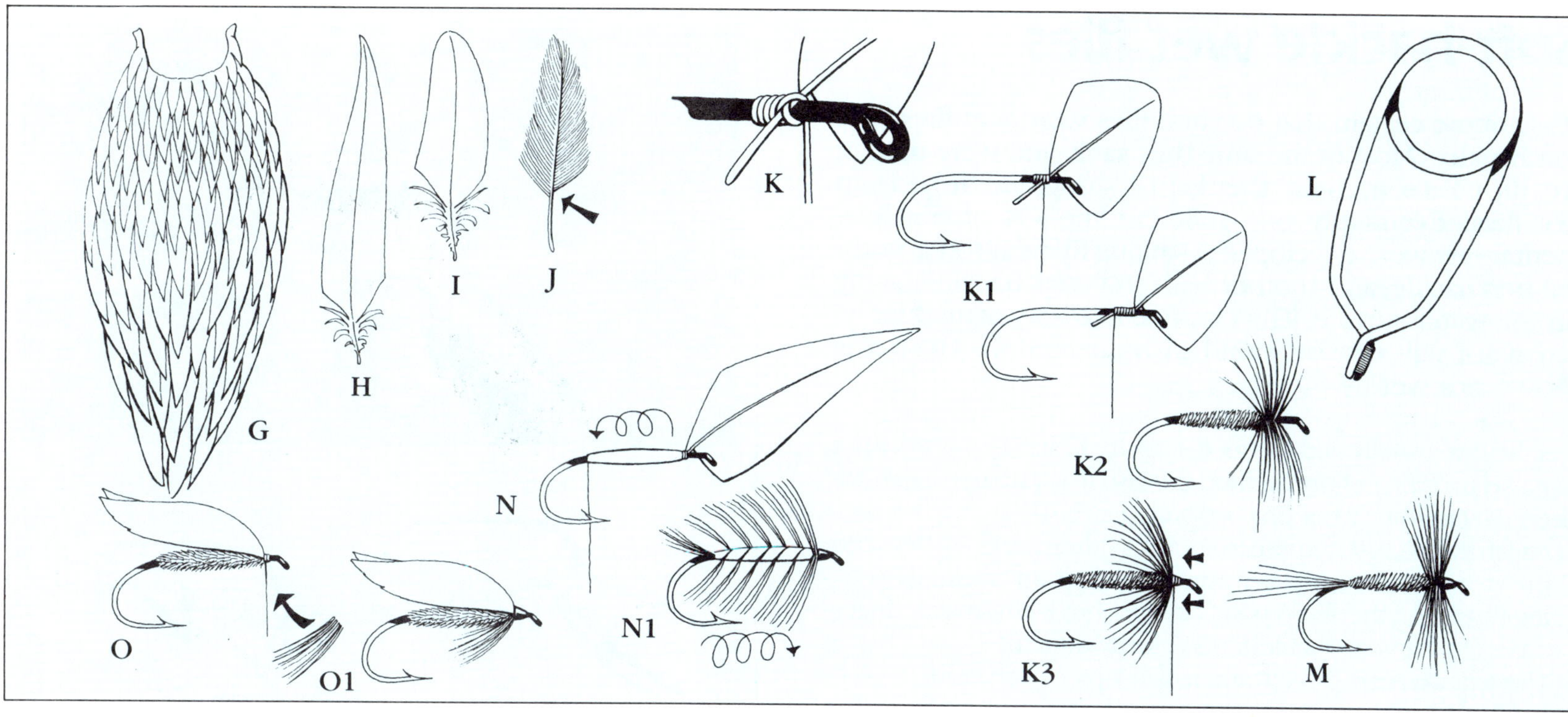

form a "coil" around the fly. On a wet fly, the practice is to press the hackle somewhat backward by a few turns of the thread at the front of the hackle (K_3). A dry fly, however, should have its fibres well spread, to give the fly as much floating support as possible (M).

Illustration N shows a fly with body hackle, or a so-called palmer hackle. You do the palmer hackle as follows. Wind a hackle with a few close turns at the fly's front, then in a sparse spiral along its body. Secure the hackle with tying thread or ribbing material, winding this through the hackle from rear to front, with a similar spiral but with turns going the opposite way.

Illustration O_1 shows a wet fly with a "false" hackle or "beard" hackle. This is simply made of a tuft of soft hackle fibres, torn from a feather and tied in underneath, just behind the fly's head. You often have to improvise. It may take two hackle feathers instead of one, to make a nice palmer hackle: one for the front part, and another for the body hackle. Likewise, you might need three small tufts of fibres to make the best false hackle: one tuft underneath, and one on each side a bit farther up.

Hooks

Among the common types of hooks reproduced here, those in the top row will be mentioned. From left, they are: wide gape, limerick, and round bend. In earlier days, up-eyed hooks for dry flies and down-eyed hooks for wet flies were the common choice. But nowadays it is normal to tie all kinds of flies on down-eyed hooks. The two filled-in hooks illustrate the difference in principle between the hooks you should choose for wet and dry flies, respectively. A wet-fly hook can be made of heavy, thick material; but a dry-fly hook should be of thinner material, to make it light.

The third row shows a hook with extra long shank. This is a streamer hook designed for fry imitations and other flies with long bodies. To the right is a hook with an extraordinarily short shank. Such a hook could well be up-eyed: on a short shank, a bigger gap between hook point and eye will make it easier to hook fish.

Further down, you can see two of the many special hooks which are found on the market. One has a bent shank, suitable for imitating caddis pupas and smaller crustaceans. The other is meant to fish upside down, thus avoiding stone bites. To the right is a specially hardened hook for salmon flies.

At page bottom is a hook scale with full-size hooks. Hooks are numbered by the sizes of their gaps. This means two or more hooks can have the same numbers but quite different shank lengths. Thus, they are experienced by the angler as being of different sizes.

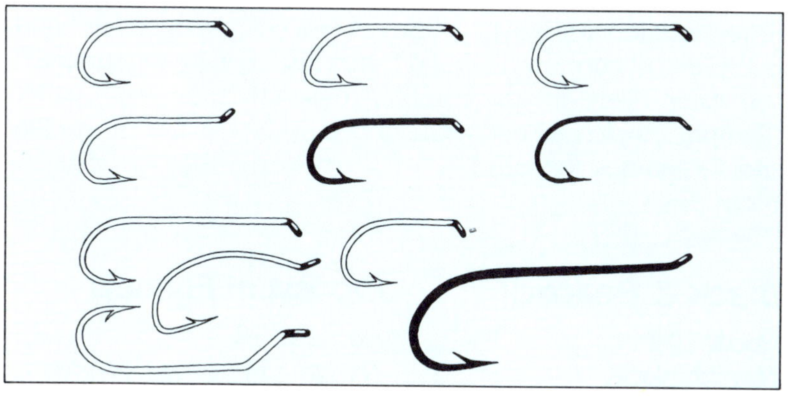

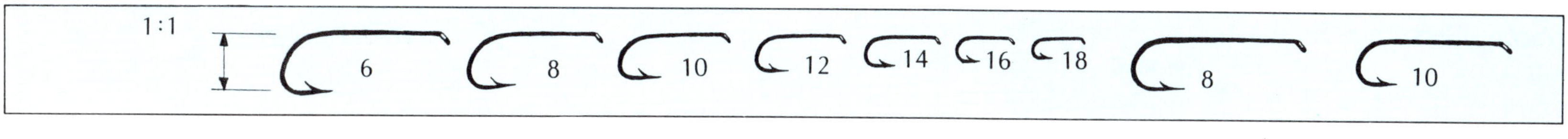

Soft-hackle wet flies

It is almost certain that our first flies were wet flies with soft hackles. Most of the time they sank, and were used as wet flies. Yet sometimes they kept floating, and turned into dry flies! Eventually two different models of that elementary fly were developed: a sinking fly with soft absorbent hen hackle, and another with stiff cock hackle floating on the water surface. The classical Red Tag, named for its red wool tail, can be found in both models. Here it is shown as a wet fly.

Wet flies are usually tied on hook sizes 10, 12 and 14. In order not to make your first efforts behind the vise frustrating, you are advised to start your tying practice with a size 10.

1. Attach the hook to the vise as shown. Hiding the point between the vise jaws (1a) certainly prevents you from cracking the tying thread on the sharp point or barb, but it also makes finger access to the rear shank unnecessarily difficult.
2. Then attach tying thread, and attach a piece of scarlet floss or wool along the entire shank to avoid a "bumpy" body on the fly. Cut the floss, leaving only a small stump as tail or tag.
3. Take two herls from a peacock's tail feather and tie them in by their tips.
4. Herls are very fragile. Twist herls and thread together to make them "stronger".
5. Wind herls and thread together in close turns toward the hook eye. Leave space for hackle and head. Cut surplus herls.
6. Tie in a brown hen hackle feather, its front side facing forward. Use hackle pliers to wind hackle, making the hackle fibres create a coil around the shank.
7. Secure the hackle point with thread, and wind thread 2-3 sparse turns through the hackle toward the hook eye. Make sure no hackle fibres are bent down by thread.
8. Form a neat head with thread and whip finish. Finally cut the remaining hackle point (see Figure 7) and varnish the head.

This is the moment of truth, as it shows whether or not you have left enough room for the hackle and head! The last thread turns may not come down over the hook eye (Figure 8a).

Red Tag is a good all-round fly and, in small sizes, it is sometimes excellent for grayling. Black & Peacock, on the other hand, is a splendid rainbow fly, when fished just beneath the surface in still water. There are also combinations of fly and nymph, called "flymphs", which are tied with dubbed bodies, soft wet fly hackle, and sometimes soft tails.

Black & Peacock

Hook: 10-14
Thread: black
Body: peacock herl
Hackle: black hen

Opossum Flymph

Hook: 12-18
Thread: light brown or grey
Body: dubbed opossum underfur
Hackle: light ginger-brown or light grey

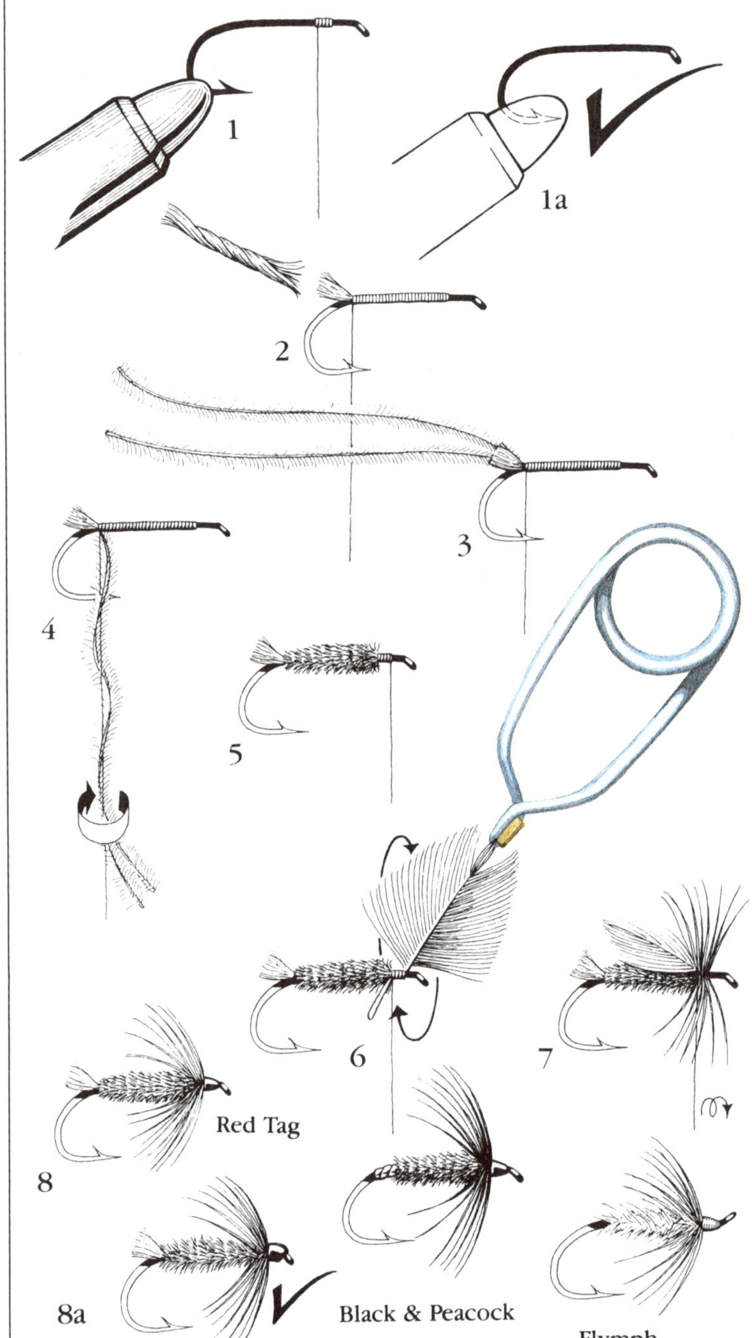

Winged wet flies

In order to make better imitations of insects with wings, flies were provided with sections from wing feathers on top of their bodies. You had the first winged wet fly! The dark Alder has always been one of my own favourites when wet-fly fishing for trout in streams. Perhaps because I got my very first fish on that fly . . .

An old Alder fly in my box has a dark claret body and a sparse spiral of peacock herl as rib (2a). But the fly is not particularly long-lasting, even though the herl is tied in from its butt (1a). Sharp fish teeth will quite easily tear the herl apart.

1. We start our fly by tying in two peacock herls by their tips.
2. Wind the herls twisted with claret tying thread along the shank. The colour of the thread will be visible—especially when the fly is wet—and by attaching the herls by their tips we get a nice, tapered body.
3. Pick two similar fibre sections from dark brown-speckled wing feathers—one left and one right—and place them side by side on top of shank.
4. Tie in the wings and cut surplus pointing forward.
5. Tear a bunch of fibres from black hen hackle and tie in as a false hackle. If necessary complete with an additional small fibre bunch on each side of the shank to get a nice and well-spread hackle. Wind the head, whip-finish and varnish.

It is important that the hackle fibres are soft, to make them move nicely in water. The fibres are not imitating the legs of an insect, as believed by many, but instead give an impression of "life" by making graceful movements when fished. Choose fibres with much flue—then the hackle will absorb water more quickly and that will make it easier for the fly to penetrate the water surface.

Worth mentioning among classical wet flies is the Butcher, a fly with dark blue wings from mallard wing feathers and with a shiny body. Flies from the Teal-series are also popular in many waters. They have wings from teal flank feather and their names—Teal and Red, Teal and Green, etc.—come from the colour of their bodies. Names of flies are often a combination of the colours and the tying materials of the fly. Black and Peacock, described above, got its name in the same way—though in this case the colour-part of the name originated from the hackle, not the body as in the Teal-series.

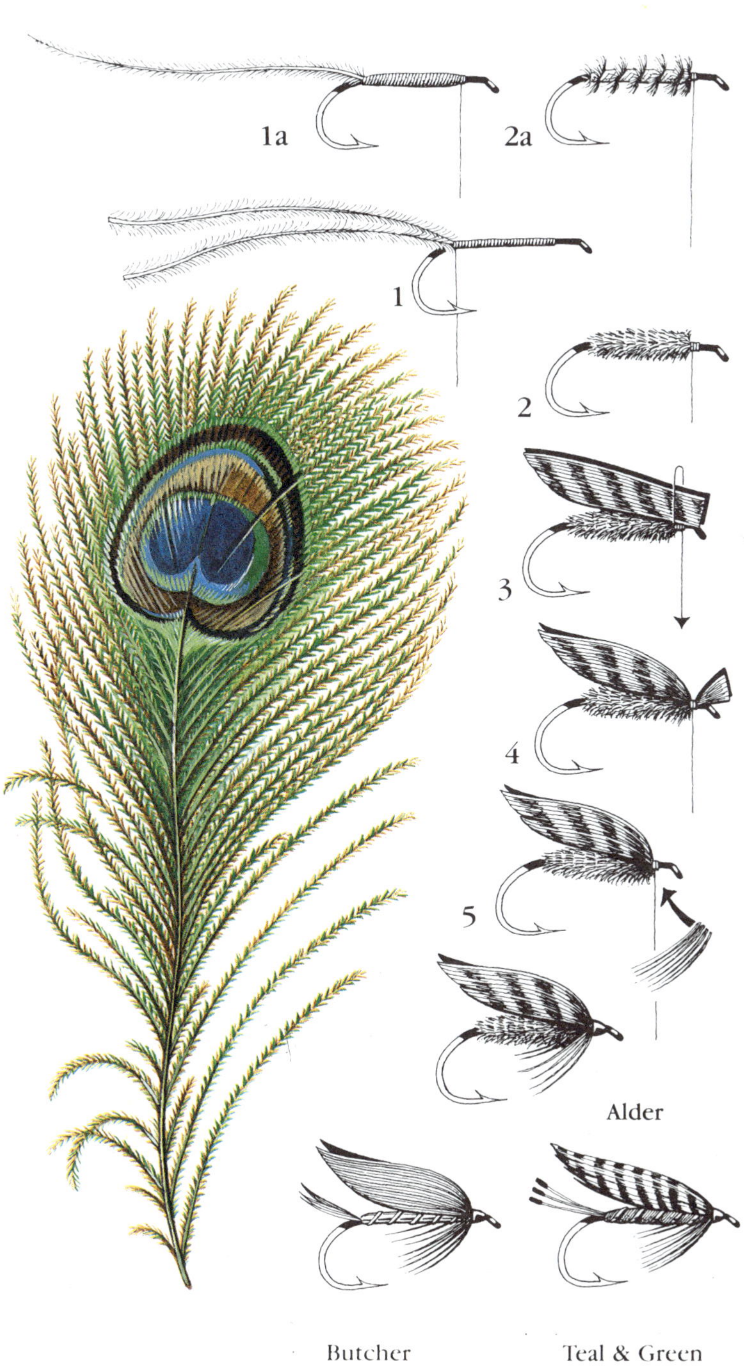

Butcher

Hook: 10-14
Thread: black
Tail: red fibres
Body: silver tinsel
Ribbing: silver
Wings: blue quill from mallard speculum

Teal & Green

Hook: 10-14
Thread: black
Tail: tippets
Body: bright green
Ribbing: silver
Wings: teal flank feather

Teal & Red

Hook: 10-14
Thread: black
Tail: tippets
Body: scarlet
Ribbing: silver
Wings: teal flank feather

Hackled dry flies

Hackled dry flies without wings are very good as all-round imitations, representing many different insects. Such a fly is easy to tie and can be altered in both colour and "dressing"— it can be made both slim and thick. Flies of this kind with neutral colours—grey, beige or brown—are often the best fishing flies. Tied in a bushy manner, a hackled dry fly maintains high floating ability even in strong rapid streams. This type of fly can also be tied small and delicate, looking like a small midge.

Being easy to tie and offering a range of variations in colours and dressings, the hackled dry fly is a very popular type. Fishing blind with dry fly, a bushy hackled fly can turn out to be the best "fish-finder".

But a hackled dry fly can also be tied with a slim body and only a few turns of hackle. This will make a thin and graceful fly resembling a mayfly or a midge. The bushy fly rather gives an impression of a caddis fly with big, fluttering wings.

1. Put hook in vise, attach thread, and tie in a cock hackle feather. Be sure to turn the blank side of the hackle forward when winding. Some fly-tiers prefer to start at step 2 and proceed to step 6—e.g. complete all of the fly's body— before they tie in the hackle.
2. Attach a bunch of long cock hackle fibres as tails. Wind thread along shank until a point straight above barb. Make sure fibres are equally long, and hold fibres firm to prevent them from sliding down the rear of the hook.
3. Bend tail straight up and make a turn of thread behind and under it.
4. Put tail back in position and make a taut turn with thread on top, right in front of previous turn. Thus the fibres will spread in a fan shape and support the fly when standing on water. Wax thread and dub it with hare's underfur or similar material.
5. Form body by winding the dubbed thread. Thin dubbing in sparse turns creates a slim body. Much dubbing and close turns makes a "fat" body.
6. Wind hackle and secure. Gently wind thread through hackle in a sparse spiral towards hook eye, making sure no hackle fibres are bent down. Form head, whip-finish and varnish.

After egg-laying the mayfly dies, wings spread and the fly floating on the surface. It is then called a "spent spinner". To imitate this, the tail and hackle of the fly are split in two equal parts using eight-turns. Illustration (a) shows the spent fly from above and (b) from the front.

Grey-brown all-round fly

Hook: 10-14
Thread: brown
Tail: cock hackle fibres, brown or grizzly
Body: hare underfur
Hackle: brown or grizzly cock

Black Gnat

Hook: 16-20
Thread: black
Body: black tying thread
Hackle: black cock

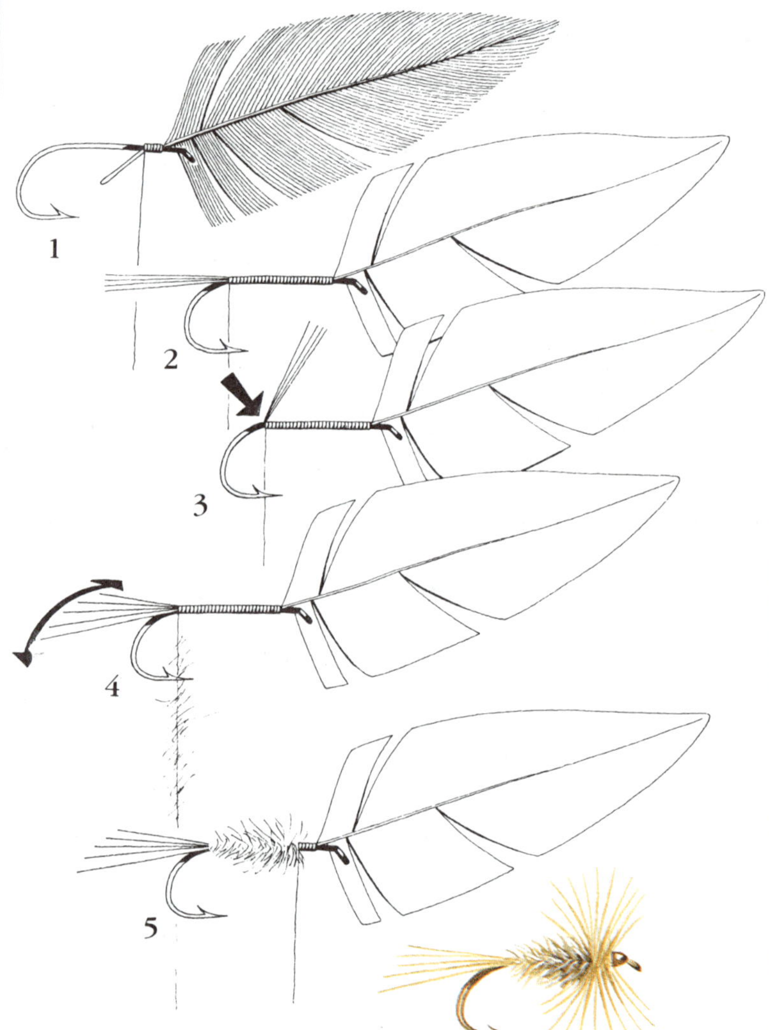

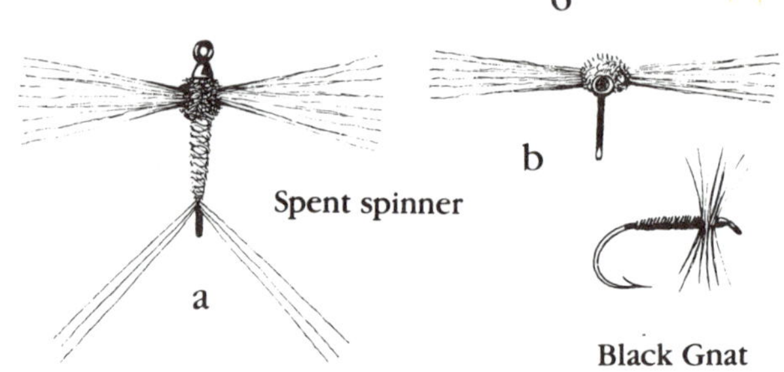

Winged dry flies

Whilst the Englishmen gave their flies quill wings, anglers in the USA developed a fly type with softer wings made of flank feather fibres from various ducks—preferably wood duck. Today it is also common to tie wings of hackle tips or synthetic hair. These wings should not be too stiff and the fly has to be symmetric—otherwise the leader will twist during casting.

The hackled dry fly is considered to be an all-round fly, while the winged dry fly is usually meant to imitate a certain insect. Therefore, choose the colours of a fly to agree with the living model.

Now we tie a winged dry fly in the American style— Light Cahill.

1. Attach thread and tie in a tuft of wood duck fibres, or a substitute. Many feathers are hard or impossible to get these days. Alternative feathers can normally be obtained in most fly-fishing shops and make perfect substitutes, if necessary dyed to the correct colour.
2. Straighten up the wing and split it in a V-shape with eight-turns.
3. Tie in tail, using the same material or light brown hackle fibres as alternative. Spread tail in a fan shape.
4. Wax and dub thread with light beige poly-yarn.
5. Form a slim, tapered body.
6. Attach hackle, wind and secure as usual. Some fly-dressers prefer to attach the hackle feather behind the wings and to wind forward, thus avoiding individual fibres to be tied down when winding the thread forward. It is hanging from the head all the time.
7. The first method gives the fly a more "split" hackle.

The pictured fly Coachman is of English style with white quill-wings (compare with the winged wet fly Alder). Adams is an American fly with hackle tip wings. Today many flies are tied with wings of poly-yarn. Most dry flies are intended to imitate mayflies. These insects have played an important part in fly-fishing throughout the ages. Mayfly eggs hatch in still or rapid waters—depending on the species—and develop into larvas. The larva grows and turns into a so-called nymph. When nymphs hatch—sometimes in great crowds at the same time—you can experience the "mating dance" performed by the adults before they lay their eggs in the water. Fish feed on mayflies in all stages— as nymphs, when hatching, as adults and as "spent spinners" after egg-laying. And every stage is imitated by various fishing flies!

Coachman

Hook: 12-14
Thread: black
Tail: brown cock hackle fibres
Body: peacock herl
Wings: sections of white wing feather
Hackle: brown

Adams

Hook: 12-14
Thread: black
Tail: brown and grizzly cock hackle fibres, mixed
Body: grey muskrat or poly-material in similar colour
Wings: grizzly hackle tips
Hackle: one grizzly and one brown cock feather

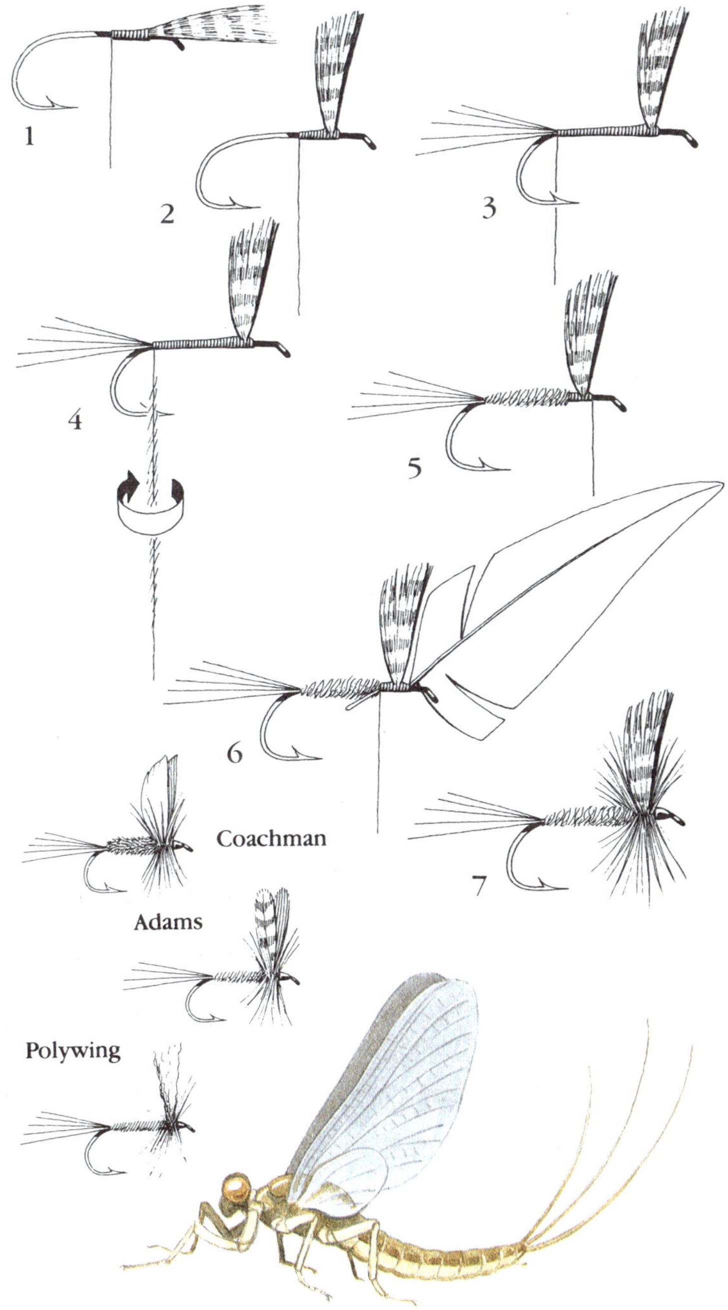

Nymphs

Many years ago Frank Sawyer gave me one of his very simple nymphs. He told me he used dark copper wire instead of tying silk. His nymph is shown here. There is no problem tying with copper wire, but most tiers prefer to first weight the hook and then use thread to tie in the material in the usual way. Sawyer made his nymphs in different variations of grey and brown.

In its submerged phase the mayfly is called a nymph. In strong-current water, we find *creeping* nymphs, which cling to bottom stones and gravel. In weak-current water, *swimming* nymphs live among water plants. Some species live in small passages through the bottom sand and are taken by fish only when they swim to the surface for hatching. Still waters also have a few nymph species.

Frank Sawyer's nymphs are weighted so that they can be fished in the intermediate water, whilst other nymphs are tied without extra weight to be fished in or just underneath the surface. The soft-hackled nymphs created by the Englishman G.E.M. Skues belong to these nymphs. Skues' nymphs caused great attention when he started to use them. He is considered to be the father of nymph fishing.

Skues' unweighted nymphs nearly always have dubbed bodies. The thorax—the front part of the body—is darker than the rear body and his nymphs have a sparse wet-fly hackle of short fibres.

The American Jim Leisenring developed a similar nymph-fishing method with his soft-hackled wet flies. His good friend and fishing mate Pete Hidy called them *flymphs*. After Leisenring's death, Pete Hidy developed flymph fishing further. He fished his flies not just sunk, or just beneath the surface, but also on the surface like a half-drowned dry fly, imitating nothing less than a hatching nymph. Also the big damsel flies have nymph phases. Their imitations are tied on long shank streamer hooks with wing cases, hackles and fibre tails.

Sawyer's Pheasant Tail Nymph

1. Weight hook with copper wire, forming a plump thorax. Tie in three pheasant tail fibres as the fly's tail.
2. Wind fibres along body.
3. Attach a small bunch of pheasant tail fibres and fold them backward over thorax. Follow with thread and secure.
4. Fold fibres forward again, and backwards . . .
5. . . . until the nymph has got plump wing cases.

Skues' Blue Winged Olive Nymph

1. Tie in three fibres from mallard flank feather on a hook 14 or 16. Tie in fine gold wire as ribbing.
2. Dub silk with brown-olive underfur . . .
3. . . . and wind . . .
4. . . . and rib rear part of body. Dub silk once more . . .
5. . . . and form a somewhat darker thorax.
6. Finally wind a speckled hackle, dyed dark olive.

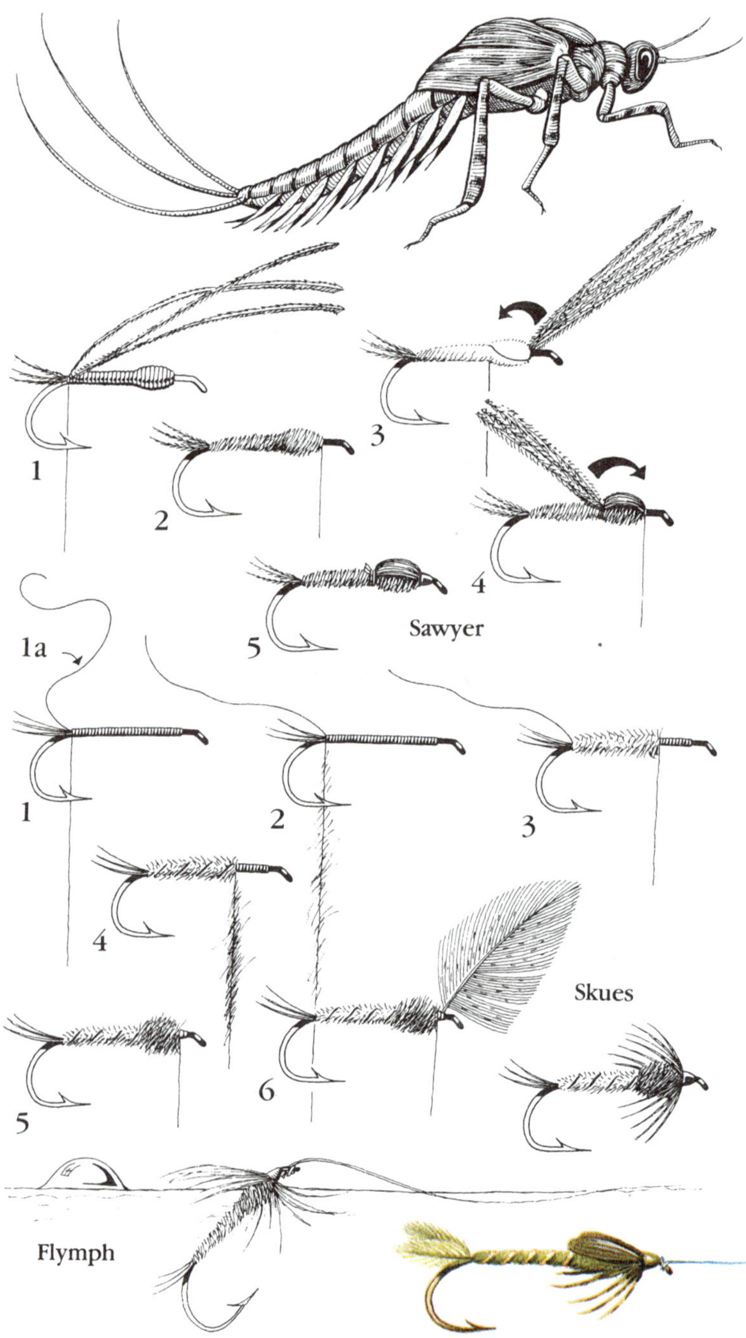

Winged Caddis flies

Both in Europe and in the USA, caddis flies have an important position in fly-fishing. In Scandinavia they are entirely dominant in many waters. My own winged caddis fly imitation is a variant of Elk Hair Caddis with body from hare and wing from elk—the American wapiti deer. The original is tied with bodies in different colours, and has a body hackle; but I leave the hackle aside and, instead, pull out a few stiffer hairs from the hare's fur.

You can find caddis flies in all kinds of waters. These insects have great adaptiveness to various environments. Caddis flies vary in colours, though most of them have bodies and wings in grey-brownish shades. As adults, caddis flies are very lively insects. On water they can swim in such an active way that they create "plough-waves" in the water. When flying they flutter very rapidly, looking just like well-dressed hackle dry flies! It is easy to recognize a sitting caddis fly, as it keeps its wings in a very typical reversed V-shape, looking like a ridge of a house.

Elk Hair Caddis Variant

1. Wind thread in close turns over shank, wax thread, and dub with the fine fur from hare's ear.
2. Form dubbed body and tie in a bunch of elk hairs as wing. Make sure the hair tips are equally long. Pull thread straight down, avoiding wing slip to rear side of hook.
3. Wind thread several turns round wing base, whip-finish and varnish. Cut surplus wing and finally pull out some of the thicker hairs from the dubbing. These hairs will do the work of a hackle.

Rackelhanen

My friend the Swedish fly-fisher Kenneth Boström has created the "Rackelhanen", a poly-fly that in just a few years has become known far beyond Scandinavia. The extraordinary floating abilities of this fly have made it extremely popular. When you pull it down into water, it immediately jumps back to the surface—creating an irresistible move to a trout's eyes.

1 Wind thread on shank, wax and dub thread with dark-brown curly poly-yarn.
2. Form a "fat" body.
3. Tie in a piece of poly-yarn as wing, same color as body. Fold back the other wing half . . .
4. . . . then secure it, dub thread again with the same poly-yarn and form thorax. Cut wings at desired length.

Green Elk Hair Caddis

Hook: 12-16
Thread: beige-brown
Body: olive wool
Body-hackle: olive
Wing: elk hair

Européa 12

Hook: 12-14
Thread: yellow
Body: grey dubbing
Ribbing: yellow tying thread
Wing: mallard (female) flank feather
Hackle: brown

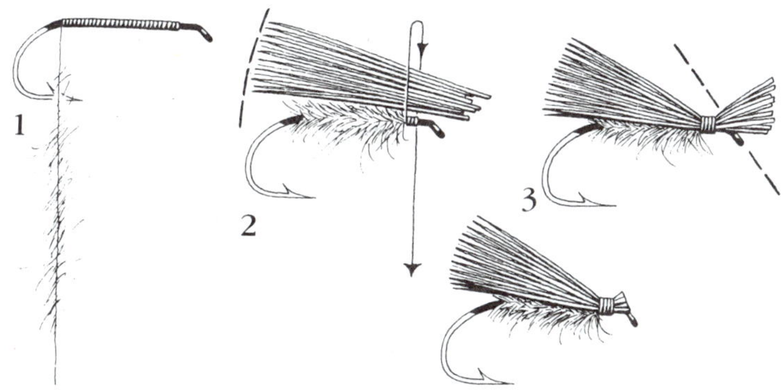

Rackelhanen

Elk Hair Caddis

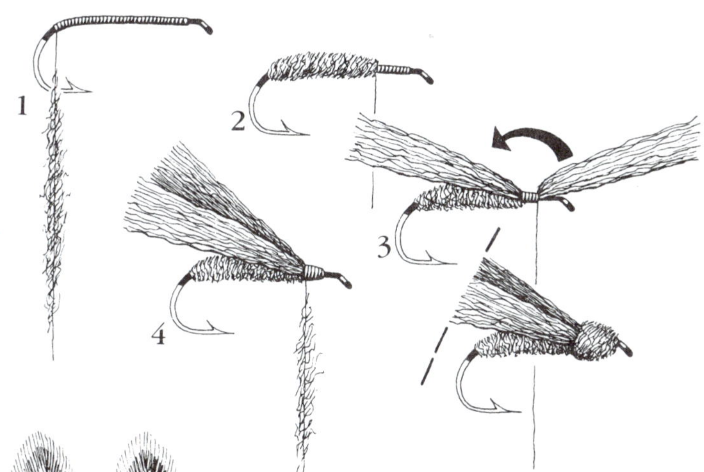

Européa-12

Pupas

Many water insects pass a pupa-phase after their larva-stage, and before they hatch and become adults. Insects with pupas most important to fly-fishermen are caddis flies and midges. Their pupas can make the fish go wild in actual rising orgies. Flies imitating pupas can be tied very simple, with just a dubbed body and a somewhat darker dubbed thorax.

Caddis-fly eggs hatch to larvas. There are many species of caddis flies: case-builders, net-spinners (a) and free swimmers. All larvae have a pupal stage, and it is as pupas (b) that they are particularly interesting to the fly-fisherman.

Midges too have larva and pupal stages (c). There are innumerable species of midges in different colour variations, but most midges have olive, olive-brown or blackish colours. On its head, the midge larva has white thread-like gills.

The smaller drawings show examples of caddis larva imitations (a_1) and midge pupa imitations (c_1). Caddis larvae can be tied as just one single body of creamed or green wool, and the long back-body of the midge pupa is best imitated by close turns of tying silk in suitable colour. Just before hatching, the midge pupa skin is filled with air, giving the pupa a silver shiny appearance in water. This can be imitated with silver tinsel, or just a silver ribbing. Thorax is made of a "ball" of dubbing—hare's ear is recommended. This makes the fly floating, as it will be fished hanging in the surface.

Caddis Pupa

1. Wind thread far down into hook bend and tie in a piece of yellow silk to be used as ribbing later on. Wax and dub thread with beige or olive-green fur or poly fibres.
2. Form body and leave enough space for thorax and head.
3. Wind ribbing and secure. You can wind the ribbing in two ways. One is masking turns in the same direction as the body material, making the ribbing "sink" into the body and be visible only when the fly is wet and semi-transparent. Or you can wind the opposite way and let the ribbing stay on top of the body material. This method will give the body a segmented appearance.
4. Shows wing cases, cut from feather sections and tied in on each side of shank. Dub thread again . . .
5. . . . and form thorax. Make a small and neat head.

Illustrations 5a and 5b show variants with legs and pulled-out hairs and fibres from thorax dubbing. Summary imitations are often enough to tempt the fish, but for his own sake the fly-tier often adds different details to his flies.

Green Caddis Larva

Hook: 10-8
Thread: brown
Body: bright green wool
Ribbing: the tying thread
Head: long and brown

Midge Pupa

Hook: 10-16
Thread: olive-green
Body: olive-green silk
Ribbing: silver
Thorax: dark brown hare

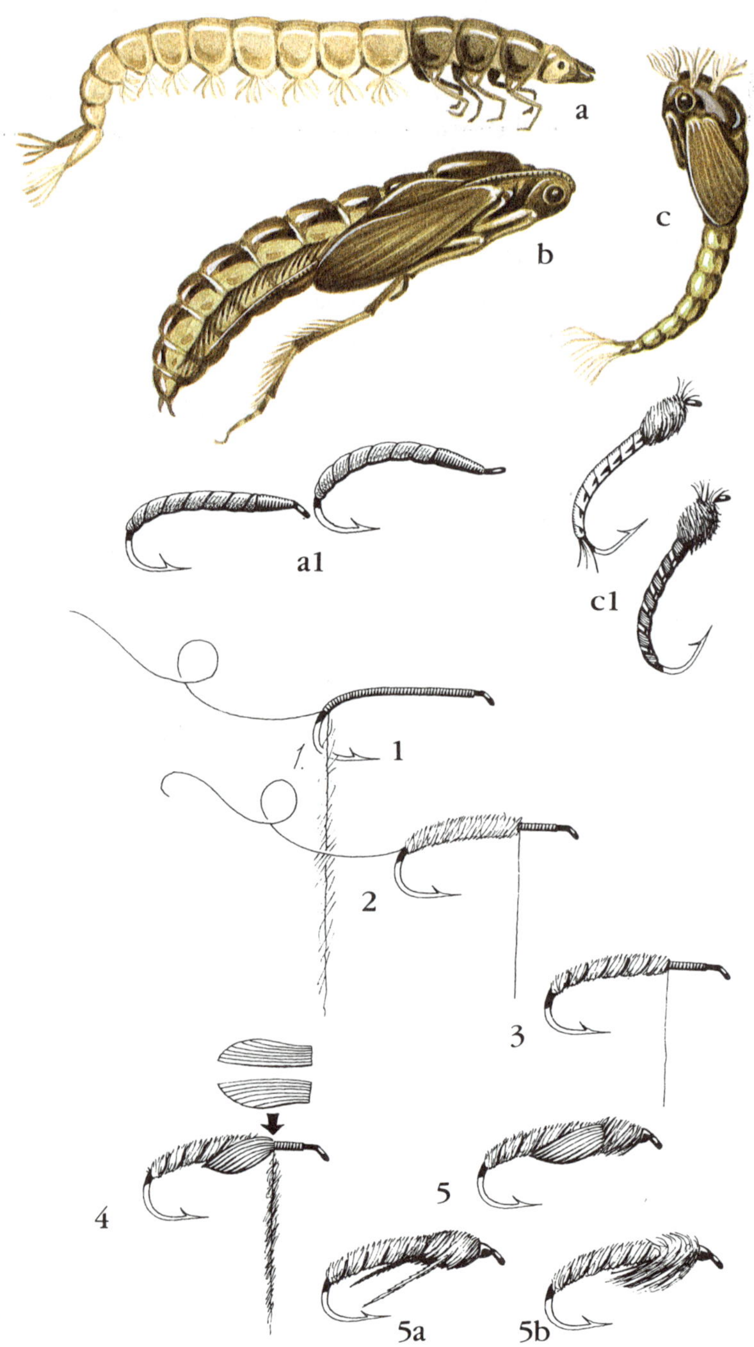

Terrestrials

Terrestrials is a collective designation for all land-living insects which now and then are blown into the water, becoming food for the fish. Small beetles, wasps, ants and grasshoppers are some of these terrestrials. Flying ants, for example, usually make the fish completely selective. In some waters, trout specialize entirely in grasshoppers. The imitation in the picture was given to me by Jack Hemingway, when we fished his Little Wood River—one of the finest brown-trout streams in the USA.

Beetle

1. Tie in a section from dark goose feather and 2-3 peacock herls, as shown in the figure. A floating imitation is tied without extra weight. Form a fat "sub-body" of wool or similar material. Wind peacock herls on top of this body.
2. Fold feather section forwards, forming a back shield over the body. Cut surplus, wind head and whip-finish. Varnish both head and back-shield.

Ant

Ants can be tied in many different ways. Two dubbed "balls" on the shank with a hackle at the "waist" between them is the most common method. However, here we will learn another variant, tied with black-coloured deer hair—a material with great floating ability, since the hairs are hollow and filled with air.

1. Attach a thick bunch of deer hairs, with hairs reaching down to hook bend. Wind thread just past middle of shank.
2. Fold hairs forward and spread them round shank. Secure with thread, forming a "waist". Keep down hairs and wind thread along the rest of the shank.
3. Tie in the hairs again, but let 4-5 hairs stick out at the waist. Fold these hairs out from the fly . . .
4. . . . imitating legs. Cut to required length.

Grasshopper

1. Attach a solid tuft of deer hair at the bend of a streamer-hook. Fold hairs forward and tie in, making three sections at *a*, *b* and *c*, using the same technique as for "ant-waist". Then attach a new hair bunch, put forward and wind thread back to point *c*.
2. Attach a brown speckled wing, rear edge cut semicircular. Place the wing flat over fly's back, bend hair and bunch back . . .
3. . . . then tie it in and trim the hairs on fly's underside. If you want legs on your fly, these can be made of feather fibres. Use knots to imitate leg joints (d).

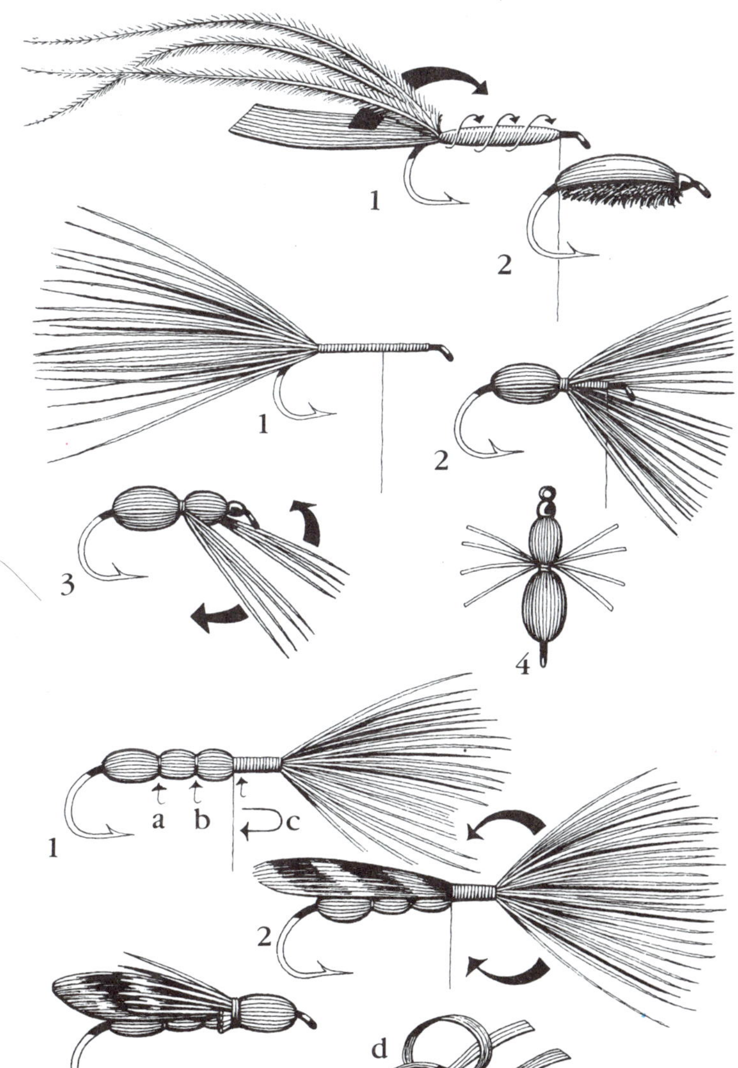

Ant (variant)

Hook: 12-14
Thread: black or brown
Body: poly-dubbing, black or brown
Waist: black or brown hackle

Grasshopper

Hook: 8-12, streamer
Thread: yellow
Body: deer hair
Backwing: light brown speckled turkey

Bucktails and Streamers

A bucktail-fly is supposed to have a wing from bucktail (!) or other hair materials, and a streamer is supposed to have long hackle feather wings. However, with the years, the word "streamer" has become a uniform name for all types of flies with long wings and tied on long-shanked hooks. The same designation is used for other special flies, such as the fly in the picture—a Thunder Creek, intended to imitate a small fish fry.

Both a traditional streamer (a) and bucktail (b) have long wings, which are attached at fly's head. While fishing this type of fly, the long wing often gets stuck underneath the hook shank just at the bend, as shown in fig. *c*. Thus the fly will rotate in the water.

To solve this problem you can put two shorter wings on the fly instead (d), one wing not reaching the bend and the rear wing also going free from the bend, depending on its position on the hook. Another variant is the Matuka streamer (e), which has two or more hackle feathers attached on top of the shank. Fibres on the side of feather facing the shank should be torn off, and the feather is not just secured at the head of the fly but attached along the shank by the ribbing.

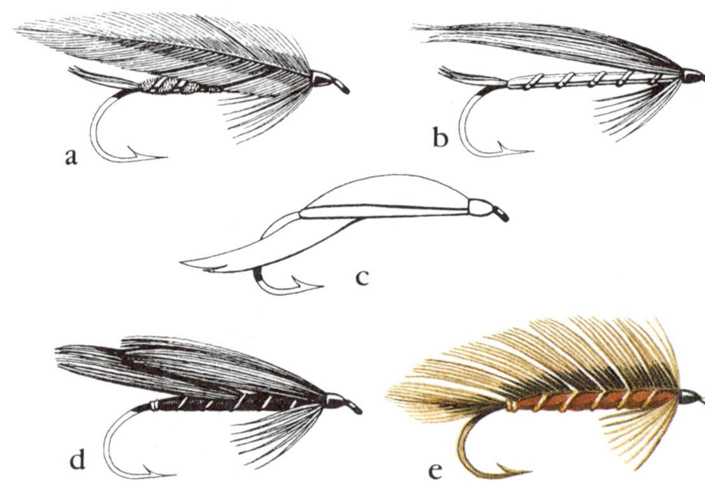

Thunder Creek

The American Keith Fulsher has created a whole series of Thunder Creek flies. These are more of a fly type than just individual fly patterns and, since they are supposed to imitate fish fry, it is a good idea to create your own colour variations, depending on what fish are present in your own waters. The original patterns are tied with bucktail hair—some of them dyed in different hues. Keith Fulsher recommends a 6X long streamer hook with a straight eye. "6X long" means that the hook has a shank answering to that of a hook with six times bigger gap.

1. Wind thread along shank in close turns and, at the same time, tie in a wide silver tinsel and a coloured body silk. Make room for a short silver tag behind the body (see figure).
2. Wind body and let tinsel folow up to two thirds of shank.
3. Attach a slim bucktail wing on top of shank.
4. Then attach a tuft of dark bucktail hairs on top and a tuft of light hairs underneath the shank. The top tuft is slightly longer . . .
5. . . . making the back longer, when the two tufts are folded backwards and secured with thread. Varnish the head several times and paint eyes on each side.

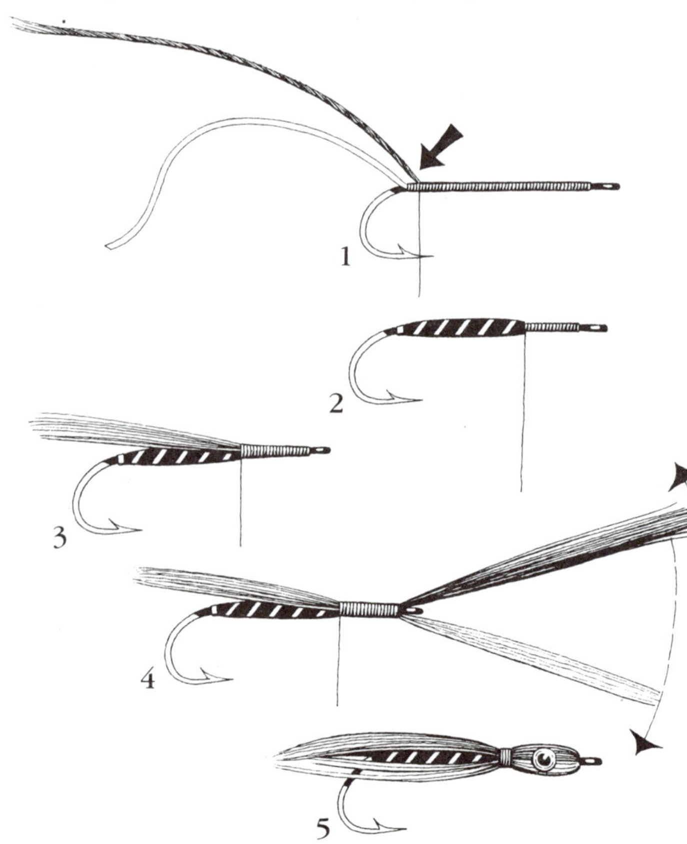

Squirrel Streamer

Hook: 8-12, streamer hook
Thread: black
Tail: red fibres
Body: silver tinsel
Ribbing: silver
Wing: dark-brown squirrel tail
Hackle: clear blue

Matuka Streamer

Hook: 8-12, streamer hook
Thread: black
Body: red wool
Ribbing: silver
Wing: brown hackle with dark middle part
Hackle: grizzly

Lures and Poppers

These are fantasy flies, intended to entice fish by tempting movements and different fishing methods. In the USA poppers, for example, are used for bass or bluegill fishing, or other fish from many species in the sunfish family.

In northern Europe, poppers are used primarily for pike fishing. This is a very interesting way of fishing. Actually, fishing with floating popper is a kind of dry-fly fishing. The pike takes the fly in the surface and the strike can be very explosive!

Marabou fibres are very soft and move easily in water. Besides, the marabou feathers are extremely light, which allows you to tie very big flies and still be able to cast, even with a one-handed rod. But the marabou fibres have one big disadvantage—they quite easily get caught around the hook bend. Consequently you have to check your fly after every one or two casts. If you give the fly metal eyes, as in figure, the fly will be slightly weighted. The fly will thus sink head-first. Using this fact the right way and manipulating your line, you can make the fly wiggle and waddle in the most tempting way through water!

Leech

Leeches (b) are not insects, of course, but can still be models for the fly-tier, since they are popular food for fish. Marabou fibres are perfect to illustrate the wiggling movements of a leech.

1. Wind thread in close turns along shank and tie in a solid bunch of marabou fibres, black or dark-brown, as tail.
2. Attach another bunch of fibres at hook bend.
3. Twist these around tying thread.
4. Wind thread and fibres forward along shank. Form a head and varnish.

Illustration 4 shows the leech-fly as we see it in the vise. When wet, the fly will be much slimmer (5). And when fished in the proper way, the fibres will open and close in water and make the fly very tempting for the fish. Thus we learn that the looks of a fly are not always as important as the qualities which the fly has when properly fished!

Poppers

Poppers can be tied with heads of trimmed deer hair, giving the fly a good floating ability. But it is more common to make a head of very light and soft wood (c). Some fish seem to prefer very colour-rich flies, so many tiers make poppers with heads painted in contrasting colours.

1. Tie in 2-4 big cock hackles at the rear on a heavy trout hook. Wind thread 4-5 mm towards head, and tie in an additional cock hackle in a contrasting colour—black or red for example.
2. Wind hackle in the form of a big collar and whip-finish. Glue the head to hook by the score underneath. Press hackle backwards and paint head and eyes. You can also paint the head before it is clued to the hook.

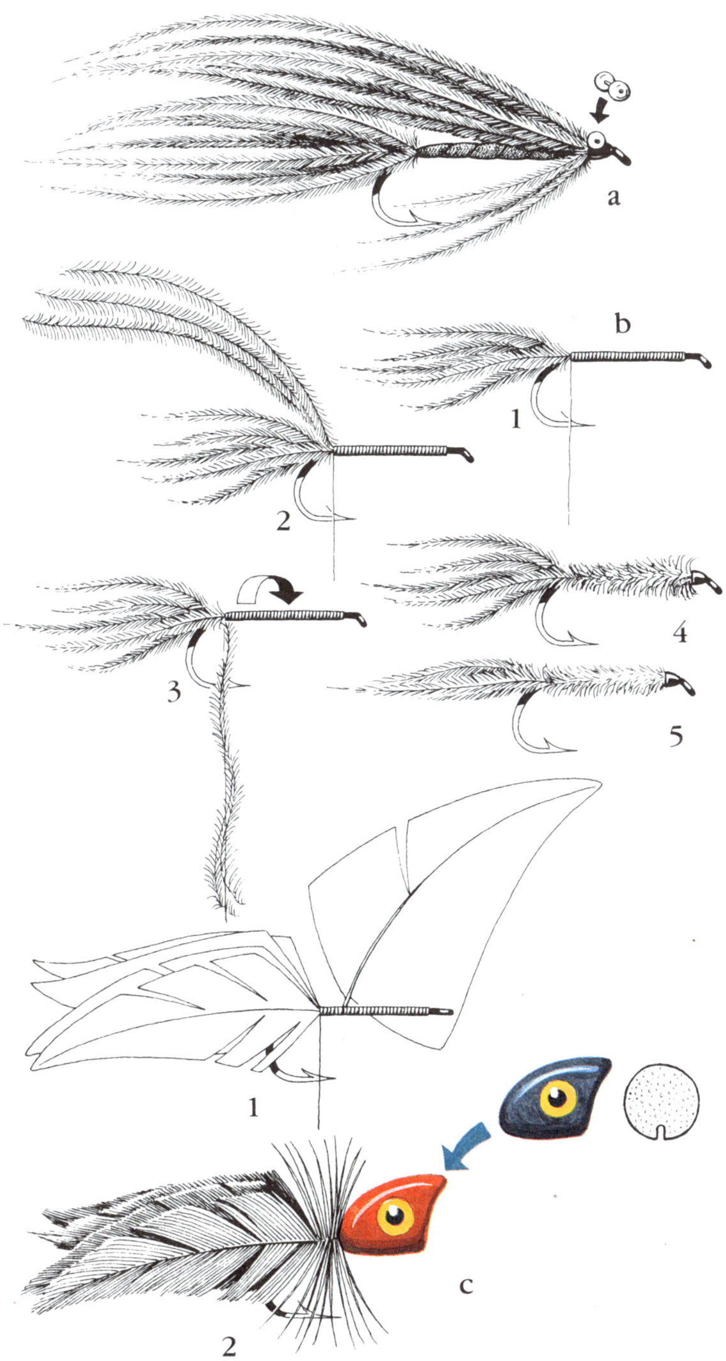

Fully dressed salmon flies

The fly in the photo is an old, fully dressed salmon fly from the end of the last century. It is tied on a hook with a loop of silk gut instead of an eye. Nowadays we use slightly up-eyed hooks and—most of all—we tie much more simple and uncomplicated flies. But the tradition of tying the old, colourful salmon flies is still alive, though today perhaps more of a handicraft.

It is not an easy task to tie a fully dressed salmon fly. You will face the first problem already when assembling materials for the fly—a lot of them are no longer available! But in most cases it is possible to get substitutes. Blue parrot, for example, can easily be replaced by fibres from blue coloured swan feathers.

The next problem is how to master the amount of materials you have to attach to the hook. The first efforts normally end up in rather clumsy creations. Let us pretend your fly consists of 30 different materials or tying moments, and you make five extra turns with the tying thread at each material or moment—just to be on the safe side, since you want your salmon fly to last. The result will be a very clumsy fly, containing no less than one hundred and fifty unnecessary turns of thread!

The same goes for how to select the amount of materials. If you take three or four extra fibres of every material included in the wing, for example, the result will be a definitely overdressed fly. And it is very easy to take too much material: normally one does not realize one's mistake before the fly is completed. Knowledge of materials and the right "how-much-sense" is something to be achieved only after eager practice behind the vise.

Yet another problem is the "styling" of a fly, i.e. proportions and character in general. A perfect fully dressed salmon fly must be well balanced and well proportioned. In fact it is a piece of art. Used for practical fishing, it has furthermore to behave in the right way. You have to know how and when to choose materials with the right softness—or stiffness—due to its purpose. For example, a soft hackle will be more alive in slow water, while a somewhat stiffer hackle is at its best in stronger current.

Tying the Black Doctor

1. Attach black thread and wind it backwards. Stop at hook bend, just above hook point. Tie in a piece of oval or round silver tinsel and wind back thread 2-3 mm to the right. Let tinsel follow in just a few close turns. Secure tinsel and cut surplus. Tie in yellow floss silk. Make a few turns with thread ending just above hook point, where the tag will end. Wind floss silk to a tag. Secure with thread and cut surplus.
2. The tail consists of golden pheasant crests with a few red feather fibres on top. Try to imagine the completed fly—dotted line symbolizing the wing—and it is easier to decide the length of the tail. To hide the joint between tag, tail and body, we give the fly a butt. It can be made of dark-red dubbing . . .

3. . . . wound as a small collar, or a dark-red ostrich herl (3a).
4. Tie in medium or heavy oval silver tinsel, one piece of black floss silk, and a big black or dark-red cock hackle feather, as shown in the drawing. Wind tying thread ahead and stop ten millimetres short of hook eye.
5. Wind black body of floss. Secure using as few turns as possible.
6. Let body hackle and silver tinsel follow. Secure, and strengthen with one small drop of varnish if you like. Tie in one or more bunches of fibres from guinea fowl, forming a throat hackle. Be sure the natural curve of the fibres follows the fly, and that fibres are evenly spread. (The throat hackle can be tied in later, when the wing is finished.)
7. Now it is time to prepare the wing. It consists of two brown sections from golden pheasant tail feather (b) on top of an underwing made of a tippet feather (c). Cut the stem on the latter to give the feather a V-shape. Fold the tippet feather along the middle and tie in. Place the brown sections on each side (ill. 7a). The wing should almost reach the tail.
8. On each side of the underwing there is an outer wing, consisting of several slim sections of feather fibres. The sections will stick together, thanks to all the microscopic barbs that sit along the edges of each fibre. The barbs will function just like the hooks in a zip fastener.

Bring out all the materials for the outer wings at one time. Counting from the top, using three fibres of each material, you join the sections in this order: light speckled turkey tail feather (d), peacock wing feather (e), yellow-dyed swan wing (f), blue-dyed swan wing (g) and red-dyed swan wing (h).

Stroke the fibres between fingers so they "zip" together. Make two equally big and proportioned outer wings and tie them in on each side of the body, as shown in figure 8a.

9. Next wing section is shorter. It consists of two materials: black striped wood-duck feather (i) and teal's flank feather. Tie as in shown at 9a.
10. Our Black Doctor is beginning to look good—but still a few materials are to be tied in. On top of the wing we tie in brownish flank feather from mallard drake (k) reaching as long as the rest of the wing (10a), then golden pheasant topping (l).

Finally form a well-proportioned head with tying thread and varnish carefully. The head should also have a red streak—use red varnish, or make a few turns with red tying silk and varnish.

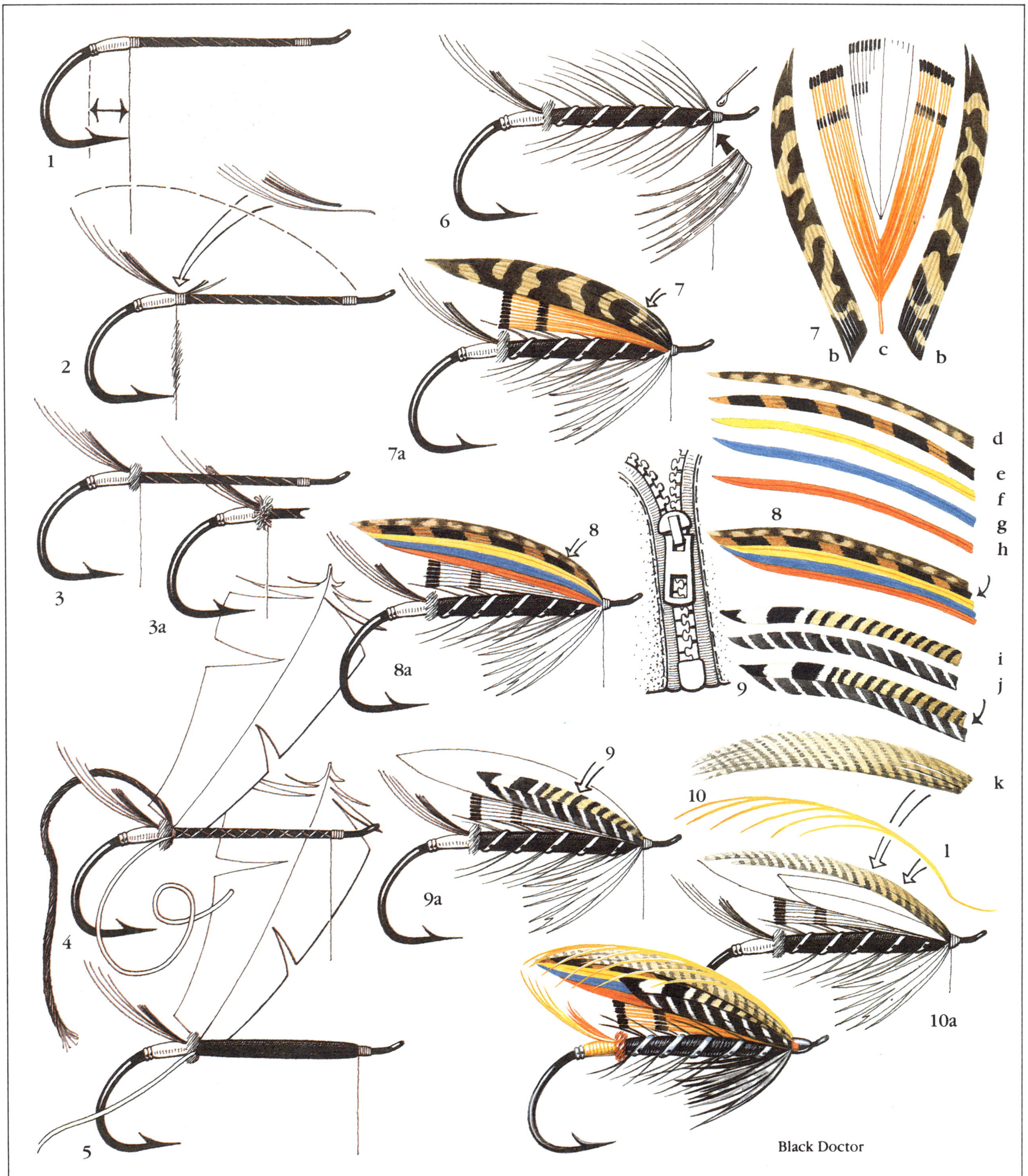
1
2
3
3a
4
5
6
7
7a
7
b
c
b
d
e
f
g
h
8
8
8a
9
9
i
j
9a
10
k
l
10a
Black Doctor

Hair-wing salmon flies

Surely a fully dressed salmon fly is a beauty—but just as time-consuming to tie. Most anglers therefore prefer more simple hair-wing flies. Besides, a softer hair-wing fly often behaves better in water. It "breathes"—its wing opening and closing—thus giving the fly more life.

Nowadays most classical salmon flies can be tied as variants with hair wings, while other flies are created as hair-wing patterns from the start. All along new flies "pop up". Some of them disappear rather quickly or are being used only locally—others stay on and, in due time, become classical themselves. Here we will tie the salmon fly Red Abbey.

1. Attach and tie in a silver tag. Tie in a thick tail of red hairs. After that, attach a strip of silver tinsel and red wool to the body. As alternative you can make a red dubbed body. In both cases the body is ribbed with five even turns by the silver tinsel.
2. Tie in a solid wing of brown squirrel tail. The fly will last longer if you make this in two smaller sections, which are secured with varnish.
3. The original pattern prescribes jungle cock feathers (3a) on each side. But the jungle cock is on the endangered species list—so we manufacture our own substitutes by painting the points of black hackle feathers with white and yellow hobby-varnish (3b).
4. Tie in a big brown hackle and wind it as a collar round the wing root.
5. Form head with thread and, at the same time, make a few turns with thread towards hackle to press this slightly backwards. Red tying thread is prescribed in order to give the fly a red head—but you can use any thread colour and then use red varnish to head.

Low-water flies

When water temperature is high and water level low, a low-water fly is better. This fly is tied on a thinner hook. The fly is smaller and has a slimmer appearance. Low-water flies can be tied with hair or feather wings, but are normally very simple patterns.

The purpose is that these flies should be fished in the surface- or midwater-area. Normally their bodies are tied much shorter than on an ordinary salmon fly—no more than half the shank is covered—and its wing should not reach further than the hook barb. Below is the fly pattern of two different low-water flies:

Sweep

Hook: 1-10, low water
Thread: black
Tag: silver
Tail: golden pheasant crest
Body: black silk
Ribbing: silver
Wing: black squirrel
Cheek: blue kingfisher
Hackle: black

Silver Blue

Hook: 1-10, low water
Thread: black
Tag: silver
Tail: golden pheasant crest
Body: silver
Ribbing: silver
Wing: teal flank feather
Hackle: blue

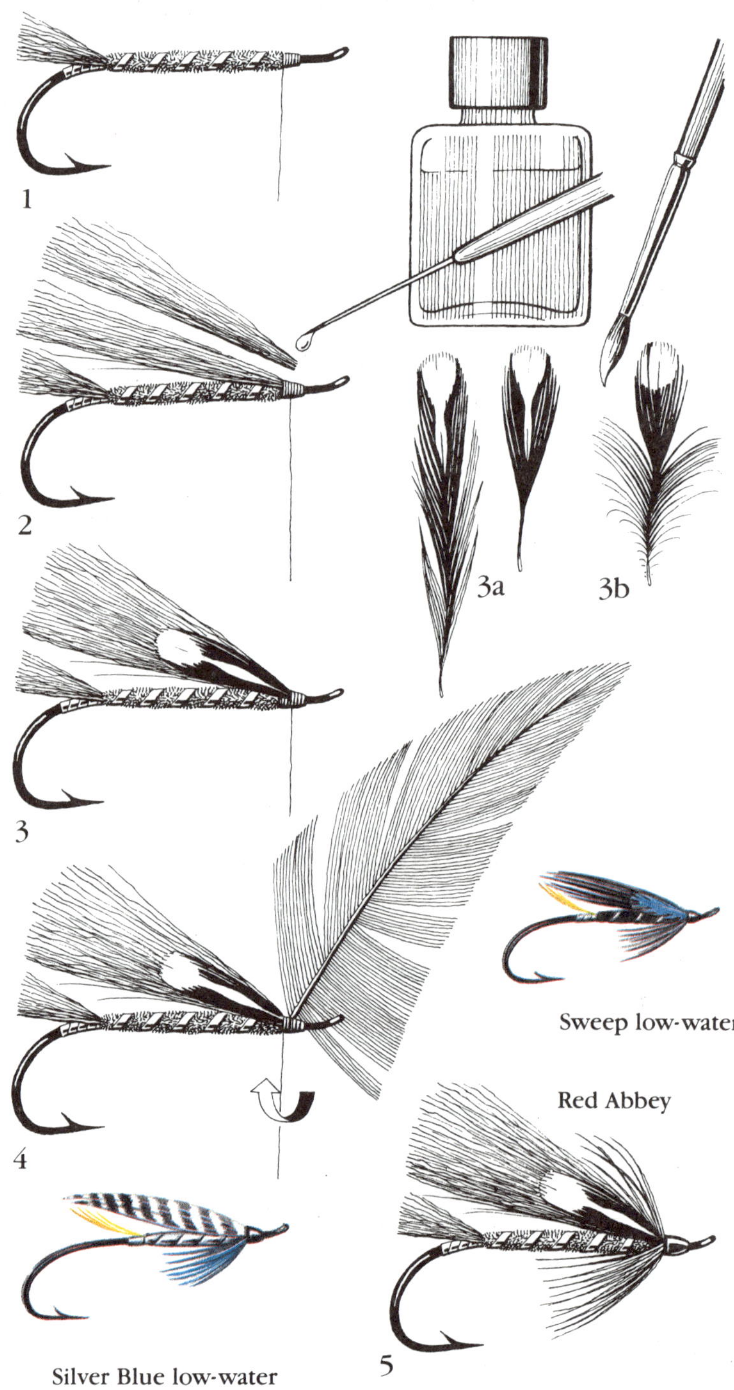

Tube flies

In many Scandinavian waters you are allowed to use flies with treble hooks, leading to an increased popularity of various tube fly models for salmon and sea-trout fishing. When spring fishing in high and cold water, it is essential to get down to the fish. Then a fly tied on a heavy brass tube is preferred. When temperature is higher, one can use a lighter plastic tube, since during such conditions fish are likely to rise to a fly.

Tube flies can be tied on either plastic tubes (a) or brass tubes (b). For the latter you put a short rubber tube on the rear of a brass tube to keep the treble in place.

Plastic tubes can be purchased in coherent lengths to be cut into desired sizes. By cautiously heating the ends until they start melting, you can form small "collars", which hinder the tying materials from slipping off the tube.

1. You cannot attach a tube directly to the vise. Start by snipping off the eye from a big salmon-fly hook. Attach eyeless hook in vise and thread tube on shank. Press tube down to hook bend—this will make it stay put.
2. Start the fly by giving the whole tube a layer of close thread turns. Tie in a silver rib. Wind thread forwards and tie in body material at marked point.
3. Wind body and let silver ribbing follow. Cut all surplus.
4. Time to tie in the wing. You can choose from a wide range of hair material, both natural and coloured. Tie in the wing in several steps as you turn the tube on the shank. Wings can be tied in bunches or spread evenly all round the body. Finally you can provide your fly with a hackle in some contrasting colour, before forming the head. Whip-finish and varnish.

To attach the treble to the tube, thread your leader through the tube starting from the front opening. Attach a treble to leader, using a clinch-knot (c). Pull leader back until treble's eye is hidden in tube's rear. This will secure the treble in the right position (d).

Tubes can be tied in many different colour combinations—for example variants of classical salmon fly patterns. Besides, salmon and sea-trout fishing tubes can be used for other kinds of fishing: for pike, for example, and in smaller sizes for trout or perch.

I will not present any special tube patterns, but think it is better to create your own patterns using your imagination. Let the tubes vary in sizes and go from light silvery to pitch dark! My own experience tells me that big yellow-white tubes with some red in them are especially tempting to pike—but the field is open to experiments.

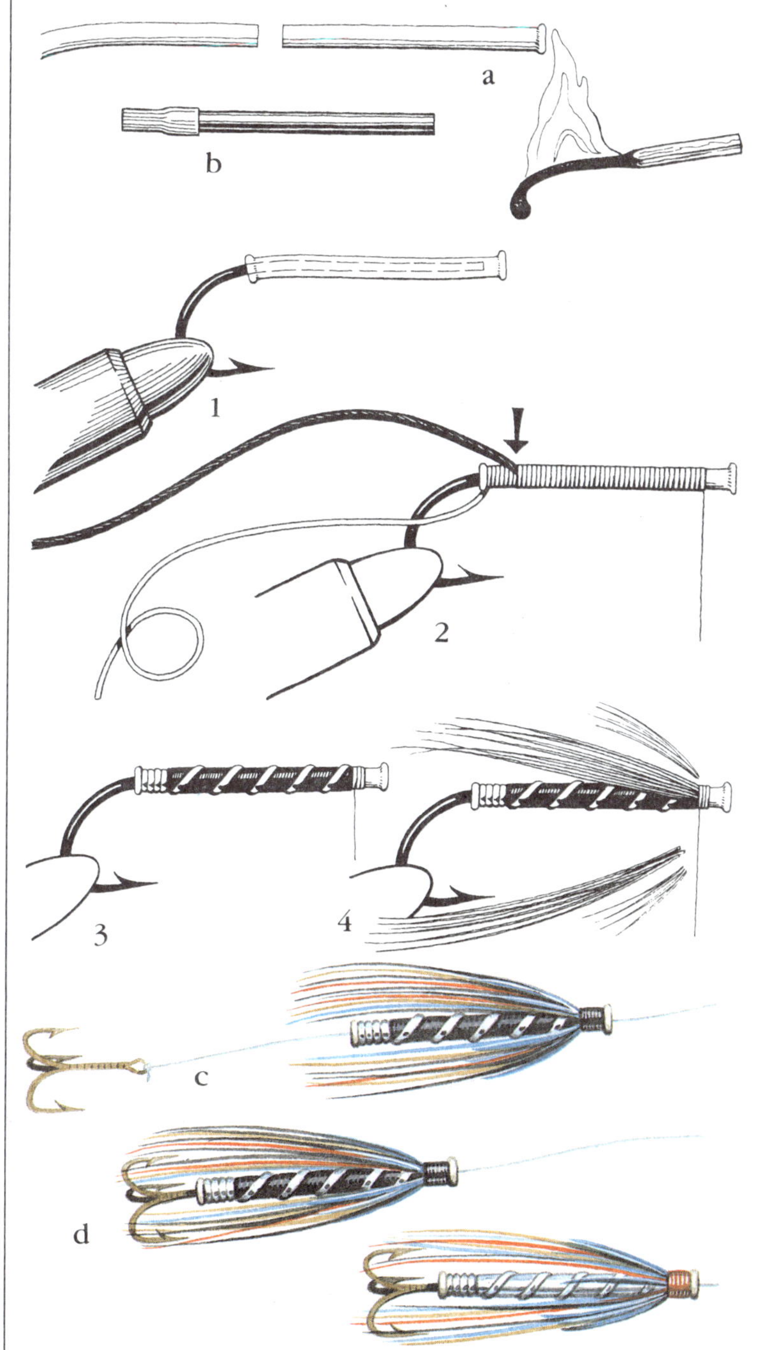

Dry flies for salmon and sea trout

In Scandinavia you can fish with a dry fly for sea trout in some rivers, while in other waters only wet flies are successful. Likewise, the American Lee Wulff has developed a dry fly in fishing for salmon on his side of the Atlantic. The photo shows one of the Danish angler Svend Saabye's creations used in dry-fly fishing for sea trout in the Norwegian river Laerdal.

Dry-fly fishing for salmon and sea trout is still relatively undeveloped. A few enthusiasts achieve good results in certain rivers, and there is every reason for more anglers to gather experience there in this field over the coming years.

In some rivers with strong current and cold water, the dry fly will presumably never be successful, while other waters are more suitable. Here one can feel an interesting development, where some success already has been achieved by those giving this kind of fishing a fair chance.

We will now tie a dry fly for sea-trout fishing.

1. Choose a strong but light hook in sizes 6-10. Tie in a bunch of squirrel hair as wings and another bunch as tail. Alternatively cock hackle fibres can be used as tail.
2. Dub thread with light fur—seal or curly poly-yarn, for example—and wind 4-5 mm on shank.
3. Then dub thread with dark-brown or black fur.
4. Wind the rest of the body. Stop a few mm behind wings to leave room to hackle. Split wings with eight-turns and fix them in a position slanting upwards (4a). They are not to stand straight up as on an ordinary dry fly.
5. Tie in two cock hackles—suitably one brown and one black. Wind thread backwards and let one hackle follow as body-hackle in a sparse spiral.
6. Secure body-hackle and wind thread forwards as shown.
7. Wind the other hackle as a front hackle, secure and complete with head and whip-finish. Finally trim the fly underneath. Then it will stand flat on the surface (7a). The slanted and split wings will make the fly always land straight.

Svend Saabye also ties his sea-trout dry flies with wings of double hackle points or poly-wings. The basic pattern can vary in colour, but the flies are always tied in a bushy fashion. They float well and, at the same time, they represent a good mouthful—well worth rising to in a trout's eyes. Below are the patterns for two of Lee Wulff's already classical dry flies for Atlantic salmon.

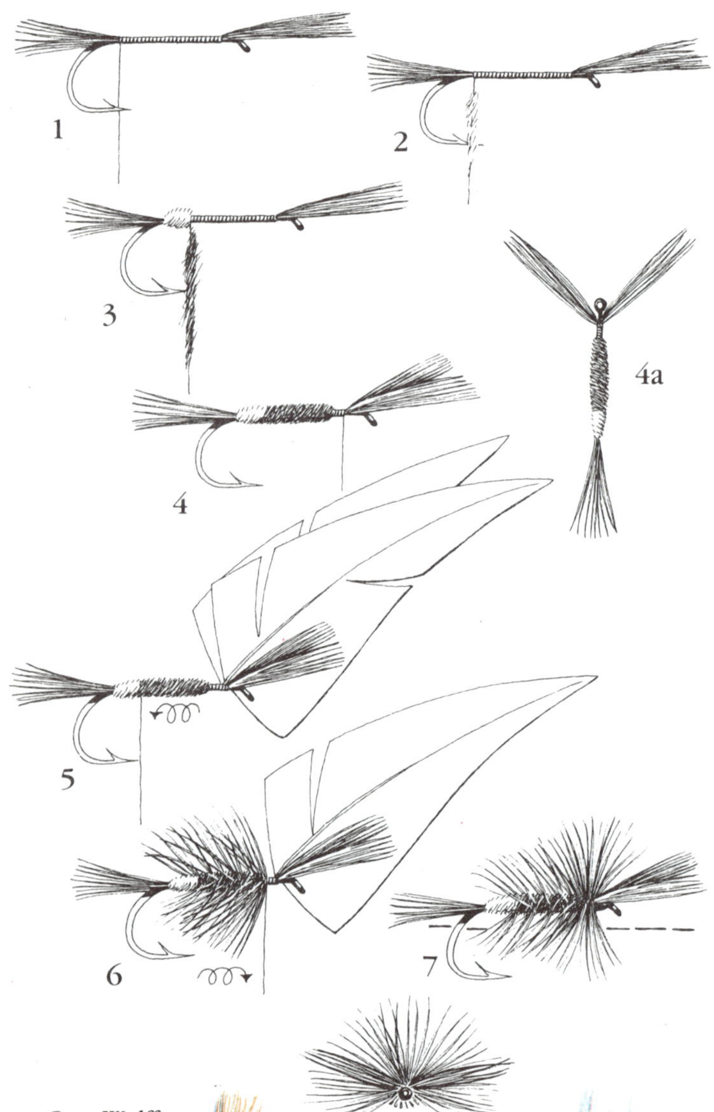

Gray Wulff

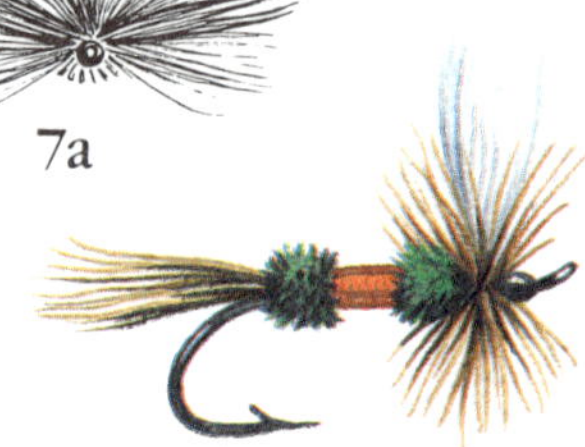

Royal Wulff

Gray Wulff

Hook: 4-10
Thread: black
Tail: bucktail
Body: grey dubbing
Wing: bucktail
Hackle: grey

Royal Wulff

Hook: 4-10
Thread: black
Tail: bucktail
Body: peacock herl/red wool/peacock herl
Wing: white calf tail
Hackle: brown

Salt water flies

While working with this fly-tying chapter, I received a letter from two American fly-fishing friends, Janet and Marty Downey, who had just returned from a fly-fishing trip to the rich waters along Florida's coast. Their goal had been tarpon and the letter included some pictures of huge fish! One weighed 70 pounds, the other 90, Janet of course having caught the biggest . . .

My own experience from fishing with salt-water flies is poor. Friends who are dedicated to this very special form of fly-fishing, however, have told me the pattern seems to be of less importance. Colours white, yellow and red are likely to be the best, but some days very dark flies take it all.

What is really important, however, is to tie the flies on stainless hook: otherwise the salty sea water will ruin the fly in no time. It is also a good idea to rinse the flies in fresh water after a day's fishing. But not just the flies— your whole equipment should be rinsed, and you should only use fly reels which are salt-water resistant.

Salt-water anglers prefer hooks with straight eyes (b). Ordinary trout or salmon hooks will not do. Also it is important that the long hackle wings don't get tangled in the hook bend (c), making the fly tumble and twist, thus ruining the fly's movements in the water.

Therefore you tie in the hackle wing at the rear of the shank (d), looking more like a long tail. True, this will cause a few fish to go for the wing and miss the hook, but most of the time fish strike so violently that they swallow the fly. In this fishing you are often dealing with really big fish!

Illustration (e) shows one type of salt-water fly, where the shank is covered with silver mylar—a synthetic tinsel that cannot rust. The fly has a "hackle" of long hairs—coloured bucktail or calf tail, for example. Today many synthetic materials are also available. Always use synthetic tying thread that won't rot.

The fly in illustration (f) has a big hackle just in front of the long tail feathers. Then the shank has been wound with tying thread in contrasting colour—red, for example. Many flies become more attractive if furnished with a few glittering mylar strips, like Flash-A-Bow, by the wing. They give the fly extra shininess and create reflexions in water.

Big hooks give bigger resistance when striking. Consequently it is essential always to have properly sharpened hooks. A small hook hone should therefore be found in every well-furnished fly-tying box—and used diligently . . .

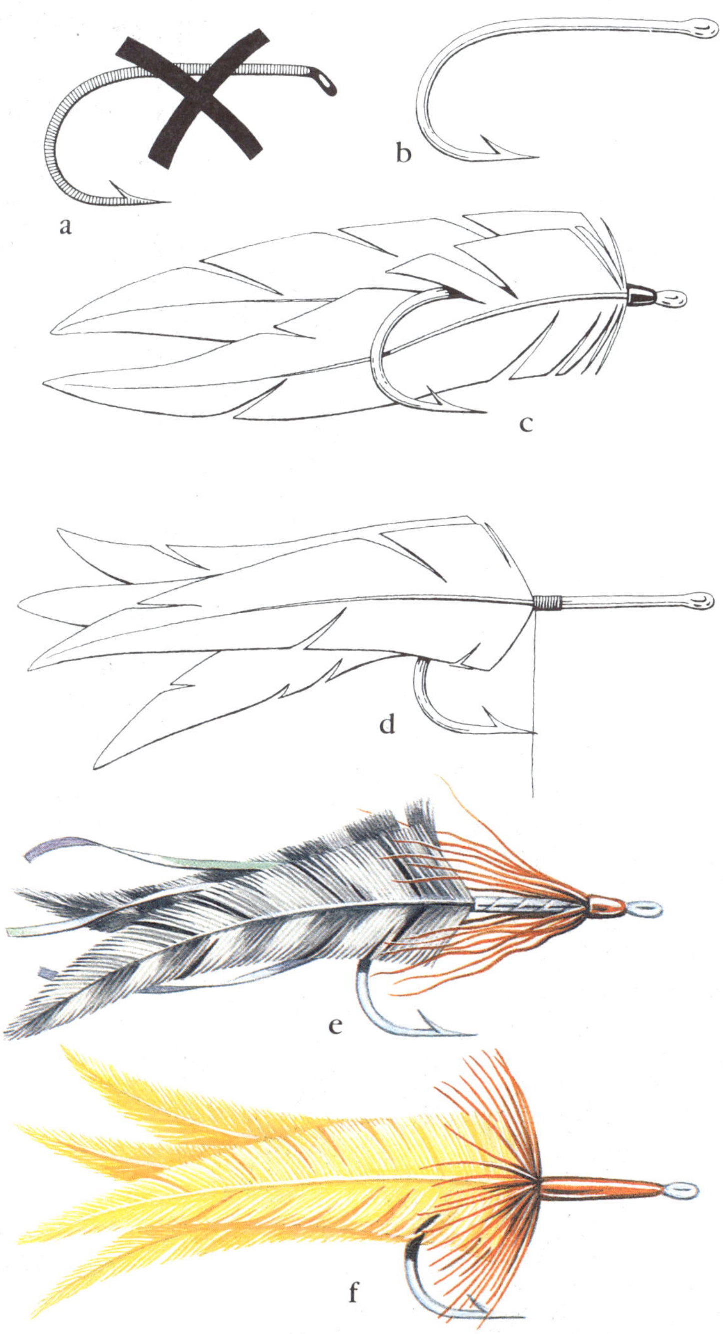

Making your own tackle

Building your own rod

More and more anglers have started building their own rods. Some see rod-building as a money-saving venture, which it certainly is if you begin with a top-quality rod blank. Most sportfishermen, however, probably think less in terms of economics and more in terms of gaining a customized fishing rod.

For most do-it-yourselfers, choosing the right blank is the most difficult decision, especially if the rod is to be used in a variety of fishing situations. If you are the least bit uncertain about which blank to choose, a reputable fishing-tackle shop should be able to provide sound advice.

Today's blanks are usually made of fibreglass, graphite, boron and kevlar. Boron and kevlar are added mainly for strengthening the blank. There are also many combinations of these materials, but it is impossible to recommend the "best", because personal preference and opinion are so important in choosing a rod.

Another material still used in manufacturing rods is bamboo. Split bamboo rods are made from specially selected bamboo poles. They are best for lightweight fly-rods of up to 8 ft (2.4 m) in length and line class 6. In the opinion of many anglers, a well-made split bamboo rod is the best fly-fishing rod available.

Placing the guides

The first step in building your rod is to decide which side of the blank the guides should be placed on. This is not always easy for beginners, and even experienced rod-builders do not all agree on how to do it.

The simplest way is to support the blank sections at the ends so that they are free to rotate and find their own center of gravity. The guides should then be mounted on the side facing down if you are constructing a fly-rod or a spinning rod, as spinning and fly-reels are attached to the underside of the rod. If you are building a rod for a multiplier reel that sits on the upper side of the rod, the guides should be placed on the upper side. Mark the side of the rod that will be used.

Mounting the cork grip

The next step is to drill holes in the cork rings for the grip. If necessary, use a file to smooth the holes, so that they are exactly the same diameter as the thickest end of the blank, where the grip will be attached.

When all the cork pieces are shaped to the right size, they should be arranged and identified in the order they will be glued together. A waterproof glue should be used.

The reel seat should be mounted at the same time as the cork grip, unless you are building a single-handed fly-rod, in which case the reel seat must be attached later. If the reel seat does not fit perfectly on the rod, the rod can be built up with masking tape until the two are level with each other. Be sure the reel seat is placed properly in relation to the guides, then use epoxy to glue the reel seat to the rod. Shape and smooth the final contours of the cork grip with a file and sandpaper. If you have access to a lathe, it can be used to shape the grip, provided you have a steady hand.

There are almost as many opinions on the best shape for a cork grip as there are do-it-yourself rod-builders, making it hard to give detailed instructions. The only steadfast rule is that every angler should construct a grip that he is happy with and that fits comfortably in his hand.

When considering the construction and shape of the reel seat, there are two important aspects to keep in mind. It must hold the reel firmly in place, and should be as lightweight as possible.

If the rod is to have a butt cap at the end of the grip, it should be attached last, after the grip and the reel seat are in place. There are three main types of butt caps. One is an aluminium fitting with a screw cast in rubber that is threaded into the grip. Another is made of solid rubber, and the third type is of plastic. Which one to choose depends on your rod and the type of grip. All three types should be glued with epoxy. On many deep-sea rods a slotted grimbal is used instead of the butt cap.

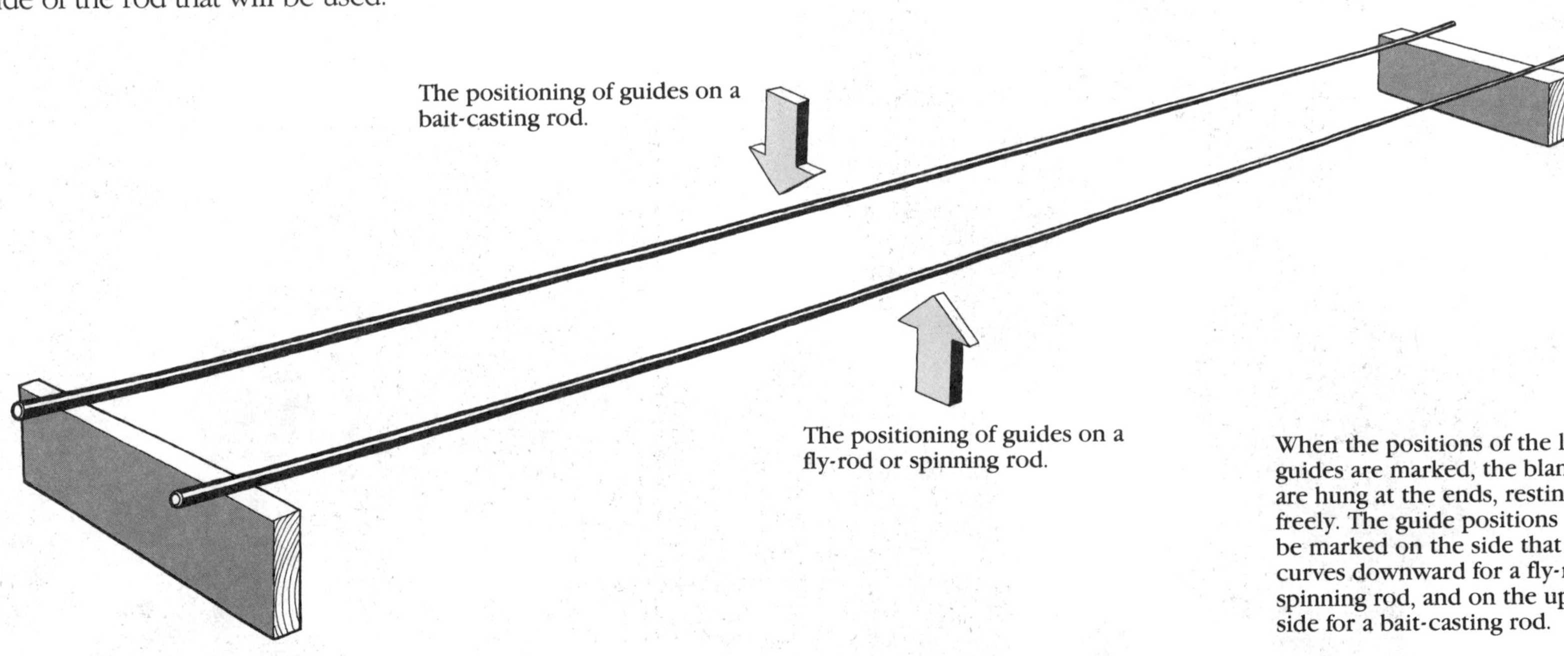

When the positions of the line guides are marked, the blanks are hung at the ends, resting freely. The guide positions must be marked on the side that curves downward for a fly-rod or spinning rod, and on the upper side for a bait-casting rod.

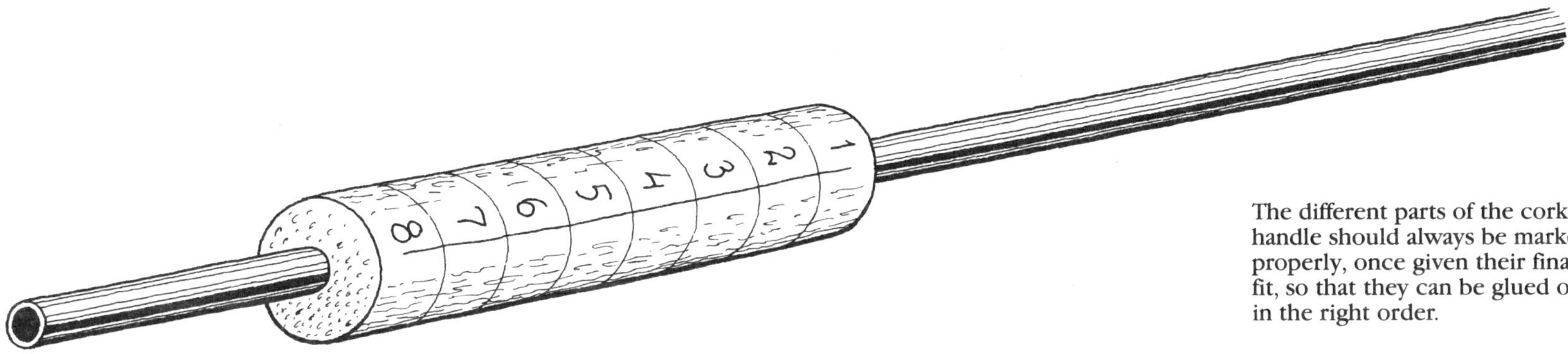

The different parts of the cork handle should always be marked properly, once given their final fit, so that they can be glued on in the right order.

Mounting the guides

The distance between guides will depend on the type of rod and the type of guides being used. Keep in mind that the purpose of the guides is to keep the line free of the rod during normal fishing conditions.

Good advice for a beginner is to request a clear description of how to place the guides when you purchase the rod. A reliable rod-and-tackle shop will also be able to suggest which guides are best for the rod blank you have chosen.

Guides are generally divided into the following categories, based on the type of rod they are made for: guides for fly-rods, for casting rods, for spinning rods, for different types of "match-fishing" rods and for boat-fishing rods. The guides manufactured today are usually of steel, hard-chromed or with inner rings of aluminium oxide or titanium oxide.

For fly-rods, three different guides are generally used: snake guides, open bridge guides, and guides with ceramic inserts. Hard-chromed snake guides are the best for most fly-rods, but sturdier bridge guides can be best for heavy-duty fly-rods that use heavier line. Ceramic guides are exceptionally good as stripping guides.

Fly-rod manufacturers often combine the three types of guides. A very resilient rod, for example, with an extremely flexible, sensitive tip, designed for the upper line classes, may have two ceramic butt guides close to the grip, followed by two bridge guides and then by snake guides. The tip-top would then be a steel guide with a pear-shaped center opening.

Hard-chromed steel guides should be used on spinning and casting rods. These lightweight guides are used on most of today's spinning and casting rods, since the combination of hard chrome and lightweight steel produces guides that are both light and strong. Their disadvantage is that they are very sensitive. Careless handling can sometimes loosen the soldering, but it is better to take that risk and gain a good rod than to mount heavier guides that lower the rod's performance. Rugged, hard-chromed guides are used on heavy-duty spinning and beach rods, often with extra reinforcement and with ceramic inserts. These heavy-duty guides can also be mounted on certain types of boat rods.

The tip-tops on almost all casting and spinning rods are usually steel guides lined with inner rings of aluminium or titanium oxide. On lightweight spinning rods the most commonly used guides have inner rings and only one foot, because this construction has the least effect on the rod's action. They are very light, but also very sensitive, which means that the guides can be easily bent or broken during transport if they are not handled with care.

The same materials are also used for the guides on rods for match fishing. What is more important than the strength or weight of the guide, though, is holding the line as clear of the rod as possible. This is most important when bottom fishing, because the thin line that is used clings to the rod when it is wet. This explains why the guides on ledgering rods have a relatively high foot. On ledgering rods the guides are made of stainless steel

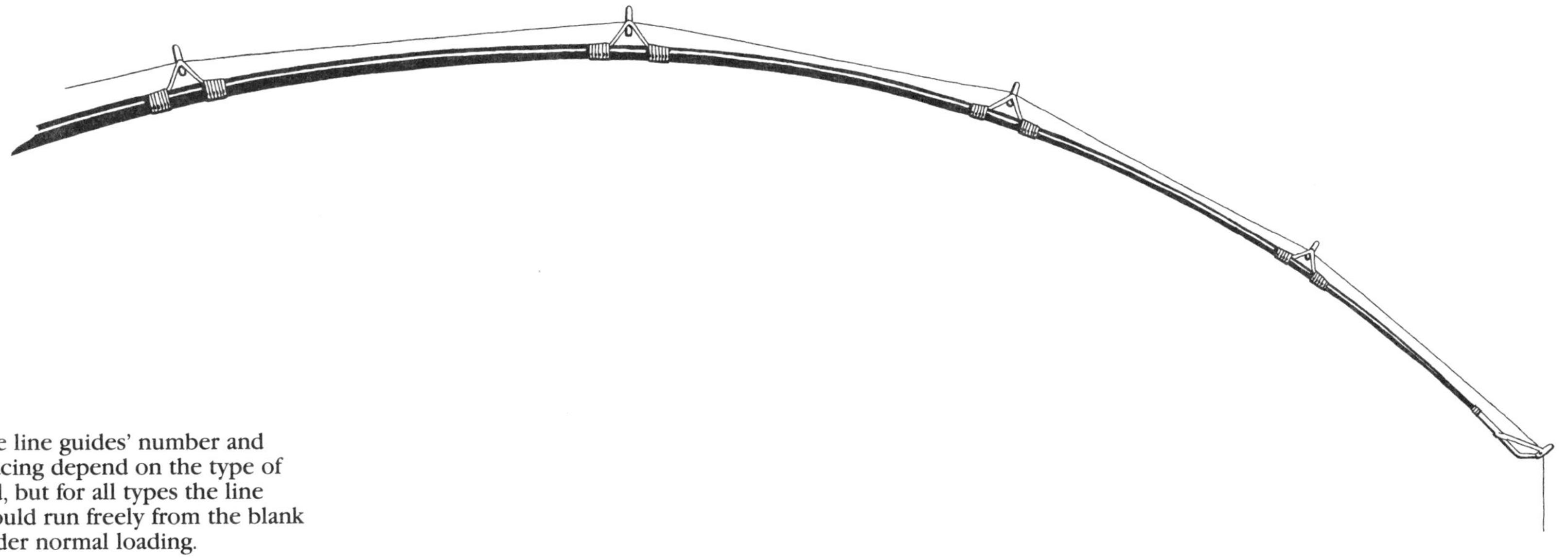

The line guides' number and spacing depend on the type of rod, but for all types the line should run freely from the blank under normal loading.

Guides for a fly-rod

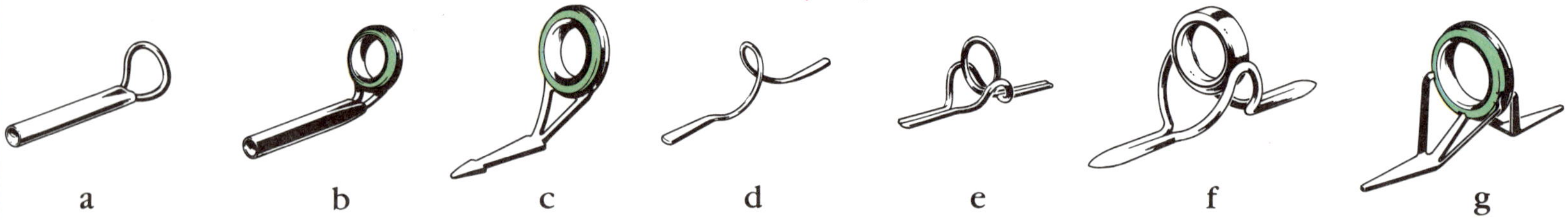

Line guides for a fly-rod: *(a)* Tip-top of pear form. *(b)* Tip-top with ceramic insert. *(c)* Intermediate guide with one leg and a ceramic insert. *(d)* Intermediate guide of snake form. *(e)* Intermediate guide of open ring form. *(f)* Stripping guide. *(g)* Stripping guide with ceramic insert.

Line guides for a spinning and bait-casting rod: *(a)* Tip-top with ceramic insert. *(b)* One-legged guide with ceramic insert. *(c)* Hard-chromed lightweight guide. *(d)* Three-legged guide with ceramic insert. *(e)* Strong hard-chromed guide with extra reinforcements.

Line guides for a "match rod": *(a)* Tip-top for a ledgering rod, with threads for swing tip and quiver tip. *(b)* High-legged intermediate guide with ceramic insert.

Line guides for a boat rod: *(a)* Roller tip-top. *(b)* Hard-chromed wide guide. *(c)* Three-legged guide with ceramic insert. *(d)* Roller.

Guides for a spinning and bait-casting rod

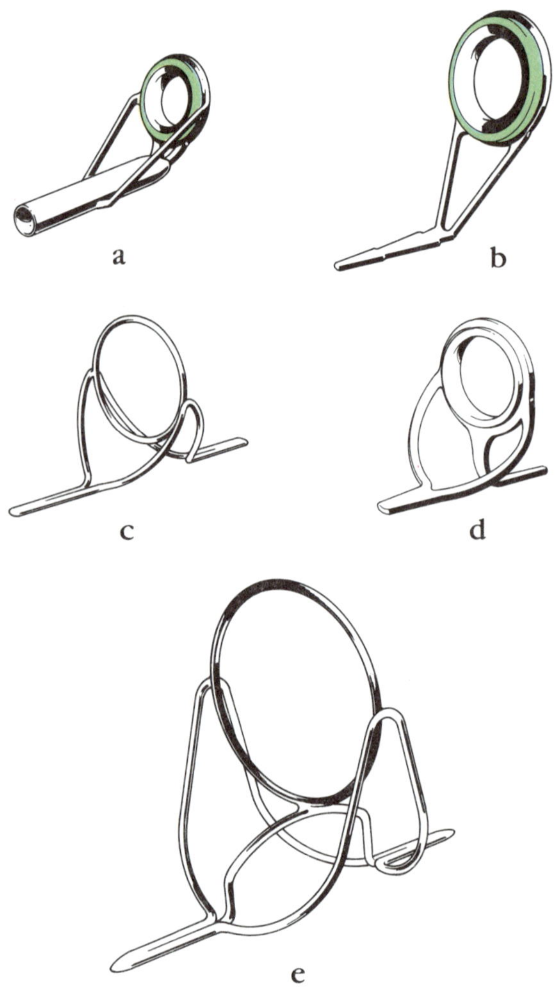

Guides for a coarsefishing rod

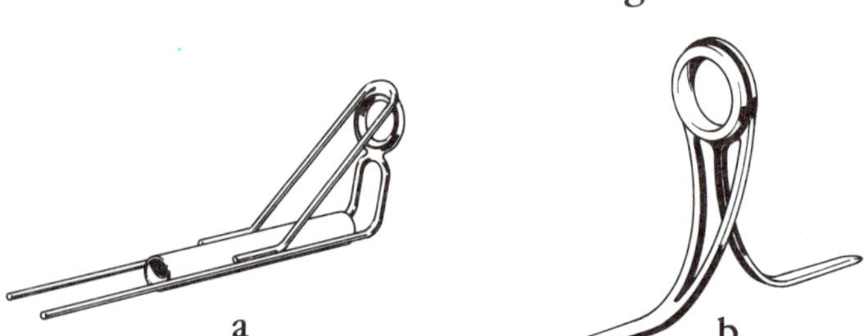

Guides for a boat rod

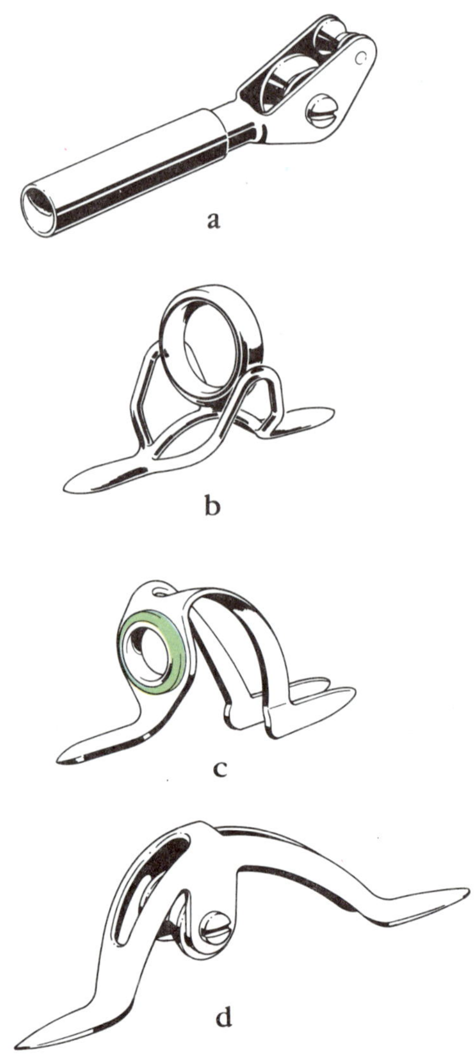

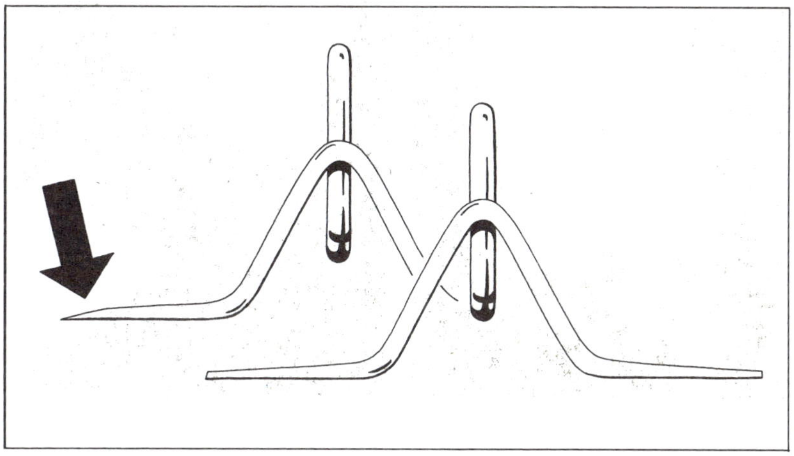

Above: The line guides should always be filed down at the ends before being wrapped tight.

Above right: When the guides are wrapped tight, the wire turns should have uniform tension and density.

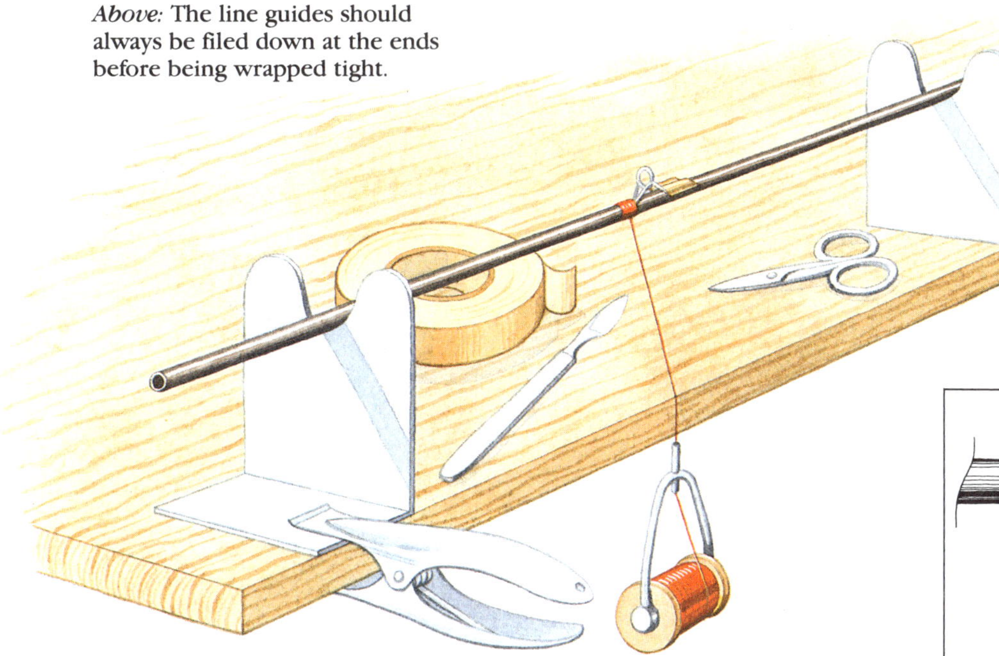

Left: Aids to wrapping the blank are a wrapping support, glue clamps, bobbin holder, scalpel, scissors and masking tape.

Below left: Beginning to wrap.
Below right: End of wrapping.

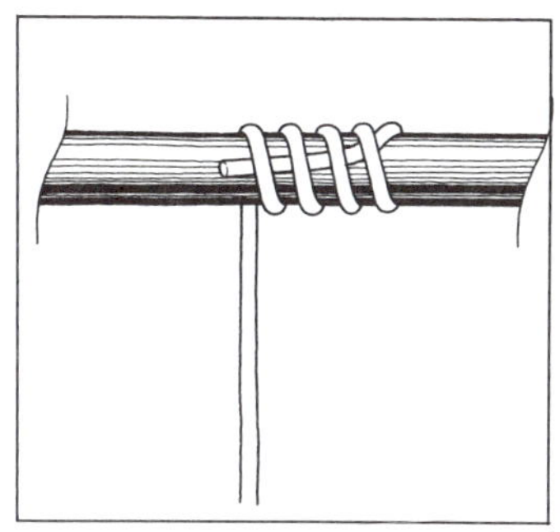

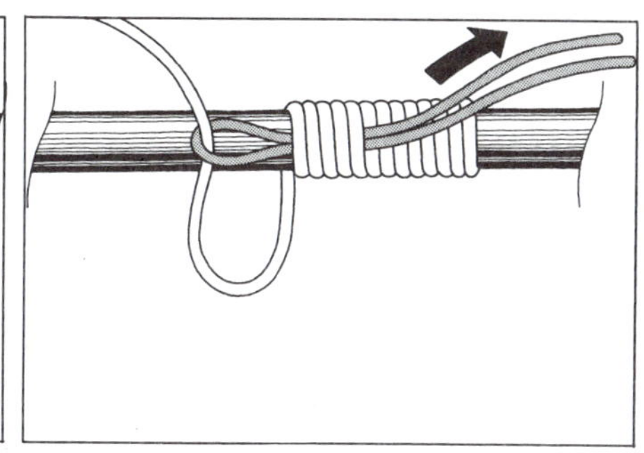

with hard-chromed center ring. The same material is used for the tip-top, but it should be threaded so that a swing tip or a quiver tip could be attached.

Rods intended for boat fishing in saltwater must be durable and corrosion-resistant, which means that the guides must be made of stainless steel. A light saltwater rod should have hard-chromed guides with wide diameters. Heavy-duty boat rods that might fish with braided line or wire is best equipped with roller guides. If you intend to use several types of line, you can compromise by using a double roller guide closest to the foregrip and a roller tip-top. Remember that fishing in cold climates at temperatures below freezing can result in ice on the roller tip-top, making fishing extremely difficult. If a rod is intended for a harsh climate it should be equipped with steel guides all along the rod.

Before binding the guides to the rod, the feet should be filed or sanded so that they are smooth and tapered. They should then be mounted on the rod one at a time at the recommended distance from each other. Make a provisional placement with tape, then adjust each guide so that they are in a straight line along the rod.

Once the exact placement is marked, the guides should be wrapped. It is extremely important that the threads are wound evenly and consistently, both in their spacing and in the tension of the thread. Be sure the threads do not overlap. When the wrapping is completed, cut off the ends of the thread with a scalpel or a razor blade, cutting as closely as possible to the wrapping. Any threads that fringe and stick up can easily be burned off with a cigarette lighter.

When all the guides have been wrapped, including the final decorative wrappings and even hook-keepers, it is time for varnishing. If you want to retain the original colour of the binding thread, however, several coats of colour preservative should be applied before the varnish. The varnish should be applied with a small paintbrush.

Although there are many suitable varnishes available, my preference is an oil-based varnish. No matter which type you use, the final result should be an absolutely smooth surface. Apply as many coats as you like, until you can run your finger over the wrappings without feeling them.

Renovating an old rod

Probably the best way to learn how to build a new fishing rod is to renovate an old one. It is probably the most economical way, too. Since it takes almost as much time to build a new rod as to renovate an old one, it can be a hefty—and often unnecessary—expense to have a rod re-built by a professional rod-maker.

A rod can be the keeper of pleasant memories, enough reason not to throw it away. Or, as in the case of a split bamboo rod, you might no longer be able to buy a similar rod. There are, without a doubt, many reasons to renovate a valuable old rod, on the grounds of both economics and sentiment.

The first thing to do when renovating an old rod is to find out when the rod was made, and who made it. A total renovation of a valuable rod built by a well-known manufacturer is not to be recommended as a first-time project. Practice first on a rod that you do not have to be too careful with, in order to gain experience and to avoid the typical faults of novices. If practicing on old rods does not induce a sense of confidence, it is probably best to leave the renovating to a professional.

There are a number of ways to find out a rod's origins and age. For American rods, Martin J. Keane's book *Classic Rods and Rodmakers* is an almost complete documentation of rod history. Rods can also be identified by looking through old manufacturer's catalogues, such as old Hardy catalogues, which are certain to help in recognizing at least Hardy rods. As can be seen, locating a rod's origins can be a very complicated piece of detective work, which is a pity.

If you have a really old, rare and valuable rod, you should think twice before you actually begin a total renovation. A thin protective coat of oil-based varnish followed by retirement to a place of honour over the fireplace is possibly the best treatment for some of these old treasures. But an ordinary rod, one that is not an antique and has no historical value, benefits from a thorough refurbishing every now and then.

The first areas to inspect are the ferrules, the reel seat and the grip. The most common problem is that the ferrule, or the ferrules if the rod is in three sections, does not fit as snugly as it should. The first thing you notice is that the sections have twisted slightly in relation to each other. If the chafing has been severe, there can also be play in the joint, although this is more difficult to see. A loose-fitting ferrule wears hard on the rod and eventually weakens it. The ferrules can be inspected by assembling the rod and holding your index finger against the ferrule as you carefully swing the rod back an forth. If there is any play in the ferrule joint it will be felt in your finger.

A small amount of play does not call for replacing the ferrule. Some contact problems can easily be solved by using a three-jawed chuck. First, wrap the female ferrule in several layers of masking tape, so that no marks will be made by the chuck. Then press gently and carefully with the chuck and continue the process until the pieces fit together snugly and the play is gone. Because the female ferrule is protected by the tape, the jaws can remain in the same position for each adjustment.

In older bamboo rods, play is common between the rod and

By holding your index finger on the spigot and, at the same time, swinging the rod carefully back and forth, you can feel whether the spigot has play in it.

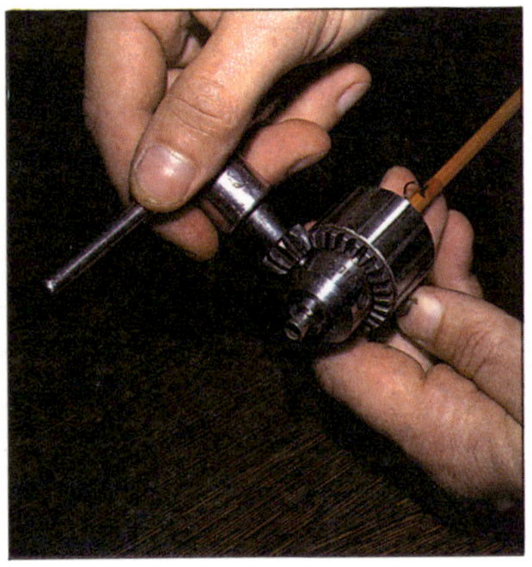

With a three-jawed chuck, you carefully adjust the female spigot until the play is gone.

the ferrule. The play usually appears as cracks in the wrappings at the edges of the ferrules. But the cracks are not always caused by play; unavoidable movements of the bamboo and the edges of the ferrules can also cause cracks in the surface.

Cracks can also be caused by one or several of the edges of the ferrules breaking apart with age, but this cannot be detected before the old wrappings have been cut off. Broken or damaged ferrules should always be replaced. This fault occurs most often in old ferrules that are made of brass.

Replacing old ferrules

Remove the old thread wrappings with a sharp knife or a razor blade. Cut very carefully, starting from the wrapping-end and cutting towards the ferrule, so the rod is not damaged.

On older rods, the ferrule is often attached with a thin plug made of German silver, a material that is still used in the United

Right: If the spigot is fastened with a pin, this must be removed before the spigot is pulled off.

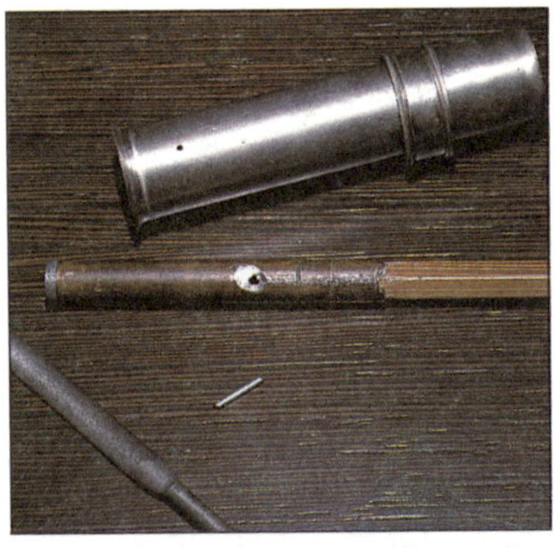

Below: If the spigot sits very tightly, it may have to be heated carefully from beneath, to loosen the glue.

States for the manufacture of fishing rods and tackle. This plug must be removed before the ferrule can be loosened. The plug is easier to remove if you gently tap around it with a sharp object and file carefully around the edges of the opening.

If you want to reuse the ferrule, it must be removed with a tool that does not scratch or damage it. The best method is to drill a hole in a piece of hard wood, the same diameter as the outside of the ferrule. Then saw through the piece of wood, exactly in the middle of the hole, so you have two identical halves. If you do not want to reuse the ferrule, the easiest way to remove it is with poly-grip pliers or a similar hand tool.

Clamp the rod section in a vice and try to pull off the ferrule. If it does not budge, heat it carefully with a cigarette lighter or a small butane flame, so that the ferrule glue or cement softens. Be sure not to heat the ferrule so much that the heat penetrates into the blank as this could damage the blank. Because the ferrule should be heated only as much as is absolutely necessary to loosen the glue, this is a job best done by two people—one to hold the flame and the other to pull on the ferrule.

Replacing old grips

The reel seat may also be attached to the rod by a plug, creating a removal problem if you intend to use the reel seat again. The reel seat should be removed using the same careful procedure that was described for removing old ferrules, keeping an eye out for plugs or nails that could damage the reel seat.

The best tool for removing an old cork grip is a knife or a file. Remember to make a good contour sketch of the old grip's shape and size, because you will need this pattern to make an exact copy of the original grip.

Replacing guides

The guides on many older rods are of poor quality and they have a tendency to wear hard on the line, particularly on fly-lines. Before removing any old guides, their positions must be marked out on the proper side of the rod. If you plan to do a total renovation and to re-varnish the rod, the reel seat's position must also be marked. The wrappings can be cut off with a scalpel or with a very sharp knife. Cut carefully just above the foot of the guide to avoid damaging the blank.

If you want to preserve the manufacturer's name or any other markings on the rod's grip, the text should be traced on onion-skin paper when the wrappings and guides have been removed, and then copied back onto the rod with a waterproof pen.

The hardest part of refinishing a rod still remains: stripping off the old varnish. This is not so difficult if you approach the work calmly and methodically. One word of warning is necessary, however—never use varnish remover. It almost always causes irreparable damage to the glued joints, particularly on split bamboo rods, and this damage is almost impossible to prevent. Use steel wool to rub away the old varnish on rods made of fibre-glass or other man-made materials. On split bamboo rods, the best equipment for removing varnish is a razor blade wrapped in masking tape. Wrap one edge to protect your fingers and leave one end free for scraping. A cabinetmaker's scraper or a similar tool can also be used, but these are really too big and clumsy to work well on slender fishing rods. A sheet of glass or plexiglass makes an excellent working surface for this tedious task, but any level work table is just as good.

Hold the razor blade between your index finger and thumb at a slight angle towards the area to be scraped. You should always

To preserve the old handle's appearance, an exact drawing of its shape and dimensions must often be made before removing it.

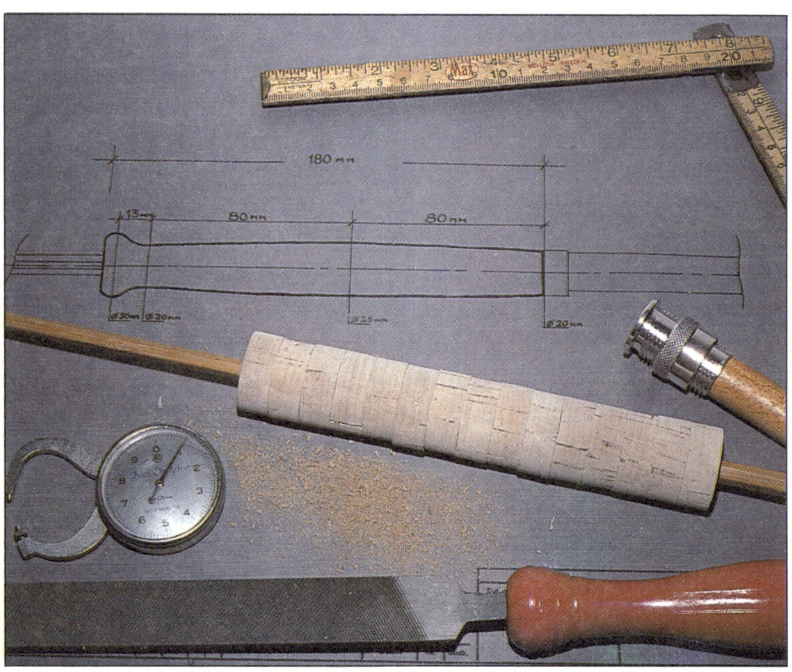

Always cut above the guide foot when the old wrappings are removed, to avoid damaging the blank.

When scraping off the old lacquer, use the ends of a razor blade, masking the sharp edges with tape to protect your fingers.

scrape from the rod's thick butt end towards the thin tip. With the outside of your hand resting on the work surface, scrape carefully and slowly, keeping the blade level. If you are working on a split bamboo rod, only one section can be scraped at a time. Use a vacuum cleaner to keep the work surface free from varnish scraps as you scrape.

Some bits of varnish can be extremely tough to strip away. Work these areas later with a piece of very fine sandpaper, the kind used for water sanding. Mount the sandpaper on a wood block, 8–10 in (20–25 cm) long and 1–2 in (3–4 cm) wide, and slide the block back and forth across the encrusted area with even pressure, again and again until the last remains of varnish have been sanded off. Finally, sand the edges of the blank smooth by wrapping a piece of the same fine sandpaper around the top and bottom of the rod, and work the rod back and forth.

If you are renovating a very old rod, it is a good idea to rub it with raw linseed oil after the varnish has been removed. It is important that the rod is just dampened, as too much linseed oil can do more damage than good.

At this point the actual rebuilding of the rod can begin. Start by varnishing the rod two or three times. Use a varnish brush or your fingers if you cannot spray the rod or dip it in varnish. Be sure the rod is absolutely dust-free before beginning to varnish.

There are many different types of varnish. In the case of a split bamboo rod that is being refurbished to its original shape, a turpentine-based oil varnish should always be used. A polyurethane varnish is a good choice for a newer rod. If you discover dust or knots after varnishing, they can be gently dislodged and the surface shined up again with car polish. Note that this procedure can be used only when the varnish is completely dry.

When the rod blank is finished and the varnish has dried thoroughly, the ferrules can be reset. If ferrules with the exact same inside diameter cannot be found, choose ferrules with the next larger diameter. Never go down in size as this can weaken the rod so much that it could even break. Glue the ferrules in place with a two-component glue that hardens slowly, and apply the glue to both the rod and the inside of the ferrule. To be certain that the ferrules are free of cooling oil, clean them with a pipe cleaner and a liquid thinner before they are glued.

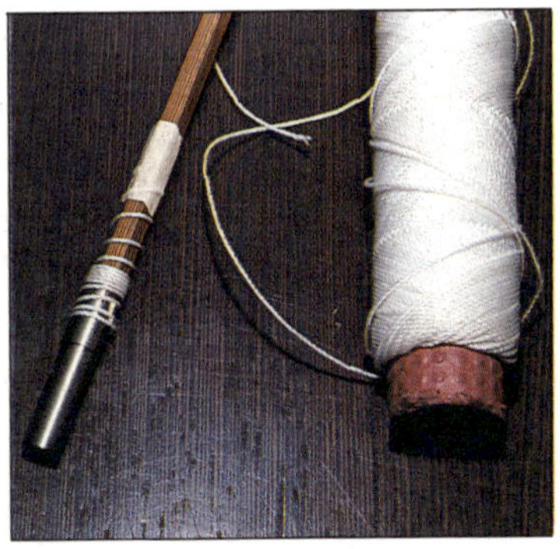

Left: Smooth off the last traces of lacquer and the blank's edges with fine sandpaper.

Above: Once the spigots are glued, fasten them with strong thread, wrapped around the edges so that these press hard against the blank.

Press on the ferrules and wipe away any excess glue that is squeezed out. Then use a strong thread to wrap the edges of the ferrules tightly against the rod so that they will set firmly.

Follow the same procedure for both the male and the female ferrules, joining the rod sections in the order you want them. Test the rod for straightness and make any necessary adjustments. This explains why a slow-hardening glue is recommended—to allow time for these final alignments. When you are satisfied that the rod is straight, leave it until the glue has hardened completely.

Once the glue has hardened, the ferrule's wrapping threads can be removed and any excess glue can be sanded off. At the same time, you can file the edges of the ferrules so that they taper towards the rod. The final step is to wrap the edges of the ferrules with two layers of wrapping silk or nylon rod-winding thread. Give them one or two coats of an oil-based varnish, and let them dry.

Making your own lures

It is not only rods that are being made by enthusiastic anglers. Since the 1970s, more and more sportfishermen have also been making their own lures. Although one reason is that lures have become more and more expensive, the main reason is probably that sportfishermen have become so competent and particular that they are often dissatisfied with the commercially made spoons, wobblers and spinners. Today's angler wants to make his own lures, and better than those that can be bought.

Plugs

Plugs, small imitation fish made of wood or plastic, are the lures most often experimented with in home workshops. A plug's body is easy to whittle, file and form. The bill at the mouth of a plug can be made of hard plastic or thin metal, the hooks can be easily mounted in screw eyes, and the surface treatment is easy to do. What makes a plug the favourite of so many anglers is not only its fish-like appearance, but also its swim. There is no other lure that looks as natural in the water as a plug. By choosing different materials and body shapes, by varying the size, angle and appearance of the bill, and by manipulating the plug's center of gravity, the plug's behaviour in the water can be controlled.

A fast, vibrating plug should be short. The longer a plug is, the calmer it swims. If a bill is placed at a wide angle to the plug's longitudinal axis, a shallow swim is created; with a nearly horizontal bill, the plug makes a steep dive to the bottom.

The balance in most plugs is achieved by soldering or glueing lead weights to them. The rule of thumb is that the farther behind the bill the weight is placed, the faster the plug swims. The opposite is also true: when the weight is placed closer to the bill, there is less movement.

The simplest plug does not have a mouth bill to direct its swaggering swim through the water. Instead, the front end of the plug

is carved or cut at the exact angle needed to produce the "right" swim.

To make a plug, start with a cylinder of wood, 3–4 in (8–10 cm) long. Shape it until the belly side has a noticeably curved shape. In a top view, the body should look a little narrower at the tail end. Next, sand the plug with fine sandpaper until it is completely smooth, and then dip it in water. Wetting the wood loosens some of the wood fibers, but a second sanding after the wood has dried will remove these loose ends.

The body should be weighted, partly for balance and partly to give it the right swim. To weight the plug, bore a hole in the belly side, around 1 in (2–3 cm) from the front end. Put a piece of lead weighing 10–12 gr in the hole, then fill it with epoxy. The placement of the screw eyes should then be marked and drilled with a 2-mm drill bit. Once the screw eyes are in place, it is time to begin the final surface treatment.

All wooden plugs need a tough and durable protection from sharp fish teeth. Otherwise the water-resistant surface leaks, the wood swells, and the enamel begins to crack. The plug would be quickly destroyed. In the long run, the proper treatment of the outer surfaces of wooden lures is always worth the time and effort it takes.

A wooden plug should first be covered with a two-layer base coat, preferably of a non-glossy enamel, in the same colour as the belly side of the finished plug. Patterns and decorations can be added in many different ways. The simplest is to paint by hand, using a very small brush. For those who do not feel confident with a paint brush, the parts that are not going to be painted can be covered with masking tape and the tape removed when the paint has dried.

The most professional results are from spray painting, especially if this is done using templates of a variety of different fish patterns. Fish scales can be reproduced by spray-painting the plug through a finely holed net, and the spots on trout, perch and other fish can be made by cutting the pattern from thick paper and using it as a template.

Eyes are easily painted using a nail with a relatively large head, first dipped in paint and them stamped on the plug. When the paint has dried, the procedure can be repeated with a smaller nail and a second colour, so that the pupil is placed correctly.

The most demanding part of making a plug is preparing the tough, water-resistant surface that was mentioned earlier. A wooden plug should be finished with five coats of clear varnish. Boat varnish is the best type, as it forms a hard, tough surface. Although the surface treatment takes time, it can be done efficiently if several plugs are produced and treated together.

Another type of billess plug was originally made by Indians, from the antlers of elk and wild reindeer. Wood works just as well, especially a piece taken from a fork in a tree, or from a branch with a bend. To make a durable plug, the thick contours of the plug body should follow the wood grain.

The same tools are used for this plug as for the ones described earlier. The weighting is, again, a lead weight glued in a hole in the body, and the surface treatment is the same. The difference is that the first 1.2 in (3 cm) of the head of this plug are

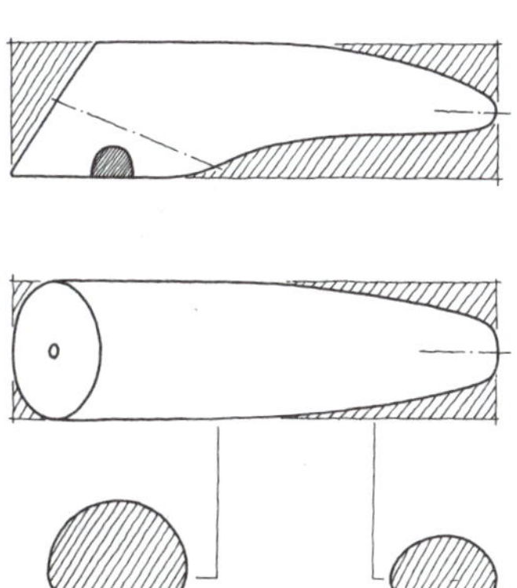

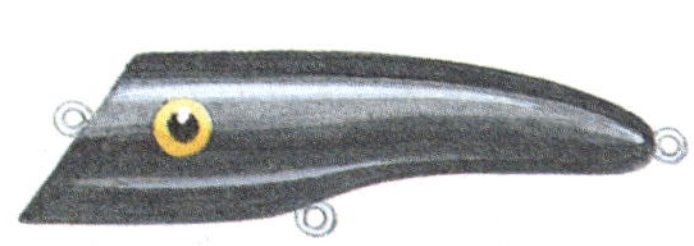

The simplest type of plug has no frontal scoop or bill. It is therefore important to have a pronounced front surface and incurved belly-side, and a lead-weighted body, so that the bait has the right wobbling movements.

This plug is made from a tree's fork or strongly bent branch. Unlike the type described earlier, it has a front surface of about 1.2 inches (3 cm) which is quite flat.

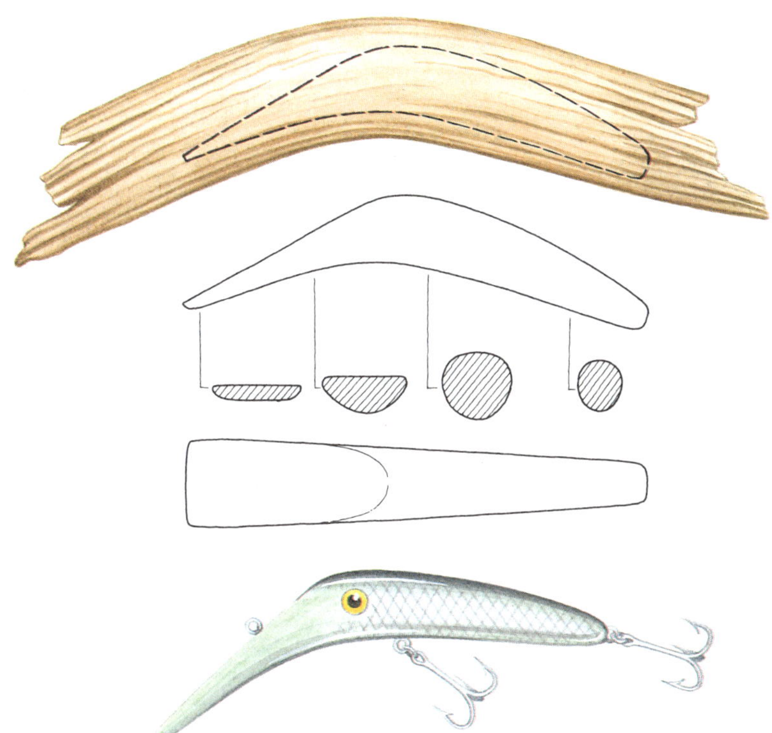

completely flat. If this is not done, the result is not a plug but a nicely painted, curved stick.

The type of plug known as the Cisco Kid is made of a light wood such as alder or linden. For simplicity's sake, the weighting can be done by drilling or sawing a hole and filling it with Plastic Padding. Remember that Plastic Padding is not as heavy as lead and it takes a lot more of it to weight the plug.

The bill on a Cisco Kid type of plug is made of metal. The best choice is 1-mm thick copper or brass sheet. The bill is attached to the body at the front, close to the abdomen, with two screws. The line eye can be made of heavy piano wire or of an old bicycle spoke.

Today's best-known plug is probably the Finnish Rapala. Although it was originally made of pine bart, the bodies of these familiar plugs are now made of balsa wood. Balsa wood is so soft that a hook cannot be attached in the hook eye as usual. Instead, you must make a long wire shaft, with an eye loop formed at the head and the tail, and glue half a plug body on each side of it. Stainless-steel wire, barely 1 mm thick, is the perfect material for the shaft. The plug's body is made from two pieces of balsa that are very loosely glued together. The only tools needed are a knife, a file and sandpaper. A slit, about half as high as the body, is sawed for the bill.

When the two symmetrical half-bodies have been cut to the shape of the plug, they are separated, and small holes are made just behind the slit for the bill. The holes should be large enough to hold several 3-g split shots. A good amount of epoxy should be mixed and each split shot glued in place. The flat sides of both Rapala half-bodies should be covered generously with glue, the wire shaft put in position, and the two bodies parts placed on either side of the shaft. The plug should then be wrapped tightly with tape until the glue hardens. If the separation between the two plug halves is almost invisible, the taping was properly done.

The bill can be cut from an appropriately curved section of a plastic bottle, usually close to the neck, where both the thickness and curvature are suitable. A pattern can be traced from a commercially made plug and transferred to the piece of plastic. When sawing the slot for the bill, remember that it must be placed vertically so that the bill does not block the wire shaft running longitudinally through the body. Glue the bill in place with epoxy. Because balsa wood is so porous, it needs more coats of paint than do most plugs. A few extra coats of varnish are also a good idea.

To make an extremely shiny plug, a piece of aluminium foil can be pressed directly onto the still-wet paint after the last coat. Use a sharp object to make a scale pattern on the foil.

When making a plug of the Rapala type, the two symmetric body-halves are glued around the wire construction only after the weights have been mounted and the frontal scoop's jacket is made. Finally the scoop is glued on and the wobbler is painted in the desired colours.

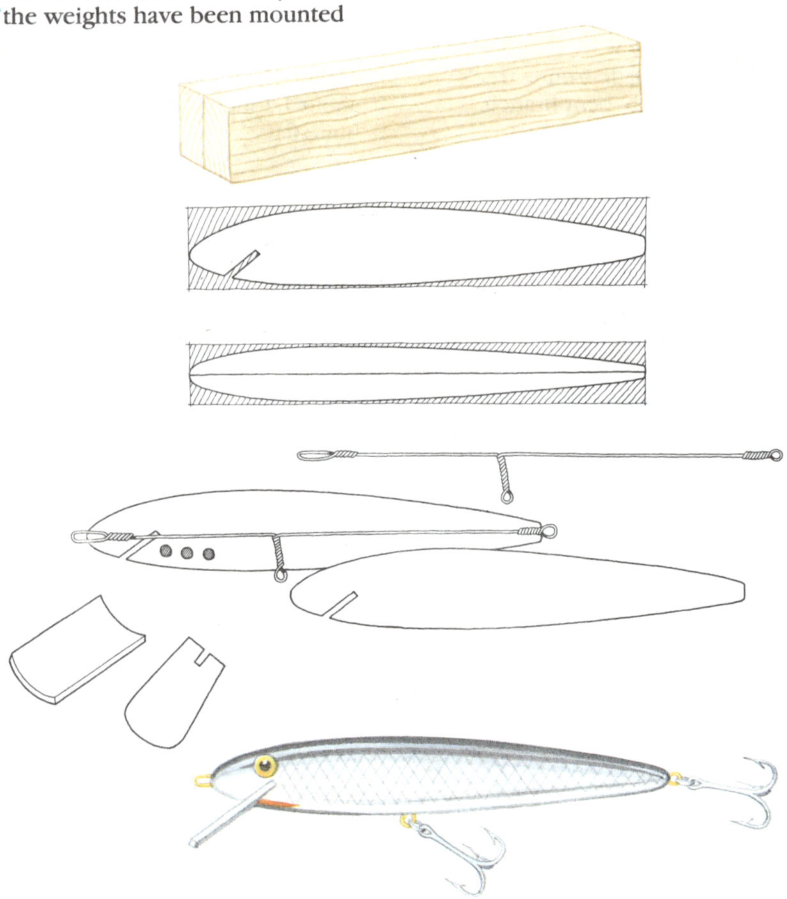

Spoons

A spoon is basically a metal sheet cut to the right size, with a hole for the split rings.

The materials usually used by do-it-yourself lure-makers are copper, brass and aluminium, as they are all easy to work with.

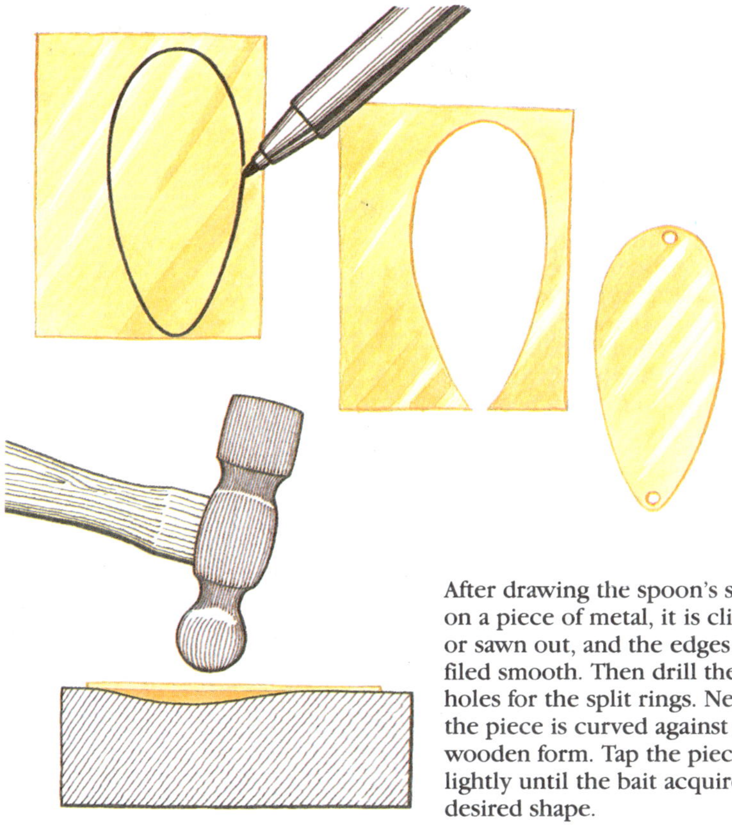

After drawing the spoon's shape on a piece of metal, it is clipped or sawn out, and the edges are filed smooth. Then drill the holes for the split rings. Next, the piece is curved against the wooden form. Tap the piece lightly until the bait acquires the desired shape.

The tools needed are a hacksaw or plate shears, a fine-edged file and a drill. If you want to make a more curved spoon that gives better control in the water, you will also need a ball hammer and a wooden mould to place under the spoon when it is hammered.

To start the work, use a waterproof marker to draw the shape you want on the piece of metal. Then cut or saw around the drawing and file the edges smooth. Be sure there are no rough edges that could cut the fishing line. Next, drill the hole for the split rings. Mark the placement by hammering an indentation with a sharp nail and then drill the hole with a 2-mm drill bit. Here, too, smooth and round the edges.

A jigging spoon has a long, slim body. When making this type of spoon, cut it about 50% longer then the finished pirk will be. The end that will carry the hook can then be bent double and the weight concentrated there. The result is a lightweight pirk that makes long casts and is therefore perfect for fishing coastal waters.

Excellent spoons of the pirk type can be made from the handles of knives, forks and spoons. By recycling these old and discarded pieces of silverware, they continue to feed their owners, but in a new way. To make one of these lures, cut off the shaft, drill a 2-mm hole in it, add split rings and a hook, and it is ready to fish.

Sometimes the lure needs to be curved or rounded to produce a more attractive swim. If the metal plate being worked with is no more than 1–1.5 mm thick, a pair of strong hands can probably twist and bend it into shape. If the material is too heavy, it can be held in a vice and bent with a hammer. The best way to get the right shape is to experiment. Metal sheeting is an inexpensive material, so you can afford to make a few mistakes.

Making deep curves in a lure is more complicated. The best spoons are made using a mould made from a hard wood such as beech, oak or teak. The metal piece is placed over the mould and hammered with a ball hammer until the spoon takes on the curved, rounded indentations of the mould. Plastic and rubber hammers are good for this, as they leave no marks on the metal.

Be sure none of the curves or indentations are exaggerated. A moderately curved spoon performs best in the water because it has a life-like, regular swim. If the shape is too compact, the spoon has a less distinctive, faster swim, while a spoon with a bulging shape can have such a heavy swim that there is little swagger or swing to attract fish.

There are several ways to colour homemade spoons so that they catch the eye of a fish. Small, round pieces of coloured electrical tape can create scales and eyes. Elongated triangles of the same material can imitate the stripes of a perch. Spoons can be painted with enamel, or they can be spray-painted just like a plug, creating a very professional look.

Zebra stripes are another popular colouration. The best way to make them is to spread a fatty substance such as butter over the parts that are not to be coloured. The lure is then dipped in liquid blueing for 30 seconds and rinsed under running water. The resulting zebra pattern is an oxidation of the metal in the spoon, and will retain its colour unless rubbed hard with steel wool. Because the blueing can cause skin irritations, rubber gloves should be worn when using it.

There are many ways of patterning a spoon. Coloured prisma tape can give a scale-like pattern, while bluing agent produces zebra stripes. With varnish paint, you can brush or spray on a variety of fish-attracting patterns.

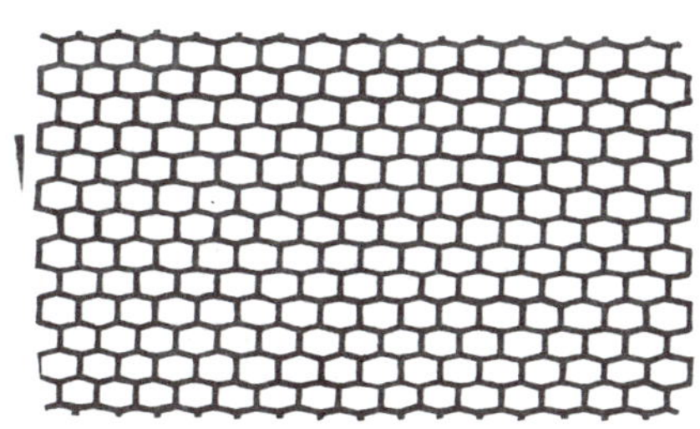

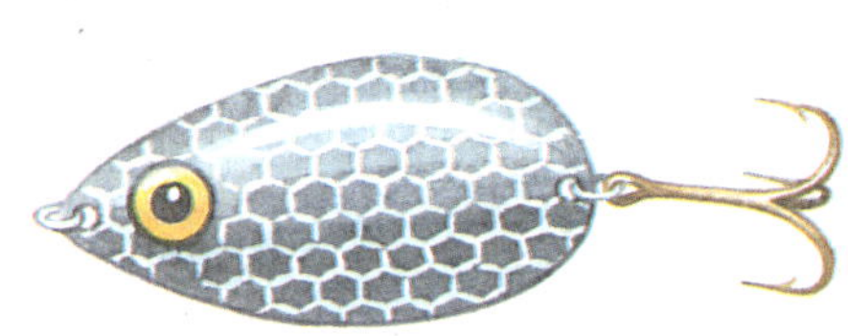

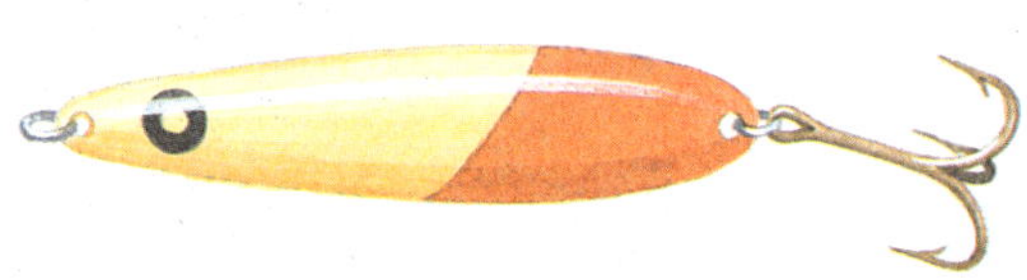

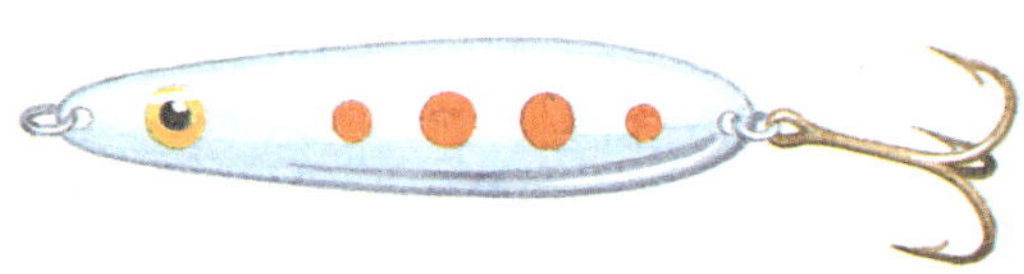

Spinners

There are seven parts to a spinner, which may make it seem like the most difficult lure to make yourself. The wire shaft which a spinner is built around has an eye loop at each end and a body that is a well-turned piece of solid brass with a hole through the center. The spoon is attached to a clevis that is difficult to duplicate at home because it is so small. A spinner is actually a masterpiece of symmetry, as there are tiny beads strung on the shaft before and after the clevis.

Most of the parts of a spinner are available in bulk in tackle shops. Another good source of supplies is to collect old, discarded lures that can be used as spare parts. Actually, because making a spinner is not so much a matter of making your own parts but of combining ready-made parts to suit your personal fishing style, the spinner is one of the simplest lures to make.

You can buy and use not only lure wire, but also electric welding wire, piano wire or, what is best, cold-drawn stainless-steel wire. The disadvantage with piano wire is that it rusts, and even though it is the best substitute, stainless-steel wire can be very difficult to find. The wire should have a diameter of about 0.80 mm.

The hook eye is made by looping the wire around a pair of bending pliers with round jaws, and the hook is mounted in the eye. The body is then strung on the wire shaft, locking the end of the wire inside the body.

The beads are used to separate the clevis and the spoon on the shaft, so that the spoon rotates freely. The first bead is positioned on the wire just after the body of the spinner. The spoon is hung in the clevis, and the clevis is added to the wire. Be certain that the concave side of the spoon is facing the spinner's body, or the lure will not function properly.

Thread one more bead on the wire after the clevis, and the forward loop can be made. Use the pliers to form a loop identical to the loop for the hook eye. The loop is finished by making two turns around the shaft, and when the wire is cut the spinner is finished. Once you know how to go about it, it takes less than two minutes to make a spinner!

By making your own spinners it is easy to incorporate the qualities you want in a lure. A deep-swimming spinner should have a heavy, elongated body and a relatively small, barely protruding spoon. A surface spinner should have a shorter, lighter body with a comparatively large, wide spoon and an accentuated bulging shape. Elongated spoons rotate close to the body and cause a lot less line twist. Short spoons behave in exactly the spposite way, but they spin better and they begin spinning sooner.

A spinner has one disadvantage—it often twists the line. A partial solution to the problem is to use slightly heavier line. Another and better alternative is to design the lure so that it counteracts line twist. Moreover, an anti-twist head can be mounted in front of the spinner. These devices can be bought in tackle supply shops, and they do actually eliminate line-twisting tendencies in spinners. Another tactic is to look in tackle shops for asymmetrical spinners which, for one reason or another, have a center hole that was not placed exactly in the center of the body.

You can make your own spinners from ready-bought components or from parts of old discarded spinners. Use pliers to shape a hook eye on the wire, then thread on the components. With the hook, body, blade and bead in place, make a frontal eye by wrapping the wire twice around itself and nipping off the end. At far left are shown two variants of spinner that behave differently.

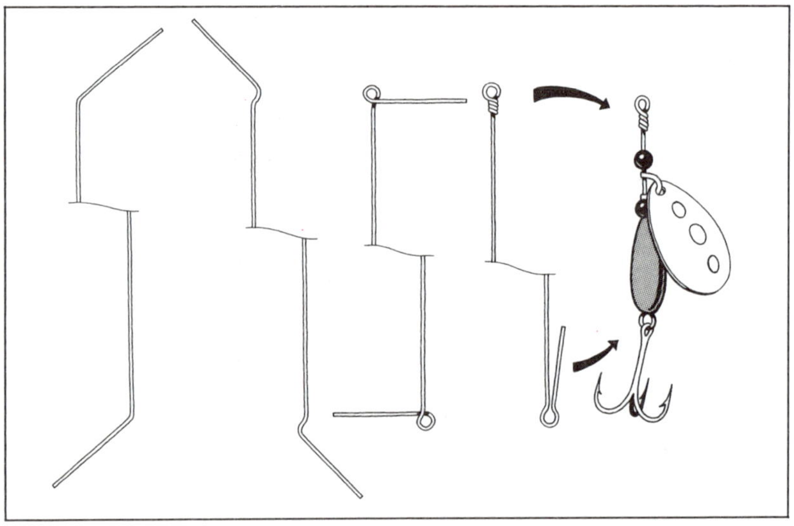

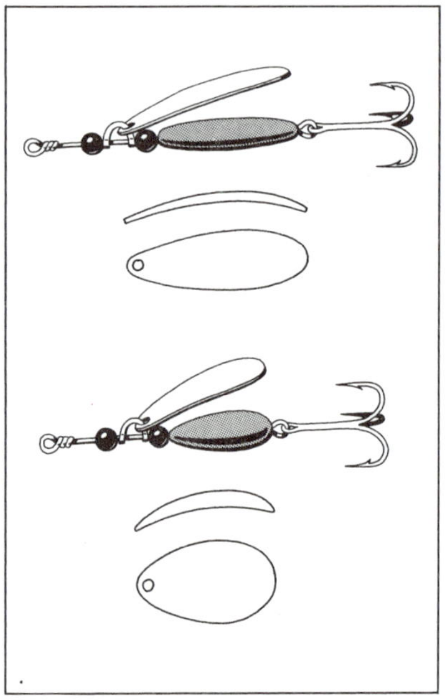

Anglers who fish with these spinner bodies seldom complain of line twist.

A spinner can also be assembled with no metal body. If you experiment with this type of spinner in a fast current, use only metal or glass beads. Attach a sinker at the end of the tackle and add a leader farther up on the line, with the lightweight and body-less spinner as a suspender. This tackle is not only very effective, but it also never twists the line.

Try attaching the hook to your spinner with a split ring. This makes changing hooks much easier when your are on the water, if the hook you are using has become dull or if you want to experiment with a fluorescent hook. A fluorescent hook actually does bring home more fish, expecially at twilight, when a fish's hunting eyesight is at its weakest.

One more hook variation worth trying is dressing the hook with a fly-tied feather. It is a well-known fact that feather-dressed hooks can sometimes be the trick to increase the catch.

Jigs

The jig is probably the oldest of all the artificial lures. A jig is very simple: it is a hook that has been weighted with a head made of lead and dressed with a tail of hair or feathers. Jigs originated on the North American west coast, where salmon fishing is widespread. Jigs were the perfect lures for the heavy tidal currents, because they were designed to stay at the depth the angler wanted to fish.

Ready-made jig bodies can be bought with the weighted metal head already in place, so the only remaining do-it-yourself work is to paint the head and bind the tufts for the tail. An enthusiast who wants to complete the entire process himself can buy pre-shaped jig hooks, a melting ladle and a mould. Casting with lead is very dangerous because of the noxious fumes, but tin is an excellent substitute for casting small objects. Tin is less expensive than lead and its fumes are much less dangerous, although good ventilation is still necessary.

The hook to be cast is placed in the mould and the melted tin is poured carefully in the funnel opening at the top of the mould. If the mould is not warm enough, the first jig may not be perfect, but don't let that disappoint you. Let the tin harden about thirty seconds before opening the mould and removing the finished jig. Place a new hook in the mould, fill it with more tin, let it cool, remove the jig and repeat this relatively simple process.

Five or six different colours should be used for painting the heads. It is certainly no secret that fish never seem to know which colour they like. Sometimes they prefer red instead of white, sometimes yellow instead of red, and so forth. Give the jigs a simple coat of paint— enamel is best—and hang them to dry for a day or two.

The tail can be made of almost any material that is soft and pliable and can be tied to the hook. (See the section on fly-tying for more details.) Long hairs from the tails of squirrels, deer and calves are excellent material. So are the fur from long-haired animals and the soft feathers from all sorts of birds. There are also many synthetic materials available for fly-tying that can be used on jigs. Silver and gold mylar and Flashabou are two examples. Even yarn in different qualities and colours can make an effective tail.

Tails made of soft, pliable plastics can be bought individually and threaded on the jig hook so that they flutter seductively in the water and lure predators to the hook. These tails come in such a wide range of colours, shapes and sizes that there is no end to the number of different jigs that can be made.

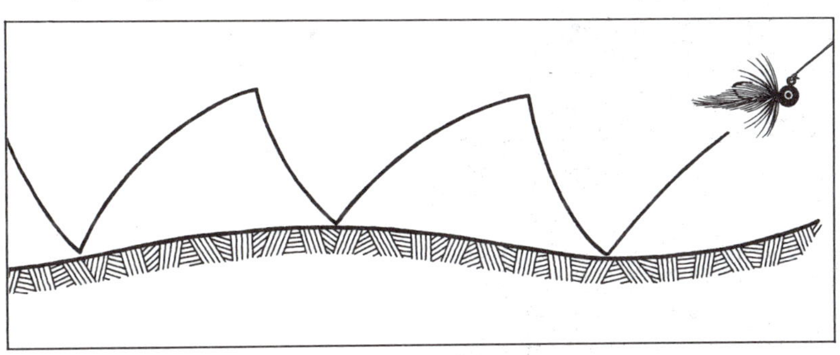

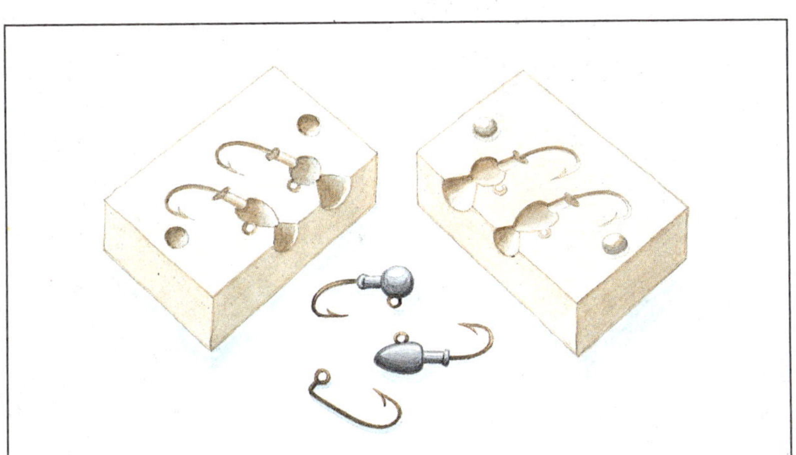

Jigs are very popular lures in many waters. They should be fished with jerks, and their lead heads make them suitable even for deep waters or strong currents. Below at left are shown moulds for casting the heads of specially bent jig-hooks. Illustrated below are some different types of skirt material which have proved rewarding.

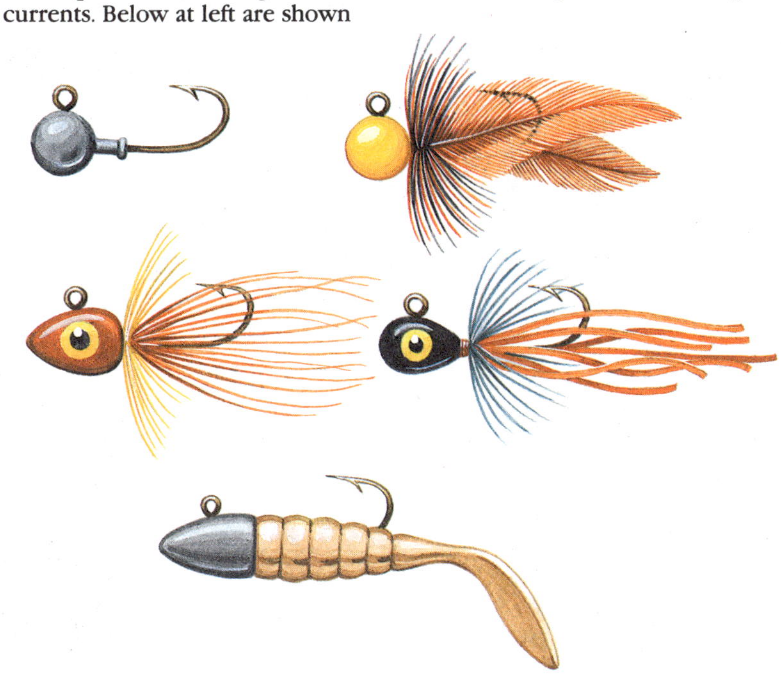

Fishing after the catch

We sportsfishermen devote a great deal of effort to planning our fishing hours, taking care of our tackle, and of course the fishing itself. Most of us probably like to eat fish, too. And what fisherman hasn't been willing to stand beside his catch for a snapshot? Some have even preserved their trophies in plaster.

But, hand on our hearts, don't we sometimes get a little careless with our catch once the fight is over and the excitement calms down? Aren't we sometimes too eager to bring in one more while they are still biting, instead of taking proper care of the one we just caught? The answer is probably that each of us has at one time or another shown little respect for the fish we caught, once it was landed.

Once a fish is out of water it is very sensitive to bacteria, especially if the air temperature is above 15°C (59°F). This is because fish normally live in an environment with relatively low temperatures. We know that fish move to deeper, cooler water when water temperatures at the surface or near land get too high, and this movement can be regarded as an indication of a fish's temperature preference.

The quick deterioration of fish when exposed to the air is not caused by the introduction of new bacteria, but is a part of a process that can be described as a self-triggered spontaneous combustion. As soon as the fish dies, the enzymes in the flesh set off this process, which causes deterioration by breaking down the cell tissues. The loosening of a fish's bones from the flesh is one of the most obvious signs that this process has gone on too long.

It is therefore very important to handle the catch carefully, partly to delay the internal-combustion process, and partly to protect the fish from bacteria. Fish that are improperly handled are limp and floppy, and have little taste. A fish that is handled properly, on the other hand, offers a gastronomic delight that is as rewarding as the fishing.

Killing and cleaning

If a fish is going to maintain its taste and consistency, there are certain rules that must be followed when killing and storing it.

To begin with, the fish should be killed *immediately* after it is caught, not only so the fish suffers as little as possible, but also to inhibit the production of lactic acid. The extreme stress of being caught results in the production of large amounts of lactic acid, which considerably reduces the quality of the fish. Allowing a fish to wiggle and flop on land until it dies is the best way to produce a more or less inedible fish.

There are several ways to kill a fish quickly and efficiently. The only equipment needed is a good knife, which is also needed for cleaning the fish. To kill the fish, stick the tip of the knife directly into the brain, which lies a few centimeters behind the eyes, and do not remove it until the last muscle spasms are over. If you want to drain the fish's blood, however, which is quite common for salmon, push the knife in under the gill cover and cut diagonally to the abdominal cavity, directly behind the gill. In this way, the artery in the throat is cut and the blood is quickly drained.

Once the fish is caught, it must be killed and cleaned as soon as possible. The innards are removed carefully so that no bacteria get inside. Then rinse the fish and take out the innermost blood vessels near the spine.

Another method, mainly for small and medium-sized fish, is to use what is called a priest. A priest is a handle about 12 in (30 cm) long, tipped with lead or brass. The fish is given a sharp knock on the head with the metal ball, just behind the eyes.

Once the fish is dead, the entrails should be removed as quickly as possible, so that the putrefactive bacteria in the intestines and the stomach do not spread to the abdominal cavity and activate a further deterioration of the cell tissue. The best way to clean the fish is to cut the skin on the abdomen, starting at the anal opening and cutting forward. Then remove the entrails carefully, so that no bacteria from the intestines or the gall can spread into the abdominal cavity.

When the fish is cleaned, rinse it in water and remove the clotted blood from the backbone. Using the tip of a knife, cut a hole in the thin membrane at the back of the abdominal cavity, so that the blood there can be scraped with a fingernail or a knife. Rinse the fish once more and the cleaning is finished.

Keeping fish fresh

If you do not intend to prepare the fish right on the beach, you must store it properly so that it does not deteriorate in quality. If you do not plan to eat it for a few days, you should rib the inside of the abdominal cavity with salt or vinegar, allowing no chance for bacteria to grow. Salt is easy to carry with you, but it has the disadvantage of drawing liquid from the fish, leaving it somewhat dry and perhaps even a little tasteless. Vinegar, on the other hand, has a bacteria-killing effect without altering the taste of the fish.

The fish should be kept dry and in the shade. Putting fish in direct sunlight is an invitation to bacteria to start the destructive process. If the fish will be cooked or frozen within a few hours, it can be wrapped in grass or paper, but for a longer time it is best to wrap it in a piece of clean cloth. Woven basket creels, proven by tradition to be good for keeping fish, work so well because they allow air to circulate. One point to remember is that fish should be kept where there is good air circulation, which is also why fish should be stored separately, whether wrapped in grass, paper or cloth.

Unfortunately, many anglers are known to toss their catch into plastic or rubber bags and then let the bag lie out in the sun or in the trunk of a car. This storage method quickly reduces the quality of the fish. This behaviour says two things about the angler. One is that he has little understanding of the effect of bacteria on fish; the other is that he has little regard for the fish once it has been caught.

A properly cleaned and stored fish should stay fresh for at least 24 hours without freezing. If you are not certain the fish is still fresh, there are several ways to find out. The flesh should have a firm consistency: if you press your finger lightly on the skin, the indentation should fill again. The fish should also maintain its natural colour, such as the red gills, and it should not look limp or soft. A fish that has spoiled is limp, has lost its colour and has a strong odor.

Preparing fish

There are an amazing number of ways to prepare fish. Some species are best fried, others taste best when boiled, some are perfect for grilling, and there are others that are exquisite when smoked. In general, smaller fish are best when they are fried, and larger fish are best when they are boiled. Fish with a lot of fat, such as salmon and eel, are excellent for grilling and smoking, but the same processes used with lean fish leave the flesh dry and tough.

The first step in preparing a fish is to scale it. It is easiest to scale a fish when it is cleaned because the skin is still soft, but scaling can also be done just before the fish is cooked. First, rinse the fish for half a minute or so, to soften the scales and the mucus. Using a knife or a fish scaler, scrape from the tail to the head until all the scales on one side are gone, then do the same on the other side. Finally, rinse away any scales and mucus that remain.

How to fillet a fish

In preparing a fish, especially if it is to be fried, the fish may need to be filleted. The equipment needed is a flat work surface such as a cutting board, and a sharp knife with a long, narrow blade, called a fillet knife. Scissors are also good to have at hand.

Place the cleaned fish on its side on the work surface and cut carefully around the head and down behind the pectoral fin. Next, make a cut at a slight angle towards the backbone, as close as possible to the head, and continue to cut all the way to the tail, using a smooth, even motion. Cut as close as possible to the backbone to avoid any needless waste. Turn the fish over and cut the other filet in the same way. If the skin is to be removed from the filets, start cutting from the tail forward.

If this is done properly, the result is two beautiful filets. It is not easy to fillet fish, but after two or three practice sessions you should be able to cut a good filet.

How to skin a fish

Sometimes a fish must be skinned. Other equipment needed besides a sharp knife and a flat work surface is a pair of scissors and a pair of tongs. Before laying the fish on the work surface, cut around the fins, about 1/2 in (or 1 cm) deep, and pull them off. Then carefully cut through the skin around the head and down to the abdomen, and along both the abdomen and the backbone all the way to the tail. Make only a surface cut, penetrating the flesh as little as possible. It is now time to put the fish on its side, grasp

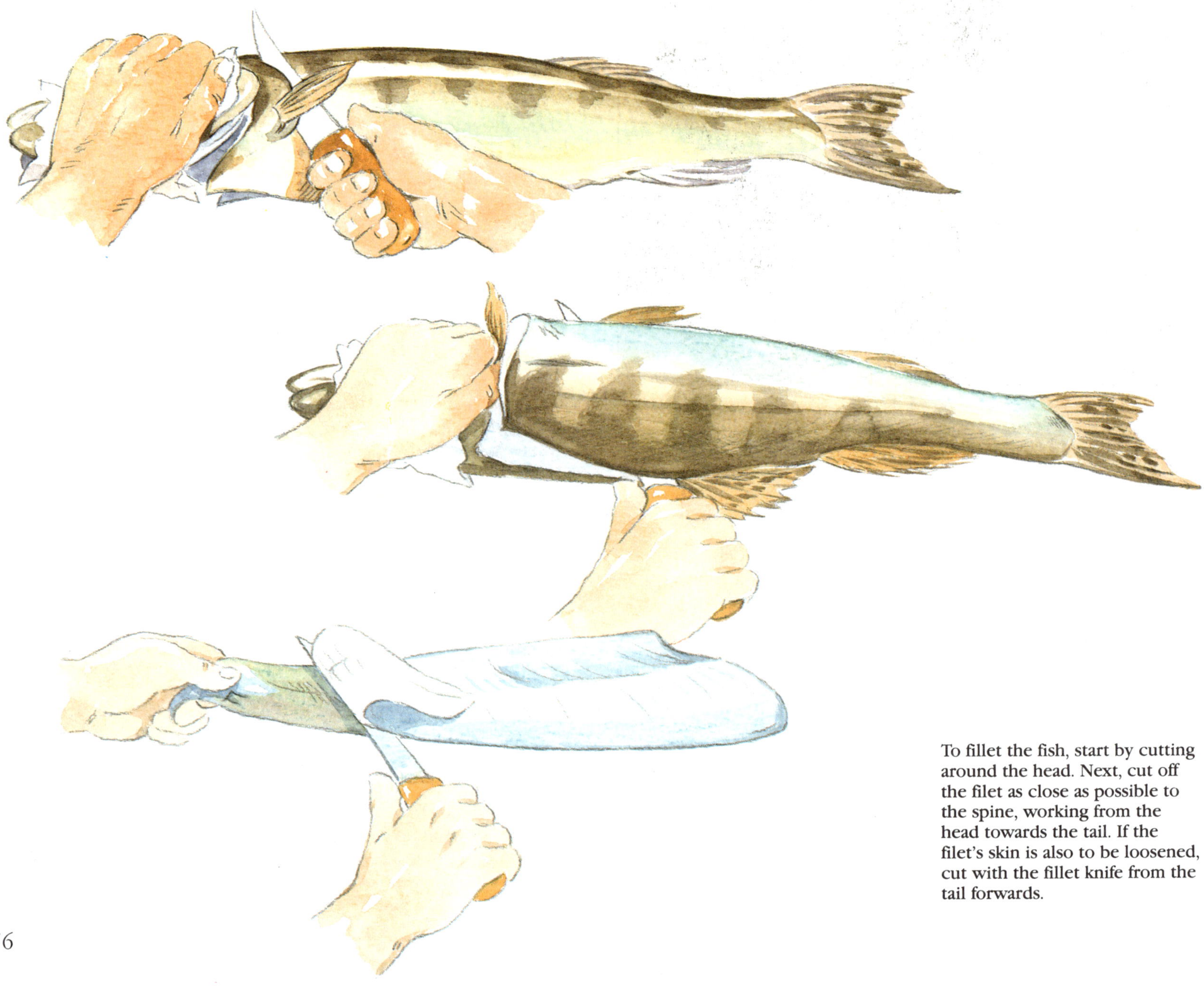

To fillet the fish, start by cutting around the head. Next, cut off the filet as close as possible to the spine, working from the head towards the tail. If the filet's skin is also to be loosened, cut with the fillet knife from the tail forwards.

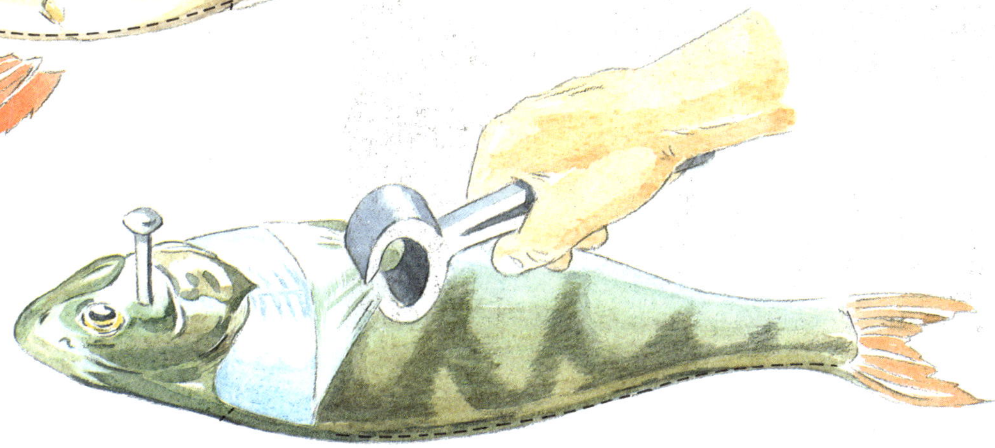

The fish is flayed by cutting its skin carefully around the fins and head, and down to the tail on both sides. Then use tongs to grip a flap of skin at the head, and pull off the skin. To get a better hold on the head, it can be nailed onto the working surface.

a piece of skin close to the head with the pliars and firmly pull the skin towards the tail. Hold the head steady with your other hand. If the fish head is too slippery, you can hold it with a piece of paper or cloth, or you can nail it to the work surface. Turn the fish over and remove the skin from the other side in the same way.

Smaller fish can usually be skinned in one section. Make a gash through the skin around the neck, lay the underside of the fish on the work surface, grasp a piece of loosened skin with the tongs, and steadily pull the skin towards the tail. This method is particularly useful when skinning eels. The last step is to cut off the head.

Grilling

How many times don't you wish you could cook the freshly landed fish right on the beach, without needing to carry half the kitchen with you? The simple solution is to grill the fish over an open fire.

Once the fire is made, carve two sharp points on a forked stick. A small fish can be skewered whole and put directly over the fire. Rotate the stick often, so that it is grilled evenly on both sides.

A fish weighing more than 2 lbs (1 kg) should be opened along the underside so that it has a giant fillet shape, and then put on the roasting stick. The fire should not be allowed to burn too low. A low fire produces less heat, which means that the grilling goes more slowly, and there is a greater risk that the fish close to the bone may not be cooked thoroughly.

The fish is ready to eat when it is brown on both sides and the bones begin to separate from the flesh. Fat fish such as salmon and eel are the best for grilling. Lean fish tend to become dry and hard, sometimes still raw on the inside and tasteless on the outside.

Grilling over an open fire.

Cooking over coals

This method can be used with both fat and lean fish. In addition, it retains the wonderful aroma of freshly cooked fish. To cook fish over coals, the fire must have died down so that only the glowing coals remain, but the coals must be very hot to cook the fish thoroughly.

Begin by cleaning and rinsing the fish well. Place it on a piece of aluminium foil, and add salt and spices. Dill or rosemary are good choices. If the fish is lean, a little fat rubbed on the foil before the fish is added will make it juicier. Wrap the package securely and place it directly on the hot coals. The fish is ready in about fifteen minutes.

This method is excellent for small fish. Larger fish can also be cooked in this way, but they should be cut into fillets first, so that the fish will be thoroughly cooked. Each fillet should be wrapped in its own package.

Marinating fish

Marinating fish is another ancient preservation method, used today mainly for salmon. Always begin the marinating process by filleting the fish and scraping off the scales. Remember to cut off the fins and to remove as many bones as possible. The materials you will need for marinating are:

1 kg fish
1/2 dl salt
1/2 dl sugar
19 white peppercorns, crushed
a liberal amount of dill

Mix the sugar and salt with the crushed peppercorns, and carefully rub this mixture into the fish filets. Chop the dill finely. Spread a layer of dill in a glass or ceramic dish with low sides that is the same size as the fish. Place the first filet, skin side down, in the dish and cover the flesh side with a layer of dill and spices. Place the flesh side of the second filet on top of the first, with the flesh sides together and the skin sides out. Cover both fish halves with dill and the rest of the spices. Finally, cover the dish with a plate or cutting board, and place a heavy weight such as a stone on top.

If several layers of fish are to be marinated, be extremely careful to arrange the fish in pairs with the skin side always on the outside. The fish should be kept in a cool place for two or three days. It is then ready to be served, but it will keep for several more days in the refrigerator.

Keep in mind that marinating does not kill parasites such as tapeworm which can be found in fish from polluted water. By freezing the fish at a temperature of about −10°C (14°F) for a minimum of 24 hours before marinating, any parasites that might have been living in the fish will be killed.

Above left: Before cooking a fish over coals, carefully clean and rinse it. Then spice it with, for example, dill or rosemary.

Below left: Wrap the spiced fish in aluminium foil, and lay the packet directly on the coals. After about 15 minutes it is ready to eat.

Left: The principles of hot smoking. With relatively simple equipment, you can build your own hot oven from, say, an old oil barrel.
Right: Cold smoking requires a fixed installation. Since the smoke must not be hotter than 95°F (35°C), it has to go through a cooling passage several meters long, before reaching the fish. Cold smoking takes one to five days, depending on the fish's size.

Smoking fish

Smoking fish demands much more preparation than grilling or cooking over hot coals because you need a smoke oven. Smoking is an ancient method of preserving fish which was used in the past for long-term food preservation. It prevents the internal spontaneous-combustion process at the same time as it slows down the growth of bacteria.

There are two methods of smoking fish: cold smoking, and hot smoking. The latter takes less time and relatively little work. Cold smoking requires a few days, more attention, and a relatively sophisticated apparatus to produce the best results.

Before the fish can be smoked by either method, the fish must be salted and dried. To do this, rub the fish with salt on both sides and in the abdominal cavity, or soak the fish in a solution of salt and spices. The fish is ready in three or four hours. Rinse it in cold water and let it dry several hours in a cool and well-ventilated spot. This process creates a membrane that keeps the fish from becoming too dry during the smoking.

Small fish can be hung by their heads while being smoked. If the fish weighs more than 2 lbs (1 kg), the head should be removed and a cut made from the belly up to the backbone, so that the fish can be split into two halves, similar to filets. Remove the backbone and place two sharp sticks crosswise through each fish half.

Hot smoking

Once the fish have dried, they should be smoked as soon as possible. The temperature in the smoke oven should be around 65°C (150°F). Hot smoking can take from two to ten hours, depending on the size of the fish, the heat from the smoke, and how heavily the fish should be smoked. The longer a fish is smoked the longer it will keep, but it also becomes a little drier.

The smoking process begins at a low temperature that increases once the smoking is underway. Coniferous branches or wood chips from hardwood trees are used as fuel. Because different kinds of fuel produce different tastes, some experimentation is recommended to discover the type of wood and the smoking time that produce the taste you prefer.

Hot smoked fish keep well for a week or two if they are kept cold. They can also be frozen and kept even longer.

Cold smoking

As mentioned earlier, cold smoking is a more arduous method than hot smoking because it must continue for at least 24 hours, preferably a few days. In addition, this method requires a permanent and more complicated smoking oven.

In terms of cleaning, salting and drying, the cold smoking process is the same as for hot smoking. Even the fuel is the same. The greatest difference between the two is that the source of heat for hot smoking is approximately one meter underneath the fish, so that the hot smoke rises directly upwards, while the smoke for cold smoking reaches the hanging fish by going through a pipe that is 3–6 ft (1–3 m) long. The cold smoking process is designed so that the smoke temperature will not exceed 95°F (35°C) when it reaches the fish, an ideal temperature being about 82°F 28°C).

Remember that the cover over the smoke oven must be very tight so only a minimum of smoke can escape. Anchor the cover with a stone or another heavy object so that it sits tightly.

Preserving trophy fish

The dream of a lifetime, the chance of a lifetime, the catch of a lifetime. The champion fish finally took the hook and the dream came true. But often, all that remains of that wonderful experience is a colour photo of the fish and the fisherman. There is another, relatively easy way to preserve the moment, by making a plaster cast of the exceptional catch. And of course if there is room on the walls at home, other memorable fish can also be preserved this way.

Making an attractive cast is actually easier than it sounds, even though it takes four or five evenings before the project is finished. Casts are usually made of plaster, latex or silicon. Latex and silicon produce a slightly better cast, but they are more difficult to work with and for an amateur, the results are not worth the extra work. Plaster is definitely the best material for beginners, and when making a plaster cast the first try can often be good enough to keep.

The actual casting is relatively easy; painting the cast is what takes time and patience, because it must reflect the fish's actual colouration. The painting is easier if you have a good colour photo of the fish, taken as soon as possible after landing. A fish's colouration and markings fade quickly, even a few hours after it is caught, so it is important to take the picture right away. The materials you will need for making a plaster cast are:

1/2 litre water per kilo plaster
a wooden or cardboard box slightly larger than the fish
sand
cardboard and pins
thin plastic wrap
a water-based floor varnish
cooking oil
a plastic bucket and a stirring stick
2 bolts, about 2 in (5 cm) long, for mounting the cast
metallic lacquer or other paint

Preparations

Fill the box with a layer of sand, about as deep as the thickness of the fish. Cover the sand with plastic wrap, to protect the fish. Prepare the *uncleaned* fish, fresh or frozen, by rinsing it, removing the protective membrane, and drying the fish with a towel or a paper towel. Arrange the fish so that almost half of it lies in the sand. If the pectoral or dorsal fins stick out too much, they can be pinned to the body. After this, cut pieces of cardboard that are slightly bigger than the dorsal fin, the anal fin and the tail fin. Place a piece of cardboard under each of the fins to support them, so they do not sink into the sand when the plaster is poured. These cardboard pieces placed between the fins and sand help to make a sharper impression. Stretch out the fins and pin them securely onto the cardboard.

If the fish has thawed before the cast is made, it is possible that the eye will sink in when the plaster is poured. To prevent this, you can place a wad of damp paper in the fish's mouth to hold the eye in place.

Making the mould

The next step is to mix the plaster. Remember to always pour the water in the bucket first, then the plaster. The amount of plaster needed is 1.5 times the weight of the fish. If there are no other instructions on the package, measure 1/2 litre of water per kilo plaster. Stir the mixture until all the lumps are gone.

Once the plaster is smooth and consistent, it can be poured over the fish. Be certain it completely covers the fish. Let the plaster harden for 30–40 minutes, then turn the mould over and carefully remove the fish. When the fish has been rinsed thoroughly, it can be prepared in the same way as any other fish.

If you want to make a solid cast of the fish, repeat the procedure using the other side.

Finishing the mould

The mould is very fragile at first, so you should wait five or six days before doing any more work on it. By then it has dried thoroughly and you can begin to scrape away the rough edges with a sharp knife. The impressions of the fins are sometimes too thin and very brittle, and they may need to be shaped with the knife. They may also need to be strengthened with a thin ridge of plaster. Build up this ridge a few centimeters beyond the edge of the fin, so that it produces a strong cast. Give the mould a final scraping to remove excess plaster around the fins and reinforce the indentations, especially the lines in the tail fin, with a knife blade.

When thoroughly dry, paint the inside of the mould with a water-based floor varnish. When the varnish is dry, go over the indentations of the head and the fins one more time. When this is dry, brush a thin layer of cooking oil over the mould.

Casting the fish

Everything is now ready to do the actual casting. Mix a new batch of plaster, this time using one kilo of dry plaster for each kilo of fish. Pour the plaster in the mould so that it comes to the top, but does not run over, and be sure the fins are completely covered. Before the plaster begins to set, place the bolts in the mould. Two or three bolts are sufficient for fish weighing up to 20 lbs (10 kg), but more bolts are needed for mounting a heavier fish securely on its backboard. One bolt should be placed immediately behind the gill cover, another at the same elevation as the anal fin, and any additional bolts should be placed between these two at intervals of about 2 in (5 cm). The bolts must be held in place for a few minutes until the plaster begins to set.

Wait five or six days before taking the cast out, so that it does not crack. When the plaster is thoroughly dry, you can begin carefully chipping the mould away. The mould usually begins to crack apart on its own as the plaster dries, but if it does not, you need to saw narrow slits in the form, about 2 in (5 cm) apart. After that, use a chisel to prise out the cast from its mould. Begin by freeing the head and proceed to chisel out the rest of the fish, ending at the tail. Take extra care so that the plaster does not crack around the fins and the tail.

Shown below are the main tasks in plaster casting. First the fish is half-buried in a sand bed. Then pour the mould, let it stiffen for 30–40 minutes, turn it over and take out the fish. Polish the mould before pouring the actual cast. After five to six days, break open the mould, with care not to damage the cast. Finally the cast is painted and varnished as naturally as possible.

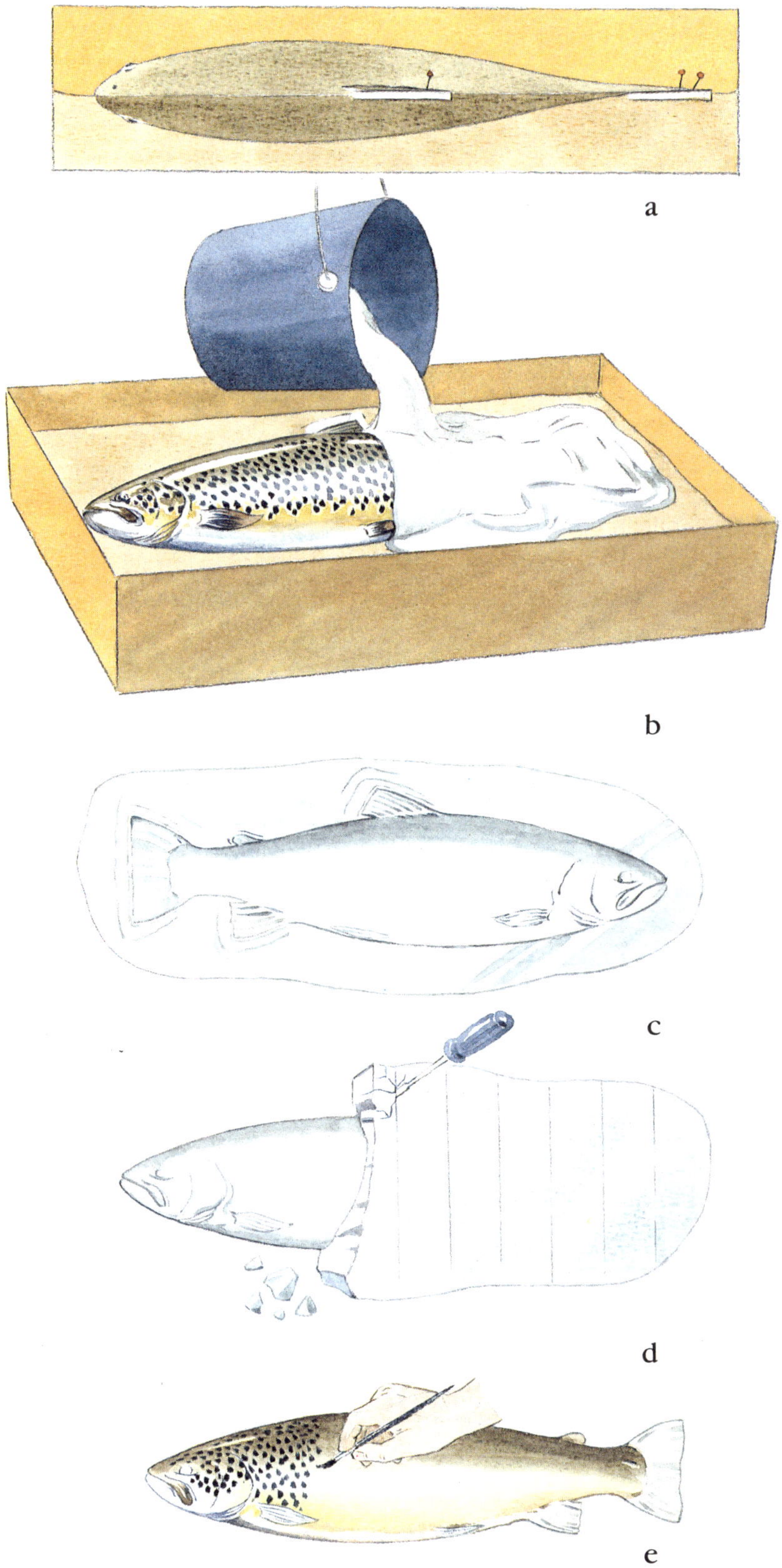

If, in spite of the gentlest handling, the cast should crack anywhere, it is easy to patch with epoxy. When the pieces have been mended and the glue has dried, fill in the crack with a thin plaster mix and let it dry. After smoothing out the break with the point of a sharp knife, it is hardly noticeable, and when the cast is painted the crack will have disappeared entirely.

Some parts of the cast may need touching up before they can be painted. Small details on the fins and the head may need to be emphasized so that they look natural. This is easily done with a knife and a small file. Small bubbles or cracks in the plaster should be filled with a thin mixture of plaster and smoothed over with a knife. When all this is finished, smooth off the back of the plaster cast so that the surface is flat and even.

Painting the cast

When the finishing work is done and the cast is thoroughly dry, it should be varnished 2–3 times so that the plaster is saturated. Then the painting can begin. This is the most difficult and time-consuming part of the project, because it takes a certain amount of experience to produce a truly natural-looking fish. But the painting is the most fun, as this is when the cast takes on its final appearance. Unless you are blessed with natural artistic talents, this is also where a good photograph of the fish is invaluable, and necessary, in capturing the fish's actual appearance and its colouration.

Oil paints, the same type used by artists, are the best to paint with, but metallic lacquers can also be used. Metallic lacquers are easy to work with and they produce a shiny surface that actually looks real. Try to find a basic colour that closely resembles the fish, and spray the cast from far enough away that there is an even merging of the colours, starting from the darker back and progressing to the lighter, glossy belly.

If you do not know how far away to hold the spray can, or how to merge the colours from the back and the belly, do some experimenting on pieces of plastic or on a flat board. If you are not satisfied with the colour of the cast when you are finished, wait until the paint dries and paint it again. The eye and markings should be hand-painted with oil paint to give the right lustre. Painting the details with very thin brushes creates a realistic effect.

When you are satisfied with the painting, let the paint dry properly and then apply several coats of varnish to give the surface the same lustre as a living fish. Once the varnish has dried to a hard surface, the fish is ready for mounting on its background. Although the choice of material and colour are personal, most people seem to agree that natural wood gives a more solid impression than plywood or other man-made wood products. In order to display the fish at its best, dark wood is generally recommended for light-coloured fish and lighter woods for dark fish.

Index